THE CHRISTIAN MILLENNIUM

Studies in Eschatological
Millennial Views

Kevin J. Conner

THE

CHRISTIAN

MILLENNIUM

Copyright © AD.2000
K.J.C.Publications

**It is illegal and a violation of Christian
ethics to reproduce any part of parts
or diagrams in this book without
written permission of the author**

ISBN 0 949829 49 8

TABLE OF CONTENTS
PART ONE
FIVE MILLENNIAL VIEWS

Foreword
Preface
Chapter   Page

1. Introducing the Millennial Problems — 1
2. Historic Pre-Millennialism + Bibliography — 4
3. Futurist Pre-Millennialism — 8
4. Dispensational Pre-Millennialism + Bibliography — 12
5. Post-Millennialism + Bibliography — 20
6. A-Millennialism + Bibliography — 26

Conclusion

PART TWO
AREAS OF ESCHATOLOGICAL CONTROVERSY

Preface — 36
Chapter

1. Daniel's Seventy Weeks Prophecy — 38
2. The Kingdom — 56
3. The Church — 64
4. The Nation of Israel — 72
5. The New Covenant — 82
6. The Mosaic Covenant Economy — 90
7. The Rapture — 104
8. The Antichrist — 113
9. The Great Tribulation — 126
10. The Second Coming of Christ — 133
11. The Binding of Satan — 138
12. The Resurrection — 147
13. The Judgment — 164
14. The Millennial Kingdom — 174
15. The Eternal States — 180

PART THREE
THE CHRISTIAN MILLENNIUM

Introduction — 190
Principles of Interpretation — 192
Chapter

1. The Weeks of the Lord — 196
2. The Days of the Lord — 200
3. Significance of One Hundred and Twenty — 205
4. The Age and the Ages to Come — 208
5. A Study in 'Thousands' — 210
6. What is NOT in a Christian Millennium — 216
7. The Christian Millennium — 224
8. Reigning on the Earth — 237
9. The Glory of the Christian Millennium — 243
10. End of Millennium Events — 248

Conclusion

Overview Chart of Millennial Views

Bibliography

FOREWORD

THE CHRISTIAN MILLENNIUM

Over the years, I have read the Book of Revelation many times and have been fascinated with its message. What an incredible book! And what an exciting message filled with hope for us who believe in the Lord Jesus Christ who is coming again! I have also read many commentators on Revelation, who were both interesting and useful, containing many important elements of truth. Many of the interpretations had been made out of either a particular system of eschatology or a particular system of interpreting Revelation. Somehow, it often left me unsatisfied. It was hard to piece these elements of truth together into a coherent whole.

Over many years I have taught with Kevin Conner "The Key of Knowledge" Seminar, which teaches Methods and Principles of Interpreting the Scriptures. One of the key sentences we have used is this, "The way the Bible was put together is the way it can be taken apart." Kevin applies these same Methods and Principles taught in " The Key of Knowledge" Seminar as he interprets the controversial subject of "**The Millennium**" in this present text.

When it comes to interpreting Revelation, Biblical balance is certainly needed. That is what I have personally found in Kevin's exposition as he grapples with the concept of the Millennium. At the break between sessions in a seminar on Revelation some while ago, one person asked me how Kevin arrived at some of those conclusions on various passages under consideration in Revelation. I explained what Kevin had taught in that session, and added, "I know **WHAT** Kevin believes, **WHY** he believes it, and **HOW** he came to those conclusions!" I make that same statement in regard to this present book. Likewise, it is important for all of us who are students of God's Word, whoever we are, and whatever our spiritual gifts and orientation might be, to know **what** we believe, **why** we believe it, and **how** we got there!

In order for you to find out what Kevin believes, why he believes, and how he got there regarding **"The Christian Millennium"**, I thoroughly recommend his earlier text book, **"Principles of Interpreting Revelation."** There he sets out clearly the principles of Biblical interpretation that should be used to interpret the Book of Revelation. He also demonstrates how these principles are applied. In addition, his book, **"The Seventy Weeks Prophecy, An Exposition of Daniel 9 "**, is well worth studying. Daniel's prophecy is a 'master key' that will unlock the door of Revelation. Daniel was told by the angel that the words he wrote were to be sealed up until the time of the end (Dan.12:4,9). We need to understand Daniel's Seventy Weeks Prophecy if we are to understand the message of Revelation. Kevin writes in the Preface of that book, "Vital issues such as Messiah's first and second coming…the Millennial Kingdom, etc., are based upon one's understanding and interpretation of this focal point of prophecy."

As a diligent Bible student, you can check out for yourself what Kevin believes about **"The Christian Millennium"**, and why he believes it, and how he got there as you read this book along with the others recommended here. As Kevin wrote in "The Seventy Weeks Prophecy" (page 140), **"The Christian Millennium"** needs a text book of its own to cover its material." Here is that textbook! Read it! Study the Scriptures for yourself! Prove all things, and be blessed by the settled hope we have as the redeemed of the Lord!

David W.Searle ,
T.S.TC., Dip.Div., L.Th., B.A.Hons., Di.Min.Couns.

PREFACE

Undoubtedly, one of the greatest areas of controversy in the field of Eschatology is that which pertains to the Millennium. The word, though not a Bible word, is a Bible truth. The word comes from two Latin words, "Mille", meaning "a thousand", and "Annum", meaning " A Year" – therefore, a thousand years.

The foundational passage upon which Millennial views are built is found in Rev.20:1-10. The period of "one thousand years" is mentioned some six times in the passage. It has become one of the most perplexing problems, as to its proper interpretation, to expositors, and this throughout Church History. What is the nature, the purpose, and the duration of this Millennium? Is it an actual and literal period of time? Or, is it simply a symbolic period of time in which various events take place and find fulfillment? Why do we even need a Millennium? If there is such a period of time, what takes place in this period? Who are the inhabitants? What is it all about, especially when there is really only one passage in the whole of Scripture that speaks of such a period and very few details about it are given? These are questions that have puzzled the best of expositors of Scriptures and still seek answers.

Basically there are three major Schools of Millennial views. Each has a system of interpretation of their own in which is set forth their exposition of Rev.20:1-10. These Schools are known as:

1. Pre-Millennialism.
   Within this School there are three categories, defined as:
   (a) Historic Pre-Millennialism,
   (b) Futurist Pre-Millennialism,
   (c) Dispensational Pre-Millennialism.
   Each believes that Christ returns **before** the Millennium.
2. Post-Millennialism.
   Post-Millennialists believe that Christ returns **after** the Millennium has been established.
3. A-Millennialism.
   A-Millennialists believe that Christ returns at the **close** of the Millennium.

It is to be recognized that there are many sincere, genuine, evangelical believers and scholars in each of these Schools and systems of interpretation. The differences do not arise out of unbelief or rejection of the inspired Scriptures. The difference is not over **revelation** and **inspiration** but it is over **interpretation** and **application!** Each School has their distinctive hermeneutical principles used to interpret Scripture. Each has a theology that affects their interpretation of Scripture. In other words, theology and hermeneutics affect each in their exegesis of the Bible.

The great doctrines of redemption have been set out systematically over Church History and are generally accepted by all that are strongly evangelical. But, when it comes to some of the finer points of the doctrine of the second coming of Christ and the future aspects of the Kingdom of God, no fixed position has been arrived at. As a result, these three major views continue to be written about and examined for further light and clarity. Other authors have examined each of these views. Each will be examined in brief in this text. The purpose of this book, however, is to present another possible view of the Millennium, that is, **The Christian Millennium!**

Most writers recognize the inadequacy of the terminology using concerning the Millennial position, whether "Pre", "Post" or "A" Millennial. Each position believes in a Millennium of some kind. The difference is as to the "when" (the time), and the "where" (the place), and the "what" (the nature) of this Millennium.

As to the time? When does this Millennium find fulfillment? Is it a present reality or is it a future period of time, a coming Utopia to be enjoyed by all? Pre-Millennialists and Post-Millennialists would say it is future. A-Millennialists would say it is a present reality.

As to the place? Is the Millennium here on earth now, or is it a future state on the earth after Christ comes? A-Millennialists would say it is here and now. Post-Millennials and Pre-Millennialists would say it is future glory here on the earth.

As to the nature? Is the Millennium a spiritual kingdom in the hearts of men here and now or is it an earthly, political and Jewish kingdom set up in earth after Christ comes? A-Millennialists would say the kingdom is here and now, in the hearts of true believes. Pre-Millennialists, of the Futurist and Dispensational persuasion would say it is an earthly kingdom predominantly of Judaistic and Jewish economy, and this is established after Christ comes the second time.

It is important to understand that the basic fundamentals of Evangelical Faith are held by each of these Schools of Eschatology. Each School has far more in common as to redemptive truths than differences as to eschatological truths. It is for this reason that Christian grace should be evidenced in expressing various opinions and opposing views as to end-time events. The things held in common by all Schools mentioned are listed here:

- Each holds that the Word of God is the final authority for all matters of faith and practice.
- Each holds to the redemptive work of Christ and His once-for-all sacrifice for sin and salvation for all men is only through faith in Christ.
- Each holds to the truth of Christ's future, personal, visible and bodily coming the second time.
- Each holds that the Word of God teaches that the eternal states of all are settled forever after the great judgment of all mankind. The righteous saints and angels will live eternally with God and Christ in heaven, and the unrighteous angels and sinners will dwell eternally in hell with Satan.

The differences are as to interpretative methods when it comes to Christ's coming and the details of the Kingdom of God in its final aspect.

Perhaps the reader has heard of the fable of **"The Blind Men and The Elephant"**. It is worth repeating here for the lesson it speaks to all expositors of the Word relative to eschatological events.

"It was six men of Hindustan, To learning much inclined,
Who went to see the elephant, Though all of them were blind,
That each by observation, Might satisfy the mind.

The first approached the elephant, And, happening to fall
Against its broad and sturdy **side**, At once began to bawl:
'Why, bless me! But the elephant, Is very **like a wall.**'

The second, as he felt the **tusk**, Cried, 'Ho! What have we here?,
So very round and smooth and sharp, To me 'tis mighty clear,
This wonder of an elephant, Is very **like a spear'.**

The third approached the animal, And, happening to take
The squirming **trunk** within his hand, Thus boldly up and spake:
'I see,' quoth he, 'the elephant, Is very **like a snake!**'

The fourth reached out his eager hand, And felt about its **knee,**
'What most this wondrous beast is like, Is mighty plain, ' quoth he:
'Tis clear enough the elephant, Is very **like a tree!**'

The fifth, who chanced to touch the **ear**, Said, 'Even the blindest man
Can tell what this resembles most; Deny the fact, who can,
This marvel of an elephant, Is very **like a fan!**'

The sixth no sooner had begun, About the beast to grope,
Than, seizing on the swinging **tail**, That fell within his scope,
'I see,' quoth he, 'the elephant, Is very **like a rope!**'

And so these men of Hindustan, **Disputed loud and long,**
Each in his own opinion, Exceeding stiff and strong;
Though each was partly in the right, They all were in the wrong!

By John Godfrey Saxe

As can be seen, each of the blind men touched a part of the elephant and thought it was the whole. None of them saw the whole and each in their blindness described what the elephant was like according to the part they touched. They disputed and argued loud and long. Each had their own stiff and strong opinions. The lesson is clear: **"Though each was partly in the right, They all were in the wrong!"**

When we all stand before the Lord it probably will be like this when it comes to the subject of eschatology. We all will be partly in the right and/or partly in the wrong. We see through a glass very dimly. We do not have perfect sight or insight into the inexhaustible Word of God. Even the apostles and writers of Scriptures did not always have this insight. Many times they had revelation given to them but they did not have illumination of the revelation they wrote under inspiration (1Pet.1:9-12).

This writer sees that each of the views has points in common and points of difference. Each endeavours to discover the truth of the Scriptures and what the writers meant when they wrote these things down. All see the glass very dimly. All will become clear in 'the perfect day'. Until that time, Christian grace and tolerance should be manifest when considering the differing views on the Millennium. There is really no place for un-Christ-like attitudes, criticism and intolerance of another's differing point of view and opposing opinion. Such things should not be found in a true Bible expositor and believer, even though one may have strong convictions about what they believe.

This writer asks for this kind of grace and Christian tolerance as the reader considers the possibility of **"The Christian Millennium."**

PART ONE

TABLE OF CONTENTS
PART ONE
FIVE MILLENNIAL VIEWS

Foreword
Chapter
1. **Introducing the Millennial Problems**
2. **Historic Pre-Millennialism + Bibliography**
3. **Futurist Pre-Millennialism**
4. **Dispensational Pre-Millennialism + Bibliography**
5. **Post-Millennialism + Bibliography**
6. **A-Millennialism + Bibliography**

Conclusion

CHAPTER ONE

INTRODUCING THE MILLENNIAL PROBLEM

In introducing the Millennial Problem, it really becomes necessary to spell out the various parts of the great eschatological jig-saw puzzle! As the writer sees it, there are some fifteen components belonging to the field of eschatological controversy. Each of them are related to end-time events. Each have their bearing on the Second Coming of Christ and a person's view of the Millennium. Each Millennial School of thought is affected in their understanding and interpretation of these things. This will be seen in the appropriate chapters.

Following are, what may be called, the parts of the eschatological puzzle. Any person who has ever put a puzzle together generally, first of all, lays out the parts of the puzzle. The parts must not be forced or else the picture in the puzzle becomes distorted. Again, none of the parts are needless, for all belong to the whole. In putting the puzzle together, one uses what has been called, 'the hermeneutical cycle', where one 'works from the part to the whole and the whole to the part'. One must not 'force' the Scriptures or else this distortion affects the whole. Every part of the puzzle should lock and interlock until the whole picture is seen in all its beauty. So it is with eschatological parts. There is much that is a puzzle to us. We want to lay the parts of the puzzle out first, considering these parts. Then we want to work from part to whole and whole to part, without forcing anything. The desire is to see everything lock and interlock until we something of the 'big picture' of end-time events and worship our God and His Christ! In much question format, we list out the major parts of the eschatological puzzle.

1. **Daniel's Seventy Weeks Prophecy**
   Basically, most every interpretation and exposition of Daniel and/or Revelation arise out of one's understanding and interpretation of this notable Seventy Weeks Prophecy. Is it totally fulfilled or unfullfilled? Or is there a 'gap' of some 2000 years between the sixty-ninth and seventieth week of the prophecy in which certain events are to take place?

2. **The Kingdom of God**
   Another great area of controversy has to do with the Kingdom of God. Did John and Jesus offer the Kingdom to Jewry as a nation? Was it a literal, material and political kind of Kingdom? Was it a spiritual Kingdom? When the Jewish nation rejected the King (Jesus) was the Kingdom then postponed to the end of this age for the Jewish nation to preach? Is the Gospel of the Kingdom different from the Gospel of the Grace of God? Is the Gospel of the Kingdom a distinct Gospel relative only to the Jewish nation?

3. **The Church**
   The subject of the Church is another area of difference. When the Jewish nation rejected the King and the Kingdom, did God have Plan B and brought in the Church? Is the Church a parenthetical purpose of God because of Jewish unbelief and the rejection and postponement of the Kingdom? Or, is the Church in the eternal purpose of God? Whatever one's understanding of the Church is affects one understanding of eschatological events also.

4. **The Nation of Israel**
   The problem of Israel, or 'the Jewish problem' is a very sensitive subject for many preachers and teachers and believers. What about Israel? What about the Jew? What about the Old Testament prophecies concerning Israel blessing the nations of earth? Is the Jew still the elect nation? What about the promises of the restoration of Israel to be head of the nations? Is this restoration national or spiritual? What about God's everlasting covenant with Abraham? These are great issues that need to be handled in the field of eschatology.

5. **The New Covenant**
   Many of God's people suffer today from what may be called, 'Covenantal confusion'. Where does the New Covenant fit in with God's scheme of things? What part does it play in the overall purposes of God? Has the New Covenant really been established with the House of Israel and the House of Judah yet? Or is it yet to be established in the end of this age or the Millennial Age? And again, if the New Covenant has been established, is it to be replaced by a return to the Old Covenant in a future Millennial Kingdom? Or, is the New Covenant the ultimate purpose of God for both Time and Eternity? These questions are of great interest in the realm of end-time events.

6. The Mosaic Covenant Economy

This area is very much related to the previous. The matter of the Mosaic Covenant economy has a very strong bearing on eschatological controversy. Is the Mosaic Covenant economy to be restored? Will the nation of Israel come to God through a restored Old Covenant or Mosaic Covenant economy? What about the restoration of a Temple? And animal sacrifices and oblations? What about the Aaronic and Levitical Priesthood? The Sabbaths and the Festival days? What about Ezekiel's Temple? What about the nations keeping the Feast of Tabernacles in a coming Millennium? Or, was the Mosaic Covenant fulfilled and abolished at Calvary? Or must we look for a restoration and reinstitution of this Covenant in a coming Jewish Millennium? Or, are all to be saved, whether Jews or Gentiles, by the power and ministry of the New Covenant? This area is a great stronghold of teaching in the Futurist and Dispensational approach to eschatology and needs to be seriously considered.

7. The Rapture

Many, many Christians are looking for the Lord to come "as a thief in the night" in a "secret rapture". What about the "secret rapture" of the Church? Is there such a thing? Does the Bible teach this as a truth? Does this "secret rapture" take place at the beginning of some seven-year Great Tribulation, or mid-way through this seven-year period? Or does the rapture take place at the same time as Christ's second coming? If there is a rapture, will the whole Church be taken up and will some Christians be left behind to experience the Great Tribulation? These questions are also pressing in the whole field of eschatology, and numerous Christians hang their hopes on "the great escape".

8. The Antichrist

The teaching of a coming Antichrist has been around for many years, but there are many questions concerning the same. Is the Antichrist a person? A system? A spirit? Is the Antichrist a world government, a world dictator or a world religious leader? What is the Mark of the Beast that the world is caused to receive? Is it actual, literal or symbolical of a diabolical system?

9. The Great Tribulation

Another point of eschatological controversy has to do with what has been "the Great Tribulation". Some teach it is a period of seven years, or three and one-half years, the seventieth week of Daniel's prophecy. Is there such a thing as the Great Tribulation? Hasn't there always been tribulation on the people of God? Is the Tribulation past, present or future? Is the Church going to go through the Tribulation or be raptured just about before it begins? Is this period seven years or three and one-half years at the end of the age before Christ comes again? What of the Christians who have been martyred over Church History in the nations of the earth? Was that not 'tribulation' for them? Or is there an end-time Great Tribulation?

10. The Second Coming of Christ

Depending on which eschatological School one belongs to, questions arise about Christ's Second Coming. How many 'comings' of Christ are there? Is the coming of Christ in two stages; one called the "Rapture" and the other called the "Revelation", which takes place seven years later? Or does the Bible simply teach one coming of Christ?

11. The Binding of Satan

An important point of controversy concerns the binding of Satan. Is Satan already bound? Is he yet to be bound? Are the nations now no longer being deceived? How can the deception that is in the world be handled if Satan is not in the Abyss, but on a long chain?

12. The Resurrection

How many resurrections are there? Are there two resurrections: the first and the second resurrection? Is there one resurrection for the righteous and one resurrection for the unrighteous? Is there an extra resurrection that takes place in the "secret rapture" and another kind of "first resurrection" for the saints who missed this rapture? Or is there but one general resurrection at the coming of Christ. This is another area of much difference in the field of eschatology.

13. The Judgment

This is related very much to the previous part of the puzzle. How many judgments are there? Is there a judgment for believers spoken of as the Judgment Seat of Christ? Is there a judgment for unbelievers, spoken of as the Great White Throne Judgment? What about Dispensationalists who speak of some five or even seven judgments to take place at Christ's coming? Or is there but one general resurrection followed by one general judgment?

14. **The Millennial Kingdom**
It is this area that is the most controversial part of eschatology. Is there such a thing as a Millennial Kingdom? Is the Kingdom of God everlasting or it is to be of limited duration during this period of 1000 years? Or, is this 1000 years a symbolic period of time between the first and second comings of Christ? Or, is there an actual period of 1000 years Kingdom of God on this earth? Is it a Jewish Kingdom, a Jewish Millennium? Is this Millennium an intermediary state between Christ's second coming and the eternal state of the New Heavens and New Earth? If there is a future Millennium, what is the purpose of it? Why do we need it? What is the character and nature of it? Who are the citizens of this Millennial Kingdom? When does this period come in? Or, are we in the Millennium now? Is Satan bound now? Are the saints reigning now? Or, can we look for a Jewish, nationalistic, materialistic and political Kingdom, with Christ reigning on the throne of David in earthly Jerusalem for 1000 years over the nations of earth? Will Christ rule in this Millennial Kingdom with a rod of iron, forcing all nations to bow to His rule and reign? These and many other questions arise concerning the Millennial Kingdom. It should be remembered: Each School believes in a Millennium – of some sort. The difference concerns the time, the place and the nature thereof. These are things subject to our consideration.

15. **The Eternal States**
It would appear that most Schools have basic agreement on the Eternal States. Each holds that, after the Great White Throne, eternal destinies are settled for peoples of earth, and all angelic beings. All the righteous will be with God and Christ and the holy angels in heaven, for eternity. All the unrighteous will be with Satan and his angels in hell, for eternity. The New Heavens and New Earth will be the eternal habitation of the righteous. The questions that arise expose the differences in the Schools as to the time element. Does the second coming usher in the eternal states? Is this present period of time "the last day" or "the end of the age?" Does eternity follow Christ's advent, with no in-between Millennial Age? Are eternal destinies of heaven and hell settled at Christ's coming again without having to wait for a supposed Millennial period to pass? Does eternity follow Christ's second coming or not?

The serious student should immediately see the inter-relatedness of these things and how they have their bearing on the Second Coming of Christ and the future aspect of the Kingdom and eternity!

Because of the many textbooks dealing with each of the views, these points will only be dealt with in brief. The reader is referred to the Bibliography for those writers dealing with such. The purpose of this book is to present a possible alternative view, seeking to present, hopefully, a balanced and Scriptural view on these issues. After considering in brief the fifteen issues in each eschatological School, the writer presents an alternative view – **"The Christian Millennium"** – for prayerful consideration. And, the reader should remember the Fable of "The Blind Men and The Elephant!"

CHAPTER TWO

HISTORIC PRE-MILLENNIALISM

The reader needs to remember that, when we speak of Pre-Millennialism, there are several branches in this field of eschatology; these being, Historic Pre-Millennialists, Futurist Pre-Millennialists and Dispensational Pre-Millennialists. The thing in common with each is that all believe in a coming and future Millennium. The differences consist of what kind of a Millennium it is. Each believes that Christ returns the second time **before** the Millennium, hence, "Pre" (before) the Millennium!

Dr. J.G. Vos (Blue Banner Faith & Life, Jan-March,1951) provides this definition of Historic Pre-Millennialism as adapted here. "Pre-Millennialism is that view of the Last Things which holds that, the second coming of Christ will be followed by a period of worldwide peace and righteousness, before the end of the world (i.e., the ushering in of the New Heavens and New Earth). This period is called the Millennium or the Kingdom of God, during which Christ will reign as King in person on this earth".

And again (as noted previously), "Pre-Millennialists are divided into various groups by their differing views of the order of events associated with the second coming of Christ. But they all agree in holding that there will be a Millennium on earth after the second coming of Christ, but before the end of the world." Pre-Millennialists believe Christ returns before the Millennium reign of Christ on earth.

We note in briefest outline the basic beliefs of Historic Pre-Millennialists as to the fifteen components of end-time eschatology. The basic points are noted without supplying many of the Scripture references used by the Historic Pre-Millennialists in support of their views. This will be so with regard to each of the Schools in **Part One** of this book. Historic Pre-Millennialists differ with Futurist and Dispensational Pre-Millennialists on several of the points under consideration.

1. **Daniel's Seventy Weeks Prophecy**
   Historic Pre-Millennialists believe that the Seventy Weeks Prophecy of Daniel have been fulfilled and this at the first coming of Christ. For this School there is no division or gaps in the prophecy. It is seen as a 'time-continuous' prophecy. That is, the seven weeks, the sixty-two weeks and the seventieth week are unbroken and fulfilled. There is no Biblical warrant or ground for any 'time-gap' of some 2000 years being placed between the seventieth week as the Futurist Pre-Millennialists and the Dispensational Pre-Millennialists teach.

2. **The Kingdom of God**
   Historic Pre-Millennialism sees that the Kingdom of God was not postponed or suspended as the Futurist and Dispensational Pre-Millennialists teach. Christ is now reigning in heaven as King, at the Father's right hand. It is a spiritual reign already inaugurated at Christ's ascension after completing the work of redemption at Calvary. He is both Lord and King now. In this reign, He sits on the throne of David in glory.
   Historic Pre-Millennialists see the Kingdom of God "now, but not yet". As people are born again they enter that spiritual Kingdom but there will be a full manifestation of that Kingdom in a future Millennium here on earth once Christ returns. There was a faithful remnant that accepted the King and His Kingdom and these became the nucleus and foundation members of the New Testament Church. There will come a time when the Son will give the Kingdom back to the Father and He Himself become subject to the Father for the Father's eternal plan.

3. **The Church**
   Historic Pre-Millennialists see that the Church was and is in the eternal purpose of God as declared by Paul in Eph.3:1-11. The Old Testament Prophets saw the coming in of the Gentiles into the Kingdom of God. Paul saw that the Mystery of God involved both believing Jews and believing Gentiles, both set in the one Body of Christ, the one Olive Tree (Gal.6:16; 3:16,29). There is only one way of salvation for Jew and Gentile, which is, by faith in Christ Jesus, apart from the works of the Law (Rom.9-10-11). Many prophecies in the Old Testament speaking of natural Israel are applied to the New Testament Church, the spiritual Israel of God. Abraham is the father of all who believe, the father of a spiritual people, a people of faith, and this means that believers are children of Abraham. It means that they are Israel in true and spiritual sense. The New Testament Church is the Seed of Abraham, spiritual Israel, the true Circumcision and people of the New Covenant. This, however, does not make them Israel after the flesh. There is a natural (national) Israel and

there is a spiritual Israel, the latter consisting of believing Jews and Gentiles – the New Covenant people of God.

4. **The Nation of Israel**
Historic Pre-Millennialists believe that there will come some visitation of God upon the Jewish nation. There will be an outpouring of the Spirit upon Israel as a nation. Under this outpouring, their eyes will be opened and they will be grafted back into the good olive tree. It will be by true faith in Christ, apart from the Old Covenant. This visitation may be in this present time, or even in the end of the age, in the early days of the final Great Tribulation (Rom.11:24-26). Some suggest it may be in the future Millennium. There is, however, no special plan of salvation for the Jews in any future age. There is only one plan of salvation for Jew and Gentile, and that is, through faith in the Lord Jesus Christ.
When the Prophets speak of a restoration of Israel, this restoration is particularly to the Lord. The Old Covenant saw a restoration of the Jew to the land, a restoration of the Temple and the Mosaic economy, but all this took place at the close of the Babylonian Captivity. Any restoration of Israel, whether in or out of 'the land' is a spiritual restoration to God, and that, through Christ and the New Covenant – not by way of the Old or the Mosaic Covenant.

5. **The New Covenant**
Historic Pre-Millennialists see that the Old Covenant has been completely fulfilled and abolished in Christ, by His redemptive work on Calvary. The New Covenant has been established, both now and eternally. It will never be replaced by any other Covenant. All believers, Jew or Gentile, are now in New Covenant relationship with God through Christ.

6. **The Mosaic Covenant Economy**
Historic Pre-Millennialism holds that there will be absolutely no re-institution of the Mosaic Covenant economy in this age or any age to come. The Old Covenant with its Temple, Aaronic and Levitical priesthood, animal sacrifices and oblations, Sabbaths, Festival days, Circumcision and so forth – all have been fulfilled and abolished in the cross of the Lord Jesus Christ. The very prophets that foretold the restoration of Israel to the Lord also foretold the cessation of the Old Covenant economy and all the ritualism pertaining to the Mosaic Covenant (Jer31:31-34). The cross dealt with the carnal and material expression of these things, bringing them to the higher level, the spiritual expression of these things in the New Covenant. To restore the things of the Mosaic Covenant is to violate the New Testament revelation of Christ's ministry and work, and would especially negate the witness of truth in the Book of Hebrews.

7. **The Rapture**
Historic Pre-Millennialists believe that there is only one coming of Christ. The rapture of the Church, along with the resurrection of the dead in Christ, takes place at the revelation of Christ in His second advent. There are not two stages of the coming of Christ, but one second coming of Christ. He comes "for" and "with" His saints at the same time. There is no secret rapture or extra resurrection seven years or less before Christ comes. The "rapture" and the "revelation" take place in the same period of time. With Futurist and Dispensational Pre-Millennialism, Historic Pre-Millennialists part company on this point.

8. **The Antichrist**
Historic Pre-Millennialism hold that Antichrist is figurative of all the evil forces of Satan arrayed against the Church, the people of God, throughout Church History. The "Antichrist" has been evidenced in Antichristal forms of governments, Antichristal systems, and in the Satanic spirit behind them, manifested in various individual dictators, as well as political and religious figures. All things pertaining to end-time Antichrist powers will be destroyed at Christ's second coming.

9. **The Great Tribulation**
Historic Pre-Millennialists basically hold that "the great tribulation" was fulfilled in AD.70 in fulfillment of Christ's prophetic word to His disciples as given in Matt.24th chapter. Tribulation and persecution, however, has been the lot of the Church, the people of God, throughout Church History. All tribulation consummates in the end of the age and will come to an end at the coming of Christ the second time.

10. **The Second Coming of Christ**
    Historic Pre-Millennialists believe that there is but one coming of Christ. As noted under **"The Rapture"**, the rapture and the revelation take place at one and the same time, at the end of this age, at Christ's coming. Christ comes personally, bodily, visibly and gloriously to the world. Every eye shall see Him in His unveiled glory.

11. **The Binding of Satan**
    Historic Pre-Millennialists understand that Satan was legally "bound" at Calvary but the full evidence and execution of this takes place when Christ returns again. This will be over the 1000 years period of time.

12. **The Resurrection**
    Historic Pre-Millennialism, along with Futurist and Dispensational Pre-Millennialists believe in two resurrections, both being physically or bodily. These resurrections, of the just and the unjust, are 1000 years apart. The Historic view holds that the righteous are raised at the coming of Christ, in the first resurrection and the wicked are raised in the second resurrection. The righteous are judged and rewarded according to their works and enter the Millennial Kingdom. The wicked are also judged and rewarding according to their works, and then cast into the Lake of Fire, after the Great White Throne Judgment. The first resurrection is for the righteous, and takes place at the beginning of the 1000 years; the second resurrection, for the wicked, takes place at the close of the Millennium.

13. **The Judgment**
    Historic Pre-Millennialists, along with the Futurist School and Dispensational School, hold that there is a judgment for the righteous and the unrighteous. Each judgment takes place at the beginning and end of the Millennial Kingdom. The judgments introduce the eternal states. For the righteous, judgments and rewards are given and the righteous enter the Millennial Kingdom, and at the close, enter the New Heavens and New Earth. For the unrighteous, judgments and rewards are given at the Great White Throne Judgment and all enter the eternal states of Hell. Historic Pre-Millennialists do not hold with the Dispensationalists on their teaching on "Seven Judgments", or, as some hold, five in all.

14. **The Millennial Kingdom**
    Historic Pre-Millennialists hold that there is an actual, literal and earthly manifestation of the Kingdom of God in the earth. This is the Millennial Kingdom where Christ will be seen as King over all the earth. Believing Jews and Gentiles (the Church) will reign with Christ. Satan is bound in the abyss in this period of time. There will be peace and righteousness in the earth. Mortals and immortals will mingle freely in earth. Sinful offspring will be born to mortals over this period of time. Evil will be suppressed. At the end of this 1000 years reign of Christ, the close of the Millennium, Satan will be loosed, and there will be an organized rebellion against Christ's Kingship. These unregenerate sinners, headed by Satan, will come against Christ and the saints. All show that the heart of man is incorrigible apart from the restraining grace of God. The Great White Throne Judgement follows this. This is "the end" when the Son gives back the Kingdom to the Father that God may be all in all (1Cor.15:24-26).

15. **The Eternal States**
    Historic Pre-Millennialists see, after the Great White Throne Judgment, the eternal states being ushered in. Here the eternal destinies of all angels and mankind have been settled. For the holy angels and the redeemed saints, there are the New Heavens and New Earth. For the Devil, his angels, demonic spirits and all the unredeemed of mankind, there will be the eternal Hell, the Lake of Fire. This ushers in the eternal states, about which there is little given, except that all will be eternal joy and bliss to live eternally with God and Christ, the holy angels and the saints of all ages.

These are the basic points of end-time events that the Historic School holds. Of course, according to the teacher of the same, there are always slight variations in understanding and presentation. For fuller details on the Historic Pre-Millennial views, the reader is referred to the Bibliography at the close of this chapter and the close of **Part One**.

BIBLIOGRAPHY

HISTORIC PRE-MILLENNIALISM

1. Alford, The Greek New Testament, 1874
2. Frost, Henry W., The Second Coming of Christ, 1934
3. Guinness, H. Gratten, The Approaching End of the Age, 1880
4. Kellogg, S.H., The Jews or Prediction and Fulfillment, 1883
5. Ladd, George E, The Blessed Hope, 1956
6. Ladd, George E., Crucial Questions About the Kingdom of God, 1952
7. Ladd, George E., A Commentary on the Book of Revelation, 1972
8. Ladd, George E., The Gospel of the Kingdom, 1959
9. Ladd, George E., The Presence of the Future, 1974
10. Reese, Alexander., The Approaching Advent of Christ, 1917
11. West, Nathaniel., The Thousand Years in Both Testament, 1880

CHAPTER THREE

FUTURIST PRE-MILLENNIALISM

Futurist Pre-Millennialism holds to the Pre-Millennial view of Christ's second coming **before** the Millennium and the establishment of the Kingdom of God over all the earth. In this, there is agreement between Historic, Futurist and Dispensational Pre-Millennialism.

There are, however, certain differences between Historic and Futurist Pre-Millennialism. On the other hand, Futurist Pre-Millennialism and Dispensational Pre-Millennialism have much more in common. The major emphasis and difference between these Schools would be the restoration of the Jew to God under the Mosaic Covenant economy and the exaltation of the Jewish nation above all nations. As a general rule, allowing for some variations as to details, Futurist Pre-Millennialists hold the following views on the fifteen components of eschatological controversy.

1. **Daniel's Seventy Weeks Prophecy**
   Futurists believe that sixty-nine of the notable Seventy Weeks Prophecy were fulfilled at the entry of Christ into Jerusalem on traditional Palm Sunday. In their understanding, there remains but one week – the seventieth week – to be fulfilled. The Church Age of some 2000 years comes in between this 'gap' of the sixty-ninth and seventieth week. This week is yet to be fulfilled and comes in at the close of this age after the rapture of the Church. It is the last seven years of this age before the actual second coming of Christ. This seventieth week is divided into two halves of 3½ years, each relative to end-time events, as seen in subsequent points here.

2. **The Kingdom**
   Futurists believe and teach that John and Jesus both came preaching the Gospel of the Kingdom during the close of the sixty-nine weeks of Daniel's prophecy. The Jew, however, rejected both the King and his offer of the Kingdom. The Kingdom offered to Jewry was an actual, literal, materialistic and political Kingdom like to the rule and reign of David; not a spiritual Kingdom. Because of Jewish unbelief and rejection, the Kingdom was taken from them and was postponed to the end of the Church Age. One notable writer believes that, had the Jew accepted the King and the Kingdom, then Christ would not have needed to be crucified. God only permitted Calvary because of Jewish blindness and unbelief. At the end of the Church Age, the Jewish remnant will accept the Kingdom and preach the Gospel of the Kingdom in the end times, possibly after the rapture of the Church. Many will be saved under the Jewish evangelists, according to Futurist interpretations of Rev.7. This preaching will usher in, after the Great Tribulation, the next aspect of the Kingdom, which is the Millennial Kingdom. Futurist and Dispensational Pre-Millennialists agree on this.

3. **The Church**
   Futurist Pre-Millennialists teach that, because of the rejection of the King and the postponement of the Kingdom, God had, as it were "Plan B", a separate plan, and that was the creation of the Church. The Church actually is a parenthetical purpose of God because of Jewish blindness and hardness of heart and the postponement of the Kingdom. The Church also, is primarily a Gentile creation of God while the Kingdom is primarily a Jewish creation of God. Therefore, according to the Futurist, the Church and the Kingdom are two separate things and must not be confused. The Church (mainly Gentile), and the Kingdom (mainly Jewish) will be two separate entities, two separate peoples of God, both in Time and Eternity.
   The Church fills the "gap" between the Kingdom offered, rejected and postponed until the Kingdom is received, proclaimed and fulfilled. The Church was not seen in the Old Testament, according to Futurist's understanding of Eph.3:1-10. The Church was another plan, a different plan, and a secondary purpose in the mind of God, only because of Jewish hardness, blindness and rejection of the King.

4. **The Nation of Israel**
   Futurist Pre-Millennialists believe that most of the prophecies of the Old Testament concerning the national glory of Israel were never fulfilled. Hence, this School finds a literal, materialistic and nationalistic kind of Kingdom to be fulfilled in the future. This involves the possession of all the land promised in the Abrahamic Covenant, to Abraham, Isaac and Jacob, as well as to the nation. For the Futurist, God has two plans; one for Israel and one for the Church. These two plans for these two peoples must be distinguished and never confused. The nation of Israel will be "the

head" and not "the tail" in the coming Kingdom Age. Futurists and Dispensationalists hold a separate and distinct future for the Jew apart from the Church. The Jew is God's earthly people, and the Church is God's heavenly people. Israel is to be restored to Palestine; Jesus will be there on the Throne of David. The Davidic Kingdom will be established once again as a literal, materialistic, political and nationalistic Kingdom, ruling the nations of the earth. Jerusalem will be the earthly headquarters of Christ and His government and the Jews will be the head of the nations. The reader is referred to Number 13 in this chapter for further detail.

5. **The New Covenant**
Futurist Pre-Millennialists along with Dispensational Pre-Millennialists hold that the New Covenant has not yet been made. It is to be made in the future by Christ with the House of Israel and the House of Judah. This will particularly done in the coming Kingdom Age of 1000 years. Refer to comments on this point under Dispensational Pre-Millennialism.

6. **The Mosaic Covenant Economy**
Futurists, along with Dispensationalists, teach that there will be a total and complete re-institution and re-establishment of the Mosaic Covenant economy. There will be a rebuilt Temple set up in the Great Tribulation period. In this rebuilt Temple, Antichrist will set himself up as God to be worshipped. Many Jews will be saved in this period of time. Many will reject he Gospel of the Kingdom.
Ezekiel's Temple, in all its glory and administrations, with its Mosaic Covenant economy, will be built in the coming 1000 years Kingdom Age in Jerusalem, as the landscape is re-arranged by Christ at His second coming. The Aaronic and Levitical Priesthood will once again offer sacrifices and offerings. Festival days, Sabbath days, circumcision, and other areas of the Law, all will be re-instituted in the coming age. The Jews will become the "Missionary Nation" to all nations. The Lord will plague Nations who refuse to come to Jerusalem for worship. All will be made to bow to the "iron rule" of Christ in this time. Worship will be enforced. This is how the Futurist and Dispensational Schools interpret Isa.2:1-4 with Zech.14th chapter, and Ezek.40-48 chapters, along with other supportive Scriptures.

7. **The Rapture**
Futurists, along with Dispensationalists, teach that there will be a "secret rapture" of the true Church. This will take place either at the beginning of Daniel's seventieth week, the beginning of seven years tribulation, or, for some, it may be mid-week. Christ could come at any moment, as all prophecies relative to the Church and world conditions have been fulfilled. The Church may expect the rapture to take place any moment, any time, anywhere, day or night. The "secret rapture" will be like the Lord coming as "a thief in the night". The world will wake up too late once the rapture has taken place. This "secret coming" involves a resurrection of the dead also, and it is based upon the interpretation of 1Thess.4:15-18 and other "thief in the night" Scriptures.

8. **The Antichrist**
Futurist Pre-Millennialists, with the Dispensationalists, hold that there will be a personal Antichrist, a world dictator, appear in the end of the age. This Antichrist will make a Covenant with the Jewish nation, according to their understanding of the Seventy Weeks Prophecy. Antichrist will break this Covenant in the middle of this seventieth week. He will set himself up in the rebuilt Temple as God and seek to be worshipped as God. This Antichrist will rule over a One-World Empire, a One-World Government of ten kings, and the spirit of Antichrist controlling all. Antichrist will, by means of his partner, the False Prophet, set up a One World Religion and all will be forced to take "The Mark of the Beast" or die. Antichrist will be Satan incarnate. He, with his ten kings, will stand up against Christ at His coming, but will be destroyed by the brightness of Christ's advent and be cast into the Lake of Fire, along with the False Prophet. They will not appear at the Great White Throne Judgment. These weighty events take place in the last seven years of this age, prior to Christ's actual coming again.

9. **The Great Tribulation**
The Futurist and Dispensational Schools hold that there will be a special time of tribulation in the end of the age. This period of "the GREAT Tribulation" is the seven years, according to Daniel's prophecy. While believing there has always been some kind of tribulation through history, this period is "Tribulation, the Great one!" In this period of time, the wrath of God will be poured out

in the seven bowls of wrath on all who dare to take the Mark of the Beast, his number or his name. At the end of the seven-year Tribulation, Christ comes again.

10. The Second Coming of Christ

Futurists and Dispensationalists believe that there are two stages of Christ's coming. There are two comings of Christ, one where He comes "for" His saints and the other when He comes "with" His saints. These two stages are seven years apart. The secret coming is at the beginning of the seven years tribulation, and the open coming at the close of this same seven years. Within these Schools, some have "Pre", "Mid", "Partial" and even "Progressive" rapture going on in this time. Because "the dead in Christ rise first" and those who "are alive and remain" are caught up together, it makes for an extra resurrection before "the first resurrection" of Rev.20:1-6. Christ's coming, however, will be personal, visible, bodily and gloriously, with His holy angels and will usher in the 1000 years of the Kingdom Age.

11. The Binding of Satan

Futurists and Dispensationalists together see that the binding of Satan has yet to be fully executed. Though Satan and all his hosts were conquered at Calvary, the actual binding and casting into the Bottomless Pit does not take place until Christ comes again. This precedes the first resurrection.

12. The Resurrection

Futurist Pre-Millennialists, along with Dispensationalists, believe that there are mainly two resurrections and these are 1000 years apart. In general, the first resurrection takes place at either the secret rapture of the Church or at the second coming of Christ at the beginning of the Millennium. Some hold "the first resurrection" to be from the rapture to the revelation of Christ in order to make it all as "the first resurrection". Only the blessed and holy have part in the first resurrection. It is a resurrection of the just. This is the first resurrection and speaks of a physical and bodily resurrection in order to enter the Kingdom Age. The second resurrection is for the unjust. This takes place at the close of the 1000 years reign of Christ here on earth. It is the second resurrection and it is a resurrection of the wicked to judgment at the Great White Throne of God.

13. The Judgment

Futurists believe and teach that there are mainly two judgments; one for the believer at the beginning of the 1000 years Kingdom Age, the other for the unbelievers at the close of this period of time. One judgment is for the saints and this takes place at the "Bema Seat" of Christ. The saints are rewarded according to their works. The other judgment is for unbelievers and takes place at the Great White Throne Judgment. The sinners are also rewarded according to their works. The saints come unto full salvation, the sinners unto full damnation. One judgment begins the Millennium, the other closes it off. There are some variations in the scenes of judgment, especially in the Dispensational School of Eschatology.

14. The Millennial Kingdom

The view of the Futurist and Dispensational Pre-Millennialists concerning the Millennial Kingdom is, without doubt, the most controversial area of eschatology. Each of the Schools believe in some kind of Millennium, but "when", "where" and "what" are the issues involved.

The Futurist believes in a literal, materialistic, nationalistic kind of Millennial Kingdom. Christ will rule from Jerusalem, on the Throne of David. It will be a Davidic and Theocratic type of Kingdom, the Jews being the head of the nations. Along with the re-institution of the Mosaic economy, Ezekiel's Temple built, Christ will rule with a rod of iron. All "sheep nations" saved over from the previous age will submit to worship festivals at Jerusalem or come under judgment. Satan is bound in this 1000 years and is not able to deceive the nations in this time. Israel, God's elect nation, will rule over the nations. The prophecies concerning the glory and supremacy of Israel, as found in the Old Testament, will be fulfilled. The curse will be lifted. Longevity of life will be experienced. Earth will be as the Garden of Eden. The Church will be God's heavenly people, as Israel is God's earthly people. It will be a 'Jewish/Judaistic Millennium'. At the close of this 1000 years, Satan will be loosed out his prison for a little season. He will deceive the nations that feigned submission to Christ. They will compass the camp of Christ and the saints. Fire comes down and destroys them. The Great White Throne Judgment takes place and eternal destinies are settled there.

15. The Eternal States
Futurists, Dispensationalists, Historic Pre-Millennialists, along with Post-Millennialists and A-Millennialists – all see the eternal states in the New Heavens and New Earth and the Lake of Fire. Eternal destinies concerning heaven and hell are all settled at the close of the Millennium – whichever way the "Millennium" is interpreted. The A-Millennialist would hold that the second coming of Christ ushers in the eternal states and settles eternal destinies for angels and mankind, without having any intermediate period of 1000 years.

It would appear that the major reason this School is spoken of as "Futurists" is because of the strong teaching that Israel is yet to experience the fullness of the Old Testament prophecies in national glory. Seeing, in this School, this has not happened, it must take place in the Millennial Kingdom. National Israel, under the Mosaic Covenant, will come to Christ and He will exalt the nation above all nations, and all the unfulfilled prophecies about Israel will find fulfillment in the future Millennium, after Christ comes the second time. Hence, "Futurist Pre-Millennial" School of Eschatology.

CHAPTER FOUR

DISPENSATIONAL PRE-MILLENNIALISM

"Pre-Millennialism" has been defined in an earlier chapter as speaking of those Schools of Eschatology who believe that Christ comes the second time **before** the establishment of the Millennium Kingdom in the earth.

"Dispensational Pre-Millennialism" concerns that School of Eschatology who believe that Time is divided into seven periods called 'Dispensations', the seventh being the Millennial Kingdom established on earth after Christ's coming. This School arose out of the Futurist School. It also includes the restoration of natural and national Israel and the re-institution of the whole of the Mosaic Covenant economy. This is the major difference between Historic Pre-Millennialism and Futurist/Dispensational Pre-Millennialism.

Dispensational Pre-Millennialism teaches that God, in each period of time, deals with the human race on some one specific principle. Dr.C.I.Scofield says that, "A Dispensation is a period of time during which man is tested in respect to obedience to some specific revelation of the will of God." The major representatives of Dispensationalism are J.N.Darby (of the Plymouth Brethren), and Dr.C.I.Scofield. Clarence Larkin is also a notable Dispensationalist, his views expressed clearly in his text, **"Dispensational Truth"**. Dr.C.I.Scofield, and more especially the Scofield Reference Bible has become, without doubt, the major dispenser of Dispensational views. The Bible has been printed in the millions, many believers taking Scofield's reference notes almost as part of the inspired text.

So, although Historic, Futurists and Dispensationalists are all Pre-Millennialists as to the second coming of Christ, there is the great difference as to the Seven Dispensations and the position of National Israel in the purposes of God. In other words, all Dispensationalists are Pre-Millennialists, but not all Pre-Millennialists are Dispensationalists!

For the Dispensationalists, the Dispensations have a beginning and an end. They are governed by specific principles of God's dealing with man in each period of time. It is also to be recognized that, although there are some variations among Dispensationalists as to details, the primary view is that of the Seven Dispensations. The Scofield Bible teaches that these Dispensations are as follows:

1. Dispensation of Innocence – from the creation of Adam and Eve and their period of time in Eden until the Fall.
2. Dispensation of Conscience – from the Fall until the Flood. Conscience is defined as the knowledge of right and wrong during this period, because conscience was man's guide.
3. Dispensation of Human Government – from the Flood until the call of Abraham.
4. Dispensation of Promise – from the call of Abraham to the giving of the Law at Mt. Sinai. The special promises given to Abraham, Isaac and Jacob embraced the promise of redemption as given in Gen.3:15, given immediately after the Fall. Now the promises are given to the nation of Israel.
5. Dispensation of Law – from the giving of the Law at Mt. Sinai through to the completion of the ministry of Christ (Jhn 1:17; Lke.16:16).
6. Dispensation of Grace – from the closing days of Christ's ministry to the second coming. Or, this period covers the period of the Church, the period of grace, from the descent of the Holy Spirit to form "the mystery" (i.e., the Church) through to the rapture of the Church.
7. Dispensation of the Kingdom – from the return of Christ to the end of His reign on earth. This covers the Millennial period of 1000 years of the Kingdom Age. The New Heavens and the New Earth and those things that pertain to the eternal states then follow this.

It is necessary to understand in some measure the Dispensationalist's scheme of things as all have a great bearing on eschatological events, as seen in the brief explanation of the fifteen components of end-time events.

1. Daniel's Seventy Weeks Prophecy

Dispensational Pre-Millennialists (with Futurists) believe that the sixty-nine weeks of Daniel's prophecy were fulfilled generally at the entry of Jesus into Jerusalem just before His crucifixion. There remains but the seventieth week to be fulfilled. This seventieth week is placed at the end of the age, just prior to the second coming of Christ.

At the beginning of this week, the Antichrist comes and makes a Covenant with the Jewish nation. In the middle of this week (that is, in 3½ years), he breaks the Covenant with the Jews and sets himself up in a rebuilt Temple in Jerusalem to be worshipped as God. For the last half of this week (the final 3½ years), he is worshipped as God and all the world is made to receive the Mark of the Beast. At the close of the seventieth week, Christ comes again. The events of the seventieth week are dealt with in Rev.4-19th chapters. That is, from the rapture of the Church, represented in Rev.4:1-2, to the revelation of Christ seen in Rev.19:11-21. Most of the components dealt with in these chapters pertain to the seventieth week.

All of this is in contrast with Historic Pre-Millennialism, the Post-Millennialists and those who are A-Millennialists, who believe that the Seventy Weeks Prophecy has been fulfilled at Christ's first coming.

2. **The Kingdom**

Dispensational Pre-Millennialists basically follow the Futurist position as to the Kingdom of God. In "**The Meaning of the Millennium**" (Four Views, by Robert G. Clouse, pages 85-86), Hermon A.Hoyt, writing of the position of Dispensational Pre-Millennialists says it this way:

"In spite of the clear teaching of Christ, the King and His Kingdom were rejected. At the time of the first announcement of the Kingdom, Christ understood there was contingency. The offer of the Kingdom was genuine, but so also was the human contingency (Matt.10:5-17; 15:24). ...One day they wanted to make Him King, but the next day, they forsook Him (Jhn.6:15,60-66). ...This (i.e., opposition) finally culminated in the death of Christ, the rejection of the Kingdom and its suspension for the present (Matt.12:38-40). Having rejected the King, the nation of Israel rejected the Kingdom Christ came to establish."

Hoyt goes on to say how Christ explained to His disciples that the Kingdom would take on a "mystery form" until His second coming, when He would establish His Kingdom in the earth. Hoyt sees the establishment of the Kingdom in the Millennial Dispensation. The Church fills in this present time of Jewish rejection of the Kingdom.

Dispensationalism, while recognizing that the Kingdom of God is eternal and universal, sees the view that, in relation to the earth, there is a mediatorial Kingdom. This aspect of the Kingdom in earth has passed through successive stages, from Adam to Israel and on through human history. When Christ came and offered the Kingdom to the Jewish nation, the nation, as a whole, rejected both King and Kingdom and so the full manifestation of the Kingdom was postponed during this present Church Age, the Dispensation of Grace.

3. **The Church**

Dispensationalists, along with Futurists, believe that the Church was brought in as a parenthetical purpose of God. This came in because of Jewish unbelief and their rejection of the Messiah of God. The Church is primarily a Gentile thing and to be formed in the "gap" between the sixty-ninth and seventieth week of Daniel's prophecy.

Dispensationalists teach that the Church was not seen in Old Testament times but was a mystery revealed to Paul. The Church was God's Plan B because of Israel's blindness, hardness of heart and unbelief. The Church was God's secondary plan and is a different purpose of God, different to that which He planned for the Jews, as His chosen nation. The Church was God's substitute plan once Jewry rejected the King and the Kingdom. As noted, this is in direct opposition to the view of Historic Pre-Millennialists, as well as the Post-Millennial and A-Millennial views. These Schools see the Church as being in the eternal purpose of God, and eternally as God's Plan A, not Plan B.

4. **The Nation of Israel**

Dispensational Pre-Millennialists, as Futurists, hold that there is a separate and distinct purpose and future for the Jewish nation, apart from the Church. Accordingly, the Jew is to be restored to the land of Palestine. The view believes that the numerous prophecies in the Old Testament concerning the glory and blessing of national Israel are yet to be fulfilled.

After the restoration to the land, and the period of the Great Tribulation, the terrors of the reign of Antichrist, Jesus returns the second time. The Jewish nation have their eyes opened to their long-rejected Messiah. The nation, as a whole, will be converted to Christ. They will enter the Millennial Kingdom as a saved nation. As Christ's brethren after the flesh, the Jews will have a special place in the earthly Millennium. Christ will set up a nationalistic, political and materialistic

Kingdom as under David's times. Christ will reign on the Throne of David over all the nations of the earth, from Jerusalem. The Jews (Israel) will be the head of the nations, and the Old Testament prophecies of Israel's glory and blessing in the earth will then find fulfillment. It will be a Jewish Millennium in the full sense of the word. Futurists and Dispensationalists hold the same general view except that the Dispensationalists major on the Dispensations of Time.

5. **The New Covenant**
Dispensational Pre-Millennialists do not make much of the New Covenant. They do not seem to see the significance of it. Because of the concept and understanding of the Old Covenant and Mosaic economy being restored, and that the Jews will come to Christ by that Covenant, the importance and relevance of the New Covenant and the Old Covenant are missed.

One Dispensational writer goes so far as to say that the New Covenant has not yet been made but is to be made in a future Dispensation; that is, in the Millennial Kingdom. Clarence Larkin, in his text, "**Dispensational Truth**" (page 151) writes:

"The New Covenant has not yet been made. This is to be made with Israel after they get back to their own land. It is promised in Jer.31:31-34. It is unconditional and will cover the Millennium and the New Heavens and New Earth. It is based on the finished work of Christ (Matt.26:28). It has nothing to do with the Church and does not belong to this Dispensation. It is the 'Eighth Covenant' and speaks of the **Resurrection and Eternal Completeness**." Comments on this view will be noted in the appropriate time.

6. **The Mosaic Covenant Economy**
Dispensational Pre-Millennialists (as Futurists) see a complete restoration and re-institution of the Mosaic Covenant economy, either in the end of this age or the Millennial Age to come. There are a number of variations in the Dispensational School as to exact details. Basically, Dispensationalists teach that there will be a rebuilt material Temple in Jerusalem during the days of the Great Tribulation. Antichrist will sit in the Temple as God, and, according to their understanding and interpretation of the Seventy Weeks Prophecy, "he will cause the sacrifice and oblation to cease". He will then demand worship as God. Many Jews, converted to Christ, will refuse to do so and will be martyred accordingly. The whole world will be forced to take the Mark of the Beast.

The Temple of Ezekiel's vision is understood to find its fulfillment in the Millennium, in the restored city of Jerusalem. The Jews will be the head of the nations under Messiah Jesus. He will rule on the Throne of David with a rod of iron. All nations, who fail to come to Jerusalem for worship in the Feast of Tabernacles, will come under Divine judgments. Old Testament prophecies that speak of a literal, nationalistic and materialistic Kingdom will find fulfillment in the Millennium. Some of the major Scriptures used to under-gird this theory are Ezek.40-48 chapters, with Zech.12-14-14 chapters, Isa.2:1-5; Mic.4:1-8; Isa.11:1-11; 65:17-25; Dan.2; Dan.7; Rev.20:1-10, as well as many others. It will be predominantly a Jewish Millennial Kingdom!

Clarence Larkin, in "**Dispensational Truth**" (pages 150-151) writes: The Mosaic Covenant was given to Moses at Mt. Sinai, shortly after the Exodus from Egypt. It ushered in the 'Dispensation of Law'. It was conditional on obedience, and may be divided into three parts.
    (1) The Moral Law (Ex.20:1-26). This consists of the Ten Commandments.
    (2) The Civil Law (Ex.21:1—24:18).
    (3) The Ceremonial Law (Ex.25:1—40:38). This includes the Tabernacle, the Priesthood, and the Order of Service. The Sign of this Covenant is the Sabbath (Ex.31:12-18).
This Covenant continued in force until the Jews were scattered at the destruction of Jerusalem in A.D.70. It will be renewed when Israel is converted and restored to their own land, and will then be known as the 'Palestinian Covenant', which Covenant ends in the 'Renovation of the Earth by Fire'." The quotation speaks clearly for the Dispensational and Futurist view of the Old Covenant.

7. **The Rapture**
Dispensationalists, with Futurists, teach that Christ could return at any moment, and by a "secret rapture" transport the true Church to glory. Dr.Robert Strong provides a good definition of the rapture. He says: "By the Rapture is meant the sudden and possibly secret coming of Christ in the air to catch away from the earth the resurrected bodies of those who have died in faith and with them the living saints" (**The Presbyterian Guardian**. Feb.25th,1942).

They hold that this rapture takes place at the beginning of the seven years Great Tribulation, and so the Church will not be here on earth in this period of time, Daniel's Seventieth Week. The Church is raptured out of the world before the Tribulation begins.

Dispensationalists (and Futurists) teach that Christ's coming is in two stages, these being "the rapture" and "the revelation". In the first stage, Christ comes "for" His saints, while in the second stage, He comes "with" His saints. This is based on their interpretation and understanding of 1Thess.4:15-18 with Rev.4:1-2. This teaching makes Dispensationalists both Pre-Tribulationists and Pre-Millennialists. That is, Christ raptures the Church out of the world **before** the Great Tribulation, and Christ also comes with the Church **before** the Millennial Kingdom is ushered in.

8. **The Antichrist**
Dispensationalists with Futurists believe that the Antichrist is an individual person. He will reign during the seven years Tribulation period. Antichrist will be ruler over a ten-kingdom empire and will conquer the world in this final period before the coming again of the Lord Jesus Christ. The Antichrist will be a world dictator or emperor, over a one-world government. The system and the spirit of Antichrist will control the world.
As already mentioned, this Antichrist makes a seven-year Covenant with the Jewish rulers and in the middle of this period of time, breaks the Covenant. He sets himself up in the rebuilt Temple in Jerusalem and all the world is caused to receive the Mark of the Beast, his Number or his Name (666), or else be killed. Antichrist, along with his co-regent, called the False Prophet, and the ten subordinate kings, will stand up against Christ, the Lamb, at His second coming. When Christ comes, He overcomes all enemies, and the Antichrist- "The Beast" – with the False Prophet, are cast into the Lake of Fire without even appearing at the Great White Throne Judgment. This takes place at the beginning of the 1000 years Kingdom Dispensation.

9. **The Great Tribulation**
Dispensational Pre-Millennialists, with Futurists, because of their understanding and interpretation of the Seventy Weeks Prophecy, see that the seventieth week becomes the period of the Great Tribulation.
While there is some variation as to detail, the general view is, as already noted, the Antichrist makes a Covenant with Jewry at the beginning of this seven-year period. The first half of this week is in peace. In the middle of this week, Antichrist breaks the Covenant, and the final half of this week is Tribulation proper. In general then, the Dispensationlists teach either a seven-year or three and one-half years Tribulation. In this period of time, all of the events of Rev.4-19 chapters find fulfillment. That is, the seven seals, the seven trumpets and the seven bowls of wrath – all these things take place within this short period of seven years. All consummate with the seven bowls of wrath being poured out on all who take the Mark of the Beast, those who worship the Antichrist.

Relative to this same period of time, the Holy Spirit, who is here in measure, uses the Jewish remnant, the 144,000 Israelites of Rev.7, who have come to Christ, to preach the Gospel of the Kingdom in the earth. Many are saved, even though the Holy Spirit has raptured the Church. Those who are saved are called "tribulation saints", seen also in the latter half of Rev.7. How the multitudes are saved when the Holy Spirit has been withdrawn is not generally explained. The Great Tribulation ends with the second coming of Christ, who destroys the Antichrist and his armies in the Battle of Armageddon.

10. **The Second Coming of Christ**
Dispensationalists, along with Futurists, hold that there are two stages to Christ's coming. Christ comes, first of all "for His saints", and then later on, "with His saints". These two stages are seven years apart. As already mentioned:
   (a) The Rapture
      This is the "secret coming" of Christ FOR His saints. There are varying views about the possible secret rapture. Some are Pre-Tribulation rapture, some Mid-Tribulation rapture, some Partial-Tribulation rapture, and even some Progressive-Tribulation rapture, but all are related to the seven years Tribulation.
      The rapture is spoken of and supported by the "thief-in-the-night" Scriptures on the coming of the Lord. He comes secretly, silently, and, as a thief, takes away the valuables to his place. With this, there is a "the first resurrection" of the saints, the dead in Christ. Again, there are varying views. Some have Pre-Tribulation rapture/resurrection, and

others, Mid-, Partial- or Progressive rapture/resurrection of saints and martyrs, all taking place in this seven year tribulation period. This is done in order to make any or all of these as part of the "first resurrection", rather than a series of rapture/resurrections before the "first resurrection". The reader may see the difficulties in this variety of beliefs in the Dispensational School.

(b) The Revelation

This stage of Christ's coming is the personal, visible and bodily coming of the Lord. He brings His saints WITH Him and this stage takes place at the conclusion of the seven years Great Tribulation period. In diagram form, it would be something like this.

The Rapture - Christ comes **for** His saints	The Great Tribulation of 7 Years Antichrist Reign	The Revelation – Christ comes **with** His saints

11. The Binding of Satan

Dispensationalism also sees that the binding of Satan and his being cast into the Bottomless Pit does not take place until Christ returns. Satan and his powers were all conquered at the cross, their total and final defeat made possible, but this judgment on Satan, this binding is fulfilled at the second coming. The nations, at present, are still being deceived by Satan and his demonic hosts.

12. The Resurrection

Dispensational Pre-Millennialists, along with the Historic and Futurist Schools, believe in two resurrections. These two resurrections are both physical and bodily resurrections and take place 1000 years apart. Each of these views hold that the just or the righteous are the ones in the FIRST resurrection and the unjust or unrighteous are those in the SECOND resurrection.

The righteous are judged at the Judgment Seat of Christ (Grk. "Bema") and rewarded according to their works, and enter the Millennial Kingdom. The wicked are judged at the Great White Throne Judgment, and rewarded according to their works. These will be cast into the Lake of Fire at the close of the 1000-year period.

This is in contrast to Post-Millenialists and A-Millennialists, who believe that the "first resurrection" is absolutely spiritual, and the "general resurrection" is a physical and bodily resurrection of both the just and the unjust. This "general resurrection" takes place at the coming of Christ.

13. The Judgment

Dispensationalists with Futurists see the two major judgments of the just and the unjust, one at the beginning of the Millennial Kingdom and the other at its close. Some Dispensationalists, however, teach that there are seven judgments in all. And again, there are variations within this School on the number of Judgments, some, as Clarence Larkin, reducing the list to five. The Scofield Bible, the textbook for modern Dispensationalism, sets forth seven judgments, which are as follows:

1. The Judgment of Believer's Sin – took place when Christ died on the cross.
2. The Judgment of Self in the believers – takes place as the believer learns to judge himself.
3. The Judgment of Believer's works – takes place at the "Bema" Seat of Christ.
4. The Judgment of the Living Nations – takes place at Christ's coming as "Sheep nations".
5. The Judgment of Israel – takes place when Christ comes and establishes the Kingdom.
6. The Judgment of Fallen Angels – takes place when Satan is finally judged.
7. The Great White Throne Judgment – takes place at the close of the Millennium and ushers in the Eternal States.

14. The Millennial Kingdom

Dispensationalists and Futurists belong in the same school of thought as to the Millennium. The teaching is that, when Christ comes the second time, He will, after destroying Antichrist and his armies, set up His Kingdom on earth. This Kingdom will be a literal, materialistic, nationalistic and Davidic kind of Kingdom, a theocratic form of government. Christ will rule the nations with a rod of iron. The Jews, as Christ's brethren after the flesh, will be head of the nations, fulfilling Old Testament prophecies of Israel's glories among the Gentiles.

Clarence Larkin, in "**Dispensational Truth**" (page 151) has this to say about Israel in this time. "This (Palestinian) Covenant was given to Israel through Moses, and is conditional on the repentance of Israel. It will go into effect after their return to Palestine. It ushers in the 'Millennial Dispensation' and ends with it."

Satan is bound in this period of 1000 years. The nations are not deceived. Israel, as God's elect nation, will rule over the Gentile nations and thus fulfill the prophecies of destination of which the prophets spoke. It will be a Jewish Kingdom in deed and in truth.

There will be longevity of life, children will be born, the curse on earth will be lifted and the earth shall be as the Garden of the Lord, a veritable Edenic Paradise on earth.

Dispensationalists vary as to full details. Some hold that the Church will possibly be "God's heavenly people" and the Jews will be "God's earthly people". There will be a mingling of mortals and immortals here on earth. Glorified saints and mortal sinners will be together.

The Kingdom that the Jews rejected at Christ's first coming and was postponed to the end of the age, will now be ushered in as to its full glory. Dispensationalists believe this is the seventh Dispensation or the Kingdom Age.

At the close of this earthly, glorious Millennial Kingdom, Satan will be loosed for a little season. The second resurrection, that of the wicked dead, takes place. Satan will deceive the nations in the four corners of the earth. These nations have submitted to Christ's iron rule and have rendered feigned obedience and worship over the years. As Gog and Magog, they have one final attempt to overthrow Christ and the camp of the saints. Fire descends. The Great White Throne Judgment takes place. Eternal destinies are settled and all find themselves in the New Heavens and New Earth or the eternal Hell, the Lake of Fire.

Dispensationalists have a general outline as to the conditions prevailing in the Millennium.
1. There will be peace on earth (Isa.2:4). Wars will cease.
2. There will be universal prosperity (Zech.8:12; Isa.60:17).
3. There will longevity of life (Isa.65:20; Zech.14:17-19). The wicked will be punished with an early death, while the good will live through the 1000 years, more or less.
4. Creation itself will be delivered from the curse (Isa.65:25; 11:8,9). There will be no storms, floods and disasters in nature.
5. Christ and His apostles will reign in the order of the Kingdom (Matt.19:28).
6. The Jews will be head over the Gentile nations, fulfilling Old Testament prophecies.
7. Christ rules all with a rod of iron, and nations are forced to worship the Lord.
8. All nations will keep the Feast of Tabernacles or be plagued (Zech.14).
9. Ezekiel's Temple and the Mosaic Covenant will be restored for all to keep.
10. Mortals and immortals will mingle together in this Kingdom. Sinless and glorified saints will be with sinful and mortal beings on earth.
11. The end of the Millennium shows man's heart is evil even under the reign of Christ.
12. Satan heads the final rebellion and then all are judged and eternal destinies settled.

15. The Eternal States
All the varying Schools of Millennial Eschatology have general agreement as to the eternal states. At the Great White Throne, eternal destinies are settled for the angelic hosts and for all mankind. The holy angels and the redeemed of mankind will enjoy eternal bliss in the New Heavens and New Earth. The Devil, the fallen angels, the demon spirits, along with the unredeemed of the human race, will suffer the torments of the damned in the final and eternal Hell, the Lake of Fire.

Lorraine Boettner, in "**The Millennium**", has given permission to use material from his text with or without credit. With credit to the author, however, we quote from pages 141-143. Boettner provides an excellent **summary** of major points of Pre-Millennialism. The reader must allow for differences between Historic Pre-Millennialism and the twin Schools of Futurist and Dispensational Pre-Millennialists. The writer felt that this would be a good summary of all the points covered in these first several chapters.

He writes: "The Pre-Millennial system is considerably more complicated than either the Post-Millennial or the A-Millennial system and, consequently, it has also been attended with greater diversity of opinion among its advocates. But despite these differences, it has been characteristic of both Schools of Pre-Millennialism to hold:

1. That the Kingdom of God is not now in the world, and that it will not be instituted until Christ returns.
2. That it is not the purpose of the present Gospel Age to convert the world to Christianity, but rather to preach the Gospel as a witness to the nations and so to warn them of and make them justly subject to judgment. Also to gather out of all nations God's elect, the Church saints.
3. That the world is growing worse and will continue to grow worse until Christ comes to establish His Kingdom.
4. That immediately preceding the return of Christ, there is to be a period of general apostasy and wickedness.
5. That we are now in the latter stages of the Church Age and that the return of Christ is near, probably to occur within the lifetime of the present generation.
6. That at Christ's coming the righteous dead of all ages are to be raised in the "first resurrection."
7. That the resurrected dead together with the transfigured living saints who are then on the earth are to be caught up to meet the Lord in the air.
8. That the judgment of all the righteous then takes place, which judgment consists primarily in the assignment of rewards.
9. That before and during the tribulation period the Jews are to be restored to the land of Palestine.
10. That at the mere sight of their Messiah the Jews are to turn to Him in a national conversion and true repentance.
11. That Christ at His coming destroys the Antichrist and all his forces in the Battle of Armageddon.
12. That after the Battle of Armageddon, Christ establishes a world-wide Kingdom with Jerusalem as its capital, in which He and the resurrected and transfigured saints rule for a thousand years in righteousness, peace and prosperity.
13. That during this reign, the city of Jerusalem and the Temple are to be rebuilt, the Feasts and the Fasts and the Priesthood, ritual and sacrificial system re-instituted, though performed in a Christian spirit and by Christian worshippers.
14. That the golden age also is to be characterized by the removal of the curse from nature so that the desert shall blossom as the rose and the wild ferocious nature of the beasts shall be changed.
15. That during the Millennium, great numbers of the Gentiles will turn to God and be incorporated into the Kingdom.
16. That while many remain unconverted and rebellious at heart, they are not destroyed, but are held in check by the rod-of-iron rule of Christ.
17. That during the Millennium, Satan is to be bound, cast into the Abyss, and so shut away from the earth.
18. That at the close of the Millennium, Satan is to be loosed for a short time.
19. That the Millennium is to be followed by a short but violent outbreak of wickedness and rebellion, headed by Satan, which all but overwhelms the saints and the holy city of Jerusalem.
20. That the forces of wickedness are to be destroyed by fire which is cast down upon them from heaven.
21. That the wicked dead of all ages are then to be raised in the "second resurrection", judged, and with the Devil and the wicked angels, cast into Hell.
22. That Heaven and Hell are then introduced in their fullness, with the New Heavens and the New Earth as the future home of the redeemed, which will constitute the eternal state.

We trust the reader will bear with this Summary as it brings together the tenets and philosophy of the Dispensational and Futurist School of Eschatology!

BIBLIOGRAPHY

DISPENSATIONAL PRE-MILLENNIALISM
(Includes Futurist Pre-Millennialism)

1. Anderson, Robert., The Coming Prince, 1969
2. Blackstone, Wm.E., Jesus is Coming, 1878
3. Brookes, James M., Maranatha, 1876, 1889
4. Chafer, L.S., Systematic Theology, 1948
5. Chafer, L.S., Dispensationalism, 1936, 1951
6. Dake, Finis Jennings., God's Plan for Man, 1949, 1977
7. Darby, John N., Synopsis of the Books of the Bible, 5 Vols, 1950
8. Feinberg, Charles L., Pre-Millennialism or A-Millennialism? 1936
9. Gaebelein, Arno C., The Harmony of the Prophetic Word, 1907
10. Gaelelein, Arno C., The Return of the Lord, 1925
11. Gray, James M., Prophecy and the Lord's Return, 1917
12. Haldeman, I.M., The Coming of Christ, Both Pre-Millennial and Imminent, 1906
13. Hoyt, Herman A., The End Times, 1969
14. Ironside, H.A., Lectures on the Revelation, 1930
15. Ironside, H.A., The Lamb of Prophecy, 1940
16. Larkin, Clarence., Dispensational Truth, 1918, 1920
17. Lindsay, Hal., The Terminal Generation, 1976
18. Lindsay, Hal., The Late Great Planet Earth, 1970
19. Lindsay, Hal., There's a New World Coming, 1973
20. Morgan, G. Campbell., God's Methods With Man, 1898
21. Pache, Rene., The Return of Jesus Christ, 1955
22. Pentecost, J. Dwight., Things to Come, 1959
23. Pentecost, J. Dwight., Prophecy for Today, 1961
24. Peters, G.H.N., The Theocratic Kingdom of our Lord Jesus Christ, 3 Vols., 1884, 1957
25. Ryrie, Charles C., Dispensationalism Today, 1965
26. Sauer, Erich., From Eternity to Eternity., 1954
27. Scofield Reference Bible, 1909, Revised 1917, New Edition, 1967
28. Scofield, C.I., Rightly Dividing the Word of Truth (Booklet, 64 pages)
29. Seiss, Joseph.,Millenialism and The Second Advent
30. Walvoord, John F., The Rapture Question, 1957
31. Walvoord, John F., The Millennial Kingdom, 1959

CHAPTER FIVE

POST-MILLENNIALISM

Loraine Boettner provides one of the most accurate, yet comprehensive definitions of Post-Millennialism, in his text **"The Millennium"** (page 4). He writes: "Post-Millennialism is that view of the last things which holds that the Kingdom of God is now being extended through the preaching of the Gospel and the saving work of the Holy Spirit, that the world eventually will be Christianized, and that the return of Christ will occur at the close of a long period of righteousness and peace commonly called the **Millennium**."

A briefer definition is, Post-Millennialists are those who believe that Christ will not return until after (Post) the Millennium has been ushered in by the ministry of the Church militant, and the proclamation of the Gospel of the Kingdom Christianizing the world. Post-Millennialism has a very simple yet positive approach to end-time events, as their view on the fifteen components of Eschatology show.

1. **Daniel's Seventy Weeks Prophecy**
    Post-Millennialists see that the notable prophecy of Daniel's Seventy Weeks has been fulfilled in the nation of Israel, consummating in the first coming of Christ. All is fulfilled in Him. Historic Pre-Millennialism would agree on this point.

2. **The Kingdom**
    As noted already, Post-Millennialism holds a very strong and positive approach, especially when it comes to the subject of the Kingdom of God. To the Post-Millennialists, the Kingdom of God is an everlasting Kingdom and the purpose of God is to establish His Kingdom in the earth through the ministry of the Church. By this ministry, the Church will usher in the Millennium. A study of the Post-Millennial view of final things is vitally linked with the message of the Kingdom preached by the Church which ushers in the coming 'Utopia' – the Millennial Kingdom, making some over-lap of this theme.

    Loraine Boettner (A Post-Millennialist) presents the position well. From the text we adapt the following points in brief outline. Post-Millennialists hold:

    - The world will be Christianized by the Church preaching the Gospel of the Kingdom. The many Scriptures which speak of "all nations" (Psa.86:9; 22:27; 2:8; 47:2-8; 72:7-17; 110:1; Isa.2:2-4; Ezek.47:1-5 with Matt.28:18-20), point to this.
    - The world will hear the Gospel. The many Scriptures, which speak of "the world", confirm this also (Jhn.3:16-17; 11:29; 4:42; 8:12; 1Jhn.2:29; 4:14).
    - The whole earth is to see the glory of God. The many Scriptures which speak of "the earth" also confirm this (Psa.47:2; 97:5; Zech.9:10; Isa.11:9; 49:6; 40:5; 45:22; Num.14:21).
    - "All flesh" is to come under the outpouring of the Holy Spirit in the last days (Joel 2:28). For the Post-Millennialist, these Scriptures point to the conversion of the world to Christ, though not every individual, of course.
    - The Gentiles will come into the Kingdom (Acts 15:17-18).
    - The Stone Kingdom of Christ will crush the Kingdoms of this world and fill the whole earth (Dan.2:44).
    - The Son of Man will destroy the Beast Kingdoms of the earth (Dan.7:27).
    - The Kingdom of Heaven will 'leaven' the whole of humanity (Matt.13:33).
    - The Kingdom of Heaven will grow like the seed of the mustard tree and will fill the whole earth (Matt.13:31-32).
    - All nations are to be blessed through the Seed of Abraham (Gal.3:7,16,29; Gen.13:16; 22:17).
    - Jesus told His disciples to make disciples of all nations (Matt.28:18-20).
    - More people will be saved than those lost according to Rev.7:9-10.
    - The world is growing better as things are considered socially, morally, economically, judicially and scientifically.
    - Earth will be blessed with fruitfulness as in the Garden of Eden as more nations are Christianized in the Millennium.
    - The Millennium will approach with imperceptible degrees, not by any sudden introduction. Just as the Church Age blends into the Millennial Age, by a long and slow process, so the

Millennium will hardly be known or noticed. The Kingdom will come without observation, just as illustrated in the Parable of the Kingdom Seed (Lke.17:20 with Mrk.4:28).

The student will see the need to spell out the Post-Millennial view of the Kingdom and its evident bearing on the coming Millennium, as seen in the eyes of Post-Millennialism.

3. **The Church**

   Post-Millennialists, as a whole, see that the Church is in the eternal purpose of God and that there is only one way to God, through faith in Christ, for both Jew and Gentile. The Prophets who spoke of the Gentiles coming into the Kingdom of God did not understand "the mystery" that was revealed to Paul, that Jews and Gentiles would be ONE BODY in Christ. Jews and Gentiles would be ONE OLIVE TREE. They saw the Gentiles coming into the Kingdom with Israel, but did not understand the Church as being the Body of Christ, made up of believing Israel and believing Gentiles.

   Post-Millennialists see that the Kingdom was taken from Jewry and given to the "holy nation" – the Church (Matt.21:43 with 1Pet.2:2-10). Post-Millennialists see Old Testament prophecies, spoken of Israel then, now applied by the New Testament writers, to the New Testament Church. The true Israel in the New Testament is the Church (Gal.2:28,29; 3:7; Eph.2:14-16; 3:1-11; Gal.6:16). The true Israel is saved by faith (Rom.11:26; 16:25-26). The cross broke down the middle wall of partition between Old Testament Israel and the Gentiles. The rent veil made way for both ethnic groupings to have access within the veil.

   The following diagram illustrates the Post-Millennialists view of the relationship of the Old Testament to the New Testament.

The Old Testament	The Work of the Cross	The New Testament
Natural, National Israel	**Calvary**	**Spiritual. Heavenly Israel**
Father Abraham		Father God
Seed of Abraham	Christ broke down the	Seed of Abraham by Faith
Nation of Israel	Middle Wall of Partition	Church – Spiritual Israel
Promised Land	between Jew and Gentile	Abraham Heir of the World
Aaronic/Levitical Priesthood		Melchisedek Priesthood
Sacrifices and Oblations	Veil of Temple Rent	Spiritual Sacrifices to God
Moral and Civil Laws	from top to bottom	His Laws – Tables of Heart
To Bless the Nations of Earth	Access to God for all	Church – Disciples all Nations
First the Natural	**"In Christ"**	**Afterwards the Spirit**
Israel – Olive Tree		**Church – Olive Tree**

4. **The Nation of Israel**

   Post-Millennialism sees that the promises given to Israel in the Old Testament have either been fulfilled in the Restoration from the Babylonian Captivity, or, they have been forfeited or cancelled by a disobedient nation. Post-Millennialists teach that there is nothing for the Jew (National Israel) outside of Christ and the New Covenant. Since the cross, the Jew has been set aside. There will never be a restoration of natural or national Israel to being a Kingdom as under Davidic times. The Kingdom of David pointed to the Kingdom of Christ, the greater Son of David, who is now on David's Throne (Psa.110; Acts 2). Wrath came on the Jews and their only hope is "in Christ" (1Thess.2:16). Some even hold that there are no true physical Jews to be found, as the race was absorbed into other races by inter-marriage, and that the so-called "restoration of Israel to the land" in these days is but a political scheme, not Biblical prophecies being fulfilled.

   Post-Millennialists understand that the promises given to Israel were conditional upon their obedience (Deut.28:13-25, 45-46; Jer.18:9-10; 1Sam.2:30. Jonah 3:4; 4:1-2). Once they broke the covenant conditions, God was not obligated to fulfill these promises. When people question the "everlasting" promises, Post-Millennialists answer that these promises never have been and never can be "everlasting" as we understand it. Examples of this are seen in these references.

   - Everlasting possession of the Promised Land (Gen.17:8; 1Kgs.4:2).
   - Everlasting Aaronic Priesthood (Ex.40:15).
   - Everlasting Feast of Passover (Ex.12:4).
   - Everlasting Sabbath (Ex.31:17).
   - Everlasting Throne of David (2Sam.7:13,16,24).

5. The New Covenant

The Post-Millennialists holds that the New Covenant, established by Christ, totally and forever replaces the Old Covenant. The New Testament writers use the New Covenant to interpret the Old Testament Scriptures. The Old Testament should not be used to interpret the New Testament, and this especially since the work of Christ on Calvary (Jer.31:31-34 with Heb.8).

6. The Mosaic Covenant Economy

Post-Millennialists agree that the Old Covenant or the Mosaic economy has been fulfilled and abolished in Christ at Calvary. It will never ever be restored or re-instituted in this age or any age to come. The Temple, the Aaronic Priesthood, the animal sacrifices and oblations, the Festival and Sabbath days – all have been fulfilled in Christ on the cross. To restore the things of the Mosaic Covenant is to violate the New Testament revelation of Christ's ministry. It would negate the whole testimony of the Book of Hebrews (Heb.10:10-14). In this point there is strong agreement between Historic Pre-Millennialism, Post-Millennialism and A-Millennialism.

7. The Rapture

Post-Millennialists see that the rapture of the Church will take place at the second coming of the Lord Jesus Christ. The rapture of the Church and the revelation of Christ take place at one and the same period of time. There is no such thing as a "secret rapture" any time before the actual, bodily, visible and personal second coming of Christ.

8. The Antichrist

Post-Millennialists believe that the Antichrist (or Antichrists) are symbolic and figurative of all the wicked leaders and hostile forces arrayed in conflict against the Church, the people of God. These Antichristal powers and spirit seek to hinder the spread of the Gospel to the nations by the Church during this present time. All will be overcome and subdued by the power of the Gospel in this era, ushering in the Millennial 'Utopia' of a better world. The binding of Satan for a 1000 years is to be done gradually as the Church ministers triumphantly and victoriously in the power of the Gospel. This "binding of Satan" is being accomplished throughout this age.

9. The Great Tribulation

Post-Millennialists hold that "the tribulation" is simply the opposition of Satan and his forces against the people of God. There has always been resistance, opposition and persecution through the ages of time, in greater or lesser degree. Some believe that "the tribulation" period was fulfilled in A.D.70 in the destruction of Jerusalem by Prince Titus and the Roman armies, according to the prophetic words of Christ in Matt.24. It also speaks of "the Great Tribulation" that the Church has endured over the ages of time. Luke wrote, "We must through much tribulation enter the Kingdom of God" (Acts 14:22). Jesus told His disciples also, "In the world, you will have tribulation, but be of good cheer, for I have overcome the world" (Jhn.16:33). Any and all tribulation will consummate in the close of history and before or at the second coming of Christ. Historic Pre-Millennialists, Post-Millennialists and A-Millennialists would agree on this point also.

10. The Second Coming of Christ

Post-Millennialists believe that there is only one coming of Christ. As already mentioned, the rapture of the Church and the coming or revelation of Christ takes place in one and the same time. There are not two stages to Christ's advent. Christ does not come "for" His saints first in a secret coming and then come "with" His saints some seven years later, or, after the Great Tribulation. There is only one coming of Christ. That is, Christ comes visibly, gloriously, bodily and personally. He comes "for" and "with" His saints at one and the same time.

Robert G. Clouse, quoting Loraine Boettner (a Post-Millennialist) speaks of eight ways in which Christ "comes" either "for" or "to" His people. They are noted and adapted in brief here.
There is:

- The coming of Christ for the Christian at the time of death (Jhn.14:2-3). This is the coming with which all individuals should be concerned.
- The coming of Christ in judgment. Christ came in judgment on apostate Israel in A.D.70 according to Christ's prophetic words in Matt.24.
- The coming of Christ to His disciples after His resurrection. Christ's post-resurrection appearances were like a literal, visible and personal coming, fulfilling Jhn.14:18,28; 16:16, where Jesus promised "I will come to you".

- The coming of Christ on the Day of Pentecost in the outpouring of the Holy Spirit on the disciples in the upper room (Acts 2).
- The coming of Christ to the Churches in Asia Minor. Christ told several of the Churches that He would "come" to them if they did not repent. He came to several and removed their lampstand (Rev.2:5).
- The coming of Christ to believers, and a presence of Christ through the Spirit with believers of all ages. This was and is a fulfillment of His promise in Jhn.14:26 with Matt.18:20.
- The coming of Christ to various cities in Palestine during His public ministry while here on earth. "The Son of Man comes" to the cities in His ministry after the Seventy had been before Him, sent out by Him two by two (Matt.10:23; Lke.10:1).
- The coming of Christ, visibly and gloriously at the end of the age.

(Refer to "**The Millennium – Four Views**", Robert G. Clouse, pages 206-208). The Post-Millennialist believes it is important to distinguish which "coming" of Christ is spoken of in the particular passage under consideration.

Historic, Post- and A-Millennialists do agree that the Rapture and the Revelation take place at one and the same time, at the end of the present age, regardless of "where" each place the Millennium. Some Post-Millennialists do not believe that Rev.19:11-21 is the actual coming of Christ but symbolizes the conflict or good and evil during the present age.

11. The Binding of Satan
Post-Millennialists believe that Satan is being "progressively bound" during the Church era. This is done by the Church's ministry, the Church militant and triumphant over all the powers of the enemy, all made possible because of what Christ did on the cross. Satan will finally be conquered in total when Christ comes the second time and Satan is cast into the Lake of Fire.

12. The Resurrection
Post-Millennialists believe that there is only one resurrection, a general resurrection. They hold that there is no "first" or "second" resurrection, as taught by Historic, Futurist and Dispensational Pre-Millennialists. The resurrection of the just and the unjust takes place at one and the same time, as seen in Jhn.5:21-29 with Rev.20:1-6.

13. The Judgment
Post-Millennialism teaches that there is but one resurrection of the just and the unjust and this is followed by one general judgment of both. This judgment takes place at Christ's Judgment Seat or the Great White Throne Judgment, one and the same thing in the understanding of Post-Millennialists. There is no such thing as two judgments, one for the believer and the other for the unbeliever, and these, 1000 years apart. It is at this general judgment that eternal destinies are forever settled. All will be judged according to their works.

14. The Millennial Kingdom
The Post-Millennial view of the Kingdom is unique and different from other Millennial positions. The Post-Millennialist view is spelled out best by one of their own writers. Loraine Boettner in his text, "**The Millennium**" (page 19), permission being given to quote freely, says:

"The Post-Millennialist looks for a golden age that will not be essentially different from our own, so far as the basic facts of life are concerned. This Age gradually merges into the Millennial Age as an increasingly larger proportion of the world's inhabitants are converted to Christianity. Marriage and the home will continue, and new members will enter the human race through the natural process of birth as at present. Sin will not be eliminated, but will be reduced to a minimum as the moral and spiritual environment of the earth becomes predominantly Christian. Social, economic and educational problems will remain, but, with their unpleasant features greatly eliminated and their desirable features heightened. Christian principles of belief and conduct will be the accepted standards. Life during the Millennium will compare with life in the world today in much the same way that life in a Christian community compares with that in a pagan or irreligious community. The Church, much more zealous in her testimony to the truth and much more influential in the lives of the people, will continue to be then as now, the outward manifestation of the Kingdom of God on earth." (End Quote)

Other points worthy of note are:

- The Millennium will not be a sinless or perfect state, but righteousness and peace prevail, as the world in general is Christian, though certainly not every individual. The world as a whole, however, will be converted (Isa.11:9).
- Rev.19:11-21 is not Christ's coming before the Utopian Millennium but symbolic of His triumph over His enemies.
- The binding of Satan is a long process that takes place over the Church era.
- The 1000 years is a symbolic number, an indefinite long period of time, but it is a limited period of time, as other numbers in Revelation signify.
- There will be a short time of final rebellion and apostasy at the end of the Millennium but it is quickly put down by Christ's judgments.
- This is "the end" when Christ delivers up the Kingdom to the Father and all flows on into the eternal Kingdom of the Father (1Cor.15:24-28).

In the understanding and teaching of Post-Millennialists, Christ comes at the **END** of the 1000 years Millennium, and **NOT at the BEGINNING** as the Historic, Futurist and Dispensational Pre-Millennialists teach. The Post-Millennial view would coincide with the A-Millennial point of view. Christ comes at the close of the symbolic Millennial period. The reader is referred to the Bibliography for fuller exposition of the Post-Millennial view.

15. The Eternal States

Post-Millennialists see the age closing off after the Millennium by the coming of Christ, a general resurrection of just and unjust and a general judgment of both. After the Great White Throne Judgment, eternal destinies are settled. All created beings are destined either for the New Heavens and New Earth with God, Christ, the holy angels and the redeemed, or else to the eternal Hell, the Lake of Fire with Satan, his angels and demons and the unredeemed of the human race. This position is the same with each Millennial School of Eschatology.

As seen in this chapter, The Post-Millennial position is a far more simple yet positive approach to the purposes of God and the eschatological scheme of things. The Futurist and Dispensational views are much more complicated. In short, Post-Millennialism sees the Kingdom of God as a spiritual reign of Christ in the hearts of the redeemed. It will conquer, in general, the whole earth, before Christ comes and receives the Kingdom, and then after an indefinite period of time (symbolic 1000 years), give the Kingdom back to the Father as all then flows on into the eternal states.

BIBLIOGRAPHY

POST-MILLENNIALISM

1. Boettner, Loraine., The Millennium, 1957
2. Brown, David., The Second Advent, 1849, Reprinted, 1953, under title, Christ's Second Coming
3. Campbell, Roderick., Israel and the New Covenant, 1954
4. Hodge, Charles., Systematic Theology. 1871
5. Kik., J. Marcellus., An Eschatology of Victory, 1974
6. Shedd, W.G.T., Dogmatic Theology, 1888
7. Snowden, James H., The Coming of the Lord, 1919
8. Strong, Augustus H., Systematic Theology, 1907
9. Warfield, B.B., The Millennium & The Apocalypse, 1904, Reprinted in Biblical Doctrines, 1929

OTHER RECOMMENDED TEXTS
(Most Dealing with the Four Views)

1. Clouse, Robert G., The Meaning of the Millennium, Four Views 1977
2. Erickson, Millard J., A Basic Guide to Eschatology (Formerly, Contemporary Options in Eschatology – A Study of the Millennium), 1977, 1998
3. Gregg, Steve., Revelation – Four Views – A Parallel Commentary, 1997
4. Pate, C. Marvin., General Editor., Four Views on the Book of Revelation, 1998

CHAPTER SIX

A-MILLENNIALISM

Dr.J.C.Vos, quoted in "**The Millennium**" (Loraine Boettner, page 4) defines A-Millennialism as follows: "A-Millennialism is that view of the last things which holds that the Bible does not predict a Millennium of world-wide peace and righteousness on this earth before the end of the world.
A-Millennialism teaches that there will be a parallel and contemporaneous development of good and evil – God's Kingdom and Satan's Kingdom – in this world, which will continue until the second coming of Christ. At the second coming of Christ, the resurrection and judgment will take place, followed by the eternal order of things – the absolute, perfect Kingdom of God in which there will be no sin, suffering or death."

The A-Millennialist sees no Scriptural evidence for a Millennium on either Pre-Millennial or Post-Millennial principles. A-Millennial simply means "no-Millennium". This, however, sometimes conveys a wrong concept to some. It is not that the A-Millennialist does not believe in a Millennium, for they do. But it is a symbolic period of time between Christ's comings, NOT after His coming and NOT an earthly, literal or Jewish Millennium, as Futurist and Dispensation Millennialists teach.

Some A-Millennialists prefer to speak of "Realized Millennialism" That is to say, they do not believe in a future, materialistic, Jewish Millennium but in a present or realized Millennium between the first and second comings of Christ. W.E.Cox prefers "Biblical Millennialism" to "A-Millennialism."

John F. Walvoord (a critic of A-Millennialists) in "**The Millennial Kingdom**" (page 6) provides a good definition of A-Millennialism. He writes: "Its most general character is that of denial of a **literal** reign of Christ upon the earth. Satan is conceived as being bound at the first coming of Christ. The present age between the first and second comings is the fulfillment of the Millennium. Its adherents are divided on whether the Millennium is being fulfilled now on earth (Augustine) or whether the saints in heaven (Kliefoth) are fulfilling it. It may be summed up in the idea that there will be no more Millennium than there is now, and that the eternal state immediately follows the second coming of Christ. As they freely recognize that their concept of the Millennium is quite foreign to the Pre-Millennial view, they have been given the title of A-Millennialists by most writers."

Following we comment on the fifteen components of Eschatology as to what, in general, A-Millennialists believe.

1. **Daniel's Seventy Weeks Prophecy**
   A-Millennialists, along with the Historic Pre-Millennialists and Post-Millennialists, believe that the Seventy Weeks Prophecy is a "time-continuous" prophecy. All was fulfilled at the first coming of Christ and somewhere about the time of the death of Stephen. The A-Millennialists argue that there are no Scriptural grounds to place a "gap" of some 2000 years between the sixty-ninth and the seventieth week of the notable prophecy. All other "time prophecies" in the Scripture continue as to their unfolding fulfillment. The same is true for Daniel's prophecy in Dan.9:24-27. With the completion of the Seventy Weeks Prophecy, the Millennium is ushered in until Christ comes the second time.

2. **The Kingdom**
   Because of the A-Millennial view of the Kingdom, the least that could be said under this caption is that they hold that the Kingdom is here and now. Christ came to usher in the Kingdom of God. It is a spiritual ruling and reigning of Christ in the hearts of men. It is a spiritual Kingdom, not a Jewish, political, literal or materialistic kind of Kingdom as was David's Kingdom. Those who are born again enter the Kingdom and become subjects of that Kingdom here and now. This is the Millennial Kingdom, the rule and reign of Christ and His saints in this age. This reigning is either in life on earth now, or reigning with Christ in heaven now. The Kingdom is between the first and second comings of Christ, after which follows eternity. Refer to comments on "The Millennium", Number 13, of this chapter. There is a close connection of thought on this matter of the Kingdom now with the Post-Millennialists, although not exactly the same.

3. **The Church**

A-Millennialists, along with Historic Pre-Millennialists and Post-Millennialists have strong convictions about the Church. Each believes that the Church is in the eternal purpose of God. Each hold that there is only one way for Jew and Gentile to be saved, and that is, through faith in Christ (Eph.2:1-10; 3:1-11). The Church, composed of believing Jews and believing Gentiles in the one good olive tree, all being there by faith (Rom.9-11 chapters). The Church is not a parenthetical purpose of God brought in because of Jewish unbelief. Since the cross of Calvary, there is only one people of God, one purpose of God, and this is the Church – the new, the spiritual and the eternal Israel of God.

4. **The Nation of Israel**
A-Millennialists, along with Post-Millennialists, hold that there is no future for the Jew as to any restoration of a Davidic, materialistic, political and literal Kingdom. The Old Testament prophecies concerning the nation of Israel have been fulfilled in Old Testament history, or in the restoration from the Babylonian Captivity. Old Testament prophecies that appear unfulfilled have been forfeited through unbelief and disobedience or have been cancelled out by reason of the same. The only restoration for Jewry (Israel) is through redemption in Christ. Most A-Millennialists see nothing in the so-called restoration of Jewry to the land of Palestine and reject the theory that there are any true and physical Jews to be found in the nations of earth. All have been swallowed up in the scattering among the nations through inter-marriage, and so forth. The Jewish issue in Palestine today is more political than Biblical.

5. **The New Covenant**
A-Millennialists agree with Post-Millennialists as to the replacement of the Old Covenant with the New Covenant. The New Covenant is everlasting. It will never be replaced by another Covenant in this age or any age to come. Christ's death forever fulfilled and abolished the Old Covenant.

6. **The Mosaic Covenant Economy**
A-Millennialists, along with Post-Millennialism, see absolutely no restoration or re-institution of the Old Covenant or any of the Mosaic Covenant economy. To restore the Temple, with its Aaronic and Levitical Priesthood, animals sacrifices and oblations, Sabbath Days and Festival occasions, along with circumcision, etc., would be a return to Judaistic religion. All these were fulfilled and abolished at the cross.
The New Covenant is established both now and eternally. To return to the Mosaic Covenant would be a violation and negation of the New Covenant ministry of the Lord Jesus Christ. It would be a total rejection of the revelation given in the Book of Hebrews to New Covenant saints. The New Covenant, and not the reverse must now, since the cross, interpret the Old Covenant.

7. **The Rapture**
A-Millennialists hold the same belief as Historic Pre-Millennial and Post-Millennial adherents. There is no secret rapturing of the Church out of this world before Christ's second advent. The Rapture and the Revelation take place at the same time.

8. **The Antichrist**
A-Millennialism believes that there will be a personal Antichrist, who is in reality the Devil and Satan incarnate. Satan will be loosed at the end of the present "realized Millennium". This will also involve a time of great persecution against the Church. Antichrist is an individual, a spirit as well as a system, representing all that is against God, His Christ and the Church.

9. **The Great Tribulation**
A-Millennialists, along with Post-Millennialists, basically teach that the "Great Tribulation" was fulfilled in A.D.70, according to the prophetic words of Christ (Matt.24). This "tribulation" was under Prince Titus and the Roman armies in the terrible destruction of Jerusalem. Beyond that, the people of God – the Church – has always experienced trouble, persecution, opposition and tribulation through its history. Any and all tribulation will consummate in the close of history, at the second coming of Jesus Christ.

10. **The Second Coming of Christ**
A-Millennialists, along with Post-Millennialists, believe that there is but one coming. The Rapture of the Church and the Revelation of Christ take place at one and the same time. All take place at

the end of this present age. Christ comes "for" and "with" His saints at His second advent. Christ comes personally, visibly and gloriously.

11. The Binding of Satan

A-Millennialists teach that Satan has already been bound by the power of the work of the cross. Jesus triumphed over him and all his Satanic hosts. As the "Stronger Man" Jesus bound the "Strong Man" – Satan- and now he is restricted in his activity. He was bound by the chain of the conquering Angel who is probably the Lord Jesus Christ Himself. Satan can no longer deceive the nations. This means, though he goes about "as a roaring lion" (1Pet.5:8), he is bound in the fact that the nations can no longer be deceived, all nations may now accept the Gospel of Christ. In the Old Covenant, only the chosen nation of Israel had access to the knowledge of God. Now all nations have access. It is in this sense only that Satan is "bound". Being in the Pit is symbolical of the restraints on him, even though he is on a long chain.

12. The Resurrection

A-Millennialism, again in harmony with Post-Millennialism, hold that there is but one general resurrection, both of the just and the unjust. This is in fulfillment of Jhn.5:25-29 with Rev.20:1-6. There is no series of bodily resurrections. The "first resurrection" is a spiritual resurrection, of believers being born again into the Kingdom of God. Believers are translated out of the Kingdom of Darkness into the Kingdom of Light. From being "dead in trespasses and sins", they are now, in Christ, "raised to life". This is their "first resurrection". The next resurrection has to do with the body, being a physical resurrection either to life or death. This is the general resurrection of all mankind who have ever lived. There are no two physical resurrections. The "first resurrection" is a spiritual, and the next resurrection is a physical resurrection. One takes place each time someone comes to Christ; the next takes place at Christ's advent.

13. The Judgment

A-Millennialists, as Post-Millennialists, also see one general judgment after a general resurrection. This is the judgment of the righteous and the unrighteous, the just and the unjust. They are separated into two classes, the saved the lost, the blessed and the damned. Following the Great White Throne Judgment, eternal destinies are settled in Heaven or in Hell.

14. The Millennium

Louis Berkhof in "**Systematic Theology**" (page 708) has this to say about the Millennium from the A-Millennialist's point of view, the content being adapted for our purpose here.

The Kingdom of God is both present and future; present in the Church, future in the eternal states. The Kingdom of God is an eternal Kingdom and not a temporal or materialistic earthly Kingdom. It is a spiritual or heavenly Millennium, not an earthly one of a literal reign of Christ on the earth before Christ's final judgment. The 1000 years has to do with the intermediate state, where believers who have died or been martyred are now reigning with Christ in heaven. The 1000 years is a symbolic period of time between the first and second coming of Christ. The Church Age is the Millennial Age.

There are some variations of the Millennium among the A-Millennialists, but basically the position is that there is no future, earthly Millennial Kingdom on earth when or after Christ comes again. A-Millennialists with Post-Millennialists believe that Christ comes at the END of the Millennium. A-Millennialists see this period of time reaching an indefinite period between Christ's first and second coming, rather than, as Post-Millennialists believe, the Church ushers in that Millennium.

Satan is bound in the sense that his power is limited. Satan can no longer deceive the nations as he did in the Old Testament times. By this is meant, that he cannot hinder the Gospel being preached in all the nations since Christ "bound" him at Calvary. As a dog is limited on a chain, so is Satan bound by the chain of the angel's power (Rev.20:16).

Because the platform and foundational stronghold of A-Millennialism is their understanding and interpretation of Rev.20:1-6, it will be helpful to provide some brief outline of their interpretation of this passage. The hermeneutics used by A-Millennialists are also used to bring some refutation of other Schools of Eschatology, especially those of the Pre-Millennial Schools. Following we note the main points of A-Millennial interpretation of this controversial Millennial passage.

A. Chronological Arrangement of Revelation
The foundational platform for A-Millennial interpretation of Rev.20 is on their arrangement of the Book of Revelation, commonly spoken of as "Progressive Revelation". In simple form, the Book of Revelation is divided into two major sections.
1. Rev.1-11 chapters – Pictures the Church being persecuted by the world unto Christ's coming.
2. Rev.12-22 chapter – Pictures from a different viewpoint of Christ and the Church being persecuted by Satan and his hosts unto the New Heavens and New Earth.

William Hendriksen in "**More Than Conquerors**" (page 48), charts the Book of Revelation in seven visions, in which each go back to the beginning of this age, the first coming of Christ, and each consummate at the close of this age, with the second coming of Christ. This view and arrangement of Revelation is that especially spoken of as "Progressive Parallelism". His view and arrangement is as follows:

PROGRESSIVE PARALLELISM

First Coming   [The Christ-indwelt Church in the World, Ch.1-3_____)   Second Coming
                                                        Lampstands

THE CHURCH
[The Church suffering trial and persecution, Ch.4-7_____)   Final Judgment
                                                      Seals

AND THE WORLD
[The Church Avenged, Protected, Victorious, Ch.8-11 _____)   New Heaven
                                                     Trumpets   New Earth

[Christ opposed by the Dragon and his helpers, Ch.12-14 _____)
                                                      Christ & Dragon

CHRIST
[Final wrath upon the impenitent, Ch.15-16 _____)
                                             Bowls

AND
[The Fall of Babylon and the Beasts, Ch.17-19 _____)
                                             Babylon

THE DRAGON
[The Dragon's Doom, Christ & Church Victors, Ch.20-22 _____)
                                                    Consummation

It is upon this arrangement of Revelation that Hendriksen states that Rev.20 takes us back to the beginning, back to the work of the cross, where Jesus "bound Satan". Also, he says that Rev.19:11-21 brings us to Christ's second coming. It is upon this basis and arrangement of Revelation that the "realized" Millennial position stands.

B. Interpreting Revelation Chapter 20
Following is a brief outline of the A-Millennial understanding and interpretation of Rev.20. Verses 1-6 are generally divided into two parts; vs.1-3 speaking of the binding of Satan for 1000 years, a scene on the earth, and vs.4-6, the reign of souls with Christ for 1000 years, a scene in heaven before the coming of Christ.

1. **The Use of Symbolic Language**
   The language of Rev.20 is symbolic. Symbols used in the chapter have to do with a chain, a key, a beast, and if these are symbolic, so must the 1000 years be a symbolic period of time. Satan and spirits cannot be bound by literal chains.

2. **The Thousand Years**
   The 1000 years is not to be taken literally. It is symbolic of an indefinite period of time from the first coming of Christ to His second coming. Just as the number 12, 144,000, etc., are figurative and symbolic numbers, so must the 1000 be seen to be figurative. Neither Jesus, nor any of the apostles or writers of Scripture ever speak of a 1000-year Kingdom reign of Christ. This is the one and only passage in the total Bible that speaks of this time period. Therefore, a

doctrine of a Millennial reign of Christ on earth cannot be built on one passage, and that being a passage using symbolic language.

A-Millennialists variously speak of this time as a "realized" or "inaugurated Millennium". It is a present period of time in which we are now. Scriptures speak of the "last days" and the "last day", all of which point to the present days in which we are living. There is no "last day" beyond the "last days" (1Jhn.2:18; Joel 2:28-32; Acts 2:16-17; Jhn.6:30-40,44,54; 11:24; 12:48). The Millennium is here and now. All will be ushered into the eternal Kingdom at Christ's advent (Lke.17:20-21; Matt.12:28; 5:3; 18:4; Rom.14:17; 1Cor.4:19-20; Col.1:13).

3. The Binding of Satan

Satan was bound by Jesus Christ at His first coming and in His work on Calvary. Jesus is the "stronger Man" who bound the "strong man" Satan, so He could spoil his house and take the captives of sin out of Satan's house. This "binding" simply means the restriction of Satan's power in earth. The Scriptures speak of Satan's being conquered by Christ (Gen.3:15; Col.2:15; 1Jhn.3:8; Matt.12:28-29; Lke.13:32; Mrk.1:34; Jhn.12:31; Heb.2:14,18; Rev.3:9-11). All this was accomplished on Calvary. Christ's first coming was the most important day in history, not the second coming. The second coming is only the ultimate of that which took place in His first coming.

4. The Abyss

Satan being "bound" in the Abyss, the Bottomless Pit, is figurative of his activities being curbed in this period of time. It is symbolic of his power being restrained. Even though he still goes around like a roaring lion, he is "bound", on a long chain, according to William E.Cox and other A-Millennial writers.

5. The Nations not Deceived

Satan being bound, the nations can no longer be deceived. This, according to the A-Millennial view, simply means that the Gospel can now go to all nations (Matt.28:18-20; Mrk.16:15-20; Acts 1:8), whereas the knowledge of God was limited in Old Testament times to the chosen nation of Israel.

6. The Enthroned Souls

The word "throne" is used some forty-seven times in Revelation, and all but three times speaks of thrones in heaven. This points to the overcomers who reign with Christ in heaven (Rev.3:21; Dan.7:22). The 1000 years is the period of the reign of the martyrs with Christ in heaven. It is a similar scene to that of Rev.6:9-11, the souls under the altar.

7. The Judgment Given

Scripture speaks of judgment being given to Christ and His saints (Rev.20:4,12; Psa.122:1; 1Jhn.4:1; Matt.18:17; Jhn.20:23; 1Cor.14:24; 5:11; Eph.5:11).

8. The Reigning with Christ

Christ is reigning as King here and now, reigning as King since His ascension. He is reigning on the Throne of David, the Throne of the Lord. He is not coming back to reign over any earthly, sinful Kingdom, or rule by force the nations of the earth, who then rebel against Him at the end of a 1000 years. The martyrs who are slain and believers who die, all go to be with the Lord and reign with Christ in heaven over the symbolic 1000 years. It is symbolic of the intermediate state of all the dead in Christ. These are the "souls" reigning with Christ spoken of in this passage.

9. The Beasts

The Beasts are symbolic of all Antichristal powers. For some A-Millennialists, the Beast pointed to Pagan Rome and the False Prophet pointed to Papal Rome; one being the political and the other being the ecclesiastical persecutions of early Church centuries.

10. They Lived and Reigned

The ones who "lived and reigned with Christ" are those who are blessed and holy. They are the ones who have experienced the "first resurrection". The "first resurrection" is a spiritual resurrection. It speaks of new birth, regeneration, from being dead in trespasses and sins and being raised to new life in Christ (Eph.2:1-6; Jhn.3:1-5; 5:25-29). The "first resurrection" speaks of all the souls of believers who have died and now reign with Christ in heaven. Some say this reigning is on earth in victory over all enemies.

The "second resurrection" (though not specifically called that) is a bodily or physical resurrection. This is the general resurrection of the just and the unjust that takes place at Christ's coming. It is spoken of in Jhn.5:28-29; Acts 24:15. It is specifically those who are "in the graves" who hear His voice and "come to life" (Grk. "**Ezesan**", Matt.9:18; Rom.14:9; 2Cor.13:4; Rev.2:8). The 1000 years then is the period of the "first resurrection", for the 1000 years is co-extensive with this Gospel Age. Every time a person is born again, they experience the "first resurrection". If they die before Christ returns, they experience their bodily resurrection at His second coming.

11. The Loosing of Satan
At the close of the present Millennium, and **before** Christ comes again, Satan is to be loosed out of his prison for a little season.

12. The Deceiving of Gog and Magog
Satan deceives the nations in the earth, those who have not responded to the Gospel over this 1000 years "realized Millennium". Their number is as innumerable as the sand of the sea. They compass the camp of the saints and the beloved city of Jerusalem. Fire comes down and destroys them. Fire comes to cleanse the earth (2Pet.3).

13. The Lake of Fire
Satan is cast into the Lake of Fire where the Beast and the False Prophet have been over the 1000 years, and these are tormented forever and ever.

14. The Great White Throne Judgment
This is the general judgment of all mankind which takes place after Christ's coming and the general resurrection. The wheat and tares grow together over this Millennial Age, and then at the Great White Throne, there comes the eternal separation (Matt.13:24-30, 36-43).

15. The Second Death
The wicked are consigned to the Lake of Fire, which is the second death.

16. The New Heavens and New Earth
The righteous go to be with God and Christ and enjoy the bliss of eternal life in the City of God, in the New Heavens and New Earth (Rev.21-22).

17. The Eternal States
A-Millennialists follow the same truth as all other Schools as to the eternal states. After the Great White Judgment, eternal destinies are settled. All the redeemed of all ages will live eternally with God, Christ and the holy angels in the New Heavens and New Earth. All the unredeemed of all ages will be cast in Hell, the Lake of Fire, and be there with the Devil, the fallen angels and demonic spirits and this for all eternity. A-Millennialists point out, that there is:

- One Harvest – Two Classes : Wheat and Tares (Matt.13:24-30, 36-43; Rev.14:14-20. Here there is total separation of the righteous and the wicked. It is complete salvation for the righteous (Heb.9:28; Rom.8:23; 1Pet.1:3-5). It is complete destruction for the wicked (Matt.24:38,39; 2Thess. 1:8,9; 2Thess.2:8). Tares are cast into the furnace; the righteous shine forth in the Kingdom (1Cor.15:20-27).

- One Resurrection – Two Classes: Just and the Unjust (Jhn.5:28,29; Acts 24:15; Matt.22:30,31; Heb.6:2. He severs the wicked from among the just.

- One Judgment – Two Classes – Two Destinies: Heaven or Hell (Matt.16:27; 25:31-46; Rev.20:11-15; Rom.14:10; 2Pet.3:7; Jhn.12:48; 2Cor.5:10; Acts 17:31; Mal.4:1-3).

- One Separation – Two Classes: Saints and Sinners (Matt.24:37-39; 25:31-46; 13:47,48; 2Thess.1:10; Phil.3:20-21; 2Tim.4:8; 1Pet.1:13; 5:4; 2Thess.1:8). Saints rewarded and the wicked are judged at the same time.

For the A-Millennialists, there is the one coming of Christ, the one general resurrection of the dead, just and unjust, the one general judgment at the Great White Throne, and then eternal destinies are settled, the righteous to everlasting life, and the wicked to everlasting damnation.

There is nothing revealed to us beyond Rev.21-22 and therefore, all Schools of Millennialism see these chapters as the ultimate revelation that God has given us. Little is known of eternal glory, except that these chapters do show that all will be bliss and peace in the presence of the Father, and the Redeemer, our Lord Jesus Christ, the holy angels and the redeemed of all ages.

As for the Pre-Millennial views, Christ comes the second time and then there comes the earthly Millennium, the final aspect of the Kingdom relative to earth.
As for the Post-Millennial view, Christ comes the second time after the ministry of the Church triumphant has brought in the Millennium.
As for the A-Millennial view, the Millennium is here and now in the present age and Christ comes at the close of this Millennium and eternity follows the final events of resurrection and judgment.

The Futurist and Dispensational views of the Millennium are far more complicated than the position of the Post-Millennialist. The Post-Millennial view is a simplified view of the whole. The A-Millennial view, arising out of their foundational interpretation of Rev.20 makes for the most unique view of them all, re-interpreting the foundational passage of all Millennialistic positions as seen above.

For the Pre-Millennial Schools, Satan is yet to be bound in the Abyss and this before the Millennium. For the Post-Millennial School, Satan is being progressively bound through Church history, ushering in a Utopian Millennium. For the A-Millennial School, Satan has already been bound and this at Christ's first coming and His redemptive work on the cross.

The "stronghold" of A-Millennialism is its exegesis of Rev.20, hence the necessity of having some understanding of their position arising out of this. It is for this reason that this chapter has given more details to the A-Millennial position.

BIBLIOGRAPHY

A-MILLENNIALISM

1. Allis, Oswald T., Prophecy and the Church, 1945
2. Berkhof, Louis., Systematic Theology., 1941
3. Berkhof, Louis., The Second Coming of Christ, 1953
4. Berkouwer, G.C., The Return of Christ, 1972
5. Bray, John L., The Millennium, 1984 (Booklet)
6. Cox, William E., A-Millennialism Today, 1972
7. Cox, William E., An Examination of Dispensationalism, 1971
8. Cox, William E., Biblical Studies in Final Things, 1967
9. Fletcher, George B., The Millennium – What it is NOT and What it IS (Booklet)
10. Graebner, Theodore., War in the Light of Prophecy, 1941
11. Grier, Wm. J., The Momentous Event, 1945
12. Hamilton, Floyd E., The Basis of Millennial Faith, 1942
13. Heerboth, L.A., The Millennium and The Bible (Booklet)
14. Hendriksen, William., More Than Conquerors, 1939
15. Hodges, Jesse Wilson., Christ's Kingdom and Coming, 1957
16. Hughes, Archibald., A New Heaven and A New Earth, 1958
17. Kuyper, A., Chiliasm, or The Doctrine of Pre-Millennialism, 1934
18. Lewis, Arthur H., The Dark Side of the Millennium, 1980
19. Masselink, William., Why Thousand Years? 1930
20. Mauro, Philip., The Seventy Weeks and The Great Tribulation, 1944
21. Mauro, Philip., The Gospel of the Kingdom, 1928
22. Mauro, Philip., Dispensationalism Justifies the Crucifixion, 1966 (Booklet)
23. Morris, Leon., The Revelation of St. John., 1969
24. Murray, George L., Millennial Studies, 1948
25. Pieters, Albertus., Studies in the Revelation of St.John, 1937
26. Pieters, Albertus., The Seed of Abraham, 1950
27. Pieters, Albertus., A Candid Examination of the Scofield Bible, 1938 (Pamphlet)
28. Schumm, F.C.G., Essay on Revelation Chapter 20 (Pamphlet)
29. Thomas, Lawrence Rowe., Does the Bible teach Millennialism? 1970, Booklet
30. Vos, Geerhardus., The Pauline Eschatology, 1930
31. Wyngaarden, Martin J., The Future of the Kingdom, 1955

CONCLUSION

As was mentioned at the beginning of PART ONE concerning Millennial views, the various Schools have far more in common on the major theological truths than differences. It is in the field of Eschatological truths that the differences are to be found. Our outlines of these Millennial views are summarized here.

1. **Daniel's Seventy Weeks Prophecy**
   Historic Pre-Millennialism, Post-Millennial and A-Millennialism agree that the Seventy Weeks Prophecy has been fulfilled at Christ's first advent. Futurists and Dispensational Pre-Millennialism disagree with the previous and believe that the final or seventieth week is yet to be fulfilled.

2. **The Kingdom**
   Historic, Post- and A-Millennialists all agree that the Kingdom is here. Futurists, Dispensationalists disagree with this view and believe that the Kingdom was offered, rejected and postponed to the end of the age.

3. **The Church**
   Historic, Post- and A-Millennialists agree that the Church was in the eternal purpose of God. Futurists and Dispensationalists disagree with this and believe that the Church was Plan B, a parenthetical purpose of God because of Jewish unbelief.

4. **The Nation of Israel**
   Historic Pre-Millennialists believe that there may be a visitation of the Lord upon the Jewish nation and they can find hope in Christ. Post-Millennialists and A-Millennialists see nothing for Israel as a nation apart from Christ. Futurists and Dispensationalists believe the eyes of the Jewish nation will be opened to Christ and they will, as a saved nation, become the head of the nations in the Millennial Age.

5. **The New Covenant**
   Historic, Post- and A-Millennialsts agree that the New Covenant was established by Christ and will never be replaced. Futurists and Dispensation Pre-Millennialists disagree and believe that the New Covenant is yet to be made in the future age.

6. **The Mosaic Covenant Economy**
   Historic, Post- and A-Millennialists agree that the Mosaic Covenant has been fulfilled and abolished by Christ never to be re-instituted. Futurists and Dispensationalists disagree with that view. They believe that the Mosaic Covenant economy is to be restored in a rebuilt material Temple in the end of the age, or else in Ezekiel's Temple in the Millennial Age.

7. **The Rapture**
   Historic, Post- and A-Millennialists agree that the rapture takes place at one and the same time, that is, at the second coming of Christ. Futurists and Dispensationalists disagree, and see a "secret rapture" seven years, or less, before Christ's second coming.

8. **The Antichrist**
   Historic, Post- and A-Millennialists basically agree that Antichrist is symbolic of all hostile forces arrayed against the Church over this age. Futurists and Dispensationalists generally disagree on this point. They see an individual and personal Antichrist arising in the end of the age, setting himself as God in a rebuilt material Jewish Temple.

9. **The Great Tribulation**
   Historic, Post- and A-Millennialists all agree that there has always been Tribulation through Church history. Futurists and Dispensationalists, in general, disagree, and see "the Great Tribulation" taking place in the end of the age, during Daniel's seventieth week.

10. **The Second Coming of Christ**
    Historic Pre-Millennialism, Post- and A-Millennialists agree that there is but one second coming of Christ, though there is disagreement as to the time Christ comes relative to some kind of Millennium. Futurists and Dispensationalists disagree with the previous view and see two stages of

Christ's coming; the rapture and the revelation, seven years apart. Both these agree that Christ comes before the Millennium begins.

11. The Binding of Satan
Historic, Futurists and Dispensationalists agree that the binding of Satan takes place at Christ's advent. Post-Millennialists see a progressive binding of Satan during the Church Age while A-Millennialists see that Satan has already been bound by the work of Christ on Calvary.

12. The Resurrection
Post- and A-Millennialists agree that there is but one general resurrection of the just and the unjust and this takes place when Christ returns again the second time. Historic, Futurist along with the Dispensationalists see that there are two resurrections, of the just and the unjust, and these are 1000 years apart.

13. The Judgment
Post- and A-Millennialists agree on this point, that there is one general judgment of the just and the unjust that takes place at Christ's coming after the one general resurrection of the dead. Historic, Futurist and Dispensation adherents disagree with the previous Schools and see two judgments, of the just and unjust, along with the two resurrections. These judgments are 1000 years apart.

14. The Millennial Kingdom
Historic, Futurists and Dispensational Pre-Millennialists agree on a future aspect of the Kingdom, though there is disagreement as to the "Jewishness" of this Kingdom. Post-Millennialists disagree with these two Schools and see that the Church militant will usher in the Millennial Kingdom. A-Millennialists see that this present age, between the first and second comings of Christ, is the Millennial period, a "realized Millennium".

15. The Eternal States
Historic, Post-A-Millennialists along with the Futurists and Dispensationalists basically agree on the eternal states; a New Heavens and New Earth for the righteous or Hell, the Lake of Fire, for the unredeemed, angelic or human beings.

The student is referred to the Bibliography on each of these Schools as the various writers have presented their case accordingly. The purpose of this text was not to repeat all that they have written but to condense the major points down to a brief outline, manageable for the final purpose of this text.

PART TWO

PART

TWO

PREFACE

Having considered the three major Schools of Eschatology (Pre-Millennial, Post-Millennial and A-Millennial), our consideration in Part Two is given to a possible alternative – The Christian Pre-Millennial View.

For the sake of consistency, the fifteen points of difference are followed as in the previous chapters. These components are dealt with in a much fuller way than in the previous chapters, owing to the many textbooks that have already dealt with these issues. The difference, however, will be seen that each of these things have a chapter given to them, while in Part Three, fuller details will be given as to why the writer holds the view he has coined and designated: "The Christian Millennium."

PART TWO
AREAS OF ESCHATOLOGICAL CONTROVERSY

Preface
Chapter
1. **Daniel's Seventy Weeks Prophecy**
2. **The Kingdom**
3. **The Church**
4. **The Nation of Israel**
5. **The New Covenant**
6. **The Mosaic Covenant Economy**
7. **The Rapture**
8. **The Antichrist**
9. **The Great Tribulation**
10. **The Second Coming of Christ**
11. **The Binding of Satan**
12. **The Resurrection**
13. **The Judgment**
14. **The Millennial Kingdom**
15. **The Eternal States**

CHAPTER ONE

DANIEL'S SEVENTY WEEKS PROPHECY

Introductory:
The reader will have already seen that one's understanding and interpretation of the notable Seventy Weeks Prophecy of Daniel 9:24-27 has a great bearing on end-time events.

The Historic Pre-Millennialist, the Post-Millennialist and the A-Millennialist each see the prophecy being fulfilled in Christ's first coming, especially consummating with His redemptive work at Calvary. The Futurist and Dispensationalist see 69 weeks of the prophecy fulfilled in Christ's first coming, and more especially at His entry into Jerusalem. For these two Schools, there remain but one week, the 70th week, to be fulfilled. This, they see, finds fulfillment in the Book of Revelation. This is seen to be the period of the Great Tribulation and the rule and reign of Antichrist over these seven years. According to these Schools, the events of Rev.4-19 chapters take place in this week of seven years.

The Rapture is purported to take place at the beginning of these seven years, and the Revelation or coming of Christ at the end of these seven years. With this "secret coming " of Christ "for" His Church, there is also a resurrection of the dead in Christ, "the first resurrection". Eschatological events are built on this interpretation of Daniel's Seventy Weeks Prophecy.

As can be seen, these varying Schools are divided. One group says the prophecy is fulfilled at Christ's first coming. The other group says the final week is to be fulfilled at Christ's second coming. Who is right? Which is the proper view, the proper interpretation?

The question may be asked: Is it possible that both are part right or both part wrong? Is there a possibility or an alternative understanding and interpretation of this prophecy, especially that which pertains to the 70th or last week? Is there another view worth considering? The writer believes there is, and this is what this chapter is about!

Daniel's Seventy Weeks Prophecy – KJV Daniel 9:24-27	Daniel's Seventy Weeks - NAS Daniel 9:24-27
24. Seventy weeks are determined upon thy people and upon thy holy city, to finish the transgression, and to make an end of sins, and to make reconciliation for iniquity, and to bring in everlasting righteousness, and to seal up the vision and prophecy, and to anoint the most Holy. 25. Know therefore and understand, that from the going forth of the commandment to restore and to build Jerusalem unto the Messiah the Prince shall be seven weeks, and threescore and two weeks: the street shall be built again, and the wall, even in troublous times. 26. And after threescore and two weeks shall Messiah be cut off, but not for himself: and the people of the prince that shall come shall destroy the city and the sanctuary; and the end thereof shall be with a flood, and unto the end of the war desolations are determined. 27. And he shall confirm the covenant with many for one week: and in the midst of the week he shall cause the sacrifice and the oblation to cease, and for the overspreading of abominations he shall make it desolate, even until the consummation, and that determined shall be poured upon the desolate.	24. "Seventy weeks have been decreed for your people and your holy city, to finish the transgression, to make an end of sin, to make atonement for iniquity, to bring in everlasting righteousness, to seal up vision and prophecy, and to anoint the most holy {place.} 25. "So you are to know and discern {that} from the issuing of a decree to restore and rebuild Jerusalem until Messiah the Prince {there will be} seven weeks and sixty-two weeks; it will be built again, with plaza and moat, even in times of distress. 26. "Then after the sixty-two weeks the Messiah will be cut off and have nothing, and the people of the prince who is to come will destroy the city and the sanctuary. And its end {will come} with a flood; even to the end there will be war; desolations are determined. 27. "And he will make a firm covenant with the many for one week, but in the middle of the week he will put a stop to sacrifice and grain offering; and on the wing of abominations {will come} one who makes desolate, even until a complete destruction, one that is decreed, is poured out on the one who makes desolate."

The student is encouraged to read several other translations of this notable passage to help further understand the import of it all.

Daniel 9 contains, without doubt, the most marvellous and amazing prophecy of all Bible prophecy; that is, the Seventy Weeks Prophecy. A clear understanding of this important prophecy will reveal that it is actually THE KEY to all Bible prophecy. It is because of mistaken interpretations and misunderstanding of this prophecy that all 'Prophetic' and 'Time element' in the Book of Daniel and the Book of Revelation have been confused. Unless this vital Scripture passage, and the 'Time element' in it is correctly understood, then it is well nigh impossible to "rightly divide the Word of Truth" (2Tim.3:15), especially in the prophetic books.

The Seventy Weeks Prophecy is THE KEY to both the Book of Daniel and the Book of Revelation. It alone unlocks the door of prophetic understanding and allows the student believer into the glorious secrets of the revelation of God as pertaining to future and end-time events. No wise student will throw away "the key" but use it as God intended (Lke.11:52).

A. The Preparation of Daniel – vs.1-23
The student should read these verses before considering the prophetic words of vs.24-27. They become the foundation of the prophetic word to Daniel. They reveal the preparation of Daniel's heart before he received and understood, in good measure (though not full measure) the wonderful prophecy. As Daniel prepared his heart before he received the prophetic word, it sets a good example for all students of prophecy to follow.

1. Study of the Word – vs.1-2
In these verses Daniel is seen studying the prophetic word of God in the prophets (2Tim.2:15). He "understood by books" – the Divine Books, the Holy Scriptures, that the Babylonian Captivity was soon to end. When the House of Judah sinned, God punished them by sending them into Babylon for 70 years. God permitted Nebuchadnezzar to destroy the city and the temple and desolate the land. All this had been foretold by the prophets, especially by Jeremiah (Jer.5:11-29; 7:1-16). The time limit of Judah's Captivity was to be 70 years only, after which they would return to the land of Judah, rebuild the city and the temple, and be there for the first coming of Messiah (Read Jer.25:9-14; 29:1-10).

The reason for this 70 year Captivity is found in the fact that Israel and Judah failed to keep the Sabbatical years as commanded in Lev.25:1-7, that every seventh year was to be a Sabbath Rest for the land. God promised that He would punish the nation with Captivity for disobedience and neglect of these Sabbath years (Lev.26:31-35). This Divine judgment was fulfilled in the Babylonian Captivity (2Chron.36:15-21).

It is worthy of note that Israel failed to keep these Sabbatical years for a period of 490 years, and, as far as Biblical Chronology is right, this takes us back to the days of King Saul. The removal from the land under the Babylonian Captivity took place about BC.606. Add 490 years to this time and its takes us back to BC.1096, the year of Saul's anointing as king. Every seventh year was to be a Sabbath. In 490 years, there should have been 70 Sabbaths, Failure to keep these Sabbaths brought about the Divine punishment of 70 years in Babylon. These Sabbaths rested the land while Judah was in Babylon. It would seem that this period of time (70x7=490 years) actually become a 'prophetic shadow' of the 490 years of the Seventy Weeks Prophecy about to be given to Daniel. It also becomes prophetic of a greater 'Captivity' and a greater 'Desolation' yet to come.

It is these facts that Daniel undoubtedly "understood by books", especially the prophecies in the Books of Leviticus (Lev.25-26), and Jeremiah (Jer.25-29).

2. Prayer and Supplication – vs.3-15
As one carefully reads the prayer and supplication of Daniel, it is evident that the language of the Seventy Weeks Prophecy actually is founded on the language of the prayer. A study of the prophetic Word drove Daniel to prayer and supplication in behalf of his people and his city.

3. Confession and Intercession – vs.16-19
Daniel's prayer reveals the ministry of a true intercessor (Isa.59:16). In this prayer, he identifies himself with the sins of the people. He shares in their punishment, even though he himself was a righteous man before the Lord. Note the "we" and the "us" in his intercessory

prayer. Daniel refers to the Law of Moses (vs.13), and the curses of the broken Law. Notice also the use of words such as "sin, iniquity, transgression, righteousness, desolations", for each of these words become the basis of the notable prophecy, and actually become the language of the prophecy. It is upon this foundation of studying the Word, prayer, supplication with fasting, that Daniel receives the revelation and great understanding of this mighty prophecy. The same principle applies to the believer today who would understand this prophecy of Daniel!

4. **Angelic Visitation – vs.20-23**
In these verses is given the account of the visitation of the archangel, Gabriel. His name interpreted means "God is Mighty" or, "Strength of God". Gabriel is always associated with Divine revelation and/or interpretation of Messianic prophecies. In all, there are four accounts of Gabriel's visitation to earth and that to three of the people of God.
- Dan.8:16-19. Gabriel visits Daniel concerning the Cleansing of the Sanctuary, or the great Day of Atonement.
- Dan.9:21. Gabriel visits Daniel in time of intercessory prayer and gives him the Seventy Weeks Prophecy, the revelation of the coming Messiah.
- Lke.1:1-25. Gabriel visits Zacharias in the Temple at the time of incense, and foretells the birth of John the Baptist, Zacharias and Elizabeth being his father and mother.
- Lke.1:26-38. Gabriel visits the virgin Mary and foretells the birth of Jesus the Messiah.

Gabriel is the angel who brings the revelation and gives the interpretation, the skill and the understanding to Daniel in the Old Testament. He is the one who appears in the New Testament to Zacharias and Mary concerning the birth of John the Baptist and then of Jesus, the Messiah of God. Gabriel's ministry is typical of the ministry of the blessed Holy Spirit. It is His ministry to bring revelation, understanding and skill to the Church in the prophetic Word. He will lead the believer into all the truth as it is in Jesus. He will show us things to come, He will reveal the future. He will make Christ real to the heart (Jhn.14:26; 16:7-15).

5. **Evening Oblation – Ex.29:38-46; 1Kgs.18:36**
It is significant that Gabriel appeared to Daniel at the time of the evening oblation. This speaks of the fact that God always works in connection with the Atonement. Only through sacrifice and oblation (the Atonement) can revelation and understanding be given to the Church in these last days. The Atonement (the Reconciliation) makes possible revelation from God about His prophetic purposes in earth.

B. **The Revelation to Daniel – vs.24-27**
In these verses are given the actual Seventy Weeks Prophecy. Prophecy is that which has to be fulfilled. It is a prediction of future events. God alone knows all things beforehand, and before they come to pass (Acts 15:18). Because of God's essential attributes, He is able to tell things beforehand. This is God's omniscience, His foreknowledge, and prophecy is God's foreknowledge as revealed to His saints. This is what this notable prophecy is as given to Daniel.

1. **Time Element**
The first word of this prophecy is: "Seventy weeks are determined upon your people and upon your holy city…" As most prophetic students of the Word know, this is literally "Seventy sevens (or 490 years) are marked off, upon your people (House of Judah), and upon your holy city (Jerusalem). Refer Amplified Old Testament also. Gabriel states that a period of 490 years was 'marked off' in which and at the conclusion of, certain major events would take place, as listed out in vs.24. Therefore, 490 years of time were allotted for the fulfillment of this prophetic word given to Daniel.

2. **Seventy Sevens**
The word "week" in the Hebrew is literally "seven". It is a Hebrew idiom (a peculiar mode of expression) and simply means "seven". Therefore, "seventy weeks" = "seventy sevens", or 490 years are marked off concerning Daniel's people and Daniel's city.
The Hebrew mind was saturated with the concept of "sevens", as God governed their whole social and religious life by these "sevens", or by these "weeks". This may be seen in the following examples of these Hebrew weeks.
- A Week of Days, or seven days (Lev.23:1-3).
- A Week of Weeks, or 7x7=49 days, or, seven weeks (Lev.23).

- A Week of Months, or seven months (Lev.23).
- A Week of Years, or seven years (Lev.25:8).
- A Week of Weeks of years, or 7x7=49 years (Lev.25).

Thus the idiomatic expression, "week" simply means "seven". The "seventy weeks" are "weeks of years", that is, 490 years in all. It is inapplicable to any of the other "weeks" as spelled out here. There is no need to apply the "day-for-a-year" theory here, as it is already clear that the "weeks" are "years". The fact that a "prophetic week" is a period of seven years is shown also in the following Scripture references (Lev.25:8; Num.14:34; Ezek.4:6). Jacob worked two "weeks of years" for his two wives, Leah and Rachel. That is, he worked 2x7=14 years to gain the wife he first loved.

C. The Six Clauses of the Prophecy – vs.24

There are six clauses in the prophetic word. These six clauses cover the scope of the prophecy, and all are to be fulfilled within the time limit or within the period of the 490 years. It should be self-evident that really only one of the six clauses has had any measure of fulfillment, although the rest were fulfilled judicially at the cross, as will be seen. This statement should be proof enough that the Seventy Weeks Prophecy is not already fulfilled or over and done with. The Church and the hosts of heaven long for and await the ultimate fulfillment of these mighty statements. The six clauses are as follows:

1. To Finish the Transgression

To "finish" means to "shut up, to restrain" rebellion and lawlessness. Transgression and the transgressors are on the increase in our generation and find their fullest expression in the close of this present age (Dan.8:3; Amos 3:13-14; 1Jhn.3:4). Note the use of these three words, "transgression, sin and iniquity" in Isa.53:5,6,10; 59:12. Jesus would be wounded for our transgressions on Calvary, but evidence in the earth shows that transgression has not been "shut up, or restrained" in the full sense of this clause.

2. To Make an End of Sins

This also means, "to finish, to seal up" sin, in both root and fruit. Though Jesus would die on the cross for our sins, yet world evidence shows that sin is increasing, sin is abounding. Sin actually consummates in Antichrist, who is 'The Man of Sin" – the Lawless One (2Thess.2:1-12). Read also Isa.13:9-11; Rom.14:23; Psa.37:28; 1Jhn.3:4. Sin and sinners are to be destroyed out of the earth, finished, sealed up, never again to pollute the universe, in God's appointed time.

3. To Make Reconciliation for Iniquity

The Hebrew thought is "to cover, to cleanse, to make atonement". It is evident that this clause finds fulfillment in Calvary. Reconciliation was made on the cross by Jesus Christ. He has committed the ministry of reconciliation to the Church, which is His Body. Mankind may now be reconciled to God (Isa.53; Col. 1:20-21; Heb.2:14-16; 10:12; Rom.5:6-21; 2Cor.5:18-20). There will come a time when this ministry will finish. On the cross, Jesus took our transgressions, our sins and our iniquities in Himself. On the cross, He made reconciliation possible for all mankind. However, even though reconciliation was made at Calvary. Transgression, sin and iniquity still abound in the earth (Matt.24:12). So, even though the means to that end was effected at Calvary, all will be brought to a total end at the close of this present age.

4. To Bring in Everlasting Righteousness

The Hebrew thought means to bring in "age-lasting righteousness", or justice and uprightness. The atonement of Jesus Christ has provided a "faith-righteousness", but righteousness has not been brought into its fulness as far as this earth is concerned. It cannot be brought in to its fulness until " transgression is finished, an end is made of sin, and all iniquity" has been dealt with. This takes place at the end of this age, though all was judicially fulfilled at Calvary. The only righteousness that God accepts today, however, is "faith righteousness" (Rom.5:1-2).

5. To Seal up the Vision and Prophecy

That is, "to complete, finish and fulfill" vision and prophecy. Joel prophesied that in the last days, God would pour out His Spirit on all flesh. They would have visions and prophesy. Vision and prophecy are still in the Church this day, and will be until that which is perfect is come, then all in part will be done away. There is no need of vision and prophecy when He who is the end of all vision and prophecy —Christ – comes! No need of prophecy when all is swallowed up in fulfillment (Joel 2:28-32; Acts 2:17-21; 1Cor.13:9-14; 14:1; Hab.2:2-3). Scripture reveals that vision and prophecy are to increase in the last days outpouring of the Holy Spirit. The "sealed book" is being opened to the Church as it was to John (Read Dan.12:8-9 with Rev.22:10).

6. To Anoint the Most Holy

"To anoint a Holy of Holies" – Amplified Old Testament. It should be kept in mind that the Temple at Jerusalem had been destroyed by Nebuchadnezzar years beforehand. This prophecy and clause was given when there was material Temple at Jerusalem. It is also important to understand that "the Most Holy" was **a place, NOT a person**! Some expositors endeavour to make this anointing of the Most Holy as referring to and finding fulfillment in the anointing of Jesus at the river Jordan, or else, on the Church, as God's Temple now. The Most Holy was a place in the Tabernacle or in the Temple. It was the "Holiest of All", the inner sanctuary (Ex.26:33; 40:9-10). It does not refer to Messiah's anointing at Jordan.

The measurements of the Most Holy Place in the Tabernacle of Moses were 10x10x10=1000 cubical content. God had something in mind when He gave these measurements. The Holiest of All, as all the Tabernacle and furnishings, had to be **anointed** first before the Shekinah Glory and Presence of the Lord came and dwelt between the Cherubim on the bloodstained Mercyseat. God inhabited the Most Holy Place. In the Tabernacle in the Wilderness, the Glory of the Lord covered, as it were, "the earth floor".

The writer believes all of this is prophetic of the coming Day of the Lord when "the **earth** shall be filled with the knowledge of the **GLORY** of the Lord as the waters cover the sea" (Hab.2:14; Isa.30:26). The 1000 cubical dimension of the Most Holy Place points to the 1000 years of the Millennial Age, which begins, with the coming of the Lord Jesus Christ. It is at that time, "The Tabernacle of God is with men..." (Rev.21:3). The earth will become the "Most Holy Place" and the earth will be anointed to stand the Glory of the Lord manifested in that Kingdom. It is at Christ's coming that these clauses find their ultimate fulfillment.

Summary of Vs.24

Transgression, sin and iniquity abound on every hand. Although Jesus died on the cross and was judged for our transgression, sin and iniquity, making reconciliation to God possible, these things have not been brought to a total end. Everlasting righteousness is available for all who believe, but in relation to earth, its fulness is not yet manifested. Vision and prophecy have not been finalized as both are still in the Church. The earth is corrupted by the evils of mankind. It has yet to be cleansed of sin and sinners. It has yet to be anointed as the Tabernacle of God with His redeemed for the 1000 years of the Kingdom Age. All of this takes place at the coming of the Lord Jesus Christ. It may be said then, that these six clauses, all pointed to Calvary, judicially fulfilled there, but find fulfillment actually in the end of the present age.

D. The Division of the Weeks

In vs.25-27 the angelic communicator and revelator, Gabriel, shows Daniel that the seventy weeks are divided into three or four sections. This is seen in the following:
- Vs.25, Seven Weeks, (7x7) or, 49 years   )
- Vs.25, Sixty-two Weeks (62x7) or, 434 years   ) Making Seventy Weeks or, 490 years
- Vs.27, One Week (1x7) or, 7 years   )
- Vs.27, This final Week is divided into two halves, or 3½ years each (2x3½ years).

Concerning this seventieth week, it speaks of something that happens "in the middle of the week", that is, the middle of the last, the final or the seventieth week.

God never does any thing promiscuously. He always has a plan and purpose in mind. The fact that the seventy weeks are divided into four sections reveals that certain specific events are to take place in those sections of time. Certain events are to take place in the first section of 49 years, the second section of 434 years, and the third section of 3½ years, and then the fourth section of 3½ years. As we follow the record of prophecy and fulfillment, it is possible to understand the important events that transpire in each of these sections.

E. **The Commandment of Commencement**
Several questions present themselves. When did the prophecy begin? When is the point of commencement? What is the "time element" for the beginning of the prophecy to come to pass? Vs.25 provides the answer. "KNOW therefore, and UNDERSTAND that FROM the going forth of THE COMMANDMENT to restore and build Jerusalem UNTO Messiah the Prince shall be seven weeks (49 years), and threescore and two weeks (434 years), the street shall be built again, and the wall, even in troublous times."
In other words, there would be 69 weeks in all, or, 483 years, unto the manifestation of Messiah, the Prince. And again, the date of commencement for the seventy weeks is FROM the going forth of the commandment to restore and build the city of Jerusalem.

The simplest way of arriving at the date of the "going forth of the commandment" is to measure **backwards** from the date of the manifestation of Messiah the Prince. In the verse under consideration there are three important events that are outlined (vs.25).
- The going forth of the commandment. This is the beginning point of the prophecy.
- The restoration and building of Jerusalem, the street, the walls and this in troublous times.
- The manifestation of the Messiah at the close of 69 weeks, or, 483 years.

We ask then: When did the commandment go forth? And, when was Messiah manifested to Israel?

It is important to establish what Gabriel meant by the "going forth of the commandment" in order to establish the proper time for the commencement of the prophecy. The problem is, there were several Decrees or Commandments given over a period of time, which, if taken as the point of commencement, will throw the whole 'Time element' of the prophecy out of line with the Messiah's manifestation, and thus distort the whole interpretation. For the benefit of the student, the following covers these various Decrees, and also helps establish which is to be reckoned as THE COMMANDMENT spoken of in Dan.9:25.

1. **The Decree or Commandment of Cyrus**
Isa.44:28; 45:1-5, 13; 2Chron.36:22-23; Ezra 1:1-11; Ezra 2:1-2,64; Neh.7:66. Under this time, about 50,000 Jews return to Jerusalem. This Decree has to do with the rebuilding of the Temple. The Temple building was hindered over the years up to the second year of Darius of Persia (Ezra.4:4,5). The Decree of Cyrus actually involved the release of the captives, the rebuilding of the city of Jerusalem and the Temple.

2. **The Decree or Commandment of Darius**
Ezra 5:1-17; Ezra 6:1-15. A letter was sent to Darius, and the Decree of Cyrus was found. Darius gave this second Decree, which simply confirmed the first Decree of Cyrus. The rebuilding of the Temple was finished under his reign.

3. **The Decree or Commandment of Artaxerxes**
Ezra 6:1-6,11-25, along with Ezra 7-8. These chapters should be read carefully. In Ezra 6:14 it brings these several Decrees or Commandments together as one commandment. "And they builded, and finished it, according to THE COMMANDMENT of the God of Israel, and according to THE COMMANDMENT of (1) Cyrus, and (2) Darius, and (3) Artaxerxes king of Persia."

4. **The Decree or Commandment of Artaxerxes**
Neh.1—2:1-20. There is a further Commandment given some 13 years or more later than Ezra, and this was in the 20th year of king Artaxerxes, This Decree is referred to in Dan.9:25 where it states, "The street shall be built, and the wall, even in troublous times." Nehemiah's book gives us the story of the rebuilding of the walls and the troublous times spoken of by Daniel the prophet, and therefore, wonderfully fulfills this clause of the prophecy.

In all, these various Decrees concern the release of the captives of Judah, the rebuilding of the city of Jerusalem and the rebuilding of the Temple of the Lord.

Without taking time and space here to answer the various arguments concerning the date of commencement, the reader is referred to Martin Anstey's "**Bible Chronology**". Martin provides the best of all chronological Bible times. He clearly confirms the fact that THE

COMMANDMENT to restore and build Jerusalem was the commandment given by Cyrus. It is Cyrus who was named years before his birth. It is Cyrus who is called "My Shepherd" by the Lord, and also "My Anointed". It is Cyrus who releases the captives of Judah, and gave the Decree for the rebuilding of the city of Jerusalem along with the rebuilding of the Temple. It remarkably fulfilled all the required details of the prophecy of Isaiah (Isa.44:26-28; 45:1-13). Though there are varying dates as to the other Decrees, Martin Anstey places the date for THE COMMANDMENT as being BC.457. Philip Mauro in "**The Seventy Weeks & The Great Tribulation**" confirms the same, even though this writer does not follow along with Mauro's final analysis.

As noted earlier, it helps us further establish the date of commencement of the prophecy if we discover the time of Messiah's manifestation to Israel. By working backward from that date, it should bring us to the date of the commencement, or when THE Commandment was given!

F. Messiah the Prince
The name or title "Messiah" means "Anointed" in Hebrew and in Greek the name or title "Christ" means "Anointed". It may be asked: When and where did Jesus of Nazareth become the Messiah (Jhn.1:41,Margin. Lke.3:23). Jesus, though He was indeed born "Christ the Lord" (Lke.2:11) actually became the Messiah at the river Jordan in water baptism (Jhn.1:33). He was not "anointed" at His birth (Lke.2:11). Nor was He "anointed" at His circumcision (Lke.2:21,26). But He was "anointed with the Holy Spirit and power" at the river Jordan as He rose from the waters of baptism under John (Lke.3:21-23). It was after this He could truly say and did say, "The Spirit of the Lord has **ANOINTED ME** to preach the Gospel ..." (Lke.4:18 with Isa.61:1). It was "the anointing" that made Him "the anointed".
God the Father (The Anointer. Grk –"**Chrio**"), anointed Jesus of Nazareth (The Anointed. Grk-"**Christos**") with the Holy Spirit (The Anointing. Grk-"**Chrisma**") – Acts 10:38.

The date of His public manifestation to Jewry and Jerusalem as the Messiah was approximately AD.26, or 483 years from THE COMMANDMENT given in BC.457. That is, the 69 weeks of the prophecy has been fulfilled when Jesus becomes anointed, or, when Jesus became Jesus CHRIST! Whether one works forward from BC.457 to AD.26 or whether one works backward from AD.26 to BC.457, the 483 years, or 69 weeks, have become history. They have been fulfilled! It is 'safe' either way, for the required years of time, regardless of several years give or take in our present calendar. The important thing is the allotted time from the "going forth of the commandment...unto Messiah the Prince", that is, 69 weeks or 483 years! That is the real issue in this part of the prophecy.

1. The Time is Fulfilled
Saying this in other words, it means that 69 of the 70 weeks were past history; they had been fulfilled when Jesus was manifested in Jordan as God's anointed One. His ministry began after the baptism and temptation in the wilderness. Therefore, 483 years of the 490 years of the prophecy were over, finished with, once Jesus began His ministry.
This leaves exactly but **ONE WEEK** (or seven years) to be fulfilled, from the beginning of Christ's ministry; no more and no less. It is around this **last week, the seventieth week**, that all the tremendous clauses of the prophecy have to do and find their fulfillment. It is also around this seventieth week that the controversy of the different eschatological Schools gathers!

The Gospel of Mark provides some very significant thoughts relative to Messiah's manifestation and ministry.
- Messiah's baptism and anointing for ministry – Mrk.1:9-11.
- Messiah's temptation in the wilderness with the originator of sin – Mrk.1:12-13.
- Messiah's commencement of ministry – Mrk.1:14-15 with Matt.4:17.

"Jesus came into Galilee, preaching the Gospel of the Kingdom, saying, **THE TIME IS FULFILLED**..." We ask: What time? The time is the 69 weeks "UNTO Messiah the Prince". The time of 483 years unto Messiah's manifestation is fulfilled. It is the beginning of Messiah's ministry. To Judah and Jerusalem, Jesus is revealed as the Messiah of God. Messiah's ministry is at the beginning of the seventieth week. Had Jewry and the religious leaders an open heart to receive Jesus of Nazareth, they would have known, or could have known by Daniel's prophecy almost the exact time of His manifestation. Only a few of the faithful remnant recognized Him in their time of visitation (Lke.2).

2. **Time for Ministry**
It was also time for Jesus to commence ministry. In Num.4, the Law commanded that those who were 30 years of age could minister in the Priesthood. So Jesus is about 30 years of age when He began ministry as our Prophet, Priest and King. He fulfills all things in Himself, for 30 is the number of consecration for service to the Lord (Lke.3:23).

G. Sections in the Prophecy
As seen earlier, the prophecy was divided into three sections, or four, if we count the division of the final week or the seventieth week. A brief comment or so on these divisions may be helpful.

1. **First Section of 49 Years**
From BC.457 we take 49 years, which brings us to BC.408. In this period of time, we have the Restoration Books, Historical and Prophetical and their details. Ezra, Nehemiah and Esther cover the Historical Restoration Books, while Haggai, Zechariah and Malachi cover the Books of Prophecy and restoration times. Malachi is the last of the Old Testament Prophets, and the final revelation of God in the prophetic Word to Judah. From this time on, God ceased to speak by the mouth of the Prophets. This period of 49 years basically covers this time and brings us to, what has been called, "the 400 silent years".

2. **Second Section of 434 Years**
From BC.408 to AD.26 we have 434 years, or, 62 weeks of the prophecy. This period of time covers "the 400 silent years". In this period of time, there was no revelation from God, no voice, no prophet, and this silence was broken by Gabriel (The Seventy Weeks Revelator) to Zacharias and Mary concerning the birth of John the Baptist, Messiah's forerunner, and then the birth of the Messiah Himself. Then 30 years later (AD.26), Messiah is manifested at the river Jordan. How wonderfully accounted for is the time. Unto Messiah the Prince, there would be 62 weeks. From Malachi, the last of the Old Testament prophetic Word, unto Messiah, THE WORD made flesh, was 434 years, or, the required time of 62 weeks (Jhn.1:1-3,14). In all, 7 weeks, plus, 62 weeks, or 483 years have been fulfilled when Jesus of Nazareth becomes the manifested Messiah.

3. **Third Section of 7 Years**
There is but one week or seven years of the prophecy to be fulfilled when Jesus begins His ministry. There is nothing in the prophecy so far that points to the Antichrist. Contrary to the Futurist and Dispensationalist point of view, the seventieth has nothing to do with Antichrist. There is but one week to be fulfilled. Antichrist has not had anything to do with the 69 weeks already fulfilled. There is but one week, and this is Messiah's week! He has to fulfill the six clauses of the prophecy – vs.24. Antichrist has nothing to do with the prophecy. The six clauses have to be fulfilled in this seventieth week as, so far, they have not been fulfilled!

H. The Seventieth Week
It cannot be over-emphasized that the first 69 weeks of the prophecy have become history. They are past, fulfilled, finished, and over and done with, when Jesus begins His ministry. There remains but the seventieth week, one week, the last week, to be fulfilled and all that is involved in the mighty clauses of the prophecy. It is in this last week, the seventieth week, that the most tremendous events take place as outlined in the prophecy, none of which have found fulfillment in the past 69 weeks! Let us consider some of the important events in the passage.

1. **The Two Princes**
In vs.25 and vs.26, two Princes are mentioned, each having something to fulfill. These Princes should not be confused, as some expositors have done.
- There is Messiah the Prince - vs.25,26.
- There is the Prince that shall come – vs.26.

The whole burden of the prophecy actually concerns the ministry of the Messiah, the Lord Jesus Christ. Only Messiah Himself can possibly fulfill the language of the prophecy. It is Messiah who will finish the transgression, make an end of sins, make reconciliation for iniquity, bring in everlasting righteousness, seal up vision and prophecy and anoint the Most Holy. No angel in heaven, no man on earth, no demon in hell, and no Antichrist could fulfill these clauses. Only God Himself in the person of Jesus Christ could do it (2Cor.5:19-21).

- Messiah's ministry – vs.24
- Messiah's manifestation and anointing – vs.25
- Messiah's crucifixion foretold – vs.26.

2. **The Middle of the Week**

   In vs.26 we are told, "And **AFTER** (it does no say at the close of, but after) 62 weeks (that is, the second section of 434 years from Malachi to Messiah), shall Messiah be cut off, but not for Himself." Undoubtedly this refers to the crucifixion of Christ. At Calvary, Jesus was 'cut off' out of the land of the living, but not for Himself, but for the sins of the whole world (Jhn.1:29,36; 3:16; Heb.9:28; 10:1-10; Isa.53:8). When was the Messiah 'cut off'? How long did Jesus minister? The answer to these questions should clarify who the person is spoken of in vs.27. It speaks of the Lord Jesus, the Messiah of God.

   The "he" of vs.27 can only refer to one of the two Princes mentioned in the prophecy. It is either Prince Messiah or the Prince that would come. Many mistaken interpretations of this prophecy have arisen because of applying vs.27 to the Antichrist. Antichrist supposedly makes a Covenant with the Jews for 7 years (the 70th week of Daniel), and in the middle of this week, he breaks the Covenant, desolates a rebuilt Temple, and sets himself up as God in the Temple to be worshipped. He becomes the false Messiah.

   All of this, however, has to be 'forced' into the prophecy by wresting the Scriptures (2Pet.3:16) and handling the Word of God either ignorantly or deceitfully (2Cor.4:2). The prophecy has nothing to do with Antichrist. Antichrist is not in view. The Antichrist is dealt with in detail in other chapters of Daniel. The whole burden of Dan.9 is that which concerns the true Messiah, Jesus of Nazareth, and all the clauses concern His redemptive ministry. Only a small portion of the prophecy deals with "the Prince that shall come". This matter will be considered in due time.

3. **The Covenant Confirmed]**

   Facts to remember:
   - Of the 70 weeks of the prophecy, 69 have already been fulfilled at Messiah's manifestation at Jordan river.
   - There remains only one week to be fulfilled, which began with the anointed ministry of Christ Jesus (Lke.4:18).
   - This final or seventieth week was to be given over to "confirming the Covenant". He shall confirm the Covenant with many for one week; that is, the seventieth week.

   When Jesus began His ministry, it was to **confirm the Covenant**. What Covenant? Which Covenant, as there were a number of Divine Covenants? It needs to be mentioned again, that, neither Antichrist nor Satan has any Covenant to make with God or man, and not one verse in the Bible speaks of such a Covenant. The Covenant of Death which is to be annulled is not to do with Antichrist (Isa.28:14-18).

   The only person who instituted Covenants in the Bible was God Himself, and all Divine covenants were to be fulfilled in and through Jesus Christ. The Scripture lists out nine Divine Covenants in which God is concerned and every one of them were made by God Himself.
   - The Edenic Covenant (Made before sin) – Gen.1-2.
   - The Adamic Covenant (Made after sin) – Gen3.
   - The Noahic Covenant (Made after the Flood) – Gen.8-9.
   - The Abrahamic Covenant (Made after Babel) – Gen.12,15,17,22.
   - The Mosaic Covenant (Made after the Exodus) – Ex.19; Deut.4-5.
   - The Palestinian Covenant (Made with the New Generation) – Deut.29.
   - The Davidic Covenant (Made after David's enthronement) – Psa.89; 2Sam.7.
   - The NEW Covenant (Made just before Christ's redemptive death) – Matt.26:26-28; Jer.31:31-34.
   - The Everlasting Covenant (Made in the Eternal Godhead) – Heb.13:20.

   All such Covenants were founded upon sacrifice. Each had their particular sign, seal or token. THE Covenant spoken of here in Daniel was THE ABRAHAMIC COVENANT. This Covenant is the great and most comprehensive of all Covenants in the Bible that God made with man. All other Covenants were comprehended in this Covenant and each were developments of the same. The Abrahamic Covenant was the Covenant of Messiah. This Covenant was not made with the Gentiles, only with the chosen nation. It is the Abrahamic Covenant alone which opens the way of blessing for ALL NATIONS, through Jesus Christ, the Seed of Abraham (Gal.3:16). Because this Covenant involves the promises of the other Covenants, this is the reason why it is seen to be the most comprehensive of all Covenants.

Daniel understood exactly what Covenant was meant in the prophecy. Daniel was told about those who "forsake the Covenant" and "do wickedly against the Covenant" (Dan.11:30,32). The Messiah would "confirm the Covenant".
"Confirm" means "to attest to, to back up, to establish". Note Rom.15:8. "Jesus Christ, a Minister, to **confirm the promises** made unto the Fathers..." He confirmed the promises made to Abraham, Isaac and Jacob, the three fathers of Israel. Jesus, as the Seed of Abraham, confirmed the Covenant in signs and wonders, miracles and revelation of the Word of the Father (Acts 10:38). He healed the sick, cast out devils, opened blind eyes, raised the dead, and preached the Gospel of the Kingdom of God. He was a Man approved of God. He was THE SEED to bless all nations. God confirmed all that Jesus Christ was, all He did, all He said. He was "the Covenant" of God personified, personally expressed (Isa.42:6; Lke.22:20; Jer.31:31-34; Heb.9:28). He is called by Malachi, "The Messenger of the Covenant" (Mal.3:1; Matt.20:28).
Read these Scriptures which speak of Christ's confirming ministry (Heb.2:3-4; Acts 15:41; Mrk.16:16-20). He fulfilled the Adamic, Noahic, Abrahamic, Mosaic, Palestinian, Davidic and the New Covenant in Himself!

The Angel Gabriel informed Daniel that "He" – that is, the Messiah – would confirm the Covenant with many for one week, that is, for seven years. He began to confirm this after His anointing. His ministry is the **beginning** of this last week, the seventieth week! How long did Jesus Christ minister? How long did He confirm the Covenant with signs and wonders? The answer is: He ministered for 3½ years.

I. The First Half of the Seventieth Week
The Gospels plainly reveal that Jesus Christ ministered for 3½ years. That is, he ministered for ½ a week, after which He was 'cut off', crucified at Calvary.
Jesus was about 30 years of age at His anointing and manifestation (Lke.3:23). He was about 33½ years of age at His crucifixion. Most Bible expositors seem to agree that Jesus ministered for about 3½ years. Two major things would point to this fact.

John's Gospel records four Passovers, the fourth being THE true Passover, the Lamb of God Himself being offered up (Jhn.2:13; Jhn.5:1; Jhn.6:4; Jhn.13:1). Luke's Gospel speaks of the fig tree that bore no fruit. Most accept that the fig tree here symbolizes the Jewish nation. When the dresser of the vineyard came seeking fruit, he found none. He wanted to cut it down. The dresser of the vineyard asked that it be left one more year. Three years plus one year equals four years in all. John the Baptist ministered for about 6 months, Jesus ministered for 3½ years, and this would make up the "three years" and "one year" spoken of here (Lke.13:6-10). The important points of identification therefore are:

1. **Messiah's manifestation and anointing**
   From the Commandment unto Messiah was 7 weeks and 62 weeks, covering time from Ezra to Malachi (7 weeks), and then from Malachi to Gabriel's announcements we have the 400 silent years. Then from Malachi to Jesus Christ there are 62 weeks, or 434 years. Thus from BC.457 to AD.26, the 69 weeks are history.

2. **Messiah's Covenant Confirming Ministry**
   Jesus confirmed the promises made to the fathers in Covenant, with signs, wonders, miracles and ministry of the Word of His Father, the Gospel of the Kingdom.

3. **Messiah's Crucifixion in the Middle of the Week**
   After 3½ years, Jesus was crucified. He was indeed 'cut off' in the land of the living, but not for Himself but for the sins of the people. There at Calvary He took our transgressions, our sins, our iniquities, He made reconciliation to God possible, He brought in everlasting faith-

righteousness. He was 'cut off' in the middle of the seventieth week. He also caused the Old Testament animal sacrifices and oblations to cease.

4. **Messiah's Sacrifice and Oblation**
The prophecy states: "He shall cause the sacrifice and oblation to cease". The "He" concerns the Messiah. It is nothing to do with an Antichrist sitting in a rebuilt Temple, breaking any Covenant with the Jews, and causing the animal sacrifices to cease. All of that has to be read into the prophecy because of missing the burden of the prophecy – Christ Himself!

Blood sacrifices and oblations were ordained by the Lord God in Eden after the entrance of sin. They continued through all the Covenants, and especially under the Law or Mosaic Covenant. Every Covenant had its own particular sacrifices as ordained by God. The Mosaic Covenant abounded in "sacrifice and oblation", under the Tabernacle and Temple dispensation. No angel in heaven, no man on earth, and no demon of Hades could "cause the sacrifice and oblation to cease". None could hinder the ministry of the atonement, as typified therein. Only God Himself who instituted it could cause it to cease, in the full meaning of this clause.

The Old Testament only begotten son, Isaac, asks the question: "Where is the Lamb for a burnt offering?" The New Testament answers the question, and it is answered by John the Baptist as he sees Jesus coming for baptism. "Behold, the Lamb of God which takes away the sin of the world!" (Jhn.1:29,36 with Gen.22). Jesus Christ, the perfect, sinless, spotless, once-for-all sacrifice and oblation, caused ALL animal sacrifice and oblation to cease when He was 'cut off' on Calvary. Here He made reconciliation for the sins of the people, in the midst of this final week (Read Heb.8-9-10). Christ Himself was THE END of the Law. **God was never pleased** with the Old Testament animal blood sacrifices, even though He commanded, ordained and blessed them. The student should carefully read these Scriptures confirming the truth of these things (Heb.10:6-8; Psa.40:6; Psa.50:8; Jer.6:20; Mic.6:6-8; Amos 5:21; Psa.51:17). But when John said, "Behold THE LAMB of God…", the Father responded, "This is My beloved Son, **in whom I am well pleased!**" (Matt.3:17).

When Jesus Messiah cried, "It is finished!" (Jhn.19:30), all sacrifice and oblation was finished. The Father now accepts His only begotten Son as THE sacrifice and THE oblation – forever! And so must all mankind, or else, perish. It is a finished work. None can add to it. None can take from it. We are reconciled to God by the death of His Son. All animal sacrifices automatically ceased to be accepted by God at Calvary. HE – the Messiah caused the sacrifice and oblation to cease. He was born under the Law, He fulfilled the Law Covenant, confirmed the Abrahamic Covenant and instituted the New Covenant.

Calvary closes off the first half of the Seventieth Week! It closes with Messiah's cutting off, His crucifixion. The Angelic interpreter, Gabriel, takes Daniel to the "middle of the week", to the cutting off of Messiah. In other words, Gabriel takes Daniel **TO THE CROSS** and leaves him there! And this was the express purpose of the Law and Old Testament ministry. "The LAW was a schoolmaster to bring us to Christ" (Gal.3:24).

Absolutely nothing is said to Daniel about the **last half of the Seventieth Week,** even though Gabriel had given the full time period of 70 weeks to him. Nothing is said of the events or details of this last week. There is only the briefest inference to it in the final clauses of vs.27. Gabriel makes no attempt to interpret the final half of the week. For any one to do so is to go beyond that which Gabriel was permitted to do at that time, for, details are not given concerning it in Dan.9:24-27.

It may well be asked: Why? The answer simply is that the revelation of the final half of this week, as to details, belonged to another dispensation, the dispensation of the Holy Spirit. It belonged to the end-times, the end of this present age. In summary of the time covered so far in the prophecy:

Seven weeks from the Commandment, Ezra to Malachi	= 49 years
Sixty-two weeks from Malachi to Messiah's ministry	= 434 years
One half a week from anointing to Messiah's crucifixion	-= 3½ years
Sixty-nine and a half weeks from the Commandment to Messiah's cutting off	=486½ years.

In all, there are 69½ weeks of the 70 weeks fulfilled at the cross! All is past history. There remains but ½ a week, or, 3½ years left to be fulfilled. Nothing less, and nothing more! From the crucifixion of Messiah, that is the only part of the time element of the prophecy yet to be fulfilled, yet to come to pass. And all the clauses have to be fulfilled by the end of this final half also, in the total fulness of what is meant by those clauses. Messiah has confirmed the Covenant with many (His disciples) for but ½ a week, not the full week, for He was cut off at Calvary. Once more, it may be asked: "Is there to be found any period of time, prophetic time, in the Bible, that appears as yet unfulfilled? The answer is: Indeed! It is found exactly where it should be found, and that is, in the Book of Revelation, in the book of the end-times. Before, however, discovering the final half of this seventieth week, there are other clauses in the prophecy given by Gabriel that need to be considered.

J. The Overspreading of Abominations

The final clauses of the prophecy emphasize three particular words needing our attention. These words are (1) Overspreading, (2) Abominations, and (3) Desolations.

1. Overspreading

Having taken Daniel to the first 3½ years, or, to the middle of the seventieth week, Gabriel has left Daniel at the cross of Jesus Christ. Gabriel then speaks of "the overspreading of abominations". What does this mean? Literally, it reads, "The WING of Abominations."

The word "overspread" means, "to spread out, to spread over, to cover" (Refer also Gen.9:19.KJV). In other words, the overspreading speaks of that which is stretched out as a wing, a period of time spread over, or over-spread. It is a stretching out of time after the first 3½ years has finished. It covers a certain period of time. From the crucifixion of Messiah, there would be an "overspreading" of time, time being stretched forth as a wing. This overspreading, the writer believes, refers to this present Church Age of some 2000 years of time.

God foreknew that Judah and Jerusalem (Jewry) would crucify their long-expected Messiah (Isa.53). Jesus Himself knew He would be despised and rejected of men, of His own House of Judah (Jhn.1:11). He foretold His own rejection and crucifixion and ascension back to the Father. He also foretold the fact that He would build HIS CHURCH (Matt.16:16-19). Both Old and New Testaments also tell of a period of time in which the Gentile nations would come into blessing through the Seed of Abraham. God spoke through the prophets that He would take out of the Gentiles a people for His name (Acts 10-11 with Acts 15:14-18; Rom.16). And because Jewry rejected their Messiah, they were rejected also of Messiah and cast forth out of their land to wander in captivity in all nations until the closing days of this age.

It is this matter of "overspreading" period of time in which Judah (the natural branches) are cut off because of unbelief, while the believing Gentiles are grafted into the good olive tree by faith in Christ. This is what Paul deals with in the vital chapters of Rom.9-10-11. Jewry has been blinded by their own unbelief. This blindness is on the nation, generally speaking, UNTIL the fulness of the Gentiles is gathered in. The Gospel went "to the Jew first" but they rejected it (1Thess.2:14-16). The Gentiles are being grafted in during this present age, during this "overspread" period. The time is limited "until the fulness of the Gentiles are come in" (Refer also Lke.21:24).

The Old Testament prophets did not see the mystery of the one Body of Christ, composed of Jew and Gentile. They did see the Gentiles coming into the Kingdom of God, into the true Israel of God. They did not see the "one Body". This was the revelation given to Paul (Eph.2-3 chapters). They saw Messiah's crucifixion, and then His glory. They saw these mountain peaks of prophecy. They saw the Gentiles coming into the Israel of God. But they did not see the details of the valley of the present Church Age between the two mountains of suffering and glory. Daniel was taken to the cross and then there comes this "overspreading" of time, or this "gap" between Christ's first and second coming. In this period, the Lord is building His Church of believing Jews and believing Gentiles. This is the Dispensation of the Holy Spirit, or "the last days" (Joel 2 with Acts 2).

"The WING" is the Hebrew thought of "Overspreading". Jesus wanted to gather Jewry under His wings, but they would not (Matt.23:37). They would not heed the danger call of the mother hen and run for safety under His wings.

The whole concept of "wings" was familiar to the Hebrew mind. With relation to the Tabernacle of Moses, the Holy Place, which measured 10x10x20=2000 cubical contents, the priests walked under the shadow of the wings of the Cherubim. The Cherubim and wings had been inwrought in the linen curtains of the Tabernacle. This is why the writers of Scripture often speak of coming under the "shadow of God's wings" (Ex.19:4; Psa.17:8; 36:7; 57:1; 91:4; Mal.4:2; Lke.13:34). Jewry rejected to come under His wings. His body was broken on Calvary, and since then, the Master's wing is being stretched out – overspread – for the Gentiles to come under (Ruth 2:12; Mal.4:2). It is between the first half and the last half of this seventieth week that this time of overspreading belongs. This points to the Church Age, the Dispensation of the Holy Spirit over these some 2000 years.

2. Abominations

The full expression is "Overspreading of Abominations". What then does this point to? Scripture lists many things that are an abomination to God. Read Deut.7:25-26; Ezek.8; Jer.7:10. An abomination is that which is detestable, disgusting, filthy, loathsome or idolatrous. Rev.17 gives us a vision of the Mother of Harlots and Abominations of the Earth. But the abominations especially spoken of here, in the light of the interpretation of this passage, distinctly refer to that which was prophesied of in Isa.1:10-15 and Isa.66:1-4. Note the vivid contrast of the latter Scripture. Here the Lord speaks of a time coming when all sacrifice and oblation would be an abomination to Him!

Heaven is My throne, Earth is My footstool. Where is the House that you build to Me. For My hands have made all these things. The Lord says through the prophet Isaiah:
"He that kills an Ox is as if he slew a Man,
He that sacrifices a Lamb as if he cuts of a Dog's Neck,
He that offers an Oblation as if he offered Swine's Blood,
He that burns Incense as if he blessed an Idol."

The Lord says He will look to the one who is poor and contrite in spirit, the one who trembles at His Word. He speaks of Israel saying, They have chosen their own ways, and their soul delights in their **abominations** (Isa.66:3).

This indeed is strange language. God was the One who ordained sacrifices and oblations. He ordained the ox, the lamb, the oblation and the incense. Now He is saying that these things have become an abomination. It is like manslaughter, or killing a dog, or offering swine's blood on His altar or even idolatry. The issue is, God is plainly saying that the time is coming when anyone who offered these things, even though He had once commanded and blessed it under the Law, all would become an ABOMINATION to Him. This is God's attitude to Temple and sacrifices since Calvary's once-for-all sacrifice.

When did this time come? It came when Jesus the Messiah became THE Ox, THE Lamb, THE Sacrifice, THE Oblation at Calvary for the sins of the whole world. God was never pleased or satisfied with animal blood under the Old Covenant, even though He had ordained and blessed it. He instituted it UNTIL His only begotten Son became the sacrifice and oblation. Therefore, for any one to continue to offer such sacrifices after Calvary's perfect and once-for-all sacrifice, THAT constituted the greatest abomination and insult to God! The greatest insult and blasphemy against God, against Calvary, is to reject the blood of the Lamb of God and offer animal blood to God for sin! For Futurists and Dispensationalists who teach that animal sacrifices and oblations will be offered again to God, this teaching is the greatest insult to Christ and His perfect, sinless sacrifice!

For this reason alone, of many, the Temple in Ezekiel's vision cannot be a literal, material Temple of stone, and wood. The sacrifices mentioned therein cannot be literal animal blood sacrifices. For God to accept such sacrifices is to go back, back to the Law Age, back to the Old Mosaic Covenant abolished at Calvary, and do despite to the blood of His only begotten Son. Such a thought is impossible. He waited some 4000 years for that precious blood and will never again accept animal blood. Any other blood offered to God is an abomination.

Jewry continued to offer these sacrifices after Calvary for 40 years. It was for this thing that God allowed the Temple to be destroyed in AD.70. Orthodox Jewry today still keeps a bloodless Passover, and Day of Atonement. They are without a Temple, without a Priesthood and without a Sacrifice! Any sacrifices, or substitutes offered by Jewry or heathen religions are an abomination to God and to His Son, the Lord Jesus Christ. Jewry invoked upon themselves and their unborn generations the curse of innocent blood, when they cried, "His blood be on us and our children." They sadly suffer under the curse of innocent blood, and that curse can only be lifted when they accept that blood of atonement for sin (Matt.27:25). How awful the guilt and how sore the punishment which befell the Jewish nation when they deliberately chose the blood of animals in preference to the blood of God's dear Son. It revealed that the Aaronic and Levitical priesthood had rejected God's sign of the rent veil. That rent veil declared to them the end of the Law Age, the Old Covenant, the Levitical Priesthood and all sacrifice and oblation (Matt.27:51).

History tells us that the Priesthood sewed up the rent veil to hide it from the people and carried on the system until God allowed it to be destroyed in AD.70.

In the light of these facts, how can any Christian believer look for a restoration of Temple and sacrifice? Such constitutes "the overspreading of abominations", covering some 2000 years of Church history. For this cause, God destroyed the Temple and scattered Jewry to the four winds of heaven. This is what Messiah spoke in Matt.24:15. "When you see, therefore, the **abomination of desolation** (spoken of by Daniel the prophet), stand in the Holy Place (Or, standing where it ought not. Mrk.13:14), let him that reads understand…"

In Isa.53 Messiah is 'cut off' but not for Himself, but for the sins of the people. In Isa.66:1-4 the abominations of continued animal sacrifices and oblations is spoken of. Once Isa.53 was fulfilled, then Isa.66:1-4 became a reality. Any further sacrifice and oblation offered to God became an abomination to Him! Daniel understood in measure what was meant by "the abomination of desolation", as his use of these terms express (Dan.11:31; 12:11). The consummation of all abominations is seen in Revelation, in (1) The Great Harlot Church, the Mother of Abominations, and (2) The Antichrist and he setting himself up as God to be worshipped by the whole earth. If the Jews rebuild any Temple and re-institute animal sacrifices and oblations, such will be only be further abominations to God. The Church Age then covers the period of "the overspreading of abominations". The student is referred to Strong's Concordance for further references on what "abominations" are in the sight of God. The overspreading of abominations as understood here is in the light of the interpretation of the content of the passage.

3. **Desolations**

The third word needing some comment is the word "desolations". The passage says, "For the overspreading of abominations he shall make desolate" (KJV). "And on the wing of abominations (will come) one who makes desolate" (NAS). There is difference of opinion on who the "he" is who makes desolate. An understanding, however, of the theme of desolation in Scripture actually provides the answer.

"Desolate" means "to deprive of inhabitant, make desert, lay waste, ruin, destitute." In Bible terms, it means to be laid desolate, devoid of the presence and glory of God. The question is asked: What is made desolate, or who makes desolate? We note the foundational Scripture upon which the theme of "desolation" is built. It may be spoken of as the "Fourfold Desolations" which were to come on Israel if they disobeyed the Laws of the Lord, the Laws of the land!

In Lev.26 the Lord warned Israel that He would punish them if they violated His Laws, Commandments and Statutes. He gave them laws for living in the land. For the Lord is the Lord of the land – He is "the Land-Lord!" For their disobedience, He told them he would:
- Desolate their Sanctuaries,
- Desolate their Cities,
- Desolate their Land,
- Desolate them as a Nation (Read especially Lev.26:31-35 in conjunction with the whole chapter.

Jesus Christ Himself simply confirms to Judah and Jerusalem the punishments and desolations of the broken Law, the broken Covenant.

- The Temple, God's Sanctuary, would be desolated (Read Matt.23:37-38; 24:1-4).
- The city of Jerusalem would be desolated (Lke.21:20-24; 23:28-31; Lke.13:35).
- The Roman armies would desolate the Land of Palestine.
- The House of Judah (Jewry) would be desolate as they were taken captive and scattered.

All of this took place in AD.70. God permitted Titus and the Roman armies to come and desolate the Temple, the city of Jerusalem, the land and the people in the terrible and horrible siege of that time. Read carefully Matt.21:37-41; 23:37-38; Lke.21:20-24; 23:28-31. Each involved the other in desolation.

When Jesus began His ministry, at the beginning of the seventieth week, He cleansed the Temple, calling it "My Father's house, a house of prayer". He came suddenly to His Temple (Mal.3:1 with Jhn2.). He cleansed it the second time at the close of His ministry. The religious leaders rejected the cleansing, and rejected their Messiah, until He in Matt.23:37-38 left the Temple saying, "YOUR house is left unto you desolate..." It was no longer His Father's house. It would become desolate – devoid of inhabitant, a waste, a ruin and desolation. Once Christ left the Temple, He never ever returned to it. Immediately in Matt.24:1-2, as the disciples show Him the glory of the Temple and its buildings, Messiah prophesies that it would be destroyed, not one stone being left unturned upon the other. Thus desolation befell the temple.

In this sense, "And HE (the Messiah) shall make it (the Temple) desolate." He was the Glory of God (Jhn.1:14-18) personified. Once He departed, the Glory of God departed, never ever to return to a material or literal Temple, even if Jewry builds another. God has forever finished with such Temples. He will never again inhabit such a place, whether Jewry builds one again or not. God never goes backward! The only Temple God is now concerned with is His Church (1Cor.3:16; 2Cor.6:16; Eph.2:19-22).

Father, Son and Holy Spirit all witnessed that the material Temple was finished. This is seen in the following comments.
- **The Father**
  The Father rent the veil of the Temple before the High Priest in connection with the sacrifice of His only begotten Son, who caused all sacrifice and oblation to cease. It was an act of God declaring that He no longer accepted the blood of animals, which He had once ordained now that He had the TRUE sacrifice. Christ's sacrifice was the sacrifice of all sacrifices! (Matt.27:1-51). The rending of the veil signifies the end of the Dispensation of the Law Covenant and all that pertained to Mosaic ritualism.
- **The Son**
  After cleansing the Temple at the beginning and end of His ministry (one half a week, or, 3½ years), Christ declared that the Temple would be destroyed and the Abomination of Desolation would be manifest. He never ever returned to the Temple after that. He saw that it was no longer the Father's house, but Jewry's house.
- **The Holy Spirit**
  On the Day of Pentecost, the Holy Spirit by-passed the Temple as Jewry kept the letter and form of the Law concerning that Feast. He went to an upper room where the TRUE Pentecost was kept, and there the TRUE Temple was dedicated – that is, the New Testament Church! If the Father and Son had finished with the Temple, so was the Holy Spirit finished with it. He came to dwell as the Shekinah Glory in the New Covenant Temple, the people of God.

The Godhead, as Father, Son and Holy Spirit each put their seal that material Temples and animal sacrifices were finished with, forever! Surely the One who made desolate was the Lord Jesus Christ Himself. Judah came to experience the desolation of the Temple, the City, the Land and the People according to the Laws of Leviticus, and the confirming word of the Lord Jesus, the Messiah.

M. **The People and Prince to come**
Comment needs to be made concerning "the people of the Prince that shall come". Futurists and Dispensationalists make this "Prince" to be the Antichrist, who makes a Covenant with the Jews, then breaks it and desolates the people. History, however, has confirmed who this Prince was and who the people of the Prince were.

The people of the Prince to come were to do certain things. They were to destroy (1) The City of Jerusalem and (2) The Sanctuary, the Temple. How can Antichrist sit in a rebuilt Temple as God and at the same time destroy the city and the sanctuary, if that view was right?

It was Prince Titus and the Roman armies who came in AD.70 and indeed fulfilled the prophetic word of Dan.9:26b, and the words of Christ. Prince Titus and the Roman armies destroyed the city of Jerusalem and the Temple, scattered Judah to the four corners of earth and desolated the land. History tells how in AD.70, Prince Titus, son of the Roman Emperor Vespasian, came to Jerusalem, with the Roman armies and besieged it. The curses of the Law fell upon Jewry until in the horrible siege, they ate their own children. The Temple was burnt. The soldiers upturned the stones of the Temple as the silver and gold melted. They did this to recover the metals, thus fulfilling Christ's prophecy. As far as Jewry – Judah and Jerusalem and Palestine is concerned, it is a time of overspreading of abominations. It is a time of desolation, both naturally and spiritually. The greatest desolation is that Jewry has been desolate of Temple, Priest and Sacrifice ever since, as well as being scattered to the four corners of earth. The city, the sanctuary, the land and the people were desolated and have been ever since. This condition is to continue until the Times of the Gentiles are fulfilled. The student should read these Scriptures in the light of these comments (Matt.24:1-2; Dan.9:26; Isa.8:7,8; 28:18; 10:23; 28:22; Psa.90:5; Deut.29:49-67 with Lev.26).

For those expositors who see that the "he who makes desolate" refers to some other than Christ, these comments may be helpful. The Lord Jesus Christ, as sovereign over all certainly prophesied the fourfold desolation. But, on the human side, He knew and permitted Prince Titus and the Roman armies to fulfill His words. The "he" of the Divine side may refer to Jesus Messiah, and on the human side, the "he" may refer to Prince Titus who fulfilled the Divine decree, the prophetic word of the desolations to come. There is no contradiction in the truth of all this.

N. The Consummation
Vs.27 tells us that condition of "overspreading of abominations and desolation" was to continue "**even until the consummation.**" The consummation of a thing is the end! In other words, this condition will obtain right through to the close of this present age, the end-time. Dan.12:9 speaks of it as "the time of the end", the end of the Church Age.
Where then does it place the final half of the 70th week? The answer should be evident. It places it right down to THE END of this age, the end of the overspreading of abominations. This is exactly where it is. It is therefore future and yet to be fulfilled. Gabriel has taken Daniel to the cross, the cutting off of Messiah in the middle of the 70th week. The order then is, the first half of the 70th week, then comes the overspreading period of time, the abominations and desolations, and then comes the consummation, the end, or the last half of the 70th week. Between the first and the last half of the week, the entire Church Age intervenes.

The verse continues. "And that determined shall be poured out upon the desolate" (vs.27.KJV). The Marginal reading says, "the Desolator." When the consummation comes, something that has been determined (Lit. "marked off") shall be poured upon the desolate. This is the only inference of what takes place at the end concerning Jewry, the people who are desolate. This is far as the Angel Gabriel interprets, and no further. Some expositors see the "Desolator" as an allusion to the Antichrist. If that is allowable, then something God has marked off shall also be poured out on him. The details of this consummation are left to the Book of Revelation, the Book of the Time of the End. The final and ultimate abomination that brings desolation is the worship of the Antichrist Beast and the taking of his Mark, Number and Name. All who do so shall suffer eternal damnation. The "pouring out" spoken of here finds fulfillment in Rev.15-16 in the vials (bowls) of wrath that are "poured out" on a desolate world of Antichrist worshippers. When people reject the "outpoured Holy Spirit" in mercy, then they have no alternative but to suffer the "outpoured wrath" of God in judgment. That is the picture portrayed for us in the clauses of the prophecy.

O. The Last Half of Daniel's Seventieth Week
In bringing our exposition of Daniel 9 to its conclusion, there are certain vital points that the student needs to remember.
- Sixty-nine weeks of the prophecy are past when Jesus was manifested as the Messiah at Jordan's river.
- One half of the 70th week is fulfilled from Jordan's river to Calvary's cross.
- Then comes the overspreading of the abomination of desolation during the Church Age.

- There remains but half a week, the last half of the seventieth week, yet to be fulfilled.
- We may expect to find the fulfillment of this final half-week in the end of the overspreading period of time, at the end or the consummation of the age.

Once again, is there anywhere in the Word of God, a period of time – prophetic time – that appears as yet unfulfilled? The answer is in the affirmative. A brief summary of the Scripture passages, which speak of this last half are listed. It will be found that this specific period of time, which completes the Seventy Weeks Prophecy also, brings to ultimate fulfillment all of the clauses involved.

As will be noted, there is absolutely no mention or suggestion of any period of seven years (One Week) to be found in the Book of Revelation, the Book of the End-Times. Revelation is the "Book of Sevens". There are some fifty-seven "sevens" in Revelation, but there is no mention of any seven years period. The only time element or specific time relative to the Seventy Weeks Prophecy of Daniel is 3½ years! No more, no less! It is this period which is the ultimate "Time of Jacob's trouble" (Jer.30:7; Dan.12:1). It is also known as the period of the "Great Tribulation" (Matt.24:21; Rev.7:14). Let us note the references to this 3½ years in both Daniel and Revelation.

1. **Daniel 7:25**
   Here in this vision, Daniel sees the Little Horn among ten horns and he wears out the saints of the Most High (the tribulation saints) for a Time, Times and Half a Time. That is, in all 3½ years, or the final half of the seventieth week. The ten horns here correspond with the ten toes on the feet of the Image dream (Dan.3). Worthy of note is the fact that, before Daniel is given the Seventy Weeks Prophecy, he is given a period of time of 3½ years of pressure on the saints by the Little Horn. This is simply half a week given to him.

2. **Daniel 12:5-12**
   Here Daniel asks "How long shall it be to the end of these wonders?" The Man clothed in linen tells him it would be for a "Time, Times and Half a Time" before these wonders come to an end. Note vs.11,12. Again Daniel is given a period of 3½ years. He, however, heard but understood not. When he asked about it all, he was told that this was shut up and sealed until the time of the end. The wise would understand in that time. In both Daniel 7 and Daniel 12 we see the same period of time, and it is simply 3½ years, not 7 years.

3. **Revelation 11:2,3**
   John sees two witnesses of Jesus Christ and they are called on to prophesy for 1260 days. This is 3½ years of ministry. The vision also concerns the "holy city" where our Lord was crucified, which is none other than Jerusalem, even though spiritually it called Sodom and Egypt. This city is to be trodden under foot for 42 months, or, 3½ years. The House of Judah will have their eyes opened to their long-rejected Messiah (Read Zech.10-11-12-13 chapters). This concerns the same period of time when that which is determined shall be poured upon the desolate, as in Rev.15-16 chapters.

4. **Revelation 12:6,14**
   John in this chapter sees a woman, pointing to the end-time Church (the Bride of Christ). This woman is given wings of an eagle so that she might fly into the Wilderness where she is preserved from the face of the serpent. This preservation is over the period of time called 1260 days or Time, Times and Half a Time. That is, exactly 3½ years.

5. **Revelation 13:5**
   The final mention of this prophetic time period is in this verse. The Beast (Antichrist) reigns for 42 months, which is, 3½ years. He is he final Desolator, Satan incarnate. The details of this period of time are actually covered in Rev.10,11,12,13,14,15,16,17,18 up to Christ's coming in Rev.19. That is, the events of this final half week, the last 3½ years of the Seventy Weeks Prophecy. At Messiah's coming, all the clauses of the prophecy come to their ultimate fulfillment. All were judicially made possible at Calvary. All are actually fulfilled at Christ's second coming.

In both Daniel and Revelation, there are eight references to 3½ years, never one to 7 years. The student is encouraged to read thoughtfully these eight references given again here (Dan.7:25; Dan.9:24-27; Dan.12:7; Rev.11:2; Rev.11:3; Rev.12:6; Rev.12:14 and Rev.13:5). No seven years is mentioned in Daniel or Revelation. All of the teaching of the "seven years tribulation" arises out of a misunderstanding and misinterpretation of the notable Seventy Weeks Prophecy.

Philip Mauro, in his excellent books (**"The Seventy Weeks & The Great Tribulation"**, page 107), in grappling with the final half of the week, attributes the apparent discrepancy to the prophet Daniel, and not his interpretation of the prophecy! He understands the prophecy to have finished with or about the time of the death of Stephen. It can be asked then: "What about the fulness of the six clauses being fulfilled? Where is the "Most Holy" that was anointed? What then of the seven or eight references to the period of 3½ years mentioned in Daniel and Revelation, as twin books? With Philip Mauro on this pint we would graciously disagree and hopefully have proved that the final half of the 70th week is fulfilled at the end of the age, before Christ comes.

Conclusion:
This then is an alternative understanding and interpretation of the Seventy Weeks Prophecy. To every thesis, there is an antithesis; the balance generally is found to be in the middle, in a synthesis. This interpretation is in between the different Schools of Eschatology. For the Historic Pre-Millennialist, and the Post-Millennialist and the A-Millennialist, who believe the Seventy Weeks was fulfilled at Christ's death or the death of Stephen, what then of these seven or eight references to 3½ years, or half a week in Daniel and Revelation? Futurists and Dispensational Pre-Millennialists, who believe the 70th week is fulfilled in Revelation, have to find that 7 years for there is only 3½ years to be found. If there is no 7 years Tribulation, then the Futurist and Dispensationalist scheme of events built on these 7 years needs to be reconsidered.

For this writer, this remarkable prophecy, and its attendant events, as yet to be seen, finds its ultimate fulfillment at the second coming of the Lord Jesus Christ. As mentioned several times, a person's eschatology arises out of their interpretation of Daniel's Prophecy, right or wrong. The key to Daniel and Revelation is found in this prophecy. Most every expositor's view of Daniel and Revelation, and the component parts, is built on this understanding. It is for this reason that much more detail is given to this prophecy. The rest of the chapters concerning a Christian Millennium are built on this interpretation of the Seventy Weeks!

CHAPTER TWO

THE KINGDOM

Another important area pertaining to end-time events is that which concerns the Kingdom of God. For the Post-Millennialists and the A-Millennialists, the Kingdom is everlasting. It is 'now' and will be seen as the Kingdom eternal when Jesus comes again. For the Historic pre-Millennialists, the Kingdom of God is everlasting, it is "now, but not yet". There is the present manifestation of the Kingdom, spiritually, in the hearts of men; but there will be an expression of the Kingdom in greater glory in the coming Millennium.

For the Futurist and Dispensational Pre-Millennialists, however, the Kingdom was offered to the Jewish nation under the ministries of John the Baptist and Jesus. The Jewish nation, regrettably, rejected the King and the Kingdom. The King was crucified, and the Kingdom was postponed to the end of the present age. Jewry, as a nation, will have its eyes opened to their Messiah, accept Him and then preach the Gospel of the Kingdom to the nations. Christ will return, and then the full manifestation of the Kingdom will be seen in the Millennium. It will be a "Jewish Millennium", when the Jews will be the head of the nations. Christ will be reigning on the throne of David in Jerusalem for 1000 years. At the end of this period, He will deliver the Kingdom back to he Father.

As the student can see, there is some imbalance and there are some extremes in the positions held here. It evidences the need for some balanced understanding of this important theme – The Kingdom of God. It is this that is the concern of the present chapter.

Introductory

The theme of the Kingdom is the most comprehensive and all-embracing subject of the Bible. It covers all Dispensations, reaching from eternity to eternity, covering all time allotted to man. An over-all understanding of the Kingdom of God should be helpful when it comes to having an understanding of the Christian Millennial aspect of the Kingdom.

A. Principle of Interpretation

When it comes to the Word of God as a whole, one needs to have sound principles of interpretation, or, sound hermeneutics. Sound hermeneutics makes for sound theology. This is true when it comes to the matter of the Kingdom of God, relative to Time and Eternity.

There is a twofold aspect of the Kingdom of God that needs to be kept in balance; that is (1) The Spiritual aspect and (2) The Literal or Actual aspect of the Kingdom. In other words, there is the Kingdom in its Spiritual, Eternal and Heavenly manifestation, and there is the Kingdom in its Literal, Earthly and Time manifestation. Both have their parallels and both run together when it comes to Time and Earth. Our overview of the theme presented here will confirm this principle.

From **"God and His Bible"** (W.H.Offiler, page 99) the following comments have been adapted as exemplifying "The Principle of the Spiritual and Literal".

"The Word of God has both spiritual and literal aspects to it. All Scripture has this dual basis stamped on it. Most of the problems of interpreting the Word of God come because expositors have 'spiritualized the Word' with disregard to the earthly or human side. One cannot properly interpret the Word of God without taking into consideration the fact that it has both spiritual and literal, Divine and human, sides to it.
God the Creator has identified Himself with man, the creature. We are born of the flesh (the human side). We are born of the Spirit (the Divine side). The birth of the Lord Jesus Christ was literal or actual (Human), and yet it was also spiritual (Divine). He was begotten from heaven, His Father God, by the overshadowing of the Holy Spirit. He was born on earth, His mother, the virgin Mary. Jesus was the Son of God (on the Divine side). He was the Son of Man (on the Human side). Jesus was Son of God and Son of Man. He was a Divine-Human Being – the God-Man! The Divine and Human natures were perfectly blended in the One person of our Lord Jesus Christ; His mother, Mary, His Father, God. Jesus Christ was Deity and Humanity, Heavenly and Earthly, Spiritual and Literal – THE WORD made FLESH! Each are brought together in the

Redeemer – the Lord Jesus Christ. It was GOD and MAN coming together to form one new creature – the Divine pattern for all new creations of God" (End of adapted comments).

The same principle is applicable to the truth of the Kingdom of God. The Kingdom of God is both spiritual and literal, heavenly and earthly, Divine yet revealed in redeemed mankind. It is not one without the other. The Kingdom has both heavenly and earthly expression and manifestation. The imbalance is when expositors take it to its extreme on the spiritual side and disregard the literal side. Or else, the other extreme or imbalance is to make the Kingdom so literal and earthly, that the heavenly and spiritual is disregarded. The balance would be to see that both aspects run parallel as far as the earth is concerned. The Kingdom is both spiritual and literal, heavenly and earthly, having Divine and human aspects to its expression.

B. The Kingdom Defined

The word "Kingdom" is made up of two words: "King's Domain" = King-Dom. It is the territory or area over which a King rules or reigns. It is the King's Domain. God's Kingdom is the reign or the rule of God, whether in heaven or earth. It is the purpose of God, the extension of God's rule. The Greek word "**Basileia**" speaks of the sway, rule and administration of a King. It is the royal reign of the Kingdom of God as far as God is concerned. The word "Kingdom" is used some 450 times in the Bible, about 160 of these references in the New Testament.

The word "Kingdom" not only involves the territory over which a King rules and reigns, it also includes the subjects over which the King rules and reigns. Both are included in the concept of the Kingdom. It is possible for a King to have territory and no subjects, but one cannot have subjects without some territory for the subjects to dwell in. When we speak of the Kingdom in these chapters, it includes both territory and subjects, whether in heaven and/or in earth!

C. The Kingdom in Eternity – Heaven

There is no disputing the truth that the Kingdom of God is everlasting – it is eternal. There has never been a time when the Kingdom did not exist. Where ever the King is, there the Kingdom is personified. The Scriptures clearly tell us that the Kingdom is from "everlasting to everlasting" (Psa.145:10-13; 2Pet.2:11; 2Tim.4:18; Dan.7:27; Rom.14:17; Psa.103:19; Dan.4:3). The Kingdom, from God's point of view has neither beginning nor end. It is sovereign and rules over the whole universe (Rev.11:15; Psa.10:16; 1Chron.19:12).

To say it again: the Kingdom of God is all-inclusive. It includes within itself, its domain, the total universe, the elect and fallen angels, heaven and all creatures as well as mankind on earth (Ex.15:18; Psa.145:10-13). This is the territory and the subjects and this constitutes THE KINGDOM OF GOD! The Kingdom is eternal, as to 'time'; it is universal as to 'place' and it includes angelic beings and human beings as to 'subjects'. And even though Satan and his angels sought to establish, as it were, a 'rival Kingdom', the Kingdom of God is over-all. It is sovereign. Sin brought confusion and chaos, but God's Kingdom is still supreme. This 'rival Kingdom' will be subdued in God's time and Satan and his angels will be confined to the eternal jail - Hell (Rev.16:10; 2Pet.2:4; Jude6).

God's Kingdom is a Kingdom of light, life and love. It is a Kingdom of righteousness, peace and joy (Rom.14:17). Satan's Kingdom is a Kingdom of darkness, death and hatred. It is a Kingdom of unrighteous qualities, and discord and sorrow (Col. 1:13; Matt.12:25-26; Rev.16:10). Whatever the King is like, so is the Kingdom!

D. The Kingdom in Time – Earth

God's purpose is expressed in the "Disciples Prayer" (Matt.6:9-13). "…Your Kingdom come, Your will be done in earth, as it is in heaven…For Yours is the Kingdom, the power and the glory – for ever. Amen!" God wanted His Kingdom to be manifested in earth. While, therefore, recognizing that the Kingdom of God is a spiritual Kingdom, a heavenly Kingdom, it also has to be seen that God wanted His Kingdom to be established in earth, in and through mankind and especially through the redeemed people of God in the nations of earth! So our considerations are given over here to the earthly expression and manifestation of the Kingdom of God. Our studies show that there will have been a seven-fold expression of that one Kingdom of God relative to earth when "Time shall be no more!" In each age there has been a further or progressive revelation of the Kingdom of God in the earth. Let us consider the seven-fold aspect of God's Kingdom as seen in time and in the earth. Each have their bearing on the final aspect of the Kingdom – the Christian Millennial Kingdom.

1. **The Kingdom of God in Eden**
   There is no question that God wanted His Kingdom to be manifested in the earth in the creation of man. Adam and his bride, Eve, were King and Queen over all creation. They were to reproduce after their kind, a race of sinless beings. In and through them the heavenly Kingdom would be manifested and demonstrated in this very earth. This was God's whole purpose in creation. God wanted His Kingdom to come in the earth as it was in heaven. He gave the man and the woman dominion, rulership and authority in the earth, under His rule and authority. They were to be instruments for the expression of God's Kingdom in earth. This Kingdom was both spiritual and literal, heavenly and earthly in its manifestation. Man was over the earth (Psa.8 with Gen.1:26-28). Tragically, they sold themselves and the unborn human race out to Satan's Kingdom – the Kingdom of Darkness. It looked as if sin had frustrated God's purpose – temporarily! God came in redemptive power and grace and covered man's sin with blood atonement. The Kingdom of God was set in the hearts of the faithful. The time period of God's Kingdom is from Adam (the father of the human race), to Noah (the father of the human race after the Flood). Great evil was manifested in the human race, but God kept the line of faith in the Godly line. Divine judgement fell on the unrighteous and all ungodly flesh was destroyed (Gen.3-9).

2. **The Kingdom of God in the Patriarchs**
   After the Flood, God revealed His heavenly Kingdom, His rule, reign, government and authority in Noah and faithful line, right through to Abraham. The highest revelation given to father Abraham was the appearance of Melchisedek, the King-Priest from heaven. This was after the battle of the nine kings of worldly kingdoms against Abraham and his servants. Divine victory was given. Melchisedek blessed Abraham, giving him communion and accepting from him tithes from the spoils. Abraham is the father of all who believe. The Kingdom in its spiritual manifestation is seen in the lives of the Patriarchs – Abraham, Isaac and Jacob, and on through the 12 sons of Jacob unto the development of the nation of Israel. Though the Kingdom was spiritual, its expression is seen in the lives of believers here on earth. God promised Abraham and Sarah that kings would be born of them in due time (Gen.17). The kingly line would be of the tribe of Judah (Gen.49:10; Num.24:7; Deut.17:18-20). The time period of the patriarchs is covered from Gen.12-50. In the patriarchs was preserved the promises of the Seed Messiah. Though these men were imperfect, yet they knew the rule and reign of God in their hearts and lives in the midst of apostate and corrupt nations about them.

3. **The Kingdom of God in Israel**
   Surely none can question that God chose the nation of Israel, as a nation from other nations, so that He could manifest and demonstrate His Kingdom in the earth through it. In Ex.19:1-6, God told the nation through Moses that He wanted them to be "a Kingdom of Priests, a holy nation".
   Israel was a theocracy. God ruled the nation. In this nation He established more fully His Kingdom, His Laws and Statutes and His Commandments (Ex.19-40). God wanted Israel to become His instrument in the earth and demonstrate His Kingdom to all nations.
   Saul (1Sam.9-10), David (1Sam.16; 1Chron.10:14), Solomon (1Kgs.1:46) were the first earthly kings to reign over a united nation. In due time, the Kingdom of Israel was divided into two houses, two kingdoms, the Kingdom or House of Israel and the Kingdom or House of Judah (1Kgs.11-12; Ezek.16; Ezek.23). Both houses had prophets of God sent to them to remind them of the Laws of God's Kingdom. The tragedy is found in the fact that Israel failed to be all that God intended them to be. For this reason, God allowed the Captivity of both houses; the House of Israel going into Assyrian Captivity and the House of Judah going into Babylonian Captivity.
   God restored a faithful remnant of the House of Judah back to the land, permitted them to rebuild the Temple and all this to hold them in the land until the birth of Messiah, the King. The Restoration Books of the Old Testament deal with these things. In spite of repeated failure, there was a manifestation and expression of God's Kingdom in the hearts and lives of the faithful remnant. The King would come. He

would present the Kingdom to the Jewish nation, and all that God really meant by His Kingdom rule in the hearts and lives of a redeemed people. However, during the Captivity of the House of Judah, the Kingdom – God's sovereign rule in the earth – would be manifested in the Gentile nations of earth.

4. The Kingdom of God in the Gentile World

During the Captivity of the House of Israel and more especially that of the House of Judah, God allowed the Gentile nations to become the instrument for the manifestation of His Kingdom, His sovereign rule and reign in the earth.

The Book of Daniel especially shows the sovereignty of God's Kingdom. He rules in the heavens and in the earth and He gives the Kingdom to whomsoever He will (Dan.2; Dan.4; Psa.9:16; Ezra.1:1-4; Dan.7:9-14,26,27; Psa.22:28,29; 1Kgs.2:15; 2Sam.16:8; 2Chron.36:22; Dan.4:17,25, 32-35). The Lord is the Lord of all the earth (Josh.3:11-13). Under the various Captivities, one may see the rise of the Assyrian and Babylonian Empire. Then came the Medo-Persian, the Grecian and the Roman Kingdoms ruling over the people of God. Over and above all rules the Kingdom of God. Through it all, GOD gives the Kingdom to whomsoever He will. Kings over the world-kingdoms were caused to admit this truth under the dealings of God.

5. The Kingdom of God in Christ

When it comes to the revelation of the Kingdom of God in Christ, there is a complete new level, manifestation and demonstration of that Kingdom. Here the Father sent His Son, the King's Son – or, the promised King. God held the House of Judah in the land of Palestine until the advent of the King, Jesus Christ. The Gospel of Matthew is especially the Gospel of the King and the Kingdom.

The Kingdom has been in Eden, then in the patriarchs, then in the chosen nation of Israel, and then in the Gentile world. The sovereign hand of God was over all. But now there would be a new expression of the Kingdom. This would be in the person of God's Son. The Kingdom would be personified in the King. He would be the clearest, fullest and most perfect demonstration of the Kingdom in human form that the world had ever seen. Beyond being seen in the hearts and lives of the redeemed, the Kingdom would be seen in the King, God's Son, the Lord Jesus Christ Himself.

It is important, however, to understand the mind-set of Jewry as a nation about the Kingdom of God, at this advent of the King. The Kingdom under Old Testament times, though spiritual in the hearts of the faithful, had **nationalistic, materialistic and political** characteristics about it. Jewry was at that time under Roman rule – the iron rule of the Kingdom of Rome. When they heard John and Jesus announce, "The Kingdom of heaven is at hand…" (Matt.3:1-2; 4:17), they only thought of a nationalistic, materialistic kind of Kingdom. The Messianic kind of King they were expecting and wanted, was a Davidic kind of King. They wanted a King who would throw off the Roman yoke and establish a Jewish Kingdom as it had been centuries before under King David. They neither understood the King (Jesus), nor the Kingdom (of Heaven) He proclaimed! The Old Testament had foretold the coming of the King and the Kingdom. They had misinterpreted them both. Only the faithful had any idea of what it was all about.

The King:
The Old Testament foretold the coming of the King. Jewry did not understand the character of the King when he came. Note these prophecies concerning the coming King.
- The Father had set His Son, His King, in Mt. Zion (Psa.2:1-9).
- The King would be a King over all the earth (Zech.14:9).
- He would sit as a King-Priest in His throne (Zech.6:12-15).
- He would be of the tribe of Judah (Gen.49:10).
- Of His Kingdom there would be no end (Isa.9:6-9).
- He would be the King, the Judge and the Lawgiver (Isa.33:22).
- He would be a righteous King, the Lord our Righteousness (Jer.23:5-6).
- He would be a King-Priest after the Order of Melchisedek (Psa.110).
- He would be the King of Glory (Psa.24:7-10 with Psa.45:1-17; 22:27-31; 1Sam.2:7-10).

- He would be higher than the Kings of the earth (Psa.89:1-52,27).
- He would as a hiding place in the storms (Isa.32:1-2).

When Jesus came, He was born the Son of David, the Son of Abraham (Matt.1:1). He was promised the throne of David, and the Kingdom of David (Lke.1:30-33). But this was not the type of King Jewry wanted. If He was a Davidic King, then He would crush their enemies as did David for Israel, and they would rally to His cause.

The Kingdom:
Jewry, as already mentioned, had a wrong concept of the Kingdom also. They were looking for "The Stone Kingdom" that would crush the iron rule of the Kingdom of Rome, according to the Daniel 2. They were looking for "The Son of Man Kingdom" that would destroy the Beast Kingdoms of this world, and establish the supremacy of the Kingdom of Israel – of Jewry, according to Daniel 7. They did not, however, realize that the "ten toes" and the "ten horns" of the last of the World Kingdoms had not yet been manifested. Their interpretation of the 'time element' was out of God's timing.

Contrary to Futurist/Dispensationalist views, the Kingdom Jesus presented to Jewry was NOT a nationalistic, materialistic or politically Davidic kind of Kingdom. Jesus Himself said, "My Kingdom is not of this world system" (Jhn.18:36). The Kingdom Jesus proclaimed was a **spiritual Kingdom in the hearts of men, here and now**. It has always been the rule and reign of God in the hearts of His redeemed! Those who believed would be governed by His Laws – the Laws of His Kingdom, as seen in Matt.5-6-7, the Sermon on the Mount!

- Repentance was necessary to enter the Kingdom (Matt.3:1-2; 4:17).
- Jesus preached the Gospel of the Kingdom (Matt.4:23; 9:35; Mrk.1:14; Acts 1:3).
- The poor in spirit would inherit the Kingdom (Matt.5:3,10,19,20).
- We are called to seek first the Kingdom of God and His righteousness before material and physical requirements (Matt.6:33).
- The casting out of demons and healing of the sick were evidences of the power of God's Kingdom (Matt.12:25-29).
- One has to have the humility and simplicity of a little child to enter the Kingdom (Matt.18:1-6; 19:14).
- The publicans and sinners would enter the Kingdom before the Scribes and Pharisees (Matt.21:31-32; 23:12-13).
- One must be born again to enter the Kingdom (Jhn.3:1-5).
- Jesus taught His disciples to pray, "Your Kingdom come…"(Matt.6:6-13; Lke.11:2).
- Jesus said the Gospel of the Kingdom would be preached in all the world for a witness to all nations before the end of the age would come (Matt.24:14 with Matt.10:7; Lke.9:2; 10:9-11),

Jesus went about preaching and teaching and demonstrating the power of the Kingdom of God. The power of the Kingdom conquered the power of Satan's Kingdom everywhere Jesus went. The Kingdom was personified in the King Himself!

The Gospels provide evidence of increasing antagonism to Christ's person (Who He was) and His teaching (What He said). Jesus was knowledgeable of His rejection. He changed His style of teaching and moved into much more parabolic kind of teaching. The King would be crucified. The Kingdom would be rejected. The parabolic teaching of Jesus now points to "the Kingdom now, but not yet", as some expositors speak of it. It would be "mystery Kingdom" in the earth, in the hearts and lives of men, and there would be mixture seen in the Kingdom through to the end of the age. There would be the **present** manifestation of the Kingdom, and there would be a **future** aspect and manifestation of the Kingdom. The following Scriptures chart this truth out for us. The references show both the present aspect and the future aspect of the Kingdom. The references have to be considered carefully to see this distinction as to the time, whether the Kingdom "now" or the Kingdom "not yet".

The Kingdom Now – Present Aspect	The Kingdom Not Yet – Future Aspect
Kingdom within you – Lke.17:20-21; Matt.12:28 Law & Prophets, then the Kingdom-Lke.16:16 Publicans enter the Kingdom – Matt.21:31-32 Repentance precedes the Kingdom –Matt.3:1; 4:17 Born again to enter Kingdom – Jhn.3:1-5 Kingdom has mixture, wheat & tares, good & bad fish, to end of age – Matt.13:1-52	Abraham, Isaac, Jacob sit down in the Kingdom while others cast out – Matt.8:1-12· Your Kingdom come – Matt.6:10 Apostates not enter Kingdom – Matt.7:21 Things that are an offence and do iniquity to be cast out of the Kingdom, the righteous shine in the Kingdom of the Father – Matt.13:1-52 Sheep enter into Father's Kingdom – Matt.25:31-46 The Man receives a Kingdom and returns – Lke.19:11-27 Remember me in Your Kingdom – Lke.23:42 Appoint you a Kingdom – Lke.22:29-30 In regeneration sit on 12 Thrones – Matt.19:28 Better to enter Kingdom maimed than whole – Mrk.9:47 Sit on right & left hand in Kingdom-Matt.20:21

After 3½ years of Covenant confirming ministry in signs and wonders, preaching and teaching the Gospel of the Kingdom, Jewry rejected the King and the Kingdom. Jesus was not the kind of King they wanted. He did not present the kind of Kingdom they looked for.

As noted in **The Seventy Weeks Prophecy**, Jewry came under the fourfold desolation spoken of in the Law. The Temple, the City, the Land and the Nation were desolated (Lev.26 with Matt.23:38; 24:1-2; 21:41-46; Ezek.10:18; 11:23; Dan.9:24-27; 2Chron.36:21). Wrath came upon them in AD.70 (1Thess.2:14-16; Rom.2:9-10). The curse of innocent blood came upon the nation, as they rejected the blood of the New Covenant in Christ (Jer.31:31-34; Matt.26:26-28). The nation was broken out of the faith-olive tree because of their unbelief (Rom.11).

What then happened to the Kingdom? Futurists and Dispensationalists teach that the Kingdom was **postponed** to the end of this present age. At this time, Jewry will have its eyes opened, accept their long-rejected Messiah and then preach the Gospel of the Kingdom to the Gentiles. In the meantime, God had Plan B and created the Church as a parenthetical purpose due to Jewish blindness and unbelief. All of this is contrary to the Word of God. It is contrary to the revelation in the Scriptures concerning the everlasting Kingdom of God. If the Kingdom has been postponed, then no true believer has been born again. Jesus said, all must be born again if they want to see and enter the Kingdom. Once a person is born again, they enter the Kingdom of God, right here and now. This, however, does not negate the future aspect of the Kingdom as already seen in the Kingdom "now but not yet" columns of Scripture references.

What happened to the Kingdom? Jesus gave the answer very clearly as He spoke to the Jews just prior to His death. "The Kingdom will be taken from you and given to a nation that will bring forth the fruits thereof" (Matt.21:42-46). That **NATION is THE CHURCH**! The Kingdom was transferred over to the New Testament Church. It was NOT postponed to the end of the age, as out next section confirms.

6. **The Kingdom of God in the Church**
There is no doubt that there is a relationship and connection between the Church and the Kingdom in the New Testament. Jesus said, "Upon this Rock I will build **My Church**…and I will give to you (Peter), the Keys of **the Kingdom**! (Matt.16:15-20).
He also said that the Kingdom would be taken from the Jewish nation and given to **"a nation"** that would bring forth the fruits thereof. A serious reading of these Scripture references tell us that this nation is none other than the New Testament Church composed of believing Jews and believing Gentiles (Matt.21:42-46 with 1 Pet.2:1-10; Ex.19:1-6; Isa.26:1-4). As will be seen, the Church now

becomes the instrument for the proclamation and demonstration of the Kingdom of God. The Church is the Messenger! The Kingdom is the Message! The Church and the Kingdom, though distinct, are related. The Kingdom, as already noted, is the universal reign of God over all creation and creatures as well as the universe of worlds. It includes in itself angels and mankind. The Church is composed of redeemed believers, out of every kindred, tongue, tribe and nation. The Church does not include the angelic hosts. It may be said that the angelic hosts are in the Kingdom of God but only the redeemed are in the Church. The Kingdom is eternal and all encompassing. The Church is God's eternal purpose but manifested in Time. It is limited to those of mankind who are redeemed by Christ. The distinction yet relationship between the Church and the Kingdom needs to be understood to avoid confusing the real issues involved in both. We do not pray, "Your Church come" but "Your Kingdom come!" Nor do we preach "The Gospel of the Church" but we preach "The Gospel of the Kingdom!" (Matt.6:6-10 with Matt.24:14). While the word "Church" is used some 115 times, the "Kingdom" is used some 160 times in the New Testament. The Church is in the Kingdom and the Kingdom – God's rule and reign – is to be in the Church. But the Kingdom is far more inclusive than the Church. The Church is a part of the Kingdom, but it is not the Kingdom in its totality.

The Book of Acts, along with other Scriptures from the Gospels, shows that the Church was the channel, the instrument, the vehicle and vessel for the expression of the Kingdom of God. It was through the Church that the Kingdom of God was to be extended in the earth, in the hearts of men. As previously said, "The Church" is **THE MESSENGER,** and "the Kingdom" is **THE MESSAGE!** In the Book of Acts we see how believers were "**born into the Kingdom**" and "**added to the Church**" (Jhn.3:1-5 with Acts 2:41-47).

We bring together some of the most salient points concerning "The Kingdom of God in the Church!" These confirm the comments that the Kingdom was taken from Jewry and given to the Church. The Kingdom continues, but the instrument for its proclamation, expression and demonstration has changed over the centuries. The student is encouraged to read these references along with the comments.

- Christ will build His Church and the Church will have the Keys of the Kingdom (Matt.16:18-19).
- Repentance and faith are the doorway into the Kingdom (Matt.3:1-2; 4:17,23).
- The Kingdom is at hand, through which one can be added to the Church (Mrk.1:14-15; Heb.6:1; Acts 2:34-42).
- One must be born again, born from above, by spiritual and heavenly birth to enter the Kingdom (Jhn.3:1-5). If the Kingdom was postponed, as Dispensationalists teach, then no one could be born again!
- Regeneration is a translation out of the Kingdom of Darkness into the Kingdom of Light and Love (Col.1:13-14).
- The Kingdom of God is righteousness, peace and joy in the Spirit (Rom.14:17; Matt.6:33).
- The Kingdom of God is not of this world system (Jhn.18:36; Matt.6:9-10; Lke.17:20-21).
- The Gospel of the Kingdom is to be preached in all the world for a witness in all nations before the end comes. This is done by the Church (Matt.24:14; Mrk.16:15-20).
- The Law and the Prophets were until John. Since then the Kingdom of God is preached and people press into it (Lke.16:16; Matt.5:17-18; 11:13; 12:28).
- The Kingdom was taken from Jewry, as a nation, and given to the holy nation, the New Testament Church (Matt.21:42-46; 1Pet.2:5-9).
- Believers are the good seed of the Kingdom in the "mystery" expression of the Kingdom in this present age (Matt.13:27-28; Mrk.5:11; Matt.8:11; Lke.1:28-29).
- We are called to seek first the Kingdom of God as our priority (Matt.6:33; Lke.21:31).
- The Kingdom of God is within the heart (Lke.17:20).
- In the Book of Acts, the Church preached and demonstrated the power of the Gospel of the Kingdom of God (Acts 1:3-6).
  Philip, the evangelist from the Church, preached the Gospel of the Kingdom (Acts 8:1,12).
  Paul, as an apostle from the Antioch Church, preached the Kingdom of God (Acts 14:22; 19:8; 20:25; 28:31).

- John and Paul, apostles of the New Testament Church, believed they were then in the Kingdom (Rev.1:9; Col.4:11; Acts 28:23,31).
- As believers were born again into the Kingdom of God, they were added to the Church (Acts 2:41-47 with 11:24 and Jhn.3:1-15).

The Church preached the Gospel of the Kingdom, for there is only one Gospel for Jew and Gentile. There are not many Gospels. This Gospel is called "The Gospel of the Kingdom" (Matt.24:14), "The Gospel of Jesus Christ" (Mrk.1:1), "The Gospel of God" (Rom.1:1), "The Gospel of His Son" (Rom.1:9), "The Gospel of the Grace of God" (Acts 20:24), "The Glorious Gospel" (1Tim.1:11), "The Gospel according to Paul" (Rom.1:17; 16:25 with Gal.1:6-9).

The Church today is the agent, the instrument for the demonstration of the Kingdom of God in the earth. Though the Church and the Kingdom, in the universal sense, are distinguishable, they are indivisible in the eternal purpose of God!

7. **The Kingdom in the Millennium**
There remains one final aspect of the Kingdom of God relative to God's purpose in the earth, and that is, the Millennial Kingdom. For this writer, it is **the Christian Millennium!**

Attention has already been drawn to the fact that Jesus taught the Kingdom as being "now, but not yet" (The reader is referred to comments on "The Kingdom of God in Christ"). By a careful reading of Lke.17:20-21 with Lke.10:11-15 the student may see the present and the future aspects of the Kingdom. Jesus had told them that the Kingdom of God is among (within) you. They were not to look for the Kingdom here or there, as the Kingdom is already here. But, as He went into Jerusalem, because some thought the Kingdom of God would immediately appear, He added another parable about the Kingdom. He told them that the Kingdom was like a man going into "a far country, to receive for Himself a Kingdom". When He received the Kingdom, He returned and took account of His servants. The interpretation of the parable should be rather self-evident. Jesus is the Man who goes into the far country, the heavenly country. He receives the Kingdom from the Father and then in due time, at the second coming, He returns to take account of His servants. The Kingdom was "now" but "not yet". It was present, and yet it was future.

Conclusion:
For the Futurist and Dispensational Pre-Millennialist, the Millennial Kingdom is a Jewish Millennium, where the Jews are exalted as head of the nations, under the restored Mosaic Covenant economy. For the Historic Pre-Millennialist, the Millennial Kingdom is basically the same as now, except that it will be a Kingdom of righteousness, peace and prosperity, Christ being King over the earth.

For the Post-Millennialist, the world will be basically a Christianized world presented to Christ through the ministry of the Church triumphant. For the A-Millennialist, the Millennium will be finished on earth, and eternity will follow the second coming of Christ.

For this writer – a Christian Millennialist - the Millennial Kingdom will be the final expression and manifestation of the Kingdom of God relative to earth. It will indeed be a **Christian Millennium**! But this has to be considered in the appropriate part of this text. It is the manifestation of the Kingdom in the earth, especially that pertaining to the 1000-year reign of Christ on the earth, that has been the cause of much controversy. It is this that the writer addresses in Part Three of this text.

In this chapter, the Kingdom has been considered in brief as to its past, present and future aspects, and this as it pertains to Eternity and Time. The Kingdom is everlasting, but, when it comes to Time relative to this earth, the Kingdom has had successive stages in the overall purpose of God. At the conclusion of the Christian Millennium, the Son gives the Kingdom back to the Father, that God may be all and in all. In the beginning God, and in the end it will be God (1Cor.15:23-28). Fuller details of this writer's view will be seen in **Part Three**, to which he reader is referred.

CHAPTER THREE

THE CHURCH

In the light of the contents of the previous chapter, and the section on **"The Kingdom in the Church"**, it hardy seems necessary to comment further. But, in order to maintain consistency, some thoughts need to be given concerning the Church as in the New Testament. Also, because some readers may be of the background teachings that the Church is a "parenthetical plan" of God, all need to see that the Church was and is in the **eternal purpose of God!**

For the Futurist and Dispensationalist Schools, each hold the belief that the Church was "Plan B" should the Jews reject the King and the Kingdom. Jewish unbelief caused the Kingdom to be postponed and caused God to drop to a secondary level, Plan B, which was the creation of the New Testament Church, predominantly a Gentile creation. Under this teaching, the Church is seen as an interlude, a mystery brought in between the first and second comings of Christ. These Schools see no continuation of God's purpose from the Old Testament Church. They teach that the New Testament Church was a mystery revealed especially to the Apostle Paul, the Apostle of the Gentiles.

While not agreeing with all that Dr.William Hendriksen says on the field of Eschatology, he does make excellent comment concerning those who hold that the Church was brought in as a parenthesis in the overall purposes of God. He writes: "There are those who maintain that the Church is a mere parenthesis, an after-thought in God's program of redemption, a valley invisible to the Old Testament prophets, who never even dreamed about it. That is, in dealing with the Church, history has left the main highway and is making a detour, and that God ignores the flight of time until He deals again with the Jews. In the sight of God, so runs the argument, the Jews are the all-important. Hebrew time is the Lord's time. Israel is like a scheduled train which has been put on the side-tracks temporarily, but will be put back on the main track again as soon as the **unscheduled (!)** Gentile-Special has passed through" (Booklet, **"And So All Israel Shall Be Saved"**, page 7).

The Church is looked upon as a stop-gap, an interlude, a parenthesis, a mystery just revealed to Paul. The Church will be removed from the earth by a secret rapture just prior to the beginning of a seven-year Great Tribulation. Some writers in this School teach that "God's prophetic clock stopped with Jewish unbelief during this dispensation". The clock will once again tick off once God has finished with the Church. He will then turn back to the Jews, His original and main purpose in time and eternity.

With this position, Historic Pre-Millennialists, Post-Millennialists, A-Millennialists and this writer – Christian Millennialist – disagree. Each School here sees the Church as being in the **eternal purpose** of God. But this is what this chapter is all about. A consideration is given to the Church in the Old Testament and the Church in the New Testament.

A. The Church in the Old Testament

It is an irrefutable fact that there was a Church in Old Testament times. It may safely be said that this was "The Church of Moses". It is clearly identified as "The Church in the Wilderness"; with Moses being the mediator. In Acts 7:37-38, it says, "It was this very **Moses** who said to the children of Israel, God will raise up a Prophet from among your brethren, as He raised me up (Deut.18:15-18). This is he who in the Assembly in the wilderness was the go-between for the Angel who spoke to him on Mt.Sinai and our forefathers..." (Amp.New Testament). The word "assembly" is the Greek word "**Ekklesia**" (SC.1577) and is translated "**Church**" 112 times in the New Testament and three times "**Assembly**". The Authorized translates it "the Church in the wilderness".

The Old Testament equivalent is the word "**Congregation**" (SC.5712, Ex.12:3,6; 19:47; 35:1). In Lev.6:26,30; Num.7:89 the word "**Congregation**" is used also (SC.4150). In the Septuagint Version of the Scriptures, the Hebrew word "**Qahal**" (or "Congregation") is translated as such some 70 times (SC.6951). This Hebrew word refers to the "congregation" as the "called and the assembled people of God". It is the Greek equivalent to "**Church**" , or "**Ekklesia**". The various words point to the people of God, and/or the place where the people of God assembled to meet with God.

In quoting from the Old Testament (Psa.22:22), the New Testament (Heb.2:12) says concerning

Christ as the leader of our worship to God the Father, "In the midst of the **Church** (or, in the midst of the Congregation) will I sing praise to You." Most translators take the words "Congregation" and "Church" to be synonymous terms. All of this proves that there was a Church in the Old Testament, and that Church was the Israel of God, the people of God.

"**Ekklesia**" is never applied to any individual believer or single person. Adam, Noah, Abraham and Sarah, Isaac and Rebekah, Jacob and Joseph, as well as many others, were men and women of faith. All were believers, but none of them were counted as "the Church". Hebrews 11 confirms they were men and women of faith. They were individual believers who walked with God, but they individually were not "the Church".

"Church" always points to and specifies an assembly or group of people. It refers to a company of people called out and gathered together to listen to and act for God. The word is used for:
(1) The elect believers of all ages, whether in heaven or on the earth. It speaks of the Church invisible, the Church triumphant, the Church universal, the Church in heaven especially, or "the dead in Christ" (Heb.12:23-24).
(2) The local congregations gathered together in some geographical place. This speaks of the Church visible, the Church militant on earth, the Church local, or "the living in Christ".

The word "**Ekklesia**" is used some 115 times in the New Testament, and ninety of these refer to the local Churches, congregations gathering together in some particular locality.

The Nation of Israel was the Old Testament Church, the people of God. They were called out of Egypt, called unto God Himself, and they gathered to listen to and act for God, as the chosen nation. They were called to be a Kingdom of Priests unto God and to demonstrate His laws in the nations of the earth. The purpose for "the Church in the Wilderness" was spelled out clearly by the Lord through Moses in Ex.19:1-6. On odd occasions, even under Old Testament times, Gentiles were blessed through the chosen nation, through the Old Testament Church. One may think of Nineveh, Daniel in Babylon, Elijah and Elisha, Ruth and Rahab, as well as other Gentiles who came into blessing by reason of the Old Testament people of God. There can be no mistaking the fact that God had a Church in the Old Testament – the Nation of Israel. There was always a faithful remnant in the chosen nation who trusted and believed God.

B. The New Testament Church
The Gospels show how "the Church of the Old Testament" ("Moses' Church"), Judaism, as a nation, rejected their own Messiah and the Kingdom of God. The Lord Jesus, knowing the will and the purpose of His Father, gave this promise and prophecy, "Upon this Rock, I will build **My Church**, and the gates of Hades will not prevail against it" (Matt.16:18). Before Paul was even thought of, Jesus spoke of building His Church. The revelation of the New Testament Church was not revealed to Paul, but before Paul, to Jesus, and to the Twelve.

Those of the Old Testament "Church of Moses", who refused to believe in their Messiah, were rejected. Those out of the Old Testament "Church of Moses" were accepted, and they moved on, in the purposes of God, into the "Church of Jesus Christ". It was, therefore, "out of Moses" and "into Jesus"; out of the Old Covenant Church and into the New Covenant Church.

The New Testament also provides a further or twofold aspect of the use of the word "Church". It speaks of:
1. The Church Universal – Matt.16:18; Eph.1:22-23; 5:25-32; Heb.12:23; Col. 1:18. Christ is the Head of the Church, which is His Body. This speaks of the Church universal.
2. The Church Local – Christ is in the midst of His people, any place they gather together in His name. He gathers with the Church (Churches) in every geographical place they meet. This speaks of the Churches local, in any given locality (Matt.18:15-20). If discipline of a member is necessary, it has to be done in the local Church and the passage here refers to the Church local, not the Church universal.

So Christ promised and prophesied to build His Church before Paul was even on the scene. This refutes the error that Paul was the one who received the revelation of the Church. This, however, will be clarified more fully in the appropriate place.

C. The Church – The Eternal Purpose of God

Paul, in the Epistle to the Ephesians, does tell us that God had an eternal purpose in Christ. This purpose in Christ concerned the Church, the Body of Christ. This is seen clearly in Eph.3:9-11, which reads: "And to make all men see what is the fellowship of the mystery, which from the beginning of the world hath been hid in God, who created all things by Jesus Christ: To the intent that now unto the principalities and powers in heavenly places might be known by the church the manifold wisdom of God, According to **the eternal purpose which he purposed in Christ Jesus** our Lord..." (KJV).

Futurists and Ultra-Dispensationalists teach that the New Testament Church was a mystery, not seen in the Old Testament, but especially revealed to Paul. These things are not confirmed by Jesus, Peter or Paul or any of the New Testament writers, as the following comments confirm.

1. The Church Prophesied in the Old Testament

One cannot have any hesitation in saying that the New Testament Church was prophesied of clearly in the Old Testament. The Old Testament prophets and writers spoke many times of the coming in of the Gentiles into Israel or into the Kingdom of God. Numerous Scriptures could be given but the student is encouraged to read fully the references provided here.

The Prophets foretold the day coming in which the Gentiles would be blessed.
- In your seed (Christ) all nations will be blessed (Gen.22:18). This seed, Paul tells us, is Christ and His Church (Gal.3:8,14-16,29).
- God spoke through Isaiah of Christ being given as a light to the Gentiles (Isa.11:1-5,10; 42:1-16; 49:6-12,22; 54:3; 60:1-5,11,16; 61:6-9; 66:19).
- Jeremiah also spoke of the Gentiles receiving blessing (Jer.16:19).
- Malachi spoke of the Name of Christ being great among the Gentiles (Mal.1:11).
- Joel prophesied of the Holy Spirit being poured out on all flesh in the last days (Joel 2:28-32 with Acts 2:17-21). Peter quoted this at Pentecost.
- Amos spoke of the Gentiles coming into the Tabernacle of David to worship, along with the believing Jews (Amos 9:11-12 with Acts 15:13-18).
- Paul quotes from the Prophet Isaiah that Christ would be a light to the Gentiles. This light would shine through His New Testament Church (Acts 13:46-47).

Ultra-Dispensationalists and Futurists seek to place the fulfillment of these prophecies of the Gentiles coming into blessing, in the "Jewish Millennium". There, as their argument goes, the Jews become the great "Missionary Nation" to the Gentile nations, and there the Gentiles enter Israel's Messianic Kingdom.

However, the Gospel, the Book of Acts and the Pauline Epistles refute such teaching. The Old Testament prophecies of the Gentiles coming into blessing are being fulfilled in this present dispensation of the Holy Spirit. It all began in the Book of Acts and still continues to the end of the age.

The student should read these references, as they are too many to quote here.
- In the Gospels – Lke.2:32; Matt.12:18-21; Jhn.12:20-24; Matt.28:18-20; Mrk.16:15-20. There the Lord spoke of His Gospel going into the entire world, to be preached to every creature, and the disciples were to make disciples of all nations.
- In the Acts – Acts 1:8; 15:13-18; 13:46-47; 9:15; 14:2-5,27; 18:6; 21:11-25; 22:21; 26:17-23; 28:28. Here we see how the Lord Jesus used the Apostle Peter to open the door of faith to the Gentiles. The Holy Spirit was poured out on the Gentiles as Peter spoke the Word. Peter and the ones with him, as well as the apostles in Jerusalem, had to recognize that the Gentiles had received the same Holy Spirit as they had, without circumcision and the works of the Law. Then Paul, as the Apostle to the Gentiles, steps into the door that Peter had opened for the Gentiles.
These things are the beginning of the fulfillment of the Old Testament prophecies of the Gentiles coming into blessing. This was NOT in a coming Millennium, as Futurists and Dispensationalists teach, but right here and NOW in this Gospel Age, the Dispensation of the Holy Spirit!
- In the Epistles – The Pauline Epistles make particular mention of the Gentiles coming into blessing, along with believing Jews. Read Rom.1:13,16; 2:9-10, 17-29; 3:9-20; 9:24-

33; 10:12-13; 1Thess.2:14-16; Gal.3:14-16. Note especially Rom.11:11,25; 16:4. Also, the reader should note how many Old Testament prophecies of the Gentiles coming into blessing are quoted by the Apostle Paul in Rom.15:9,10,11,12,16,18,27

The Book of Acts may be divided between Peter (Apostle to the Jews, the Circumcision), and Paul (Apostle to the Gentiles, the Uncircumcision). Acts 1-12 concerns the ministry of Peter to both Jews and then the opening of the door of faith to the Gentiles, and Acts 13-28 concerns the ministry of Paul, the Apostle to the Gentiles who enters that door for ministry.

The Gospel indeed went "to the Jew first", as Rom.1:16; Jhn.1: 11; Matt.10: 5,18; Acts 11:19-21; 13:5; 14:1-5; 16:3,20; 17:1,5,13,17; 18:2-5,19; 18:24-28; 20:21; 21:26-27 clearly reveal. The early Church actually consisted first of believing Jews; 3000, then 5000, then multitudes of men and women. Then, in Acts 10-11, Peter witnesses the Spirit outpoured on the Gentiles, and later on, Paul steps in as the Apostle to the Gentiles. In time, the Jews as a nation, reject the Gospel through the New Testament Church, and God causes Paul to turn to the Gentiles more fully (Read carefully Acts 13:46; 28:29 with 1Thess.2:14-16).

Enough has been written to show that the Old Testament prophecies of the Gentiles coming into blessing were prophecies of the New Testament Church. These prophecies were NOT pointing to any fulfillment in a Jewish Millennium, but prophecies to find fulfillment here and now! These prophecies were the Old Testament language speaking of the New Testament Church. The New Testament Church may have been, in that sense, "a mystery" to the Old Testament Prophets, but there was no mystery about the Gentiles coming into blessing under Messiah and the true Israel of God. Without question, the Old Testament prophesied of the New Testament Church. Those in the Old Testament Church (Israel, Acts 7:38) prophesied of the New Testament Church, under the ministry of the coming Messiah!

It is WHAT HAPPENS to believing Jews and believing Gentiles that constitutes "the mystery" as revealed to the Apostle Paul. This is seen more fully and very clearly in Ephesians Chapter 3:1-7, as quoted here in full:

" For this cause I Paul, the prisoner of Jesus Christ for you Gentiles, If you have heard of the dispensation of the grace of God which is given me to you-ward: How that by revelation He made known unto me the mystery; (as I wrote before in a few words, Whereby, when you read, you may understand my knowledge in the mystery of Christ), Which in other ages was not made known unto the sons of men, as it is now revealed unto his holy **apostles** and **prophets** by the Spirit; **That the Gentiles should be fellow-heirs, and of the same body**, and partakers of his promise in Christ by the gospel: Whereof I was made a minister, according to the gift of the grace of God given unto me by the effectual working of his power."

The Church is not "the mystery". The Church is not "the mystery Gentile Church". **"THE MYSTERY"** is that believing Jews and believing Gentiles would be equal before God, as members in the **ONE BODY OF CHRIST! THAT is the mystery revealed to Paul!** It is the truth that there would **not** be two bodies, a Jewish Body and a Gentile Body. There would be **one Body** composed of believing Jews and believing Gentiles. This is what the Council in Jerusalem was all about: What to do with the believing Jews and what to do now with the believing Gentiles. James shows both Jew and Gentile would come into the Tabernacle of David (Acts 15:15-18), and worship the Lord together as one. Paul writes, "By **one Spirit** are we all baptized into **one Body**, whether we be Jews of Gentiles and have all been made to drink into **one Spirit**" (1Cor.12:13). The Church was indeed prophesied of in the Old Testament. The Old Testament prophets and the New Testament apostles had the same truth about Gentile blessing.

2. **The Church Typified in the Old Testament**
Not only was the Church prophesied of in Old Testament times, but it was also typified in the Old Testament. Even some of the Dispensational School see pictures or types of the New Testament Church in the Old Testament, while at the same time teaching that the Church was not seen back there. This certainly becomes contradictory! Only a few types or pictures can be mentioned, as there are so many once the truth has been seen.

- The Church is the "Eve" of the Last Adam, Christ (Gen.2 with Eph.5:23-32).
- The Church is the "Rebekah" of the New Testament only begotten Son (Gen.22, Gen.24 with Eph.5:23-32).
- The Church is the Temple of God (2Chron.5 with Eph.2:19-21).
- The Church is God's Olive Tree (Rom.11:17-18).
- The Church is God's Flock, His one fold (Jhn.10 with Psa.23).
- The Church is God's Lampstand, His Light-bearer (Zech.4 with Rev.1:20).
- The Church is God's Vine (Psa.80 with Jhn.15:1-16).

Old Testament Israel typified the New Testament Church; for Israel was "the Church in the Wilderness" (Acts 7:38). This is why Paul could say that so many things happened to Israel for types and examples and they were written for our admonition upon whom the ends of the ages had come (1Cor.10:6,11).

Each of these things above are Old Testament pictures. All related to Israel, God's Old Testament Church back there. All are applied to the New Testament Church, here and now, for the Church is built on the foundation of the prophets (Old Testament Prophets), and the apostles (New Testament Apostles), (Eph.2:19-22 with 2Pet.3:1-2). The Old Testament Church, Israel, under the Old Covenant now merges into the New Testament Church, through coming into the New Covenant. One was the type and shadow, the other is the antitype and the substance.

Much more could be written. The purpose of this chapter, however, is not to be a complete text on the New Testament Church. The New Testament Church was never ever Plan B in the mind and the purposes of God. God foreknew, He foresaw, He foretold His purposes in and through the Old Testament writers and the prophets.

The New Testament Church was in the eternal purpose of God. Before there was ever a Jew, an Israelite or a Gentile in existence, God had in mind a Bride for His only begotten Son, Jesus. This Bride, the Body of Christ, was not a last minute creation of God. The Old Testament was all a part of the one purpose of God, the on-going purpose of God. Each Dispensation was a step towards His ultimate purpose. Way back in the eternities past, God wanted a Bride for His Son. This Bride was the New Testament Church, redeemed by His own blood, composed of believing Jews and believing Gentiles. It is by the one Spirit that all were baptized into the one Body, whether Jews or Gentiles (1Cor.12:13). All of this was prophesied of and typified in the Old Testament by the Prophets and the Nation of Israel. These things were NOT to be fulfilled in any Jewish Millennium but in this present Gospel Age as the Gospel of the Kingdom is now going to all nations before the end comes (Matt.24:14).

D. The Church and National Israel

One other area needs to be covered in this chapter, and that is, the relationship of the New Testament Church to the Old Covenant Nation of Israel. The Nation of Israel will be dealt with in the next chapter. But this chapter needs to conclude with what happened to the nation of Israel once the New Covenant Church was brought in. It is to the Apostle Paul that we owe the revelation as given to him by the head of the Church, the Lord Jesus Christ.

In a summary statement it may be said: The Old Covenant Church, Natural Israel, once its members accepted Christ Jesus, became members of the New Covenant Church, Spiritual Israel. This Church becomes the true Israel of God entitled to the spiritual promises of the Abrahamic Covenant. This Church is taken out of every kindred, every tongue, and every tribe and nation. Whereas the Old Covenant Church was basically one nation, Israel, now the New Covenant Church is from all nations. Abraham was to be the father of many nations, not just the one chosen nation (Gen.12:2-3; 17:1-8). Abraham was to be the father of all who believe, whether of Israel as a nation or the Gentile nations. Rom.4 shows that Abraham was the father of the Circumcision and the Uncircumcision, that is, believing Jews and believing Gentiles.

Futurists and Dispensationalists charge other Millennial Schools of thought of "robbing Israel of her inheritance" and "teaching replacement theology, that the Church replaces Israel". This is not the case. Israel's true inheritance was "in Christ" and those of Israel or Judah who accepted Christ continued on in their inheritance in the New Testament Church. The Church does not "replace natural or national Israel". The New Covenant Church is the continuation of the true and believing

Israel of God from Old Covenant times. However, it is in the higher level of the New Covenant, the Old having been fulfilled and abolished at the cross. It is the unbelieving Jew or Israelite who actually robs himself when he rejects Christ as his Saviour.

Paul shows that:
(1) Believing Israel/Jews pass through the cross into being believers in the Church, which makes them now spiritual Israel, the real Israel of God in true sense, and
(2) Unbelieving Israel/Jews are still natural or racial Israel, but are not the Israel of God, spiritual Israel, and
(3) Believing Gentiles pass through the cross into membership in the New Covenant (Testament) Church, making them also spiritual Israel, and
(4) Unbelieving Gentiles are still Gentiles in the flesh and are not the Israel of God.

Paul, therefore reduces the Jew and Gentile to the same level in God's sight in Romans. Both Jew and Gentile are all under sin, all are sinners, and Jew and Gentile need God's salvation. Both must come God's way, through Christ, or both are lost. This is Biblical truth. People should not seek to deceive the unbelieving Jew that he is still the special and chosen race in God's sight. People should be honest with the Jew and the Gentile and tell them God's way to salvation is through Christ or all are lost.

There is no difference between Jew and Gentile. There was an advantage. The Jew, as seen in the next chapter, had all the advantages of the Law, the Covenants, the Glory of God, the Prophets, the Messiah and many other things. Greater privileges also mean greater responsibility before God. The Gentiles had none of these advantages.

Paul shows that there is (1) a natural Israel, the national, the earthly, the fleshly or the sand seed, and he also shows that there is (2) a spiritual Israel, the heavenly, the spiritual and the eternal Israel of God, the star seed. It is first the natural, then afterwards that which is spiritual (1Cor.15:46). The natural came first but is superceded by the spiritual. Natural Israel had to do with birth after the flesh. The spiritual Israel has to do with birth after the Spirit (Jhn.3:1-5; 1Pet.1:23). Jesus told the Jews, who were Abraham's seed after the flesh, that they were of "their father, the Devil" as to their spiritual state (Jhn.8:33-45). Therefore, though natural Israel (Jews), they were not spiritual Israel (Jews). We note a number of Scriptures in brief that speak of the true Jew, the true Israelite, and the spiritual Israel of God.

1. Rom.9:6-8. Paul says, though they may be of Israel naturally, they are not all Israel spiritually. "They are not all Israel which are of Israel, Paul says. The flesh seed is not counted for THE seed, but only that which is of the promise, that which is of the Spirit. It is not the natural or national birth that counts, but only the heavenly and spiritual birth that counts. Nicodemus, a Jew and teacher in Israel was told he must be born again. He had been a Jew. He needed to be born from above (Jhn.3:1-5). To exalt the natural or national birth above the heavenly and spiritual birth is to exalt the flesh above the spirit. It is to exalt the natural Israel before God above the spiritual Israel, which is contrary to God's Word.

2. Rom.4:16-22. Abraham was called the father of many nations, not just the chosen Israel nation. Abraham is the father of ALL who believe, whether Circumcision (Jew) or Uncircumcision (Gentile).

3. Gal.3:6-9. All those who are children of faith are children of Abraham.

4. Gal.3:16, 29. Christ is the Seed of Abraham, but also, all who believe in Christ are the Seed of Abraham. That is, there are not many "seeds" (plural), but the "Seed" (singular) of Abraham, which together constitute Christ and His Church, a many-membered Seed to bless all nations.

5. Gal.6:16. The Israel of God are those who are new creatures in Christ, where neither circumcision nor uncircumcision counts.

6. Rom.2:17-29. He is a Jew which is one inwardly, not outwardly. It is of the heart and spirit and not of the flesh. There is the physical Jew, but there is the spiritual Jew. Paul was a Jew

physically, but he was a true Jew inwardly, in the heart and spirit. Jesus spoke of those Jews who were saying they were Jews but were liars and of the Synagogue of Satan (Rev.2:9; 3:9).

7. Rom.11:17-24. The unbelieving Jews were broken off out of the faith-olive-tree, while the believing Gentiles were grafted in among the Jews who remained in faith. The olive tree is not the natural or national unbelieving Israel, but the true believing Israel of God, including the believing Gentiles. The olive tree is the spiritual Israel of God. Believing Jews and believing Gentiles are all part of the one tree, partaking of the same sap. If Jews do not persist in their unbelief, they can be grafted back into this faith-olive-tree. It is one and the same olive tree. There are not two olive trees.

8. Ephesians 2:11-19. Jesus broke down the middle wall of partition between Jew and Gentile. Where once there were two ethnic groupings, one was in and the other was outside of Covenant, now both are made one in Christ. There is but one new man. The old man was either Jew or Gentile. The one new man is "in Christ". It is one body in Christ. Believing Jews and Gentiles belong to the one Commonwealth of Israel. To separate believing Jews and Gentiles is to get away from the cross, and re-erect the middle wall of partition that Jesus broke down. He reconciled both unto God in one body by the cross.

9. Gal.3:28-29. In Christ there is neither Jew nor Gentile, but only the new creation.

10. Col.3:9-11. In Christ there is the new man, which is neither Jew nor Gentile, bond nor free, circumcision nor uncircumcision. Christ is all and Christ is in all, uniting all as one in Himself.

11. Eph.3:1-9. The Jew and Gentile, baptized into one Body, is "the mystery" revealed to Paul. This was "the mystery" not understood by the Old Testament Prophets, even though they saw the Gentiles coming into blessing back there. There would not be two bodies, a Jewish Body and a Gentile Body, but ONE Body. National distinctions cease to exist in the one Body of Christ. National distinctions make people either Jews or Gentiles. The "old man" is either Jew or Gentile. The "new man" is the new creature in Christ. The "new man" is the Israel of God. In Romans Paul deals with Jew and Gentile as being the true Israel of God. In Ephesians Paul deals with Jew and Gentile being one Body in Christ. The new man is not a Jewish man or a Gentile man, it is a NEW man in Christ. It is the union, by the Spirit, and by spiritual birth, of all nations in one new nation, the Church, the Israel of God. The Body of Christ is not national, international, but a complete new nation in Christ.

12. 1Cor.12:13. By one Spirit are we all baptized into one Body, whether we are Jews or Greeks, and have all been made to drink into one Spirit. It is the Holy Spirit who settles the issue in the Book of Acts. There was not to be a Jewish Church and a Gentile Church. There would be one Church, one Body. This was the revelation given to the Apostle Paul.
All were cleansed by the same blood of Jesus, baptized into the same Name, filled with the same Holy Spirit, and therefore, all were in the same Body! The Jews received the Spirit (Acts 2), and the Gentiles received the Spirit (Acts 10-11), therefore all belonged to one and the same Body. There was no exaltation of the Jew, by natural birth, above the Gentile, by natural birth, but it was the spiritual birth that counted before God.

13. 1Pet.2:9. All those "in Christ" are now counted to be the holy nation, a royal priesthood, a holy and peculiar treasure to God. This is language once given to natural Israel (Ex.19:1-6).

14. Matt.21:43. The Kingdom was taken from the Jewish nation and given to the Church, God's holy and new nation. This was the righteous nation that would keep the truths of God (Isa.26:1-2). This was the nation not yet called by His name (Isa.65:1; Rom.10:20-21).

15. Gal 4:21-31. Paul's allegory shows that the Jerusalem, which now is in existence, is likened to Hagar and Ishmael, that is, children of bondage, born after the flesh. He shows that the believers in Christ are likened to Sarah and Isaac, the child of promise, born after the Spirit. The earthly city of Jerusalem is in bondage to legalism and works of the flesh. The heavenly city of Jerusalem is the free woman and is of the Spirit. Believing Jews and Gentiles belong to

the "mother which is above", and not to the "mother below". This repudiates the earthly city as the city of God. Read also Rev.11:8.

16. Heb.12:22-24. The Jerusalem, which is above, is the place where the names of the Church of the Firstborn are written. Those who have been born from above, born again of the Spirit, have their names in the Lamb's Book of Life (Rev.13:8; 17:8).

17. Acts 15:15-18. The believing Gentiles would be set in the Tabernacle of David, not the Tabernacle of Moses, along with believing Jews. If they were set in the Tabernacle of Moses, then the Gentiles would have been under the Old Law Covenant. But now, believing Jews and believing Gentiles are under the New Covenant, in Christ. This releases believing Jews from the legalism and works of the Old Covenant (Heb.8:8-13; Jer.31:31-34).

This chapter can only conclude with the truths that the New Covenant Church was prophesied of in the Old Testament; it was also typified in the Old Testament, and those believers of the Old Covenant Church come into the New Covenant Church, through Christ! Therefore, the true Israel of the Old Covenant continues on in the New Covenant Church, the spiritual Israel of God.

In the Book of Acts, 3000, 5000 and multitudes of men and women, of the Jewish nation, were the first converts in the New Covenant Church. They constituted the continuing true and spiritual Israel of God, and then the believing Gentiles are brought in by grace through faith. This is not "robbing Israel of her inheritance". This is not "replacement theology". This is New Testament revelation of the New Covenant Church, the eternal and spiritual Israel of God. It is this Israel of God that enters into the Bride-City through the twelve gates with the twelve names of the true Israel upon them. The true Israel of God is spiritual and eternal (Rev.21:12).

For full treatment on this subject, the student is referred to:
"The Church in the New Testament" (Author)
"The Vision of an Antioch Church" (Author)
"The Book of Acts" (Author), and
"Interpreting the Scriptures" (Ch.13, The Ethnic Division Principle) – Conner/Malmin

CHAPTER FOUR

THE NATION OF ISRAEL

Without doubt, one of the greatest areas of controversy in the realm of Eschatology has to do with the Nation of Israel, commonly referred to as the Jewish nation. Numerous questions are asked. What about the Jews? What about natural and national Israel? Where do they fit in the plan of God? Has God got some special plan for the Jews in the end of this age, or in a coming Millennial Age? Is God about to finish with the Church and turn again to the Jews to fulfill His purposes in earth? Will the Jewish nation be the head of all the Gentile nations in the Millennium? Many, many other questions are asked. For many of God's people, it is a very sensitive issue, and in some cases, a very divisive issue in the Body of Christ. This chapter seeks to deal, within as brief and reasonable comment as possible, on this subject.

To remind the reader of the Millennial Schools and their position as to the Nation of Israel, we note the following.

The Historic Pre-Millennialist sees that the Jewish nation will experience a visitation of God somewhere in the end of the age. Their eyes will be opened to their long-rejected Messiah and they will be grafted back into the good olive tree.

The Post-Millennialist and the A-Millennialist basically hold that the nation of Israel has basically forfeited the promises of God through national unbelief. There is no hope for the Jewish nation apart from Christ. Some hold that the Jews have been swallowed up in the nations of earth and have really lost their national identity because of their sin, and especially the greatest sin in the rejection of their long-promised Messiah, Jesus Christ. These Schools hold no hope for the Jew except in and through Christ.

The Futurist and Dispensational Schools of thought hold that the Jews will have their eyes opened to their rejected Messiah in the end of the age, under the ministry of the Two Witnesses (Rev.11). They will become the great Missionary Nation to the Gentile nations, especially in the coming Millennium. In this Millennium, the Mosaic Covenant economy will be restored and it will be basically a Jewish Millennium with Christ on the throne of David, ruling and reigning from Jerusalem over all the earth.

The position of this writer, as a Christian Millennialist, would hold basically the same position as the Historic Pre-Millennialist. The Jews will experience a fresh outpouring of the Spirit in the end of this age, and under that, their eyes will be opened. They will be grafted, by faith, back into the good olive tree. They will not be a special or elect people, but, with believing Gentiles and believing Jews, all will be **one olive tree**, and **one Body in Christ**. National barriers cease to exist in Christ. "In Christ, there is neither Jew nor Gentile…" (Gal.3:28). This however, is spelt out more fully in this chapter. Hopefully, the chapter will present a balanced view between those Schools that would 'deify the Jew' above the Church, or those Schools that 'damn the Jew' as being totally hopeless and without any identity.

A. Threefold Ethnic Divisions in Earth
Paul in writing to the Corinthian Church speaks of three ethnic divisions in earth relative to the human race, or the nations of earth. He says, " Give no offence either to (1) the Jews, or to (2) the Greeks (Gentiles), or (3) the Church of God" (1Cor.10:32). All the nations of earth are divided into one or more of these three ethnic groups. All belong either to the Jewish nation or to the Gentile nations, or, by spiritual birth, regardless of national birth, they belong to the Church of God. The Word of God needs to be rightly divided when it comes to these three classes of people.

B. A Brief History of Israel and Judah
At the risk of being somewhat technical, a brief history of the Nation of Israel should be helpful here, especially when it comes to dealing with the modern day Jewish Nation, or the State of Israel as it is known today.

Abraham, Isaac and Jacob were the fathers of the chosen nation of Israel. Abraham, Isaac and Jacob were not Jews, nor were they Israelites, as oftentimes expositors mistakenly speak of them. They were Hebrews (coming from Eber). Abraham is spoken of as a Hebrew (Gen.14:13). The infant nation was also spoken of as Hebrews, the Hebrew Nation (Ex.1:15-19). Therefore the three fathers were not "Jews" as some speak of them. Also, Abraham, Isaac and Jacob were not "Israelites" even. It was Jacob whose name was changed to Israel who became the first "Israelite" in strictest sense of that word. Jacob's descendants became known as Israelites. It was after this that his twelve sons became known under the corporate name, "Israel". This was the Hebrew nation or the nation of Israel. It was not called the "Jewish nation" but the Hebrews (Ex.1:15-19). Israel was only ever an individual name when given to Jacob. From then on it became a corporate name of twelve tribes, never any single tribe. There was never any called "Israel". There were the tribes of Israel as a nation.

It was Judah, the fourth son of Jacob, who became the father of the Jews, or the tribe of Judah. When the division came in Israel, and the twelve tribes were divided, then the two tribes of Benjamin and Judah (also Levi, the priestly tribe) became known as "the House of Judah", or "Jews". The ten tribes became known as "the House of Israel". One was the Southern Kingdom, and the latter the Northern Kingdom. In the technical sense, all Jews are Israelites but not all Israelites are Jews. The fact of the matter is that the first use of the word "Jew" in the Bible is at a time when the two Houses of Israel and Judah are at war with each (2Kgs.16:6). The word "Jew" is actually a corruption of the word "Judah". The words "Jew" or "Judah" are never ever applied to the House of Israel, that is, to the ten tribes. "Strictly speaking, the name ("Jew" or "Judah") is appropriate to the subjects of the Kingdom of the two tribes after the division and separation from the ten tribes" (BC.975. **Young's Concordance).**

Who then is a Jew? A Jew is (1) a descendant of Judah, the fourth son of Jacob, or one of the tribe of Judah, and (2) a member of the House of Judah, consisting of the tribes of Judah, Benjamin and Levi.

The nation of Israel remained a united nation for some centuries. After the death of Solomon, however, and the accession of his son Rehoboam, the nation divided and has been that way from that day to this time. In 1Kgs.12 and 2Chron.10-11 we have the details of the division of the nation into the two houses; the House of Israel and the House of Judah. The Bible provides the two distinct records and histories of these two houses, these two kingdoms or dynasties unto their two distinct captivities. Chapters such as found in Zech.11; Ezek.37, Ezek.23 with Jer.31:31-34 spell out the distinctions between the two houses.

It is necessary for serious students of the Word to recognize these facts, for the Major and Minor Prophets speak to the two houses as the Lord commands them. It is necessary to understand which house the Prophet is speaking to and what Divine utterance is being spoke to that house. Otherwise there is, and has been, endless confusion and contradiction between the Prophets and their utterances. All this is because many Bible expositors do not understand which house is being spoken to and what the prophecies are about.

The House of Israel was taken captive and dispersed to Assyria (BC.721). The House of Israel, as a whole, never returned to Palestine, but was scattered to the four winds of heaven to wander in the nations of earth, according to the utterances of the Prophets. They became known as "the lost ten tribes", though they are not lost to God. The House of Judah was taken captive to Babylon (BC.606). The House of Judah did return to the land of Palestine 70 years later. It is noted then, the two houses were taken into captivity at two different periods of time, to two different places and by two different nations about 100 years apart.

The Books of Ezra and Nehemiah deal with the return from the Babylonian Captivity of the House of Judah. It is the restoration to the land after 70 years Babylonian Captivity. Though the corporate name of "Israel" is mentioned, the only tribes mentioned in these books are the tribes of Judah, Benjamin and Levi, or, more plainly, the tribes belonging to the House of Judah, the Jews! Why? Plainly because the House of Israel had been taken captive to and dispersed through Assyria some 100 years or more earlier.

All of this is necessary to provide a clearer understanding of the purpose of God concerning the Jew. When we deal with the Scriptures pertaining to the Jew in the New Testament revelation, it helps us to understand more clearly that God is speaking more particularly of the two-tribed House of Judah, which had been restored to Palestine from Babylon. God wanted to hold Judah in the land until the birth of Messiah and on through AD.70 at which time they would be scattered to the four winds of heaven. They would remain that way until the "last days" in which a remnant would be caused to return to the land and be there for the second advent of the Lord Jesus Christ, their rejected Messiah and King.

(**Note:** For the purposes of simplicity and convenience, the words "Jew" and "Israel" will be used interchangeably from this point on. At least, the student will understand in measure some of the technical terminology used above).

C. **The Jew's Privileges in the Purposes of God**
Probably the most important chapters in the **NEW Testament** concerning the Jewish nation (or, Israel, to be more exacting!) are the chapters of Romans 9-10-11 where Paul deals with the so-called "Jewish problem".

In Rom.9:1-4 Paul expresses his burden for his own nation of Israel. He has great heaviness and sorrow for the Jews as they, as a nation, have rejected Christ and have become enemies of the Gospel of Christ. Paul himself is a Jew, of the tribe of Benjamin, an Israelite indeed, yet he is sent by the Lord to be a missionary to the Gentiles. Underneath this call, there was a continual burden for his own Jewish nation, even as God places the burden of various nations on those He calls to be missionaries (so to speak) to that nation.

In Rom.9:4-5 with Rom.3:1-2, Paul lists out a list of the national privileges that were given to the nation of Israel when chosen by God out of the nations of earth. There are at least nine major privileges given to Israel. These reveal why God chose the nation and why He preserved them. What were these things? The list here shows the things that pertained to Israel.

1. The Adoption – Ex.4:22-23. They were adopted as a nation from nations to be God's son.
2. The Glory – the visible manifestation of the Shekinah Glory, His visible presence with them.
3. The Covenants – the Abrahamic, the Mosaic, the Palestinian, the Davidic and finally the New Covenants were the Covenants God made with Israel.
4. The Giving of the Law – that is, the Moral, the Civil, the Ceremonial, and Food and Health Laws were given to this nation.
5. The Service of God – the order of approach to God in the Tabernacles of Moses and David and the Temple of Solomon.
6. The Promises – concerning the Seed (Sand Seed and Star Seed), especially Messiah.
7. The Fathers – Abraham, Isaac and Jacob, the three fathers (Ex.3:6).
8. The Messiah – Rom.1:3. As concerning the flesh, Christ was born of Israel, of Judah, of Mary (Gen.49:8-12; Isa.9:6; 7:14; Lke.1:30-33). Jesus was born a Jew, having a Jewish body but not Jewish blood, as the blood was from His Father, God (Acts 20:28).
9. The Oracles of God –The sacred Scriptures were entrusted to this nation.

D. **Reasons for God's Choice of Israel**
The Lord spelt out very clearly why He chose the nation of Israel. He told them that He did not (1) choose them for numbers as they were a small people as to numbers, and He did not (2) choose them for their righteousness, as they were a stiff-necked people. The reason He chose them was:
1. Because He loved them as the seed of the three fathers, and
2. Because of the Covenant He had made with the three fathers, and
3. Because He wanted to use them to bless all the nations of the earth (Read carefully Deut.7:6-9; 9:4-6 with Gen.12:1-3; 22:18). In Abraham's seed all nations were to be blessed. God foreknew that Judah would reject their own Messiah, but He used their failure to bring salvation and blessing to the Gentile nations.

This basically was the purpose, plan and will of God in the election of this nation. The distinctive promise of the Messiah was given to Judah, the fourth son of Jacob, and to the House of David who was of the House of Judah. God became incarnate in a Jew, not any other nationality. The virgin Mary was a Jewess. None ever wrote under inspiration infallible Scripture but those of the House of Judah, or those of the elect nation of Israel. God's prophets were of the chosen nation. The twelve apostles were of the House of Judah. The Jew was used to preserve the oracles of God. All owe the New Testament predominantly to Jewish writers. It was Jerusalem and Jewry who witnessed the first coming of Christ and the outpouring of the Spirit. Salvation is of the Jews, Jesus said. It was from Jerusalem and Judah that the Gospel would spread to all nations (Matt.28:18-20;

Mrk.16:15-20; Acts 1:8; Lke.24:47-49). All these things the whole world owes to God through the chosen nation of Israel, and to the Jew.

E. To the Jew First – Rom.1:16

The Lord's purpose in bringing the House of Judah back to the land after the Babylonian Captivity was to hold them there until the manifestation of the Messiah. The Gospel was to go "to the Jew first" and then later on, to the Gentile. This is seen in the Gospel and then in the Book of Acts.

1. In the Gospels

Jesus was born as King of the Jews (Matt.2:2).
He came unto His own (House of Judah, the Jews), and His own received Him not (Jhn.1:11).
Salvation is of the Jews (Jhn.4:9,22).
The Twelve were sent to the lost sheep of the House of Israel, not to the Gentiles (Matt.10:5,18).
After some 3½ years' ministry, the Jews rejected their King and crucified Him. Their answer was the cross. John the Baptist and now Jesus Messiah were rejected of their own nation. The Gospel indeed went "to the Jew first", before the death, burial and resurrection of Christ.

2. In the Book of Acts

After the death, burial and resurrection and then the ascension of Christ, the Gospel still went "to the Jew first". They were given, as it were, another 40 years of grace until AD.70 when the nation was scattered to the four winds of heaven for their sinful rejection of their Messiah.

- Peter went to the Jew first
  The Gospel must begin at Jerusalem, then Judea…to the Jew first (Acts 1:8; Lke.24:47).
  Jews out of every nation came and heard and received the Gospel at Pentecost. There were 3000 Jewish converts. Peter uses the keys of the kingdom Christ gave to him (Matt.16:18-19), as he opens the door to the New Testament Church.
  Another 5000 were added to the Church in Acts 4:4. Then multitudes of men and women were added to the Lord (Acts 4:32; 5:14; 6:1).
- Paul also went to the Jew first
  Saul, a converted Jew, witnessed to the Jews about Christ (Acts 9:1,22-23).
  They preached the Word to none but the Jews only (Acts 11:19-21).
  The Word was always preached first in the Synagogues of the Jews (Acts 13:5).
  Paul went to the Jew first, and went to every city where there was a Synagogue of the Jews (Acts 14:1-5; 16:3,20; 17:1,5,10,13,17).
  Paul would reason with the Jews in the Synagogue (Acts 18:2-5,19; 18:24-28; 20:21).
  Thousands of Jews believed the Gospel of Christ (Acts 21:26-27).

Here we see, after the death, resurrection and ascension of Christ, and under the outpouring of the Holy Sprit, thousands of Jews came to Christ. Peter and Paul preached "to the Jew first". The early Church was primarily a Jewish Church up to this point of time. Jerusalem, then Judea…was to the Jew first. This was Divine order. In Acts 28:17-19,29, Paul also spoke to the Jews first even at Rome.

The Gospels and the Acts show that the Good News was indeed preached to the Jew first, both before and after Calvary and Pentecost. The Jews had the Son of God Himself, the second person of the Godhead, to minister to them, as well as John the Baptist, His forerunner. They had the apostles and the ministry of the disciples also who had received Christ.

Then after Pentecost, they had the ministry of the Holy Spirit; the third person of the Godhead, to minister to them through the apostles and the believers in the Church, by mighty signs and wonders. But, sad to say, they also rejected the ministry of the Holy Spirit. Note the following Scriptures.
"Unto you **first**, God having raised up His Son Jesus…" (Acts 3:16).
"It was necessary that the Word of God should be spoken to you **first**…" (Acts 13:46).
"The Gospel is the power of God unto salvation… to the Jew **first**…" (Rom.1:16).
"To the Jew **first**, tribulation and wrath…" (Rom.2:9-10).

Paul, at the close of Acts, tells the Jews that the salvation of God is now sent to the Gentiles, and they, in contrast to the Jews, will hear it. The Book of Acts covers time from approximately

AD.33-60 in which time the Gospel was given to the Jew first, but only a faithful and believing remnant receive it. The rest reject it. About 10 years later, in AD.70, God rejected Jewry and scattered the nation to the four-corners of the earth.

The whole Book of Acts centres around two apostles in the main, that is, Peter and Paul. It also centres around two classes of people, two ethnic divisions of the human race; the Jews and the Gentiles, the Circumcision and the Uncircumcision, those within the Law and those without the Law. These two apostles have their distinctive callings of the Lord with relation to the Jew and the Gentile.

As noted in our previous chapter, God sent Peter down to the Gentiles and, under a sovereign outpouring of the Holy Spirit, the door of faith is opened to the Gentiles (Acts 10-11). Peter uses the keys of the kingdom to open the door and let the Gentiles in (Matt.16:16-19 with Acts 10:45; 11:1,18). God granted the Gentiles repentance unto life and the gift of the Holy Spirit. The Jewish brethren, who contended with Peter going to the Gentiles, were convinced after Peter shared the vision and the results with them. It settled the contention.

However, in Acts 15, there is the great Council in Jerusalem concerning the Gentiles coming into blessing. The Judaizers wanted to make the Gentiles as the Jews, under circumcision and the law. The Jews, however, did not want to become like the Gentiles. The answer came in vs.14-15. God was visiting the Gentiles to take out of them a people for His name.

In Gal.1-2 Paul rebukes Peter on his trip to Antioch and after the Conference for his compromise with the Jewish Judaizing brethren. Peter was the apostle to the Circumcision, and Paul was the apostle to the Uncircumcision. Peter's revelation limited him to the truth of the Kingdom of God in Israel, and that all converts of the Gentiles should be received as proselytes into that Kingdom, with Jesus as the King. There was great conflict and contention and confusion over the issue. It almost brought about two Churches, two bodies; a Jewish body and a Gentile body. There would have been a Jewish Church, accepting the Messiah and holding to the Law of Moses. There would also have been a Gentile Church, accepting Christ and not holding to the Mosaic Law Covenant. What was God's answer to the problem? Was there to be two separate Churches? It is Paul's revelation, given by the Spirit that settles the matter.

F. Paul and the Jew and Gentile

It is to the apostle Paul that so much is owed as we consider his ministry to both Jews and Gentiles and then finally, the revelation given to Him by the Lord about the "one body" of Jews and Gentiles. The reader will bear some overlapping of this and the previous chapter. Both are certainly inter-related in their truths. Here some consideration is given to Paul's ministry to these ethnic divisions, to which he never wanted "to give offence". In the appropriate place, we will consider the revelation given to Paul about these two ethnic groupings.

The Ministry of the Apostle Paul	
To the Jew First	**And also to the Gentile**
Acts 9:1,22-23. Saul convinced the Jews of Christ	Acts 9:15. Paul an apostle to the Gentiles
Acts 11:19-21. Word to none but Jews only	Acts 13:42-48. Word to Jew first, now we turn to he Gentiles
Acts 13:5. Word preached in Synagogue to Jews	Acts 14:2-5,27. Door of faith open to Gentiles
Acts 13:46. Necessary Word to the Jews first	Acts 18:6. Henceforth we go to the Gentiles
Acts 14:1-5. Word in the Synagogue to Jews	Acts 21:11-25. What God has done in the Gentiles
Acts 16:3,30. To the Synagogues	Acts 22:21. I will send you far to the Gentiles
Acts 17:1,5,13-17. Word to the Synagogues	Acts 26:17-23. Deliver you from the Gentiles – to be a light to the Gentiles
Acts 18:2-5,19. Paul went to the Synagogue first	Acts 28:28. Salvation of God sent to Gentiles
Acts 18:24-28. To the Synagogue of the Jews	
Acts 20:21. To the Synagogue	
Acts 21:26-27. Thousands of Jews that believe	
Acts 28:17-19,29. Paul spoke to the Jews at Rome	
Rom.1:16. Gospel is power of God – to Jew first	
Rom.2:9-10. To the Jew first	
Acts 13:46. Necessary Word to Jew first	

Paul ministered to both Jews and Gentiles but had the greatest response among the Gentiles. The Jews became Paul's greatest opposers of the Gospel given to him. He was called then to turn to the Gentiles. It is not necessary to claim (as some do) that the Gospel is to go "to the Jew first", for this has already been fulfilled, as seen in the Book of Acts. The Gospel went "to the Jew first", and they judged themselves unworthy of eternal life, and so God sent Paul then to the Gentiles. There was "an election of grace" out of the chosen race in the Book of Acts. Paul himself is evidence of that. But Paul, as a converted Jew, was then sent to the Gentiles to preach the Gospel of salvation by grace through faith.

G. Blessing on the Gentiles

There are many promises of the blessing that would come on the Gentiles. This blessing spoken of in the Old Testament would come on the Gentiles through the chosen nation, Israel.
Gen.22:18. In Abraham's seed, all nations were to be blessed (Gen.26:4).
Gal.3:8,14-16. The Gospel of blessing was preached to Abraham and that upon the Gentiles.
Isa.2:2-4. All nations are to flow to the mountain of the house of the Lord in the last days.
Isa.11:10. The Root of Jesse is the Root that the Gentiles would seek (vs.1-5).
Isa.42:1-16. God's Servant, the Messiah, would bring forth judgment to the Gentiles.
Isa.49:6-12,22. I will give You as a light to the Gentiles, My salvation to the ends of the earth.
Isa.52:15. Messiah to sprinkle many nations with His blood.
Isa.54:3; Isa.60:1-5,11,16; 61:6-9; 62:2. The Gentiles shall see your righteousness. They will declare My glory among the Gentiles (Isa.66:19). Many prophecies of blessing to the Gentiles are given through the Evangelist-Prophet, Isaiah.
Jer.16:19. The Gentiles shall come to you from the ends of the earth.
Zech.2:11. Many nations will be joined to the Lord in that day.
Mal 1:11. My Name shall be great among the Gentiles.
Psa.22:27-28. All kindreds of the nations will worship You.

The New Testament confirms the same promises of blessing on the Gentiles as those in the Old Testament.
Lke.2:32; 1:32-33. The Lord Jesus would be a light to lighten the Gentiles. Christ came as the fulfillment of the Abrahamic Covenant, as the Seed of Abraham. He came to the Jew first. He also came that the Gentiles would be blessed and that He might bless all nations.
Matt.12:18-21. In His Name shall the Gentiles trust.
Jhn.12:20-24,32. The Gentiles would be blessed through the corn of wheat that fell into the ground and died. Through His death, others would be brought to life.
Gal.3:14. That the blessing of Abraham might come on the Gentiles.
Matt.28:19-20. Make disciples of all nations, not only the chosen nation.
Mrk.16:17-20. Go into all the world, and preach the Gospel to every creature.
Acts 1:8. You will be witnesses to Me, beginning at Jerusalem, Judea, Samaria and the uttermost parts of the earth.

It is worthy of note that the three sons of Noah (Gen.10:5, the isles of the Gentiles), were Shem, Ham and Japheth. The Shemite races were the chosen races of Israel and Judah. The Hamite races were the servant races. The Japhethic races were the enlarged races. All were to be blessed in the Tents of Shem – the chosen nations, Israel and Judah.

In Acts we see the Shemite race (believing Jews), blessing the Hamite race (Acts 8, the Ethiopian), and the Japhethic race (Acts 10-11, Cornelius and household). The curse is lifted as they come into blessing in Christ.

Even in the Gospels, various Gentiles reached over the racial barriers and received blessing from Christ. They stepped by faith into the dispensation of Gentile blessing, even though it was not quite the time for them.
The Syrophoenecian woman received healing for her child from Jesus (Matt.15:21-28).
The Roman Centurion received blessing for his servant (Lke.7:1-10). The Lord had not seen such faith even in Israel, His own nation.
The Samaritan woman received salvation through Christ at Jacob's well and became a witness for Christ to her own city (Jhn.4). Jesus had forbidden the apostles to go to any city of the Samaritans, yet this woman received blessing. The full blessing would come in Acts 8 as Philip went to the city of Samaria and preached Christ to them.

Each of these became shadows of the coming blessing and responsive faith of the Gentiles after the rejection of Christ by Jewry, and after the cross and the outpouring of the Holy Spirit.

H. The Jews and the Gentiles
The Epistle to the Romans was written several years before Paul went to Rome. This book deals with the development of Pauline revelation concerning both Jews and Gentiles, as no other Epistle does. It shows how there is an unfolding revelation being given to Paul concerning his ministry to Jew and Gentile, and then the coming in of the Gentiles. This revelation took shape, by the Holy Spirit, in Paul's mind, as he was ministering to the Churches mentioned in the Book of Acts, over AD.58-60. The Book of Romans follows the Book of Acts. But it is important to understand that the revelation concerning the Jew and Gentile in the plan of God is unfolded very fully here. It all consummates in the revelation of "the one olive tree" in Romans 11. Note the emphasis throughout the Epistle on "the Jew and the Gentile".

Rom.1:13,16. To the Jew first, and then to the Greek, with the Gospel.
Rom.2:9-10. To the Jew first, and also to the Gentile will come wrath or blessing. Compare with 1Thess.2:14-16 where that wrath has come on the Jew to the uttermost. Fulfilled AD.70.
Rom.2:17-29. The true Jew is one inwardly, not outwardly. It is of the spirit and not of the flesh. Note those who are of the Synagogue of Satan in Rev.2:9 and 3:9.
Rom.3:1-2. What advantage has the Jew? Much every way, chiefly because God gave them the Oracles of God, the sacred Scriptures.
Rom.3:9-20. God has concluded both Jew and Gentile – ALL are under sin.
Rom.9:24-33. God calls both Jew and Gentile to Himself.
Rom.10:12-13. There is no difference between the Jew or the Greek, for the same Lord over all is rich unto all that call on Him.
Rom.11:11. Salvation has come to the Gentiles through the unbelief of the Jew.
Rom.11:25. Blindness is happened in part to Jewry until the fulness of the Gentiles is come in.
Rom.16:4. The Churches of the Gentiles.
Rom.15:9,10,11,12,16,18,27. The student should compare these verses with each of the quotations from the Old Testament concerning the blessing to come on the Gentiles. Note also Gal.3:14-16. The blessing of Abraham was to come on the Gentiles through faith.

The climax of Paul's revelation concerning Jew and Gentile is found in Rom.11:16-24. Here Paul presents the symbol of the Olive Tree. It is a **FAITH OLIVE TREE**. It does not refer to natural or national Israel in unbelief. The three major roots are found in Abraham, Isaac and Jacob. These three fathers were all men of **faith**! Those in the trunk, the branches or the tree, as a whole, were those who were of **faith**! When Christ came, those Jews who were of **faith** remained in the Olive Tree and those who were cut off as branches out of the tree were cut off because of **unbelief**! It is that simple to see.

The Gentiles, who came to **faith** in Christ through the Gospel, were now grafted into this **faith olive tree,** the true Israel of God. Believing Jews and believing Gentiles were then growing together in the **ONE Olive Tree – the FAITH OLIVE TREE!** This faith olive tree then is the spiritual Israel of God, not the unbelieving Israel.

It is asked, What about the Jewish problem, and what about Israel as a nation? The answer is given very simply here. **"If they abide not still in unbelief, God is able to graft them back again into the olive tree!"** Unbelief is the problem for both Jew and Gentile. Faith brings Jew and Gentile into the blessings of God through Christ. The Scriptures are clear. The 'natural branches' (Israel and Judah) were broken off the faith-olive-tree because of unbelief. The 'wild branches' (Gentile nations) are grafted into the faith-olive-tree by faith in the Messiah of God. However, before continuing on, some other things need to recognized.

I. The Fourfold Desolation of Jewry
Having followed through as briefly as suitable the history of Israel and Judah to the time of Christ, and then God's purpose in forming the Church out of believing Jews and believing Gentiles, we need to consider what happened to the Jewish nation as a whole. There was a faithful remnant elected according to grace that believed, but the rest of the nation fell into blindness and hardness of heart to Christ and His Church. Because of this, Jewry, as a nation, came under the fourfold desolation spoken of in Lev.26. The student should especially read the whole chapter, as it can

only be covered in brief here. The Lord promised His chosen nation that, should they disobey His laws, statutes and judgments, then desolation would come on them. This desolation was fourfold.

1. The desolation of their Sanctuary (the Temple).
2. The desolation of their Cities (Jerusalem and Judea).
3. The desolation of their Land (Palestine),
4. The desolation of their people (Jewry as a nation). Note especially verses.32-34.

Jesus Himself confirmed the same desolation. He foretold the desolation of the Temple (Matt.23:38—Matt.24:1-2), the desolation of the city of Jerusalem, the Land and also the People (Lke.21:20-24), all of which took place in AD.70 under Titus and the Roman armies. It was a repeat of the desolation that happened under the Babylonian Captivity. Jewry had rejected their Christ, His Church, composed of believing Jews and Gentiles, and resisted the Holy Spirit. There was nothing left but the fourfold desolation of the Law, confirmed by their rejected Messiah. "He came unto His own, but His own received Him not, but to as many as received Him, to them He gave power to become the sons of God..." (Jhn.1:11-12).

J. The Present State of Jewry and Jerusalem

What then is the present state of the Jewish nation, the modern State of Israel or Jews outside of Christ, where ever and whatever nation they are in? It is a sad state as the student reads these Scripture references given here.

1. Jer.3:6-11; Isa.50:1. They are a 'divorced' people because of spiritual adultery. Read also Ezek.16 with Ezek.23.
2. John 8. They are not Abraham's seed after faith and after the Spirit. They are 'sand seed' (the earthly, the natural and national flesh seed), not the 'star seed' (the heavenly and spiritual seed of Abraham). The axe has been laid at the root of the tree (Matt.3:10). If they were truly the seed of Abraham, they would believe Christ. They have Abraham as their father after the flesh, but not after the Spirit. Unbelief makes a person a child of the Devil, the father of lies.
3. Rom.10:1-4. They are ignorant of God's righteousness, going about to establish their own righteousness. They have not submitted to the righteousness of God, which righteousness is found in Christ. Self-righteousness is as filthy rags in God's sight (Isa.64:6 with Phil.3:1-10).
4. Rom.9:32-33 with 1Cor.1:23. They have stumbled over the "Stumbling Stone" – Christ. They stumbled over the truth of "faith-righteousness" and stumbled over a "crucified Messiah."
5. Rom.10:21. They are a Word-resisting people, hard to win for the Gospel of Christ. Any who do come to Christ are immediately grafted back into the **faith olive tree**!
6. Rom.11:7,8,25. Blindness and hardness of heart is their portion as a nation until the fulness of the Gentiles have come in, until the number of Gentiles that are to be saved is completed.
7. Rom.11:28. They have become the enemies of the Gospel of Christ. They were Paul's greatest opposers everywhere He went.
8. Rom.11:16-24. They have been broken out of the olive tree because of unbelief. They can be grafted back into that tree the moment they receive Christ. Every Jew who has ever believed over Church history has been grafted back into that tree, along with believing Gentiles. It has to be remembered that it is a **FAITH Olive Tree**!
9. Gal.4:21-30. Earthly Jerusalem, which now is in existence, is in bondage with her children. In allegorical sense, they are children of Hagar/Ishmael, children of the flesh, and not children of the Spirit, of Sarah/Isaac. The bondson and the bondwoman are to be cast out. They are not the heirs of the promise.
10. Rev.11:8. Earthly Jerusalem, where our Lord was crucified, is spiritually Sodom and Egypt. Sodom had two witnesses and was destroyed by fire and brimstone. Egypt had two witnesses and was destroyed by plagues under Moses. Earthly Jerusalem is not the city that Abraham, Isaac and Jacob are looked for. They look for a city whose builder and maker is God. This city is seen in Rev.21-22 chapters. Earthly Jerusalem is to be trodden down of the Gentiles until the Times of the Gentiles is fulfilled (Lke.21:20-24).
11. Matt.27:19-25 with Deut.19:10 and Num.35:33. They are under the curse of innocent blood. When they cried, "His blood be on us and on our children" they invoked the curse of the laws concerning innocent blood. The curse of innocent blood cannot be lifted until they accept the cleansing of that blood and come into blessing. Without the shedding of blood, there is not forgiveness (Heb.9-10 chapters). The tragic history of Jewry has proven the truth of this self-imposed curse of the Law.

12. Deut.28. They are under the curses of the broken Law of God. Obedience to God's laws means blessing and disobedience means cursing. Study the list of blessings and cursings in this great chapter. In rejecting the New Covenant, they remain under the curses of the Old Covenant.

It is a grief and sadness of heart to read these Scriptures and see the state of Jewry in the world today. Each time a Jew accepts Christ as His Lord and Saviour, he comes out from under these things and is a New Covenant believer, a member in the Body of Christ, with believing Gentiles. This is why Jewry needs the Gospel today, as never before.

K. The Restoration of Israel and Judah

Does the Bible teach any restoration of the Jewish nation in these end-times? If so, what is this restoration about?

The Post-Millennialists and A-Millennialists would say that there is no restoration for Jewry today, only in Christ. The Futurist and Dispensationalist would say there is restoration to God through the Mosaic Covenant economy and in the end of the age, and especially in the Jewish Millennium. The Historic Pre-Millennialist would say that there is to come a Divine visitation on Jewry where their eyes will be eyes to their long-rejected Messiah. They will be grafted back by faith into the good olive tree. It is with this latter view that this writer agrees, the reasons for this given here.

1. Israel/Jewry can still be accepted by grace through faith under the New Covenant that Christ established at His first coming (Matt.26:26-28 with Heb.8:6-13). The Lord Jesus made this Covenant with the House of Israel and with the House of Judah and fulfilled the word spoken through the prophet Jeremiah (Jer.31:31-34).
2. Israel/Jewry will experience a final outpouring of the Holy Spirit on them as a nation. The prophet Zechariah especially speaks of the Spirit of grace and supplication that is to be poured on this generation. They will mourn for the only begotten Son and look on Him whom they pierced. There they will see the fountain opened for sin and uncleanness, that fountain opened years ago at Calvary (Read carefully Zech.12:10-14; 13:1-6). God has promised to pour out His Spirit on all flesh – on all nations (Joel 2:28-32). The prophet Ezekiel speaks of this outpouring of the Spirit on them in Ezek.39:39. The Jewish nation was the first nation to be there for the first coming of Christ and to receive the first outpouring of the Spirit (Gospels and Acts). Over their period of scattering, God has been visiting the Gentile nations and pouring out His Spirit on the Gentile nations. It would seem evident from these Scriptures that the Jewish nation will have another great outpouring of the Spirit and get their eyes opened to their rejected Messiah. Many will be saved through faith in Christ. When it speaks of "all Israel shall be saved", this salvation is only possible in Christ, as for Jew and Gentile (Read these verses on being saved. Rom.9:27; 10:1,9,10,13,26; Mrk.16:15-16; Eph.2:5,8; Jhn.3:17; Isa.45:22; Rom.11:4; Rom.5:9,10; Rev.21:24). All are saved by grace through faith, not of works. Paul also tells us that they are not all Israel who are of Israel. That is, they are not all spiritual Israel who are of natural Israel. The true Israel of God is the believing Israel along with believing Gentiles (Rom.9:6-9; Gal.6:15-16).
3. Israel/Jewry will be grafted in again to the olive tree by faith once the full number of Gentiles has been saved that are to be saved (Rom.11:15-32). It is entirely by faith in Christ. This Scripture would indicate that there is to come a time of visitation on the Jew once God's purpose in the Gentile nations has been completed. It points to the end of the age.
4. Israel/Jewry will be saved by faith, not by works of the Law. They will come out from the Old Covenant, which they are still under, and come into relationship with God, through Christ and the New Covenant (Rom.11:26; 9:6,27; 10:1,9-13; 11:4; Isa.45:22).
5. Israel/Jewry will come to God under some Divine visitation when the Times of the Gentiles and the treading down of Jerusalem is completed (Lke.21:20-24 with Rev.11)

This restoration of the Jew is NOT to the Mosaic Covenant economy, which was abolished at the cross. It is a restoration to God, through Christ only, and by the body and blood of the NEW Covenant. The same message that Jesus gave to Jewish leader, Nicodemus, is the same message for all Jews and for all Gentiles today. "You must be born again, born from above, to enter the Kingdom..." (Jhn.3:1-5). In the understanding of this writer, there will be a Divine visitation on the Jewish nation. This will be before the beginning of the final Great Tribulation period. The veil will be taken away from their hearts and minds in the reading of the Old Testament (2Cor.3). Many will accept Christ as their eyes are opened. Many will probably become martyrs under the rule and reign of the Antichrist. There is no special task or mission for the converted Jews. Once they accept Christ, they are in the one Body of Christ. In Christ there is neither Jew nor Gentile, but all are one "in Christ" (Gal.3:28). Those who reject will appear before the Great White Throne in due time and be judged eternally for that rejection.

The very prophets who foretold the restoration of Israel to God, through Christ, also foretold the cessation of the Mosaic Covenant economy and the ritualism of the Old Covenant (Jer.31:31-34). The Old Covenant was fulfilled and abolished at the cross. The cross was the transition from the old to the new, from Moses to Christ. There is no future plan of God for the Jew in any future age, as there is only one plan of salvation for Jew and Gentile. In Christ, national distinctions cease to exist. There is no difference between Jew or Gentile, says the Lord, so Christians should not make a difference. All have sinned. All need salvation. All may come to God through Christ Jesus, by grace and faith. All may be in the one olive tree, the one Body of Christ. This is the message for the nation of Israel and for all nations.

CHAPTER FIVE

THE NEW COVENANT

The chapter following this one actually precipitated the necessity of this chapter. The next chapter has to deal with those Millennial Schools who believe that the Mosaic Covenant economy is to be restored, and this will be a Jewish Millennium. The Futurists and Dispensationalists hold to this belief. Such a teaching arises out of what this writer calls, "Covenantal confusion."

Each of the other Millennial Schools, whether Historic Pre-Millennialism, Post-Millennialism as well as A-Millennialism believe that God has established the New Covenant. There will never ever again be any restoration or re-institution of the Mosaic Covenant.

One has to understand the basic distinctions between the Covenants, especially the Old Covenant given to Moses and Israel and the New Covenant given to the true Israel of God by the Lord Jesus Christ. Once a believer understands the New Covenant, he will never look back to the Old Covenant to be restored as such was fulfilled and abolished by Jesus Himself at Calvary.

One of the most prominent Dispensational teachers is Clarence Larkin. As an author, there is much in his textbooks that is theologically sound. But, when it comes to a proper understanding of the matter of the New Covenant, there is great misunderstanding and misinterpretation. It is this that this present chapter seeks to deal with. But first of all, let the writer, Clarence Larkin, speak for himself, as his particular words about Covenant are repeated once again here.

In "**Dispensational Truth**" (page 151), he writes: "The New Covenant has not yet been made. This is to be made with Israel after they get back to their own land. It is promised in Jer.31:31-34. It is unconditional and will cover the Millennium and the New Heavens and New Earth. It is based on the finished work of Christ (Matt.26:26). It has nothing to do with the Church and does not belong to this Dispensation. It is the 'Eighth Covenant' and speaks of the **Resurrection and Eternal Completeness**" (End quote. Emphasis, C.Larkin).

Dispensational Pre-Millennialists do not make much of the New Covenant. They do not seem to see the significance of it. This is because of the concept and their understanding of the Old Covenant, the Mosaic Covenant, being restored, and that the Jews will come to Christ by that Covenant. So the importance and relevance of the New Covenant to the Old Covenant are missed.

It is not the purpose of this chapter, in any way, to write a textbook on "The Covenants." The reader's attention is drawn to several textbooks on this subject at the conclusion of comments given here. It is the relevance, especially, of the Old Covenant and the New Covenant with which this and the following chapter have to do. But first of all, some consideration needs to be given to the greatest of all Old Testament Covenants, and that is, the Abrahamic Covenant.

A. The Abrahamic Covenant
   The most comprehensive Covenant in the whole Bible is that which is defined and recognized as the Abrahamic Covenant. It includes in itself each of the Covenants gone before and it includes in itself each of the Covenants that follow.

   The major promises of the Abrahamic Covenant fall into five categories and each of the Biblical Covenants find their place in one or the other of these categories. These five groupings are:

   1. The Seed Promises
      These "Seed Promises" include those made in the Adamic Covenant (Gen.3:15), and the Noahic Covenant (Gen.9:25-27). These seed promises continue on through the Abrahamic Covenant, the Mosaic, Palestinian and Davidic Covenants and into the New Covenant. The seed promised to Abraham was to be twofold. One line would be as "the sand" of the sea (Gen.13:16; 22:17). The other seed line would be as "the stars" of the heaven (Gen.15:1-5; 22:17). The sand seed spoke of the earthly, the fleshly, the natural and national Israel that would come from Abraham's loins. The star seed pointed to the heavenly, the spiritual Israel that would come from Abraham's loins. Jesus recognized these seed-lines in John 8 very

clearly and saw that, though the Jews were Abraham's seed 'after the flesh', they were not Abraham's seed 'after the Spirit'.

2. The Land Promises
If there is seed, then it necessitates land in which the seed could dwell. The Mosaic Covenant especially concerned the seed of Abraham, as a nation. It was the Palestinian Covenant that concerned the land for that seed, and the laws for living in that land. They would possess the land as long as they obeyed the laws of God's land. God promised the land of Canaan to Abraham. It found its fulfillment in the Palestinian Covenant, and in due time, Israel fully possessed that promised land.

3. The Kingship Promises
To Abraham, to Sarah and to Jacob's son, Judah, were given the promises of Kingship (Read carefully Gen.17 and Gen.49:8-12). The Davidic Covenant is the fulfillment of these promises of the Abrahamic Covenant. David was of the tribe of Judah. The promise finds its fulfillment in the kings of the House of Judah, and finds it ultimate fulfillment in Christ, the greater Son of David – King of Kings and Lord of Lords (2Sam.7; Psa.89; Psa.132; Matt.1:1).

4. The Messianic Promise
The greatest promise in the Abrahamic Covenant was the promise of the Seed that would bless all nations of the earth. Paul unmistakably says that that seed was Christ (Gal.3:16). It also included the Church. He writes, "If you are Christ's, then you are Abraham's seed" (Gal.3:29). It is Christ and His Church who are the true seed of Abraham.

There were national and natural promises of blessing given to Abraham in the Covenant. These have found fulfillment in natural Israel. But there were also spiritual promises in that same Covenant. These find fulfillment in the Lord Jesus Christ. So it may be said, the greatest promise of the Abrahamic Covenant was the New Covenant. This was the promise of the Messiah who would redeem mankind from sin and Satan's dominion. The New Covenant was therefore in the Abrahamic Covenant.

5. The Gospel Promises
Included in the Abrahamic Covenant was the promise of blessing to ALL NATIONS, all the families of the earth. Paul clearly states that, when God promised Abraham blessing on all the nations, this was counted as the preaching of the Gospel to Abraham (Gal.3:8). The Gospel is 'good news'. It is the good news of redemption in Christ for all nations – Jews or Gentiles. All nations are to hear the Gospel of the Kingdom. This Gospel is to be preached to every creature and the disciples were to make disciples of all nations (Matt.28:18-20; Mrk.16:15-20; Acts 1:8). Those who believed and received, out of every kindred, tongue, tribe and nation, would constitute the New Covenant Church (Matt.16:15-19; Rev.5:9-10).

This confirms the fact that the New Covenant was in the Abrahamic Covenant. The promise that Abraham was to be "a father of many nations" is seen in Jews and Gentiles, Circumcision and Uncircumcision, coming into faith (Rom.4 with Gen.17:1-2).

On the basis of these things, it should be seen that the Abrahamic Covenant is surely the most comprehensive and all-inclusive Covenant in the Bible. It included within its bounds the Adamic, the Noahic, the Mosaic Covenants, as to the Seed promises. It included in itself the Palestinian Covenant, as to the Land promises. It included in itself the Davidic Covenant, as to the Kings of Judah and the King of Kings, the Lord Jesus Christ. It also included in itself the New Covenant, the promise of the Messiah blessing all nations through the Gospel of redemption. Such is the importance and significance of the Abrahamic Covenant in relation to all other Covenants.

B. The Old and the New Covenants
Of all the Covenants made by God, all fall under two headings, so to speak. These are either Law or Grace. The Covenants of Grace may be identified as the Adamic, the Noahic, the Abrahamic, the Davidic and the New Covenants. The Covenants of Law may be identified as the Mosaic and the Palestinian Covenants.

Just a cursory glance over these two groupings emphasizes that the two dominant Covenants are (1) The Mosaic Covenant, the Covenant of Law, and (2) The New Covenant, the Covenant of Grace. It is, undoubtedly, for this reason, that our Bible has been divided into "The Old

Testament" and "The New Testament", even though there are other Covenants in Scripture. It is because the compilers saw that the two grounds of God's dealing with mankind are either on the ground of LAW or the ground of GRACE! If man falls from grace, then he falls to the ground of the law and the dealings of God accordingly.

C. Promises of the New Covenant

The Law Covenant, spoken of as the "Old Covenant", was made by God with Israel at Mt.Sinai some 1500 years before Christ came. It was a Covenant of Law and Works. "Do and Live" was the sum of it all. It was committed to the nation of Israel by the hands of Moses, the Mediator of the Old Covenant.

Because of the weakness of the flesh and the sinful propensities of Israel, God used the Law as a Schoolmaster to bring them to Christ (Gal.3:24-25). No one could be justified by the works of the Law. It was a ministration of death. The Law works wrath and Divine judgment to all who fail to keep it perfectly. It necessitated God coming in grace and making a NEW Covenant with the people. It would be a Covenant depending on his promises and grace through faith, not a Covenant depending on the promises of the people and works of self-effort!

So, woven throughout the Old Testament prophets and their writings, there are promises of the coming New Covenant. The prophets, even though they themselves were under the Old or the Mosaic Covenant, prophesied of the New or Christ's Covenant. Some of these prophecies are noted here from the prophetic writings.

1. **Jer.31:31-34**
   "Behold, the days are coming, says the LORD, when I will make a new covenant with the house of Israel and with the house of Judah--not according to the covenant that I made with their fathers in the day that I took them by the hand to lead them out of the land of Egypt, My covenant which they broke, though I was a husband to them, says the LORD.
   But this is the covenant that I will make with the house of Israel after those days, says the LORD: I will put My law in their minds, and write it on their hearts; and I will be their God, and they shall be My people.
   No more shall every man teach his neighbor, and every man his brother, saying, 'Know the LORD,' for they all shall know Me, from the least of them to the greatest of them, says the LORD. For I will forgive their iniquity, and their sin I will remember no more." (NKJ)

   Archibald Hughes in "**A New Heaven And A New Earth**" (page 117) writes concerning this prophecy of Jeremiah, saying:
   "This prophecy foretold (1) The reunion of the then divided nation under one New Covenant, (2) The breach of the Old Covenant and its abolition, and (3) The effective power and eternal purpose of the New Covenant, and (4) Defines the salvation to be brought to them as being spiritual and not material, with an intimate knowledge of the Lord" (End quote). Read also Jer.50:5 in connection with these words.

2. **Ezek.37:24-27**
   "David My servant shall be king over them, and they shall all have one shepherd; they shall also walk in My judgments and observe My statutes, and do them.
   Then they shall dwell in the land that I have given to Jacob My servant, where your fathers dwelt; and they shall dwell there, they, their children, and their children's children, forever; and My servant David shall be their prince forever.
   Moreover I will make a covenant of peace with them, and it shall be an everlasting covenant with them; I will establish them and multiply them, and I will set My sanctuary in their midst forevermore. My tabernacle also shall be with them; indeed I will be their God, and they shall be My people. The nations also will know that I, the LORD, sanctify Israel, when My sanctuary is in their midst forevermore." (NKJ)

   Ezekiel also prophesies of the reunion of the two sticks, the House of Israel and the House of Judah, in the hand of the Son of Man. They would have one shepherd (Christ, the greater Son of David). The Lord would make a Covenant of Peace with them. It would be an everlasting Covenant. He would be their God and they would be His people (Isa.54:10).

This all finds fulfillment in the New Covenant, the everlasting Covenant in the blood of the Lord Jesus Christ (Heb.13:20-21). There would be one fold for believing Jews and believing Gentiles under Christ in the New Covenant relationship (Read Jhn.10:16 with Hos.1:10-11; Rom.9:23-26; 1Pet.2:9-10).

3. **Ezek.16:59-62**
"For thus says the Lord GOD: "I will deal with you as you have done, who despised the oath by breaking the covenant.
Nevertheless I will remember My covenant with you in the days of your youth, and I will establish an everlasting covenant with you.
Then you will remember your ways and be ashamed, when you receive your older and your younger sisters; for I will give them to you for daughters, but not because of My covenant with you.
And I will establish My covenant with you. Then you shall know that I am the LORD, that you may remember and be ashamed, and never open your mouth anymore because of your shame, when I provide you an atonement for all you have done," says the Lord GOD." (NKJ)

Again there is the promise of the coming New Covenant that God would make with the Israel of God, the true and spiritual Israel who respond to His grace. This finds fulfillment in the New Covenant, not the Old or Mosaic Covenant.

4. **Isa.42:6**
"I the Lord have called You in righteousness, and will hold Your hand; I will keep You and give You as a Covenant to the people, as a light to the Gentiles..." This again points to the Lord Jesus Christ, who was given by the Father as a Covenant to Israel and a light to the Gentiles in darkness. The same promise is confirmed in Isa.49:8 and quoted by Paul in Acts 13:46-48 when the Jews rejected the Gospel, while the Gentiles responded to it.

5. **Isa.55:3.**
"Incline your ear, and come to Me. Hear, and your soul shall live. And I will make an everlasting Covenant with you, even the sure mercies of David ...". Here again it points to Christ Jesus, who is the greater Son of David. Paul again quotes this and applies the sure mercies of David to the resurrection of Christ (Acts 13:33-35).

6. **Isa.59:21**
"As for Me," says the LORD, "this is My covenant with them: My Spirit who is upon you, and My words which I have put in your mouth, shall not depart from your mouth, nor from the mouth of your descendants, nor from the mouth of your descendants' descendants," says the LORD, "from this time and forevermore." (NKJ) Once more, Isaiah points to and prophesies of the New Covenant. This Covenant involves God's Spirit and God's words and finds its fulfillment in the Lord Jesus Christ and the Holy Spirit in the New Covenant Church, composed of believing Jews and believing Gentiles.

7. **Rom.11:25-27**
"For I do not desire, brethren, that you should be ignorant of this mystery, lest you should be wise in your own opinion, that blindness in part has happened to Israel until the fullness of the Gentiles has come in.
And so all Israel will be saved, as it is written: "The Deliverer will come out of Zion, and He will turn away ungodliness from Jacob; For this is My covenant with them, when I take away their sins." (NKJ) Paul is clear. The only way "all Israel" will be saved is by the New Covenant, through faith in the Lord Jesus Christ, who is the Deliverer in Zion. When Israel comes to faith in Christ, they experience the taking away of their sins and come into New Covenant relationship with God through Christ. There is no salvation for Israel apart from Christ Jesus.

8. **Matt.26:26-28**
"And as they were eating, Jesus took bread, blessed and broke it, and gave it to the disciples and said, "Take, eat; this is My body." Then He took the cup, and gave thanks, and gave it to them, saying, "Drink from it, all of you, for this is My blood of the new covenant, which is shed for many for the remission of sins." (NKJ)

Who can question that the Lord Jesus made the New Covenant with the Twelve who were then representative of the twelve tribes of Israel? He presented to them in symbolic form, His body and His blood. The writer to the Hebrews confirms that, once a testament is made, it necessitates the death of the testator. So Christ confirmed his own death once He said, This is the NEW Testament (Covenant) in My blood (Heb.9:15-17).

9. **Hebrews**
One can only provide brief quotations from the Epistle of Hebrews, the Book of the New Covenant in contrast to the Old Covenant. The writer to the Hebrew believers abundantly confirms that the New Covenant has been made. It is available for all to enter into its promises and blessings, through faith in Christ Jesus. Note the following quotations.

Jesus is the "Surety of a better testament" (Heb.7:22).
He is also the "Mediator of a better Covenant, established upon better promises" (Heb.8:6).
The first Covenant had its faults, and necessitated the second Covenant (Heb.8:7).
The fault was with the people of Israel. So God promised to "make a NEW Covenant with the House of Israel and the House of Judah" (Heb.8:8).
It would not be like the Covenant He made with them when He brought them out of the Egypt. It would be a Covenant in which He would write His laws in their hearts and minds, and not on tables of stone. It would be internal, not external (Heb.8:9-12). He would be merciful to them and their sins would be forgiven them. Read Heb.10:15-18, which confirms the same.
This New Covenant necessitated the death of the Testator, Jesus Christ. After His death the New Covenant promises would come into effect (Heb.9:15-17). He is the Mediator of the New Covenant.
The believer in Christ is come to "...Jesus, the Mediator of the New Covenant..." (Heb.12:22-24). He is the great shepherd of the sheep, raised from the dead, and He will make us perfect and complete through His blood, the blood of the everlasting Covenant (Heb.13:20-21).

The NEW Covenant has been made and this by Christ Jesus Himself. All believing Jews and Gentiles come into New Covenant relationship with God through Christ. It is in this dispensation, and not in a coming Millennium. Whether Jews or Gentiles, the Covenant is available for all to enter into, by faith in Christ Jesus, our risen Lord and Saviour. The Old Covenant prophets clearly point to the New Covenant that Christ was to make in this age, not in another age.

D. **The Old Covenant and the Cross**
The issue that needs to be settled is: "What happened at the cross to the Old Covenant, once Jesus established the New Covenant?" It comes down further to the matter of Law.

"The Law" is an expression that may encompass all the laws, statutes and judgments given to the nation of Israel. For the sake of simplicity, "the law" may be divided into several parts.

1. **The Moral Laws**
The Ten Commandments, written on tables of stone (Ex.20).
2. **The Civil Laws**
The laws, statutes and judgments, all an amplification of the Moral Law, and written in the Book of the Law (Ex.20-31 with Leviticus and Deuteronomy).
3. **The Health and Hygiene Laws**
Dealing with the food laws and basic laws of physical hygiene and cleanliness, also written in the Book of the Law.
4. **The Ceremonial Laws**
Dealing with the Priesthood, the sacrifices and oblations, the Sabbaths, the Festival days, the rite of circumcision and the Tabernacle/Temple ordinances and services.

What then happened to "the Law" at the cross? When the New Covenant was ratified in the body and blood of Jesus, this is what happened to the various parts of the Law, which is simply covered in brief here.

The Moral Laws, under the New Covenant, are now written on our hearts and minds, and no longer on tables of stones (Jer.31:31-34; Heb.8:8-13).

The Civil Laws, in many places, still hold in Courts of Law and as basic rules governing a society, especially where some kind of 'Christian' or Judeo/Christian ethic under-girds that society.
The Health and Hygiene Laws still hold, in principle, as God wants His people to be healthy and clean in body, soul and spirit (Heb.10:22).

When it comes, however, to the **Ceremonial Laws**, all were fulfilled and abolished at the cross of Jesus. When Jesus died, His sacrifice brought all Old Covenant (Old Testament) sacrifice and oblation to an end. When Jesus died on the cross, the veil of the Temple was torn from top to bottom. It signified the end of the old order, the Temple order, and all the ritual and ceremony of the Law or the Mosaic Covenant. It signified the opening of a new way, a new dispensation, with access within the veil into the presence of God. When Jesus died on the cross, He was our High Priest after the Order of Melchisedek. His Priesthood forever cancelled out the Order of Aaron and the Levitical Priesthood. When Jesus died on the cross, His body was broken, His blood shed. He was, as the Prophets Isaiah and Daniel said, "cut off" out of the land of the living, for our sins. He therefore fulfilled all that was symbolized in the rite of circumcision, and the "cutting of" of the flesh and the shedding of blood thereby.

He was the Passover Lamb, fulfilling all previous Passover Festival seasons. In His resurrection, He fulfilled the Sheaf of Firstfruits. When He poured out His Spirit at Pentecost, He fulfilled all that was typified in the Mosaic 'Pentecost Feast'.

All these things belonged to the Mosaic Covenant, and the ceremonial part of "the Law". All were fulfilled and abolished by fulfillment, never to be re-instituted again, in this age or any other age to come. The Book of Hebrews fully attests to these things, as well as other New Testament references. Believers, since the cross, are under the New Covenant, whether believing Gentiles or believing Jews. Once a person comes into faith and into Christ, they are in New Covenant relationship with God, through Christ. Any other teaching becomes, indeed, a confusion of the Covenants!

E. **Abraham's Two Sons**
Paul, using an inspired allegory of Abraham's two sons, Ishmael and Isaac, said that these "two sons are two covenants", the Old Covenant and the New Covenant. As Hagar and Ishmael were cast out of Abraham's house in the appointed time, so the Old Covenant Israel were "cast out" in the appointed time. It was Sarah and Isaac who became the heirs of the promise. It is the Israel of the New Covenant who remains in the house of the Father. Ishmael, the child of the flesh, mocked Isaac, the child of the promise. So the conflict came between the Old and the New Covenant people, as seen in the Book of Acts and on through several Pauline Epistles. Ishmael and Isaac could not live together in the same house. One had to go at the word of God.

Once the New Covenant had become ratified and sealed, the Old Covenant was finished. As the separation came between Ishmael and Isaac, so the separation came between the Old (Mosaic) Covenant and the New (Jesus) Covenant. Why then, it may be asked, would God want to put Ishmael (the Old Covenant), and Isaac (the New Covenant) back together in Abraham's household, the household of faith? This will never be!

F. **The Better Covenant**
Hebrews tells us that the New Covenant is "the better Covenant". This is the key word in the Epistle to the Hebrews. The Old Covenant was "good" but the New Covenant is "better". Why leave the "better" and go back to the "good", especially when it has become old and decayed and has been discarded? Note the list of "better things" in Hebrews.

- Jesus has a "better name" than the angels (Heb.1:4).
- The writer was persuaded "better things" of the Hebrews believers than a return to the Old Covenant and its abolished ceremonials (Heb.6:9).
- Melchisedek is "better" than Abraham, as it is a "better priesthood" (Heb.7:7).
- The Gospel provides a "better hope" (Heb.7:19).
- The New Covenant is a "better Testament" (Heb.7:22).
- The New Covenant has a "better Mediator" than Moses or Aaron (Heb.7:22).
- It is a "better covenant" established on "better promises" (Heb.8:6,6).
- The New Covenant has a "better sacrifice" than the Old Covenant sacrifices (Heb.9:13-23).

- Believers have a "better" inheritance in heaven than on earth (Heb.10:34).
- Believers, like the patriarchs, look for a "better country" than Palestine (Heb.11:16).
- Believers die in faith of a "better resurrection" (Heb.11:35).
- God has provided "better things" for us than materialistic things (Heb.11:40).
- The blood of Jesus speaks "better things" than the blood of Abel (Heb.12:24).

In "**A New Heaven And A New Earth**" (page 119), Archibald Hughes provides an excellent contrast and comparison between the Old and the New Covenants. It is adapted and arranged for our purposes in this text.

	The Old Covenant	**The New Covenant**
1.	Law – Jhn.1:17	Grace and Truth – Jhn.1:17
2.	Of the Letter which kills – 2Cor.3:6	Of the Spirit which gives life – Rom.7:6
3.	Earthly – Heb.9:19-23	Heavenly – Heb.9:24
4.	Can only condemn - Gal.2:21; Rom.3:20	Can make righteous – Rom.5:19; 3:21,22
5.	Law offence abounds – Sin reigns unto death – Rom.5:20	Grace reigns through righteousness unto eternal life by Jesus Christ our Lord – Rom.5:21
6.	Carnal ordinances and commandment – Heb.7:16; 9:10	Spiritual sacrifices – Heb.13:15; 1Pet.2:5. Law of the Spirit of Life – Rom.8:1-4
7.	Sealed with the blood of bulls and goats – Heb.9:19,20	Sealed with the precious Blood of Christ – Heb.9:9,26; 1Pet.1:19
8.	"Come not nigh" – Heb.12:20	"Made nigh" – Heb.12:22; Eph.2:13
9.	Heavy yoke of bondage – Acts 15:10	Light yoke of liberty – Gal.6:2; Matt.11:30
10.	Fading glory on the skin of Moses' face –2Cor.3:13	Permanent light of glory in the face of Jesus Christ – 2Cor.4:6
11.	Only a shadow of good things of the future – Heb.10:1-4,11	Now the substance – Heb.10:34; 9:23,24
12.	Weak and powerless – Rom.8:3,4	Perfect, acceptable – Heb.7:19; 8:8-13
13.	Faulty, decaying, waxed old, ready to vanish away – Heb.7:19; 8:7,13	Never to decay, wax old, but eternal
14.	Priesthood Levitical – carnal commands - Heb.7:11,18,19	Priesthood Melchisedek – Power of and endless life – Heb.7:16
15.	Memorial – Passover Lamb – Ex.12:3	Memorial – Bread and the Cup of Christ – Lke.22:20; 1Cor.11:25
16.	Law only preparatory until The Seed should come – Gal.3:19	Is permanent – Christ has come – Heb.9:11,12
17.	The first covenant "taken away" – Heb.10:9	The second covenant "established" – Heb.10:9
18.	Done away entirely – 2Cor.3:14	Eternally present – Rom.7:1-6

The New Covenant is now present. It transcends and supercedes permanently all the past Covenants which it now fulfills.

In Conclusion:
In the light of these things, how can there be any doubt in the mind of any Dispensationalist who teaches that the New Covenant has not yet been made? Or, that it is to be made in the Millennium? Or, that it has nothing to do with the Church?

The New Covenant has been made with the House of Israel and the House of Judah, represented in the Twelve Apostles of the Lamb (Matt.26:26-28; Rev.21:12; Matt.19:28). It is not yet to be made in the Millennial Age. It has already been ratified by the sacrifice of the body and blood of Jesus. It has been sealed by the Holy Spirit. Ishmael is gone; the Old Covenant has been "cast out". Isaac remains, the New Covenant remains "in the house".

Paul confirms to a Gentile Church, at Corinth, that each time they share together in the communion of the bread and the cup, they are celebrating the NEW Covenant in reality (1Cor.11:23-32). If the New Covenant has not yet been made, then no one should be celebrating the Communion as in the Lord's Table! The Covenant has been made and all, believing Jews and believing Gentiles, are one in Christ and in Covenantal relationship with God, through Christ, and with each other!

Recommended Textbooks on "Covenants".
1. The Covenants (Conner/Malmin)
2. New Covenant Realities (Conner)
3. The Two Covenants (Andrew Murray)
4. God's Covenants and Our Times (Guy Duty)
5. The Blood Covenant (E.W.Kenyon)
6. The Divine Covenants (A.W.Pink)
7. The Blood Covenant (H.Clay Trumbull)
8. Israel and the New Covenant (Roderick Campbell)

CHAPTER SIX

THE MOSAIC COVENANT ECONOMY

When it comes to the subject matter of this present chapter, the Historic Pre-Millennialist, the Post-Millennialist and the A-Millennialist are in full agreement. That is, there will never be a restoration or re-institution of the Mosaic Covenant economy. With this, the Christian Millennialist is completely in agreement, as the previous chapter explained.

Dispensational Pre-Millennialists, as also Futurists, see a complete restoration and re-institution of the Mosaic Covenant economy, either in the end of this age or the Millennial Age to come. There are a number of variations in the Dispensational School as to exact details. Basically, however, Dispensationalists teach that there will be a rebuilt material Temple in Jerusalem during the days of the Great Tribulation. Antichrist will sit in this rebuilt Temple of God, and, according to their understanding and interpretation of the Seventy Weeks Prophecy, "he will cause the sacrifice and oblation to cease." He will then demand worship as God. Many Jews, converted to Christ, will refuse to do so and will be martyred accordingly. The whole world will be forced to take the Mark of the Beast.

Various Dispensationalists also see a Temple built in the Millennium in order to fulfill the Vision of Ezekiel in Chapters 40-48 along with other prophecies of Isaiah and Zechariah. In Ezekiel's Temple, there will be a complete restoration of the Mosaic Covenant economy. But these things are the matters with which this chapter is concerned.

Enough has been written in Chapter Five on the New Covenant and its relation to the Old Covenant. The important point needing fuller development here is that which pertains to that part of the Law known as "the Ceremonial Law." Textbooks on the Futurist/Dispensational Millennial point of view are too many to mention here. The most prominent writers are J.N.Darby, Clarence Larkin, William R.Newell, J.A.Seiss, C.I.Scofield, and Walter Scott. Many others could be mentioned. Each presents the same basic view of the Millennium in Revelation, and the restoration of the Mosaic Covenant economy.

For the purpose of this chapter, the two writings of Clarence Larkin and Finis Jennings Dake will be more particularly noted as representing the Futurist/Dispensational Schools.

Clarence Larkin, in "**Dispensational Truth**" (pages 150-151) writes: "The Mosaic Covenant was given to Moses at Mt.Sinai, shortly after the Exodus from Egypt. It ushered in the 'Dispensation of Law'. It was conditional on obedience, and may be divided into three parts.
  1. The Moral Law (Ex.20:1-26). This consists of the Ten Commandments.
  2. The Civil Law (Ex.21:1—24:18). This is an amplification of the Moral Laws of God.
  3. The Ceremonial Law (Ex.25:1—40:38). This includes the Tabernacle, the Priesthood and the Order of Service. The Sign of this Covenant is the Sabbath (Ex.31:18).

This Covenant continued in force until the Jews were scattered at the destruction of Jerusalem in AD.70. It will be renewed when Israel is converted and restored to their own land, and will then be known as the 'Palestinian Covenant', which Covenant ends in the 'Renovation of the Earth by Fire'. (End quote). The quotation speaks clearly for itself and the Dispensational/Futurist view of the Old Covenant and its renewal in the end of the age and into the Millennial Age."

Finis Jennings Dake, in "**God's Plan For Man**" (pages 965-969) further provides a sample of Dispensational teachings of a restored Judaism in the Millennial Age. Dakes Bible Comments follow the same basic details. His textbook on the Millennial section is in the form of Catechism, "Asking questions and providing answers", from which his questions will be adapted as appropriate for our present chapter. The reader will see that both writers use especially the passages from Ezekiel and Zechariah as their major passages, along with some other Scripture references. These are used to support the view of a material Temple being built and the re-institution of the whole of the Mosaic Covenant economy.

The Temple of Ezekiel's vision is understood to find its fulfillment in the Millennium, in the restored city of Jerusalem. The Jews will be the head of the nations under Messiah Jesus. He will rule on the Throne of David with a rod of iron. All nations, who fail to come to Jerusalem for worship in the Feast of Tabernacles, will come under Divine judgments. Old Testament prophecies that speak of a literal, nationalistic and materialistic Kingdom will find fulfillment in the Millennium. Some of the most important Scriptures used to under-gird this theory are Ezek.40-48 chapters with Zech.12-14 chapters, and Isa.2:1-5; Mic.4:1-8; Isa.11:1-11; 65:17-25; Dan.2; Dan.7 and Rev.20:1-10, as well as many others. They teach it will be predominantly a Jewish Millennial Kingdom under the Mosaic Covenant economy.

(**Note:** Finis J.Dake teaches that the "Old Covenant was entirely abolished" (Pages 574-596), yet also teaches that the nation of Israel will be under the Mosaic Covenant in the Millennium! This seems so contradictory to his own writings!)

(**Note:** Clarence Larkin in "**Dispensational Truth**" (pages 93-94) deals with Ezekiel's Temple vision and various parts of his comments are noted along with Finis Dake's comments in the following).

A. **What Dispensationalists Teach**

    There are a number of points needing consideration as to Dispensationalist's teachings from Ezekiel and Zechariah, along with some other Scripture references. For sharper focus and succinctness, these points are set out in the following order. The response to each of them, basically, will be considered at the end of this chapter. The reader is also referred to "**The Temple of Solomon**" by this author for some details woven in this chapter (Refer Text, pages 220-232).

    1. **The Land**

        Concerning "the land" Larkin writes: "The Royal Grant of land that God gave to Abraham and his descendants extended from the River of Egypt unto the Great River, Euphrates (Gen.15:18)...This Royal Grant was not conditional and was never revoked. It is eight times as large as that formerly occupied by the twelve tribes. This Royal Grant is to be divided among the restored twelve tribes in parallel horizontal sections..."

        Dake also confirms this point of view. He writes that the Promised Land will be divided in wide strips running east and west. There will be twelve great strips, one for each of the twelve tribes. He also says that the city of Jerusalem will be twelve miles square and will be a miniature of the New Jerusalem (Ezek.48:1-35).

    2. **The Holy Oblation**

        Concerning "the holy oblation" C.Larkin writes: "The holy oblation is a square tract on the west of Jordan, 25,000 reeds, or 50 miles on a side...The holy oblation is divided into three horizontal sections...It is called the 'Levite's portion'. South of it is the 'Priest's portion' of equal size. South of the Priest's portion is the section for the 'City' with its suburbs and farming sections (Ezek.48:15-19).

    3. **The Temple**

        Finis Dake asks: "Will the Jews have a Temple during the Millennium?" His answer is Yes. It will be located in the Priest's portion of the holy oblation. The Temple and its enclosure are called "the Sanctuary" (Ezek.45:1-4). It will be one mile square (Ezek.40:1-45:14). He goes on to say that it will not be the Temple that will be built in the last days before the second coming of Christ and in which the Antichrist will sit during the last 3½ years of the age of grace (Matt.24:15-22; 2Thess.2:4; Rev.11:1-2). This one will be destroyed at the second coming of Christ. The Millennial Temple will be built by Christ Himself when he comes to the earth to set up His Kingdom (Zech.6:12-13). It will be the place for Christ's earthly throne forever (Ezek.43:7)." (End quotes)

        Clarence Larkin has this to say. "The Temple or Sanctuary will not be rebuilt in the 'New City' but in the middle of the 'Holy Oblation' (Ezek.48:10,20,21). This will locate it at or near the ancient Shiloh, when the Tabernacle rested after Israel conquered the land, and where it remained until the Temple of Solomon was built. A highway, about 12 miles long, will connect Sanctuary and City (Isa.35:8). This 'New Temple' will occupy a space of 500 reeds on a side or nearly a mile square (Ezek.42:15-20). The old Temple was not a mile in circuit." (End quotes). The argument is that Ezekiel's Temple does not refer to any formerly built Temple. Nor does it refer to Zerubbabel's or Herod's Temple. The Jews have had no Temple since AD.70. Therefore, according to Dispensational teaching, Ezekiel's Temple must refer to a future Temple, in this age or the age to come.

4. **The City**
Clarence Larkin has this to say concerning the city of Jerusalem. He writes that the city will be located in the centre of the third section and will be located on the site of the old. This 'New City' will be much larger than the old. It will be 9 miles square and with its half-mile suburbs on each side will make 10 miles square. It will have a wall around it with three gates on each side like the New Jerusalem (Ezek.48:15-18,30-35). The gates will be named after the twelve sons of Jacob. The name of the city will be Jehovah-Shammah, 'The LORD is there' (Ezek.48:35). He notes that the present Jerusalem is to be trodden down until the Times of the Gentiles are fulfilled (Lke.21:24). Then it will be rebuilt. This city will be the seat of Christ's government in the Millennium.

5. **The Living Waters**
Both writers, along with various others, see that this Temple will have a river flowing from its centre, from the throne of God. C.Larkin uses Zech.14:8 along with Ezek.47:8-12 and Rev.22:1-2 to speak of the 'Living Waters' flowing, not from Jerusalem, but from the Sanctuary. Ezekiel in vision saw these waters from the threshold of the door, flowing past the altar of burnt offering, on the south side, until the stream was deep enough to swim in. Larkin notes that, for such things to happen, great physical changes will have to take place in the land surface of Palestine. He quotes Zech.14:1,10,11 and Mic.1:3,4 as support for this. Such physical changes will level the land surface of Palestine and make room for the 'New City' and raise the Dead Sea for the waters to flow into the Red and Mediterranean Seas (End quotes).

Finis Dake confirms the same thoughts in his writings. He says: "There is to be a literal river flowing out from this Temple eastward and from the south side of the altar. It will then turn and run southward through Jerusalem and immediately south of Jerusalem it will be divided. Half of the river will flow westward into the Mediterranean Sea and half will flow eastward into the Dead Sea. There will also be trees on both sides of the river whose lead shall not fade, neither shall the fruit be consumed. The trees will bring forth new fruit according to their months, which shall be for meat and preservation of natural life for the nations. This river is not the same as the one in the New Jerusalem, for that does not come down to the earth until the New Earth after the Millennium (Rev.22:1-5). The Dead Sea into which one branch of the river flows is to be healed so that multitudes of fish will be found in it (Ezek.47:1-12; Zech.14:8). When Christ sets His feet on the Mt of Olives, there is to be a great earthquake and the whole country will be changed (Zech.14:4-5). The Dead Sea will be raised so that it will have an outlet to purify the stagnant waters, which have been shut up for all these centuries. These will be marshes left to provide salt" (End quote).

6. **The Temple Worship**
Once again, C.Larkin speaks of the Temple and its order of worship in this period of time. He says that the Temple or Sanctuary will be located in the centre of the 'Holy Oblation' and the full description of the Temple and its courts is given in Ezek.40:1—44:31). No Temple like Ezekiel's has ever been built. It cannot refer to Zerubbabel's Temple or Herod's Temple, and there is no Temple in Jerusalem as present. Therefore his point is that it must refer to the Millennial Temple. It cannot refer to the New Heavens and New Earth for there is no Temple there and no more sea.
Clarence Larkin goes on to say that the Aaronic Priesthood will be re-established, the sons of Zadok will officiate in the sacrifices (Ezek.44:15-31). He mentions that, in the new Temple, there will not be the Ark of the Covenant with its Golden Pot of Manna, the Rod of Aaron that budded, the Tables of the Law or the Cherubim and Mercy-Seat. Neither will there be the Golden Lampstand, the Table of Shewbread, the Altar of Incense, the Veil or Holy of Holies into which the High Priest alone enters to make intercession and atonement for sin.

He suggests that maybe Christ will be performing the offices of King and Priest according to Zech.6:12-13. The Levites will perform Temple services but not priestly because of their past sins (Ezek.44:10-14). The daily 'morning sacrifice' will be offered, but not the 'evening sacrifice' (Ezek.46:13-15). The Burnt, the Meal, the Drink, the Sin, the Peace and Trespass offerings will be offered (Ezek.45:17; 42:13). The Shekinah Glory that departed from the Temple at the time of the Babylonian Captivity will again takes up its residence in the new Temple (Ezek.10:18-20; 11:21-23 with Ezek.43:1-5).

7. **The Priesthood**
Finis Dake asks: "Will there be Priests in the Millennial Temple?" He answers. "There will be earthly priests in the future Temple just as there were in the first Temple (Ezek.43:19-27; 44:9-11). The Levites who went astray with the Northern Kingdom of the ten tribes will not be permitted to do the most holy work, but shall serve in other parts of the Temple. That is, their descendants will serve in the future Temple worship. The sons of Zadok who remained true to the house of David will do the most holy work (Ezek.43:19-27; 44:9-31. See 1Kgs.1:39; 2Sam.8:17; 15:24; 20:25).

The Priesthood of the Law of Moses was an eternal one (Ex.29:9; 40:15; Num.25:11-13; 1Chron.23:13). This would seem to conflict with Heb.7:11-28 where the writer speaks of a change in the law and priesthood of old. There is really no conflict. However, as far as the means of approach and the way of salvation and mediation to God are concerned, there has been a change. Men under the law had to come through the priests and offer certain sacrifices as a token of their faith, but today Christ, our Passover, has been sacrificed once and forever for us by the which we can individually draw nigh to God any time we desire (1Cor.1:7). Nevertheless, there will still be the earthly priesthood and offerings in the future age for earthly peoples – not for salvation – for the blood of bulls and goats did not take away sins even when they were offering, but for a memorial or object lesson to demonstrate that the people believe in what has been done for them through Christ.

There is no question but what God intends to have a Temple, an earthly priesthood, sacrifices and feasts in the future. For, that is what He revealed to Ezekiel (Ezek.40:1—48:35), and promised Israel when He gave them ordinances to be observed throughout all their generations forever, as we shall see below. These outward observances will not supercede the present individual salvation, or the means of approach to God, but will be added for earthly peoples to satisfy the natural instincts in man for something outward in religion" (End quotes).

It has already been seen that Larkin confirms the same thing of the restoration of the Levitical and Zadok Priesthood in service in the Millennial Temple.

8. **The Sacrifices and Offerings**
With regards to the sacrifices and offerings, Finis Dake, supplies us with the following comments. He asks: "Will there be offerings in the future Temple?" His answer? "Every offering mentioned in the law was to be observed by Israel forever as is proved by the following statements in the law, which are found from two to eight times in a single chapter in the Book of Moses:
Dake quotes several parts of verses, such as. "It is a statute forever", and "This shall be an everlasting statute unto you", or " A perpetual statute", and so forth, to confirm his thought that these offerings are to be forever. He mentions that these statements in connection with the offerings and feasts of the law can only be taken in a literal sense.

In the same section, he mentions the various offerings to be offered in the future Temple where Christ is going to reign in Israel forever (Ezek.43:7). Both Larkin and Dake list the offerings which are to be offered in Ezekiel's Temple, these being:

- Burnt offerings (Ezek.43:24-27; 45:17-25; 46:1-4 with Lev.7:16 and Lev.1).
- Sin offerings (Ezek.43:19-23; 45:17-25; 46:1-24 with Lev.4:14-21 and Lev.4).
- Meal offerings (Ezek.45:17-25; 46:1-24 with Lev.6:14-23 and Lev.2).
- Trespass offerings (Ezek.46:20 with Lev.7:1-10; 14:12 and Lev.5).
- Peace offerings (Ezek.43:27; 45:17; 46:1-24 with Lev.7:11-38 and Lev.3).

Finis Dake admits that, to some, it seems unreasonable that the old sacrifices and ceremonial law will be established in the Millennium and forever. His argument is that neither Jews nor Gentiles ever kept the law perfectly, in the heart as well as externally. He says that these ordinances are not a means to salvation any more than in Old Testament times (Heb.9:12-15; 11:4). Both Larkin and Dake and some other Dispensationalists say that the sacrifices to be offered in the Millennial Temple are "memorials" just like the Lord's table and water baptism are for believers in the Church today. These are but outward observances of what has been actually done spiritually. They are not means of salvation but acts of obedience having spiritual significance. Dake says that water baptism is an outward symbol of what has been done in the believer's heart, and the Lord's table is a memorial of what was done on Calvary. He uses the statement of Ezekiel that these things were to be "a perpetual ordinance unto the Lord" (Ezek.46:14 along with other references from Exodus and Numbers).

9. **The Feasts of the Lord**
Most all the Dispensationalists see a re-institution of the Feasts of the Lord in the Millennial Kingdom and Temple. Clarence Larkin and Finis Dake mention the various feasts as in Ezekiel, which will be observed in the Millennium. The following set these Festival occasions out according to Ezekiel and Zechariah, more especially.

- Feast of Passover (Ezek.45:21 with Lev.23; Ex.12; 1Cor.5:7). Larkin says there will not be any Passover Lamb offered as Christ fulfilled this.
- Feast of Unleavened Bread (Ezek.45:21 with Lev.23 and 1Cor.5:8).
- Feast of Firstfruits Sheaf (Ezek.44:30 with Lev.23 and 1Cor.15:20-23).
- Feast of Pentecost or Feast of Weeks (Ezek.46:9 with Lev.23 and Acts 2:1). This will fulfill the promise of the outpoured Spirit on all flesh.
- Feast of Trumpets (Ezek.44:5; 45:17 and Lev.23 with 1Cor.15:52; 1Thess.4:16).
- Feast Day of Atonement (Ezek.45-46 chapters with Lev.23; Lev.16 and Heb.8-10).
- Feast of Tabernacles (Ezek.45:25; Zech.14:16-21 with Lev.23). This Feast is to be kept by all nations under penalty of drought and plagues.

The passage in Zech.14:16-21 is the passage used most to support the keeping of the Feast of Tabernacles in the Millennium by all nations, under penalty of no rains, drought and various plagues falling on them for disobedience.

Dispensationalists see that the Jews will be the head of all nations in the Millennial Kingdom. They teach that the converted Jews will be "missionaries" to all nations in this time. They will teach the principles and practices of the laws of God. The Holy Spirit will then be poured on "all flesh" in greater way than ever in human history (Joel 2:28-32; Ezek.36:25-27; 39:28-29; Isa.32:15-20; 44:3; 59:21; Zech.12:10—13:1). There will be a universal knowledge of the Lord on the nations (Isa.11:9; Hab.2:14; Zech.8:22-23). There will be peace and prosperity in all the earth. There will be one universal religion. The glory of God will be manifested in the earth as all nations fulfill their required yearly pilgrimage to Jerusalem to keep the feast (Zech.14:16-21 with Isa.2:1-5; 35:8-9; Mal.1:11; Zech.8:22-23). New moons, Sabbath days and Festival days will be kept in this age of Millennial bliss and order (Isa.66:22-24; Ezek.44:5; 45:17; 46:1-3). The rite of circumcision will be re-introduced so that no uncircumcised person dare come near the Sanctuary of God (Ezek.44:7-9).

But enough has been given on the Dispensationalist teaching on the re-institution of the Mosaic Covenant economy in the Millennial Kingdom Age! The student is referred to the many texts that deal with these things. It has been, however, necessary to provide a reasonable coverage of what Futurists and Dispensationalists teach on this subject before seeking to provide some Scriptural refutation of these things. As mentioned earlier, there are some slight variations but this is the teaching on the whole.

B. **What the Bible Teaches**
There are two major problems with the whole of the Dispensational view of the things discussed in this chapter. The first is Geographical/Material, and the second, which is the greatest, is the great Theological problems in the Dispensational teachings. The first can only be touched on in brief. The second is dealt with more fully.

1. **Geographical/Material Problems**
In brief, to have a rebuilt material Temple of the size and proportions given in Ezekiel and built on by the Dispensationalists provides great problems. The student is referred especially to other more qualified writers on this matter.

J.Sidlow Baxter in "**Explore the Book**" (Ezekiel, pages 31-35) presents some major objections to a literal/material interpretation of the Ezekiel chapters. The student should weigh carefully the arguments presented here as against those of the Dispensational School as they are set forth here following the general order as laid out there.

(a) The Land Area
The land area for the twelve tribes, distributed in equal proportions, without respect of numbers, and these in parallel sections running from east to west presents great problems. The separate tribe portions limits all to about four to five miles of territory, seven of the tribes being north and five tribes to the south of the allotted area. This is certainly a very small land inheritance without respect of increase of numbers, if this be geographically so. If Israel is to be as numberless as the sand and the stars, then this is a very limited land area and so presents geographical problems.

(b) The Holy Oblation Area
The holy oblation or threefold sacred land area for the Temple, the Priests and the Levites covers a vast land area (Ezek.42:15-20; 45:2; 48:20). It measures 25,000 by 25,000 reeds square, or about 47 square miles. About 19 square miles of this is a reserved portion for the Priesthood, and again, about 19 square miles is a portion reserved for the Levites, and this without respect for numbers (45:3-5; 48:10,13). This is a lot of land just for one tribe, the Priestly tribe of Levi, and again presents another geographical problem.

(c) The Temple Area
The area allotted to the Temple itself covers all the area allotted to the old city of Jerusalem, that is, about one mile square. In other words, the Temple is as large as the whole of the ancient city of Jerusalem (Ezek.45:6; 48:15-19). The outer court of the Temple is 500 reeds long by 500 reeds wide (Ezek.42:15-20; 45:2). This Temple could not be contained on the Mt Zion or Mt Moriah area of Jerusalem.

J.Sidlow Baxter writes: "Take the size of the temple and the sacred area with it. The 'outer court' of the temple is 500 reeds long by 500 reeds wide (42:15-20; 45:2). And as the reed is about 10 feet, this court is one mile long by one mile wide, which means that the temple covers a space as large as the whole city enclosed by the walls of old Jerusalem. Certainly, **this** temple could not possibly be contained on Mt Zion, inside Jerusalem. But when we pass from the temple area to the sacred area, or 'oblation' of land, going with it, we find this to be 25,000 reeds long by 25,000 reeds wide (48:20). That is, 47 miles north to south, and the same east to west, covering an area between six and seven times that of modern London! Of this an area 47 miles by 19 is reserved for the priesthood alone (45:3,4; 48:10), and an area the same size for the Levites (45:5; 48:13). There is also a third area, in which, although small compared with the whole 'oblation', is a 'city' with a circuit of 20,000 reeds, or nearly 38 miles (45:6; 48:15-19). Josephus reckoned the circuit of Jerusalem in his day at only four miles! Now is it thinkable that there is to be a literal counterpart to this temple which itself is as large as the whole of Jerusalem, and in a sacred area of over 2,200 square miles?

Moreover, this sacred area is **physically impossible** – unless the river Jordan be moved further east! The boundaries of the land are the Mediterranean on the west and the Jordan on the east (47:18). And this great square of 47 miles by 47 cannot be put between the two, for the distance between them in places is scarcely 40 miles. Even if we bend the great square to the slope of the coast, we cannot get it in – the less so because on each side of the square, in Ezekiel's vision, is an **additional** area called 'the portion for the prince' (45:7; 48:21,22). Admittedly, God could move the Jordan, but is it thinkable that we are meant to infer this?" (End quote, pages 31-35).

(d) The City Area
The third portion of the sacred area is reserved for the new city. The city has a circuit of 20,000 reeds, or approximately 38 miles (Ezek.45:6; 48:15-19). The old city of Jerusalem had a circuit of approximately four miles. That means that this new city is as large as the whole frame of the land between Jordan and the Mediterranean Sea. The city area reaches to the Dead Sea. Again we note the comments of J.S.Baxter on this matter.

"There is further difficulty that although this great area is 47 miles by 47, **it does not include the site of Jerusalem**, so that this 'city' which Ezekiel sees is not Jerusalem. If then, we are to take this vision literally, what of all those other prophecies which speak of Jerusalem as the glorified centre of the coming new order?

Ezekiel's vision also places the new temple 500 reeds (some nine and a half miles) **away north from the 'city'**, in fact, fourteen and a quarter miles from the **centre** of it. Now the connection between the temple and Jerusalem is so deeply laid, both in the Scriptures and in the thought of the Jews, that to interpret literally a vision which separates them without giving the slightest reason seems again unthinkable. As C.J.Ellicott says, 'A temple in any other locality than Mt Moriah would hardly be the temple of Jewish hope.' Hard as we find to picture Ezekiel's mile-square temple spread over the variety of hill and valley which the country presents, we find it even harder to think of the new city away from Jerusalem, and the new temple still another fourteen miles north, and, in fact, well on the way to Samaria."

(e) The Living Waters

A further problem (and objection) has to do with the river which flows from the Temple threshold by way of the altar of sacrifice. An actual river flowing from a material Temple by way of a material altar of sacrifice in a great high mountain into the Dead Sea presents a problem also. This river parts into two main streams and becomes unfordable within 4,000 cubits from its source. One final quote from Baxter shows the truth of these things.

"Another problem in the way of a literal interpretation is found in the waters which Ezekiel saw flowing beneath the eastern threshold of the temple (47:1-12). To quote C.J.Ellicott again, 'These waters run to the east country, and go down to the sea, which can only be the Dead Sea. But such a course would be physically impossible without changes in the surface of the earth, since the temple of the vision is on the west of the watershed of the country. They had, moreover, the effect of 'healing' the waters of the sea, an effect which could not be produced naturally without providing an outlet from the sea. No supply of fresh water could remove the saltiness while this water was all disposed of by evaporation and Ezek.47:11 excludes the idea of an outlet. But above all, the character of the waters themselves is impossible without a perpetual miracle. Setting aside the difficulty of a spring of this magnitude upon the top of a very high mountain (40:2), in this locality, at the distance of 1,000 cubits from their source, the waters have greatly increased in volume. And so, with each successive 1,000 cubits, until at the end of 4,000 cubits (about a mile and a half), they have become a river no longer fordable; or, in other words, comparable to the Jordan. Such an increase, without secondary streams, is clearly not natural. But, beyond this, the description of waters themselves clearly marks them as ideal. They are life-giving and healing; trees of perennial foliage and fruit grow upon their banks, the leaves being for 'medicine' and the fruit, although not food, never wasting" (End quote). (Emphasis – J.S.Baxter's)

(f) The Temple Materials/Furniture

Other objections to the literalness of Ezekiel's Temple have to do with the material and the furniture. In contrast to the Tabernacle of Moses and the Temple of Solomon, there is practically no mention concerning Temple materials. So many chapters and details are given for this Temple, yet there is almost total silence concerning materials for the Temple or its furnishings. The only specific mention of materials is the appearance of "the man as brass" (40:3); the tables for the burnt offering of hewn stone (40:42), and the doors, posts, windows, and incense altar of "wood" (41:16,22). There is no mention of gold, silver or brass as specified so much in the Tabernacle and Temple structures of the previous times. Surely the lack of mention has some significance, unless Ezekiel's Temple was a repeat of Solomon's Temple!

Then there is the matter of furnishings, or the lack of mention of such. If this Temple is to exceed the glory of Solomon's, Zerubbabel's and Herod's Temple, then why is there no mention of the furniture? It is like a house without furniture. There is no mention of the Ark, even though 'the glory' fills the house. There is no mention of the Golden Pot of Manna, Aaron's Rod, the Tables of the Law, the Cherubim and MercySeat, the Golden Lampstand, the Table of Shewbread, the Incense Altar of Gold, all of which were given much detail in the previous structures. The student should remember that the final mention of the Ark of the Covenant is found in Jer.3:14-15. It has not been seen since.

Will God place it in a material Temple in the Millennium? We believe not, as a careful reading of Jer.3:14-15 confirms.

These are the Geographical and Material objections that need serious consideration when teaching that Ezekiel's Temple is a literal and material Temple to be built by Christ in the Millennium! We proceed now to the Theological problems which this kind of Temple presents.

2. **Theological and Covenantal Problems**

One of the most important principles of Biblical interpretation is "The Covenantal Principle", in which it is vital that the believer understands the difference between the Covenants of Law and Grace, or, the Old and the New Covenants in particular. The Covenantal Principle affects one's theology and theology also affects one's understanding of the Covenantal Principle of interpretation.

This is to say, we do not use the Old Testament to interpret the New Testament but we use the New Testament to interpret the Old Testament, **passing all through the cross**! The cross is the key. The cross becomes what we have called 'the hermeneutical filter' of the Old Testament economy, especially those things which pertain to the Law or the Mosaic Covenant. It should also be remembered that the New Testament apostles are the infallible interpreters of the Old Testament prophets. The test of everything since Calvary is the NEW Covenant. Believers are under the NEW Covenant, not the OLD Covenant. The Old Covenant has become old, it is decayed, it has vanished away and it has been totally replaced by the New Covenant. All believers, Jews or Gentiles, are 'in Christ', not 'in Moses'. There cannot be two Covenants. Moses and Jesus cannot rule together. Moses pointed to Christ. The Old and the New cannot work together, as the Galatian Church endeavoured to do, with Moses in one hand and Jesus in the other hand. The Law (Moses) and the Prophets (Elijah) must give way to the New Covenant (Jesus). "This is My beloved Son, HEAR HIM!" This is the Father's word out of the cloud of glory on the Mt of Transfiguration (Matt.17:1-8). Dispensationalists would have two Covenants, two mediators and two peoples in their future Millennium. This will not be! The cross has settled it – forever!

Sound theology and sound hermeneutics expose the problems of Dispensationalism!

C. **The Old and New Covenants**

The New Testament abundantly proves that there will never be a restoration or re-institution of the things belonging to the Mosaic Covenant economy. The contrasts presented here should suffice to confirm these facts. The New Covenant writers take the things of the Old Covenant, pass them through the cross, and bring them all to a greater and higher level than ever before. They move from "first the natural, and afterward into the spiritual" (1Cor.15:46). We take the various things presented under the Old Covenant, in Ezekiel's vision, and through the cross, see what they mean to New Covenant believers, now and on into eternity.

1. **The Promised Land**

Ezekiel's vision pointed to the inheritance of the land. Unless the Lord brought about great geographical changes in the land, as it is now, the inheritances of the twelve tribes could not be as in Ezekiel's vision. Inheritance points to the believer's inheritance in Christ (Eph.1:3). Paul shows that the greater promise to Abraham was that he should be "heir of the world", not just Canaan land (Rom.4:13). Believers, as kings and priests unto God, shall reign on the earth. This is the time when the saints possess the kingdom (Rev.5:9-10 with Dan.7). In the Christian Millennium, the saints indeed inherit the earth, as the Lord promised and not merely the geographical land of Palestine. The Church is the true Israel of God (Rom.9:1-6; Gal.6:15-16), and not the Israel after the flesh.

2. **The Sacred Oblation**

The whole earth is to be filled with the Glory of the Lord as the waters cover the sea. The whole earth will be like "the Most Holy" or "the Holiest of All" in the Christian Millennium. All will be sacred unto the Lord, not merely a local geographical part of the earth as Palestine. The Scriptures speak of God's glory to cover the whole world (Num.14:21; Psa.72:19; Hab.2:14).

3. **The Temple**
   The New Covenant writers all teach that the New Covenant Temple is now the believer individually and the Church corporately. Ezekiel, as well as Isaiah, pointed to Christ who would be "a little Sanctuary" to His people where ever they would be (Ezek.11:16; Isa.8:14-18; Rev.21:22). The Lord God and the Lamb are the eternal Temple in the City of God, the New and Heavenly Jerusalem. Father, Son and Holy Spirit set their seal to the rejection of a material Temple in the Gospels and the Acts. The Godhead will never return to any material Temple when the reality is now in Christ and His Church (Matt.21:12-14; 23:38; 24:1; 27:51; Acts 2:1-4; Isa.66:1-4; 1Cor.3:16; 2Cor.6:16; Eph.2:19-22). The Church is God's New Covenant house (1Pet.2:1-10).

4. **The City of God**
   Ezekiel saw a vision of the City of God, Jehovah-Shammah, "The LORD is there." Abraham, Isaac and Jacob looked for a city whose builder and maker is God (Heb.11:10-16). That city is certainly not the earthly city of Jerusalem. The earthly city of Jerusalem is in bondage with her children, and is likened to Hagar and Ishmael, in Paul's inspired allegory (Gal.4:21-31). To John, earthly Jerusalem is spiritually Sodom and Egypt, where our Lord was crucified (Rev.11:8). This was not the city Abraham looked for. The city is the heavenly and New Jerusalem coming down from heaven, adorned as a glorious bride (Rev.21-22). The twelve tribes of the true and spiritual Israel of God will enter through the gates of that city, and the saved nations, the redeemed of all ages, will walk in its light. That will be the eternal city, and its name will be Jehovah-Shammah in truth, for "the LORD is there". The writer to the Hebrews told the believers they had no city on earth, but they looked for one to come; the Jerusalem which is above (Heb.12:22-24; Heb.13:14). Believers do not look forward to living in the old Jerusalem, but the New Jerusalem which is from above.

5. **The Living Waters**
   In Ezek.47, he sees the river of God flowing from the threshold of the house. Where ever the river flowed, there was life, health, healing and a great multitude of fish. The geographical problems have been considered previously. The vision of the river of God can only find its fulfillment in that which is spiritual. Jesus stood in the Temple and spoke of the rivers of the Holy Spirit flowing. This He said at the Feast of Tabernacles (Jhn.7:37-39). The rivers of the Holy Spirit bring life, healing and health. Multitudes of souls are saved when the river is flowing from the house of God by way of the altar of the cross of Jesus. This river replaces all that was symbolized in the waters of the Molten Sea and the Brazen Lavers in Solomon's Temple. Its ultimate is the river flowing from the throne of God and the Lamb (Rev.22:1-2; Psa.46; Joel 3:18; Zech.14:8).

6. **The Temple Worship**
   Ezekiel speaks of the order of worship in his visionary Temple. In John 4:20-24 Jesus foretold the truth. He said to the Samaritan woman that the time would come when worship would no longer be acceptable only in the earthly Jerusalem, as a place. True worship would be in spirit and in truth, wherever true believers would be found. This statement of Jesus forever repudiated external and formal worship at Jerusalem. How then can nations be forced to worship God and His Christ in a Millennial Age unless born of the Spirit? The final specific mention of earthly Jerusalem is Rev.11:8 where the city is "spiritually Sodom and Egypt, where our Lord was crucified." God does not accept forced or feigned worship, in this age or any future age.

7. **The Priesthood**
   Ezekiel's vision speaks of the Priesthood of Zadok and the Levitical Priesthood in service. When Jesus died on the cross, the veil of the material Temple was torn in two, from top to bottom, and this by God Himself. It was done in conjunction with the body and blood of Christ on Calvary. It sent a message to the Aaronic and Levitical Priesthood that this order was forever abolished. Jesus is after the order of Melchisedek. The Melchisedek Priesthood for ever abolishes the Aaronic and Levitical Priesthood. In the Old Covenant, only one tribe was chosen to be the Priestly tribe, in behalf of the twelve tribes. Under the New Covenant, all believers, whether men or women, Jews or Gentiles, are called to be priests unto God and His Christ (Rev.1:6; 5:9-10; 1Pet.2:5-10). God will never re-establish the Old Covenant

Priesthood in this age or any age to come. The Church is joined to the risen head, and Christ and His members are the order of Melchisedek, "kings and priests unto God". Jesus is King-Priest on His throne (Zech.6:12-15). What an insult to Christ and His Church to have the Aaronic and Levitical Priesthood functioning again!

8. **The Sacrifice and Oblation**

Ezekiel also mentions sacrifice and oblation. If there is a functioning Priesthood, then it is necessary to have sacrifices and oblation to offer. Priesthood and sacrifice are all part of the Covenant. As the student compares Dan.9:24-27 with Heb.9-10 chapters, he will see that Christ's once-for-all sacrifice and oblation on Calvary caused all animal sacrifice and oblation to cease. Neither will it suffice to say that the sacrifices will not be offered for sin in the Millennial Temple, but only as a "memorial" now of Christ's death and resurrection. Will God forsake the Lord's Table and the bread and the cup and go back to animal body and blood for a "memorial"? The body and blood of Jesus for ever repudiates animal body and blood. To have any other sacrifices is to deny the all-sufficiency and efficacy of the sacrifice of Jesus. It has been said, "He who sacrificed before confessed Christ, but he who sacrifices now solemnly denies Him." Any return to animal sacrifices is an insult to the sacrifice of Jesus Christ. It would be the greatest insult to Christ's offering for His Father God to go back the other side of the cross of Calvary to animal offerings!

Loraine Boettner in "**The Millennium**" (pages 92-98) has some significant comments about the cessation of the Old Covenant sacrifices and oblations. Boettner has given permission to quote him with or without credit. Even though this writer does not follow Boettner's Millennial philosophy, there is total agreement with his writings on the cessation of animal sacrifice and oblation.

He writes concerning "**The Old Testament Sacrificial System**", saying: "The writer of the Epistle to the Hebrews has much to say about the endless repetition and the futility of the ancient sacrifices. He shows that their only value was to symbolize and point forward to the one true sacrifice that was to be made by Christ. 'We have been sanctified,' he said, 'through the offering of the body of Jesus Christ **once for all**. And every priest stands day by day ministering and offering oftentimes the same sacrifices which can never take away sins. But He, when He had offered one sacrifice for sin for ever, sat down on the right hand of God; henceforth expecting till His enemies be made the footstool of His feet. For by one offering He has perfected for ever them that are sanctified" (Heb.10:10-14).

Harold Dekker, one of the speakers on 'The Back to God Hour' radio program, says concerning the futility of the animal sacrifices and the finality of Christ's sacrifice as set forth in this passage: "Continually, day by day, year after year, God's people made their sacrifices according to the Old Testament law. The writer calls to mind the mountains of herbs and grains and meal offerings which had been brought before the Lord, the rivers of blood which had flowed from millions of sheep and goats and droves of cattle. And then he raised the question, Why the constant repetition? Why the endless pilgrimages to Jerusalem? Why the interminable fires upon Israel's altars? The reason, says the inspired writer, is that none of these brought lasting relief to troubled consciences. So on and on went the sacrifices."

But of Christ's sacrifice on Calvary he says, "He was surely the sacrifice to end all sacrifices. Let the blood now dry on the horns of the altar. Let the ovens that bake meal offerings now be cooled. Let the sacrificial animals go back to pasture. Final atonement is accomplished! Let all men everywhere now look to the one sacrifice of Christ finished on the cross!"

Boettner says that "In its doctrine of an earthly Kingdom with a restored Temple, Priesthood and sacrificial system, Pre-Millennialism (think Dispensationalism–this writer) is a recrudescence of Judaism!"

In quoting James H. Snowden ("**The Coming of the Lord**", pages 206-209), he continues to write: "It is one of the plainest universal teachings of the New Testament that the sacrifices of the Mosaic economy were fulfilled in Christ. And they were then done away as vanishing shadows that prefigured the substance, or as morning stars that heralded the sun and were then lost in its light." And again, "Pre-Millennialism (think Dispensationalism-this writer) is therefore required by its own logic to take the prophecy of Ezekiel, chapters 40-48, in which an idealized vision of the Temple is set forth, including the Passover and all the bloody offerings which are expressly commanded (45:21-25), and transfer it bodily and literally to the Millennial Kingdom in Jerusalem after the second coming of Christ. And this system must do the same thing with all similar prophecies, such as Isa.66:20,23 and Zech.14:16.

Lewis Sperry Chafer, also says that after the Church age has run its course there is to be "the regathering of Israel and the restoration of Judaism" ("**Dispensationalism**", page 46).

Merrill F.Unger says, "At the second advent Christ will restore the Judaistic system with far greater glory and spirituality than it ever had in the Old Testament period until its complete dissipation with the destruction of Herod's Temple in AD.70. The heart and centre of re-established Judaism will be the Millennial Temple, in connection with which Judaism will enjoy its final state of development" (**Biblotheca Sacra**, Jan-March,1950).

Scofield explains, "Doubtless these offerings will be memorial, looking back to the cross, as the offerings under the Old Covenant were anticipatory, looking forward to the cross." Boettner continues, "In any event, the re-institution of a sacrificial system could not do other than dishnour the sacrifice that Christ made on Calvary, which the Scripture represents as "once for all" sacrifice (Heb.9:27). The New Testament has absolutely nothing to say about such memorial sacrifices, nor anything about rebuilding the Temple. Furthermore, all memorials are unnecessary when the one to be memorialized is present in person, as Christ will be after His second coming.

Oswald T. Allis ("**Prophecy & The Church**", page 248) says, "The thought is abhorrent that after Christ comes, the memory of His atoning work will be kept alive in the hearts of believers by a return to the animal sacrifices of the Mosaic law, the performance of which is so emphatically condemned in passages which speak with unmistakable plainness on this very subject."

Enough has been noted in this section on sacrifice and oblation. To re-institute Mosaic Covenant sacrifice and oblation is a return to Judaism. Paul himself testifies how the Lord Jesus Christ converted him from "**the Jews' religion**" (Lit. "**Judaism**") to "reveal His Son in me, that I might preach HIM among the heathen" (Gal.1:13-16). To return to Judaism or the Mosaic and Old Covenant is to return to the weak and beggarly elements of the Old Covenant when believers are now and eternally under the New Covenant, by grace, through faith, and not of law or the works of religious and unregenerate and sinful flesh!

9. **The Altars**
Ezekiel mentions "altars" in his vision. The cross of Jesus for ever fulfilled and abolished by fulfillment all Old Covenant altars of sacrifice and incense. The Lord's Table is the symbol in the New Testament Church of that eternally efficacious sacrifice. The only incense that God accepts now is the prayers and intercessions from the heart of the believer. Even the Old Covenant prophets foretold the time would come when incense and sacrifice would actually be "an abomination" to God, even though He ordained it once. Since the cross of Christ and His sacrifice, and since He is the Mediator and Intercessor for all who come to God by Him, all sacrifice and incense is an abomination (a detestable thing) to God (Read carefully Isa.1:10-15; Isa.66:1-5 with Psa.141:1-2; Rev.5:9-10; 8:1-4).

10. **The Feasts of the Lord**
The Feasts of the Lord find their fulfillment in the LORD Jesus Christ. Ezekiel mentions various festival days. However, all feast days were fulfilled in Christ and then find fulfillment in the Church. Christ is our Passover Lamb (1Cor.5:6-8). The Holy Spirit came in fulfillment of the Day of Pentecost to write God's laws on our hearts and minds (Acts 2:1; 2Cor.3 and Heb.8:6-13; Jer.31:31-34). The believers will enjoy the fulness of the Feast of Tabernacles. The Book of Hebrews clearly shows that Christ has fulfilled the great Day of Atonement in Himself and in the true and heavenly Sanctuary above (Heb.9-10 chapters). He has entered within the veil of the heavenly Sanctuary as our Forerunner (Heb.6:19-20).

God will not re-institute the letterism and ceremonialism of these Feasts when they have been abolished at the cross and find their spiritual fulfillment in the experiences of the true believer in Christ (Col.2:14-17). They were shadows of good things to come. The 'good things' have come in Christ. He is the substance and reality of all truth shadowed forth in these Feasts of Israel. For this reason, there is no need for a material Temple, an earthly Priesthood, or animal sacrifice and oblation. All is "**in Christ**".

It is for this reason that the passage in Zechariah (14:9-20) concerning the nations in the Millennium going to Jerusalem to keep the Feast of Tabernacles cannot be interpreted in its Old Covenant literalness. Since the cross, the Old Covenant literalness is swallowed up in New Covenant spiritual reality. Old Covenant language is now interpreted through the cross by New Covenant language. To interpret Zechariah's prophecy literally necessitates a restored material Temple, animal sacrifices, a restored Levitical Priesthood and all the other things belonging to the Mosaic Covenant ritualism and ceremonialism. The language of Zechariah has to be seen spiritually this side of Calvary!

Zechariah speaks of worship, the Feast of Tabernacles, the rains, plagues for disobedience, heathen nations such as Egypt and the Canaanites. He also speaks of altars, pots and bowls along with sacrifice in the house of the Lord, at Jerusalem. All these things belong to the Law Age, to the Old Covenant. Enough has been seen in this chapter, that, in order to take these literally, then there has to be a restoration of the Mosaic Covenant economy. All this would be contrary to the New Covenant. Therefore, the keeping of the Feast of Passover is found in Christ, the Passover Lamb (1Cor.5). The keeping of the Feast of Pentecost is found in the Holy Spirit's ministrations (2Cor.3 with Acts 2). The keeping of the Feast of Tabernacles, with its Trumpets, Day of Atonement, and Feast of Ingathering – all must now, this side of the cross – be **IN CHRIST**! Can it be that, in a future Millennium all the intricate details of Exodus and Leviticus concerning the sacrifices, the oblations, the Priesthood, the various ceremonies of the Feast days, and entrance within the veil on the Day of Atonement, all is going to be re-established? The New Covenant and the teaching of the Book of Hebrews cry out aloud that this will never be so!

11. The Sabbaths and New Moons

Ezekiel also mentions Sabbaths and New Moons, as does Isaiah (Ezek.46:1 with Isa.66:23). The Sabbath was the sign and seal of the Mosaic Covenant. Sabbaths and New Moons belonged to the Old Covenant. All such were nailed to the cross, with other ordinances, so why should they be unnailed and taken down from the cross to be re-established again in the future (Col.2:14-17; Heb.8-9-10 chapters)? Paul was concerned about the Galatian believers who wanted to "observe days, and months, and times, and years" (Gal.4:10 with Rom.14:5-7). The believer is not to go back to these beggarly elements of the Law. If Paul were here in our generation, he would have the same concern for the Dispensationalists who teach that in the Jewish Millennium Sabbath days and New Moons will be observed again. True Sabbath Rest is in a person, in Christ, not merely the observance of any special day. Believers serve the Lord Jesus Christ seven days a week. To re-institute the Sabbath day again, in this age, or the future age, is to take the sign and seal of the Old Covenant and place it on or alongside the sign and seal of the New Covenant. The sign and seal of the New Covenant is the ministry of the blessed Holy Spirit, not Sabbath days or New Moons!

12. The Rite of Circumcision

Ezekiel also mentioned those who have failed in the rite of circumcision. The uncircumcised cannot minister in the house of the Lord (Ezek.44:7-9). Paul very clearly shows that New Covenant circumcision is of the heart, and of the spirit. It is not of the flesh and the letter of the law (Rom.2:24-29; Col.2:12-17). Even the Old Testament writings show that God really wanted that spiritual circumcision which is of the heart. Even though Israel was circumcised "after the flesh", they were actually "uncircumcised in heart". Because of this they were, in God's eyes, "Gentilized!" Read carefully Jer.9:25-26.

Circumcision was the sign and seal of the Abrahamic Covenant (Gen.17:10-14,23-27; 21:4; Acts 7:8). So serious was the rite that no one could keep the Feast of Passover unless circumcised (Ex.12:44-48; Josh.5:1-7). Great problems arose in the Book of Acts when the Judaizers wanted to circumcise the Gentiles who came to faith in Christ (Acts 15). Abraham was the father of all who believe, whether circumcised (Israel) or uncircumcised (Gentile) for it was the heart that counted before God (Rom.5:11). Paul tells the Corinthians that circumcision and uncircumcision is nothing in the sight of God since the cross (1Cor.7:18-19). The Galatian Church was troubled by the Judaizers over this rite (Gal.6:12-13). So Dispensationalists link arms with the Judaizers and seek to have the rite of circumcision brought in again in the Millennial Jewish Kingdom! Why, in the light of the New Covenant, seek to re-introduce this rite, which was the sign and seal of the Abrahamic Covenant, on a people in a future age when such was abolished at the cross in the "cutting off" of Christ Jesus? To do so is to yield to the Judaistic spirit and the Galatian Church philosophy!

13. The Shekinah Glory

Ezekiel also mentions the return of God's glory to this Temple even though the Ark of God is not mentioned (Ezek.43:1-3). As mentioned previously, the Glory of God never ever returned to any materially built Temple. Why should it then return to one in a future age? Will God forsake the Church, His New Covenant Temple, to which all material habitations of God pointed, and return to a material Temple? Once the Glory of God forsook the material Temple of Solomon, it has not been seen since in a material one. The "glory" of the New Covenant Temple is, "Christ in you, the hope of glory" (Col.1:27-28). The Holy Spirit in the believer, and in the Church, replaces forever the Old Covenant manifestation of "the Shekinah Glory" (Eph.2:19-22; 1Pet.2:5-9). God always wanted His presence and glory to be in His people. Will He leave them to go and dwell in a material Temple again? This will never be, for He will dwell eternally in and with His redeemed!

14. The Old and New Covenants

Ezekiel's vision is entirely founded on the language of the Old Covenant. While not agreeing with all that W.J.Grier writes in his text, "**The Momentous Event**", relative to the matter of the Old and New Covenants, there is agreement. On pages 30-31 Grier writes, "If you are still puzzled because the prophecies of the re-building of the Temple and the restoration to the land seem, on the face of them, to be literal, put the question to yourself. If the prophets had spoken of the New Testament Church, not under figures of Israel of old, but in terms of New Testament grace and truth, would they have been understood? If they had heralded the glories of Christ's people, not under the figures of the land, the temple, and the sacrifices, but in the richness and fulness of New Testament language, it would have meant nothing and conveyed nothing to the Old Testament saints...Only by things known, such as the land, the temple and the sacrifices, could the prophets picture the unknown" (End quotes).

This is so true. Another way of saying this is that this is the language even of the New Testament writers. The New Testament writers lived, as it were, at the overlapping of Dispensations. They lived that side of the cross, and then came through the cross into New Covenant realities. So we see the New Covenant writers often using Old Covenant language to describe New Covenant realities, but passing all through the cross. So the New Covenant writers speak of "the Temple", "spiritual sacrifices", "the Lamb of God", and "the royal Priesthood" (Rev.1:6; 5:9-10; 1Pet.2:5-10; Jhn.1:29,36). When we read these words, we do not take them in the literal sense that Old Covenant saints would. We see them in spiritual sense, since the cross of Calvary. So the same is true, in principle, of Old Covenant prophets and writers. They use Old Covenant language, but such becomes New Covenant realities, passing all through the cross, as the "hermeneutical filter". If the student understands this Principle of Interpretation, it will help his understanding of many of the apparently unfulfilled prophecies of Old Testament times.

The New Testament writers abundantly confirm the fact that the Old or Mosaic Covenant was fulfilled and abolished at Calvary, as to its ritualism and ceremonialism. It will never be re-instituted in this age or any future age. God will never, so to speak 'backslide' to the other side of the cross to restore the Mosaic economy which He abolished and cancelled out at and after Christ's death, burial, resurrection and ascension to His right hand.

The believer is eternally under the New Covenant in Christ (Jer.31:31-34). He said He would make a New Covenant and it would not be like the Old Covenant He made with Israel when He brought them out of Egypt. If this is true – and it is – then why would He re-establish the

Old Covenant again in the Millennium when He has made the New Covenant? Read 2Cor.3 and Heb.8:1-13.

To take these things mentioned in Ezekiel's Temple vision and see all restored in a material Temple is to do violence to the teaching and revelation of the New Testament writers and to give insult to the work of the Lord Jesus on Calvary's cross.

In Conclusion:
In bringing this lengthy chapter to its conclusion, some final statements need to be made. The New Testament writers are the infallible interpreters of the Old Testament prophets. There is absolutely no mention by any New Testament writer of any return to the Mosaic economy. The things of the Old Covenant were temporal. The spiritual truths therein are eternal (2Cor.3:18; 1Cor.15:46-47; Rom.2:20). To know the truth is to be set free from covenantal confusion!

The truth bears repetition. God has forever finished with Old Covenant types and shadows seen in the ritualism and ceremonialism of the Law or Mosaic Covenant. The New Covenant fulfilled and abolished by such fulfillment all such things. To have these things restored, re-established or re-instituted in any form would mean that God goes back to the other side of the cross. As mentioned, this would be the greatest insult from God the Father to His blessed Son's suffering sacrifice, and redemptive work on the cross at Gologotha's hill.

Even the Old Covenant writers constantly affirm that, even though God ordained and appointed such sacrifices and ceremonies, He was never pleased with them. They also prophesied of the very cessation of these things once the Messiah came. Why then will New Covenant believers teach a restoration of these things when even the Old Testament writers saw their cessation and when the New Testament writers showed their cessation in Christ? God was pleased with "the Lamb of God that takes away the sin of the world", as He spoke from heaven, "THIS is My beloved Son, **in whom I am well pleased**!" Read carefully these references in the light of these statements (Matt.3:16-17; Heb.10:6-8; Psa.40:6; Jer.6:6-8; Amos 5:21; Psa.51:17; Isa.1:10-15; Isa.66:1-4; Jhn.19:50; Matt.26:26-28,51-52).

The only way the Futurist and Dispensationalist Schools of thought endeavour to justify the re-institution of the Mosaic Covenant economy is to have "two peoples of God." The New Covenant Church is one people of God, the heavenly people; the Old Covenant Israel is the other people of God, the earthly people. The Church is under the New Covenant, while Israel is under the Old Covenant. This, however, is totally foreign to New Testament revelation. In Christ there is neither Jew nor Gentile. There is only ONE PEOPLE of God, ONE olive tree, ONE family of God and ONE body, composed of believing Jews and believing Gentiles (Eph.2:11-22).

The middle wall of partition dividing Jew and Gentile was broken down at Calvary, and God the Father attested to that fact by rending the Temple veil in two from top to bottom (Matt.27:50-52). To make "two peoples of God" in a future Millennium is to re-erect that middle wall of partition. It is to sew up the torn veil again! The Old Covenant and the New Covenant cannot be in the same house of faith, no more than Ishmael and Isaac could remain in Abraham's house, who is the father of all who believe (Gal.4:21-31).

The cross is the key. Everything of the Old Covenant must pass to the cross. At the cross, the ceremonial law was done away with, fulfilled and abolished. The cross becomes, what this writer terms, "the hermeneutical filter" for temporal things of all previous Covenants. Proper hermeneutics will not allow these things abolished at the cross to continue this side of the cross!

There can never be – and never will be – a return to the Mosaic Covenant. The New Covenant is an everlasting Covenant, and its spiritual realities are eternal. Knowing and understanding this truth indeed lifts away any covenantal confusion!

(**Note:** This chapter has been rather full because it deals with one of the greatest issues of the Futurist/Dispensationalist School of Millennial teaching. Historic Pre-Millennialists, along with the Post-Millennialists and A-Millennialists all agree on the position taken in this chapter. This is also the position of this writer also, as a Christian Millennialist!)

CHAPTER SEVEN

THE RAPTURE

Attention has already been drawn to the teaching of the Millennial Schools when it comes to the subject of the Rapture. For the Historic Pre-Millennialist, the Post-Millennialist and the A-Millennialist, the rapture takes place at the second coming of Christ, at His revelation and glory. For the Futurist and Dispensationalist, there is a "secret rapture" that takes place seven years before the actual coming and revelation of Christ. This "secret rapture" is said to be Christ's coming "as a thief in the night", when He takes His saints – His precious jewels – out of the world into His heavenly home. The student will remember that the "secret rapture" is built on the Futurist/Dispensationalist interpretation of the Seventy Weeks Prophecy of Daniel.

Each in the Dispensational School hold either a (1) Pre-Tribulation Rapture, or (2) Mid-Tribulation Rapture, or (3) Post-Tribulation Rapture or (4) Partial Rapture. A very few Ultra-Dispensationalists believe in some five raptures – "progressive raptures". One preacher wrote of:
1. Rapture of the Living Church (Rev.4:-2),
2. Rapture of the Two Witnesses (Rev.11),
3. Rapture of the Manchild Company (Rev.12:5),
4. Rapture of the Tribulation Saints (Rev.15:1-5), and
5. Rapture of the Resurrected Dead in Christ (1Thess.4:15-18).

These are the things under consideration in this chapter. For the purpose of this chapter we consider the Scriptures that speak of Christ's coming for the Church as a "thief in the night", as well as other passages in the Word that are used to base a "secret rapture" on.

Also, it does need to be said at the start of our deliberations, that, **all Schools** believe in a rapture. The issue is, the **time** and the **kind** of rapture of which the Bible speaks. Does the Bible teach a "secret" or "open" rapture?

A. The Secret Rapture Theory
To repeat: " By the Rapture is meant the sudden and possible secret coming of Christ in the air to catch away from the earth the resurrected bodies of those who have died in faith, and with them the living saints" (Dr. Robert Strong. "The Presbyterian Guardian" – Feb.25th,1942).

Futurists and Dispensationalists define the secret rapture basically as follows. Christ will come secretly as a thief in the night. There will be a resurrection of the dead saints and a change over of the living saints. Both will be caught up together to meet the Lord in the air. This is the "secret rapture" (or, "secret coming") when Christ comes "for" His saints. The world will not know until after the event. Antichrist will appear on the scene, make a Covenant with the Jewish nation for seven years, setting himself up as God in a rebuilt Temple. At the close of this seven years Great Tribulation, Christ will come "with" His saints and set up the Millennial Kingdom on earth for 1000 years.

B. Source and Origin of the Theory
As far as various authors and expositors can trace, it seems that the "secret rapture" theory originated in the early 18th Century. About the time of the Reformation and onwards, several views of the Book of Revelation were held forth.

1. **Historical Interpretation – Present History View**
The Reformers generally saw Revelation being fulfilled in their time, in Rome and the Papacy.

2. **Praeterist Interpretation – Past History View**
Aleazar, a Spanish Jesuit Priest, writing for his time, applied the Book of Revelation for the Apostle John's time only, Nero being "the Beast" and Roman persecutions as the enemies of the Church.

3. **Futurist Interpretation – Future Prophecy View**
Another Jesuit Priest, by the name of Ribera, taught that the Book of Revelation and its events were primarily to be fulfilled in the end of this age. It was out of this view that the Futurist Scheme of Eschatology arose. Following are some of the main channels through which this view continued to our time and generation.

- In the early 1800's, Emanual Lacunza wrote a book entitled, "The Coming of Messiah in Glory and Majesty". He followed the Jesuit Futurist scheme of interpretation. In his book, the "secret coming" of the Lord some years before His actual coming was seeded. He wrote under a pseudo name of a converted Jew, Rabbi Ben Ezra.
- The Librarian for the Archbishop of Canterbury (London), Dr.Maitland, got hold of Lacunza's book which had been translated into English, and through it promulgated its Futurist ideas (AD.1826-).
- Edward Irving (Founder of the "Irvingites", or "Catholic Apostolic Church"), accepted in one of his meetings a false utterance concerning a "secret coming" of Christ "for" His saints before His coming "with" His saints.
- About AD.1833 and onwards, J.N.Darby, and many other notable names of the Brethren Movement (too many to mention), became major influencers and promulgators of the "secret rapture" theory.
- Dr. C.L.Scofield and the Scofield annotated Bible has become the most influential propagator of the "secret rapture" and Futurist scheme of interpretation of Revelation and end time events. Some new believers even read his comments, footnotes and references as being part of the inspired text!

(The reader is referred to Bibliography for fuller details and sources of the above). Our considerations now are drawn to the main passages upon which the theory of a secret rapture and secret coming of Christ are built.

C. The Thief in the Night

There are about eight references in the New Testament that speak of Christ coming as a "thief in the night". These Scriptures are often used to provide further foundation for Christ's "secret rapture" for the Church prior to the Great Tribulation. A careful study of these references show that they have nothing to do with any secret rapture theory, as our study will show.

1. **Matt.24:42-44** – Jesus, in speaking of His second coming (not any secret rapture), tells His disciples to watch. They will not know the hour when the Lord will come again. If a householder knew when the thief would come, he would be constantly watching so as not to be caught unawares. Believers should always be watching for the Lord's return. It is sudden and when least expected.

2. **Lke.12:39-40** – Luke's Gospel confirms the same truth as Matthew's Gospel. Believers need always to be watchful and waiting for the Lord's unknown, yet soon return.

3. **1Thess.5:1-11** – Paul reminds the Thessalonian believers that the Day of the Lord (not a secret rapture) will come as a thief in the night (vs.2). But, if they are children of the light and of the day, then that Day will not overtake them as a thief in the night. The characteristics of the children of light, the children of the day, are watchfulness and soberness. In contrast, the characteristics of the children of darkness, the children of the night, are those of sleepiness and drunkenness (vs.4-8). The Lord Himself comes as a thief in the night to an unwatching world. But, if a believer is looking for the Lord to come as thief in the night, then it means that this believer is in darkness. Paul clearly says, "BUT you are not in darkness, that that day should overtake YOU as a thief..."

4. **2Pet.3:1-10** – Peter confirms the things that Jesus and Paul have said. He writes to the believers that the Day of the Lord (not any secret rapture) will come as a thief in the night. So cataclysmic is this coming of the Day of the Lord, that the heavens are to pass away with a great noise and the elements and the earth are burned up also. There is certainly nothing quiet or secret about the "thief in the night" coming

of the Lord and His day here. It is a very noisy and frightening event to those who know not the Lord, as the whole passage shows.

5. **Rev.3:3** – The Lord, in writing through John to the Church at Sardis, encourages the believers in that local Church, and also warns them. If they do not repent, then He would come on them as a thief in the night, that is, suddenly and unexpectedly. This warning is to a Church that has a name that it is a live Church, but it is spiritually dead, devoid of Divine life.
The history of the city of Sardis (with the local Church there) records how the city of Sardis was taken by advancing enemies on several occasions because they were caught unwatching. The enemy armies came on the city, high on a plateau, as a thief in the night and the people were taken by surprize. There was a false security about their position. They believed they were virtually impregnable. The warning the Lord gave to the Church here would be very meaningful. However, it has nothing to do with any "secret rapture" but points to the actual coming of the Lord in the end of this age.

6. **Rev.16:15** – This is the final specific reference to Christ's coming as a thief in the night. With it there is a blessing and with it there is a warning. "Blessed is he who watches, and keeps his garments, lest he walk naked and they see his shame." If there has been a secret rapture of the Church already, as supposed to take place in Rev.4:1-2, why is this warning given here? This is given in the days of the rule of the Antichrist, under the outpouring of the seven bowls of the wrath of God. Or have some saints been left behind because of some Dispensationalists "partial-rapture" theory? One would have to 'force' a secret rapture on this verse as well as any of the other references.

For the careful student, every "thief in the night" reference refutes any teaching of a secret rapture where the Lord comes "for" His saints. Christ will indeed come as a thief in the night. It will be suddenly, unexpectedly, to those Sardis-like believers who are not watching and waiting for His coming. Christ comes as thief in the night also to the godless, unwatching and unbelieving world.

The Day of the Lord will come as a thief in the night also. But, as Paul wrote, there will be no such thief-like coming to the watching, waiting and ready saints. That Day will not come on them as a thief in the night. They will be walking in the light, in soberness of mind, watchfulness of spirit, and waiting for the coming of their Master and Lord.

The thief in the night Scriptures belong to the actual second coming of the Lord, NOT to any "secret rapture" or "secret coming" of the Lord. Such a teaching has to be 'forced' into these Scripture references. The LORD comes as a thief in the night, and the DAY of the Lord comes as a thief in the night, but only to the unwatching and drunken world, or unwatching Christians! That is what each of these verses teach, as spoken or written by Jesus, by Paul, by Peter and by John!

D. The Ones "Taken" and "Left"

Other passages of Scripture used by those expositors and preachers to build the "secret rapture" theory on, are those events that speak of the Days of Noah and the Days of Lot. In Noah's days, there were those who are "taken" and those who were "left". The same was true in Lot's days. It is taught that the righteous will be "taken" in the secret rapture of the Church, while the wicked will be "left" for the seven years Great Tribulation. In Noah's days and Lot's days, the wicked were left to judgment, the righteous escaped. Let us consider these passages.

1. **The Days of Noah – Lke.17:26-27**
Jesus told His disciples that the time of His coming would be like the days of Noah. The people ate and drank, married and were given in marriage and carried on life as usual. All continued like this while Noah prepared the ark of safety and preached the word of righteousness, in the middle of the convicting ministry of the Holy Spirit.
The Flood, however, came on a day when the people least expected and destroyed them all. It was sudden judgment on an unbelieving world. Noah and his family were "taken" into the ark and preserved

"through" the Flood, or "from" it, in the safety of the ark. The wicked were "left" to destruction. Their day of salvation was over.

These things took place in the same period of time: the preservation of the righteous and the destruction of the wicked. The separation took place at the same time, the day Noah entered the ark. There was nothing secret about this day that came. Jesus said it would be the same at His coming. There would be a day when Christ would come. In that day there would be a separation of the righteous and the unrighteous. There was preservation of the righteous and destruction of the wicked. So this takes place at the coming of the Lord, NOT any "secret rapture" some seven years, or less, before He comes! One cannot build any secret-coming-rapture on this passage of Scripture!

2. **The Days of Lot – Lke.17:28-30**
Jesus also said the days and the day of His second coming would be as it was in the Days of Lot. Again, people carried on life as usual; eating and drinking, buying and selling, planting and building. All continued as normal until the very same day Lot left Sodom and fire and brimstone fell on the cities and destroyed them all.
The same day Lot and his family left Sodom, and the separation took place between the righteous and the wicked, the same day the fires of destruction fell. There was nothing secret about that day! Jesus said it would be like that in the day He comes. The events relative to Sodom and the surrounding cities took place on the same day, in the same period of time, not some years before hand. The separation and the judgment took place on the same day.
So it will on the day Christ comes again. The righteous will be "taken" and the wicked will be "left" for judgment. Lot was "taken" out of Sodom and the wicked Sodomites were "left" to judgment and destruction. Again, one cannot build any secret coming rapture theory on this passage either!

3. **"Taken" and "Left"**
Questions are sometimes raised as to who really is "taken" and who really is "left". Some say the wicked are the ones who are "taken" and the righteous are "left". Others say the righteous are "taken" and the wicked are the one who are "left".

A consideration of the passages in both Luke and Matthew show that he righteous were the ones "taken" to safety and the wicked were the ones "left" to destruction. There is, on the other hand, the thought that the wicked were "taken" away in judgment, and the righteous were "left" to continue a fresh life. It is one of those truths in Scripture that could be true in both ways, as the following confirms.

1. **The Days of Noah - Lke.17:26-27**
Noah was "taken" into the ark and was safely preserved through the Flood. The wicked were "left" to destruction. On the other hand, it could be said that, Noah was "left" alive to return to a cleansed earth after the Flood, while the wicked were "taken" away in judgment. It is true either way. The words of Jesus, however, emphasize the former way.

2. **The Days of Lot – Lke.17:28-30**
Lot was "taken" out of Sodom and was safely preserved from the fire and brimstone. The wicked were "left" to destruction by fire. On the other hand, it could be said, that, Lot was "left" behind to continue his life while the wicked were "taken" away in a terrible judgment. Both aspects may be true without contradicting each other. The words of Jesus, however, do emphasize the former way, the same as in the days of Noah.

3. **The Days of the Son of Man – Lke.17:20-37**
When Jesus comes the second time, there will be, as in the Days of Noah and he Days of Lot, a separation of the righteous from the wicked. The righteous will be "taken" to meet the Lord in the air. The wicked will be "left" to destruction.

"Two shall be in one bed – one will be "taken", the other will be "left" (vs.34).
"Two shall be grinding at the mill – one will be "taken", the other will be "left" (vs.35).
"Two shall be in the field – one is "taken", the other will be "left" (vs.36).

When the disciples asked Jesus, Where, Lord? He said, Wherever the body is, there the eagles will be gathered together! The prophet Isaiah confirms the same idea. "The righteous perishes, and no man lays it to heart; Merciful men are taken away, while no one considers that the righteous is taken away from the evil to come" (Isa.57:1). Refer also Psa.10:12; 59:12; Prov.11:6.KJV.

Note the use of the word "days" in the plural and the word "day" in the singular in the passage of Luke. He speaks of :
1. The "Days of Noah" and "the Day" Noah entered the ark.
2. The "Days of Lot" and "the Day" Lot left Sodom.
3. The "Days of the Son of Man" and "the Day" that Christ comes the second time.

The Days of Noah and the Days of Lot cannot be used to base any "secret rapture" or "secret coming" of Christ on. The judgments were not secret, but open, visible and sudden. All pointed to the actual second coming of the Lord Jesus Christ. The righteous and the wicked will be separated and judged in that day according to their works before the Lord. It all takes place at the second coming, not seven years before a Great Tribulation period.

E. Parables of the Kingdom
The Parables of the Kingdom do not give any indication of any secret coming of the Lord before His actual coming. Two examples are given which indicate very clearly that the separation of the righteous and the wicked takes place at the coming of the Lord the second time.

1. Parable of the Wheat and Tares – Matt.13:24-46
In the Parable Jesus taught His disciples that there would be mixture in the Kingdom right through to the end of this age. The wheat and the tares would grow together until then. The separation would come when Christ comes again to establish he next aspect of His Kingdom. It is to be noticed that the word was "bind **first** the tares into bundles" and after that, gather the wheat into the heavenly barn (vs.30). If there was a "secret rapture" some years before Christ comes again, then the wheat would have been gathered **first** into God's heavenly barn. But the tares are bound into bundles first. There is no thought of the secret rapture here. As in the Days of Noah and the Days of Lot, so it is here. There is mixture and then separation and all this takes place at the second coming of the Lord.

2. Parable of the Good and Bad Fish – Matt.13:47-50
The same truth is found in the Parable of the Good and Bad Fish. The Gospel net gathers in both or all kinds of fish. There is mixture in the Kingdom Net. The separation takes place at the end of the age, not some years beforehand by any secret rapture.
It is the same truth as in the Days of Noah and the Days of Lot. The mixture of righteous and wicked are seen to the end of the present age, then comes the separation and the coming of Christ and His Kingdom.

F. A Study of Greek Words
There are several Greek words that speak of the "coming" of the Lord. Those who hold for an any-moment rapture endeavour to use Greek words to justify their position. A study of these Greek words, however, in no way justifies this claim.

Greek word "Parousia" translated "Coming"	Greek word "Epiphaneia" translated "Appearing"	Greek word "Apokalupsis" translated "Revelation"
SC.3952. "A being near, advent (by implic) physically, aspect. Arrival, presence, coming	SC. 2015, "A Manifestation, ie., specially the advent of Christ (past or future); Appearing, Brightness, Give light, Become visible	SC. 602. To take off the cover, ie., disclosure; Appear, coming, lighten, manifest, be revealed, revelation
Matt. 24:3,27,37,39 1Cor 15:23. 1Thess.2:19; 3:13; 4:15; 5:23 2Thess.2:1,8,9 Jas.5:7,8 2Pet.1:16; 3:4,12; 1Jhn.2:18 This word is used 17 times of Christ's coming, and once of the coming of Antichrist (2Thess.2:9)	2Thess.2:8, Brightness of Coming 1Tim.5:14 2Tim.1:10; 4:1,8 Tit.2:18 This word is used six times concerning the coming of Christ	1Cor.1:7 2Thess.1:7 1Pet.1:7,13; 4:13 Rev.1:1 This word is used six times of the coming of Christ, of His unveiling

Futurists/Dispensationalists use the word "Parousia" as applicable to a secret coming of the Lord "for" His saints. This is not so. As already mentioned, a careful study of each of the Greek words above, in their surrounding context, shows that each word points to the actual, open and visible coming of the Lord Jesus Christ the second time. Paul uses them without making distinctions or difference. They each refer to events pertaining to one and the same coming of Christ, whether He comes "for" or "with" His saints, it all refers to one and the same coming. "The Coming", "The Appearing" and "The Revelation" all speak of the same eventful time, just showing different aspects of the same coming!

The momentous events that take place with reference to most every passage given here clearly show that there is no "secret rapture". There is nothing secret or silent about any of these Scriptures, but there is suddenness, unexpectedness for the world, and no preceding announcement! There is the shout, the voices, the flaming fire, the archangel, the angelic hosts, a resurrection of the saints and the transformation of the living. There is nothing secret about any of these events, or of them taking place seven years before Jesus actually comes again! But this brings us to those Scriptures that do deal with the Rapture, as found in 1Thess.4:15 with 2Thess.2:1, to which our attention must now be given.

G. The Pauline Revelation of the Rapture

It is to Paul, especially, that we turn and see what revelation the Lord gave to Him about the Rapture. The teaching of a secret rapture and secret coming is based upon a misunderstanding of what was revealed to Paul and misinterpretation of his words. The three most important passages concerning the Rapture are 1Thess.4:15-18 with 1Cor.15:51-52 and 2Thess.2:1. The truth of the rapture was a distinct revelation given to the Apostle Paul.

The background of the passage in Thessalonians is the concern of the believers for those who had died, or 'fallen asleep' in Jesus. The Thessalonians misunderstood Paul's teaching on the second coming and expected Christ to return in their lifetime. They thought they would be alive to His coming. Christians, however, were dying and the living, believing Thessalonians were worried about them missing out on the Lord's return. Paul's word to them was to settle their hearts. We note the important points of Paul's writing.

1. Paul desired to enlighten their ignorance about those saints who had 'fallen asleep' in death. They were not to grieve for them as others grieve, as having no hope beyond the grave (vs.13).
2. Because Jesus died and rose again, those believers who had died would also rise again. God would bring them with Jesus when He comes. For God to do that necessitates their bodily resurrection (vs.14).
3. Paul then proceeds to tell them of a revelation the Lord had given him. He spoke by "the word of the Lord". This is the New Testament equivalent of the authoritative "word of the Lord" that came to the Old Testament Prophets (vs.15).

4. There are two companies or groups of people that will experience mighty and miraculous changes at the coming of the Lord (vs.15). Those who are alive and remaining to the coming of the Lord; that is, all the Christians who are alive at Christ's return, and then, those who have previously fallen asleep in death. In other words, (a) The dead in Christ, and (b) The alive in Christ. As far as believers are concerned, at Christ's advent, all are in one company or the other – Dead or Alive!

5. Paul now tells of the order of change that will take place with regards to these two companies of believers. First of all, the dead in Christ will rise first. This involves a bodily and physical resurrection – a great miracle. Then, all the alive in Christ will be changed. The living saints will not precede the dead in Christ saints. The dead rise FIRST, then the living are changed next (vs.15).

6. At the coming of Christ, there are some momentous happenings that accompany His coming.
   (a) The Lord Himself descends from heaven. This is His actual, bodily and visible coming, not any secret coming or secret rapture.
   (b) With a shout.
   (c) With the voice of the Archangel; possibly Michael, the Archangel of the Resurrection.
   (d) With the trump of God. This trumpet corresponds with "the last trump" of 1Cor.15:51-52, and "the seventh trumpet" of Rev.11:15-19. In each of these "trumpets" a resurrection is involved.
   (e) In the clouds. Christ comes in the clouds of heaven and the saints are caught up in the clouds to meet Him. Clouds speak of Divine and supernatural transport, the chariots of God.
   There is certainly nothing quiet or secret about these attendant events accompanying Christ's coming!

7. Paul then talks about the order as far as the saints, dead or living are concerned.
   (a) The dead in Christ rise first – vs.16. Those who have fallen asleep in Jesus, asleep in death, as to their physical body – these experience resurrection power. They receive a resurrected physical and glorified body like unto their Lord's body (Phil.3:20-21). This is the FIRST resurrection of Rev.20:1-6, the resurrection of Rev.11:15-19 and 1Cor.15:51-52. The dead IN CHRIST RISE FIRST. Blessed and holy is he that has part in the FIRST resurrection. It is here that corruption puts on incorruption. It is the resurrection of the just! NOTE: Paul does not say "the dead" as if there is a general resurrection of all the dead here. He does say, "the dead IN CHRIST rise first...." Read also Isa.26:19; Dan.12:2; Lke.14:14; Jhn.5:28-29; 6:40,44,54.
   (b) The alive and remaining saints will be changed. It is here, for them, that mortality puts on immortality and death is swallowed up of life (2Cor.5:1-10 with 1Cor.15:51-52; Col.3:4). The living saints experience what Enoch and Elijah experienced in Old Testament times. They experience the change over to immortality and are glorified as to their bodies. They never die. They escape their appointment with death (Heb.9:27). They are taken out of this world without dying (Gen.5:24; Heb.11:5-6; 2Kgs.2:11).
   (c) BOTH companies of believers are **caught up** together to meet the Lord in the air. The dead in Christ and the alive in Christ are together in resurrection, immortalization and translation as they meet the Lord in the air. The living believers ("the alive and remaining") are caught up with the resurrected believers ("the dead in Christ") to meet Christ in the air. Christ comes to raise the dead, change the living and together they rise to meet and greet Christ in the clouds, in the air. He brings the spirits of those saints who have died in past ages up to that period of time, and they are united with their new, resurrected and glorified bodies, and also united with the living and glorified saints (Jhn.14:3). One company experiences resurrection and immortality. The other company experiences the change over to immortality. Both companies experience rapture or translation. This is the "gathering together unto Him" of which Paul speaks in 2Thess.2:1. It takes place at His coming. The resurrection precedes the rapture. The rapture of the living Church cannot be separated from the resurrection of the dead in Christ. They belong to each other.

These are the words with which the Thessalonians were to comfort one another – the words of the Lord.

H. Resurrection and Rapture

As mentioned, resurrection and rapture belong to each other. One cannot happen without the other, according to the revelation given to Paul. Resurrection, immortality and translation are linked. The dead in Christ are raised first. This is resurrection. The living in Christ are changed. This is immortality. Both groups experience the glorification of their bodies. Then after this, both are translated to meet Christ in the air. This is translation, or "the rapture". A comparison of the relevant Scriptures sharpens our focus more on these things.

1Thess.4:15-18	1Cor.15:51-52	2Thess.2:1
1. Lord Himself descends from heaven	1. Show you a Mystery – Not all sleep, not all die	1. The coming of our Lord
2. With a shout	2.	2.
3. With voice of Archangel	3.	3.
4. With the trump of God	4. The Last Trump sounds	4.
5. Dead in Christ rise first, those who sleep in Jesus God will bring with Jesus	5. Dead raised incorruptible, or corruption puts on incorruption and death swallowed up in victory	5.
6. Alive and remain not precede the dead in Christ	6. Living shall be changed, the mortal puts on immortality	6.
7. Both caught up together	7. Grave has lost its victory	7. Our gathering together unto Him
8. In the clouds		
9. Meet the Lord in the air		
10. For ever with the Lord		

Paul only speaks here of the "dead in Christ" being raised FIRST. He does not mention any "general resurrection" of the just and the unjust. This is the resurrection of the dead saints. It corresponds with John's word in Rev.20:1-6. The FIRST resurrection is of the blessed and the holy – the saints! Resurrection precedes and belong to the Rapture!

The passage in 1Thess.4 is the major passage on which the whole teaching of rapture in the Bible is built. The "gathering together unto Him" in 2Thess.2:1 would be the accompanying reference dealing with the truth of rapture.

The expression "caught up" comes from the Greek word "**Harpazo**". It means "to snatch away, to catch away, catch up, pluck, pull, or take by force, to take violently or by force" (SC.726). It is used of Philip, the evangelist, when he was 'caught away' by the Spirit of the Lord (Acts 8:39). It is used of Paul's experience when he was 'caught up' to the third heaven (2Cor.12:2,4). It is also used of the Manchild in Rev.12:5 which was 'caught up' (Lit. snatched up) to God and His throne at birth. It is used here of the translation of the resurrected and immortalitzed saints (1Thess.4:15).

Thayer's Greek Lexicon (SC.726) says it means:
1. To seize, to carry off by force.
2. To seize on, to claim for oneself eagerly,
3. To snatch out, or to snatch away.

Therefore, although the word "rapture" is not in the English Bible, it is still a Bible truth. The Latin word "**Raptus**" is the basis for the English word "**Rapture**", and translated by the words "**caught up**".

The whole of the coming of the Lord is attended with greatness. There is the descending Lord. There is the shout. There is the voice of the archangel. There is the trump of God. There is a resurrection of all the dead in Christ, from Adam down to the last saint that died. There is the change over of the living saints. There is the catching up of all believers, resurrected and changed. There are the clouds. And all these things are in the same passage of Scripture, the one upon which the "secret rapture" has been mainly built.

If there is a "secret rapture" and "a resurrection" at the beginning of a seven year Great Tribulation, then what of all the saints who die in this seven year tribulation period? It would necessitate another coming of the Lord, another resurrection of the Tribulation saints, and another rapture of both companies. This would make at least "two comings", "two first resurrections" and "two raptures", all of which is contrary to the Word of the Lord. How can here be a "first resurrection" before "the first resurrection?" Of course, some

Ultra-Dispensationalists have a "series of progressive raptures" and a "series of progressive resurrections" spread out over a seven year Tribulation in order to justify their position that it is all involved in "the first resurrection!" But, as has been mentioned, if there is no seven year Tribulation, which is based on a misinterpretation of Daniel's Seventy Weeks prophecy, then there is no "secret rapture" at its beginning!

The revelation of the rapture, and its attendant events, was given to Paul. The "SECRET rapture" and its attendant Futurist events may be traced to Ribera and Lacunza, Spanish Jesuit Priests of the late 17th and early 18th Century.

All Bible believing expositors believe in "the Rapture" as given to Paul, but not to a "secret Rapture" as propagated by the Futurist/Dispensationalist School of Eschatology. The resurrection of the dead and the rapture of the living take place at the actual second coming of Christ. The coming of the Lord "for" His saints (the Rapture) and "with" His saints (the Revelation) take place at one and the same period of time.

Summary:
1. Historic Pre-Millennialists believe that the Rapture and the Revelation of Christ takes place at one and the same second coming of Christ. The resurrection of the dead, and the change over of the living and the translation of both companies takes place when Christ returns. This is Post-Tribulation and Pre-Millennial.

2. Post-Millennialists and A-Millennialists believe in one second coming of Christ at the end of this age. The resurrection and the rapture take place at His advent. The Post-Millennialists, however, believe that Christ comes as the Church ushers in the Millennium, while the A-Millennialists believe Christ comes after the symbolic Millennium. One is Post-Millennium, the other A-Millennium.

3. Futurists and Dispensationalists believe that there are "two comings" of Christ, one "for" His saints in a secret rapture, then a period of seven years Great Tribulation, rule of the Antichrist, and then Christ "with" His saints at the end of this seven years. At this time, Christ ushers in the Jewish Millennium. Both Schools are therefore Pre-Tribulation and Pre-Millennial.

4. Christian Millennialists believe in one coming of Christ. The resurrection of the dead in Christ, the immortalization of the living saints, and the translation (the rapture) of both take place at the coming of the Lord. Christian Millennialists are therefore Post-Tribulationists and Pre-Millennialists.

There is absolutely no mention or indication of any seven year Tribulation, or any secret rapture at its beginning. Paul teaches us that there is only one rapture at Christ's one coming. The dead in Christ rise first, the living saints are changed. Together all are immortalized and glorified, rising together to meet the Lord in the air. So shall they ever be with the Lord. This all takes place at His second coming and before the Millennium begins.

(Refer to Chapter 10, on "**The Second Coming**").

CHAPTER EIGHT

THE ANTICHRIST

This present chapter deals with the varying views concerning what the Bible teaches about the coming of an Antichrist. Is the Antichrist a spirit? Or is it a system? Or is it speaking of an actual person or a line of persons, such as the Roman Popes? Or is it speaking of a World Dictator or succession of World Dictators? Most of the views concerning the Antichrist fall under these varying interpretations. Is it possible that there may be some fragment of truth – at least in principle – in each of these theories? As has been noted in the course of our studies, antithesis is the opposite of thesis, and generally the balance is in the middle, which is called synthesis!

The position held by each Millennial School is noted in brief here.

Historic Pre-Millennialism sees all the forces who oppose God and His Christ as 'Antichristal forces". All will be destroyed at Christ's second coming. Futurist and Dispensationalism see the Antichrist as an individual person, a world Dictator, supported by his accomplice, the False Prophet. Both are cast into the lake of fire at Christ's advent. The Antichrist, according to the theory, is to make a Covenant with Jewry for seven years, breaking it in the middle of this period of time. This is purported to be the seventieth week of Daniel's notable prophecy. The last half of this week is the period of Great Tribulation, at the close of which Christ returns.

Post-Millennialists and A-Millennialists both see Satan and all his wicked forces warring against Christ and His Church as Antichristal. Some A-Millennialists and some Post-Millennialists would also hold to the view of a personal Antichrist, or many antichrists seen through Church History. Some would hold that the Papacy, the Pope or a line of Popes, is "the antichrist". Both Schools, however, hold that all things Satanic and Antichristal are put down at the return of Christ. The writer, as a Christian Millennialist, lays out the view he believes in this present chapter.

A. Scripture References – John

There are four specific Scripture references to the Antichrist. Each are found in the Epistles of the apostle John. They are noted in full here from Authorized Version.

"Little children, it is the last time, and as you have heard that **antichrist** shall come, even now there are **many antichrists**; whereby you know that it is the last time" (1Jhn.2:18).

" Who is a liar but he that denies that Jesus is the Christ? He is **antichrist** that denies the Father and the Son" (1Jhn.2:22).

"And every spirit that confesses not that Jesus Christ is come in the flesh is not of God: and this is that **spirit of antichrist**, whereof you have heard that it should come; and even now already is it in the world" (1Jhn.4:3).

"For many deceivers are entered into the world, who confess not that Jesus Christ is come in the flesh. This is a deceiver and an **antichrist**" (2Jhn.7). (Emphasis author's)

"Anti" means "against" and "Christos" means "the anointed". Antichrist then speaks of one or any one who is over against the true Christ. They are Christian apostates who forsake the Lord Jesus Christ and turn to heresy concerning Him and His person, words and work. John says that they went out from the Church. They forsook the teaching of the apostles. They went out that they might be manifested, or exposed for what they were and how they had fallen inside (1Jhn.2:19). They especially denied that Jesus Christ was God manifest in the flesh; denying His Deity in His humanity. John calls them liars, deceivers and antichrists. The Scriptures teach that Jesus is truly God and truly man. He came down from heaven, lived a perfectly sinless life, was crucified, buried, rose again from the dead, ascended to heaven and is now set down at the right hand of God the Father. To deny these redemptive truths is to become antichrist. This same Jesus who went into heaven will return in like manner as He went into heaven (Acts 1:9-11).

As our study continues, the reader needs to keep in mind that the Bible is somewhat like a Divine jigsaw puzzle. The parts of the puzzle need to be laid out first, not forced together, but each part locking and interlocking together until the full picture is seen. This is so when it comes to what the Bible teaches about the Antichrist.

B. The Threefold Cord – Eccl.4:12

The Preacher tells us that "a threefold cord is not quickly broken" (Eccles.4:12). A consideration of John's several references to "antichrist" presents a "threefold cord" that needs to be kept together in order to see what John is saying.

1. The Many Antichrists

There can be no doubting John's words. Though he refers to Antichrist as an individual, he says that there are "many antichrists." He tells the believers that these many antichrists "went out from **us**, but they were not of **us**; for if they had been of **us**, they would no doubt have continued with **us**; but they went out, that they might be manifest that they were not all of **us**" (1Jhn.2:18-19).

In 1Jhn.4:1-3, John also warns the believers not to believe every spirit, but test them, whether they be of God or not. Many false prophets were out in the world denying that Jesus Christ was God manifest in the flesh (1Jhn.4:1-3). Again, in 2Jhn.7, John speaks of "many deceivers" who are antichrists. If that was so in John's time, much more is it true in our times, the end times. Church History has revealed many, many antichrists; apostates from the faith once and for all time delivered to the saints (Jude 3-4).

Jesus Himself forewarned His disciples that there would be "false Christs" and "false prophets". This would equate with John's "many antichrists", and "many false prophets" and the "many deceivers". When Jesus spoke of this religious and apostate company, He also warned His disciples against deception. Religious deception is one of the most powerful forms of deception (Matt.24:4,5,11,24).

For those Millennial Schools who hold that there are "many antichrists", their view is soundly based on John's words, as well as the words of Jesus. The difference would be in the seeking to identify this company of antichrists. Some would see the Pope or the Papacy as the line of succession in the "many antichrists". They would be the ecclesiastical representatives of great religious deception. Others would see various individual Dictators as individual antichrists, being the political representatives of Satan deception.

There is no question but that the apostle John, with Jesus, is dealing with the religious thing in the "many antichrists". They have become apostates from the faith. In their apostasy, they would be characterized by the things listed in Hebrews where the writer deals with those qualities of apostates.

Hebrews 6:4-8	Hebrews 10:26-29,32
1. They were once enlightened	1. They were once enlightened
2. They have tasted the heavenly gift	2. They had the knowledge of the truth
3. They were partakers of the Holy Spirit	3. They despised the Spirit of Grace
4. They tasted the powers of the Age to come	4. They were once sanctified
5. They fall away	5. They sin wilfully
6. They cannot be renewed to repentance	6. There is no more sacrifice for sin
7. They crucify to themselves afresh the Son of God	7. They trample under foot the Son of God
8. They put Him to an open shame	8. They count the Blood of the Covenant an unholy thing
9. They are like cursed thorns, rejected and to be burnt in the fire	9. They draw back and end up in a state of Perdition

"Antichrist" in Biblical meaning of the word, is more applicable to the religious person, especially a Christian who apostatizes from "the faith". It is not totally applicable to an unregenerate person, who simply rejects Christ as his Lord and Saviour. The "many antichrists" have known Christ and, beyond backsliding, have apostatized. "They fall away" from true faith and turn against the true Christ. This is "the falling away" (Grk. Lit. "**apostasia**") spoken of by Paul in connection with the revelation of "the Man of Sin" (2Thess.2:1-10). There ought not to be any difficulty in seeing that there are indeed "many antichrists", and these will continue to increase in the last of the last days, right through to the second coming of the Lord Jesus Christ.

2. The Spirit of Antichrist

Not only does John speak of the "many antichrists", he also speaks of "the spirit of antichrist", as seen again in these verses.

"Beloved, believe not every spirit, but try (test) the spirits whether they are of God: because many false prophets are gone out into the world. Hereby you know the Spirit of God. Every spirit that confesses that Jesus Christ is come in the flesh is of God. And every spirit that confesses not that Jesus Christ is come in the flesh is not of God. And this is that **spirit of antichrist**, whereof you have heard that it should come; and even now already is it in the world…Hereby know we **the spirit of truth, and the spirit of error**" (1Jhn.4:1-3,6).

Just as the Scripture speaks of the Holy Spirit as "the Spirit of Christ", so here it speaks of "the spirit of antichrist". It is the contrast between "the spirit of truth" and "the spirit of error" (1Jhn.4:6 with Rom.8:9). It reveals that there are primarily two spirits at work in the earth. One is the "Spirit of Christ" and the other is the "Spirit of Antichrist". People either respond to the Holy Spirit, as the Spirit of Truth and the Spirit of Christ, or they respond to Satan, as the Spirit of Error and the Spirit of Antichrist. Both head up under "the Mystery of Godliness" or "the Mystery of Lawlessness" (1Tim.3:16 with 2Thess.2:1-4).

The "many antichrists" had done despite to the Spirit of Christ and had opened their hearts and lives to the Spirit of Antichrist. They have turned from the life of true Christianity and to the death of religion. It can safely be said that there is a spirit of antichrist at work in the world, just as the blessed Holy Spirit, the Spirit of Christ, is at work in the world and in all nations.

3. The Antichrist

Not only does John write of the "many antichrists", and "the spirit of antichrist", he also speaks of '**THE Antichrist"** (1Jhn.2:18). The believers had heard that antichrist would come, even though there were the many antichrists around. They went out from the Church, all of which confirms that antichrist comes from the Church, and then is manifest in the world.

Most translations of 1Jhn.2:18 place the article "the" before "antichrist". The context of the verse points to an individual person as the coming antichrist, as well as the many other antichrists. There would be "the one" and there would be "the many".

"You have heard that antichrist shall come, even now there are many antichrists" (KJV).
"And as you have heard that Antichrist (he who will oppose Christ in the guise of Christ) is coming, even now many antichrists have arisen" (Amplified New Testament).
"You have heart that antichrist is coming, even now many antichrists have arisen" (NAS).
"You have heard that the antichrist is coming, even now many antichrists have come" (NIV).
"You were told that an Antichrist must come, and now several antichrists have already appeared" (Jerusalem Bible).

The very sentence construction points to an individual Antichrist, as well as the many antichrists. John's writings are about AD.96 or thereabouts.

There can be no doubt that, throughout Church History, there have been a number of individuals, both Ecclesiastical and Political, who have been "Antichrist", as well as the many. This is all part of Church History. But, in the light of John's Revelation, Pauline revelation and Daniel's prophecies, there is to be a final manifestation of THE Antichrist and his company just prior to and at Christ's coming again.

The Early Church saw the Roman Emperors as "Antichrists". Some held Nero, whose name in Hebrew numerics = 666, as the Antichrist. Some saw Prince Titus, when he entered "the Holiest of All" of the Jerusalem Temple as "Antichrist – the Abomination of Desolation". Then over the years, Mohammed was Antichrist, the Popes (or Papacy) was Antichrist – according to the Reformers. The Pope's Title came to the numerical value of 666, the number of the Beast. Napoleon, Hitler, Mussolini – all have been pinpointed as "the Antichrist". Some expositors simply hold that Satan himself is the Antichrist.

The fault of expositors is to identify some evil person, religious/political style, and say they are "THE Antichrist" – the final one. However, most all of these have been assassinated, or died by various causes and none have lived to stand up against Christ at His second coming! In every generation there have been "Antichrists". Undoubtedly, each and every one of them are pointers to the ultimate manifestation of that Antichrist; person, system and spirit. The Scriptures do speak of an Antichrist, who will stand up against Christ at His return, and be destroyed by the brightness of His coming. This is THE Antichrist at the end of the age, along with his company of antichrists. Most expositors would generally hold to this position, though details would vary.

The Principle of Comparison and Contrast is the way to sharpens one's focus on Biblical truths. The following provides us with this "threefold cord" about the True Christ and the False or the Antichrist.

The True Christ of God	The Anti-Christ of Satan
1. Christ – The One Head (Eph.1:22-23; 5:23; Col.2:19)	1. Antichrist – The One Head (1Jhn.2:18-19; 2Jhn.7; 1Jhn.2:22)
2. Christians – The many members of Christ's Body, the company of Saints (1Cor.12:12-27; Rom.12:1-8)	2. Antichrists – The many members of the Antichrist's Body – the company of the antichrists (1Jhn.2:18-19)
3. The Spirit of Christ – who joins Head and Body members together as one (1Cor.12:13; Rom.8:9; 1Pet.1:11)	3. The Spirit of Antichrist – who works in and joins together Head and Body members as one (1Jhn.2:18-19; 4:1-3)

Is Antichrist a person, an individual? Yes! Are there many antichrists? Yes! Is there a spirit of antichrist that works in a world system and apostates from the faith? Yes! It is not one against the other, or one without the other. The complete picture is threefold, and each cord is a part of the whole.

This writer believes that there will be an individual person, who will be THE Antichrist in the ultimate sense and meaning of that term. He will be the one who is alive at Christ's coming. He is the one who will seek to withstand Christ at His return and will be destroyed by the brightness of His coming! This, hopefully, brings a balance between some extremes in teaching on this controversial area.

Having then, hopefully, seen that THE Antichrist is "head" (the one), and "body" (the many), joined together by the same spirit (the spirit of antichrist), our consideration is now given to what other Bible writers have to say, beyond what John has written on "the antichrist" and "the antichrists" here.

C. Bible Prophecies of The Antichrist

The Scriptures under consideration here now all point to **an individual** person who many expositors understand to be "**THE Antichrist**" who is in existence at the end of the age and up to the coming of the Lord Jesus Christ. The visions point to an individual and not just a company of persons, as we have seen in John's writings.

It is especially to the Prophet Daniel of the Old Testament, and to the Apostles Paul and John in the New Testament, that we turn for a fuller revelation of THE Antichrist. Comments have to be somewhat restricted in order to be suitable for a chapter like this, and not fall into a complete textbook on the subject.

1. Daniel's Vision of Beast Kingdoms – Dan.7

In Daniel 7th chapter, the revelation of the Beast Kingdoms of this world was given in vision to the prophet Daniel. It was given in the first year of the reign of Belteshazzar, who was also the last of the Babylonian Kings. The Babylonian Empire fell in the time of Daniel.

In vision, Daniel saw four beasts. The interpretation given to him was that these four beasts represented four successive world kingdoms. Their rule extended from Daniel's time right through to the second coming of Christ. This provides the "time element" or frame in which these Kingdoms hold power. Such becomes important in interpreting prophecy and prophetic visions. Here the vision has to do with eschatology – the time of the end. Both Daniel and John link arms in the matter of the vision given in this chapter of Daniel.

The First Beast – Babylonian Kingdom
The first beast was like a lion, with eagle's wings, which were plucked off in the vision. This beast was lifted up from the earth and made to stand on its feet like a man, and man's heart was given to it. Most expositors see this beast as representing the Babylonian Kingdom and its rulers.

The Second Beast – Medo-Persia Kingdom
The second bear was like a bear raised up on one side, having three ribs in its mouth. It was told to devour much flesh. Most expositors see this beast as the Medo-Persian Kingdom, which followed after the fall of Babylon.

The Third Beast – Grecian Kingdom
The third beast was like a leopard, having four heads, and the wings of a fowl. Dominion was given to it. Some suggest the leopard is a hybrid between the lion and the panther. Again, most expositors see history unfolding and the leopard pointing to the Grecian Kingdom, the four heads pointing to its division into four Kingdoms after the death of Alexander the Great.

The Fourth Beast – Roman Kingdom
The fourth beast was dreadful and terrible and totally diverse from all the beast-kingdoms before it. It was exceeding strong, having iron teeth, and nails of brass. But this beast had ten horns on its head, out of which came another "little horn" speaking presumptuous things and making war against the saints. As far as the identification of this beast, the majority of Bible expositors see this to represent and symbolize the Roman Kingdom – "the iron rule of Rome", which Kingdom was coming into fuller existence at Christ's first coming.

The Ten Horns – Antichristal Kingdom
Daniel was especially concerned and troubled about this fourth beast, the ten horns on it, and also the little horn that arose out of these ten horns. Full details of interpretation were not given to Daniel, but enough was given to him to show him some connection between the Dream of the Image given to Nebuchadnezzar and the Vision of the Beasts given to Daniel. The ten horns corresponded to the ten toes of the image. They represented ten kings that would be in existence at Messiah's coming. This is confirmed clearly by John in Revelation in Rev.12,13,17 chapters and the details therein. The ten horns point to the coming Kingdom of the Antichrist. These ten kings stand up and oppose Christ at His coming, as King of Kings and Lord of Lords (Rev.19:11-21).

The Little Horn – Antichrist Himself
Daniel had much concern over this little horn and his activities. This little horn uprooted three of the ten horns in his rise to power. He makes war with the saints and prevails against them. He wears out the saints of the Most High. He speaks words against the Most High. He thinks to change times and laws. His power is limited in time to a time, times and half a time, which is simply 3½ years of his reign. By way of anticipation, this is the final half of Daniel's Seventieth Week, even though Daniel does not receive the full time period of "Seventy Weeks until Dan.9:24-27. If the Antichrist were to rule for "seven years", then this would have been the place in vision to tell John that period of time. However, this little horn simply prevails against the saints for 3½ years – not 7 years!
A comparison of Dan.7 with Rev.13 will show that "the little horn" of Daniel is "the beast" of John's revelation. Both make war with the saints, both reign for half a week of years, and both are destroyed by Christ. They are one and the same person.

The Ancient of Days – The Father God
The Ancient of Days sits upon the throne. The books are opened for judgment. Thousands of thousands minister before Him.

The Son of Man – Christ Jesus
The Lord Jesus draws near to the throne of the Father. A Kingdom is given to Him, and all nations, languages and peoples serve Him (vs.14). At this time, the saints – not the sinners – possess the Kingdom, and reign with Him (vs.27 with Rev.11:15). The fourth beast is slain and his body given to the burning flame. The rest of the beasts are not destroyed, but their lives are prolonged after their dominion is taken away. In Rev.19:19-20, the Antichrist, or the

Beast, along with the False Prophet, are both cast into the Lake of Fire. The rest of the wicked are judged at the close of the 1000 year period, before being cast into the Lake of Fire (Dan.7:12 with Rev.19:19-20; 20:11-15).

(**Note:** Some expositors endeavour to make this fourth beast, the ten horns and the little horn, all fulfilled in the first coming of Christ, and God's judgment on Pagan Rome (the Beast), and then on Papal Rome (the Little Horn). However, the vision brings us to the **second coming** of Christ, not to His first coming!).

2. **Daniel's Vision of the Ram and He-Goat – Dan.8**
   In the previous vision, Daniel is given a revelation of four successive world kingdoms. In this vision, Daniel is given further and fuller details on the Medo-Persian and Grecian Kingdoms. This vision was given in the third year of the reign of Belteshazzar.

   The Vision of the Beasts
   Daniel saw a ram with two horns. Then he saw a he-goat coming from the West with a notable horn between its eyes. This notable horn of the he-goat was broken, and then four horns came up in its stead. After there was another little horn that came up after them. This little horn magnifies himself against the Prince of the Host, casts down stars to the ground but in time is "broken without hand". The interpretation of the first parts of the vision is given to Daniel.

   Vision of the Ram
   In vs.3-4 with vs.20 we have the vision and its meaning as given to Daniel. The ram with two horns, one higher than the other, pushing westward, northward and southward, doing what it liked, and no one being able to resist it, was the Medo-Persian Kingdom. Darius the Mede, and Cyrus the Persian reigned, but Cyrus became greater in power. No nation could stand before the Medo-Persian Empire, which continued, from BC.538-BC.336.

   Vision of the He-Goat
   In vs.5-8 with vs.21-22 the meaning of the he-goat vision is given to Daniel. This he-goat from the West, with the notable horn, spoke of Alexander the Great, and the Grecian Empire. Alexander, as the he-goat, moved with great power and overcame the Medo-Persian Empire. But the notable horn (Alexander the Great) was broken, and four horns came up in its stead. When Alexander died at the age of 33 years (BC.323), the Grecian Kingdom was divided among his four generals, remarkably fulfilling the prophetic vision given here to Daniel.

   The Notable Horn
   Out of one of these horns came up a notable little horn. This horn waxed great towards the "pleasant land" (Palestine), and against the host of heaven. He cast down some of the stars of heaven, magnified himself against the Prince of the Host (the High Priest). By this notable horn, the daily sacrifice was taken away, and truth was cast down to the ground, and evil prospered.
   In vs.9-12 are given these details, but in vs.23-25 the interpretation is given. This notable horn would be a King of fierce countenance, but very understanding. He would have great power, but it would not be own, but of Satanic origin. He would stand up against the Prince of Princes and bring about an apostasy ("falling stars"). Saints would be killed by him. But in due time, he would be "broken without hand".

   Many expositors see a "dual application" and fulfillment in this "notable horn". There are those who see that Antiochus Epiphanes IV, came to the throne, desecrated the Temple at Jerusalem, changed the Jewish laws, and caused many to apostatize from the Jewish faith. He caused the daily sacrifice to cease and enforced all manner of abominations to be placed on the Jews. This was a "first fulfillment" and application of "the notable horn".
   There are those who also see the ultimate fulfillment of this "notable horn" as the final Antichrist. He rises up against the Church in the last days, brings about an apostasy, but he will be "broken without hand" by the power of Christ, and the sword of His mouth at His coming. This notable horn stands up against Christ, who is "the Prince of Princes", the Lord of Lords and King of Kings, but is destroyed by the brightness of Christ's advent (2Thess.2:1-8).

A careful study and consideration of the activities of this notable horn certainly seems to point to the final Antichrist, rather than to Antiochus Epiphanes IV, as some of the details are far more appropriate to the end-time Antichrist.

3. **Paul's Revelation of the Man of Sin – 2Thess.2:1-12**

   Paul, in writing to the Thessalonian believers about events pertaining to Christ's second coming provides an order that was to take place first. He says that the coming of the Lord Jesus Christ and the gathering of the saints to Him would not take place until two prominent things took place. The first was "the great falling away", or literally, "the apostasy", which we have already alluded to. The second thing was "the Man of sin" being revealed. In other words, Antichrist would come **before** Christ would come with and for His saints.

   It does not seem proper interpretation to say that "the Man of Sin" was a Roman Emperor, or the Papacy (line of Popes), or that this is all over and done with. The order Paul gives has to do with the second coming of Christ at the end of the age, NOT in the early century of Church History!

   It is worthy to notice the various designations that Paul gives concerning this person who was to be destroyed by the brightness of Christ's coming, His second coming in person, not 'a coming' in some national judgment back there! Names and titles in Bible times always had great meaning. The name or title spoke of the nature, the character and function of the person.

   - **The Man of Sin**
     Just as the Lord Jesus Christ is "The Man of Righteousness", the Sinless Man, the Antichrist is "the Man of Sin", or Sin's Man! Christ was the embodiment of Deity, so the Antichrist is the embodiment of Satan. Christ was God incarnate in human flesh. The Antichrist is the embodiment of the Devil in human form. As the Godhead found complete expression bodily in the Lord Jesus Christ, in the same way, Satan and sin will find its complete expression in bodily form in the Antichrist, the Man of Sin.

   - **The Son of Perdition**
     The only other person in Scripture by this name is Judas Iscariot, the betrayer, the thief, and this has great significance. Jesus said that Judas was a devil (Jhn.6:70). In Acts 1:25 we are told that Judas committed suicide and went "to his own place". Judas was one of the Twelve, sold himself out to Satan and became incarnate by the Devil when, as an apostate from the faith, he sold Christ out. He was the son of Perdition, the offspring of Satan, in spiritual nature. In his nature, he was of the pit, and returned to this place. In Jhn.13:2 it says that the Devil put it into the heart of Judas to betray Christ. In vs.27, with Lke.22:3 Satan entered into Judas and caused him to betray Christ. Satan, the prince of demons, takes over in Judas' life to sell Christ out to the priests of Judaism. The Antichrist is like Judas. Probably a fallen apostle, who will open his life to Satanic possession and sell out to the Devil and end in perdition.

   - **The Man-Exalted-God**
     Paul says that this Man of Sin will exalt himself as God, setting himself up in the Temple of God, and seek to be worshipped as God. It is the sin of Lucifer, where he exalted himself to be "like God" and desired worship due only to God (Isa.14:12-14). This issue was self-will, self-exaltation, self-deification, self-enthronement to become like God. The Antichrist is the opposite of Christ who was God, who became Man – the God-Man! Antichrist is the Man-God, the Man who seeks to become God, and is worshipped as God. This is fulfilled in Rev.13 when the whole world worships the Beast, receives his mark, his number and name, as they worship his image!

   - **The Mystery of Iniquity**
     Antichrist is the Mystery of Iniquity, or the Mystery of Lawlessness. He is the Lawless One. He is a law to himself. He makes laws that all should worship him, or be killed. He is the total antithesis of the Lord Jesus Christ, who is the Mystery of Godliness (1Tim.3:16 with 2Thess.2:8). He arises out of lawlessness, yet he himself is the Lawless One. He is not subject to the laws of God. He is Satan incarnate, the Lawless Devil.

- **The Wicked One**
  When Jesus comes again He will slay "the Wicked" with the breath of His mouth (Isa.11:4). As the Wicked One, Antichrist is the antithesis of Christ, who is the Righteous One. He is the apostate one, and heads up the apostasy in himself.

- **The Strong Delusion**
  Because people do not have a love for the truth, God will send them "a Strong Delusion". This "strong delusion" is personified in the Antichrist, the Man of Sin. People are being deluded on every hand in this generation because of not having a love for what is true.

- **The Lie**
  As Jesus Christ is "the Truth" personified (Jhn.14:6), Antichrist is "the Lie" personified. If people do not believe the Truth, then they will believe the Lie. Jesus told the Jews of His day, "I am come in My Father's Name, and you receive Me not. If "Another" come in his own Name, him you will receive" (Jhn.5:43). All the world will believe something, or someone – either the Truth of God in Christ or the Lie of Satan in Antichrist!

- **The Deceiver**
  Paul warns against deception, as does Jesus and John and other New Testament writers. The Antichrist is the ultimate Deceiver, for "the Devil, who deceives the whole world" indwells him in the end of the age. People will have believed or they will be deceived. There is no neutral or middle ground between these two grounds. Antichrist will perform lying signs and wonders, false miracles, and bring about great religious deception. Because mankind has rejected the truths of God, then they will be ensnared by deception. The miracles of Jannes and Jambres in Egypt caused the Egyptians to be deceived. The children of Israel believed the truth through Moses and Aaron. So shall it be in the end of the dispensation unto the coming of Christ.

This is Pauline revelation of the Antichrist even though he does not use the term. His revelation is of the Man of Sin and equates with John's revelation of Antichrist.

4. **John's Revelation of The Beast**
   We have already considered John's use of the word "Antichrist" (peculiar to John). It has been seen that Antichrist is one, yet also a many-membered body of antichrists, having the same spirit in them (Refer again to 1Jhn.2:18-19,22; 4:1-3,6; 2Jhn.7-11). We turn to the Book of Revelation and consider the person John speaks of as "the Beast". A careful reading and correspondence of Daniel's vision (Dan.7) and John's vision (Rev.13) confirms that both the Old Testament Prophet and the New Testament Apostle are seeing one and the same person, in the ultimate form, and that is "THE Antichrist", or "The Little Horn" or "The Beast". Each is synonymous of one and the same person, as the following clearly shows.

Daniel Chapter Seven	Revelation Chapter Thirteen
1. Four Beasts arise out of the Sea	1. One Beast arises out of the Sea
2. First Beast – Like a Lion, Eagle's Wings	2. Has the mouth of the Lion
3. Second Beast – Like a Bear	3. Has the feet of the Bear
4. Third Beast – Like Leopard with four heads, and wings of a Fowl	4. Has the body of the Leopard – combining in one Beast majesty, cruelty, agility
5. Fourth Beast – Terrible Description and having Iron Teeth, crushes whole earth	5. Terrible Beast to describe, and conquers the whole world
6. Having Ten Horns (In all, Seven Heads)	6. Has Ten Horns and Seven Heads
7. Little Horn arise out the Ten Horns	7. The Beast governs the Ten Horns
8. Speaks great blasphemies against God	8. Speaks blasphemies against God
9. Makes war with the Saints and prevails	9. Makes war with and overcomes the Saints
10. For Time, Times and Half a Time	10. For 42 months, or 3½ years
11. The Son of Man destroys the Beast and casts it to the Burning Flame	11. Stand up against Christ, King of Kings and is cast into the Lake of Fire
12. The Saints possess the Kingdom forever	12. The Saints rule and reign with Christ

Who can fail to see that the "Little Horn" of Daniel 7 is "The Beast" of Revelation 13? They are one and the same person, the individual Antichrist. The difference is, Daniel saw four world Kingdoms, while John is seeing ONE WORLD KINGDOM, which is the embodiment of all world Kingdoms preceding. John is seeing " a one world government". The Antichrist and his ten-kingdom empire devours the whole earth (the mouth of the lion), treads down the world (crushing feet of the bear), and rules with iron power (the iron teeth of the indescribable beast), and moves with the swiftness and agility (body of the leopard). The whole world wonders after the Beast, and receives his mark, his number, his name, as they worship his image.

For John, this person is "The Antichrist" or "The Beast". For Daniel, this person is "The Little Horn" or "The Notable Horn", and for Paul, this person is "The Man of Sin, the Mystery of Iniquity, the Lawless One." It is all one and the same individual as his activities confirm.

D. Antichrist in the Temple of God

The question is asked: Where is the Antichrist to be revealed? Paul answers: In the Temple of God, setting himself up as God, to be worshipped as God. The question again is: What Temple? Is this a material and rebuilt Temple in Jerusalem or a spiritual kind of Temple?

Many expositors of the Futurist/Dispensation Schools teach that the Jews will rebuild a material Temple, and it is this Temple in which the Antichrist sits, revealing himself to be God, and seeking worship accordingly. The Scriptures, especially the New Testament Scriptures, speak of another Temple beside a material Temple. (**Note:** Even if the Jews rebuild a material Temple, God's glory will never return to the same, as has been commented on in previous chapters. It will be destroyed at Christ's coming if one is built. God no longer dwells in Temples made with hands!).

The Bible reveals, once again, a "threefold cord" of revelation when it comes to the pattern of "The Temple of God" (Eccles.4:12). As this pattern is considered, it will show that Antichrist does sit in the Temple of God, but this Temple in the last of the last days, points to the Church, in which the apostasy takes place. We consider this pattern, for in this pattern of things will be seen (1) The Temple, and (2) The Antichrist, and (3) The Apostasy.

1. The Heavenly Temple Pattern
   (a) The Temple in Heaven
   There is a heavenly Tabernacle or Temple (Rev.11:19; 15:1-5 with Heb.9:1-10) This was the original Temple, of which all on earth were but shadows.
   (b) The Antichrist
   The first and original 'Antichrist' is none other than Satan himself. He rose up against God and His Word, wanting worship of the angelic hosts. He was the Anointed Cherub who covered the throne of God. He was apparently one of the Twelve Archangels in heaven, and rose up in revolt, anarchy and rebellion against Divine authority and order. He is the first 'Antichrist', and none can deny that. This Antichrist wanted to sit in the heavenly Temple of God showing himself that he was God, wanting the worship and the adoration due only to the Father, Son and Holy Spirit.
   (c) The Apostasy
   When Lucifer fell, he also caused the first and original apostasy in heaven. It is assumed that a third of the angelic hosts apostatized in heaven with Satan. They exercised their free will as self-will which was, in reality, Satan's will, against God's good, perfect and acceptable will. The heavens therefore, are not clean in God's sight. Sin began in heaven (Job.15:15; Isa.14:12-14; 2Pet.2:4; Jude 6; Rev.12; Jhn.8:44). It was in the heavenly Temple that Satan and his angels rose up against God in their apostasy. Satan and the angels that sinned with him are to be cast out of the heavenly Temple to earth, then, after the Great White Throne Judgment, into the Lake of Fire for all eternity.

Thus we have the prototype, the archetype of all types, of the heavenly Temple, the first and original Antichrist, and the first and original Apostasy of sinning angels!

2. The Earthly Temple Pattern
   (a) The Temple in Earth
   Solomon's Temple was but the pattern and shadow in earth of the heavenly Temple. The pattern was revealed to David who wrote it down under inspiration of the Holy Spirit.

King Solomon built according to that heavenly pattern. This became the central place of Israel's worship as a nation (2Chron.1-5 with 1Kgs.5-8 chapters).

(b) The Antichrist
There were various kings in Israel/Judah who actually were 'Antichristal' in word, deed and spirit. These godless kings profaned the Temple of the Lord, and caused the people of God to fall into idolatry. Even though Manasseh did finally come to repentance, his abominations and the evils in Jerusalem were never cleansed (2Chron.33:1-10; 2Kgs.21:6-7). King Ahab also could be mentioned, along with other wicked and evil kings who defiled the Temple of God.

(**Note:** Antiochus Epiphanes set an idol in the Temple and caused many in Jewry to fall away, and turn from the faith, from the Mosaic Covenant and Judaism in great apostasy..

Roman Emperors also in their various pagan temples set themselves up as god, and all sought worship from others, causing people to turn from the true God. They often set up an image of themselves to be worshipped).

(c) The Apostasy
Israel and Judah's history show how the chosen nation, under evil kings, turned from the Lord God, lapsing into wholesale idolatry and immorality and other evil practices. They committed all manner of abominations and turned from the living God, His laws, statutes and commandments. Time after time there were great periods of apostasy. Godly kings sought to bring Israel and Judah back to faith in the true God of Israel.

The pattern of heaven is repeated in the earth. There is the Temple God, the Antichrist Kings and then the Apostasy of the people of God!

3. The Spiritual Temple Pattern
(a) The Temple of God
The New Testament writers abundantly teach us that the Church is God's New Covenant Temple. Jesus spoke of the Father's house when He ministered in the earthly Temple at Jerusalem. In due time He prophesied its destruction in AD.70. The material Temple was left desolate (Jhn.2:19-21; Matt.21:12-16; Matt.23:38—24:1-2). After the veil was rent, God testified that He was forever finished with dwelling in any material Temple. The New Testament writers all point to the Church as God's Temple (1Cor.3:16; 6:19; 2Cor.6:16; Eph.2:19-22; 1Pet.4:17; 2:5-9; Rev.11:1-2).

(b) The Antichrist
Paul tells the Thessalonians that the Man of Sin would set himself up in the Temple of God, as God, and seek to be worshipped as God (2Thess.2:1-12). So instead of looking for the Antichrist in a material Temple, Paul points to the Church as the Temple of God in which the Lawless One is manifested. In other words, the Antichrist will come from the Church. As seen previously, John said the Antichrist was to come, and even now there are many antichrists. Where did they come from? "They went out from US…that they might be revealed that they were not all of US…" (1Jhn.2:18-19). Again, in other words, the many antichrists came from the Church. They went out as apostates from the faith. Consistency then would point to the fact that THE Antichrist will come from the Church, the Temple of God, even as in the heavenly Temple, and the earthly Temple patterns!

(c) The Apostasy
The 'falling away' from the faith has already been covered. Read again Heb.6:1-9; 10:26-28; 1Tim.4:1-5; 2Thess.2:1-4; Matt.7:15-23; Lke.13:23-30. In the last days, there will be great apostasy, a turning from the faith once delivered to the saints. Those who are sinners or unregenerate have nothing to 'fall away' from, as they are not in Christ. It is believers who 'fall away', apostatize and fall from faith. This is what happens again in a great way in the end of the age under the Antichrist.

The pattern is threefold! First in heaven, then in Israel and finally in the Church. There is the Temple of God, there is the Antichrist setting himself up in the Temple, and there is the Apostasy – the threefold cord that is not easily broken! The student is encouraged to meditate on these things.

E. The Pattern of Twelve
There is another pattern revealed in Scripture that points to the revelation and manifestation of the Antichrist as coming from the Church, as the Temple of God. This is the "pattern of the twelve", to which is given our attention. The pattern is revealed that, in the order of Divine government, God

has "the Twelve" and one of these falls, or becomes an apostate from God, drawing others with them in their fall. The consistency of the pattern once again points to the Antichrist in the Church, and this is "the Temple of God" to which Paul referred in 2Thess.2. Let us consider this "Pattern of the Twelve". The complete order is three, twelve, seventy and then the hosts.

Heavenly Order	Israel's Order	Church Order
Father, Son and Holy Spirit	Abraham, Isaac and Jacob	Father, Son and Holy Spirit
Twelve Archangels	Twelve Sons of Jacob	Twelve Apostles of Christ
One of the Twelve Falls (Lucifer)	One of the Twelve falls (Rueben)	One of the Twelve falls (Judas)
Seventy Prince Angels	Seventy Souls into Egypt	Seventy Disciples sent out
Multitude of Angelic Hosts	Multitude of Israel's Hosts	Multitude of Christian Hosts

The pattern is consistent throughout the Scriptures. In the pattern of twelves revealed in the Words of God, there is that one of the twelve who 'falls away', becomes an apostate, and also leads others in his apostasy. There are many types of this woven throughout the Bible. But, "in the mouth of two or three witnesses shall every word be established" (Deut.17:6; 19:15; 2Cor.13:1). There are those expositors that believe that Judas, as a fallen apostle, called the 'Son of Perdition', is a type of the Antichrist, who is also called by the same designation. He was close to Christ. He sold Christ out for money he never lived to spend. He became an apostate from Christ, and 'heads up' the great company of apostates in early Church times. He is a shadow and pointer to the last day Antichrist who will follow likewise in the steps of Judas. There is the possibility of there being "twelve last day apostles", who are the "twelve stars" on the Church, the bride of Christ (Rev.12:1). One of this twelve will fall, as did Lucifer, as did Rueben, as did Judas, and become "THE Antichrist" of the end of the age! At any rate, that which is Antichristal always comes from within the household of faith! These things are worthy of serious consideration as the apostasy increases in various 'church-denominations'.

F. The Christ and The Antichrist

There are many contrasts between the true Christ and the false Christ, between the Christ of God and the Antichrist of Satan, as our series of contrast show.

The Christ of God	The Antichrist of Satan
1. Christ is the Bright Morning Star – Rev.22:16	1. Antichrist is a Fallen Star – Isa.14:12-14
2. Christ is the Seed of the Woman – Gen.3:15	2. Antichrist is the Seed of the Serpent-Gen.3:15
3. Christ receives the Bruised Heel – Gen.3:15	3. Antichrist receives a Bruised Head – Gen.3:15
4. Christ came from heaven above – Jhn.6:38	4. Antichrist comes from the Abyss – Rev.17:8
5. Christ came in His Father's Name – Jhn.5:43	5. Antichrist comes in his own Name – Jhn.5:43
6. Christ is the Man of Righteousness – Jer.23:1-5	6. Antichrist is the Wicked One – Isa.11:4
7. Christ is the Sinless Man – Jhn.8:46	7. Antichrist is the Man of Sin-2Thess.2:1-8
8. Christ humbled Himself as Man – Phil.2:8	8. Antichrist exalts himself as God – 2Thess.2:4
9. Christ is the Kingdom of Light – Jhn.8:12	9. Antichrist is Kingdom of Darkness-Rev.16:10
10. Christ came to do the Father's will – Jhn.6:38	10. Antichrist does Satan's will – Dan.11:36
11. Christ is the Truth – Jhn.14:16,	11. Antichrist is the Lie –2Thess.2:11
12. Christ is the Son of God – Lke.1:35	12. Antichrist is the Son of Perdition-2Thess.2:3
13. Christ is the True Vine – Jhn.15:1	13. Antichrist is the False Vine – Rev.14:18
14. Christ is the Good Shepherd – Jhn.10:1-15	14. Antichrist the False Shepherd – Zech.11:16,17
15. Christ came to seek and save – Lke.19:10	15. Antichrist seeks to destroy the lost – Jhn.10:10
16. Christ is the Man of Sorrows – Isa.53:3	16. Antichrist is the Man of Satan – 2Thess.2:3
17. Christ is the Image of God – Col.1:19; 2:9	17. Antichrist sets up his own Image – Rev.13:14
18. Christ is the Mystery of Godliness-1Tim.3:16	18. Antichrist is the Mystery of Iniquity-2Thess 2
19. Christ was despised of men – Isa.53:3	19. Antichrist is worshipped of men – Rev.13:3,4
20. Christ ministers for 3½ years – Dan.9:24	20. Antichrist rules for 3½ years – Rev.13:5
21. Christ had true signs & wonders – Lke.4:18	21. Antichrist has false signs & wonders –Rev.13

Enough contrasts and comparisons have been listed to convince the student of the total opposites in the manifestation of the Christ of God and the Antichrist of Satan. Christ was a person. Antichrist is a person. Christ has many followers – Christians. Antichrist has many followers – Antichrists. Many more comparisons could be given but enough are provided here for the reader to be convinced.

In Conclusion:
Some concluding remarks are given to close off this chapter on "The Antichrist".

1. **His Coming**
   Paul speaks of two persons who are to come (Grk. "**Parousia**"); that is, Antichrist and Christ (2Thess.2:1,8,9). The same Greek word is used for the coming of Antichrist and the coming of the true Christ.

2. **His Revelation**
   Paul also speaks of two persons who are to be revealed in the same period of time; that is Antichrist and Christ. The Greek word "**Apokalupsis**", is "revelation" or "unveiling". So Antichrist is to be revealed and then the true Christ is to be revealed (2Thess.1:7 with 2:3,6,8).

3. **His Manifestation**
   Many Christians look for Christ to come first, before the Antichrist comes. The Scriptures show that Antichrist comes first, and then the true Christ. Rev.13 precedes Rev.19. Rev 13 is the manifestation and appearance of the Antichrist, and then he stands against the true Christ who comes in Rev.19 on the white horse. The pattern of Scripture also confirms this truth as to who comes first.
   - Cain came before Abel (Gen.4).
   - The Raven left the Ark of Noah before the Dove (Gen.7).
   - Ham came before Shem (Gen.9).
   - Nimrod came before Abraham (Gen.10-12).
   - Hagar was fruitful before Sarah (Gen.16).
   - Ishmael came before Isaac (Gen.16, Gen.21).
   - Esau was born first before Jacob (Gen.25).
   - It is always first the Natural, afterwards that which is spiritual (1Cor.15:46).
   - The Tares were bound in bundles first, then Wheat was gathered in the barn (Matt.13:30).
   - Antichrist comes first, and then the True Christ (2Thess.2:1-10).

4. **His Time**
   According to Rev.13, along with Dan.7:25, the time that Antichrist rules and reign as a world dictator, both ecclesiastical and political, is 3½ years, which is the final half of the Seventieth Week of Daniel's prophecy (Dan.9:24-27). He is the desolator of mankind. There is no mention of a period of seven years, but simply half that period of time.

5. **His Image**
   Antichrist has an accomplice called the False Prophet. The False Prophet causes an image to be made of the Beast and to the Beast. He causes all the earth to worship the image. To worship the image is to worship the man before the image, that is, Antichrist. And to worship the Antichrist is to worship the one behind the Antichrist and that is Satan, or the Devil himself. Satan has wanted the worship of mankind. He receives this through the Antichrist. Even as true believers worship God through Christ, so the unregenerate worship the Devil through the Antichrist (Rev.13:11-18). It will be a time of great evil and persecution against the people of God. Many will become martyrs rather than surrender to the worship of Antichrist. God will preserve His true Church through it.

6. **His Number**
   The number of the Antichrist = 666. This is his number, his name and his mark. All the world is destined to receive this mark. Upon refusal to do, then none can buy or sell without this seal of Satan. The numerical value of the name of JESUS = 888, the number of resurrection to spirit, soul and body. The number of the Antichrist ("The Beast") is = 666, the number of damnation to spirit, soul and body. Beasts were created on the sixth creative day. Man was created on the sixth day (Gen.1). So Antichrist is the MAN who becomes THE BEAST and his number = 666. There are many pointers towards this coming number, with credit cards, the microchips and numerous other identification creations. There is no need to 'spiritualize' the literalness of this number. 'Plastic

Money' will soon pass, plus Bank notes, silver coins, etc. A system of invisible marking on the hand or the forehead is to take their place. The number six through the Book of Daniel and Revelation always signifies the number of "the Man who becomes the Beast" at the close of the sixth Day of the Redemptive Week.

7. **His Character**
The character of this evil apostate person will be the character of Satan himself. All those who follow him, worship his image, receive his mark, number and name will be like him. It is the nature of self-will, independence of God, pride and lawless, stubbornness and iniquity, rebellion and insubordination, along with sin's deception – all this will be manifested in Antichrist and his followers.
As Christ and His people manifest the nature of the Lamb so Antichrist and his followers manifest the nature of the Beast! They will experience Satanic transformation. This is the "mystery of iniquity" at work in their lives (2Cor.11:13-15; 2Thess.2:8; Prov.16:18-19; Lke.10:18-20). The light in them has now become darkness (Lke.11:33-36).

8. **His Battle**
Rev.11-19 provides the details of events in this final 3½ years, under the reign of Antichrist and his ten kings. In Rev.19:11-21, the Beast stands up against Christ on the white horse. This "Beast" is the end-time Antichrist, the person who is actually alive at Christ's coming again. This shows that it does not refer to any previous "Antichrists", for this person is an individual even as is the False Prophet, is alive at Christ's coming. This is his final battle. He gathers with his armies to make war against Christ and His armies. The victory is already assured, because of Christ's redemptive work on Calvary's cross. It is the war to end all wars. It is the Battle of Armageddon.

9. **His Judgment**
What is his judgment? When Jesus comes the second time, He destroys the Antichrist with the brightness of His coming (2Thess.2:1-10). The Antichrist, along with the False Prophet, is cast into the Lake of Fire – eternally. These two persons (not systems!) are the first to be cast into the Lake of Fire, so incorrigible are they that they do not even come up for judgment. Their judgment is already settled because of their evil time in the end of the age (Rev.20:10). Worthy to note that God took two men – Enoch and Elijah – to heaven without dying. Here two men – The Beast and The False Prophet – are cast into the Lake of Fire without dying!

This writer, as a Christian Millennialist, believes in a coming personal Antichrist, as a world ruler and dictator, embodying in himself both ecclesiastical and political powers. He will rule over a ten-kingdom empire, a one-world government. "The Antichrist" then will be "head" and "body" and "spirit" joined in one against the Lord and His Christ. He is the Little Horn, the Notable Horn, the Man of Sin, the Antichrist and the Beast! He is all that Daniel, Paul and John wrote about him. But he is destroyed by the coming of Christ and then eternally consigned to Gehenna. The Roman Papacy over the centuries has shown the absolute power and influence of ONE PERSON to control ' a world' with the combined powers of ecclesiastical and political authority. Millions upon millions have come under the power of this one man. This, however, shadows forth in small measure, the power of the end-time Antichrist, Satan incarnate!

CHAPTER NINE

THE GREAT TRIBULATION

Our chapter has to do with a period of time called "the Great Tribulation." The very mention of believers going through "Great Tribulation" strikes fear into their hearts. This is often because of what has been taught on the subject through fear or sometimes ignorance of what the Word of God teaches. The subject needs to be considered from a Biblical viewpoint.

The basic view held by the various Millennial Schools of Eschatology is noted here in brief. The Historic Pre-Millennialist sees that the Church, the people of God, have always suffered tribulation. Post-Millennialists hold to the same view. The A-Millennialist position sees that "the Great Tribulation" was fulfilled in AD.70, in the Fall of Jerusalem, as well as the fact that the Church has always experienced some kind of tribulation.

For the Futurist and Dispensational Schools, they hold that "the Great Tribulation" is a period of seven years (or at least half this period of time), at the end of the age, prior to Christ's advent. They teach that it is the seventieth week of Daniel's notable prophecy, in which the Antichrist makes a Covenant with the Jews. He breaks this Covenant in the midst of the week and sets himself up as God in a rebuilt Temple, to be worshipped as God. The reign of Antichrist turns to terror and the last half of this week, at least, is the period of Great Tribulation. All must receive the Mark of the Beast or perish. The writer's view, as a Christian Millennialist, is spelt out in this chapter.

A. Word Definitions
It is important to give proper definition and clarification of the word "tribulation" right at the start of our study here.
According to Strong's Concordance (SC.2347 from SC.2346), the Greek word "**Thlipsis**" is defined as "pressure (lit. or fig). It is translated in the A.V. by the words "afflicted, affliction, anguish, burdened, persecution, tribulation and trouble."

The Latin word for "tribulation" is "**tribule**", meaning "to thresh, to beat." The Roman "tribulum" was an instrument used to beat or thresh chaff from the wheat once the wheat had come out from the milk stage into harvesting maturity. Noah Webster's Dictionary (AD.1828) defines the word meaning as, "Severe affliction; distress of life; vexations." In Scripture, it often denotes the troubles and distresses which proceed from persecution. "When tribulation or persecution arises because of the Word, he is offended" (Matt.13:21). "In the world, you shall have tribulation" (Jhn.16:33).

B. Tribulation in General
It is just a matter of Scripture that tribulation, in general, is the lot of the Church, the people of God. God's people, throughout all ages, and on through Church History, have always experienced "pressure, affliction, trouble, persecution" or "tribulation."

The Latin word "tribulum" provides an interesting concept of the word. The "tribulum", as noted already, was an instrument for threshing the chaff off mature wheat. Wheat in its milk stage would not be able to take the beating or the threshing. It would bruise it or destroy it. But when wheat is mature, the chaff is taken off by the "tribulum." So God, in His sovereign purposes, uses tribulation, pressure, affliction, persecution and trouble to remove the "chaff" from His Church. His purpose is not to destroy but to take off the "chaff", which is now unnecessary once the wheat comes to full maturity.

The Scriptures confirm the truth of tribulation, in general; that it is a part of a believer's life, whether by physical, mental or emotional means, or whether more sophisticated means. Note these Scripture references.
"...tribulation or persecution arises because of the Word..." (Matt.13:21; Mrk.4:7).
"...persecution that arose upon the death of Stephen..." Acts 11:19).
"In the world you shall have tribulation..." (Jhn.16:33).
"We must through much tribulation enter the Kingdom of God" Acts 14:22).

Paul knew that "afflictions" were his portion (Acts 20:23). Paul wrote about "tribulation" (2Cor.1:4), and "affliction" (2Cor.2:4; 4:17; 6:4), and "tribulations" (Eph.3:13; 2Thess.1:4) in these and various other passages.

"We glory in tribulations…" (Rom.5:3). "Tribulation works patience" (Rom.5:3).

John on the isle of Patmos was a companion with the saints "in tribulation" for the Word of God and the testimony of Jesus Christ (Rev.1:9).

Each of these references attest to the fact that the saints of God, all believers, the Church as a whole, will experience some form or kinds of tribulation and pressure during their life time. This is tribulation, in general. Of the some forty-five times this Greek word is translated by the various English words, it most often refers to pressure and trouble that Christian believers experience in serving the Lord.

C. The Great Tribulation – AD.70

There is another aspect of tribulation spoken of as "the Great Tribulation." It is an aspect which most Futurist/Dispensationalist folk seem to miss or pass over. That is, the tribulation that took place in AD.70 in the Fall of Jerusalem.

Jesus spoke of this tribulation to His disciples on Mt.Olivet, foretelling them of this period of time. A study of Jewish History shows that there was a fulfillment of this "great tribulation" in AD.70 when Jerusalem was destroyed, the Temple burnt, and the Jewish nation desolated, in death and taken into captivity. Note some of the specific references in Scripture to this time of "great tribulation."

"…they shall deliver you up to be afflicted…"(Matt.24:9).
"…for then shall be great tribulation…" (Matt.24:21).
"…after the tribulation of those days…" (Matt.24:29).
"…in those days there shall be great affliction…"(Mrk.13:19).
"…after that tribulation…" (Mrk.13:24).

The complete passages given to this tribulation need to be read. They are Matt.24:1-31; Mrk.13:1-37; Lke.19:41-44; 21:5-36 along with Deut.28 and Dan.9:24-27. These chapters are all in the context of the destruction of the Temple and the city of Jerusalem being desolated. These things were particularly to come on "**this generation**", according to Jesus. Note how often "this generation" is used in these references (Matt.11:16; 12:41,42,45; 23:36; 24:34; Lke.21:32). "This generation" takes us to AD.70, where "these things" did come on that generation about 40 years after the ascension of Christ and the birth of the New Testament Church. Here there was, at least, a partial fulfillment of Christ's words in the Gospels.

Josephus, the noted Jewish Historian, provides the most hideous details and account of the siege of Jerusalem and the "end" of Judaism. The reader is referred to Josephus' works, "**Antiquities of the Jews**" and "**Wars of the Jews**" (Book V, Ch.1:3; 10:2-5; 11:1 along with Book VI, Ch.3:4 and 9:3-4). There are too many details to quote in the brevity of this chapter.

Following we note the Local and partial fulfillment of Christ's Olivet Discourse on some thirteen notable points.

1. **Temple Destroyed**
   Titus, the Roman Prince and the Romans armies, destroyed the Temple, leaving not one stone unturned upon another, as the gold and silver melted between the stones of the burnt Temple. This remarkably fulfilled the word of Jesus in AD.70 as seen in Matt.24:1-3; Lke.21:5-6.

2. **False Christs & Great Deception**
   The accounts of the historian Josephus provides abundant evident of the false Messiahs, the false prophets, magicians and other religious leaders who seduced the people as to Divine deliverance from the Roman armies. This never took place and numerous Jews were deceived by these false teachers (Matt.24:4-5,11,23-26; Lke.21:8).

3. **Wars & Rumours of Wars**
In this period of time, there was great trouble and threats of wars against the Jews by several Roman Emperors, as well as several other nations (Matt.24:6-8; Lke.21:9-10).

4. **Famines**
Agabus foretold a famine in Acts 11:28 (AD.46), which also came to pass. There were famines also in Rome, Greece as well as Palestine. The siege of Jerusalem, AD.70, tells of the worst famine when Jews even cooked and ate their own children because of the terribleness of the Roman destruction (Matt.24:7; Lke.21:11).

5. **Pestilences**
History records outbreaks of pestilences and plagues in Babylon (AD.40), and in Rome, Italy (AD.66) where thousands of people perished (Matt.24:7; Lke.21:11).

6. **Earthquakes**
Jesus also said that there would be earthquakes in various places. History speaks of earthquakes that took place in Rome, and later on in the cities of Laodicea, Hieropolis and Palestine (Matt.24:7; Lke.21:11).

7. **Persecution**
The Book of Acts records the persecutions that Jewish Christians suffered by the hands of their unbelieving Jewish people. Paul spoke of the Jews opposition to the Gospel everywhere he went. The Jews became his greatest opposers (Matt.24:9-13; Lke.21:12-19 with 1Thess.2:14-16).

8. **Fearful Sights & Signs in Heaven**
Josephus speaks of some supernatural signs in the heavens over Jerusalem for some time, warning Jewry of great impending dangers and judgments coming on the nation (Lke.21:11).

9. **Abomination of Desolation**
Christ Jesus spoke of the desolation of the Temple, the city, the land and the people. This desolation took place under Titus and the Roman armies. To Jewry, the presence of the Romans was the fulfillment of the "abomination of desolation", or "the abomination that makes desolate", which the Romans did (Matt.24:15; Lke.21:20-24).

10. **Flight of Jews & Christians**
Jesus warned His disciples to flee once they saw Jerusalem compassed about with armies. In AD.66, when Prince Vespasian came with the Roman armies in the first siege of Jerusalem, the Christians took this as the sign Christ spoke of. Josephus records that the Christians fled away from the city as from a sinking ship. He records that not one Christian was known to have lost his life in the final siege under Prince Titus, some 3½ years later, in AD.70. Many Jews also fled the city, while untold thousands were slaughtered in its fall (Matt.24:16-22; Lke.21:21-24). This is why Jesus told them that they were to pray their flight was not on the Sabbath day, as the gates were shut for trade and they could only go but a Sabbath's day journey without breaking the Sabbath Laws of the Old Testament.

11. **The End of Judaism**
The disciples had asked Jesus when "the end would be". He told them the Gospel of the Kingdom would be preached in all nations for a witness and then "the end" would come. The Gospel had been preached in the then-known world (Col.1:5-6 with Rom.1:8). "The end" of which Jesus spoke was the end of the State of Jewry, the Temple, the city and Judaism as a system.

12. **The Great Tribulation**
Of all the sufferings of the Jewish people, none could compare with that which they suffered in the siege of Jerusalem in AD.70. Paul speaks of the Jews sufferings as "wrath come on them to the uttermost" (1Thess.2:16). The student is referred once more to Josephus. This was for them "the great tribulation" spoken of by Jesus that would take place in "those days" (Matt.24:21,29; Lke.21:22 with Deut.28:15-68).

13. Times of the Gentiles
Jerusalem was to be trodden down of the Gentiles until the Times of the Gentiles were fulfilled (Lke.21:24). From AD.70 to AD.948 and onwards, Jerusalem has been what the prophet Zechariah said, "a burdensome stone" and "a cup of poison" to all who touch it (Zech.12:1-3). It will be so until God's appointed time in His dealings with the Jewish nation. **(Note:** Some expositors suggest that the Times of the Gentiles is a period of 2520 years, or "Seven Times", and runs from BC.604 to AD.1917. The subject is too vast to develop any further here).

A consideration of these things indeed points to a local and partial fulfillment of Christ's prophetic Olivet Discourse. For Jewry, AD.66-70 was the period of "the Great Tribulation", and Christ came in judgment on the nation, using Prince Titus and the Roman armies as His sword of punishment. Titus was the "Prince that shall come" and the Roman armies were "the people of the Prince" who destroyed both city and sanctuary (Dan.9:24-27). But this brings us to the end of the age and the second coming of Christ!

D. The Final "Great Tribulation"
Unquestioningly, there was a local and partial fulfillment of "the Great Tribulation" in AD.70, but the ultimate or the "final Great Tribulation" will take place in the end of this age. Why can this be said? The answer is because certain events in the Olivet Discourse were NOT fulfilled in AD.70. The two most notable ones were (1) the signs in the sun, moon and stars, and (2) the actual second coming of Christ, to which some consideration is given at this point.

1. Signs in Sun, Moon & Stars
In Matt.24:27-31 and Lke.21:25-28 Jesus says that His coming would be as the lightning, shining from east to the west. He also said that there would be signs in the heavenly bodies. The sun would be darkened, the moon would not give her light, and the stars of heaven would fall from the sky, with the powers of the heavens being shaken. These signs would take place **immediately after** the tribulation of those days. The sign of the Son of Man would appear in heaven, all nations would mourn. All would see the Son of Man coming in the clouds of heaven with power and great glory. Then the sound of a great trumpet would be heard, gathering the elect from the four corners of the earth unto Himself. None of this took place in AD.70!

The Historicist position, in order to justify his belief that the Olivet Discourse was fulfilled in AD.70, slips into a kind of allegorization on these signs and His coming. Accordingly, "the sun, the moon and the stars" and "the earthquake" are simply made to mean great shakeups in earth's governments and authorities, whether they be political or ecclesiastical. "The coming of Christ" is made to symbolize Christ's "coming in judgment" on the Jewish nation in the Fall of Jerusalem. Historicists see some actual and historical fulfillment in the thirteen points of local fulfillment of Christ's Discourse, yet fall into a kind of spiritualizing or allegorizing on the signs in the sun, moon and stars, and Christ's coming!

Students and expositors of the Word need to constantly remind themselves of "The Golden Rule of Interpretation". This rule is, "When the plain sense of the Scripture makes common sense, seek no other sense. Therefore, take every word at its primary, usual, literal meaning unless the facts of the immediate context, studied in the light of related passages and aximatic and fundamental truths, indicate clearly otherwise." Or to say it again, "When the plain sense of Scripture makes common sense, seek no other sense, or one will fall into nonsense!"

There is no Scriptural reason why the signs in the sun, moon and stars, and the earthquake cannot be taken as actual signs in these heavenly bodies and in earth; at least, not in these passages under consideration. The prophets all link these signs with the coming day of the Lord (Joel 2:10; Amos 8:9; Ezek.32:7; Mrk.13:24; Acts 2:20). John also sees signs in the sun, moon and stars. The Book of Revelation was written in AD.96, some twenty years after the Fall of Jerusalem (Rev.6:12-17; 8:12; 16:8-9). Signs in these heavenly bodies are signs to God's people of coming redemption, but to the unregenerate they are signs of Divine judgments (Lke.21:28).

So the sun was darkened at Passover when Jesus hung on the cross (Matt.27:45 with Amos 8:9-10). Joshua commanded the sun and moon to stand still while he won the victory for the Israel of God (Josh.10). There was a sign in the sundial for the witness of Hezekiah's healing and his 15 years extension of life (2Kgs.20 with Isa.39). These are to be taken as they actually happened, not looked at in a figurative or spiritualized manner! These heavenly bodies were not affected in AD.70, showing that Matt.24; Mrk.13 and Lke.21 did not find total and complete fulfillment at that time. The sun was not darkened and the moon did not become blood-red, nor did the stars fall from heaven. It must be pointing then to a future time, to the end of the age and the coming day of the Lord Jesus Christ.

2. **The Coming of Christ**
The next thing to note is that Christ did not actually and personally come the second time in AD.70. He did "come in judgment" on the Jewish nation, but that "coming" was not the fulfillment of those references to Christ's coming as found in Matthew's Gospel alone.

The words "come" and "coming", speaking of or referring to Christ's actual return are used some twenty times in the Gospel of Matthew. The majority of these are used in Matt.24-25. Only one of the references to His "coming" is used in a figurative sense, all the rest speaking of His actual second coming. The references are listed here with a brief quote from the verse.

- Matt.16:27. The Son of Man shall come in the glory of His Father, with the holy angels.
- Matt.16:28. Some disciples standing there who would not death until they see the Son of Man coming in His Kingdom. Here His coming is used in figurative sense, and found its fulfillment in "the coming Kingdom" demonstrated on the Mount of Transfiguration (Read 2Pet.1:16-18).
- Matt.24:3. What will be the sign of Your coming?
- Matt.24:27,27. As the lightning comes from east to the west, so shall the coming of the Son of Man be.
- Matt.24:30. Coming of the Son of Man.
- Matt.24:37. Coming of the Son of Man.
- Matt.24:39. Coming of the Son of Man.
- Matt.24:42. Know not when his Lord comes.
- Matt.24:43. What hour would the thief come.
- Matt.24:44. Son of Man comes.
- Matt.24:46. The Lord, when He comes.
- Matt.24:48. My Lord delays His coming.
- Matt.24:50. Lord comes in a day when he is not looking.
- Matt.25:6. The bridegroom comes, go out to meet Him.
- Matt.25:13. Watch, know not when the Son of Man comes.
- Matt.25:19. After a long time, the Lord of those servants comes.
- Matt.25:27. Usury, at My coming.
- Matt.25:31. When the Son of Man shall come in His glory, and the holy angels with Him.
- Matt.26:44. The Son of Man sitting on the right hand of power, and coming in the clouds of heaven.

The reader will pardon the brevity of these references. They are noted to show the importance of His "coming" and that Christ's "coming in judgment" on the Jewish nation in AD.70 was NOT His actual, personal and bodily coming as He was talking about in all these verses except the one figurative use in Matt.16:28.

The "coming" of Christ cannot be allegorized, spiritualized or figuratively applied to Christ's coming in judgment on Jewry in AD.70. They speak of His second coming in reality at the end of the Church age. It is this fact, along with the signs in the sun, moon and stars, that lend weight to the position that the end of the age will see another and final "Great Tribulation".

When the Apostle John sees the great multitude, which no one could number, he does not know or recognize who they are. He is told that "these are they who have come – and are coming – out of tribulation, the great one" (Rev.7:14). This vision is some twenty years later than "the great tribulation" of AD.70.

All Pre-Millennialists believe that there is to be a period of great tribulation in the end of the present age. The issue is whether the Church goes through that tribulation or is raptured out of it before it begins.

It is the Dispensational School that teaches the Church will not go through "the Great Tribulation" but will be taken out by the Lord in a "secret rapture" seven years before Christ returns. All other Schools see the Church has always suffered tribulation and will suffer intense persecution in the end of the age. If the Church is not to experience tribulation, what has happened over the centuries of Church History? What of the 10+ million killed under the Pagan Roman Emperors? What of the 50+ million killed under some of the Papal Roman Popes in the Spanish and Italian Inquisition periods? What has happened and is happening in the various nations of the earth in recent decades? Think of the millions of Christians slaughtered – martyred – in Communist Russia, China, the Muslim countries and other Communist nations! Tell them that the Church will not suffer tribulation! Christians suffer the "fiery trials" for the Word of God and the testimony of Jesus (1Pet.4:13; Rev.1:9; 2:9,10)!

E. Tribulation & Wrath

One of the questions most often asked is: Why would the Lord allow the Church, His Bride, to suffer "the Great Tribulation?" Why should the Church experience the wrath of God? In answering this question, one needs to understand the difference and distinction between "tribulation" and "wrath". The New Testament writers do not use the words as being synonymous.

The definition of the word "Tribulation" has already been noted earlier in our chapter. The Greek word "**Orge**" (SC.3709 from SC.3713), translated "**wrath**" means "desire (as reaching forth or excitement of the mind),i.e., by analogy, violent passion, by implic. Punishment. It is translated by the words: anger, indignation, vengeance, wrath. The Greek word "**orgizo**" (SC.3710 from SC.3709) means "to provoke or enrage, become exasperated." Another Greek word "**Thumos**" (SC.2372) means "passion, breathing hard", and is translated in the AV., as "fierceness, wrath and indignation". These are the words used in the Book of Revelation when speaking of the wrath of God on the ungodly and unrepentant of mankind.

We note Paul's use of the words "tribulation" and "wrath in his Epistles to the Thessalonians, "The Second Coming Epistles".

Greek word "Thlipso" – Translated as Pressure, Affliction, Anguish, Tribulation, Persecution and Trouble	Greek words "Orge" and "Thumos" – Translated as Anger, Indignation, and Punishment, Vengeance, Wrath and Fierceness
1Thess. 3:4 Tribulation	1Thess.1:10. Wrath
1Thess.1:6 Affliction	1Thess.2:16. Wrath
1Thess 3:2. Afflictions	1Thess.5:9. Wrath
1Thess.3:7. Affliction	
2Thess.1:6. Tribulation…Trouble	
2Thess.1:7. Troubled	
2Thess.1:4. Tribulations	
2Thess.1:6. Tribulations	
The Church will suffer Tribulation	**The Church will not suffer the Wrath of God**

The fact of the matter is: The Church will and does suffer tribulation and pressure at the hands of God's enemies, but the Church does not, and will not suffer the wrath of God. This is the difference between "tribulation" and "wrath". It could be said that "tribulation" is Satan's rage against the people of God, but "wrath" is God's anger, indignation and punishment against the wilful, God-hating, Christ-rejecting, Holy Spirit-blasphemous world. The student should carefully read the Scriptures in the light of these comments.

The Book of Revelation uses the word "tribulation" about five times. Four times it speak of present tribulation that the people were suffering or would suffer (Rev.1:9; 2:9,10,22). One time it speaks of those coming out of "great tribulation" (Rev.7:14). The word "wrath" is used about eight times in Revelation. It refers to the wrath of the Lamb, the great day of wrath and indignation on a God-defying world, a Christ-rejecting world and an Antichrist-worshipping people of earth. It consummates in the wicked being cast into the winepress of the fierceness of the wrath of Almighty God (Rev.6:16,17; 11:18; 14:10; 16:10; 19:15). But the saints will never experience the wrath of the Lamb for they have accepted the blood of the Lamb. God has NOT appointed us to wrath, Paul says (1Thess.1:10; 5:9). It is the broken and violated Law of God that brings the wrath of God on the unregenerate and the unrepentant (Rom.4:15).

The saints, however, will suffer tribulation. They always have, and always will, until Jesus returns. The end of the age will be somewhat like the beginning. It will close with a period of "Great Tribulation" on the Church, but God will bring deliverance by the "better resurrection" (Heb.11:37-30).

Matt.24; Mrk.13 with Lke.21 will find total fulfillment prior to the coming of Christ. Signs will be seen in the sun, moon and stars. The earth will experience earthquakes in various places. The Son of Man will come with the sound of the trumpet. The dead in Christ will rise first, the living saints will be caught up together with them in the air, and all shall be forever with the Lord. The Book of Revelation is the consummation of all that Christ spoke in the Gospels in the Olivet Discourse.

In Summary:
From the Christian Millennialist's point of view:
- There has always and always will be tribulation on the saints of God. This is part of the Christian life. The Lord uses it to thresh off the chaff in a believer's life as he comes to maturity in Christ.
- There was a local and partial fulfillment of "the Great Tribulation" that took place in AD.70 and in the destruction of Jerusalem, the Temple, the land and Jewry as a nation.
- There will be a final "Great Tribulation", a time of pressure, trouble and affliction on the Church in the end of the age, intensifying as the coming of Christ draws nearer.
- The reign of Antichrist and the pressure and persecution of the saints will be for " a time, times and half a time" (3½ years), the final half of Daniel's seventieth week (Rev.13:5). Rev.11-18 chapters cover the details of this period of time and pressure, when the saints are called to be faithful unto death. There is a theology of martyrdom. God, however, will preserve His Bride in the midst of it all. Though the tribulation saints are temporal victims, they are eternal victors!
- This will be another "time of Jacob's trouble" (Jer.30:7-8), and "the time of trouble" spoken of in Dan.12 relative to "the end" and the "time, times and half a time" to the end of these wonders. The bowls of wrath will be poured out on the Antichristal worshippers in this time. This "Great Tribulation" will not be for seven years, but for 3½ years, and the world experiences "the wrath" of Almighty God.
- Christ returns the second time at the end of these things!

CHAPTER TEN

THE SECOND COMING OF CHRIST

When it comes to the subject of this chapter, the various Millennial Schools simply fall into two categories, as noted here.

1. **One Coming of Christ**
   Historic Pre-Millennialists, Post-Millennialists, A-Millennialists and Christian Millennialists all hold the view that there is only one coming of the Lord. Christ comes for and with His saints at one and the same time. There is no 'secret coming', but one 'open coming', as Christ returns victoriously and gloriously.

2. **Two Comings of Christ**
   Futurist and Dispensationalists hold that there are "two comings" of Christ. There is a 'secret coming' of Christ 'for' His saints. This is supposed to take place at the beginning of seven years Great Tribulation. Christ raises the dead in Christ first, and the living saints are caught up together with them to meet the Lord in the air. The 'open coming' of Christ is at the end of this seven-year tribulation period, when Christ sets up His Millennial Kingdom here on earth. As seen in previous chapters, this is a Jewish Millennium. These Schools teach that the events of Rev.4-19 chapters all take place after the rapture of the Church, over a period of seven years tribulation. The following diagram illustrates the Dispensationalist's view of Christ's "two comings".

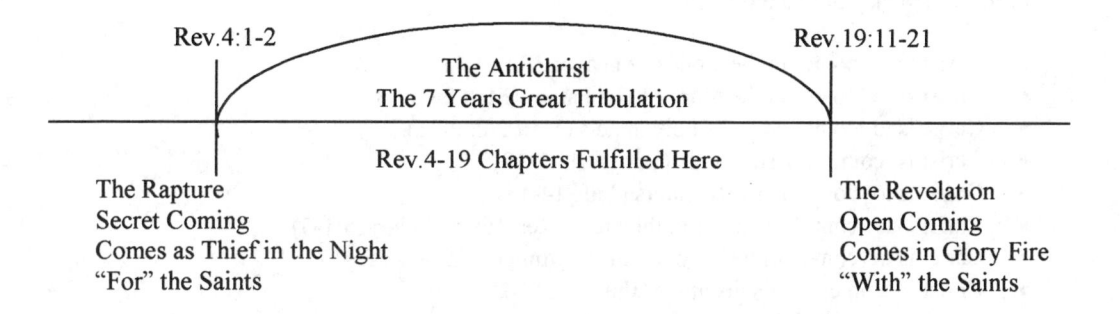

```
   Rev.4:1-2                                           Rev.19:11-21
       |⌒⌒⌒⌒⌒⌒⌒⌒⌒⌒⌒⌒⌒⌒⌒⌒⌒⌒⌒⌒⌒⌒⌒⌒⌒⌒⌒|
       |         The Antichrist                        |
       |      The 7 Years Great Tribulation            |
───────|───────────────────────────────────────────────|───────
       |      Rev.4-19 Chapters Fulfilled Here         |
       |                                               |
   The Rapture                                     The Revelation
   Secret Coming                                   Open Coming
   Comes as Thief in the Night                     Comes in Glory Fire
   "For" the Saints                                "With" the Saints
```

Much of the material concerning this subject has already been covered, so there is no need to overlap too much in this chapter. The reader is recommended to refresh himself on the contents of Chapter 7 on "The Rapture", as Chapters 7 and 10 actually belong to each other. However, to provide continuity of thought and content for this chapter, an outline of "The Doctrine of the Second Coming" is presented. Much of the material here is adapted from "**The Foundations of Christian Doctrine**" (pages 226-231), and "**An Exposition of The Book of Revelation**" (Rev.19:11-21), by this author.

It should be remembered that each of the Millennial Schools believe in the actual, personal, bodily, glorious and triumphant second coming of the Lord Jesus Christ. The differences are not over the **truth** and **fact** of His coming, but over the **events** and **details** of His coming! On the fundamental redemptive truths, all are united as one. On eschatological details, there are differences. For this reason, there is no cause for unChristlike attacks on any person's understanding of end-time events. There is no place for pride and arrogance as the Lord is working to His plan regardless of what any School believes. Grace and tolerance should be manifested in dealing with the differences as to details.

A. The Proton & The Eschaton

A helpful exercise to commence our study with is to understand the significance of "the proton" and "the eschaton". One speaks of the first, the beginning, and the other speaks of the last, the ending. One refers to Christ's first coming and the other to His second coming.

In the Old Testament, there were some 330 prophecies given concerning the first coming of Christ. Most of them were fulfilled within the short time of His death, burial and resurrection. The difficulties the Scribes had was the interpretation of some of the details about His 'coming' The following are just ten of these references to His 'coming' the first time.

- He was to 'come' as a Star out of Jacob (Num.24:17).
- He was to 'come' out of the tribe of Judah (Gen.49:11).
- He was to 'come' out of Bethlehem (Mic.5:2).
- He was to 'come' out of Egypt (Hos.11:1).
- He was to 'come' out of Nazareth (Matt.2:19-23).
- He was to 'come' out of Galilee (Isa.9:1-2 with Jhn.7:40-43).
- He was to 'come' to the city of Jerusalem riding on a donkey (Zech.9:9).
- He was to 'come' in the Name of the Lord (Psa.118:25).
- He was to 'come' suddenly to His Temple (Mal.3:1-6).
- He was 'come' as the early and latter rain to His people (Hos.6:3).

The interpreters of the Old Testament Scriptures could not reconcile all these details about His 'coming'. The prophecies seemed so unchronological. What happened? When Christ came the first time, He arranged in order, by historical fulfillment, all the apparently un-chronological prophecies of the Old Testament about His first coming! This was "the proton".

The same is true about the details of Christ's second coming. There are some 318 prophecies in the New Testament concerning Christ's 'coming' again. They seem to be rather un-chronological. When Christ comes the second time, He will again arrange in chronological order, by historical fulfillment, all the apparently un-chronological prophecies and details of the New Testament about His second coming! This will be "the eschaton". Following are some examples of references to His second coming that need some Divine order for fulfillment, and which God does have in His order, which may not be our order.

- Christ is to 'come' in the clouds of heaven (Rev.1:7).
- Christ is to 'come' in the glory of His Father (Matt.24:30-31).
- Christ is to 'come' with the holy angels (Matt.24:30-31).
- Christ is 'come' for His saints (1Thess.4:13-18).
- Christ is to 'come' with His saints (Jude 14-15).
- Christ is to 'come' as a thief in the night (Rev.16:15; 1Thess.5:1-5).
- Christ is to 'come' with the sound of the trumpet (1Cor.15:51-57).
- Christ is 'come' to His disciples (Jhn.14:3,15-23).
- Christ is to 'come' in flaming fire and take vengeance on the unregenerate (2Thess.1:7-10).
- Christ is the 'come' with a shout, with the voice of the archangel (1Thess.4:13-18).
- Christ is to 'come' in like manner as He went away to heaven (Acts 1:11).

The New Testament expositors have the same difficulties, as did the Old Testament expositors. How do we reconcile all these details without contradiction? It is out of trying to harmonize and reconcile these Scriptures on Christ's 'coming' that the various Millennial Schools have risen. History always proves prophecy! Just as all the intricate details of Christ's first coming ("Proton") were fulfilled, so will all the intricate details of Christ's second coming ("Eschaton") be fulfilled, and this, regardless of what any Millennial School believes!

B. Prophecies of Christ's Second Coming
The doctrine of the second coming is mentioned about 318 times in the 216 chapters of the New Testament. That is, one in every 25 verses makes some reference to it. Some entire chapters are given over to it, and, at least three New Testament writers wrote books concerning it (Matt.24; Mrk.13; Lke.21; 1Cor.15 with 1Thess, and 2Thess, Jude and Revelation. Not one New Testament writer fails to speak of the Lord's coming again. There are actually more references to the coming of Christ than to any other doctrine. The reason for this is evident, in that His coming consummates all other doctrine. It consummates that which was begun in the first coming. Often the Bible writers linked the first and second comings together in one verse. History, however, has proven that there is some 2000 years between these comings (Job 19:25-26; Zech.14:4; Mal.3:1-2; Dan.7:13-14; Gen.49:10).

The coming of Christ is foretold in both Old and New Testaments. As the burden of the Old Testament writers was particularly the first coming of Christ, so the burden of the New Testament writers is the second coming. The New Testament shows the detailed historical fulfillment of the first coming, so the Old and New Testaments together speak in details about Christ's second coming. We note some of the saints who foretold this great event.

1. **The Old Testament Saints**
   Many of the Old Testament saints and writers foretold the coming of the Lord Jesus Christ.
   - Enoch, the seventh from Adam spoke of Christ's coming (Gen.5:21-24 with Jude 14-15).
   - The patriarch Jacob foretold Christ's coming (Gen.49:10).
   - Balaam, the Soothsayer Prophet spoke of it (Num.24:7,17-19).
   - Isaiah foretold His coming, as the Evangelist-Prophet (Isa.59:20; 63:1-5; 13:6-9).
   - Jeremiah, the weeping Prophet, foretold His coming (Jer.23:5-6; 25:30-33).
   - Ezekiel, the Prophet of Vision, spoke of Christ's coming (Ezek.34:23-29; 37:17-29; 43:7).
   - Daniel, the Statesman Prophet spoke of Christ's coming as the Smiting Stone and the Son of Man setting up the Kingdom (Dan.2:44-45; 7:13-14).
   - Joel, the 'Pentecostal Prophet' prophesied of the outpoured Spirit when Messiah came (Joel 2:28—3:21).
   - Micah prophesied of Christ's first and second coming (Mic.3:3-4; 2:12-13; 4:1-5,7).
   - Nahum spoke of it (Nah.1:5-6).
   - Habakkuk also (Hab.2:1-14).
   - Zephaniah spoke of His coming (Zeph.1:14-18; 3:8-9).
   - Haggai, the Prophet, foretold His coming (Hag.2:6,7,21-23).
   - Zechariah spoke of both first and second comings of Christ (Zech.2:10-13; 3:8; 6:2-10; 8:2-23; 12:4-14; 13:1-9; 14:1-2).
   - Malachi spoke of His coming (Mal.3:1; 4:6).
   - David, the King and Prophets foretold Christ's coming (Psa.37:9-20).
   - The Book of Proverbs points to it (Prov.2:21-22).
   - The patriarch Job foretold His coming (Job 19:25,26).

   Each of these utterances point to Christ's coming and His Kingdom, and these over hundreds of years, without any contradiction. The same Spirit of Christ was in them all (1Pet.1:10-12).

2. **The New Testament Saints**
   All of the New Testament writers spoke of the second coming of the Lord Jesus Christ. The early Church held strongly to the doctrine of the Lord's return. The watchword of the early believers was "Maranatha", or "The Lord cometh" (1Cor.15:22), or, "Come, Lord Jesus" (Rev.22:20). The doctrine of Christ's coming almost faded into oblivion in the period of the "Dark Ages", but the recovery of the truth has been especially evident in the last century.
   - The Lord Jesus Himself foretold His second coming (Matt.16:27; 24:1—25:46; Lke.17:22-37; 21:1-33; Jhn.14:3; 21:22-23; Matt.24:27; Rev.16:15; 1:7; 22:20).
   - The two witnesses in shining garments said Jesus would come again in like manner as they saw Him go into heaven (Acts 1:10-11).
   - The apostle Peter spoke of His coming (Acts 3:19-21; 2Pet.3:3-9; 1:16; Matt.17:1-5).
   - The apostle Paul provides much detail on His coming again (Phil.3:20-21; 1Cor.11:26; Tit.2:13; Heb.9:28; 1Thess.4:13-18; 2Thess.1:7-10; 1Cor.15:22-23).
   - James, the apostle and brother of the Lord spoke of His advent (Jas.5:7).
   - John, the beloved apostle, wrote much on it (1Jhn.3:2;2:28; Rev.1:7; 19:11-21; 22:7,12,20). The Book of Revelation is the Book of Eschatology – the Book of End-Times and attendant events.
   - Jude also spoke of Christ's advent (Jude 14-15). He quotes the prophecy of Enoch.

   Every New Testament writer speaks in some way of His coming. Every time a believer partakes of the Lord's table, he is telling forth the Lord's death until He comes again (1Cor.11:26). The Lord's table points back to the first coming and forward to His second.

C. **The Manner of Christ's Coming**
   There are many Scriptures that speak of the manner of Christ's coming again. These, as parts of the Divine puzzle, should be placed in with Rev.19:11-21 where Christ's actual coming takes place. They belong to His coming again, even though John does not mention any of them or their details in this chapter. As to the manner of Christ's second coming:

- He will come personally – Acts 1:10-11; Jhn.14:3; 1Thess.4:16-17; 2Cor.11:4.
- He will come visibly – Acts 1:11; Heb.9:28; Matt.24:24,25,26,27,30; Rev.1:7.
- He will come suddenly - Rev.22:20; Mrk.13:36.
- He will come quickly – Rev.22:7,12,20.
- He will come unexpectedly – Matt.24:39; 1Thess.5:2; Rev.3:3; 16:15.
- He will come publicly – Matt.16:27; 24:26,27; 1Thess.4:16,17; 2Thess.1:7; Rev.1:7.
- He will come in the clouds of heaven with great power and great glory – Matt.24:30; Psa.97:1,2; Matt.17:5; 26:64; Mrk.14:62; Rev.1:7; Dan.7:13-14.
- He will come in the glory of His Father – Matt.25:30; 16:27; 25:31.
- He will come with the holy angels – Matt.16:27; 25:30-31; Mrk.8:38; 1Thess.4:16; 2Thess.1:7.
- He will come in His own glory – Matt.16:27; 19:26; 25:31.
- He will come in flaming fire and great brightness – 2Thess.1:7,8; 2:3-12.
- He will come with a shout, the voice of the archangel and the trump of God – 1Thess.4:16.
- He will come with His saints – 1Thess.3:13; Jude 14; Zech.14:5; 2Thess.4:15-18.
- He will come for His saints – 1Thess.4:13-18. The dead in Christ rise first, and the saints who are alive and remain to His coming will be caught up together with them to meet the Lord in the air, and so shall they ever be with the Lord.
- He will come as a thief in the night to the unwatching believers and the unregenerate world – Rev.16:15; Rev.3:1-4; 1Thess.5:2-3; Matt.24:37-39; Lke.17:26-37; 2Pet.3:10; Lke.1:34-35.
- He will come as the lightning – Matt.24:27; Zech.14:1-5.
- He will come as the Sun of Righteousness – Mal.4:2.
- He will come as the Bright and Morning Star – Rev.22:16.
- He will come in the Father's appointed time. No man knows the day nor the hour but believers will know the times and the seasons – Acts 1:7; 1Thess.5:2; 2Pet.3:10; Acts 3:19-21 with Mrk.13:32-37.
- He will come riding on a white horse, King of Kings and Lord of Lords, and His Name is THE WORD of God – Rev.19:11-21.

A careful reading of these Scriptures points to the fact that there is only ONE coming of the Lord. There is no 'secret coming' in a 'secret rapture'. The resurrection of the dead saints, the rapture of the living saints and the revelation of Christ in glory all take place at one and the same time.

Christ's coming will be visible, bodily and personally. There is but one coming. He comes for and with His saints at the same time. Paul's writings are clear on this point. When Christ returns, the dead in Christ rise first, then the living saints are changed, and both are then raptured ("caught up") to meet the Lord in the air. These events take place at the "last trump" (Paul), which is the "seventh trump" (John). The student is reminded that when John does write of the actual coming of Christ on the white horse, he does not bring together all the – so to speak – "loose ends" of the prophetic utterances and details of Christ's coming in this passage (Rev.19:11-21). The student, however, should understand that all the details of Christ's coming have to find fulfillment at this point, or at His coming.

D. Practical Value of the Doctrine

Often the doctrine of Christ's coming again is challenged as to be of any practical value. The end of all doctrinal teaching is practical godliness. The proper application of the truth concerning Christ's return is one of the greatest challenges to godly living. This will be especially true for that generation which will be alive at His coming. The New Testament writers applied this doctrine practically to the lives of all believers in their day, even as did Jesus Himself. If it was true then, it is true in our day.

1. The doctrine of Christ's coming is a comfort and purifying hope which encourages the believer to live a holy life (1Jhn.3:2-3; Acts 23:6; 26:6-8; Rom.8:20-25; 1Cor.15:19; Gal.5:5; Tit.2:13; 2Pet.3:9-12). It is the hope of the Church.

2. The doctrine of Christ's second coming is called to remembrance every time a believer partakes of the Table of the Lord. The Church is commanded to do this "until He come". The Table of the Lord points back to the first coming and forward to His second coming (1Cor.11:23-32 with Matt.26:26-29).

3. The doctrine of the second coming challenges the believer to watchfulness and prayer (Matt.24:42-44; 25:13; Lke.21:34-36).

4. The doctrine of Christ's second coming challenges the believer to be supplied with the oil of the Holy Spirit, have his lamp burning brightly and watch for the coming of Christ, the heavenly Bridegroom (Matt.25:1-13).

5. The doctrine of the second coming challenges believers to be faithful and use the talents the Lord has given, as all will give an account of their use at Christ's return (Matt.25:14-30; Lke.19:11-27; 2Cor.5:10-11; 1Cor.3:1-15).

6. The doctrine of Christ's coming challenges the believer not to fall into a condition of spiritual sleep and lethargy, lest he be caught unawares at His coming (Mrk.13:32-37; Rom.13:11-12; 1Thess.5:1-10).

7. The doctrine of the Lord's advent encourages the believer in times of trial and persecution (Heb.10:32-37; 2Tim.2:12; Jas.5:7-12).

8. The doctrine of Christ's coming also serves as a warning to the ungodly. It stirs the Church to evangelism as "the harvest is the end of the age" (Matt.13:24-30,36-43 with 2Thess.1:7-10; Matt.25:31-46).

The second coming of Christ consummates all that which was begun in Christ's first coming. There is nothing new that happens in the second coming that was not already in "seed-form" in Christ's first coming. That was the inauguration. This is the consummation. As the believer and the Church applies the truth of the "blessed hope" of Christ's return, it will have a practical and purifying effect on one's life, and thus prepare the Church as His Bride for His return!

Obedience to the doctrine of Christ's advent is indeed of great practical value! Its purpose should be far more practical than merely eschatological! Its truth should change the heart and life, not merely change the mind on end-time events! Christ will return! "Maranatha" – The Lord is coming! "Even so, come Lord Jesus!" is the cry of all true believers in this end of the age.

CHAPTER ELEVEN

THE BINDING OF SATAN

"The Binding of Satan" is another area of controversy among Millennial Schools. For some, Satan is yet to be bound, while for others, especially A-Millennialists, Satan has already been bound.

The Post-Millennialist sees that Satan is being progressively bound during this present age. Boettner, as a Post-Millennialist, writes : " We hold rather that the binding of Satan is a process continuing through this dispensation as evil is more and more suppressed, as the world is more and more Christianized, and as there is therefore less and less occasion for God to use the Devil as an instrument in the punishing of sinners" (**"The Millenniun", page 127**).

The Historic, Futurist and Dispensational Pre-Millennial Schools see Satan bound at the second coming of Christ, though there are some very slight differences as to the full effect that this "binding" really is. For the A-Millennialist, Satan was bound at Calvary by Christ at His first coming.

The Christian Millennialist position would have more in common with the Historic, Futurist and Dispensational view when it comes to the binding of Satan for 1000 years. But, there are differences within these Schools when it comes to some of the finer details. It is with some refutation of the A-Millennial position that "Satan is bound now" that this chapter has to do.

In order to dispose of any future Millennium, and to justify a "present Millennium" between the first and second comings of Christ, as well as provide a basis for the Book of Revelation to be arranged in "Progressive Parallelism", A-Millennialists have to prove that Satan is bound here and now. There is no future binding of Satan at Christ's coming, only his destiny in the Lake of Fire and Brimstone. But it is better to let the A-Millennial writers speak for themselves on this matter before tackling their position and their major points. Several of their most important writers are quoted at reasonable length so as not to misconstrue their views.

1. **William E.Cox – "A-Millennialism Today"**
   The reader will bear with the rather full quotation from this writer, as there is no intention of quoting any writer "out of context" as to what is really being said. On pages 57-58, Cox provides a good and ordered outline on what A-Millennialists believe as to eschatology. Because such relate to the interpretation of Revelation, Chapters 20,21,22, the outline is arranged and set out here accordingly.

"The A-Millennial teachings here are clear and orderly on all basic points. We believe essentially the following order of events constitutes New Testament eschatological teaching.

(1) At His first advent, our Lord met Satan on his own ground and, in fulfillment of Scriptures such as Gen.3:15, defeated Satan. Satan now lives on probation until the second coming. In the meantime, his power is definitely limited, especially in regards to God's people.
(2) Having bound Satan, our Lord ushered in the Millennial Kingdom of Revelation 20. This Millennium commenced at the first advent and will end at the second coming, being replaced by the eternal state.
(3) Though God presently reigns in the hearts of His people (spiritual Israel), the Church was forewarned by her Lord that she would face tribulation so long as she remains on the earth. This tribulation will grow progressively worse until it finally consummates in the appearance of the antichrist. While God has cautioned His people that tribulation would be their lot, He also has promised to protect them through every persecution they must face. The Church militant is assured of becoming the Church triumphant.
(4) Satan, who is now bound in one aspect of his power, will be restored to complete power for a short period of time. This loosing of Satan will come near the end of the present Millennium, and he will be put down by the second coming of Christ.
(5) The Lord will appear the second time in a literal bodily manner. This coming will bring to completion everything set in motion at the first advent. At this second coming, Satan will be cast into hell.
(6) At the second coming there will be a general resurrection of all the dead of all time.

(7) This will be followed immediately by a general judgment, resulting in the final separation of the righteous and the wicked. The saints will be present, but will be judged only to ascertain their rewards since their salvation has already been decided.
(8) The earth will be cleansed and purified with fire.
(9) The eternal state pictured in Revelation 21 and 22 will become a reality, and will last forever.
(10) All saints of all time will reign in this eternal state, glorifying God, throughout eternity. The wicked will spend eternity in hell.

Briefly stated, this is the A-Millennial belief on eschatology. Let us now treat these events in Scriptural detail" (End quote).

Cox continues on pages 58-62 to provide fuller explanation of the A-Millennial view on the binding of Satan. He explains that the word "bound" as used in the New Testament is used in both a literal and figurative sense. Under the caption "**Satan is Bound and Doomed**", he writes:

"What is meant by the binding of Satan? When John speaks in Revelation 20, of Satan being bound for 1000 years – does John mean that there will be a period of time during which Satan is completely immobilized? Does being bound, in the Scriptural sense, mean that Satan would be so trussed that he could no longer oppose God? Or that he could no longer go about like a roaring lion?

Pre-Millenarians have read more into this figure than the Scriptures will allow. The binding of Satan fixes a false image in the minds of many people. So much so that when someone suggests that Satan is bound today, these people immediately think this suggestion borders on the edge of lunacy. How, they ask incredulously, can anyone look about him at all the evil workings of Satan and yet say that Satan is bound? Can a being that is bound and cast into a bottomless pit commit such acts?

The correct answer to the above questions depends on just what is depicted by the binding of Satan. If his being bound means that he cannot move a muscle against God, then the answer is obvious: he most certainly is not bound today. If he were bound in this literal sense, then the earthly utopia looked for by the Millenarians would be upon us. If, on the other hand, Satan's binding refers (in figurative language) to the limiting of his power, then he could well be bound already.

What saith the Scriptures? (a) Satan was bound at the first advent, and (b) Satan still goes about like a roaring lion seeking whom he may devour. Satan is the archenemy of God and he is the ultimate cause of every sin and trouble. These are not contradictory statements. Both are taught in the New Testament" (End Quote).

Cox uses Scriptures found in Matt.12:28-29; Acts20:22; Rom.7:2; 1Cor.7:27 to show both literal and figurative uses of the word "bind" or "bound". He uses Scriptures found in Heb.2:14; Col.2:15; Eph.4:8; 1Jhn.3:8 with Lke.10:18 to show how Christ conquered Satan at Calvary and in His first advent. Cox further says as to Christ being "the Stronger Man" who bound "the Strong Man" – Satan – "In this case, our Lord Himself said that He bound Satan, yet we know that Satan was not literally bound to the extent that he became immobile. Therefore, the context tells us that Jesus spoke of a figurative binding…to be bound does not indicate immobility in all cases…So it is with Satan: He is bound, yet he has freedom of movement and is free to tempt, debauch, and ruin lives in spite of this binding (1Pet.5:8-9; Eph.2:12; 6:12)".

Further, Cox tells us that the first advent, in general, and the death, burial and resurrection of Christ in particular, bound Satan and that he has been doomed ever since. Satan is under a suspended sentence. The binding of Satan is tied in with the cross of Christ, where the prince of this world was judged (Jhn.12:31-33 along with Rev.12). Satan was defeated at the first advent and now turns his wrath against the Church as pictured in this chapter of Revelation.

2. **Archibald Hughes – "A New Heavens & A New Earth"**
Another A-Millennial writer has this to say in this text (pages 56-57) concerning the binding of Satan: "Further He states that He bound the 'strong man' (Matt.12:28-29; Lke.11:21-23). These further references all speak of the same fact, the 'binding' and so the binding and control of the Devil's activity (Matt.4:1-11; Lke.10:17-20; Jhn.12:31-33; Col.2:15; Rev.12:5; 1Jhn.3:8; Eph.4:8; Lke.9:1). Some might argue from 1Pet.5:8, saying, 'Does not the Devil, going about as a roaring lion contradict this viewpoint?' …In respect to 'the nations', the result of this binding is that he can deceive the nations no more. Prior to the birth of

Christ and the advent of the Kingdom of God, the nations were in darkness. Only the Jews, as a nation, had light from a revelation of God…"

3. George L. Murray – "Millennial Studies"

Murray (pages 175-180) has these comments on Rev.20. "It is our contention that the Gospel plainly reveals what is meant by the binding of Satan." Murray then expounds Matt.12:28-29 on the binding of the strong man (Satan) by the stronger man (Jesus). He continues: "There are many people who find it difficult to believe that Satan is bound today when there is such widespread evidence of his influences…The place into which Satan is cast is called the bottomless pit, or the abyss. This is his present place of abode from which he carries on his activities…"

He continues: "Satan was restrained for a certain period and yet not altogether taken away. One of the chief prohibitions laid upon him was that he should deceive the nations no more until the end of the period symbolized by the 1000 years, and representing the Gospel age. No other effect upon human life on earth other than the deceiving of the nations is mentioned. Nothing is said of universal peace or abounding prosperity, nor of the restoration of the Hebrew economy. Satan is merely restricted in his work of deceiving the nations. It is an interesting fact that from that day until recent years, the Gospel has been having free course to all nations. At present, however, we have a different situation. There are nations being deceived by Satan, living in superstition and antagonistic to the Gospel, even passing legislation to prohibit its propagation. One wonders if this does not suggest the possibility that Satan is now being loosed for a little while to go out deceiving the nations which are in the four corners of the earth. The least that can be said is that few of our prophets predict, even a decade ago, the present state of affairs"

4. William E. Cox – "A-Millennialism Today"

One further quote from Cox will suffice to show the position held generally by all A-Millennialists as to the "binding of Satan". Refer pages 61-63 of his text.

"Having shown from Scripture that Satan already has been bound, in a figurative sense, let us see how this squares with Revelation 20. After all, this is the only passage in dispute concerning the alleged future binding of Satan. The question arises, then, whether John means to portray a literal binding or a figurative one? If he speaks of a literal binding, indicating that Satan will be completely immobilized so that he can carry on no activities at all, then our dispensational friends are correct; this would mean that the predicted binding of Satan has not yet taken place. If, on the other hand, John spoke of a figurative binding of Satan, the problem dissolves itself. For we have shown conclusively that Satan is bound in this manner". Cox quotes the passage from Rev.20:1-3.

He continues: "It should be borne in mind that the Bible often uses the word "bind" to designate the limitation of power. This is the sense in which John uses the term as the context bears out. John definitely is speaking in figurative language since a spiritual being (Satan) certainly could not be bound with physical keys, chains, and the like. John says that Satan is bound in a particular respect, i.e., "that he should deceive the nations no more." This is the only sense in which this passage says that Satan is bound. In other words, it merely says that one portion of his power has been limited for a period f time.

To understand what is meant by Satan's inability any longer to deceive the nations one merely needs to let his mind take a cursory glance at the teachings of the Bible. In the beginning God placed man in the Garden of Eden, and gave man dominion over the earth. At the fall of man in the Garden, Satan took over this dominion from man and became the Prince of this world. Even at that time, God promised that His Son would some day take this dominion away from Satan (Gen.3:15). Before our Lord defeated Satan at the cross, Satan was able to "deceive the nations (Gentiles)" and to hold sway over their souls. On the cross, our Lord said, "It is finished." Then and there Satan had this world's dominion wrested from his grasp. He can no longer deceive the nations by keeping the Gospel from them. Following His victory on the cross, our Lord could say, "…all authority is given to Me in heaven and on earth. Go therefore, and make disciples of all nations…" (Matt.28:18,19). Satan's power to deceive the nations had been limited, because all authority had been given to Christ" (End Quote).

The student will note that each A-Millennial writer sees that the "binding of Satan" is **figurative rather than literal**! This binding took place at Christ's first advent. Probably this helps to sharpen the position of this writer more clearly, which is the exact opposite to this A-Millennial position. Christian Millennialists believe that the binding of Satan is **literal** and takes place at Christ's second coming! Though recognizing that Satan was conquered and dealt with at the cross by Christ, "the Stronger Man", we do not see that Satan was cast into the bottomless pit at Calvary!

Our attention can now be given to what this writer believes Rev.20:1-3 is saying about the binding of Satan. All Schools have reasonable agreement on Satan being loosed for a little season at the end of the 1000 years, regardless of their position on that period. It is the disagreement about when Satan was bound and is he already bound or yet to be bound – this is the point of difference here!

"And I saw an angel come down from heaven, having the key of the bottomless pit and a great chain in his hand. And he laid hold on the dragon, that old serpent, which is the Devil, and Satan, and bound him a thousand years, And cast him into the bottomless pit, and shut him up, and set a seal upon him, that he should deceive the nations no more, till the thousand years should be fulfilled: and after that he must be loosed a little season" (Rev.20:1-3 . KJV).

And I saw an Angel – Most expositors see this angel-messenger to be none other than the Lord Jesus Christ Himself. Satan opposed THE WORD from eternity past and all through time. God the Father could have kept this binding act and given it to any ordinary angelic spirit being. But the One most suited to bind Satan would be the One who was bruised at Calvary by the serpent, but who also bruised the serpent's head, conquering all his power (Gen.3:15; Col.2:14-15; Heb.2:14; Jhn.12:31-33). The angel-messenger here is a real being, not merely a symbolic being!

Come down from heaven - Christ comes down from heaven at His second advent. This is seen in Rev.19:11-16 where He comes riding on the white horse, conquering the Antichrist and his hosts. There He deals with the Satanic trinity; the Antichrist and the False Prophet, and now here with Satan himself. He came from heaven the first advent, and He comes from heaven in His second coming (Matt.24:30).

Having the Key of the Bottomless Pit –Keys, all keys speak of absolute authority and supremacy and power. All power is given to Him in heaven and in earth (Matt.28:18-20). It is the key of the bottomless pit, the abyss, which is called a pit and a prison. Jesus has all the keys necessary to fulfill His ministry. It is recognized that this key speaks of spiritual power and authority, not a material key as we understand it. Nevertheless, the key, though symbolic, does speak of spiritual realities.

And a great chain in His hand – The chain is also of spiritual nature to bind a spirit being, to bind Satan. However, though symbolic things are spoken of here, it does not deny reality. Satan is a real spirit being, a fallen angel. The Angel who binds is a real being, possibly Christ Himself. Jesus cast out demons by the Spirit of God. He is the "Stronger Man" than the "Strong Man" – Satan. He conquered Satan and his hosts at Calvary. The strong man (Satan) is bound first, and then his house is spoiled (Matt.12:28-29). If demons are cast out, this is the evidence that the Kingdom of God has come. This binding of Satan was made possible judicially at Calvary, but it is done actually and literally at Christ's second coming.

And He laid hold on the Dragon, that Old Serpent, which is the Devil and Satan – Laid hold, or "Gripped and over-powered" (Amp.N.T.). Note the four names of this evil angelic being.
1. The Dragon – the beastly nature of this fallen angel. He is a beast, cruel, ferocious and terrifying.
2. The Old Serpent – old as the Garden of Eden, from the creation of man, from primeval times (Amp.N.T.).
3. The Devil – the evil one, the slanderer and the liar.
4. The Adversary – which is the meaning of 'Satan'. He is the adversary and opposer of God and Christ and the saints.

And bound him – Or, securely bound him. Jesus said that the stronger man would bind the strong man and then spoil his house. The 'house' here may be likened to planet earth, for Satan is the god of this world system (2Cor.4:4). So the earth with its inhabitants, slaves of sin and Satan, has to be 'spoiled' as people are delivered from the kingdom of darkness into the kingdom of light. This 'binding' will be commented on more fully in due time in our comments on this passage.

And cast him into the Bottomless Pit, and shut him up, and set a seal upon him – Note the related actions of the binding Angel in this verse.
1. Laid hold – Or, literally, gripped and overpowered Satan.
2. Bound him – Tied him up, wound him up, fastened him.

3. Cast – Hurled him into the Abyss, the Bottomless Pit. This place is an actual place in the spirit realm, in the spirit world, not merely a symbolic place. It is spoken of as being a jail or a prison.
4. Shut him up – Closed it, like closing a door, locking Satan up in the Abyss. Satan is incarcerated, locked up in a prison.
5. Set a seal on him – That is, sealed this Abyss above him, like as the Romans sealed Christ in the tomb when He was buried so that none could tamper with the seal of Rome or steal His body (Matt.27:60-66). None dare break that seal on pain of death.

If words mean anything, and if words are to be taken at their plain, common sense meaning, then there is no way to water these phrases or words down to mean anything less than what they say. If words make common sense, then any other sense make nonsense. These words cannot be spiritualized or allegorized away or made to mean something different.

Satan is here gripped and overpowered. He is bound or tied up. He is hurled into the Abyss, the pit and prison of the spirit underworld. He is shut up. He is closed up in this prison for 1000 years. He is sealed in this prison, just like Daniel was sealed in the lion's den with the king's seal and none could tamper with the king's seal to loose Daniel out of that prison. He could not escape without someone breaking the seal and taking him out of the lion's den. So a seal is set on the Bottomless Pit so that Satan cannot get out, and none can get him out.

The A-Millennialist says all this was done at Christ's first coming and in His redemptive work on Calvary. As has already been seen, the major foundational Scripture used for this theory is based on Matt.12:28-29 and Lke.11:20-22. It has been argued that Satan is "the Strong Man" and Jesus is "the Stronger Man". When Jesus died on he cross, He bound Satan and was able then to spoil his house (i.e., Satan's Kingdom) and take his goods i.e., souls in captivity to Satan). And again, the A-Millennialist holds that, after Satan's defeat on Calvary, he was bound by a chain. That is, his activities were restricted as far as the hindering of the Gospel going forth to the nations of the earth was concerned. They hold that Satan was bound at Christ's first coming and will be loosed for a little season before Christ's second coming. The diagram illustrates this.

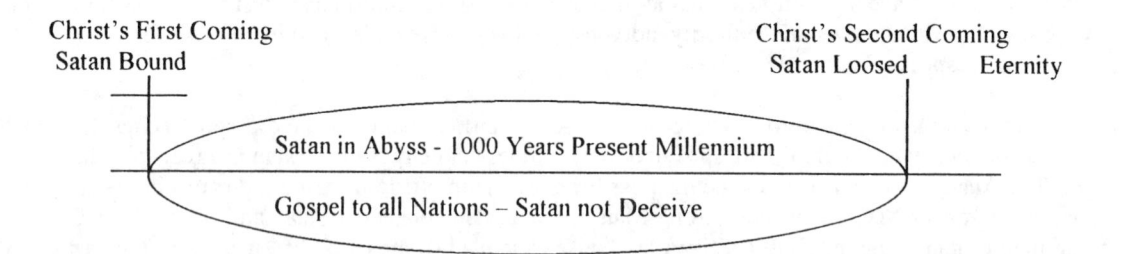

```
Christ's First Coming                                      Christ's Second Coming
Satan Bound                                                Satan Loosed      Eternity
    |_____|
         ( Satan in Abyss - 1000 Years Present Millennium  )
         ( Gospel to all Nations – Satan not Deceive        )
```

In refutation of this position, most theologians see a distinction between what is referred to as "judicial truth" and "experiential truth". Judicial truth speaks of all that happened at Calvary, all that God did in Christ judicially or legally on the cross. An end was made of sin, disease, death and Satan and all his hosts were conquered at Calvary. Jesus was made a curse for us and God judged Christ in our stead. Sin was judged, death was conquered, and Satan's power was broken. God's holiness and righteousness were upheld. All that happened at Calvary, judicially and legally in the plan and purpose of God.

But "judicial truth" has to become "experiential truth". The legal has to become actual. What Christ did for us legally at Calvary has to be done in us experientially. This is done by the power of the Holy Spirit as we walk "the bridge of faith and obedience". Paul tells us that Christ "abolished death, and brought life and immortality to light through the Gospel" (2Tim.1:9-11). Jesus destroyed him (Satan) who held the power of death; that is, the devil. He delivered us from the fear of death (Heb.2:14-15). On the other hand, Paul also tells us that the last enemy to be destroyed is death (1Cor.15:22-28,26).

If sin, sickness, disease, death and Satan and his hosts have been truly (actually, literally, experientially) bound at Calvary, why do Christians still sin and need the cleansing blood of Jesus daily, and why are Christians sick and diseased and why do Christians die? It is because judicial truth has not come to fully realized and experiential truth. Objective truth is what God has done for us in Christ at Calvary. Subjective truth is what God does in us by the power of the Holy Spirit (Phil.2:12-13). We work out our salvation with fear and trembling as God works in us to will and to do of His own good pleasure.

The FIRST COMING was THE SEED and was the most important day in the universe up to that time. The SECOND COMING, however, will be the most important day since that day in the universe. It consummates all that was done in that first day, His first coming. The first and second comings are linked together as one in the mind and purpose of God. Nothing new happens in the second coming that was not introduced or inaugurated at His first coming. We are saved by FAITH as we look back to the first coming. We are saved by HOPE as we look forward to the second coming.

In diagram form we note the distinction yet inter-relatedness of what has been called "the proton" (the beginning), and "the eschaton" (the ending).

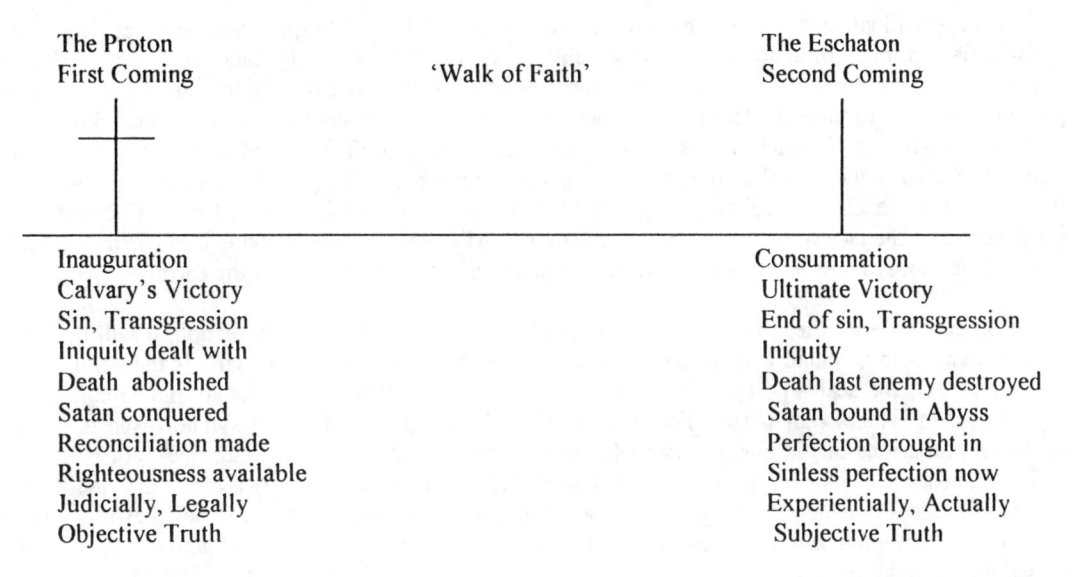

The Proton First Coming	'Walk of Faith'	The Eschaton Second Coming
Inauguration		Consummation
Calvary's Victory		Ultimate Victory
Sin, Transgression		End of sin, Transgression
Iniquity dealt with		Iniquity
Death abolished		Death last enemy destroyed
Satan conquered		Satan bound in Abyss
Reconciliation made		Perfection brought in
Righteousness available		Sinless perfection now
Judicially, Legally		Experientially, Actually
Objective Truth		Subjective Truth

In the light of these things, it may be said that Satan was bound judicially, or legally, at Calvary, but is actually bound at Christ's second coming. To say that Satan has been gripped and overpowered, bound and tied up, hurled into the Abyss, shut up in this prison and sealed over the Church era of a "symbolic Millennial period" is not doing justice to plain words!

A-Millennialists, on the whole, seem to ignore the place where Satan was hurled. Satan was hurled into the Abyss, the Pit, the Prison in the underworld, in the spirit realm. To say that Satan is on a long chain and can still operate from his prison during the 1000 years (the symbolic time between first and second comings of Christ) does despite to plain words and the meaning of these words. Satan is sealed over so he cannot operate from his prison as some prisoners in our jails have done. This is to force a meaning on words that is not there. Any expositor should be consistent in his interpretation and definition of words. Church History shows an increased activity of Satan and his demonic hosts. It is increasing more and more in this end of the age. It shows that Satan has not been actually bound in the truest sense and Christ's first coming.

The Greek word "**Deo**" is a primary verb; meaning "to bind (in various applications, literally or figuratively), and is translated as "bind, be in bonds, knit, tie, wind" (Rev.9:14; 20:2). It means to make secure; to fasten, as with a band or a rope. It means to make a prisoner and thereby restrain the activities of that person. The word is used in these sample references given here.
1. The Stronger Man will bind the Strong Man. Jesus will bind Satan in he appointed time (Matt.12:28-29; Mrk.3:17).
2. The tares were to be bound in bundles first, and the wheat gathered into the heavenly barn. This binding of the tares takes place at Christ's second coming, even as Satan is bound at the same time (Matt.13:30).
3. An unrepentant Church member is to be bound by the act of excommunication as long as he remains in a state of unforgiveness (Matt.18:15-20).
4. The Church is given the ministry of binding and loosing by using the keys of the Kingdom (Matt.16:18-19).
5. Lazarus was bound hand and foot and totally immobilized when he was super-naturally resurrected out of the grave by Christ. He had to be loosed by the disciples accordingly (Jhn.11:43-44).
6. The servant who was unwilling to forgive his brother was bound hand and foot. He was therefore, immobilized (Matt.22:13).

7. The demoniac could not be bound by chains as long he was possessed of demon spirits (Mrk.5:3).
8. Saul, as a Pharisee, bound both men and women who called on the Name of the Lord Jesus Christ and caused them to be cast into prison (Acts 9:14).
9. The prophet Agabus took Paul's girdle and bound him with it, demonstrating in prophecy that Paul would be bound by the Jews when he was in Jerusalem (Acts 21:11).
10. There are four angels bound at the river Euphrates that are to be loosed in the appointed year, month, day and hour, to torment and kill men (Rev.9:14).
11. Satan is also to be bound at Christ's second coming and cast into the Abyss (Rev.20:2).

How do A-Millennialists handle these Scripture references? By holding the position that Satan was bound at Christ's first coming **figuratively – not actually!** It may be asked: If Satan is bound and cast into the Bottomless Pit, then who is carrying on his work? Is he controlling all the fallen angels and the demonic hosts from his prison as do some modern day prisoners from their jails? To say he is simply 'like a dog on a long chain but he is restricted in his reach' is to take away the full meaning, definition and effect of the words and phrases used in Rev.20:1-3 about his binding! It seems incongruous that the King of the Kingdom of Darkness, the God of this world system, is locked away 'figuratively' in the Bottomless Pit but still wields powerful influence in every nation on the face of the earth! But, even some A-Millennialists are thinking and writing that maybe Satan may be being loosed now with so much deception taking place in the nations of the earth!

As the student re-reads the comments and quotes of the several writers in this section, it will be seen how their position that Satan is bound is justified by saying that it is "figurative, not actual". Is the Abyss, the chain, the key, the Angel, the seal all 'figurative' only? Is there nothing that is real, actual and literal. If these are all symbolic, then symbolic of what? For the reality is always greater than the symbol used to symbolize it. It would seem that one of the major reasons for making the binding of Satan figurative, rather than actual, is to justify the position of placing this binding back at Christ's first coming, at Calvary, and thus nullify any possible 'future Millennium', which is a reaction against a 'Jewish Millennium'. The writer believes it is possible to hold to a future Millennium, but not a Jewish one, but one in which Satan is truly and actually bound and the saints possess the Kingdom.

This, in a nutshell, is the difference on this matter between most all of the other Schools of Eschatology. The view of Christian Millennialists is that Satan was **conquered judicially** at Calvary but he is **bound actually** at Christ's second coming! All that was begun at the first coming is completed at the second coming. The first coming was the inauguration of redemption. The second coming is the consummation of redemption.

That he should deceive the nations no more until the 1000 years should be fulfilled – There remains one other major thing to be dealt with as far as these several verses are concerned on the binding of Satan. That is, Satan was bound so that he could no longer deceive the nations of earth. The position is held that, not only is Satan laid hold of, bound, cast into the Abyss, shut up and sealed there, he can no longer deceive the nations of earth over this period of 1000 years.

It is here that it would appear the A-Millennialist position shows a great weakness. The A-Millennialist holds that the only way that Satan is bound is with regard to the going forth of the Gospel. It is argued that the Gospel could not go to all the nations under Old Testament times, only to the chosen nation of Israel. Since Christ's triumph over Satan at Calvary, and since Christ, "the Stronger Man" bound Satan, "the Strong Man" on the cross, now the good news of redemption can go to all nations. Jesus told His disciples to go and make disciples of ALL nations and preach the Gospel to every creature (Matt.28:18-20; Mrk.16:15-20).

A-Millennialists consistently point out that this is the one and only aspect in which Satan is bound, "that he should no longer deceive he nations over the 1000 years". This is made to simply mean that the Gospel can be preached everywhere now, to all Gentile nations, not just to the Israel nation. Nothing more, nothing less, and nothing else, is all that this phrase means. It is only on this point that Satan is bound, for he still goes about like a roaring lion (1Pet.5:8-9).

In this writer's understanding, it seems very contradictory for A-Millennialists to say that Satan is bound on the one hand, and yet Satan still goes about like a roaring lion. How can Satan go about like a roaring lion, seeking to devour the people of God, and yet be locked up, incarcerated, in the Bottomless Pit? To say this binding is 'figurative' only is to violate plain and common sense meaning of the words, as we have already commented. It is to place an interpretation on the words that are there, and also to take away the full meaning of the words.

But further, there are some other warnings in Scripture that would nullify the point that "the nations are not being deceived by Satan" in this period of time between the first and second comings of Christ.

Most every book in the New Testament warns us against deception. Deception is Satan's master weapon. It was the first weapon he used in the Garden of Eden when he deceived the woman, Eve (1Tim.2:14 with Gen.3:1-6). It is his last weapon used in the end of the age, as seen in the Book of Revelation. If words mean anything, then the fact that Satan cannot deceive the nations means the nations cannot be deceived. But one thinks of the nations throughout Church History which have rejected the Gospel. There are nations that are still deceived and even now forbid any evangelization of their peoples on pain of death or deportation from the country. Even if this was the only aspect in which Satan is bound, it is not so in real life. Nations are deceived and being deceived. Proper hermeneutics will not re-interpret this phrase to mean something that it does not mean. The warnings in the New Testament are written generally to Spirit-filled believers, warning them against deception, let alone "nations being deceived".

The Amplified New Testament says: "...so that he shall no longer lead astray and deceive and seduce the nations until the 1000 years were at an end..."(Rev.20:3). The Greek word for deceive has the meaning of "to roam from the truth, to seduce, to stray, cheat, delude, beguile, lead into error or to wander" Refer to Strong's Concordance. SC.4105, 4106, 4108). Note some of the major warnings against deception. There are some fifty references in the New Testament to this Greek word.

1. Jesus warned against deception by false Christs and false prophets (Matt.24:4,5,11,24). If possible, even the very elect would be deceived. Read also Lke.21:8.
2. Mark's Gospel confirms the warning against deception in these days (Mrk.13:5,6).
3. Paul warns against those who would bring division by deception to the hearts of the simple in the Church (Rom.16:18).
4. Believers who continue to live in sin deceive themselves (1Cor.3:18).
5. Paul in Ephesians warns against those teachers who would seek to deceive those who do not have sound doctrine (Eph.4:14; 5:6 with 2Cor.6:18; Tit.1:10).
6. Sin deceives people (Rom.7:11).
7. Antichrist will be the Man of Sin who will deceive the whole world and the nations on earth by means of the miracles, signs and wonders done through his false prophet (Rev.13 with 2Thess.2:3).
8. A believer could become self-deceived over sin (1Jhn.1:8).
9. John warns against the coming of many antichrists, who would deceive people (1Jhn.3:7).
10. The Pharisees, who were extremely religious, were deceived (Jhn.7:47).
11. Paul often tells the believers "be not deceived..." (1Cor.5:33; Gal.6:7; 1Cor.6:9-11).
12. The serpent deceived Eve in the Garden of Eden when she was as yet perfect (1Tim.2:14).
13. There are those who are deceivers and being deceived (2Tim.3:13 with verses 8-9).
14. Deceivers serve their various evil lusts (Tit.3:3).
15. Antichrists and deceivers deny that Christ has come in the flesh (2Jhn.7).
16. Babylon has deceived the nations of the earth by her sorceries (Rev.18:23).
17. Satan and the Beast and False Prophet deceive the whole world into receiving the Mark of the Beast and worshipping his image (Rev.19:20; 20:10 with Rev.13).
18. Fornicators, unclean persons, covetous people and all who live in sin, even as professing believers, will not inherit the Kingdom of God. Believers need to be warned against being deceived by false words (Eph.5:1-7 with 1Cor.6:9-10).
19. There are certain philosophies that deceive people (Col.2:8).
20. When Satan is actually bound, he will no longer be able to deceive the nations of earth. This binding takes place when Christ returns and sets up His Kingdom for 1000 years (Rev.20:3,8).

If Satan was bound at Calvary, cast into the Pit, then who has been responsible for the millions of people in all nations on the earth being deceived? And why all these warnings against deception, even to Spirit-filled believers? This deception has been going on for some 2000 years, let alone some "symbolic 1000 years" period between first and second comings of Christ! Satan worship, demon worship, occultism, demon activity, drug activity and all manner of deceptions continue in every nation. If Satan is bound in his prison, operating like a criminal from his prison, and he is bound, then what will he do differently to what is taking place now, once he is loosed? No! We believe that Satan is the God of this world system. He controls the fallen angels. He controls the demonic spirits. All obey his will. He is the Prince of the power of the air. He is the King of the Kingdom of Darkness. He is working by the power of deception as never before. He knows he has a short time left before he is to be hurled into the Abyss for 1000 years. Men deceive men. Sin deceives. People are self-deceived.

Satan, however, is the source of all deception. He is the Master Deceiver! To accept the A-Millennial position that Satan is bound, only with regard to the Gospel going to all nations, is really to ignore reality. It becomes a kind of 'mental gymnastics' to ignore all these warnings against deception, individually, corporately, nationally and internationally!

And after that he must be loosed a little season – There does not seem to be any major disagreement as to the loosing of Satan at the end of the 1000 years, whatever one's view may be on this period of time. All Schools of Eschatology have general agreement that Satan is to be loosed again and will deceive nations once again. Whether one is Historic Pre-Millennial, Post-Millennial, A-Millennial, Futurist/Dispensational Pre-Millennial, or Christian Millennial, all just accept the fact that, for some Divine reason, God allows Satan to be loosed from his prison in a final deceptive work over the nations. Comments on this cannot be covered here. The major purpose of this chapter was to deal with the issue whether Satan is bound now or is yet to be bound.

In Summary:
From the understanding of this writer, as a Christian Millennialist, the details of Rev.20:1-3 may be set out in the following manner.

1. The Angelic-Messenger is possibly the Lord Jesus Christ.
2. The coming down from heaven is His second coming, under the figure of the white horse and rider seen in Rev.19:11-16.
3. The key and the chain are of spiritual nature to bind Satan, who is a spirit and an angelic being.
4. The Bottomless Pit is the Abyss, a jail, a prison, an actual place in the spirit realm.
5. The Dragon, the Old Serpent, the Devil and Satan, though described under symbolic names, is an actual and real angelic spirit being.
6. The binding of Satan is an actual reality, not merely figurative. This binding of Satan is a total limitation on all his activities in the earth as he is locked in the Abyss.
7. This shutting up and sealing in the Abyss is the total locking up of Satan in the prison of the spirit realm. By implication, because Satan is the King of the Kingdom of Darkness, then this binding would include Satan's hosts of fallen angels and demon spirits, who are also confined in this time period.
8. The nations are not deceived by Satan in this 1000 year period of time. Deception has been Satan's master weapon since Eden, and continues to increase its influence in the end of this age. No deception implies no sin, for sin deceives.
9. The 1000 years is an actual period of time, even as the Angel, Satan, the Abyss, the souls on throne are real and actual beings – not merely symbolic – and this period is ushered in at Christ's second coming, not His first coming.
10. The loosing of Satan is as actual/literal as is his binding, not figurative. If the binding is figurative, then the loosing would be figurative, in order, at least, to be consistent in interpretation!

This binding takes place when Christ comes again, at the close of this present Church age and at the close of the 3½ years Great Tribulation. With this "binding" Historic, Futurist and Dispensationalists generally agree.

This writer sees that Christ conquered Satan and all his works and hosts at Calvary, judicially, legally, making possible Satan's actual binding at His second coming. The words are taken to mean what they say, not to be spiritualized or allegorized into a figurative meaning. The multiplied activities of Satan and his angelic and demonic hosts in the nations of the earth are all evidence of the deception he carries on, even though the Gospel can go to the nations, where possible. It would be blindness to ignore the fact of deception going on in the nations, even though the Gospel is being proclaimed wherever possible in the nations!

CHAPTER TWELVE

THE RESURRECTION

Our studies bring us to the subject of the Resurrection. The Millennial Schools, once again, fall into two major categories: Those that believe in one general resurrection, and those who believe in, at least, two resurrections.

The reader needs to be reminded that ALL Millennial Schools do believe in a bodily resurrection of the just and the unjust. The difference is a matter of the "time element", as to WHEN both companies are actually raised. Is there but one general resurrection of the righteous and the unrighteous at one and the same time. Or is there a period of time, of 1000 years, between what is called "the first and second resurrection?" The issue then, is not a personal issue, or not even a doctrinal issue. All believe in the **truth** of the resurrection of just and unjust. It is an issue of the **time** of the resurrection of both companies. The two groupings:

1. **Two Resurrections**
    Historic Pre-Millennialists, Futurists, Dispensationalists, and this writer – Christian Millennialist – all believe that there are two resurrections 1000 years apart. The first is the resurrection of the righteous, who are rewarded by Christ at this time. This is at His second coming. The second resurrection is that of the unrighteous, who are judged at the Great White Throne at the close of the 1000 years period. Eternal destinies are settled then.

2. **One General Resurrection**
    The Post-Millennialists and the A-Millennialists both believe in one general resurrection of the righteous and the unrighteous. This general resurrection takes place at the second coming of Christ. For the Post-Millennialist, this general resurrection takes place at Christ's advent. For the A-Millennialist, it takes place at the second coming of Christ, at the close of the "present Millennial age", the period of time between Christ's first and second comings.

The positions of the two categories of Millennialists, as to the resurrection, need some examination, which is the purpose of this chapter.

A. **The Doctrine of the Resurrection**
    Before examining the views as to the **time** of the resurrection of the just and unjust, it will be beneficial to review what the Bible teaches as to the **truth** of the resurrection.

    In Hebrews 6:1-2, the writer lists "the principles of the doctrine of Christ", the fifth one being "the resurrection of the dead", which is then followed by "eternal judgment." This principle is one of the greatest in the Word of God. In actual fact, it is the foundational doctrine of Biblical Christianity. It is the foundation stone of the Gospel of the Lord Jesus Christ. "If Christ is not risen from the dead", then there is absolutely no Gospel of salvation. The Gospel of the Resurrection is a Gospel of Life, Resurrection and Immortality through the Lord Jesus Christ (Acts 4:1-3; 23:1-11).

    The doctrine may be considered in a twofold manner (1) Spiritually – a resurrection of the spirit of man from being dead in trespasses and sins, and (2) Bodily – a resurrection of the human body from the grave of death and corruption. The word "resurrection" means "to be made alive, or to be quickened, raised to life from a state of death." It is applied in Scripture both spiritually and physically. There can be no resurrection without death. In order to appreciate the doctrine of the resurrection, it is necessary to understand death. Death is the absence of life, whether spiritual life or physical life.

B. **The Entrance of Death**
    In Genesis we have the account of the entrance of death. God placed man in the Garden of Eden, an earthly Paradise, in a garden of trees. Before him were two special trees, the tree of eternal life and the tree of the knowledge of good and evil. These two trees spoke of eternal life or eternal death. The tree of the knowledge of good and evil represented death. The tree of life represented eternal life (Gen.2:8-17; 3:1-4; 2:22-24 with Deut.30:15-20).

The Lord said to Adam, "You can eat freely of all the trees of the garden, but the tree of the knowledge of good and evil, in the middle of the garden, you are not to eat of it, for in the day you eat of it, you shall surely die" (Gen.2:17). Or, more literally, "in dying, you shall die", which meant, "in dying spiritually, you shall die physically." Human history provides the tragic results of Adam and his wife eating of the forbidden tree. "By one man SIN entered the world, and DEATH by sin, and so death passed upon all men", for in Adam all sinned and all die. By man came death, for in Adam all die (1Cor.15:21-22).

Scripture gives a threefold aspect of death. Death is not a state of non-existence, or annihilation, or a state of unconsciousness (Read Rev.6:9-11; Lke.16:19-31). It is a state of separation, as these three aspects of death confirm.

1. **Spiritual Death**
   The moment Adam sinned, he 'died' spiritually. Spiritual death is the separation of the soul from God from sin. Adam died as a living soul in the 24-hour-day he sinned. He was cut off, separated from God by sin (Gen.2:17; Ezek.18:4-32,20; Eph.2:1-6; 1Tim.5:6; Col.2:13; 1Jhn.3:14). The student should read these references. Each records the fact that all men are dead in trespasses and sins. They are "dead, while they live". That is, they are spiritually dead to God and the things of God.

2. **Physical Death**
   Physical death is the separation of the soul and spirit from the body of flesh. Adam died physically later than he died spiritually, yet he died within "the day" that the Lord had said. "In THE DAY you sin, you will surely die". That is, a day unto the Lord, which is 1000 years, according to Moses, who wrote Psa.90:4 with 2Pet.3:8. Physical death pertains to the body of man (Rom.5:12,14-21; 6:3-23; 7:5-13,24; Heb.9:27). All men are appointed to die and after this comes the judgment. All men have a death-doomed (mortal) body. God said, "In dying (spiritually), you will die (physically)" (Marginal reading of Gen.2:17). He died spiritually in the 24-hour-day he sinned, and he died physically in the 1000-year-Day of the Lord. Sin gave to man a body of death (Rom.7:24). It is between "spiritual death" and "physical death" that God gives to every one "space to repent" or time to come to repentance, none knowing how long that "time" may be (Rev.2:21). This is God's grace indeed!

3. **Eternal Death**
   In Rev.2:11; 20:6,10-15; 21:8 it speaks of the "second death", and this pertains to eternal death; that is, eternal separation of the spirit/soul of man, unredeemed man, from God for all eternity. In death man becomes a naked or disembodied spirit. Unless redeemed in this life, man becomes separated from God and His eternal Presence and all that means. God is the source of all life, light and love. Apart from Him there is death, darkness and hate. Man's spirit separated eternally from God is "the worm that never dies" (Isa.66:24 with Mrk.9:44-48). Man's spirit is undying, and when unredeemed becomes unredeemable and this for all eternity. Eternal separation from God is eternal death, the second death.

Adam tasted the first death, in the first two aspects of spiritual and physical death, but he escaped the "second death" through the atonement, when he accepted the coats of skin provided by God through a substitutionary blood/body sacrifice. He was clothed by God through this innocent, sacrificial victim. He experienced a "time-separation" but not "eternal separation" from God. The Tree of Eternal Life is to be restored in the end of the age to all who overcome and do His commandments (Rev.2:7; 22:2,14).

The flaming sword at Eden's Gate barred the way to the Tree of Eternal Life. To go through this sword would mean death. God killed a lamb providing an atonement for Adam and Eve. They could either accept or reject the lamb and its death for them. Accepting this lamb made it possible for God to restore eternal life to them in the appointed time. But they had to die physically. They were, however, given eternal life, spiritually, and have the promise of resurrection life and immortality (Gen.3:15). They, along with all saints, "died in faith", and they did not "die in unbelief."

So it is today. Jesus Christ went through the sword of God, through death and made the way open to the tree of eternal life for all mankind. Man must accept God's lamb to receive life or experience eternal death, the second death after judgment (Jhn.8:21-24; Lke.1:79; Matt.4:16).

Note how often "the death bell tolled" in Gen.5:5,8,11,14,17,20,27,31, as it records, "And he died...". They all died in faith of the resurrection of the body. The student is encouraged to read these Scriptures references as they are too many to quote in any way in this chapter (Gen.6:17; 7:21; Rom.5:12-21; 6:3-23; 1Cor.15:21,26; Rom.7:5-24; 2Cor.3:17; 1Cor.15:55-56; Heb.2:14-15; Psa.68:20; Jas.1:15; Ezek.18:4-32; 33:7-20; 3:18-20; Jer.21:8; Psa.118:8; 116:8; 33:19; 102:20; 79:11). A simple diagram may help illustrate the truth dealt with here.

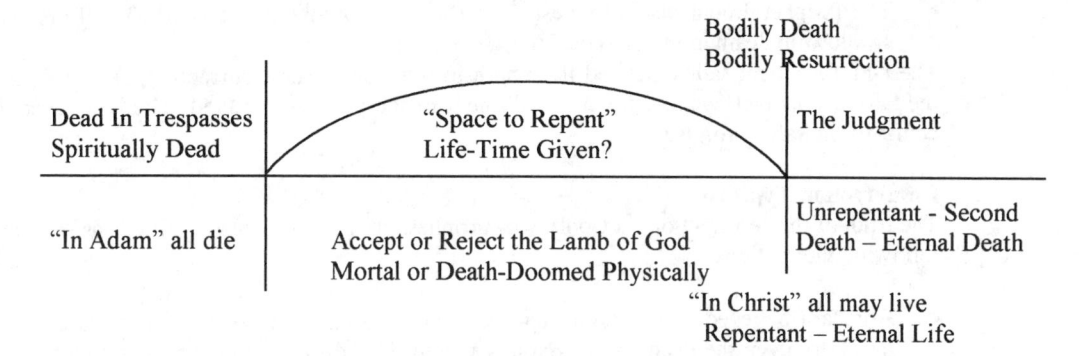

```
                                      Bodily Death
                                      Bodily Resurrection
                    _____
Dead In Trespasses /  "Space to Repent" \      The Judgment
Spiritually Dead  /   Life-Time Given?   \
─────────────────┼────────────────────────┼──────────────────
                 │                        │  Unrepentant - Second
"In Adam" all die│ Accept or Reject the   │  Death – Eternal Death
                 │ Lamb of God            │
                 │ Mortal or Death-Doomed Physically
                                            "In Christ" all may live
                                            Repentant – Eternal Life
```

"In dying (spiritually), you will die (physically)" - Lamb accepted -- Promise of Tree of Life

The Death of the Believer
For the believer, there is hope of eternal life in Christ. "Precious in the sight of the Lord is the death of His saints" (Psa.116:15; Rev.14:13; Jhn.5:24). The believer dies in faith (1Jh.3:14; Heb.11:13; Rev.2:11; Eccles.3:21; 7:1; Lke.20:36). The righteous have hope in death (Prov.14:32; 10:2; 11:4; Ezek.3:21; 18:21).

The Death of the Unbeliever
The death of the unbeliever, the unrepentant sinner, is terrible and beyond words. The sinner dies in unbelief, without hope, and awaits the Great White Throne Judgment. The end result of that judgment is the second death, which is eternal separation from God (Isa.66:24; Mrk.9:44-48; Ezek.18:23; 33:7-11; Rev.20:8-15; 14:9-11). The resurrection of the sinner is but for one purpose – to bring judgment (Heb.9:27), and then the second death. All men are given "time" or "space to repent". However, no one knows how long that "space" or "time" is! NOW is the appointed time, and NOW is the day of salvation (2Cor.6:2).

C. **The Entrance of Resurrection**
"By man came death...by man came also the resurrection of the dead...in Adam all die, in Christ all shall be made alive..." (Rom.5:12-21 with 1Cor.15:21-22; Gen.3:15). The promise of life, resurrection and immortality has been brought to light through the Gospel of our Lord Jesus Christ (2Tim.1:9-10). Christ died to redeem mankind from death, spiritually, physically and eternally. He died to redeem mankind from Satan, the author and power of death (Heb.2:9-15).

As proof of the promise of resurrection for all who believe in Christ, God caused 'resurrection truth' to be prophesied, typified and demonstrated in Old Testament New Testament times.

1. **Resurrection Prophesied**

    - Gen.3:15. Death came by sin and Satan. The Seed of the Woman was to crush the Serpent's head. This crushing would destroy him who had the power of death, that is the Devil himself (Heb.2:9-14). Resurrection is by implication here in this first promise.
    - Ex.3:15. The Name of God as given to Moses is "I AM WHO I AM". This is the God of Abraham, the God of Isaac and the God of Jacob. Jesus said He is the God of the living, not of the dead, for all live unto Him. It is the Name of resurrection life (Matt.22:31-32).
    - Job prophesied, Though worms destroy my body, yet in my flesh I shall see God. Job knew the Lord as his redeemer (Job.14:14; 19:25-27). He spoke of physical resurrection.

- Enoch, the seventh from Adam, prophesied of coming judgment, which involves the bodily resurrection of men (Heb.11:5 with Jude 14-15). Enoch did not experience death himself but passed over from mortality to immortality.
- Joseph believed in a resurrection to life (Gen.50:24-26; Heb.11:22; Josh.24:32).
- David also prophesied of the resurrection of the Messiah (Psa.16:8-11; 17:15; 2Sam.12:23; Acts 2:29-32).
- The Prophet Daniel foretold the resurrection to life and to shame, or the resurrection of the righteous and the unrighteous (Dan.12:1-2,13).
- The Prophet Hosea saw that God would redeem man from death and ransom them from the power of the grave (Hos.13:14).
- The Prophet Isaiah also prophesied of the resurrection of the dead. The Lord would swallow up death in victory (Isa.26:8,19).

The Old Testament saints attested their faith in the God of the resurrection, and they died in the faith of this fact, waiting for the fulfillment of the promises of God. The New Testament confirms the same promises.

2. **Resurrection Typified**

The truth of the resurrection, not only was prophesied, but it was also typified, as seen in the following illustrations.

- Abraham believed in the resurrection power of God. He considered not his body now dead, not even the deadness of Sarah's womb. He considered God who raised the dead. From this 'death' came Isaac, the Old Testament only begotten son. It was through faith in the resurrection power of God (Rom.4:16-25).
- Abraham also proved his faith in the typical death and resurrection of his only begotten son, Isaac, when he offered him on Mt. Moriah, from whence he received from the dead, in a figure (Grk.Lit. "**tupos**", a Type). Heb.11:12-19 with Gen.22:5. Abraham said, I and the lad will yonder and worship and come again..." This was his faith in the resurrection of Isaac after his typical sacrifice on the altar.
- Jonah's experience of death in the great fish foreshadowed the death and resurrection of Christ Jesus. Jonah experienced 'death and burial' in the fish. He experienced the power of 'resurrection' when the fish returned him to land after thee days and three nights. Then he preached repentance to Nineveh (Jonah 2:1-10 with Matt.12:39-40). Jesus said this was A SIGN of His own death, burial and resurrection and future ministry among the Gentiles.

The resurrection was therefore prophesied and typified in the Old Testament, all founded on the word and promises of the Lord God. Many of the promises of God could only come to pass by a resurrection, and these saints all "died in faith, not having received the promises, but having seen them afar off..." (Heb.11:13-16).

3. **Resurrection Demonstrated**

Both Old and New Testaments confirm the truth of resurrection from death by the number of those that God raised from the dead. These become the proof and sample of what God will do in the resurrection of all mankind to judgment. In all there are nine resurrections noted here, without too many details. In every Dispensation, God has demonstrated His power in resurrection by raising some to life. These resurrections have witness of His promise and power to each Dispensation and gave ground for the faith of the saints for their future resurrection to life.

Resurrections in the Old Testament	**Resurrections in the New Testament**
1. Moses died, God buried Him, and God raised him from the dead. This is why the Devil contended with Michael over the **body** of Moses (Deut.34:5-6; Jude 9; Matt.17:1-9).	1. Jesus raised Jarius' daughter from the dead (Matt.9:18-26).
2. Elijah manifested the resurrection power of God when he raised the widow's son (1Kgs.17:17-24).	2. Jesus raised the widow's son from death also (Lke.7:11-23).
3. Elisha raised a widow's son to life in	3. Jesus raised Lazarus to life again (Jhn.11:43-44; 12:1,9,17).
	4. After Christ's resurrection, a company of saints rose from the dead also (Matt.27:51).
	5. Peter raised Dorcas from death (Acts 9:36-

resurrection power (2Kgs.4:18-37; 8:5). 4. A man was raised from death when his body touched the bones of the Prophet Elisha (2Kgs.13:20-21).	42 with Matt.10:8. 6. Paul raised a young man from death (Acts 20:7-12).

In the Old Testament we have four resurrections. In the Gospels, we have three resurrections. In the Book of Acts we have two resurrections. There are a total of **nine** resurrections, which is the number of Holy Spirit power in raising people from death to life. Each of these resurrections points to the resurrection of the saints and of all mankind. Read these Scriptures as they pertain to the Doctrine of the Resurrection (Matt.22:23,28-33; Mrk.12:18,23-25; Lke.20:27-36). The very Name of God as 'The I AM' is the Name of resurrection life and power.

The Sadducees deny the resurrection of the body, and apostates seek to overthrow the faith of some about it, but the Word of God stands sure. The fact of resurrection is as sure as the Word of God (Jhn.5:19-29; Rom.1:1-4; Heb.11:35-40; 2Tim.2:15-19; 1Tim.1:20).

D. The Resurrection of Christ

The very 'hub' of the wheel of truth concerning the resurrection is the fact of the resurrection of the Lord Jesus Christ. The resurrection of Christ is the sure foundation stone and actually becomes the surety of the resurrection of all mankind, believers and unbelievers alike, each in his own order (1Cor.15:1-23; Acts 17:30-31). The resurrection of Christ is the sure proof of the resurrection of all men, Paul said to the Athenians.

Jesus Himself is THE RESURRECTION and THE LIFE (Jhn.11:25). Resurrection is the glory and power of God (Rom.6:4-6; Jhn.11:40; Eph.1:19-21; 2Cor.13:4; 1Pet.1:5; Rom.1:3-4). The Resurrection is a person, Christ Himself. It is IN HIM that resurrection power and life resides (Jhn.14:6; 17:1-3; 11:25; 10:10). Outside of Him there is nothing but death. He had demonstrated His power over death, and He has demonstrated resurrection life, by the three resurrections He did in His earthly ministry. It is a perfect testimony (Matt.11:5).

Jesus Himself tasted of death for every one. Isaiah says "He made His grave with the wicked, and with the rich in His **deaths**..." (Isa.53:9). The Hebrew thought of the word is "deaths" in its plural form. It foretold the fact how Jesus Messiah would suffer the various aspects of death when "he tasted death for every man." He suffered spiritual and physical death for us, and by dying conquered death (Heb.2:9-14). He experienced that terrible separation from God on the cross when He was made sin for us and was forsaken by the Father. He experienced death in its three aspects.

1. He experienced separation from God when He was made sin for us on Calvary. This was a 'spiritual death' (Isa.53). His soul was made an offering for sin.
2. He experienced physical death, when His spirit/soul left His body and His body was placed in the grave, while His spirit was with the Father.
3. He 'tasted' that separation from God when He was forsaken of the Father. This was a 'taste' of the eternal death, the second death that the unregenerate and unredeemed will experience for all eternity. That will be Hell indeed.

He experienced those 'deaths' (separation) in soul, body and spirit at Calvary! This was for us that we might no longer experience such, but come into resurrection life in our total being (1Thess.5:23).

Jesus also predicted His own resurrection. He told the disciples He would be crucified, buried and raised from the dead. This was his confession of faith in which the Father declared He would raise Him from death, after paying the price of redemption from sin for mankind (Matt.16:21; 17:23; 27:63; Jhn.20:9; Lke.24:7,46; Mrk.9:9-10).

Father, Son and Holy Spirit were each involved in death and resurrection (Jhn.3:16; 10:17; Heb.9:14; Psa.2:7; Acts 13:33; Col.1:18; Acts 2:32; Gal.1:1; Rom.8:11). The resurrection of Christ is founded on the everlasting Covenant in the counsels of the eternal Godhead (Heb.13:20).
- He was resurrected to justify sinners (Rom.4:25).
- He was resurrected to be our Intercessor (Rom.8:34).

- He was resurrected to be Lord of both the dead and the living (Acts 2:29-36; Rom.14:9).
- He was resurrected to be Judge of all mankind (Jhn.5:22-27; Acts 17:30-31; 2Tim.4:1).
- The resurrection is the sure proof of the resurrection of all mankind to come up for judgment (Acts 17:30-31).

There were numerous witnesses of the resurrected Christ. It is not that any person actually SAW Christ raised from the dead, but hundreds SAW the resurrected Christ after He was raised from the dead (Acts 10:41). God showed the resurrected Christ to chosen witnesses. The resurrected Christ was seen of His disciples over some 40 days before His ascension into heaven. Many Scriptures attest to this truth (Jhn.20:17-18; Matt.27:62-66; Lke.24:54-56; 24:1,33-34; Jhn.21:19-24; 1Cor.15:6; Mrk.16:19, etc).

Even in ascension glory, the resurrected Christ was seen in 'post-resurrection' appearances by Stephen, Paul and John (Acts 7:54; Acts 9:7; 22:9; Gal.1:18; Acts 9:1-9; Rev.1:7,10-16).

Every recorded sermon in the Book of Acts is wrapped about the death and resurrection of Christ. It was the cornerstone of all apostolic preaching and teaching. Signs, wonders and miracles were done in the power of the name of the resurrected Son of God. His name would be powerless were He not raised from the dead. A dead man's name does not have living power in it (Acts 4:1-33 with Acts 5:30-32; 13:22-39; 10:38-43; 17:16-33; Rom.10:9-10). If Christ is not risen from the dead, then preaching is all in vain, and we are all as yet dead in our trespasses and sins. Read the great 'Resurrection Chapter' written by Paul (1Cor.15).

Enough has been written on the Doctrine of the Resurrection to reaffirm the believer's faith in Christ, the Son of the Living God. The student is reminded that ALL Millennial Schools have faith in the resurrection of the dead. It is the matter of whether there be one general resurrection of the just and unjust or whether there be two resurrections separated by 1000 years, to which our attention now needs to be given.

E. The Resurrection of the Just and Unjust

In this section of our chapter, attention is given to the two major views of the Millennial Schools. Is there one general resurrection or are there two resurrections, when it comes to the righteous and the unrighteous?

As a reminder:
- Post-Millennialists and A-Millennialists hold that there is one general resurrection of the just and the unjust.
- Historic Pre-Millennialists hold that there are two resurrections, 1000 years apart, called the first and the second resurrections. The Old and New Testament saints are raised at Christ's coming to reign with Him. The wicked dead are raised at the close of the 1000 years and come up for judgment and condemnation.
- Futurists and Dispensationalists hold that there are two resurrections, 1000 years apart between the first and second resurrections. With the demands of this system, however, several resurrections would be required, over some period of time, as seen in the following:
  (a) The resurrection of the saints at the secret rapture, where "the dead in Christ rise first" and "the alive and remaining " are caught up together to meet the Lord in the air. This resurrection is taught to be seven years before the Lord's coming, at the beginning of the Great Tribulation.
  (b) The resurrection of the saints who either died or were martyred during the seven years Tribulation period.
  (c) The resurrection of all who lived and died during the Jewish Millennium, whether good or evil, at the end of the Millennial reign of Christ. This is because this School sees death in the Millennium (Isa.65:20).
  (d) The resurrection of the wicked dead of all ages at the end of the Millennium to appear before the Great White Throne Judgment.
  As can be seen, the Dispensational system requires these several resurrections to justify their teaching
- Christian Millennialism holds the belief that there are two resurrections, the first resurrection of the righteous, and the second resurrection of the unrighteous, the points under discussion in this section.

Our attention and comments need to focus more especially on the Post-Millennial and A-Millennial position of the one general resurrection. The A-Millennial position will take the precedence as to their position and their understanding and interpretation of the controversial passage in Rev.20:1-6 which speaks of "the first" and, by implication, "the second" resurrection.

F. A-Millennialism on Rev.20:4-6

The chief passage of Scripture, and the most controversial passage on "resurrection", used for support of two (or more) resurrections is found in Rev.20:4-6, which is quoted here in full.

"And I saw thrones, and they sat on them, and judgment was committed to them. Then I saw the souls of those who had been beheaded for their witness to Jesus and for the word of God, who had not worshiped the beast or his image, and had not received his mark on their foreheads or on their hands. And they lived and reigned with Christ for a thousand years. But the rest of the dead did not live again until the thousand years were finished. This is the first resurrection. Blessed and holy is he who has part in the first resurrection. Over such the second death has no power, but they shall be priests of God and of Christ, and shall reign with Him a thousand years." (NKJ)

The varying Millennial views about "one general resurrection" and "two resurrections" are based on a person's interpretation and understanding of this passage. It, therefore, necessitates a verse by verse exegesis in an endeavour to understand what John is saying here. John would in no way contradict Paul and Paul and John would in no way contradict what Jesus taught on the resurrection. Let us consider here what A-Millennialism understands this passage to mean. The A-Millennial School practically stands alone in its interpretation of Rev.20:4-6. The salient points of the passage are:

- The ones sitting on thrones, judgment being given to them.
- The souls who have been martyred under the Beast and are now reigning with Christ for a 1000 years, as priests unto God and His Christ.
- The blessed and holy ones in the first resurrection and on whom the second death has no power.
- The rest of the dead who live not again until the 1000 years are fulfilled.
- The 1000 years period of time itself.

Because of some differences among A-Millennialists, one can only quote some brief statements which, at least, will provide some general idea of the position held as to Rev.20:4-6.

Arthur H. Lewis, in "**The Dark Side of the Millennium**" (page 58) writes" "The Christian passes from 'death to life' when he believes, according to John 5:24, and the new life in Christ is frequently called 'a resurrection' (Rom.6:11; Eph.2:4,5; Col.3:1). But here John observed glorified saints who had died yet had remained alive and were able to sing the praises of the Lamb."

In "**A-Millennialism Today**" (pages 100-103), William E.Cox has this to say. "As a result of the first resurrection, and his part in it, the believer has spiritual life (Jhn.5:24); behold, all things have become new (2Cor.5:17); he is now a citizen of heaven (Phil.3:20; Heb.13:14); he has already begun to reign with Christ (Eph.2:6; Col.1:13; Rev.1:6); he has already been delivered from the power of the second death (1Thess.1:10; Rev.20:6). All these blessings will reach fruition at the second resurrection. However, each has already begun as a result of the believer's participation in the first resurrection, i.e., his becoming joint heir with Christ (through the new birth), who Himself is the First Resurrection (Jhn.11:24; 1Cor.15:20)... We are interested in the spiritual resurrection, which we take to be the new birth...Actually, then, our Lord Himself is the First Resurrection. Let us reconcile this statement with our previous statement, that the new birth is the first resurrection for the Christian. Before conversion, every person is spiritually dead (Cf. Eph.2:1,5,6 with 1Jhn.3:14). Paul teaches that the believer is partaker of Christ in the crucifixion and also in His resurrection (Rom.6:6; Col.3:3). Thus, to be born again is to have partaken in the first resurrection" (End quotes).

George L.Murray, in, "**Millennial Studies**" (pages 182-184), has this to say relative to the saints reigning with Christ over the 1000 years. "They (the martyrs) are not dead. They live and reign with Christ. Let it be remembered that John saw only the souls of those martyrs. Their souls lived and reigned with Christ, while their bodies rested in unknown graves, until the resurrection...These passages (Rev.14:4,13) seem to teach that there is a heavenly state of bliss entered by the souls of those who die in the Lord, a state in which they shall live and reign with Christ until the time set by God for Christ to return and reap the harvest of the earth...The foregoing would seem to justify the conviction that John actually saw, and described, the pre-resurrection state of Christ's martyrs...The disembodied souls of this vision lived and reigned with Christ...John describes believers as having been made 'kings and priests'. This is their status in this present life, although their priesthood is more in evidence than their kingship...The reign of these disembodied souls with Christ is said to be for a period of 1000 years...It is the cycle of time extending from our Lord's first advent to the day of His return. It consists of the period during which the souls of the departed saints reign with Christ. That is what they are doing now. This heavenly reign of theirs is described as the first resurrection."

Dr. Louis Berkhof, "**Systematic Theology**" (page 715), writes: "The only Scriptural basis for this theory (of the two resurrections) is Rev.20:4-6, after an Old Testament content has been poured into it. This is a very precarious basis for various reasons.

(1) The passage occurs in a highly symbolical book and is admittedly very obscure, as may be inferred by the different interpretations of it.
(2) The literal interpretation of this passage, as given by Pre-Millennarians, leads to a view that finds no support elsewhere in Scripture, but is even contradicted by the rest of the New Testament. This is a fatal objection. Sound exegesis requires that the obscure passages of Scripture be read in the light of the clearer ones, and **vice versa**.
(3) Even the literal interpretation of the Pre-Millennarians is not consistently literal, for it makes the chain of vs.1 and consequently also the binding in vs.2 figurative, often conceives of the 1000 years as a long but undefined period of time, and changes the souls of vs.4 into resurrection saints.
(4) The passage, strictly speaking, does not say that the classes referred to (the martyr saints and those who did not worship the beast) were raised from the dead, but simply that they lived and reigned with Christ. And this living and reigning with Christ is said to constitute the first resurrection.
(5) There is absolutely no indication in these verses that Christ and His saints are seen ruling on the earth. In the light of such passages as Rev.4:4; 6:9, it is far more likely that the scene is laid in heaven.
(6) It also deserves notice that the passage makes no mention whatever of Palestine, of Jerusalem of the Temple, and of the Jews, the natural citizens of the Millennial Kingdom. There is not a single hint that these are in any way concerned with this reign of a 1000 years" (End quotes).

One more quote from Prof. Floyd E.Hamilton as he writes in "**The Basis of Millennial Faith**" (page 117). "The first resurrection is the new birth of the believer which is crowned by his being taken to heaven to be with Christ in His reign during the interadventual period. This eternal life which is the present possession of the believer, and is not interrupted by the death of the body, is the first resurrection and participation in it is the Millennial reign." He continues:
"In John 5:24-29 we have two resurrections brought together in the same paragraph. 'He that heareth My word, and believeth Him that sent Me, hath eternal life, and cometh not into judgment, but is passed out of death into life. Verily, verily I say unto you, the hour cometh and now is, when the dead shall hear the voice of the Son of God; and they that hear shall live...Marvel not at this: for the hour cometh in which all that are in the tombs shall hear His voice, and shall come forth, they that have done good, unto the resurrection of life; and they that have done evil unto the resurrection of judgment.'
Now, though the word 'first resurrection' is not used in this paragraph, clearly the fact is taught inescapably. What else can we call passing 'out of death into life' but resurrection? Notice that it is contrasted with the resurrection which takes place when the dead bodies of all men are raised. Notice also that it is said that **all** that are in the tombs shall hear the voice of Christ and come forth. Then, as they come forth from the tombs, the separation takes place into the resurrection of life and the resurrection of judgment. The use of these two terms, 'resurrection of life' and 'resurrection of judgment' in connection with the previous statement that **all** hear Christ's voice and come forth for the separation into the resurrection of life and the resurrection of judgment, in no way indicates a separation in time of a 1000 years, as the Pre-Millennialists claim, for it distinctly says that all, good and bad, hear the voice and come forth" (End quotes).

So it is, that "the first resurrection is not to be taken literally, and Rev.20:4-6 in no way supports the Pre-Millennial doctrine of two or more physical resurrections!

Enough quotes have been given to lay out clearly the A-Millennial position on "the first resurrection", the saints who live and reign with Christ for a 1000 years, and what this period of 1000 years is, as being the period of time between Christ's first and second comings.

To summarize the points under discussion, from the A-Millennial aspect:
1. The ones sitting on thrones, judgment being given to them, are the saints of God.
2. The souls who had been martyred and who are reigning with Christ for a 1000 years, as priests to God, are the saints who have died over the centuries and are now in heaven in the intermediate state. They are 'souls' and not 'bodies' that John sees.
3. The first resurrection is the new birth, those who have been regenerated by the Holy Spirit. It is a spiritual resurrection from being dead in trespasses and sins to spiritual life in Christ (Col.2:12; Eph.2:5; Rom.6:4,13; Jhn.11:25-26). These ones are blessed and holy and the second death will have no power over them.
4. The 1000-year period is symbolic of that unknown period of time between the first and second comings of the Lord Jesus Christ.
5. The implied 'second resurrection' is the resurrection of all the dead, the just and the unjust, at the second coming of Christ. All are raised from the dead for one general judgment, at the Great White Throne of God.

For the A-Millennialist, there is one coming of Christ, one general resurrection, and one general judgment of the righteous and unrighteous, the just and the unjust, the good and the evil. Satan is bound in the abyss and the period of time in which the saints reign in heaven is that time between Christ's first coming and His second coming.

It is here, however, that in the understanding and interpretation of Rev.20:4-6 that this writer parts company with the A-Millennial point of view. This necessitates the writer's exegesis of the controversial passage in Revelation.

G. Christian Millennialism on Rev.20:4-6 – The Resurrections

The writer's consideration and response to the A-Millennial point of view is seen in the comments here. These comments are not necessarily in the order as dealt with in the above summary of the A-Millennialist position, though each will be dealt with in the course of our comments.

1. The New Birth – A Resurrection

Most theologians would agree with the A-Millennialist on the fact that the new birth is a spiritual resurrection. The difference would be that they would not designate it as being equated with "the first resurrection".

As already commented on in the first section on "**The Doctrine of the Resurrection**", when God created man, He placed him in an earthly Paradise to enjoy life in fellowship with His Creator. Adam was permitted to eat of all the trees in the Garden, but one. This was the Tree of the Knowledge of Good and Evil. A death penalty was decreed upon man's disobedience to God's one commandment of prohibition (Gen.2:16-17). The moment Adam sinned, he died spiritually. Disobedience brought death on himself and so sin and death have passed onto all mankind (Rom.5:12-21). Adam died physically 930 years later. Since then, all of Adam's race are born "dead in trespasses and sins" (Eph.2:1-6; 1Jhn.3:14; Col.2:13; 3:1; 1Tim.5:6). When a person believes and receives Christ, he passes from 'death to life'. He experiences a spiritual resurrection. He is raised with Christ, who is his life (Col.3:1; Jhn.11:25; 1Jhn.5:12).

Regeneration is a spiritual resurrection by which one is raised to eternal life. No one can raise himself, but Jesus, who is the Resurrection and the Life, raises one from a state of death by faith in His miraculous power. This, however, should not be made, as the A-Millennialist says, "the first resurrection", for reasons which shall be seen.

The major passage of Scripture used by the A-Millennial position to say that the new birth is a believers "first resurrection" – a spiritual resurrection – is found in Jhn.5:24-29; The same passage is also used for the physical resurrection of the just and the unjust. The "first resurrection" is spiritual and the implied "second resurrection" is physical, or, so it is claimed. The passage is quoted here in full.

"Most assuredly, I say to you, he who hears My word and believes in Him who sent Me has everlasting life, and shall not come into judgment, but has passed from death into life.
"Most assuredly, I say to you, the hour is coming, and now is, when the dead will hear the voice of the Son of God; and those who hear will live.
"For as the Father has life in Himself, so He has granted the Son to have life in Himself,
"and has given Him authority to execute judgment also, because He is the Son of Man.
"Do not marvel at this; for the hour is coming in which all who are in the graves will hear His voice and come forth-- those who have done good, to the resurrection of life, and those who have done evil, to the resurrection of condemnation." (NKJ) The passage here speaks of a spiritual resurrection and a physical resurrection. To focus the words more sharply, we place them in two columns accordingly.

A Spiritual Resurrection – Jhn.5:24-27	A Physical Resurrection – Jhn.5:28-29
"Verily, verily, I say to you, **the hour is coming, and now is**, when the dead shall hear the voice of the Son of God, and they that hear shall live. For as the Father has life in Himself, so has He given to the Son to have life in Himself, And has given Him authority to execute judgment also, because He is the Son of Man."	"Marvel not at this: For the hour is coming, in the which **all that are in the graves** shall hear His voice, And shall come forth; they that have done good, unto **the resurrection of life**; and they that have done evil, unto **the resurrection of damnation.**

There is no doubt that Jesus is referring to regeneration, or new birth, which is a spiritual resurrection, in Jhn.5:24-27. Mankind is dead in trespasses and sins. The hour comes, with Christ, and **now is**, in this present time, when those who truly hear His voice in the Gospel, and believe, shall live. They receive eternal life. They are raised to life by the power of the Gospel. This resurrection life is imparted to their spirit and soul. It is NOT a physical resurrection. Read Gen.2:17; Eph.2:1,5,6; 1Jhn.5:12; Col.2:8,13; 1Tim.5:6; 1Jhn.3:14 once again to confirm these things. Note also Jhn.4:20-24, especially vs.23 and the similar expression, "**the hour comes and now is**" when the Father seeks true worshippers. This refers to this present time, this present age, for both true worship and spiritual resurrection to life. With this spiritual resurrection most theologians agree. But to make this "the first resurrection" of Rev.20:4-6 is the point of disagreement. It just does not follow, as will be seen in due time.

2. **The Physical Resurrection**
As the student considers the next couple of verses in the appropriate column, the words distinctly point to a physical resurrection. For the Post-Millennialist and A-Millennialist, this speaks of a bodily and physical resurrection, a general resurrection of the righteous and the unrighteous, of the good and evil. One class is the good and the other is the evil. Without question, this resurrection points to the physical and bodily resurrection. The good have a resurrection to life, and the evil have a resurrection to judgment. Because of these verses here, they see no need, or Scriptural reason or justification, to place a 1000 years between, and make two resurrections out of them. In diagram form, it would be like this.

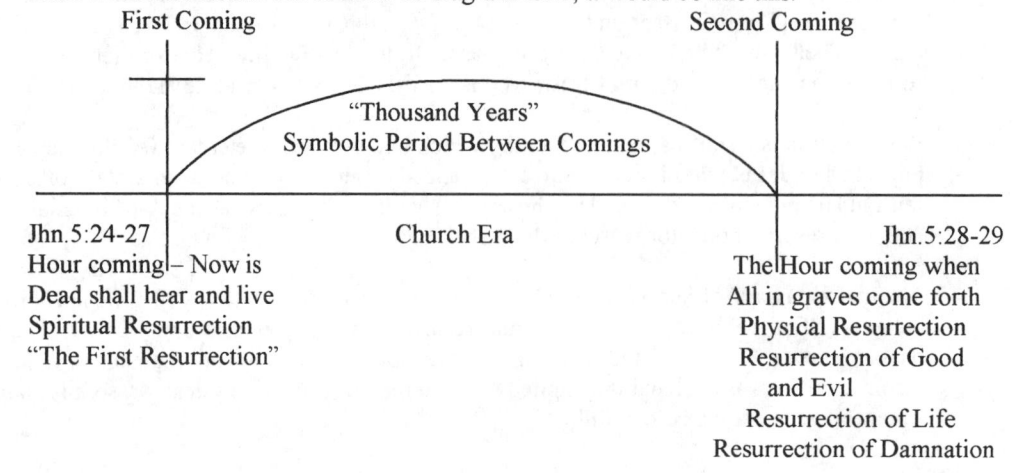

First Coming | Second Coming

"Thousand Years"
Symbolic Period Between Comings

Jhn.5:24-27 | Church Era | Jhn.5:28-29
Hour coming – Now is | | The Hour coming when
Dead shall hear and live | | All in graves come forth
Spiritual Resurrection | | Physical Resurrection
"The First Resurrection" | | Resurrection of Good
 | | and Evil
 | | Resurrection of Life
 | | Resurrection of Damnation

For the A-Millennial and Post-Millennial teachers, John 5:24-29 becomes a foundational passage for understanding and interpreting the Rev.20:4-6 passage.

For this writer, holding a Christian Millennial view, there is more agreement with the Pre-Millennial position, as to these resurrections. That is:

(a) Spiritual Resurrection or New Birth – Jhn.5:24-27
As noted several times, theological students agree with this, but would not identify it as "the first resurrection" of Rev.20:4-6. It is "**a resurrection**", not "**the first** resurrection."

(b) Physical Resurrection – Two Resurrections – Jhn.5:28-29
Whereas the position of the A-Millennialist uses Jhn.5:24-29 to interpret Rev.20:4-6, this writer would use Rev.20 to help interpret Jhn.5. One cannot be used to contradict the other. John wrote both the Gospel and the Revelation. He does not oppose himself. He received things in the Gospel of John. He received further things in Revelation. Revelation cannot be used to contradict John or John to contradict Revelation. Both are part of the whole as given to the Apostle John. The following diagram illustrates this viewpoint.

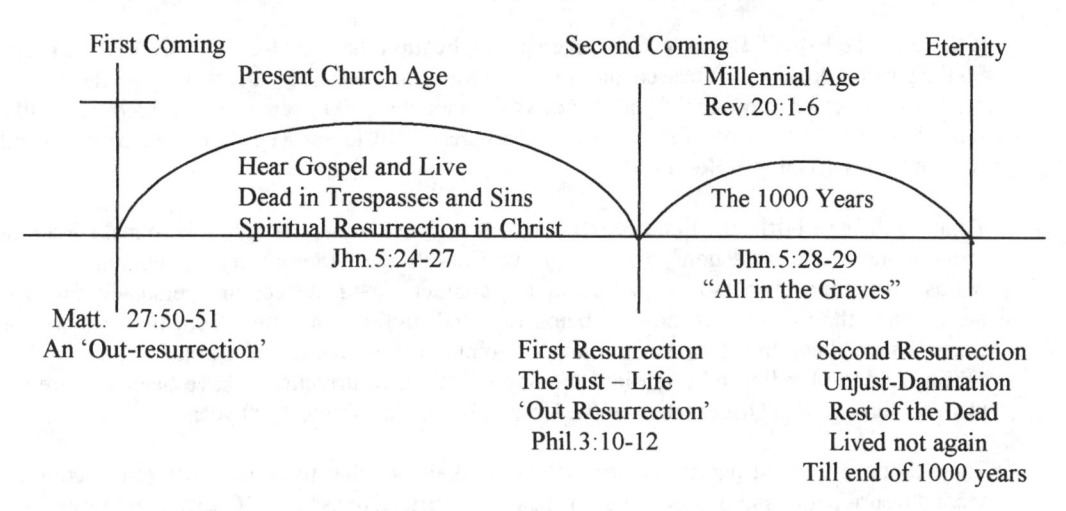

```
First Coming                    Second Coming              Eternity
    |     Present Church Age    |    Millennial Age           |
    |                            |    Rev.20:1-6              |
    |    Hear Gospel and Live    |                            |
    |    Dead in Trespasses and Sins |  The 1000 Years        |
    |    Spiritual Resurrection in Christ |                   |
    |        Jhn.5:24-27         |      Jhn.5:28-29           |
    |                            |     "All in the Graves"    |
  Matt. 27:50-51
  An 'Out-resurrection'        First Resurrection      Second Resurrection
                                The Just – Life         Unjust-Damnation
                                'Out Resurrection'      Rest of the Dead
                                Phil.3:10-12            Lived not again
                                                        Till end of 1000 years
```

It may genuinely be asked: How can placing a 1000 years between resurrections be justified when John places the resurrection of the good and evil all in the one verse? The answer is: John himself does it! While in Jhn.5:27-28, he speaks of the resurrection of the good and evil, in one verse, and either to a resurrection or life or a resurrection of damnation, it is John himself who places a 1000 years between these resurrections in Rev.20:4-6. The two resurrections are implied in Jhn.5:28-29, while they are seen clearly in Rev.20:4-6, by the use of the words "FIRST resurrection", and, by implication "a SECOND Resurrection", where John tells us that "the rest of the dead lived not again until the 1000 years were finished!"

The two resurrections are implied by Jesus in John's Gospel, by Daniel also, by Paul also and then by John himself in Revelation, as the following columns infer.

The First Resurrection	**The Second Resurrection**
1. The Resurrection of the Good – Jhn.5:28-29	1. The Resurrection of the Evil-Jhn.5:28-29
2. The Resurrection to Life	2. The Resurrection to Damnation
3. The Resurrection to Life – Dan.12:2	3. The Resurrection to Shame and Contempt
4. The Resurrection of the Just-Acts 24:15	4. The Resurrection of the Unjust-Acts 24:15
5. Blessed and Holy is he that has part in the First Resurrection.	5. The Rest of the Dead – The Wicked Dead Lived not again – The Second Resurrection
6. They are Kings and Priests to God and reign with Christ a 1000 years	6. Until the 1000 years were fulfilled

John is not confusing what he had written in Jhn.5:24-29 about the spiritual resurrection and making it the first resurrection. John, under inspiration of the Holy Spirit, is giving further revelation about the resurrection. In Jhn.5:28-29, John speaks of the "resurrection to life" and the "resurrection to damnation." The TWO RESURRECTIONS are implicit here. Paul does the same in his writings. Daniel also does the same. In Rev.20:4-6, John defines these resurrections as "the FIRST resurrection", and, by implication, "the SECOND resurrection."

It has been argued that John does not mention the words "second resurrection", and this is read into the passage. The argument from silence is really no argument. The argument is by implication. The writer to Hebrews provides an example, as seen in Heb.8:8,13. When God spoke through Jeremiah of "a NEW Covenant", even though the words "OLD Covenant" are not specifically used, they are there implicitly. "In that He made a **NEW Covenant**, He has made the first **OLD**. Now that which decays and waxes **OLD** is ready to vanish away." In Heb.8:7 is given another example. "For if that **FIRST Covenant** had been faultless, then should no place have been sought for the **SECOND**." In Heb.10:9, he writes, "He took away the **FIRST** (The Old Covenant) to establish the **SECOND** (The New Covenant)."

The same argument, by implication, can be applied also to Rev.20:4-6. It is the Law of Opposites as constantly used in Biblical interpretation. If there is light, then there is darkness. If we are to "put off" the old nature, then we are to "put on" the new nature. If there is "old", then there must be "new", and if there is a "first", then there must be a "second".

If there is "the **FIRST Resurrection**", then by implication there is "the **SECOND Resurrection**". So the passage speaks of "Blessed and holy" are those of the first resurrection, but "the rest of the dead" (the "cursed and unholy") lived not again until the 1000 years were fulfilled, or, until "the second resurrection". This is sound, Biblical exegesis and logic! The first resurrection is indeed "the better resurrection" (Heb.11:35)!

To make the new birth "the first resurrection: - as in A-Millennial thought – is to make it a kind of "continuous first resurrection", all through the Church age, "the present Millennium". In other words, every time any person is born again, it is another "first resurrection", personally for them! It means that "the first resurrection" is being repeated millions of times, from the first coming to Christ's second coming! It makes millions of points of time, instead of a point of time at Christ's coming and the binding of Satan into the abyss. "First resurrections" have been and are taking place all through this Dispensation of the Holy Spirit, the symbolic 1000 years!

The School of thought that this writer belongs to believes that there is a first resurrection and a second resurrection, and that both are physical or bodily resurrections. On what authority or basis can the first resurrection be made a "spiritual resurrection" and the implied second resurrection a "physical resurrection?" This has come about, partially, by re-arranging the order and chapters of the Book of Revelation into "progressive parallelisms", and not reading it as it is written, basically in chronological order – as John is seeing it – like a "continuous Divine video", so to speak.

Instead of reading Revelation Chapters 19,20,21,22 in order, as written, Rev.20:1-6 is taken back to the beginning of the Church era, to the cross, and Satan being 'bound at Calvary' and cast into the abyss back there. If Satan was actually bound back there, then that justifies the theory that "the Millennium" also began back there, and we are now in that Millennium! Also, it would seem to this writer that this is also a reaction against a future "Jewish Millennium". In order to get rid of such an unScriptural kind of Millennium, it seems right to place the Millennium is some other time-zone, rather than the future after Christ comes. The place and time most suitable is the present age, the Church age! But, such an arrangement takes Rev.20 right out of its writing order; that is, after Rev.19, the second coming of the Lord Jesus Christ!

In closing off this section on the "two resurrections", the first and second resurrections, it is worth considering Paul's two passages where he speaks of the resurrection of the saints. In both passages, he speaks only of the resurrection of the people of God. There is no mention of the resurrection of the unrighteous, the wicked or the unjust. If there was (or is) to be one general resurrection, then these two passages would also have been appropriate to mention both groups of mankind; the redeemed or the unredeemed! The matter is, ALL the passages on the doctrine of resurrection need to be brought together, compared and reconciled with each other.

In 1Cor.15:22-26 Paul writes, "For as in Adam all die, even so in Christ shall all be made alive, but each in his own order; Christ the firstfruits, afterwards they that are Christ's at His coming. Then comes the end, when He shall have delivered up the Kingdom to God, even the Father; when He shall have put down all rule and all authority and power. For He must reign, till He has put all enemies under His feet. The last enemy that shall be destroyed is death." The only ones mentioned relative to resurrection here is "they that are Christ's" – the believers only. There is no mention of the wicked coming up in resurrection in their order. John does this for us in Revelation, where he says "the rest of the dead (the wicked dead) lived not again until the 1000 years were fulfilled".

Another passage Paul deals with relative to the resurrection of the saints is found in 1Thess.4:13-18. There he writes that "the dead in Christ shall rise first, then we which are alive and remain unto the coming of the Lord shall be caught up together with them to meet the Lord in the air, and so shall we ever be with the Lord." There is no mention of "the dead who are NOT in Christ". There is no mention of the wicked dead noted here. It is to do with the saints in Christ, dead or living. Paul would not have forgotten that he spoke in Acts 24:15 of a "resurrection of the just and of the unjust". Here in Thessalonians he is encouraging the saints concerning **their** resurrection at Christ's coming, the same as he does in Corinthians. "The rest of the dead (the wicked dead) lived not again until the 1000 years were finished". This is John's word concerning the resurrection of the saints and the sinners, the righteous and the unrighteous.

In Luke 14:14 Jesus speaks about being recompensed at "the resurrection of the just", but, in this account, "the unjust" are not mentioned, as they are in other passages.

H. Christian Millennialism on Rev.20:4-6 – The Souls Reigning
Because of their inter-relatedness with "resurrection", attention needs now to be given to "the souls reigning with Christ for 1000 years".

There are some slight variations among A-Millennialists as to "the souls who live and reign with Christ" over the 1000-year period, the period between the first and second coming of Christ. According to their teaching, Satan was bound in the abyss at Christ's coming, on Calvary. The 1000-year symbolic Millennium began at His first coming also. The souls who live and reign with Christ also began at His first coming, and continues over Church History through to Christ's second advent.

Some A-Millennialists point to the fact that this living and reigning with Christ is right here on **earth**, as victorious Christians reign over the world, the flesh and the Devil. Some A-Millennialists teach that this living and reigning with Christ takes place in **heaven** the moment a Christian dies and goes to be with the Lord. The same basic Scriptures that speak of the saints "reigning in life" are used for both positions (Refer Rom.12:21; Rev.14:1; 5:9-10; 1:6; 1Jhn.5:4; 2:14; Rom.5:17; Lke.10:19).

The view is held that the passage in Revelation speaks of "**souls**" that lived and are reigning, not "**bodies**" reigning. Therefore, it is a spiritual resurrection, not a physical or bodily resurrection that is meant here. A serious consideration, however, of WHO these "souls" are provide some clue as to WHEN "they lived and reigned with Christ for a 1000 years". It seems that there could be two groupings of people mentioned in Rev.20:4.

1. **The "They" Company of Saints**
   The Scripture says, "And I saw thrones, and they sat upon them, and judgment was given unto them." The Amplified says, "Then I saw thrones, and sitting on them were those to whom authority to act as judges and pass sentence was entrusted…"

2. **The "Souls" Company of Saints**
   "And I saw the souls of them that were beheaded for the witness of Jesus and for the Word of God, and which had not worshipped the Beast, neither his image, neither had received his mark on their foreheads or in their hands; and they lived and reigned with Christ a 1000 years (Rev.20:4b). The Amplified says, "Also I saw the souls of those that had been slain with axes (beheaded) for their witnessing to Jesus, and for preaching and testifying the Word of God, and who had refused to pay homage to the Beast or his statue and had not accepted his mark or permitted it to be stamped on their forehead or on their hands. And they lived and ruled with Christ, the Messiah, a 1000 years."

There are the "they" sitting on thrones, and the "souls" of the martyrs who lived again and reigned with Christ. Identification of the both classes are saints of God, whether it be "they" or "souls". Whether there are two companies of saints here or not, they are all the people of God. They are His and they are one with God through Christ.

The identification of the "souls" should not be difficult. There should be no mistaking who they are. The "time element" of their sufferings has been identified for us. That is, it was during the period of time in which THE BEAST, the Antichrist, ruled and reigned. In our chapter on "**Daniel's Seventy Weeks Prophecy**" this reign was dealt with. The reign of the Antichrist is simply 3½ years at the end of this age, and immediately prior to the second coming of Christ. It is the final half of Daniel's seventieth week. It is the time when the False Prophet instituted the worship of Antichrist's image, and the receiving of the Mark of the Beast, on pain of martyrdom. All who would not bow to his image, take his mark, number or name in their hand or forehead, would be killed. The details of these things are covered in Rev.13,14,15,16 chapters. These "souls" are the tribulation saints, the martyrs of the reign of Antichrist.

It is the final half of the seventieth week prophecy of Daniel. It is at the close of the Church age, preceding the coming of the Lord Jesus Christ. **THAT is the 'time element'** – NOT at the first coming of Christ, or at the beginning of some symbolic 1000 year period. If this was what took place at the first coming of Christ, then who was "the Beast" and "the False Prophet" back there? For, when Christ came on the white horse, He cast them both into the Lake of Fire for eternity! This act is seen taking place in Rev.19:11-21, not in Rev.20, for there, those who did not have their names in the Book of Life were cast into the Lake of Fire, "where the Beast and the False Prophet are". Also, what was "the Mark of the Beast" back there at Christ's first coming if these "souls" were slain there and have been throughout this Church era? To avoid clear answers to these things, many times a kind of allegorization or spiritualization is resorted to, and all these things become 'figurative', not having any actualities of some kind!

These "souls" that lived were the martyrs of the 3½ years reign of the Beast. There can be no honest way of exegesis to say these "souls" are simply those believers who have conquered "the Beast system" of Church History, the symbolic 1000 years and are now ruling and reigning with Christ in heaven!

As seen in our chapters on "Tribulation", "Antichrist" and "Daniel's Seventy Weeks Prophecy", the 3½ years is at the end of the age. These "souls" are martyred during this time, at the close of this age. These "souls" live and reign with Christ at the end of the 3½ years. This is the first resurrection. The 1000 years follows the 3½ years, at Christ's advent. The Millennium follows the reign of the Beast. A-Millennial teaching makes the 3½ years a symbolic period of time, also covering the whole of the Church age. The Beast is symbolic of the Antichrist system. The 1000 years is made to be symbolic of the Church age. By over-symbolization, events in Revelation are made to fit in with the symbolic time-period of the Millennium between Christ's first and second comings.

It bears repeating again. A-Millennialists hold that when these "souls lived and reigned with Christ" it was a spiritual resurrection – new birth – and constitutes the "first resurrection". The emphasis is that the first resurrection is **spiritual** and the second resurrection is **physical**. In order to be consistent in exegesis, it ought to be said, if the first resurrection is spiritual, then, so the second resurrection should be spiritual. Or, if the second resurrection is physical, so the first resurrection should be physical. This would be consistency, at least!

Most Greek expositors admit that the same Greek thought used in "**lived**" to speak of resurrection is also used in "**lived not again**", pointing to a physical first and second resurrection. If the first resurrection is new birth, why not make the second resurrection the same? Consistency of thought in Revelation makes both resurrections either spiritual or physical. The only way this is done is by using Jhn.5:24-29 to interpret Rev.20:4-6 and make the first resurrection a spiritual one, by new birth.

We note a number of things said about these "souls" in the particular passage here.

1. These **souls** had been beheaded (been axed). That is, they had been slain bodily, or physically beheaded. They had been martyred.
2. These **souls** were beheaded for (a) the witness of Jesus, and for (b) the Word of God (Compare Rev.6:9; 12:17).
3. These **souls** had not (a) Worshipped the Beast, nor (b) Worshipped his image.
4. These **souls** have not received the Mark of the Beast in their forehead or their hand.
5. These **souls** lived and reigned with Christ over the 1000 years.
6. These **souls** were in the first resurrection.
7. These **souls** do not suffer the second death. They had experienced physical death, martyrdom, under the Antichrist in the last 3½ years tribulation.
8. These **souls**, being in the first resurrection, were blessed and holy. Amplified says, "Blessed (happy, to be envied) and holy – spiritually whole, of unimpaired innocence and proved virtues – is the person who takes part (shares) in the first resurrection."
9. These **souls** became kings and priests to God and Christ, and reign with Him over the 1000 years. That is, they were part of the Order of Melchisedek, as seen in Rev.1:6; 5:9-10 with Heb.7. "If we suffer with Him, we shall also reign with Him" (2Tim.2:12 with Isa.61:16; 1Pet.2:5,9.

We take these "**souls**" to be "**persons**" who have been resurrected and they live and reign with Christ in the Millennial Kingdom, and not just speaking of the human soul after death. Although the word "soul" may speak of the human soul (or spirit) after death, it also is used in numerous occasions as "persons" – living, human beings. So in Noah's ark, there were few, "that is, **eight souls** saved by water" (1Pet.3:20). And on the Day of Pentecost, "**three thousand souls**" were added to the Church; that is, three thousand living, human beings (Acts 2:41). The things that are spoken about the "souls" in Revelation are most suitable to be applied to people who have been raised from the dead physically in the first resurrection, and now live and reign with Christ in His Kingdom.

I. Dispensationalism on the Resurrections

A few comments need to be made as to the Futurist/Dispensationalist teaching on the Resurrection. The several resurrections mentioned at the beginning of this chapter, as to the Dispensational view, need proper re-evaluation. If there is no "secret rapture", then there is no extra "first resurrection" seven years before Christ returns. If there is only one coming of the Lord, for and with His saints, then there is no need for another resurrection to raise the Tribulation saints. If there is but one FIRST resurrection, then ALL the righteous dead are raised at Christ's advent, whether Old Testament saints, and all the New Testament saints, right to the last of the saints from the Tribulation period. Seeing the resurrection of "the dead in Christ", and the rapture of the living saints with them, taking place at the coming of Christ, this fulfills the FIRST RESURRECTION and there is, therefore no need to add any 'extra resurrections'.

Summary of Order of Events:

In bringing this lengthy chapter to a conclusion, and because of the inter-relatedness of end-time events up to and at the second coming, it will be helpful to provide some outline of the order of events to Christ's return. It has to be kept in mind that, in dealing with second coming events, John does not bring all the Scriptures pertaining to them and write them in Revelation. But, the details of which Jesus speaks, and the Synoptic Gospels, as well as Paul's writings – these details have to be brought together in harmony with John's writings. This has to be done without any contradiction of events. So, although John tells us Jesus comes the second time riding on the white horse (Rev.19:11-21), he does not bring in and write down all the details that, for instance, Paul writes. John does not say about "the shout, the voice of the archangel, the trump of God" as well as what Jesus said about "the holy angels, the glory of the Father" and so on. Yet we know those details belong to the actual second coming. It is the work and art of the interpreter is to bring all these details together in the advent of Christ, without forcing the parts, distorting the picture or contradicting anything in the Scriptures about Christ's advent. Following is set out some reasonable outline and order of events at Christ's coming. A number of these have been covered in the various chapters of our text.

1. Christ's second coming is seen as the rider on the white horse (Rev.19:11-14). He comes with the armies of heaven, the angels and the saints (Matt.16:27; 25:31; 26:64; Mrk.8:38; Lke.9:36; Dan.7:10; Zech.14:5; Jude 14-15).

2. The Antichrist and his armies are defeated and destroyed by the sword of His mouth. Antichrist is paralyzed by the brightness of Christ's coming (Rev.19:15-21 with 2Thess.2:1-12).

3. The Antichrist and the False Prophet are taken and cast alive into the Lake of Fire of brimstone (Rev.19:20 with Rev.14:9-11).

4. Satan is arrested, bound and hurled into the Bottomless Pit, or the Abyss, and his prison is sealed. He is locked up there for a 1000 years. He can no longer deceive the nations. All loose and fallen angels and demonic spirits are representatively bound with him also (Rev.20:1-3). Note: Satan is not cast into the Lake of Fire until the end of the 1000 years, after the Great White Throne Judgment. The Antichrist and the False Prophet have already been there 1000 years, having been thrown alive into it at Christ's coming. Compare with Rev.19:20 with Rev.20:10.
A-Millennialists hold that the beginning of the symbolic 1000 years was at Christ's first coming. Antichrist and the False Prophet are thrown in the Lake of Fire at Christ's second coming. Then it needs to be explained how Satan can be cast in the Lake of Fire at the end of the 1000 years, where the Antichrist and the False Prophet have been for this 1000 years already!

The Beast and the False Prophet are cast into the Lake of Fire when Christ comes riding on the white horse. Is this the first or second coming? Most expositors see Rev.19:11-21 as Christ's second coming. It is at His second coming that the Satanic trinity is dealt with by Christ, not at His first coming!

- The Beast, the Antichrist, is cast alive into the Lake of Fire (Rev.19:20).
- The False Prophet is cast alive into the Lake of Fire (Rev.19:20).
- The Devil or Satan is cast alive into the Bottomless Pit, the Abyss (Rev.20:11). The Beast and the False Prophet are eternally judged in the Lake of Fire at **the beginning** of the 1000 years, at Christ's coming again. The Devil, however, is eternally judged and cast into the Lake of Fire after the Great White Throne Judgment at **the end** of the 1000 years Millennial Kingdom.

Their eternal judgments are the same, in the Lake of Fire, but these judgments are 1000 years apart. The places also differ for the 1000 years. The Beast and False Prophet are cast alive straight into Gehenna, the Lake of Fire, but not into the Bottomless Pit or the Abyss. The Devil is cast into the Bottomless Pit for the 1000 years, at the beginning of the 1000 years. There are two different places of judgment and confinement for the Satanic trinity. At the end of the 1000 years, the evil trio are all seen in the same place of judgment and confinement for all eternity!

5. The first resurrection, the resurrection of the righteous takes place, along with the rapture of the living saints. There are a number of significant events that take place at Christ's coming. It should be remembered that a number of these take place simultaneously. Paul provides us with some sort of order in his Thessalonian Epistles.

- The Lord comes from heaven with a shout, with the voice of the archangel (possibly, Michael), with the trump of God (1Thess.4:13-16 with Matt.24:29-30).
- The dead in Christ rise first (1Thess.4:16; 1Cor.15:23; Rev.11:15-19). They rise at the trump of God, the seventh trump, which is the last trump. This is the first resurrection. It will include all the righteous dead from Adam down to the last tribulation saint or martyr. All the dead in Christ, all believers of all ages who have died in faith, will be raised at this time – the first resurrection. They will receive a resurrected and glorified body like unto the Lord's (Phil.3:20-21; 1Cor.15). These are the "they" and the "souls" who lived again in Rev.20:4. The qualifications for those being in the first resurrection are that they are "blessed and holy" (Rev.20:4-6).

    Note: There is no resurrection or rapture until Christ's coming again. To have another or extra resurrection and a secret rapture seven years before Christ's advent is to have another or 'extra first resurrection'. This has been mentioned previously. Christ's coming, His actual revelation, is at the close of 3½ years tribulation, when the events noted here take place.

    The first resurrection includes all those who refused to take the Mark of the Beast in the tribulation period. They loved not their lives unto death (Rev.12:11). The first resurrection includes all the saints of Old and New Testament times who died in faith that they might receive "a better resurrection" (Heb.11:13-16,32-40). The first resurrection is the 'out-from-among-the-dead', or 'the out-resurrection' that Paul looked for (Phil.3:9-11). The first resurrection saints are called "the children of the resurrection". They neither marry nor are given in marriage, neither can they die any more. They are like the angels and are the children of the resurrection. Abraham, Isaac and Jacob and the other patriarchs will all be raised in this first resurrection; the physical, bodily resurrection of glorification (Lke.20:27-38).

6. The rapture of the living saints. Paul continues to say that, after the dead in Christ are raised, then those who are alive and remaining to the coming of the Lord, will be caught up (Lit. "seized up, snatched up, raptured") to meet the Lord in the air (1Thess.4:17-18). It is here we have the first resurrection of "the dead in Christ", and the rapture of the living saints, those saints still alive at Christ's coming. The coming of Christ, the first resurrection of the dead saints and the rapture of the living saints all take place in the same period of time – that is, simultaneously! Together, both companies of saints are translated to meet the Lord in the air and will be for ever with the Lord!

Who are the saints who are still alive at the coming of the Lord? Who are the saints who experience rapture and translation without dying? It is the Church, the Bride of Christ, preserved during the 3½ years tribulation, these are the ones still alive at His coming. There may be other saints that have escaped the sword of the Antichrist who are alive at His coming (Rev.12:1-17; 13:7-10; 14:12-13; 16:15).

All the resurrected dead in Christ will receive an incorruptible body. All the living in Christ will receive a glorified body. At the coming of Christ, "this corruption will put on incorruption, and this mortal will put on immortality" (1Cor.15:51-57). Here death is swallowed up in victory. Here death loses its sting, which is sin. The dead in Christ are the "corruptible, who put on incorruption". The living in Christ are the "mortal who put on immortality". Mortality is swallowed up of life, for which all believers receive the earnest of the Spirit (2Cor.5:1-5). This is the redemption of the body that Paul spoke about (Rom.8:23 with Eph.1:13-14; 4:30).

Then follows the Millennial Kingdom order, where the saints possess the Kingdom. This, however, is to be developed more fully in Part Three of our text.

7. At the close of the 1000 years, the second resurrection takes place, and this of the wicked. The whole purpose of resurrection is for all to appear at the Great White Throne Judgment. There eternal destines of the wicked are settled forever! But this brings us to our next chapter on "**The Judgments**".

Once more it is good to remind the reader that, all Schools believe in the Doctrine of the Resurrection, so this is not the issue. The issue is the difference as to the time of the resurrection, whether it is one general resurrection, or two resurrections 1000 years apart. It is to be hoped that this chapter has addressed these things.

The following diagram illustrates the summary order of events as outlined here (Not to scale).

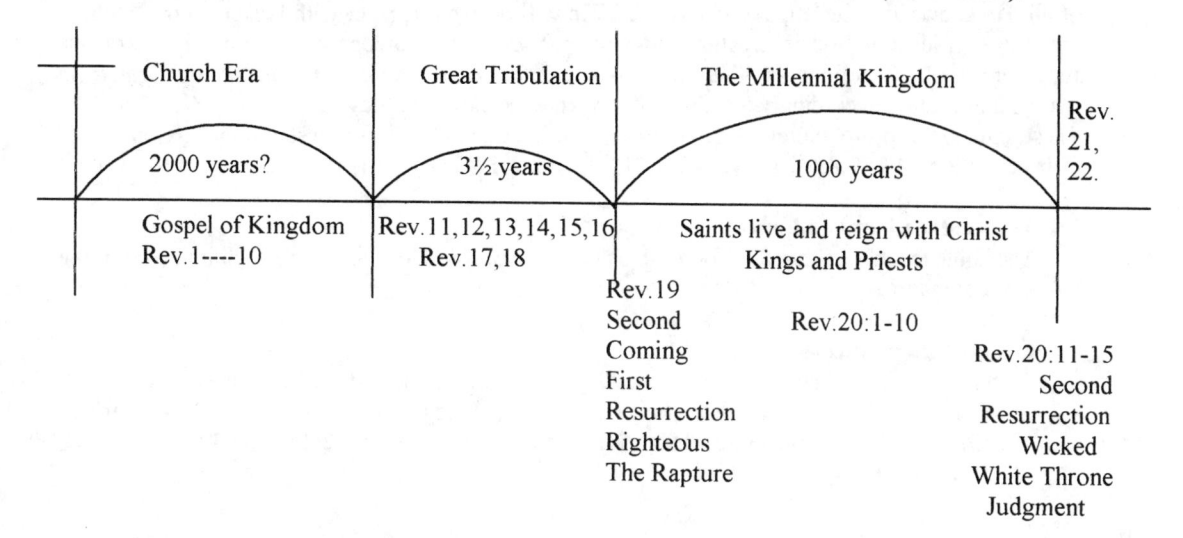

Church Era	Great Tribulation	The Millennial Kingdom	
2000 years?	3½ years	1000 years	Rev. 21, 22.
Gospel of Kingdom Rev.1----10	Rev.11,12,13,14,15,16 Rev.17,18	Saints live and reign with Christ Kings and Priests	
		Rev.19 Second Coming First Resurrection Righteous The Rapture	Rev.20:1-10	Rev.20:11-15 Second Resurrection Wicked White Throne Judgment

CHAPTER THIRTEEN

THE JUDGMENT

When it comes to the subject of "The Judgment", the Millennial Schools fall, once again, into two major categories, as the reader is reminded in brief here.

Historic Pre-Millennialists, Futurists and Dispensationalists each believe in a judgment at the beginning and end of the Millennial Kingdom. The first judgment is for the righteous and the final judgment is for the wicked, at the end of the Millennium. For the Dispensational School, however, the teaching involves anywhere from five to seven judgments. These are spelt out more especially in the Scofield Reference Bible. There are, however, variations as to the number of these judgments within the Dispensational School of thought. The reader is referred to comments on Dispensational Pre-Millennialism in Part I, Ch.2.

The Post-Millennialist and A-Millennialist teach that there is one general judgment, which follows on the one general resurrection, considered in our previous chapter. The position of this writer – a Christian Millennialist – is developed and set out in this chapter.

Following the same approach in this chapter as on "**The Resurrection**", we consider "**The Doctrine of Eternal Judgment**", and then conclude with the "Final Judgments" of the righteous and the unrighteous. Through the course of our study, some areas of Dispensational teaching will be considered as to its proper validity.

A. The Doctrine of Eternal Judgment

The writer to the Hebrews, in listing out "the First Principles of the Doctrine of Christ", speaks of the fifth and sixth principles as "the Resurrection" and "Eternal Judgment" (Heb.5:12-6:2). Both of these doctrines are foundational principles of the oracles of God. There are several aspects of Divine Judgment in the Word of God, as will be set forth in this chapter, but there is a final judgment, which is declared to be "**Eternal Judgment**."

The very fact that God is just, righteous and holy in His nature and being, demands that God judge all unrighteousness in His creatures. The whole purpose of the resurrection of all mankind is for judgment. Resurrection precedes judgment. Judgment follows resurrection (Acts 24:25; 17:30-31). It is appointed unto man once to die, and after death, the judgment (Heb.9:27).

All things foreign to God and things pertaining to sin and Satan are judged eternally by God. A Judge is one who speaks with authority because of discerning right from wrong. One who hears, sees, perceives, discerns is the one who the ability to judge. God Himself is the true and final Judge of all. There is no possible chance of mistaken judgment, for all the facts of every case are clearly before Him. There is no possible chance of deception. God is just. God is righteous. God is holy. God is love. He is omnipotent, omnipresent, and omniscient. He can do all things. He is everywhere present at all times. He sees all things. His justice and judgments are perfect. As Judge of all, He knows all, sees all, and discerns all. He will do what is right with His creatures. He will not judge or deal with His creatures in any manner that is inconsistent with His character. Judgment has been defined as "that which is sifted, discerned thoroughly; discerning right from wrong, and dealing accordingly; or, the sentence and decision of a Judge."
These sample Scripture references ought to be read in conjunction with these thoughts (Gen.18:25; Heb.12:23; Psa.94:2; 9:8; 96:13; 98:9; Jer.11:20; 1Pet.1:17; Psa.89:14; 19:7-9).

1. The Godhead and Judgment
The Bible teaches us that the Godhead, as Father, Son and Holy Spirit are each involved in the work of judgment.

- **God the Father is Judge**
  God is a God of law and order. His ways, His statutes and commandments will be upheld, and any violation of these things is open to judgment, as these Scriptures affirm (Psa.50:6; 75:7; Isa.33:22; 1Sam.2:10; Psa.110:6; 82:8; Isa.2:4; Rom.3:6; 1Cor.5:13; Rev.6:10; Isa.30:18).

- **The Son of God is Judge**
  The Scriptures are too many to quote. These sample Scriptures clearly teach that the Father has committed all judgment over to His Son (Mic.5:1; 4:3; 2Tim.4:1,8; Jas.5:9; Isa.11:1-10; Jhn.5:22-30; 8:15-16,26,50; 12:47-48). Jesus Himself says that the Father judges no man, but has committed all judgment over to the Son. And again, even the Son Himself judges no one, but **The Word** that He has spoken will judge us in that day. Why? For it is the Word of the Father which Jesus has spoken. As the perfect Judge, He will not judge after the sight of His eyes, or the hearing of His ears, nor after the flesh, for He is not judging after the natural senses. He will judge righteously, and that by the Spirit (Acts 17:31; Rom.2:16; 1Pet.4:5-6; 1Cor.4:4; 11:31-32; Rev.19:11; Isa.9:6-7; 42:1-4; Jer.33:15; Jhn.9:39). Christ has been ordained of the Father to be the Judge of all men in the appointed day (Acts 17:30-31; Heb.9:27).

- **The Holy Spirit is Judge**
  The Holy Spirit is not only the Spirit of Grace, He is also the Spirit of Judgment and Burning (Isa.4:4; Jhn.16:7-11). The Holy Spirit comes to convict the world of sin, and of righteousness and of judgment (Acts 24:24-25). He is the one who convicts, reproves, judges sin, speaking of righteousness, and judgment to come. The judgment of the Holy Spirit is according to the Word of Christ, which is the Father's Word!

B. **Two Aspects of Divine Judgment**
The Bible also shows that are two major aspects of Divine judgment in His dealings with mankind; that is, the aspects of restoration and damnation.

1. **Judgment unto Restoration**
   This aspect of judgment is corrective. It is Divine discipline, with a view to restoration. God judges us with a view to our restoration to Himself through redemption. God chastises, punishes and corrects, even as a father does His own children, in order that He may restore man to fellowship with Himself (Read 1Cor.5:1-5,12,13; 6:1-11; 11:23-32; 1Pet.4:17; Gal.6:1). One can read the Letters to the Seven Churches and see the Lord's desire to restore His Church where sin is dealt with (Rev.1-2-3).

2. **Judgment unto Damnation**
   This judgment is punitive, final, and unto damnation. If man refuses God's judgment in this world, and continues wilfully in sin and lawlessness, then there is only one alternative in judgment. That is, eternal judgment unto damnation in the world to come. This judgment is eternal and fixed. It is unchangeable when once executed by God (1Pet.4:17-18; Jhn.5:24-29; 1Cor.11:31-32. Amp.NT; Jhn.3:36; Isa.66:24; Rev.14:9-11). This judgment will be executed on the Day of Judgment, as will be seen in the final section of our study here. If God spared not his wrath when His only Son was made sin for us, what will those who are wilful and rebellious experience when they reject God's Son? If people reject restoration, the only other alternative is damnation!

C. **Examples of Divine Judgment**
There are numerous examples of Divine judgment recorded in the Word, and all have been set forth as examples unto us, and they are written for our admonition (1Cor.10:1-10; Jude 7). The Prophet Isaiah says, "When Your judgments are in the earth, the inhabitants of the earth will learn righteousness…" (Isa.26:8-9).

1. **In Eden's Garden**
   In Gen.3:1-24, we have the entrance of sin, and God's first pronounced judgments. Note the order here.
   - Judgment on the serpent – the curse uttered upon Satan. The serpent in creation is evidence spiritually of the Divine judgment. The curse and judgment was uttered on the very source and fountainhead of sin (Rev.20:11-15).
   - Judgment on the man – the head of the human race. Not a curse, but judgment of sweat and toil in his labour, unto death. "In Adam all die."
   - Judgment on the woman – the first sinner, deceived by the serpent into sin. Judgment by sorrow, subjection and in childbirth.

- Judgment on the earth – earth is cursed with thorns and thistles, and the animal creation is affected also.

Note: There is a judgment unto damnation upon the Serpent, Satan; his head is to be crushed (Gen.3:15 with Rev.20:1-15). And there is a judgment unto restoration available for the man and the woman (Gen.3:15,22-24; Rev.12).

2. **In Noah's Day** – judgment came upon the world of ungodly flesh by the Flood (Gen.6-8).
3. **In the Tower of Babel** – judgment came on lawlessness by the confusion of tongues and the scattering of Noah's sons (Gen.10-11).
4. **In Sodom and Gomorrah** – God judged these twin cities with fire and brimstone (Gen.18 with Jude 7).
5. **In the Nation of Egypt** – Ex.6:6; 7:4; 12:12; Acts 7:7. The ten plagues were the judgments of God on the gods of Egypt, seeking to bring the nation to repentance, as well as the release of Israel.
6. **In Babylon** – God judged the great city of Babylon (Dan.5 with Jer.50-51).
7. **On Cain** – Cain was judged by God placing a mark on him as he went out from the presence of the Lord (Gen.4).
8. **On Achan** – God judged Achan and his family for their sins (Josh.7).
9. **On Korah and his company** – Read Num.16 with Psa.106:30. God judged this rebellion.
10. **On Golden Calf worshippers** - Ex.31-32-33. God judged idolaters by death.
11. **On Israel and Judah** – The two houses of Israel and Judah were judged by God under the Assyrian and the Babylonian Captivities. The curses of the law came on the nations for their disobedience (Deut.27-28). The Fall of Jerusalem in AD.70 was also Divine judgment (Matt.24:1-3; Lke.21:20-24).
12. **On Uzziah** – In 2Chron.26 is the account of Uzziah's judgment with leprosy for presumption.
13. **On the Sorcerer** – Acts 13:11. Paul smote him with blindness because of his resistance.
14. **On the whole world** - when Christ returns the second time, it will be a time of judgment on the whole world (2Thess.1:7-10).

The Scriptures abound with examples of Divine judgment. There is (1) personal judgment, and (2) local judgment, as well as (3) worldwide judgment, all of which took place right here in this life. But, **Eternal Judgment** speaks especially of that final judgment, yet to come, all of these previous judgments being pointers to that final judgment of God!

Mankind, individually and collectively, have been in God's Courtroom. The verdict of "Guilty" has been declared. The death penalty has been pronounced. Mankind has been convicted by the evidence, the testimony of the witnesses, and now the sentence has to be executed. But, God, through Christ, comes in grace and offers to pay the penalty for man's sin, to bear the death-sentence, which is on mankind. It is entirely of grace. There is nothing in man to deserve, to earn or merit it. It is all of grace. Man can either accept it or reject it. This is the story of the Book of Romans (Rom.1-5 chapters).

The Bible, as a whole, therefore, speaks of a threefold judgment relative to all mankind: Judgment Past, Judgment Present and Judgment Future. Our considerations are given to this now.

D. Judgment Past
As far as the believer in Christ is concerned, he has already been judged. This what may be called "judgment past." Christ was judged for our sin at Calvary (Jhn.3:16-18,36; 5:24; Rom.5:16,18; Jhn.16:7-11).
The Scriptures clearly show this truth. Note especially the Amp.NT., on Jhn.3:18. "He who believes on Him – who clings to, trusts in, relies on Him – **is not judged** – he who trusts in Him **never comes up for judgment** – for him there is no rejection, no condemnation, he incurs no damnation. But he who does not believe, nor cleave to, rely on, trust in Him, **is judged already**: he **has already been convicted**, has **already received his sentence**, because he has not believed on and trusted in the Only Begotten Son of God – he is condemned for refusing to let his trust rest in Christ's name" (Note also Jhn.18-11).

Thus the one who receives Christ as his Saviour, his Mediator, Barrister and Solicitor, does not come into judgment, but passes from death to life. The sentence has been executed on Christ, his substitute. The death penalty has been carried out. The Law of God is satisfied, its demands have been paid. Judgment has been executed (Rom.2:2,3; 5:16; Acts 8:33; Heb.9:27; Jhn.18:28-33). Christ has borne the judgment that was due to us.

This judgment is past. This judgment is as a sinner, in the cross. The repentant thief on his cross is typical of the repentant sinner, who believes on Christ, and thus passes out of death into life, from judgment and condemnation into salvation. The unrepentant thief is judged already, already convicted, and already has received his sentence. He is already condemned because he believes not on the Son of God. He will come into "Eternal Judgment" (Rom.8:34; 1Cor.11:32; Jhn.3:17-18; Acts 13:27; Psa.109:31). "There is now no condemnation (judgment) to them which are IN Christ Jesus" (Rom.8:1).

E. Judgment Present

There is also a judgment that is going on now; it is a "present judgment." The believer's judgment for SIN is PAST, and this was settled on the cross of Calvary. Here we were dealt with as **sinners,** but judgment present is in relation to our position as **sons** of God by new birth. The believer is not made perfect by new birth, and therefore still has the tendency to sin. This involves confession of the Lord Jesus Christ (1Jhn.2:1; 1Jhn.1:9). Christ is the believer's Advocate. This "present judgment" involves chastening from the Lord oftentimes for unconfessed sins (Heb.12:5-11). The Lord deals with us in chastisement as His sons.

Paul writes to the Corinthians, "If we would judge ourselves, we would not be judged, but when we are judged, we are chastened of the Lord that we should not be condemned (judged) with the world."

This 'self-judgment' is symbolized in the Tabernacle of Moses, in the Brazen Laver. Brass speaks of judgment against sin. The Brazen Altar symbolized judgment past; the Brazen Laver typifies judgment present. The Priest had been dealt with as a sinner at the Brazen Altar, where the sacrificial substitute had been offered, where the blood was shed. This was fulfilled in Jesus Christ as our sacrifice. But now, the Priest must judge himself, lest he be judged, by the daily washings and cleansing at the water of the Brazen Laver (1Jhn.5:7-8). Sin had been dealt with, but now 'self' must be dealt with. Both these articles were of brass, both concerned judgment, but the first was as a sinner, and then the second as a son (Ex.30:17-21; Jhn.13:1-26).

This "present judgment" of the believer is a very important one, and will save the believer from much in the judgment to come, the future judgment (Read 1Cor.11:23-32; 1Cor.5; 1Pet.4:17; 1Tim.5:24. Amp.NT). This present judgment is in relation to the Lord's people (Heb.10:30-31; Psa.50:4,5). In 1Cor.10 Paul gives us various examples of Divine judgment on the Lord's people as the chosen nation of Israel. They are all set forth as warnings and admonitions for us, examples and types unto the Church, as well as to the believer personally.

Because of the importance of this "present judgment" of the believer, which is so often overlooked by preachers and teachers, further consideration is given in the following comments.

(a) The Lord shall judge His people

Peter tells us that judgment must begin at the house of God (1Pet.4:17), and if the righteous scarcely be saved, where will the sinner and the ungodly appear? There are numerous Scriptures which speak of the Lord judging His people, discerning what is right and wrong and dealing with His people as necessary (Dt.32:36; Psa.7:8,11; 50:4; 54:1; 72:1-4; 135:14; 9:1-4,8; 26:1; 67:4; Jas.2:12-13; Isa.1:27; 3:13-14; 4:4; 28:5-6; 33:5; Mal.3:1-6; Jhn.16:8-11). The Lord loves His people as they are, but He loves them too much to leave them as they are. His work is to purify and sanctify to Himself a holy people for His name.

(b) The High Priest in Israel

In Israel, God appointed and anointed Aaron as the High Priest. Part of the holy garments of the High Priest was the Breastplate of Judgment. In this breastplate were the two mysterious stones, called Urim and Thummin, or "Lights and Perfections". These were used to judge sin in the people of God as well as being associated with atonement for sin (Ex.28:15-30; Num.27:21; Lev.8:8; Deut.33:8; 1Sam.28:6; Ezra 2:63; Neh.7:65; Ezra 7:10; 2Chron.19:1-11). The High Priest was chosen for the people of God, Israel, which was God's Church in the

Wilderness. The blood of atonement was available for sins of ignorance (Lev.4; Num.16:22-29). All pointed to the ministry of the Lord Jesus Christ, our Great High Priest.

In Rev.1-2-3, we have the antitypical fulfillment, where we see Jesus Christ, the Great High Priest, in His Church, in the midst of the sanctuary of God in the earth. He stands as the High Priest, with the Breastplate of Judgment in Himself, and the robes of glory and beauty. He is about to begin judgment at the house of God. There is no chance of deception with Him. All "Lights and Perfections" of insight, omniscience, omnipotence and omnipresence are in Him, our Great High Priest, after the Order of Melchisedek. The very fact of His standing in the midst of the seven golden Lampstands reveals the "present judgment" going on in the Church. He is judging, sifting, discerning, and dividing asunder of the flesh and the soul activities in His people, and all with a view to restoring His Church to be all He intended it to be, in the midst of the dark world.

(c) **The Ministry of Judges in Israel**
In Ex.18:1-27, Moses is given a word of wisdom from Jethro, his father-in-law. He is to choose judges from the people of Israel, who would stand with Moses in discerning various cases between the Israelites. They were to be able men, men who feared God, men of truth, hating covetousness, and these would qualify to help Moses in his ministry of oversight in Israel (Deut.1:9-18 also). They were to be men of wisdom, understanding, knowledge and discernment, as well as being known in the tribes. The qualifications are similar to that of elders in the New Testament Church (1Tim.3:1-16; Tit.1:5-9)

(d) **The Discipline in the Church**
In the Church there is to be judgment and discipline when necessary. It has already been mentioned, but the Corinthian fornicator had to be dealt with by the Church. Paul, in writing to them said, "I have already judged…" concerning this person (1Cor.5). The offender is to be brought before the Church and the saints were called to judge in the matter. The believer does not judge the sinner outside the Church. God does that. But he is to judge those who are within the Church. The purpose of Church discipline (or judgment) is restoration. In due time, the excommunicated Corinthian came to genuine repentance and was restored to fellowship (2Cor.2:6-8; 7:8-12; 12:20-21).

- Brothers who refuse to be reconciled have to come under discipline and be put out from the Church (Matt.18:15-20).
- Elders at times have to be disciplined (Tim.1:18-20; 5:19-20).
- Teachers are to give account of their teaching, as greater judgment is on them (Jas.3:1).
- Heretics are to be judged (Tit.3:10-11; 2Jhn.9-11).
- Many stripes will be given if we fail to do God's known will (Lke.12:41-48).
- Members need to be restored in a spirit of meekness (Gal.6:1).
- We are to mark those who cause divisions in the Body (Rom.16:17-18).
- Brothers who walk disorderly are disfellowshipped (2Thess.3:6-11).
- Sectarianism and carnality have to be dealt with also (1Cor.3:1-3; 1Jhn.1:5-7).
- Judgment came on members who failed to discern the Lord's Body in other members (1Cor.11:23-32). If we would judge ourselves, we would not be judged, Paul said.
- A spirit of unforgiveness brings one into the hands of the Judge (Matt.5:25; Lke.12:58).
- Some unforgiving members are delivered to the tormentors (Matt.18:21-35).

It is clear from these many references that various things have to be dealt with, or judged, in the Church, in this present time and age. This is what is meant by "present judgment". Many things that do escape judgment now will be judged at the coming of Christ. The Scripture encourages the believer to judge himself now, in this present time, so that he will not be judged by the Lord in this time or His coming. To judge oneself, and confess the things that need to be confessed, brings cleansing, and therefore nothing comes up for judgment "in that day!" John writes to the believers exhorting them that they should have "boldness in the Day of Judgment" (1Jhn.4:17 with 1Pet.4:17).

There is a difference also between "sins of ignorance" and "sins of presumption" (Num.16:22-29 with Num.16:30-31).

F. Principles of Divine Judgment

God Himself always deals in "**judgment and justice**", Many court rooms on earth exercise "judgment" but there is not always "justice". God calls us to exercise "justice in judgment". The Psalmist writes, "Justice and judgment are the habitation of Your throne; mercy and truth shall go before Your face" (Psa.89:14). God's judgments are always righteous. He wants the same in us.

All judgment must be according to the Word of God, for, in the final analysis, it is **THE WORD** that will judge all God's people, as well as the unbeliever (Jhn.12:47-48). Moses and the Levites were responsible to teach the people of the Lord, His laws, His judgments, His statutes and His commandments (Deut.4:1-4,45; 7:11-12; 11:1,32; Ex.21:1; Psa.119; Psa.19:7-9; 36:6; 72:1-2; Isa.51:4-5). We list some of those Principles of Divine judgment, which the Lord desires in His people here. He tells us what NOT to do and what we MUST do.

- Not to judge after the flesh, or by outward appearance (Jhn.7:24,51; 8:15).
- Not to judge another man's conscience on foods, or the keeping of any day (Col.2:16; 1Cor.10:29-33; Rom.14:1-7).
- Not to judge others, lest we judged (Matt.7:1-5; Lke.6:37; Lke.19:11-28).
- Not to judge the Law of God but let it judge us (Jas.4:10-12).
- Not to judge any man's personal liberty, or motives, for the Lord will do that His own appointed time (1Cor.4:1-5).
- Must judge all things by the Word, even false ministries (2Cor.11:13; Rev.2:2; Matt.24:11; 2Pet.2:1).
- Must always have mercy with judgment (Jas.2:12-13; Lke.17:2-4; Lev.19:17).
- Must have true and righteous judgments (Zech.7:9-10; Ezek.44:17-24; Isa.32:1,6; 16:5; Psa.122:5).
- Must always balance out justice with judgment (Psa.89:14; Prov.1:3; 21:3).

These principles have to do with "present judgment" in the people of God, in order to be what the Lord wants His people to be. When Christians say we are not to "judge people", and misuse Matt.7:1 to justify this, this needs to be balanced out with numerous other Scriptures that call us to judge things in our own lives, or areas of Church discipline. This has been abundantly proven in our comments in this chapter. Understanding the Biblical overview of "The Doctrine of Eternal Judgment" will help balance out any Dispensationalist extremes on this wonderful truth.

G. Judgment Future

Having considered "judgment past" and "judgment present", it is appropriate to give some attention to "judgment future". It is around this third area that Millennial Schools have their variations. "Judgment Future" falls into two parts, these being (1) Judgment Future – For Believers, and (2) Judgment Future – For Unbelievers.

1. Judgment Future – For Believers

That there is also a "future judgment" for the believer is clearly taught in the Scriptures. Historic Pre-Millennialists, Futurists and Dispensationalists see, at least, two major judgments; one for the believer and the other for the unbeliever, and these 1000 years apart. The Post-Millennialist and A-Millennialist see but one general judgment of all mankind at the throne of God. The "Judgment Seat" of Christ and the "Great White Throne" of God are seen as being one and the same throne. As a Christian Millennialist, the writer sees two resurrections and associated with these, two judgments, as laid out here. The "two judgments" are the point of controversy as are the "two resurrections".

We note several Scriptures which speak of future judgment for the believer.
"We must all appear before the Judgment Seat of Christ and give an account of ourselves..." (2Cor.5:10-11).
"That we may boldness in the Day of Judgment" (1Jhn.4:17).
Idle words must be given an account of in the Day of Judgment (Matt.12:36-37).
All are to stand before the Judgment Seat and give an account of all we have done (Rom.14:10-12).
The words that Jesus has spoken will judge us in that Day (Jhn.12:47-48 with 2Tim.4:1,8).
The time came when the righteous dead should be judged and rewarded (Rev.11:18).

The "Judgment Seat" of Christ here is the "**Bema Seat**". The custom was, after the Olympic Games, the various runners, wrestlers and contestants assembled before the Seat of the Judge, or the Judge's Stand, on which the Umpire sat, and there the winners received a corruptible crown of laurel leaves. Some had no reward, no victor's crown. But there was no punishment either; simply they received no reward. This is the picture to which Paul alludes in his mention of the "Judgment Seat of Christ".

It is not a judgment in the sense of a Trial, to see whether the believer is saved or lost. That has already been settled. It is a judgment for believers only, as in the Grecian Games. There the Judge stood at the end of the race and he distributed rewards and a garland crown for the winners of the race (1Cor.9:24-27). The result of the race is not 'salvation' or 'damnation' but 'reward' or 'loss'. That is the issue. It is not a judgment for sin, but a judgment for works.

This is especially noted in 1Cor.3:11-15; 2Cor.5:10. The believer's works and motives are assessed before the Lord. Worthless deeds are counted as "wood, hay and stubble", fit for the fire, reduced to ashes. "Gold, silver and precious stones" are valuable, and will abide the fire, but be purified and rewarded. Note that Paul takes the Ordinance of War Spoils from Num.31:21-24, concerning those things that "may abide the fire" and go through "the waters of separation" and be suitable for the service of the Lord. The great tragedy in that Day will be for the believer who has 'stacks of hay' and 'tons of wood' and acres of stubble' as his works unto the Lord. All that will be left after the fire-test will be nothing but ashes – worthless and useless ashes to present to the Lord. There is no loss of salvation, but there is no reward. It will better to have a little 'gold, and silver and precious stones', which will stand the fire-test, for there is the Lord's reward.

For the believer then, this is:
- Judgment Past –as a Sinner (At the cross, and the Brazen Altar and Laver in symbol).
- Judgment Present – as a Son (At the Lord's Table, the Table of Shewbread in symbol).
- Judgment Future – as a Servant (At the Judgment Seat of Christ, the Ark in Symbol).

The New Testament speaks of five crowns as rewards for the believers.
- The Crown of Life – Jas.1:12; Rev.2:10.
- The Crown of Glory – 1Pet.5:2-4
- The Crown of Rejoicing – 1Thess.2:19-20.
- The Crown of Righteousness – 2Tim.4:8.
- The Crown of Incorruption – 1Cor.9:25-27; 1Jhn.2:28.

2. **Judgment Future – For the Unbeliever**
The Judgment Seat for believers should not be mistaken for the Great White Throne of God. The first takes place at he beginning of the 1000 years Millennial reign of Christ, and the latter takes places at the close of that period of time. The first is for the righteous, and the second is for the wicked dead, for the unbeliever. All Millennial Schools of thought are agreed on this judgment.
The Book of Revelation is actually a Book of Judgment. Judgment begins at the House of God (the Church), and then it ends with judgment on all the wicked, at the Great White Throne, as our outline would show.

- Rev.1. The Divine Judge, the Lord Jesus Christ Himself, our Great High Priest and Judge.
- Rev.2-3. Judgment in the Churches by Christ as He deals with sins in the Churches.
- Rev.4-5. The Seven-Sealed Book.
- Rev.6-7. The first Seven Seals of Judgments in the earth.
- Rev.8-9-10. The Seven Trumpets of Judgments.
- Rev.11,12,13,14. The Judgments of the Great Tribulation of 3½ years.
- Rev.15-16. The Judgments of the Seven Bowls of Wrath in the earth.
- Rev.17. Judgment on the Great Whore, the Harlot Church, Mystery Babylon.
- Rev.18. Judgment on Commercial and Political Babylon.
- Rev.19. Judgment on the Antichrist, the False Prophet and the armies of earth.
- Rev.20. The Great White Throne judgment.
- Rev.21-22. The Eternal States of the Saints and Sinners.

The Great White Throne comes into view at the end of the 1000 years of the saints reigning with Christ as kings and priests (Rev.20:11-15). Who will be there?
- The people of Sodom and Gomorrah will be there (Matt.10:15; 11:20-24), along with Tyre and Sidon, and Capernaum. It will be more tolerable for some in that Day of Judgment than for others, Jesus said. This is according to the Divine grace manifested on earth, and rejected by these peoples.
- The people of Ninevah will be there. They will rise up in the judgement and condemn the generation of Jewry that rejected Christ. They would have repented had they seen the signs and wonders Jesus did (Matt.5:21-22; 12:38-42).
- The peoples of all nations will be there, from Adam down to the last tribulation unbeliever, who rejected Christ.
- The fallen angels will be there to be judged by God, Christ and the saints (Jude 6; 2Pet.2:4-9; 1Cor.6:1-3).
- Demonic spirits will be there, along with Satan, their Prince and Leader (Gen.3:15; Rev.20:11-15; Jhn.12:31; 16:11). Though Satan was 'judged' at Calvary, this throne has to do with 'eternal judgment' on all created beings, angelic or human (Eccles.3:17; 11:9; 12:14; Psa.1:5; 9:7,16; Rev.14:7; 1Tim.5:24; Heb.9:27; 10:27; Rom.2:5; Psa.149:1-9).
- The Lord has prepared His throne for judgment (Psa.9:7,16; Acts 24:28). Daniel says, "The judgment was set and the books were opened…" (Dan.7:9-14,21-28 with Rev.20:11-15).
- The Lord has appointed A DAY in the which He will judge the world by THAT MAN whom He has appointed, even the Lord Jesus Christ (Acts 17:31; Rom.2:16). All the secrets of men will be judged. It will be a fearful thing to fall into the hands of the living God. All the thoughts, the motives, the desires, the words, the deeds, and the character of mankind will be judged in that Day! For the unredeemed it will a great and terrible Day! To stand before God, before Christ, the Lamb they rejected for their salvation, the holy angels, all the redeemed of the human race, and the saints whose testimonies and witness has been rejected, and the preachers and teachers who taught the Bible – all will be there. That will be the beginning of 'eternal torment' spoken of in Rev.14:10-11!
- Enoch, the seventh from Adam prophesied of the Lord's coming and judgment also (Jude 14-15).
- The Twelve Apostles of the Lamb will sit on twelve thrones in the regeneration judging the twelve tribes of Old Testament Israel, who were unredeemed, though in the chosen nation (Matt.19:28).

There will be no appeal from the Divine Verdict. This is **Eternal Judgment!** The first resurrection then is for the believer, at the Judgment Seat of Christ. The second resurrection is for the unbeliever, at the Great White Throne Judgment of God.

H. **The Time of the Judgment**
As in "The Doctrine of the Resurrection", so with "The Doctrine of Judgment", we have established what the Bible teaches on these subjects. The issue for all Millennial Schools then, is not the **fact** of judgment, but the **time** of judgment. This is the area of controversy and difference. Is there one general judgment, for all mankind, or are there two judgments, one for the righteous and the other for the unrighteous, and these, a 1000 years apart?

This writer holds to **two resurrections** and associated with these are **two judgments**. The first judgment is associated with the first resurrection and is for believers at the Judgment Seat of Christ. The second judgment is associated with the second resurrection and is for unbelievers at the Great White Throne Judgment of God. As already noted, for the believer it is a matter of rewards, not of salvation. The second judgment is a matter of eternal destinies. Here the rewards of the wicked are meted out, for their evil works and the great and damnable sin of unbelief in the Lord Jesus Christ. This is "the resurrection of judgment" (Jhn.5:28-29). But this brings us to a principle of interpreting the Word.

The Breach Principle
A question often asked is, How can it be justified to place a time of 1000 years between the resurrections and judgments when they are often seen in one and the same verse? This is a good question. In seeking to answer it, attention is drawn to a hermeneutical principle of Scripture interpretation called, "The Breach Principle". From "**Interpreting the Scriptures**" (Conner/Malmin, pages 117-128). We adapt the following material.

"The Breach Principle" has been defined as "that principle by which the interpretation of a certain verse or passage of Scripture is aided by a consideration of certain breaches of promise and time." A "breach" has been defined in Webster's Dictionary as:
- A state of being broken; a rupture; a break; a gap,
- A hole or opening, as in a wall or fence, made by breaking or parting,
- An interruption of continuity; a blank space.
- A break or interruption in friendly relations.

Terms used in our day speak of "a breach of promise", which is a failure to keep a promise; or "a breach of faith", a failure to keep faith; or, "a breach of trust", and so forth.

In the Hebrew Concordance, there are a number of different Hebrew words used to speak of "a breach", several of which we note here. There is "**Bedeq**" = a breach (2Kgs.12:4-8,12), and "**Baqa**" = to make a breach (Ezek.26:10), "**Parats**" = a breach (Gen.38:29), and "**Sheber**" = broken (Lev.21:19). These are but a few examples. The words have a wide variety of applications, but the basic meaning that links them all is the thought of a **division or gap**!

The Scriptures speak of two especial kinds of breaches, (1) A Breach of Promise and (2) A Breach of Time, to which consideration is given.

1. **Breach of Promise**
   The nation of Israel experienced a "breach of promise" when it came to entering the Promised Land of Canaan. This first generation forfeited the land of promise because of their unbelief (Num.13-14 with Heb.3-4). Forty years later, the promise of God was fulfilled to the new generation. It was not that God broke His promise. He did postpone it because of unbelief. Note AV., on Num.14:26-28 where God told the people, they would "know My breach of promise!" Other examples are found in the recommended textbook.

2. **Breach of Time**
   There are a number of examples of a "breach of time in prophetic fulfillment", in both Old and New Testaments. By "breach of time" is meant the span or period of time between the fulfillment of certain prophecies. This is not to say that "God's prophetic time-clock stopped", for it never has. But because the writers of Scriptures were often caught up in what is spoken of as "the prophetic perspective", they would group together in certain verses or passages events involving the past, the present and the future. Because God is the great I AM THAT I AM (Ex.3:14-15) time past, present and future are as one eternal present before Him.

   When the prophets were 'in the Spirit', they saw things from God's eternal present. History, however, which is the fulfillment of prophecy, shows that there was or is "a breach of time" or "time periods" for these prophetic details of events to unfold. "A breach of time" is not to be confused with "a breach of promise". The Old Testament could not always understand their own prophecies concerning the coming of Christ. They searched what these things meant. They tried to understand the **time** of which the Spirit of Christ in them was speaking. It was revealed to them that many of their utterances were not just for themselves or their generation but for another generation (1Pet.1:10-12).

   Various passages in the Prophetical Books view mountain peaks of events as being all together, with no valleys in between. Their historical fulfillment has proven that is there is a "time gap" or "a breach of time" involved in their fulfillment. This is especially true concerning the events pertaining to the first and second comings of Christ. It is this area of "time element" that makes interpretation of prophecy so difficult, as well as those areas of eschatology involving 'time element'. Some examples of these are given here.

   - **The First and Second Comings of Christ**
     A comparison of Isa.61:1-2 with Lke.4:16-21 implies both the first and second comings of Christ. When Jesus entered the synagogue at Nazareth, He was given the Book of Isaiah. He opened it to Isa.61 and began to read. He read the clauses of vs.1 and the first clause of vs.2, concerning "The acceptable year of the Lord." At this point He stopped reading and closed the book. It may be asked why He did not continue to read. The next clause speaks of "the day of vengeance of our God." The first coming was indeed "the acceptable year of the Lord," and His ministry in the Gospels, from His anointing in

Jordan to His crucifixion, certainly fulfilled the clauses of vs.1 (2Cor.6:2 with Isa.49:8). There was no vengeance in His heart then, for He asked His Father to forgive those who crucified Him. It is the second coming that is "the day of vengeance of our God" (Isa.63:4 with 2Thess.1:7-9). Though the prophet Isaiah spoke of these two events in the same passage, history proves that there is **a breach of time** between them, extending from the first coming to the second coming.

- **The Day of the Lord**
  The prophets spoke much about "the Day of the Lord" that was to come. A consideration of any of these prophetic utterances, in the light of historical fulfillment, clearly shows that "the Day of the Lord," with its surrounding events, was used to refer to both the first and the second comings of Christ. Some 2000 years have elapsed between these two comings, therefore, constituting **a breach of time**.
  Mal.3:1-2 speaks of Messiah's first coming as the Messenger of the Covenant, preceded by the ministry of John the Baptist (Mrk.1:2 also). It is spoken of as "The Day of His coming."
  Mal.4:1 speaks of Messiah's second coming. This is also spoken of as "the day that comes." It is a time of complete judgment on the wicked.
  Therefore, between Mal.3:1-2 and Mal.4:1, there is an intervening Messianic era – **a breach of time** between the first and the second comings of the Lord. (**Note**: No one in the Old Testament, on the whole, could see that there would be some 4000 years between Adam and Christ. No one seemed to understand that there would be some 2000 years between Christ's first and second coming, as both were 'rolled into one verse', so to speak!)

- **The Two Resurrections**
  The same "breach principle" may be applied here when considering John's word on "the resurrections" (Rev.20:4-6). There are several other verses of Scripture that speak of the resurrection, both of the righteous and the wicked. These are also 'rolled into one verse', and a surface reading of them would suppose that the resurrection of the righteous and the wicked was to take place in 'one general resurrection', as the Post-Millennialist and the A-Millennialist believe.

  Daniel speaks of some who awake to everlasting life, and some who awake to everlasting shame and contempt (Dan.12:2). Jesus speaks of those who are raised to the resurrection of life, and those who are raised to the resurrection of damnation (Jhn.5:28-29). Paul also speaks of the resurrection of the just and the resurrection of the unjust (Acts 24:15). On the surface reading of these verses, it would appear to teach that all, both righteous and wicked, are raised in a general resurrection, for a general judgment.

  By referring to Rev.20:4-6, however, we discover that there is **a breach of time** between these resurrections. There is a breach of 1000 years between the resurrections. There are two resurrections. There is "the first resurrection", and this is for the blessed and holy. And there is "a second resurrection" implied by the use of the words, "the rest of the dead lived not again until the 1000 years were finished." The previous verses must harmonize with what John writes here. There can be no contradiction made of Scripture. John wrote his Gospel. John wrote the Revelation, and he would not contradict or misinterpret the one with the other. Though the previous several verses speak of the resurrection of just and the unjust, there is implied in them **a breach of time**, as is clearly stated in the Book of Revelation.

  If this is so, it would also be applicable to other things that Jesus taught in the Gospels, in both parable and in truth.

- **The Wheat and Tares Parable**
  The wheat and tares grow together to the end of the age. At the coming of Christ, the great separation takes place. The wheat is taken to Christ's barn, and the tares are burned in the fire (Matt.13:24-30,36-43).

- **The Good and Bad Fish Parable**
  The Gospel Net brings in the good and the bad fish. They are in the same net until the end of the age. The separation into vessels takes place when Christ returns (Matt.13:47-50).

- **The Sheep and the Goats Parable**
  At Christ's coming, He sits on the throne of glory, and the people of the nations are separated into two companies, sheep and goats. The sheep are the believers, the righteous ones, and the goats are the unbelievers, the unrighteous. They cannot be judged as "nations" but as individuals. Christ told His disciples "to make disciples of all nations", and this can only be applied to individuals in the nations, not nations as a whole! The sheep are taken into the Father's Kingdom, and the goats are sent to everlasting punishment, with the Devil and his angels (Matt.25:31-46). It is on this matter that the Dispensationalists teaching needs adjustment.

- **The Good and Evil in Resurrection**
  Jesus spoke of the time when all who are in the graves would hear His voice and be raised from the dead. The good would be resurrected to life, and the evil would be raised to the resurrection of damnation (Jhn.5:28-29).

- **The Two Resurrections**
  John wrote about "the first resurrection" and "the rest of the dead" who lived not again until the 1000 years were finished (Rev.20:4-6). The language makes common sense, and points to two resurrections, a 1000 years apart. One is the resurrection of the righteous and the other of the unrighteous. This is **a breach of time** between the resurrections!

Summation of Breach Revelation
The things revealed in Scripture concerning "breach of time" confirms the truth that God both transcends and controls TIME. The breaches of time are not to be viewed as having caused God's time-clock and His eternal purposes to stop running. Though time may be lost to man, time is never lost to God. His purposes and promises are sure, and so is their fulfillment. Because God is eternal, He was able to inspire the writers of Scripture to write of events, even though there was to be a breach of time in these events. God wove these things throughout His Word, and "it is the glory of God to conceal a thing, but the honour of kings to search put a matter" (Prov.25:2).

In diagram form, using "The Breach Principle" or "the breach of time", as dealt with here, it would appear somewhat like this.

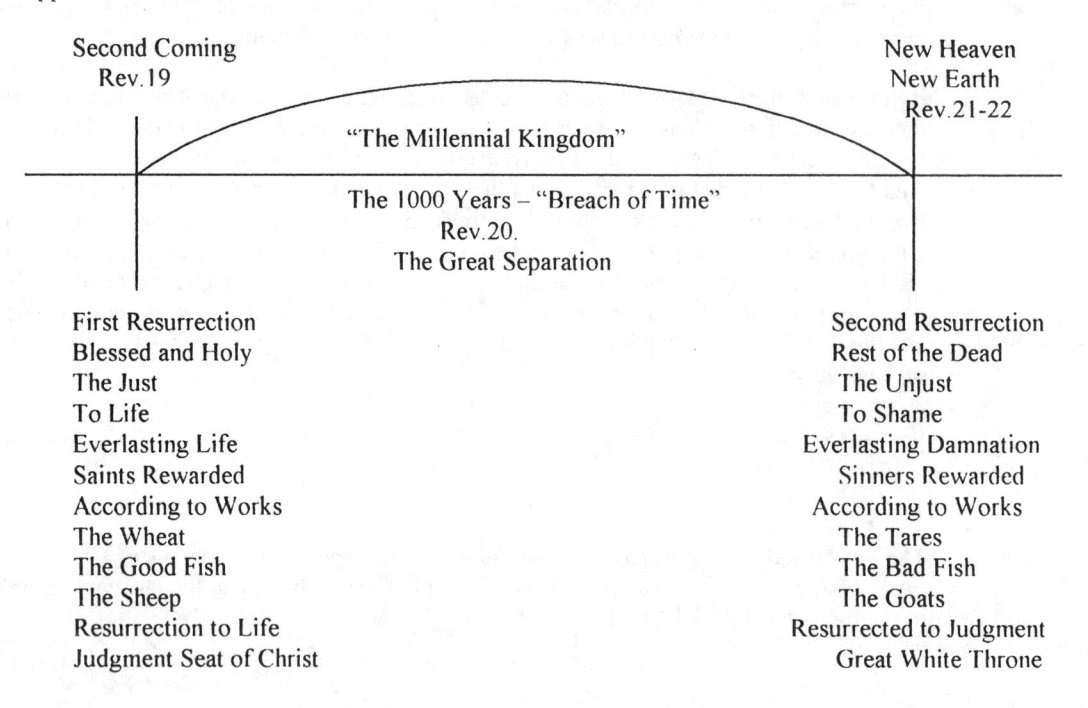

Second Coming Rev.19		New Heaven New Earth Rev.21-22
	"The Millennial Kingdom"	
	The 1000 Years – "Breach of Time" Rev.20. The Great Separation	
First Resurrection		Second Resurrection
Blessed and Holy		Rest of the Dead
The Just		The Unjust
To Life		To Shame
Everlasting Life		Everlasting Damnation
Saints Rewarded		Sinners Rewarded
According to Works		According to Works
The Wheat		The Tares
The Good Fish		The Bad Fish
The Sheep		The Goats
Resurrection to Life		Resurrected to Judgment
Judgment Seat of Christ		Great White Throne

Conclusion:
In bringing this chapter on "The Judgment" to its conclusion, we note a wonderful picture from the Old Testament of the Throne of God. It concerns the Throne of Solomon. The details are given in 1Kgs.7:7; 1Kgs.10:18-20 with 2Chron.9:17-19).

The Throne of Solomon was a Throne of ivory and overlaid with pure gold. It speaks of the Great White Throne of God, and the Glory of God. This throne has six steps to it, with a footstool of gold fastened to the Throne. Two lions were by the supports on the right hand and the left hand. Revelation speaks of two witnesses of the Lord in Rev.11 with Zech.4.

Then upon the six steps, on either side, there were six lions, making twelve lions in total. There was no Throne ever made like it. These twelve lions point to the Twelve Apostles of the Lamb. There is no Throne in the universe like the eternal Throne of God. It was from the Throne that Solomon executed judgment in the wisdom of God.

This is a great symbolic picture of the "One greater than Solomon", even our Lord Jesus Christ. He is King of Kings, and Lord of Lords, and with Him, in His judgment, is perfect wisdom. The two witnesses in Revelation will be on His right hand and left hand, and with Him, associated in His Throne shall be the Twelve Apostles of the Lamb. The six steps to the Throne may be prophetic of the 6000 years of Time allotted to man. Heaven is God's Throne and earth is His footstool.

ALL SIN will be judged. SATAN and his kingdom of darkness will be judged. All rebellion shall be put down, and all outside the Lamb's Book of Life will be judged eternally in the Lake of Fire. There can be no appeal from the verdict of the Throne of the Most High God. His judgment will be just, His judgment is perfect and eternal.

If men refuse to accept Christ, who was judged in their stead, for their sins at Calvary, then they must bear their own judgment and sin's judgment eternally. The Throne of Grace will then become the Throne of Judgment (Heb.4:16). All individual, or local judgments, in the history of mankind, are but pointers to that great Day of Judgment, the final and eternal judgment, from which none escape. The Lake of Fire is eternal judgment. Heaven is eternal blessing (Matt.25:41; Isa.66:24; Rev.20:11-15; Rev.21-22 chapters).

CHAPTER FOURTEEN

THE MILLENNIAL KINGDOM

The student is referred to Chapter Two and comments there on "**The Kingdom**". The revelation of the Kingdom of God in its various aspects and manifestations were considered in that chapter, as it pertains to both Time and Eternity. As has been seen, the Kingdom is an everlasting Kingdom, but, when it comes to God's purposes in the earth, there will have been a seven-fold expression of that Kingdom in time. The reader will bear with the repetition of the outline from Chapter Two, especially as the Kingdom relates to the earthly manifestation in time.

A. The Kingdom in Eternity – Past (Psa.145:10-13).
B. The Kingdom in Time – Present.
    1. The Kingdom in Eden (Gen.1:26-28. Adam to Noah).
    2. The Kingdom in the Patriarchs (Gen.6-22. Noah to Abraham).
    3. The Kingdom in the Nation of Israel (Ex.19:1-6).
    4. The Kingdom in the Gentile World (Dan.1-7).
    5. The Kingdom of God in Christ (Psa.2; Psa.22; Psa.110; Heb.7).
    6. The Kingdom of God in the Church (Matt.16:15-19).
    7. The Kingdom of God in the Millennium (Rev.20:1-6).
C. The Kingdom of God in Eternity - Future (2Pet.2:11).

From eternity to eternity the Kingdom of God rules and reigns. God is he King of all the earth and the universe of worlds. His Kingdom rules over all creation and creatures. The Kingdom rules in time, progressively being manifested through some 7000 years of God's time which He has allotted to man (Psa.145:10-13; 2Pet.2:16; 2Tim.4:8; Dan.7:27; Rom.14:17).

It is about the seventh expression of the Kingdom of God in the earth with which this chapter has to do. For the present chapter, consideration needs to be given to the fact that there is a future aspect and manifestation of the Kingdom of God here on the earth. This is spoken of as the Millennial Kingdom. Fuller details will be covered in **Part Three** of this text.

A brief reminder, however, of the Millennial views:
Historic, Futurist, Dispensationalist Pre-Millennialists, along with this writer – Christian Pre-Millennialist – each see a future aspect of the Kingdom of God here on this earth. Post-Millennialists believe the Church militant and triumphant will usher in a Millennial Kingdom for Christ's return. A-Millennialists see no future aspect of the Kingdom in or on the earth.

Historic, Futurist, Dispensational and Christian Millennialists all believe that Christ's second coming ushers in a Millennium of some kind. A-Millennialists believe that Christ's coming ends the present Millennium and ushers in eternity. All agree on some future aspect of the Kingdom after Christ returns. The question is whether this is a Kingdom of 1000 years followed by eternity, or whether Christ's coming ushers in eternity, the Kingdom everlasting.

It is the A-Millennial position with which there is more to deal when it comes to the contents of this chapter. The A-Millennialists, as has been noted, see no future aspect of he Kingdom as it concerns the present earth. Of the approximate 160 references to "the kingdom" in the New Testament, the A-Millennialist sees that all these are speaking of "a spiritual kingdom". It would seem that, in an over reaction to a "literal, earthly,, Jewish Millennium" and a reinstitution of the Mosaic economy, A-Millennialists throw out, ignore or disregard any literal aspect of the Kingdom of God.

When we speak of the "literal" aspect of the Kingdom, we mean that human side of the Kingdom. The Kingdom is not something that is only spiritual, abstract and unreal. It involves both the Divine and the human, God and man, heaven and earth, spiritual and literal, unseen and seen, in the heart and in the earth (The reader is referred back to comments on this in Chapter Two).

A-Millennialists also take these approximately 160 references to the Kingdom in the New Testament and place them into two major categories. They see these Scriptures as either applying to the spiritual Kingdom in the hearts of believers here and now, or else, apply them to the eternal state, the Kingdom in eternity. For their position, eternity follows the second coming of Christ, NOT any 1000 years manifestation of the Kingdom of God on the earth. In emphasizing the truth of the everlasting Kingdom, they believe that a 1000 year future Kingdom here on earth is placing a limitation on God's everlasting Kingdom. Yet, they do the same, in principle, by saying that the 1000 year Millennial period is a symbolic period of time between the first and second comings of Christ!

The position presented here is that the Scriptures teach there is a future manifestation of the Kingdom of God, here on earth, and this fulfills the final step of God's plan of redemption relative to this earth, before ushering in the eternal states. This, as previously noted is spoken of as "the Kingdom now, but not yet." Enough has been written in Chapter Two on the Kingdom in its present manifestation. The following presents some of the Scriptures that point to a future aspect of the Kingdom, from the Lord Jesus Christ Himself, and the Prophet Daniel.

A. **The Words of Jesus**
   Jesus Himself spoke of both the present and future aspect of the Kingdom of God. Of some 160 references to the Kingdom, we look at some of the most important ones that point to a future aspect of the Kingdom as it pertains to earth.

   1. **Matthew 7:21-23**
      Jesus tells of a day when professors of religion and apostates from the faith will stand before Him. Many will have called Him 'Lord', they will have prophesied, cast out devils and done miracles in His name, but they have been workers of iniquity, lawless ones. The Lord told them to depart from Him. They could not enter the Kingdom. It is evident they were in the Kingdom in its present state but they would not enter the future Kingdom.

   2. **Matthew 8:11-12**
      Jesus, after seeing the faith of a Gentile Centurion, told His disciples of the future aspect of the Kingdom. He said, "Many will come from the east and the west and sit down with Abraham, Isaac and Jacob in the Kingdom of Heaven. The sons of the Kingdom will be cast out into outer darkness. There will be weeping and gnashing of teeth." Believing Jews and believing Gentiles will sit with the patriarchs, Abraham, Isaac and Jacob in the coming Kingdom. One cannot spiritualize these Scriptures to only mean God's Kingdom, His rule and reign, in the heart.

   3. **Matthew 13:24-50**
      The Parables of the Kingdom that Jesus taught show that there will be mixture in the Kingdom until the end of the age. The Parable of the Wheat and Tares, the Parable of the Good and Evil Fish each teach mixture. At the end of the age and the second coming of Christ, separation takes place. In the coming Kingdom there will be no mixture. The words of Jesus in Matt.13:30,41-43 are particularly to be noted, as they are very clear as to this matter. "The Son of Man shall send forth His angels, and they shall **gather out of His Kingdom** all things that offend (Lit. 'scandals') and them which do iniquity (practice lawlessness)...Then shall the righteous shine forth as the sun **in the Kingdom of the Father**." This certainly teaches both the present and future aspect of the Kingdom of God.

   4. **Matthew 19:28**
      Jesus also promised the twelve apostles that, because they have followed Him in His time on earth, "in the regeneration, when the Son of Man shall sit on the throne of His glory, you shall also sit upon twelve thrones, judging the twelve tribes of Israel." This promise was not in heaven but pertains to the second coming of Christ and His Kingdom here on earth, reigning over those who are redeemed Israel. Read also Lke.22:29-30. Here Jesus says to the Twelve, "I appoint you a Kingdom, even as My Father has appointed one for Me; that you may eat and drink at My Table in My Kingdom, and sit on thrones judging the twelve tribes of Israel." This certainly teaches a future aspect of the Kingdom as they were already in the Kingdom in its then present manifestation.

   5. **Matthew 25:31-34**
      When Jesus comes the second time, He will sit upon the throne of His glory. The nations will be gathered together before Him. He will separate them as sheep and goats are separated by the shepherd. The sheep are the righteous. The goats are the unrighteous. Once the judgement is finished, the Lord, as

the King on His throne, says to the righteous, "Come, you blessed of My Father, inherit the Kingdom prepared for you from the foundation of the world." (vs.34). The goats are banished to everlasting fire which was prepared for the Devil and his angels. This separation is the same separation as seen in he Parables of the Wheat and Tares and the Good and Bad Fish. The Apostle Paul also speaks much about those who "will not inherit the Kingdom of God" (Eph.3:3-6; 1Cor.6:9-10; Gal.5:21; 2Tim.4:18). This speaks of the future aspect of the Kingdom, beyond its present manifestation.

6. **Luke 19:11-15 with Luke 17:20-21**
Jesus in these passages showed His disciples both the present and the future aspects of His Kingdom. He told them that they were not to look for the Kingdom here or there. The Kingdom does not come with observation. The Kingdom of God was right there, here and now, among them. Jesus, however, had to teach them a further word about the Kingdom future. As Jesus entered Jerusalem, He added and spoke another Parable to them (a) Because He was near Jerusalem, and (b) Because they thought the Kingdom of God should immediately appear. He told them the Parable of the certain nobleman going into a far country **to receive for himself a Kingdom**. In due time, he received the Kingdom, and **having received the Kingdom, he returned** to take account of his servants. The interpretation of the Parable should be evident. The Nobleman is the Lord Jesus Himself. The far country is heaven. He receives the Kingdom from His Father. He returns in His second coming. He takes account of His servants, the believers, and rewards them accordingly. This corresponds with Daniel's vision (Dan.7). Sufficient it is to see both the present and future aspect of the Kingdom. (The student could also read Mrk.9:47; Matt.20:21; Lke.23:42 which point to the future Kingdom).

B. **The Words of Daniel**
The Book of Daniel is a Book of the Kingdoms, the Kingdoms of the Gentile World, and the Kingdom of God, both everlasting, but revealed in time relative to God's sovereignty in earth over the affairs of men. Two notable chapters are considered as both show the present and future aspect of Kingdoms, of this world and of the heavens above and manifested in the earth.

1. **Daniel 2**
In this chapter is given the details of the Dream of King Nebuchadnezzar. The dream foretold the coming of successive Gentile Kingdoms right through to the setting up of the Kingdom of God here on earth. All were seen in the image of deified man, degenerating, deteriorating and finally disintegrating to nothingness. The Gentile Kingdoms here on earth are as follows:
- The Head of Gold – Babylonian Kingdom
- The Breast and Arms of Silver – Medo-Persian Kingdom
- The Belly and Thighs of Brass – Grecian Kingdom
- The Legs of Iron – Roman Kingdom
- The 10 Toes of Iron and Clay – Antichrist's Kingdom
- The Stone cut out of the Mountain without hands – Kingdom of God in Christ.

The Stone crushes the feet of the image and the whole of the image of world kingdoms disintegrates to nothingness. It then becomes a great Kingdom and fills the whole earth – not heaven! The Kingdom is the Stone Kingdom and fills the whole world, crushing all the Kingdoms of this world. It is recognized that Christ is the smiting stone. However, He was not in that role in His first coming, when He preached that "the Kingdom of heaven is at hand" (Matt.4:7 with Matt.3:1-2).

Because the Jews had a mistaken concept of the Kingdom of God, they rejected the King and His Kingdom. Refer again to Chapter Two. The 'time element' was not fulfilled when Jesus came the first time. The ten-toe-Kingdom was not yet in existence when Christ came the first time. The ten-toe-Kingdom pointed to the Kingdom of Antichrist which will be in existence at Christ's second coming (Read Rev.12-13 with Dan.2-7). The smiting stone is prophetic of Christ's coming again. As the Stone Kingdom filled the whole earth, so it points to the future aspect of the Kingdom as it pertains to this earth, not heaven! Jesus also confirms this message about the Stone Kingdom in Matt.21:3-44. It cannot be applied merely to "a spiritual Kingdom in the hearts of men". There is that which is spiritual and actual in this Stone Kingdom.

2. **Daniel 7**
In this chapter, Daniel is given a vision. The vision corresponds with the dream of Nebuchadnezzar in chapter two. It is a vision of the successive Gentile Wold Kingdoms right through to the Kingdom of

the Son of Man. In this vision, however, God shows that the Kingdoms of this world are like wild, cruel and rapacious beasts of earth, in contrast to the Son of Man, the Lord Jesus Christ and His Kingdom.
- The Lion with Eagle's Wings – The Babylonian Kingdom
- The Bear – The Medo-Persian Kingdom
- The Leopard with four Heads – The Grecian Kingdom
- The Non-descript Beast – The Roman Kingdom
- The Ten Horns – The Kingdom of Antichrist
- The Little Horn – The Antichrist King himself
- The Son of Man – The Lord Jesus Christ, King of Kings.

The Kingdoms of this world are beastly in nature and character and behaviour. The Kingdom of God is likened to A MAN, the Son of Man, the Lord Jesus Christ. When the Son of Man comes, having received the Kingdom from the Father, He destroys those Beast Kingdoms.

It is to be noted how the phrase "the saints possessed the Kingdom" is used in verses 18,22,27. It is an everlasting Kingdom. The Kingdom will not be left to other people. It will not be succeeded by other Kingdoms as were the Gentile Kingdoms. The time came when the saints possessed the Kingdom. The vision has to do with the future aspect of the Kingdom here on earth when the Son of Man returns the second time. The truth is linked here with the Parable in Luke 19:11-15, where the Nobleman went into the far country and received the Kingdom. Having received it, He returns again to take account of His servants, the believers in the Kingdom in its present time.

As mentioned earlier, there are some 160 references to the Kingdom in the New Testament. Most of them speak of the Kingdom in this present time and age. Others speak of the future Kingdom. In Chapter Two, on "The Kingdom", we saw how some expositors speak of "the Kingdom now, but not yet". When reading the Scripture references that speak of "the Kingdom", one needs to discover whether they speak of "the Kingdom now" or "the Kingdom not yet". Is it or are they speaking of the Kingdom present or the Kingdom future or the Kingdom everlasting?

For those Schools who see the future Millennial Kingdom of God in earth, the words of Jesus and the words of Daniel are the clearest words confirming this truth. Both New and Old Testament writers give witness. For the A-Millennialist, these same Scriptures are taken to mean the Kingdom of God everlasting, the Kingdom in eternity. All Schools hold that there is a future Kingdom. It is a matter of whether it is a Millennial Kingdom here on earth, or the Kingdom everlasting! The student has to discern which view is the proper view.

For this writer, there is a future Millennial Kingdom here on earth where the Scriptures considered in this chapter find their fulfillment. This is the final manifestation of the Kingdom of God in the earth. It completes the plan of redemption as it pertains to earth. The Christian Millennium, for this writer, is the prelude to eternity, bringing the redeemed to the everlasting Kingdom. The Kingdom is "now, but not yet."

CHAPTER FIFTEEN

THE ETERNAL STATES

When it comes to the final or Eternal States, its seems that, whichever School of Eschatology one belongs to, there is basic general agreement. In order, however, to complete Part Two of our text, some differences will be noted and briefly commented on.

For the Post-Millennialist and A-Millennialist, Christ's second coming ushers in a general resurrection, and a general judgment and then Eternity. For the Historic Pre-Millenialist, the Futurist and Dispensationalist, the close of the Millennial Kingdom ushers in Eternity. This, of course, comes after the Great White Throne Judgment. Eternity brings us to the New Heavens and New Earth and the final Hell. The writer, holding a Christian Millennial position, would follow the same position.

The difference in these Schools, once again, has to do with the 'time element'. This has already been mentioned in previous chapters, relative to the Resurrection and the Judgment. Our attention is this present chapter is given over the eternal destinies of the saved and the lost, the righteous and the unrighteous, the redeemed and the unredeemed, the believer and the unbeliever. It is at the Great White Throne Judgment that the eternal destines of all created beings, angelic or human, are settled.

In simple language, the eternal destiny of the wicked is Hell, or Gehenna, and the eternal destiny of the righteous is Heaven, the dwelling place of God. Much of the material following best sets out the eternal state of the unredeemed and redeemed, and is condensed and adapted from the author's text, "**The Foundations of Christian Doctrine**" (pages 301-308). In outline form, we see what the Scriptures teach us about these two places, for the character of the inhabitants is according to these two places. There is no heaven without a hell, and heaven and hell are as eternal as the God who created them. Every person has their choice as to which eternal habitation they choose to dwell in.

A. Hell – Eternal Dwelling of the Unredeemed

Hell is the place or state of final punishment of the wicked; of all who die in their sins and unregenerate state. After the Great White Throne Judgment, all whose names are not found in the Book of Life are consigned to Hell (Rev.20:11-15).

1. Hell is an **actual place**, as surely as heaven is a place (Matt.5:22,29,30; 10:28; 18:9; 23:15). Many like to believe that heaven is an actual place while rejecting hell as a place. One does not exist without the other. Just as God has a place of happiness for the redeemed who serve Him, so God has a place of punishment for the rebellious who serve the Devil. Jesus, the perfect compassionate One, spoke more about Hell than all other Bible writers put together. This is no wonder, for He came to save mankind from this terrible place.

2. Hell was not made for mankind but it was actually prepared **for the Devil and his angels**. If men, however, choose to serve the Devil in this life, then they will dwell eternally with the Devil in hell (Matt.25:41).

3. The Scriptures speak of **three divisions** in the underworld and each find their divisions swallowed up in Gehenna, which is the final Hell. These various Greek words are all translated by the word 'Hell' in English translations.

    (a) Sheol or Hades

    Sheol or Hades is generally recognized as being "the place of departed spirits", or "the unseen state." Sometimes it is spoken of as referring to the grave.

    The Hebrew word this place is "Sheol" and is translated as "Hell", "Grave" and "Pit" in various Scriptures (Deut.32:22; Psa.18:5; Job 26:6; Jonah 2:2; Isa.14:9,15). As the student reads these verses, it will show that Sheol is "down", "in the depths", "beneath" and it is a place of pains and sorrows, while the righteous in the Old Testament are promised deliverance from such.

    The Greek word "Hades" is translated "Hell" and one time as "Grave" (Matt.11:23; 16:18; Lke.16:23; 1Cor.15:55). Hades is seen to be "down", having gates, and is seen to be the place for departed spirits. It will lose its victory over the righteous and then Hades is to be cast into the Lake of Fire, the final Hell (Rev.20:13-14).

Old and New Testament confirm each other in the information given, that Sheol or Hades is the place of departed spirits, especially the departed spirits of human beings under Old Testament times.

(b) Tartarus

The Greek word "Tartarus" is used but once in the New Testament. It is translated "Hell" (2Pet.2:4). This verse, along with Jude 6, shows that Tartarus is a prison, a jail, specifically for sinful angelic spirit beings. It is also "down" and it is a place of darkness where these fallen angels are reserved and held until the time when angels are to be judged at the Great White Throne Judgment (1Cor.6:3; Rev.20:11-15 with 2Pet.2:4 and Jude 6).

(c) Abyss

The third division in the lower down departments of the earth (Psa.63:9; 139:15; Eph.4:9) is called the Abyss, the Deep, or the Bottomless Pit.

The Hebrew word "Abaddon" is translated "Destruction" in the Old Testament and "Abaddon" in the New Testament (Job 26:6; 28:22; Psa.88:11; Prov.27:20; Rev.9:11).

The Greek word "Apollyon" is translated "Destruction" and "Apollyon" in the New Testament (Matt.7:13; 2Pet.2:1; 3:16; Rev.9:11).
"The Deep", as in Rev.9:1-3; Rom.10:7; Lke.8:31 is also the Abyss.
"The Bottomless Pit" (Rev.9:1-3; 20:1-3,7) is also the Abyss.

By reading these particular references, it is found that Sheol and the Abyss are connected. It is especially called "a prison." The Bottomless Pit is seen to be a dungeon, a jail, and this is the abode of demon spirits, a deeper pit than Sheol or Hades. The Abyss is Destruction, Abaddon, Apollyon, The Deep or the Bottomless Pit.

Meditation on these references will show that each place or department of "Hell", the underworld or spirit world, is a prison or jail for different created beings, who have sold themselves out to evil. The place of Sheol or Hades is a place for departed human spirits, especially for the unsaved, since the resurrection of Christ, as well as for Old Testament unregenerate persons. The place of Tartarus is a place for fallen angelic spirit beings. The place of the Abyss or Bottomless Pit is a place for demon spirits. Men place accused criminals and offenders in different cells, according to their crime, where they await their sentence and final judgment of their case. So God has various jails in which He locks up prisoners until the Great White Throne Judgment, when all will be tried and sentenced eternally to the final Hell, Gehenna.

(d) Gehenna

The final and eternal Hell is seen in the Greek word "Gehenna." "Gehenna" means, "The Valley of Hinnom." It is translated "Hell", at least 12 times, as seen in some of these references (Matt.5:22,29,30; 10:28; 18:9; 23:15,33; Mrk.9:43-47; Lke.12:5; Jas.3:6). It is also translated "The Lake of Fire" some five times (Rev.19:20; 20:10,14,15; 21:8).

It should be remembered that it was the Lord Jesus Himself who spoke more of this final Hell than all other Bible writers. When this terrible place is seen in Scripture, it is used to symbolize the final state of the wicked in the final Hell, which God really prepared for the Devil and his angels – not for mankind.

The Old Testament equivalent is found in the Hebrew word "Tophet" or "Topheth" which means "Altar." The Greek word "Gehenna" is founded upon this Hebrew concept of "Hell". Tophet or Gehenna shadowed forth all that Hell will be to the wicked. When Israel fell into idolatry, and began to worship Baal, they used a certain part of the valley on the east side of Jerusalem to burn their children alive, and also to burn the refuse of the city with fire and brimstone. This part of the valley was called "Tophet" or "Valley of the Dead Bodies." Here wicked kings made their children pass through the fire unto the gods of Baal and Molech, the "Sun" and "Fire" gods (Lev.18:21; Deut.18:10; Ezek.23:27,39; 1Chron.28:3-4; 33:6; Jer.7:31; 19:1-12). These thousands of children were placed on the hot metal hands of the great idol, and, as they were being roasted alive, cymbals and the shouts of the frenzied worshippers drowned their agonizing screams. They also beat drums to drown out the cries of the children. The valley was called:

- The Valley of Hinnom (Josh.15:8; Neh.11:30; Josh.18:16).
- The Valley of the Children of Hinnom (2Kgs.23:10).
- The Valley of Dead Bodies (Jer.31:40).
- The Valley of the Groans of the Children (2Chron.28:3-4; 33:6).
- The Valley of the Son of Hinnom (2Chron.28:3; Jer.32:35).

The second thing about this place was that it became the place of all the refuse of the city of Jerusalem. The godly King Josiah defiled this place so that the abominations would not be carried on and from this time on it became a place for the filth and impurity of the place. This fire was kindled by brimstone. Brimstone is a horrible substance in its action on human flesh and it becomes torturous when thrown in with fire. Worms fed on the garbage out of reach of the fire, and vultures gloated over the scene continually. From this valley there arose stenchful and horrid smoke continually (2Kgs.23:10; Isa.30:33).

The Gehenna of the New Testament then, is equivalent to the Old Testament Tophet. The Lord Jesus uses the two major features of this horrible place as a fitting symbol of the final Hell, the Lake of Fire. Hell is a place where the wicked are cast, and the smoke of their torment ascends up for ever and ever. That "Gehenna" was outside the earthly city of Jerusalem. The eternal "Gehenna" is outside the Heavenly City of Jerusalem, the Holy City of God. If it is argued that such things are only symbols, then it should be remembered that the reality is always worse than the symbol used to symbolize it. If the symbols of Hell are so terrible, then the reality will be far more terrible. Thus the Lord Jesus, the One of infinite love and compassion, spoke more of Hell than anyone did, because He is the One who came to save mankind from this terrible place. Note how the New Testament describes this place of terror and horror.

The New Testament provides a terrible and frightening description of what this final Hell, Gehenna, will be like.

- Hell will be the valley of the dead bodies and souls of the unregenerate (Matt.5:29-30; 18:9; Lke.12:5).
- Hell will be the valley of the groans, weeping and wailing of the lost of Adam's race (Matt.13:42,50).
- Hell will be a place for the hypocrites, serpents and vipers in character (Matt.23:14,15,33).
- Hell will be a place of fire and brimstone (Rev.19:20; 20:10,14-15; 21:8).
- Hell will be a place of continually ascending smoke (Rev.14:10-11).
- Hell will be a fire which is never to be quenched (Mrk.9:43-49).
- Hell is a place where "the worm" of conscience never dies (Isa.66:24; Psa.21:9; Job 24:20 with Acts 12:20-23; Mrk.9:43-48). It will be terrible torment to have lusts which cannot be satisfied and a conscience that torments of past guilt and rejected grace.
- Hell will last eternally. The same Greek word "Aion", translated "Ages" is used about twenty times in the New Testament. It is used at least sixteen times pertaining to God, another time of the eternal bliss of the saints, and three times of eternal punishment of Satan and the inhabitants of Hell. Eternal punishment is as long as eternal life (Matt.25:46; Dan.12:2; Rom.6:23; Jude 7; Rev.14:11).
- Hell is the place where the wicked and unregenerate are "salted" as sacrifices on an altar (Mrk.9:48-49). Rejecting God's sacrifice on Calvary's altar, they become sacrifices on this altar, the "Altar of Tophet."
- Hell will be some place or planet in the universe as an eternal jail for the wicked of mankind and criminal angels. God will not cause the righteous to remember such things (Isa.66:22-24; Rev.14:9-11; Isa.65:17).

- Hell was prepared for the Devil and his angels. The unredeemed there will find it a place of vile company (Isa.30:33; 2Pet.2:4; Jude 6; Matt.25:41,46; Rev.21:8).
- Hell is for all whose names are not found written in the Book of Life (Rev.2:11; 20:11-15; 21:8).
- Hell is called the second death (Rev.2:11; 20:11-15; 21:8).
- Hell will be outside the new and Heavenly Jerusalem (Rev.21:8; 22:14-15).
- Hell will be a place of shame and everlasting contempt (Dan.12:2; Rom.2:16).
- Hell will be a furnace of fire (Matt.13:42,50; 25:41,46).

At present, Hell is unoccupied. The fallen angels and the wicked dead and demonic spirits are in their various prison houses, awaiting the Day of the Great White Throne Judgment. After this, all will be cast into the Lake of Fire, including their respective prisons or cells.

- Hell is described by various names, each indicating what the place is like. These are too many to mention here, so only several can be named. Hell is "Destruction" (Matt.7:13), "Perdition" (Heb.10:39), "Outer Darkness" (Matt.24:51; 25:30), "A furnace" (Matt.13:41-42, "Damnation" (Mrk.16:16), "The Lake of Fire and Brimstone" (Rev.21:8).
- Hell will be a terrible place of separation from the presence of God, the rejected Lamb of God, the holy angels and the redeemed. No light, life, peace, joy, righteousness, only darkness and torment of conscience will be suffered there for all who have rejected and despised the grace of God in Christ. This is the Hell that Jesus Christ died to save us from.
- Hell is neither annihilation nor a place of temporary punishment. It is not a state of probation or a state of non-existence. Hell is a place of eternal punishment. Hell is a self-chosen and self-inflicted curse, the inevitable outcome of sin. Rejecting God, rejecting Christ and resisting the Holy Spirit, the inhabitants of Hell have chosen to live a life of sin here on earth. God leaves them to the choice they have made and to live eternally with the sins they have chosen. God will not force any to be saved or to go to heaven against their will. Yet God is not willing that any should perish (1Tim.2:4; Jhn.5:40; Matt.23:37; Jer.8:5-6; 2Pet.3:9). God's banishment of the wicked to a place where sin and iniquity can no longer defile others is just. Hell is therefore God's eternal jail for criminals of the universe, never to be let loose to wreck God's New heaven and New earth, or to defile the New Jerusalem, or to corrupt the angels and the saints.

4. Hell has various occupants or inhabitants, seen by the Scripture references presented here.
    - The Antichrist and the False Prophet are the first two persons to be cast alive into the Lake of Fire (Rev.19:11-21 with Rev.20:1-10).
    - The Devil himself is cast into the Lake of Fire at the close of the 1000 years Millennial period (Rev.10:11-15).
    - The fallen angels are also to be cast into Gehenna (2Pet.2:4; Jude 7).
    - The fallen demonic spirits also will be cast into Hell (Lke.8:26-31).
    - The unredeemed and unregenerate of mankind will be cast into Hell, the Lake of Fire after the Great White Throne Judgment. All whose names are not written in the Book of Eternal Life are cast there (Rev.14:9-11; 20:11-15).
    - Then finally Death and Hades/Sheol, Tartarus and the Bottomless Pit are all cast into this final Hell, the Lake of Fire and Brimstone. The jails will then have served their purpose (Rev.20:14; Hos.13:14; Isa.25:6-9; 1Cor.15:26, 54,55).

5. The Location of Hell is somewhat uncertain. Two major views are held as to where this final Hell as a place might be. One view holds that it is some special place somewhere in the universe, where God will confine the damned criminals of heaven and earth. The other view is that this present earth will become the final Hell at the close of the Kingdom period and God's plan relative to this earth. This view would seem to be the more consistent, as a consideration of 2Pet.3:3-9 with Rev.20:11-15 and Rev.21:1 would indicate.

Satan has always desired to have this planet earth. Men have lived and died here, and sold themselves to Satan here on this earth. Jesus came from heaven to earth to take the redeemed to a New Heaven and a New earth wherein dwells righteousness. Thus it seems fitting that this planet earth will be the jail of the universe of worlds that witnesses to all creatures that "sin does not pay!" Wherever Hell may be, it is a place to shun and to warn all to escape from it, turning them to the grace of God manifest in the Lord Jesus Christ (Isa.65:17; 66:22-24).

B. Heaven – Eternal Dwelling of the Redeemed

Heaven is the dwelling place of God, and the elect angels. It is the everlasting home of the redeemed of mankind. The Hebrew word "Shamayin" means "heavens, or the heaved up things." The Greek word "Ouranoi" is translated "the heavens, the skies."

1. Heaven is **an actual place** (Gen.2:1,4; Deut.10:14).

2. Heaven is spoken of as **God's dwelling place** (2Chron.6: 25,33,35,39; Heb.1: 10; 4:14; Dan.4: 26; Zech.12: 1).

3. The heavens were **created by the Lord** (1Chron.16: 26,31; Job 9:8).

4. The Scriptures speak of **three heavens**, and that these three heavens are the reality of the shadow cast on earth in the three places in the Tabernacle of Moses and the Temple of Solomon. The earthly Sanctuary was the shadow of the heavenly Sanctuary, as the Book of Hebrews and the Book of Revelation set forth (Heb.8:1-5; 9:1-28; Psa.19:1-6; Amos 9:6; Rev.11:19; 15:1-5). Jesus Christ is the minister in the heavenly Temple as our Great High Priest (Heb.7).

    ### (a) The Third Heaven
    The third heaven, or the immediate Presence of God, is called Paradise. It is heaven's 'Holiest of All', or, 'The Most Holy Place'. It is the very throne-room of the eternal Godhead, and the place of the brightness of God's glory. It is the original or the archetype of all that has ever been shadowed forth on earth, in the Tabernacle of Moses and the Temple of Solomon. This is why it is variously called:
    - The third heaven (2Cor.12:1-4).
    - Paradise (Lke.23:43; Rev.2:7; 2Cor.12:1-4).
    - Heaven itself, the Presence of God (Heb.9:24).
    - Heaven, God's dwelling place (2Chron.6:30-35).
    - The Heaven of Heavens (2Chron.6:18; 2:6).
    - Heaven, the Throne of God (Matt.5:34; Rev.4:1; Acts 7:47-50; Isa.66:1-4).

    It is this heaven which is the very centre of the universe, the universe of worlds, and all revolve in obit according to God's will, according to the power of this eternal throne (Heb.1:1-3; 4:14; 9:23; Job 15:15; Heb.8:1-5; Rev.12:12). It is this heaven which the saints and the prophets looked into when they had "open heavens" (Matt.3:16; Acts 7:56; Ezek.1:1; Rev.4:1; Jhn.1:51; Psa.11:4; Matt.6:9; 2Cor.12:1-4).

    ### (b) The Second Heaven
    The second heaven, the central one, is the planetary heaven. It corresponds with the Holy Place in the earthly Sanctuary of Moses. It is that heaven which has in it untold millions of planets, galaxies, star-worlds and suns, blazing and moving according to their God-willed orbits in their various glories. It is these heavenly bodies that the prophets speak of being darkened in the Last Days in judgment, prior to the coming of the Lord Jesus Christ (Joel 2:10,30; Hag.2:6; Isa.50:3; 51:6; Isa.13:13; 34:4). This heaven is to be shaken.

    ### (c) The First heaven
    The first heaven, from man's point of view, is the atmospheric heaven. It is the heaven immediately above and surrounding this planet. It is the atmospheric heaven that man depends upon for breath, sustenance and earth produce, by wind, sun and rain. It corresponds to the Outer Court of the Tabernacle of Moses. This heaven is to be followed by a New Heaven and a New Earth in due time. It is to be rolled up as a scroll and melt with fervent heat (Gen.1:8; 2Pet.3:5-16; Rev.21:1-2). It is this heaven that is "shut up" and withholds the rain from man when he sins against God (Read 2Chron.6:26; 1Kgs.17:1; Deut.8:23; Lev.26:19; Job 1:16; Rev.6:13-15; 20:11; 21:1; Job 15:15;

Rev.12:7-12). It is this heaven that is also polluted by the presence of Satan and his angels until they are cast out. Then will the heavens be completely cleansed.

5. The Bible shows that in time there will be a New Heaven and a New Earth. This will then be the eternal dwelling place of the redeemed. From here shall all eternal activity proceed. The New Jerusalem will be the new capitol of the universe and the place where the redeemed gather for worship and service (Rev.21-22 chapters with Isa.65:17; 66:22; 2Pet.3:13). The Scriptures give some indication of the character of this New Heaven and New Earth and New Jerusalem, for it is this which provides us with the best description of our future heavenly dwelling place.

- It will be a **New Heaven and a New Earth,** for the former are to pass away (Gen.1:1 with Rev.21:1).
- There will be **no more sea**, which speaks of separation and division of land (Rev.21:1).
- There will be a **New Jerusalem**, a holy city, in contrast to the old and former Jerusalem, which became a filthy city. The New Jerusalem is the city that Abraham looked for, whose builder and maker is God (Heb.11:10-16; 13:14; Gal.4:26; Rev.3:12; 21:2).
- This city will be **the Tabernacle of God**, God's dwelling place with His redeemed people. He will be their God and they will be His people, thus fulfilling the spiritual promises of the Abrahamic Covenant as well as those of the New Covenant (Ex.19:4-6; Jer.31:31-34; Rev.21:3).
- There will be **no tears**, sorrow, crying or pain there (Rev.21:4).
- There will be **no more death**, which is the wages of sin, for the last enemy has been destroyed, and these things belong to the earth and the unredeemed man (Rev.21:4).
- The city is filled with **the Glory of God**, and His Presence, even as the Tabernacle of Moses and the Temple of Solomon were filled with the Glory-Presence as his dwelling place on earth (Rev.21:10-21).
- Everything will be transparent; that is, **no shadows** or darkness or uncertainty will be there (Rev.21:21).
- The worship will centre around God and the Lamb eternally instead of any earthly Temple and sacrifice (Rev.21:22).
- All will be **eternal light** in the New Heavens and New Earth. The New Jerusalem has no darkness or night there (Rev. 21:23-26; 22:5).
- **No unrighteous** or unholy person shall ever enter this city. It is a righteous and holy city for those redeemed of like character (Rev.21:27; 22:15).
- The **river of life** will be there, proceeding from the throne of God and the Lamb (Rev.22:1,7).
- The **tree of eternal life** will be restored to man in this heavenly Paradise. Man lost it through disobedience and failing to keep God's commandment. Now it is restored to all who obey His commandments (Gen.2:17 with Rev.22:2,14; 2:7).
- All the redeemed shall **see His face** and His name shall be in their forehead. Man was driven out from the face of God because of sin. Sin is no more there (Gen.3:22-24; Rev.22:4; Gen.4:14-16; Matt.5:8; 2Cor.3:10-18; Ex.33:20-33). No man can see the face of God and live, but all in this city will have 'died to sin and self', and now will be able to behold the glory of God in the face of Jesus Christ.
- The redeemed shall worship and serve God and the Lamb eternally as **King-Priests** after the Order of Melchisedek (Rev.1:6; 5:9-10; 22:5).

6. Description of Heaven
God uses figurative and material glories to describe spiritual realities. Even as Hell is described under various names and designations, so is heaven. Heaven is "the Father's house" (Jhn.14:2), "a place prepared" (Jhn.14:2-3), "with Christ" (Phil.1:23), "heaven" (Matt.6:19-20), "Paradise" (2Cor.12:2-4), "the third heaven" (2Cor.12:2-4), "the city of God" (Heb.11:10-16; 13:14; Rev.21:1-2), "the heavenly country" (Heb.11:10-16), and "the New Heavens and New Earth" wherein dwells righteousness, and "the New Jerusalem" (2Pet.3:13; Isa.65:17; Rev.21:1-2).

Here the believer is promised "the tree of life" (Rev.2:7) and not to be hurt of the second death (Rev.2:11). He is promised a stone with a new name in it (Rev.2:17; authority with Christ (Rev.2:26-27); a white garment and his name in the Book of Life (Rev.3:4-5). He is to know security in the city of God (Rev.3:12), and ruling and reigning in the throne of God and the Lamb (Rev.3:21).

All this can only be a description of heaven, the dwelling place eternally for the redeemed of all ages. Jesus told His disciples He was going to prepare a place for them, and that He would come again, and receive His own to Himself. Where He was, they would be (Jhn.14:3). Where ever Jesus is, that is heaven. Heaven will be a place of light, love, holiness, righteousness, worship, service, joy, peace and life eternally because Jesus the Redeemer will be there. There will be no darkness, hatred, sin, unrighteousness, sorrow, discord or death there. Without these things, it will be heaven indeed. What a wonderful and worthy reward of the God who redeemed us! After considering heaven and its alternative – hell – it is only 'spiritual insanity' to turn from God and His Christ!

C. The Kingdom to the Father

Attention has already been given to the theme of "The Kingdom." There it was seen that the Kingdom of God is an everlasting Kingdom, but, in relation to earth, there has been a progressive manifestation of that Kingdom.

The final aspect of the progressive revelation and manifestation of that everlasting Kingdom of God is that which takes place at the close of the 1000 year period of time, called the Millennial Kingdom. Paul speaks of the coming of the end, when the Son will deliver up the Kingdom to the Father. Here the cycle is complete. The everlasting Kingdom has been manifested in its sevenfold expression in the earth, reaching from eternity to eternity in its completeness.

A careful study of Paul's word in the Corinthian Epistle seems to provide us with some kind of Divine order with regards to final things. The language covers time from Adam to Christ's resurrection and on to the close of the Millennial Age. This calls for some running comments on the passage in 1Cor.15:22-28, and each of its important clauses.

1. **"In Adam all die"** – this takes us back to Gen.3:1-24 where sin entered Eden's Paradise, and sin and death were passed on to all men (Rom.5:12-21).

2. **"In Christ all shall be made alive"** – this brings us to Christ's redemptive work on Calvary. As any one accepts Christ as Lord and Saviour, they are taken out of being "in Adam" and placed "in Christ". God sees but two representative men. All of the human race are either "in Adam" or "in Christ". There is no neutral ground.
But Paul goes in thought beyond that exchange of 'Federal Headship' to the resurrection of the body. All those "in Christ" shall be made alive; that is, resurrected from death.

3. **"Every one is raised in his own order"** – This speaks of an order that will be seen in the resurrections. This "order" can be seen in the first and second resurrections. The righteous will be in the first resurrection; the unrighteous in the second resurrection. This is how all will be raised in his own order. Even in the resurrection, there is Divine order.

4. **"Christ, the Firstfruits"** – Refer vs.20,23. Christ, as head of the Church, takes pre-eminence in the resurrection and glorification of His body. In Passover Feast, there was the sheaf of the firstfruits presented to God in His Tabernacle (Lev.23). Christ rose after three days and three nights. He rose first, and then after His resurrection, a company of saints were raised bodily, and appeared to many in Jerusalem (Matt.27:50-51). He is the Firstborn from death, and He is the First Begotten of the dead (Col.1:18; Rev.1:5). He Himself is THE Resurrection and THE Life (Jhn.11:25).

5. **"Afterwards, they that are Christ's at His coming"** – This clause brings us to the first resurrection of the righteous at His second coming. Paul says, "They that are Christ's" will be raised at His advent. He makes no mention of those who are not Christ's. This resurrection here would include the rapture and translation of the dead in Christ with the living saints (1Thess.4:13-18).

6. **"Then comes the end"** – The first coming was "the end" of the Old Testament age (Heb.9:26). And Paul speaks of "the end" of the ages coming on us (1Cor.10:11). The second coming of Christ will be "the end" of the New Testament era (Dan.12:6,8,9 with Rev.22:10,20). In AD.70 there was "the end" of Judaism in the destruction of the Temple and city of Jerusalem (Matt.24:1-3). The Gospel of the Kingdom is to preached to all nations during this era and then shall "the end" come (Matt.24:14). This shows us how the words "the end" are used. It should answer the question as to "How many 'ends' can there be?"
As this writer understands this passage, "the end" here refers to the close of the 1000 year period when the Son returns the Kingdom back to the Father, as the next clause indicates.

7. **"He shall have delivered up the Kingdom to God, even the Father"** – As understood, this is referring to the Millennial Kingdom. Daniel 7 along with Luke speaks of the Son receiving from the Father ("Ancient of Days") a Kingdom. When He receives the Kingdom, He returns to take account of His servants (Lke.17:20-21 with Lke.19:11-27). In the Millennium, "the saints possess the Kingdom", and Christ reigns as King of Kings and Lord of Lords. But, at the end of the 1000 years Millennial Kingdom, the Son delivers it up to the Father God (Psa.145:11-13; 2Pet.1:11; Dan.4:3,34; 7:14,27; 2Tim.4:18). This completes the cycle of the manifestation of the Kingdom in earth.

8. **"He shall have put down all rule and all authority"** – All rule and authority given to the Son is now returned to the Father God.

9. **"He must reign"** – Christ is indeed reigning now in this present aspect of the Kingdom. He is sitting at His Father's right hand. He reigns as King-Priest after the Order of Melchisedek (Zech.6:12-13 with Psa.110; Psa.2 and Heb.7). He will continue to reign over the Kingdom in the 1000 years. With the crushing of the ten toes of the Image (Dan2), and the smiting of the ten horns of the Beast Kingdom (Dan.7), He is the "Smiting Stone" and the "Son of Man" ruling in the Kingdom.

10. **"He must reign until He has put all enemies under His feet** – The Last enemy to be destroyed is death"** – At Christ's second advent, all enemies will be forever crushed under His feet. But, once Satan and his hosts are judged and cast into the Lake of Fire – that is the ultimate fulfillment of this promise (Psa.110). Then, after the Great White Throne Judgment, "death and Hades" are cast into the Lake of Fire (Rev.20:11-15). This fulfills, "the last enemy to be destroyed is death."

11. **"For all things have been put under His feet"** – That is, the Father is the One who has put all things under the Son's feet. Think of Joshua telling the Israelites to put their feet on the necks of the enemy kings in Canaan Land. It was a sign of total victory over all enemies (Josh.10:20-27; Psa.107:40; Isa.26:5-6; Mal.4:3 and Rom.16:20). God will bruise Satan under your feet shortly, Paul wrote to the Roman believers.

12. **"But when He says all things are put under His feet, it is manifest that He is excepted, which did put all things under Him"** – By "all things" being placed under the feet of the Son, it is evident that the Father God is not subject to the Son. The Son is subject to the Father, not the Father to the Son. There is order in the Godhead: Father, Son and Holy Spirit. The Father has put all things under the Son's feet, but He is not under the Son's feet. This is what Paul is saying here.

13. **"When all things are subdued unto Him, then the Son Himself also will become subject to Him who put all things under Him"** – When the time comes that everything is subdued to the Son, then the Son becomes subject to the Father. It would appear from Rev.20 that this is the time when eternal destinies are settled that this happens. Satan, the fallen angels, demonic spirits, unredeemed mankind, death and Hades – all are cast into the Lake of Fire. It is the absolute end of sin and the source of sin. All enemies are subdued. This is at the close of the Millennium. Here the Son gives the Kingdom back to the Father. The work of redemption is complete. Here the Son subjects Himself to the Father for whatever eternity holds. This is "the end" of which Paul speaks. The truths here are vastly superior to our limited and finite minds, as to what was revealed to Paul on this matter.

14. **"That God may all in all"** – The cycle is finished. It brings us back to Gen.1:1. "In the beginning God…" and it will be, "In the end God…".

This brings us to the eternal states – to eternity! Beyond this, God has told us nothing. Rev.21-22 chapters tell us what the eternal states of the righteous and the wicked will be. These chapters close off the Bible story of Creation and Redemption. "In the beginning God…" are the words with which the Bible opens (Gen.1:1). "The grace of our Lord Jesus Christ be with you all. Amen" are the words with which the Bible closes (Rev.22:21). Here the New Heavens and the New Earth replace the old creation of the old Heavens and Earth! Here is eternity with God and the Lamb, and the holy angels and the redeemed! This will be heaven indeed – heaven without end. Amen!

In a diagram overview of this passage, it would appear something like this:

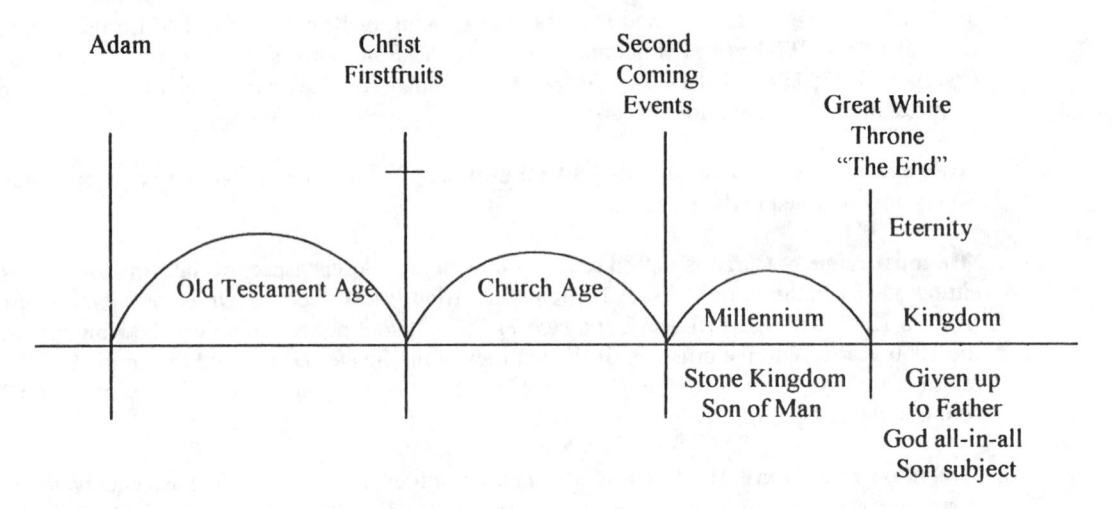

```
Adam              Christ            Second
                  Firstfruits       Coming
                                    Events
                                                  Great White
                                                  Throne
                                                  "The End"

                                                  Eternity
        Old Testament Age    Church Age
                                        Millennium    Kingdom

                                    Stone Kingdom    Given up
                                    Son of Man       to Father
                                                     God all-in-all
                                                     Son subject
```

Conclusion:

In bringing this chapter of "The Eternal States" to its close, the most fitting would be to see the wonderful and glorious contrast and comparison between Genesis and Revelation. In these two books, Moses (the beginning) and John (the ending) join hands, completing the links between Creation and Redemption, as the following chart confirms.

The Book of Genesis	The Book of Revelation
1. Creation of the Heavens and the Earth	1. The New Heavens and New Earth
2. Creation of Adam and his Bride, Eve	2. Last Adam, Christ and His Bride-Church
3. The Rivers in the Garden Paradise	3. River of Life in the City of God
4. Tree of Knowledge of Good and Evil in the midst of the Garden – Forbidden	4. No Tree of Knowledge of Good and Evil – ended in history of human race
5. Tree of Eternal Life in the midst also	5. Tree of Eternal Life near the River of God
6. The Garden of God, Garden of Delight	6. Trees of Life along the Banks of River
7. The Edenic Covenant	7. The New Covenant
8. The Serpent in Paradise	8. The Serpent in the Lake of Fire eternally
9. Entrance of sin and death	9. No more sin and death
10. Sorrow, pain, sadness and tears	10. No more sorrow, pain or tears
11. Tree of Life forfeited by disobedience	11. Tree of Life restored by obedience
12. The Beginning – Moses the Prophet as writer of Genesis	12. The Ending – John the Apostle as writer of Revelation

The Preacher truly said: "Better is **THE END** a thing than **THE BEGINNING**" (Eccles.7:8). Genesis is the beginning. Revelation is the end. Revelation is indeed better than Genesis!

PART THREE

PART THREE
THE CHRISTIAN MILLENNIUM

Introduction
Principles of Interpretation
Chapter
1. The Weeks of the Lord
2. The Days of the Lord
3. Significance of One Hundred and Twenty
4. The Age and the Ages to Come
5. A Study in 'Thousands'
6. What is NOT in a Christian Millennium
7. The Christian Millennium
8. Reigning on the Earth
9. The Glory of the Christian Millennium
10. End of Millennium Events

Conclusion

Overview Chart of Millennial Views

Bibliography

THE CHRISTIAN MILLENNIUM

INTRODUCTION

Our text in **Part One** and **Part Two** has worked through the fifteen areas of Eschatological controversy in relation to the differing Millennial views. It has been a necessary exercise to work through these areas. The serious student will have seen their inter-relatedness and how each have some bearing and effect on the other, some more and some less. Whatever one's view of one or more or all of these things determines which School of Eschatology in which they place themselves. That is, they place themselves in either Post-Millennial, Historic Pre-Millennial, Futurist and/or Dispensational Pre-Millennial or the A-Millennial School. The same is true of the present writer, with some great differences.

Hopefully, this writer has provided some clear response, more or less, to each of the fifteen areas under discussion. It is now appropriate in **Part Three** to develop more fully what the writer has coined "**The Christian Millennium**".

At the risk of being charged with bias, bigotry, conceit or arrogance, the following comment is made. After many years of study, a reading of numerous books and a careful consideration of the various Millennial Schools of thought, the writer believes that there is a mixture of truth and error in them. In this text, we have endeavoured, with Christian grace, to deal with the problems and not attack the persons involved. It is a matter of working through doctrinal issues and not personal issues, as each School seeks to come to a clearer understanding of end-time events.

In **Part Two, Chapter 14**, the major truth the writer wanted to communicate was that there is a future aspect of the Kingdom of God relative to earth. This is generally referred to as the Millennial Kingdom. Regarding the previous Chapters (Part One/Part Two), it can be seen that the Historic Pre-Millennialist, the Post-Millennialist and the A-Millennialist position have much in common with the Christian Millennialist position. Regarding the Futurist and Dispensational Pre-Millennialist, which have the most in common, there are some areas with which the Christian Millennialist agrees.

There will be, and are, however, some very sharp differences with each School of opinion on some areas. This will be seen more especially in **Part Three** of this text and chapters on "The Christian Millennium". Some of these differences have already been noted when dealing with the fifteen areas under discussion.

The writer has found over time that, on the one hand, the Futurist/Dispensational School attributes A-Millennialism to him. On the other hand, because the writer still holds to a future Millennium, the A-Millennialist attributes Dispensationalism to him. The writer does have many friends in each of these Schools of Eschatology and, at times, have enjoyed discussion on these issues, without coming to complete agreement.

The writer believes that it is very likely that one extreme resists the other extreme and both react against the other's point of view. It has already been said that, to every thesis, there is an antithesis, and the balance is often down the middle, that is, synthesis. The view set forth here, hopefully, is a balance between two apparent extremes. Is it possible to hold to a future Millennium, but take out of it what has been, without any Scriptural basis, placed in it? This writer believes so! Because the opinion is that there are some extremes in each School, the author has sought to come to and present a balanced Scriptural view, according to his limited and imperfect understanding. This is so on each of the fifteen points of controversy, and more especially on the Millennium.

To remind ourselves:
The Post-Millennialist sees a future Millennium, ushered in by the Church militant and triumphant, where life will be much like it is now. It will, however, be a Christianized world, a Utopian period of righteousness and peace.
The Historic Pre-Millennialist sees a future Millennium, much like life is at present, but there will be mortals and immortals, unredeemed and redeemed co-mingling together. It will be a Kingdom of righteousness, peace and prosperity under the reign of Jesus Christ.
The Futurist and Dispensational Pre-Millennialist see primarily an earthly, Jewish Millennium, where the Mosaic Covenant economy will be re-instituted. The Jews will be head of the nations of earth and Christ Himself will rule in Jerusalem on the throne of David.

The A-Millennialist sees "a realized Millennium" as being fulfilled in this present age, between the first and second comings of Christ. There is no future earthly or Jewish Millennium. Eternity is ushered in by the return of Jesus Christ.

Because of some contradictions, apparent extremes and reactions in each School over end-time and Millennial issues, and because the writer believes that there is a future Millennial reign of Christ on earth, he wanted to come up with some designation that defined his position. Therefore, the designation "**Christian Millennium**" was coined. The author believes in a Millennium, but it is not a 'Jewish Millennium', or a Millennium where mortals and immortals co-mingle and where so many things have been unScripturally placed. It is, as the title says, **"The CHRISTIAN Millennium!"**

Most preachers, teachers, and Christian expositors of the Word exclaim: " A Christian Millennium – What is that?" Students of prophecy and end-time events have heard of a Utopian Millennium (Post-Millennial), and a Realized Millennium (A-Millennial), and a Jewish Millennium (Futurist/Dispensational), and a Blessed Millennium (Historic Millennial), but A CHRISTIAN Millennium – what kind of a Millennium is that? **Part Three** seeks to answer that question and present a possible alternative to each of the other Millennial views.

The reader is encouraged to read the whole of **Part Three** through first, considering the arguments and contents presented before forming some opinion and coming to some conclusion. The writer of Proverbs says, "He that answers a matter before he hears it, it is a folly and shame to him" (Prov.18:13).

Because, for many readers, there will be some different concepts presented on a Christian Millennium, the author believes it would be helpful, right at the beginning, to set out a rather full proposition, definition and summary of the position of the Christian Millennialist. It summarizes the teaching in the respective chapters of **Part Three**.

"The Christian Millennium is a Millennium established by Christ at His second coming. It is the reign of Christ here on the earth. It will be an actual yet spiritual revelation and manifestation of the Kingdom of God on the earth for 1000 years, closing off God's Week of Redemption as it pertains to this earth. It is the final expression of God's everlasting Kingdom relative to earth.

At Christ's coming, the dead in Christ rise first (the first resurrection), the living saints are changed and caught up together with them to meet the Lord in the air. The saints are rewarded and in their various glories find their place in the order of the Kingdom. The saints possess the Kingdom. Only Christians, that is, the redeemed, enter this Kingdom. This is why it is called a Christian Millennium. Christ reigns as King of Kings and Lord of Lords. The earth is filled with the knowledge of the glory of the Lord as the waters cover the sea.

There will be no unconverted Jews or Gentiles, no unredeemed or mortal sinners in the Millennial Kingdom as all are destroyed at the second coming of Jesus Christ. There will be no re-institution of the Mosaic Covenant economy. There will be no restoration of the nation of Israel over the Gentile nations. Only the redeemed of the earth will enter that Kingdom.

Satan will be bound in the Abyss, and with him all his angels and demonic hosts. There will be no sin, sickness, disease or death. Sorrow and pain will be no more. There will be no marriages, no births and no deaths. The earth will keep its Sabbath Rest as the Devil is bound, the source of all sin and evil. The whole earth will be as the Garden of Eden, the Paradise of the Lord on the restored earth.

At the close of the 1000 years, Satan is loosed from his prison, the wicked dead are resurrected (the second resurrection). Satan deceives them into a final attempt against the saints of God. Fire comes down from heaven. There is the Great White Throne Judgment on Satan, all his hosts, and all the unredeemed of all ages of mankind's history. All whose names are not in the Book of Life go to the Lake of Fire, eternally. The redeemed go to the New Heavens and New Earth. Eternal states are ushered in. The Son gives the Kingdom back to the Father so that God may be all and in all (1Cor.15:20-28). The Christian Millennium is 'heaven on earth' but is the prelude, the preface to the eternal order."

The following chapters in **Part Three** provide the details and are an explanation and amplification of the propositional summary as given here.

PRINCIPLES OF INTERPRETATION

In "**Interpreting the Scriptures**" (Conner/Malmin. Foreword), the writers hold that, "Generally speaking, Bible believing Christians are united in accepting the facts of revelation and inspiration. However, the major divisions concern interpretation and application. The problem then is, not over **revelation and inspiration** as much as it is over **interpretation and application**."

This is true when it comes to the different views of "The Millennium." On the whole, all Millennial Schools are Bible believers. There is no attack on the infallible and inspired Word of God. The difficulty has to do with hermeneutics, or Biblical Principles of Interpretation.

There are a number of Hermeneutical Principles when it comes to rightly interpreting the Word of God, the Holy Scriptures. When it comes to the Millennium, as presented in this text, there are two most vital principles of interpretation that divide the varying Eschatological Schools of thought. These have to do with that which is Theological and Hermeneutical. The first is the Covenantal Principle and the second major area is the Literal Method of Interpretation.

1. **The Covenantal Principle**
   All Schools of Millennial interpretation divide at the point of Covenants. The Covenants fall into two major streams; the Covenant of Law and the Covenants of Grace. The foundational premise of this text is that, at the cross, the Old or the Mosaic Covenant was fulfilled and abolished. The New Covenant is now in effect. Therefore, the principle of interpreting the Word is never to use the Old Testament to interpret the New Testament, but to use the New Testament to interpret the Old, passing all through the cross. The cross becomes, what may be called, "the hermeneutical filter" for interpreting the Scriptures. To understand the Covenantal Principle, one will not teach or believe that the Old Mosaic Covenant is to be re-established in this end of the age, or any future age. Believers are under the New Covenant, and this is an everlasting, irrevocable Covenant. This principle is one of the most vital principles under-girding a number of chapters in the text, especially under Part Two and Part Three. The cross is the key, and any and all Old Testament Scriptures must now, since the New Covenant was ratified in the blood of Jesus, pass through the cross!

2. **The Literal Method**
   Defining "the literal method" of interpreting the Scriptures, has become a kind of 'battle zone' for Millennialists. What does the word "literal" mean? Should the Scriptures be interpreted "literally" or "figuratively" and who is the authority to say which should be used? What is literal, and what is figurative? What is to be interpreted actually and what is to be interpreted symbolically? If one does not understand or explain clearly what is meant by the use of "the literal method", then much difference of opinion and interpretation is the result.

   This writer uses the literal method of interpretation throughout this text. But this needs some explanation and qualification. This has been ably explained in the text already mentioned (Conner/Malmin, page 18), which is adapted and amplified for the purposes here.

   A. Origin: In relation to Scripture, the literal method of interpretation is the oldest in existence. It is said to have originated with Ezra, the Father of Hermeneutics. Its history may be traced through the Palestinian Jews, through Christ and His Apostles, the School of Antioch, and the Reformers, to the fundamental Conservatives of the present time.

   B. Definition: The literal method assumes that the words of Scripture in their plain evident meaning are reliable; that God intended His revelation to be understood by all who believe; that the words of Scripture communicate what God wants man to know; and that God based the communication of truth on the regular laws governing written communication, thereby intending for it to be interpreted by those same laws. This is not to deny the Holy Spirit's involvement in both the production and the interpretation of the Bible.

   The expression "literal sense" may be defined as: the usual, customary, and socially accepted meaning conveyed by words or expressions in their particular contexts. It involves that which a particular word meant to the original writer and readers. It recognizes that a word may have different meanings in different contexts and thus must be interpreted in the light of its contextual usage. It contends that, though a word may possibly have several meanings, in any one particular usage, it generally will have but one intended meaning.

According to Tan ("**The Interpretation of Prophecy**", page 29), "To interpret 'literally' means to explain the original sense of the speaker or writer according to the normal, customary and proper usages of words and language." He notes that this method is also called the Grammatico-Historical method because, in order to determine the normal and customary usages of Bible language, the accepted rules of grammar and rhetoric must be considered and the historical and cultural aspects of Bible times must be taken into consideration. Tan develops and expands his understanding into four areas which are adapted and amplified here.

(1) The Literal Sense does not exclude the Figurative

Pre-Millennialists place strong emphasis on the literal interpretation of the Scriptures. Post-Millennialists and A-Millennialists accept the literal but place stronger emphasis on the figurative and symbolic language of Scripture. Some interpreters have used the term figurative in opposition to the term literal, as though the figurative meaning of words were opposed to their literal sense. However, in that figurative language is a part of normal communication, it also is encompassed by the literal system of interpretation. The literal includes the figurative. God intended some words to be used figuratively. Actual is the opposite of figurative. The figurative is to be included in the literal or actual. The figurative meaning arises out of and is consistent with the actual meaning of the word or words. The word 'actual' mean "real or effective, or that which exists truly or absolutely." The word 'actual' is used to say "what the words really and truly mean." The words "literal" or "actual" could be used interchangeably.

The prophets used words that literally and actually mean what they are, but use them in a figurative sense.

"The trees clap their hands, and the mountains break forth into singing" (Isa.55:12). Taking these words in their literal and actual meaning, trees are trees, and mountains are mountains, but here the prophet uses the literal in a figurative sense. But the figurative is based upon the literal meaning of those words. Otherwise, one lapses into allegorization of words, that trees and mountains really do not mean that. Trees and mountains are something else!

"Herod, that old fox" (Lke.13:22). A fox is a fox, but Jesus uses the literal and actual fox to be figurative or symbolic of Herod in his sly, cunning and killing nature and character.

The blood out of the winepress of God's wrath flowed to the horse's bridles (Rev.14:20). The blood of the grapes was a literal and actual result of treading out the life of grapes in the winepress. Here God uses the literal/actual in a figurative and symbolic manner to describe the total crushing of the wicked in God's winepress of wrath. But the figurative arises out of the literal.

The Devil goes about "as a roaring lion" (1Pet.5:8). God uses the literal or actual lion – for that is what the word means – in a symbolic and figurative manner to describe the workings of the Devil. The figurative arises out of the literal and actual use and meaning of the word. So the literal and actual are used in a figurative and symbolical way in numerous Scriptures in the Bible. The literal method, therefore, does not exclude the figurative sense of Scripture.

(2) The Literal Method does not exclude Spiritual Meaning

Some interpreters have used the term "spiritual" in opposition to the term "literal" as though the spiritual meaning of Scripture were opposed to its literal meaning. Under the title of "the spiritual method" some interpreters have spiritualized Scripture to mean something other than what it says. The literal method, though rejecting spiritualization (and allegorization), does admit the spiritual substance and nature of the Scriptures. The Bible is a spiritual book conveying spiritual truth and therefore must be spiritually interpreted. This can be done through accepting as sufficient the illuminated meaning of the words.

Paul provides an example of this for us in 1Cor.10:1-4. He writes about the Israelites passing through the Red Sea, and eating of the Manna and drinking waters from the Rock that followed them. He speaks of the Cloud that led Israel to the promised land. But then he goes on to say that the Red Sea was "a baptism into Moses," and the Manna and Waters from the

Rock was "spiritual meat and drink". Then he says that the Rock that followed them was "Christ." What is Paul doing here? These things were literal and actual things in Israel's history and experience. Paul says they were "spiritual", and they were "types and examples" for us and our admonition. Paul is not spiritualizing away the miracles that happened back there, literally and actually. These things were not "types" to them. They are types to us. But Paul is drawing from the literal and actual historical accounts, some spiritual lessons for the believers at Corinth, and for the Church today. The literal must not be confused with the spiritual nor the spiritual with the literal. The spiritual is firmly founded on the literal understanding of the words. The literal method does not exclude the spiritual.

The Literal and Actual	The Spiritual and Typical
1. Baptized unto Moses in the Red Sea	1. Water Baptism of Nation to Mediator
2. Baptized in the Cloud of Glory	2. The Holy Spirit to lead them to Canaan
3. Ate of the Manna	3. Spiritual Meat and Food
4. Drank of the Waters	4. Spiritual Drink
5. From the Rock that followed them	5. That Rock was Christ (Anointed)

In "**Harmonies of Divine Revelation**" (page 90), W.H.Offiler has this to say about the Word of God. Comments are adapted here. "The Word of God is not only capable of a "Literal" interpretation, for a "Literal" interpretation is absolutely necessary to a correct understanding of the Scripture of Truth.

Jesus said, My Word is Spirit and My Word is Life. All Scripture MUST be interpreted on this dual basis. Great harm has come, and much misunderstanding, and false teaching have come by spiritualizing THE WORD, with an utter disregard of its human, or earthly side. Jesus Christ, the Son of God, was as definitely Man in the flesh. Son of God and Son of Man are the Divine titles applied to Him, and as representing the Divine and Human parts of His nature. His Mother Mary, His Father GOD. Deity and Humanity; Heavenly and Earthly, Spiritual and Literal – THE WORD made FLESH. The birth of Christ was as literal (human) as it was spiritual (Divine). He was begotten from heaven. He was born on the earth.

Truth concerning salvation must have these characteristics. We are born again – Born of the flesh and born of the Spirit. God and Man coming together to form one New Creature. This is the Divine pattern, and so through all the revelations of the Word of God. God has identified Himself with His creatures. Were this not true, MAN could never understand His Maker GOD." (End adapted quotes) The Literal Method does not exclude spiritual meaning, but spiritual meaning must be firmly grounded upon the proper, the literal and actual use of the words of Scripture. This is an important qualification of the use of the literal/spiritual.

(3) The Literal Method does not exclude Application
Some interpreters confuse interpretation with application. John Calvin said, "The Word of God is inexhaustible and applicable at all times, but here is a difference between explanation and application, and application must be consistent with explanation." The task of literal interpretation is first to discern the meaning of God's Word, and then, upon that basis, to apply it. A general rule of the literal method is: "There is one interpretation, but many applications."

Many preachers and teachers often proceed into application in their 'Sermons' when they fail to give proper interpretation of the passage or verse under consideration. Explanation precedes application. Application must be based on proper interpretation. Application must not contradict or violate or be confused with interpretation. Interpretation should precede application in the use of the literal method.

An example of this is seen in Num.13-14 with Heb.3-4. The literal and actual account in Numbers is the failure of Israel to enter into Canaan land because of unbelief. The spiritual application the writer to the Hebrews gets from this is, believers may also fail to enter into God's rest because of the same sin of unbelief. But the application of truth is solidly based on the proper understanding of the actual and historical occasion in Israel's history. The writer is not spiritualizing or allegorizing away the historical account. He provides explanation and then weaves this proper application throughout.

(4) The Literal Method does not exclude Depth of Meaning

Some interpreters believe that the literal method greatly limits the believer in discovering the Divine depths of truth latent in Scripture. Indeed, some definitions of this method do, but here it is defined to include depth of meaning within certain necessary limitations. In that God is the virtual Author of Scripture, some truths therein are patent, outward and obvious, while others are latent, inward and hidden. Historical events do have spiritual significance, and certain figures of speech, such as types, symbols and allegories, do have hidden meaning. However, this meaning is solidly based on the earthly sense of the words and necessitates that interpretation remain within the proper boundaries of truths plainly revealed in God's Word.

"It is the glory of God to conceal a thing, but the honour of kings is to search out a matter" (Prov.25:2). Job tells us: "Surely there is a vein for the silver…" The gold, silver, precious stones of the earth, and pearls of the sea – all have to be mined for, or explored for in the depths of the sea. These precious gems are not to be found on the surface. Many Christians 'surface read' the Scriptures but never 'dig deep' to find God's hidden treasures of truth that are beneath the surface reading of the inexhaustible Word of God. The Literal Method includes depth of meaning for those serious students of the Scriptures (2Tim.2:15).

The Tabernacle of Moses and the Temple of Solomon provide much depth of meaning by using proper hermeneutical principles beyond just the surface reading of the materials used to build these Divinely planned habitations of God.

The student is referred to "The Figures of Speech Group of Principles" that deal with ways of 'digging deep' into the treasure field of God's Word ("**Figures of Speech in The Bible**", E.W.Bullinger). These Principles include the Symbolic, the Numerical, the Typical, the Parabolic and Allegorical Principles of Interpretation. These things are woven throughout the way to interpret Prophecy, Eschatology and other interrelated Books of the Bible.

In the Literal Method then, there is the Literal and the Spiritual, the Actual and the Figurative, the Interpretation and Application, the Surface Meaning and also Depth of Meaning.

Conclusion:

The Literal Method is that which is used in this textbook. Included in the use of the Literal Method is the breakdown of the things dealt with in this chapter. It is a safe and sound and sensible approach to the interpretation of Scripture, and when used properly, will save the expositor from much extreme. It is upon the literal method that this text is built.

The Golden Rule of Interpretation

When the plain sense of the Scripture makes common sense, seek no other sense; therefore, take every word at its primary, ordinary, usual, literal meaning unless the facts of the immediate context, studied in the light of related passages and aximatic and fundamental truths, indicate clearly otherwise!

Or, in other words, When the plain sense of Scripture makes common sense, seek no other sense, or one lands into non-sense!

Finally, **Sound theology** united with **sound hermeneutics** makes for **sound exegesis** of the Scriptures! The writer has sought to follow these things throughout the text.

CHAPTER ONE

THE WEEKS OF THE LORD

The Scriptures provide a number of prophetic foreshadowings and types of the Christian Millennium. A careful consideration of these various pictures all add some weight of truth concerning a future Millennium. The student should weigh carefully the Scripture references, the prophetic import in them and how they find fulfillment in the period of time – the Kingdom Age – of 1000 years which ushers in eternity.

One of the most significant patterns of Scripture, if not the 'foundational pattern', is that which appertains to God's Sevens, "The Weeks of the Lord". This pattern of God's Weeks has become, for the writer, one of the most convincing foundations in Scripture for believing in a future Millennium, a Christian Millennium.

The Prophet Jeremiah, in referring to the Feasts of the Lord, complained about the rebellious heart of the people of Judah. He lamented the fact that they did not say, "Let us now fear the LORD our God, that gives rain, both the former and the latter, in his season: He reserves unto us the **appointed weeks** of the harvest" (Jer.5:24). The Hebrew words for "**week**" here simply means "**seven**". The "appointed weeks" are literally speaking of "the appointed sevens". The Hebrew mind was saturated with the concept of the "Weeks of the LORD". The whole context of Scripture shows indeed that God was shadowing forth the "Redemptive Week" in the patterns of the sevens given to the chosen nation of Israel. The whole of Scripture shows a seven-fold revelation of these Weeks, the ultimate being manifested in the Week of Redemption. This is seen in the following.

1. **The Week of Creation – Gen.1:1—2:3**
   The Book of Genesis provides for us the account of creation. Here in these first chapters we see how God worked for six days, whatever the length of those 'days' were. Some expositors see a 24-hour day, and others see a time period in those 'days'. The matter is, God worked six days in creation. On the seventh day, He rested. He sanctified this seventh day as the crowning glory on the work of the previous six days. The man and woman He created actually began their time on earth with this seventh day, as they were created at the close of the sixth day. This is the first "week" or the first "seven" to be revealed in the Bible. It sets the pattern for all the following "weeks" or "sevens". This is designated as "The Week of Creation". It is God's creative week; six days work, and the seventh day – Rest, Sanctification and Blessedness!

2. **The Week of Days – Ex.31:12-17; Lev.23:3**
   In this passage, we see the LORD calling his chosen nation, Israel, to work for six days and then to rest on the seventh day. The seventh day was the holy Sabbath to the LORD and no manner of work was to be done on this day, on pain of death. Man's days were 24-hour days. But God, in commanding Israel concerning this "week" pointed back to the first "week" – His work and week in creation. He Himself had worked six days in creation, then He rested on the seventh day. Israel was therefore, to follow God's pattern in a similar manner. They were to work for six days, then rest the seventh day according to God's commandment and His own example. Read also Ex.20:8-11, which confirms these thoughts. God's week in creation became a pattern week for Man's week in Israel. Six days work, then the seventh day is rest!

3. **The Week of Weeks of Days – Lev.23:15-22**
   Remembering that the word "week" simply means "seven", we see here again in the Feast of Pentecost the pattern of a week of weeks, or a seven of sevens. The Israelites were told to count from the day of the waving of the Sheaf of Firstfruits 49 days, or 7 x 7 = 49 days. This is, 7 weeks. Seven Sabbaths were to elapse. Then the day following, which was "the morrow after the seventh Sabbath" was the fiftieth day. On this day, they kept the Feast Day of Pentecost. The Feast of Pentecost was founded on "the Week of Weeks". Pentecost was actually called "the Feast of Weeks" in the Old Testament because of this time. Thus, seven weeks of seven days were 49 days, or, the pattern of the Week of Weeks of Days, Pentecost being the fiftieth day. The seventh Sabbath along with the fiftieth day was a sacred seven. Sufficient to note that God repeats the pattern of His week, but in this case it is the week of weeks. Surely He was wanting to communicate some truth to His people Israel.

4. **The Weeks of Months – Lev.23:1-14**
   The next order in the number seven relative to the weeks of the Lord is that which is seen in the Feasts of the LORD in this chapter. The Feasts of Passover, Pentecost and Tabernacles were encompassed within the

"week", that is, within seven months, or "a Week of Months". Passover took place in the first month, Pentecost was in the third month, and Tabernacles was held in the seventh month. This seventh month was the most sacred month of the year. In this month was the Feast Day of the Blowing of Trumpets, the great Day of Atonement and the Feast of Tabernacles proper. Here again there is this cycle of the "seven" or the "week". The seventh month, as mentioned, was the most sacred month. It was sanctified or set apart from the previous six months. Because the Feasts of the LORD took place within the cycle of seven months, it is called "the Week of Months".

5. **The Week of Years – Lev.15:1-7; Ex.21:1-6**
Here again the LORD repeats to Israel His pattern of "seven". This time it has to do with years. "The Week of Years" has to do with the rest for the land and the liberation of all slaves in Israel. The LORD commanded Israel to work the land for six years, but the seventh year was to be a year of rest, a Sabbath for the land. No sowing nor reaping was to be done. The land was to rest from all work on it. Failure to keep the Sabbath years of Rest for the land brought about the Babylonian Captivity for 70 years. This Captivity became the 70 Sabbaths for the land (2Chron.36:21; Dan.9:1-2). Again we have a "week", the "Week of Years"; work for the land six years, and the seventh year rest. This surely points to the "seventh Millennium" when this earth shall keep her Sabbath Rest, with the curse lifted and Satan bound. That will be rest indeed.

Relative to this same period of time, this "week" or "seven", we have the Lord's word concerning the slaves. If an Israelite bought a slave, then the slave was to work for his master six years, but in the seventh year, he was to be set free, unless he desired to be a love-slave to his master – for ever! The slave understood what this "Week of Years" meant. This seventh year was called the year of release (Deut.31:10). It certainly was, in the mind of any Israelite, or any slave, a very blessed and sacred year. It pointed to God's seventh Millennium when all the slaves of Satan, who are redeemed, are totally released from all that sin brought on them. Once Satan is bound, there is full release for the earth and for those who were once slaves of sin. Once again, there is God's pattern of the "week", impressed here on the Week of Years, even as this pattern has been impressed on the days and months previously. Who can ignore God's pattern of sevens?

6. **The Week of Weeks of Years – Lev.25:8-17**
Once again the LORD re-emphasizes to Israel something that He has in mind concerning His Weeks. Here the pattern is seen in a "Week of Weeks of Years". This week of weeks of years follows a similar pattern to that which was seen in he Feast of Weeks and Pentecost. There it was 7 x 7 = 49 days, then the fiftieth day was Pentecost. In this pattern, there is 7 x 7 = 49 years, then the fiftieth year was a Jubilee Year. The forty-ninth year was the seventh Sabbath year, and then the year following was also a sacred year, the year of Jubilee. It is a "week of weeks of years" or "seven sevens", making the 49 years in all. The Jubilee Year actually began on the Day of Atonement, which was the tenth day of the seventh month. These patterns are too great to ignore or discard. God spoke to Israel through these "Weeks", and surely they have some significance for the true Israel of God, the Church. The earth will keep its Sabbath when Satan is bound. The earth will keep her Jubilee, as some of the old Gospel Songs taught.

7. **The Week of Millenniums – The Whole Bible**
Each of the previous patterns of "weeks" or "sevens" shadow forth the total purpose of God relative to man and this earth. God has been at work in the week which is called "the Week of Redemption". Since the Fall of Adam, God has been working some six days, that is, 6000 years. "A day unto the Lord is as a 1000 years and 1000 years as a day" (Psa.90:4; Gen.2:17; 2Pet.3:8; Job.24:1). Sin broke God's rest as well as man's rest. There can be no true and perfect rest while sin abounds. Hence God began to work again. As He worked in Creation, now He works in Redemption. This time is given to redemption. Jesus said, His Father worked and He was working. Now we are living in the dispensation when the Holy Spirit is working (Jhn.5:17; 19:30). Jesus came to bring man to rest (Matt.11:28-20). The believer enters into spiritual rest now by entering into the spiritual Feasts of the Lord. The full rest is yet to come.

The writer to the Hebrews speaks of the fact that "there remains yet a rest (Grk. Lit. a Sabbath) to the people of God" (Heb.4:9). The Millennial Day will be this "Day of Rest" – a Sabbath, a seventh day. The New Heavens and the New Earth will be to redeemed mankind, what was typified in Israel, "the eighth day", a new beginning. It was typified in "the morrow after the Sabbath". It will be eternal rest from Satan and sin and all evils that came on the earth when man fell.

All of the sevenths pointed to the seventh day of the Lord. The seventh day, the seventh month, the seventh year, etc., all pointed to God's seventh day, the Millennial Age. Each of these "weeks" or "sevens" prophetically pointed to the Week of the Lord, the Week of Redemption. All were shadows and prophetic of the eternal rest (Lev.23:3; Col.2:17)

All the weekly Sabbaths pointed to the Millennial Sabbath and each of "the morrow after the Sabbath" pointed to eternal rest.

True and complete rest will only come to man and to the earth when an end is made of all sin, transgression is finished, reconciliation for iniquity has been fully realized. This will be when Satan and his evil hordes have been cast into the Bottomless Pit, and then at the end of the 1000 years, into the Lake of Fire for eternity. This will be rest indeed (Dan.9:24-27).

In the light of these "Weeks" we see how God's work and Week of Creation shadowed forth the work and the Week of Redemption. The Weeks of the LORD in Israel also were typical and prophetic of these greater Weeks. They pointed back to the Week of Creation, yet pointed forward to the Week of Redemption.

The seventh day of the Lord is revealed to be 1000 years (Rev.20:1-6). The previous six days have each proved to be about 1000 years, making some 6000 years in all, time as known to God. From Adam to Christ's first coming, there is some 4000 years, or four days of the LORD. Then the last 2000 years are designated as "the last days". These 4000 years and 2000 years make "six days of the LORD", the present age being the Dispensation of the Holy Spirit. In these six days, God, as Father, Son and Holy Spirit have been at work. The seventh day will be rest – the Sabbath of the LORD, rest for God, the redeemed and the earth.

Following is the relationship between the seventh day Sabbath and the morrow after the Sabbath, and their typical and prophetic import, for Israel and ultimately for the Church, the true Israel of God.

The Sabbath Rest – Millennial Rest	The Morrow after the Sabbath – Eternal Rest
The Seventh Day	The Eighth Day
The Natural and Old Creation	The Spiritual and New Creation
The First Man, the First Adam and Bride	The Second Man, Christ and His Bride
The Sabbath Rest	The Eternal Rest of God and the Redeemed
Physical Work – For Israel	Spiritual Work – for the Redeemed
Sabbath – sign of the Mosaic Covenant	Rest in Christ – Sign of the New Covenant
The Command of the law	The Blessing of Grace
A Covenant of Works – then Rest	The New Covenant of Faith – then Rest
The Curse lifted from the present earth	No more curse – New Heavens and New Earth

The Millennial Kingdom consummates God's plan relative to the work and Week of Redemption in the earth. It fulfills the seventh day, the holy Sabbath of the Lord and His redeemed.

The New Heavens and the New Earth fulfills the morrow after the Sabbath and ushers in the fulness of eternity. It is the fulfillment of the eighth day, the day of new beginnings. In this all things are made new. There is the New Heavens and the New Earth, the New Jerusalem and the whole of the New Creation. A careful reading of Rev.21-22 chapters in connection with these remarks confirm the truth of these things.

The Divine pattern of "Weeks" is, to this writer, one of the greatest arguments for a Seventh Day Sabbath, a Millennial Rest for earth and for the redeemed of mankind. The writer finds it difficult to understand how some preachers, teachers and expositors of God's Word see and accept God's sevenths, or:
1. The Week of Creation, six days work, then the seventh day, rest,
2. The Week of Days, six days work, and the seventh day, rest,
3. The Week of Weeks of Days, six weeks, and the seventh week, rest,
4. The Week of Months, six months, then the seventh sacred month,
5. The Week of Years, six years work, and then the seventh year, rest,
6. The Week of Weeks of Years, 49 years, and the seventh by seventh year, rest, and then reject or discard,
7. The Week of Redemption, 6000 years of the Lord's work, and the Millennial Sabbath Rest!

The number seven always speaks of fulness, completeness in that which is temporary. It speaks of perfection. It is the number of end-times and relates to the coming of Christ. It points to the consummation of all things that pertains to the earth and the redeemed. At times, those who reject any future Millennium ask the question, Why do we need a Millennium, what is it for, what is it all about? These are good questions. But, the same questions could be asked about God's Week of Creation. Why did God work six days, whatever these days were, and why did God need the seventh day as a day of rest? Was God tired and weary of His work in creation? Or did He have some purpose and plan in mind? The answer should be self-evident. So it is with the Week of Redemption. God worked for six days to redeem mankind and to redeem the earth as man's lost inheritance. The Christian Millennium is God's seventh day of Sabbath Rest and at the close ushers in Eternal Rest! It completes God's plan of redemption as far as earth is concerned and before the New Heavens and New Earth is brought in.

CHAPTER TWO

THE DAYS OF THE LORD

Another wonderful theme that runs throughout the Scripture, is that which pertains to "The Days of the Lord". This theme, as all themes belong to the theme of God's Weeks. Both are inter-related and really cannot be separated, as both are supportive and confirmative of the same truths.

The theme of the Days of the Lord is spoken of as "the 1000 year-day theory". It is a Biblical theory relating to the Weeks of the Lord as mentioned. If the theory is right, it adds further weight to the matter of a future aspect of the Kingdom of God, the Millennial Kingdom, or the Christian Millennium, here on this earth. This is not a matter of setting any dates, for that is contrary to Scripture. The matter is, however, that GOD has His calendar and He knows when years begin and end according to His calendar. Man does not know God's calendar or see His time-piece, hence the danger of man setting any dates relative to end-time events and Christ's coming again. A consideration of the Days of the Lord is explored here.

The Patriarch Job asks a good question. "Why seeing TIMES are not hidden from the Almighty, do they that know Him not see HIS DAYS?" In this chapter we seek to understand God's Times and God's Days.

1. **What Moses Said – Psa.90:4**
It is a significant fact that Moses is purported to have written Psalm 90. As one reads the Psalm, one can see its link with the Book of Genesis, also attributed to Moses as the writer. The Psalm tells of God being God from everlasting to everlasting. He is the Eternal. He is not limited to or by Time. He does work in Time. In vs.4, Moses states, "For a 1000 years in Your sight are like yesterday when it is past, and like a watch in the night". Moses seems to be the first writer in Scripture that uses this 1000 year time element as a theory for our consideration.

2. **What Peter Said – 2Pet.3:8**
The apostle Peter, when he wrote his Epistle to Spirit-filled believers, writes, "But, beloved, do not forget (or be ignorant) of this one thing, that with the Lord, one day is as 1000 years and 1000 years as one day." From where did Peter quote this? From the Psalm that Moses wrote. One day with man is but 24 hours. One day with the Lord is as 1000 years. This is God's time-clock, not man's time-clock. It is time as known to God as to both its beginning and its ending and it is foolish for man to try and establish any set dates. All time is known to God. He only allows His people to know the "times and the seasons" but not "the day nor the hour" (1Thess.5:1-5 with Matt.24:36-37).

3. **What God Said – Gen.2:16-17**
Moses also, under inspiration of the Holy Spirit, wrote the Book of Genesis. When God created Adam, He commanded him not to eat of the tree of the knowledge of good and evil. He could eat of any of the other trees in the Garden of Paradise. God said, "In **the day** you eat thereof, you will surely die" (Gen.2:16-17). It may be asked, Did Adam die in "the day" he sinned? The answer is, Yes and No! He died **spiritually** in "the day" he sinned; that is, in the 24-hour day. But he died **physically** 930 years later. That is, he died within "**the day**" according to the Lord, within the 1000-year day. The fact of the matter is, nobody has ever lived "a day", that is, according to God's day – 1000 years. All the patriarchs, even Methuselah who lived the longest of all, 969 years, died within "the day" according to God's calendar (Gen.5).
This is another foundation Scripture that lends weight to the 1000-year-day theory. One day with the Lord is as a 1000 years and 1000 years as a day (Psa.90:4; 2Pet.3:8 with Job 24:1).

The Hebrew word for "day" in Genesis, as well as in Old Testament use is SC.3117 "**Yowm**" and it comes from an unused root meaning to be hot; a day (as the warm hours), whether literal (from sunrise to sunset, or from one sunset to the next), or figurative (a space of time defined by an associated term). So the Hebrew word for "day" is used sometimes in a literal sense and sometimes in a figurative sense. It is associated with a space of time whether a literal day or figurative day.

The context of Gen.2-3 shows that Adam died spiritually within the 24-hour day he sinned, but he died physically within the 1000-year day of God's calendar. It is worthy of note that all believers who enter the seventh Day of the Lord (the Christian Millennium) will live that Day and forever. This seventh Day of the

Lord is the 1000 years of which John speaks in Rev.20:1-6. Satan is bound for 1000 years, the one who had the power of death. The saints experience resurrection once the source of death, Satan, is bound. The saints lived and reigned with Christ 1000 years. This fulfills all that Adam lost and more, for the saints will live on through the Millennium into eternity. Jesus told His disciples that those that enter into that Kingdom are the children of the resurrection. They do not marry, neither can they die any more (Lke.20:34-36). The last enemy, death, has been conquered for them (1Cor.15:25-26). The death that came by Satan and sin in Adam has been dealt with in the Lord Jesus Christ and His righteous life and resurrection power. The tree of life is restored to man, which was lost in Adam. All of this gives much weight to the coming 1000-year Day of the Lord; lost in the first man, Adam, but restored in the second Man, the Last Adam, the LORD from heaven.

4. **What Hosea Said – Hos.6:2**
The Prophet Hosea uses the Hebrew word for "day" in prophetic sense also. He says, "After two days, He will revive us; on the third day, He will raise us up that we may live in His sight." Is the prophet talking here about man's 24-hour days or God's 1000-year days? Undoubtedly he is speaking of the longer picture, God's calendar. These "two days" would point to the "last days" (i.e., some 2000 years of the Church Age). The "third day" would point to the Millennial day (i.e., the 1000 years of the fulness of the Kingdom Age). He will bring revival in the end of the two days. He will bring resurrection life. He will "raise us up", on the third day, and we shall live in His sight in resurrection glory. The prophecy of Hosea cannot be applied to any literal 24-hour days of man. It refers to God's days, and "a day unto the Lord is as 1000 years and 1000 years as one day."

5. **What Jesus Said –Lke.11:31-33**
Because the words of Jesus relate to the words of Hosea concerning "days", it is quoted here for the student's consideration.
"The same day there came certain of the Pharisees, saying unto him, Get out, and depart hence: for Herod will kill thee. And he said unto them, Go and tell that fox, Behold, I cast out devils, and I do cures **today** and **tomorrow**, and the **third day** I shall be perfected. Nevertheless I must walk **today**, and **tomorrow** and **the day following**: for it cannot be that a prophet perish out of Jerusalem."

What is Jesus saying? What does He mean by "today, tomorrow and the third day?" It can be seen that it is one of those prophetic words similar to what the Prophet Hosea spoke to his generation. It cannot be merely applied to literal 24-hour days (3 days) of Christ's ministry in Jerusalem and Judea. It has dispensational implications. The "today and tomorrow", point to the "last days", the Church Age, and the "third day" would point to the Millennial Age. It is the same truth as implied in Hosea's prophecy. A day unto the Lord is as a 1000 years and 1000 years as one day.

6. **The Four Days of the Passover Lamb – Ex.12:1-6**
One of the most remarkable shadows of God's days is that which is seen in the instructions concerning the Passover Lamb and its death for Israel. The Lord told Israel to take a lamb on the tenth day of the first month and keep this lamb for **four days**. On the evening of the fourteenth day, the Passover Lamb was to be killed, its blood sprinkled on the lintel and side posts of the door. The body was to be roasted and eaten inside the house. What did God have in mind? Did any Israelite ever ask themselves, Why does God want us to keep the appointed lamb for four days before its death for Israel?

It is an important principle of understanding Scripture, that, "in the Old Testament, God often got people to do typically what He Himself was going to fulfill actually in the New Testament". This is true of what took place in the Passover Feast. The four days in which Israel kept the lamb were four 24-hour days. Without doubt, these four 24-hour days of man became prophetic of God's four 1000-year days, a greater calendar than that of man.

When Adam sinned, God set His Lamb, the Lord Jesus Christ, aside. He was foreordained to die. From Adam to Jesus we have some 4000 years of time, or four Days of the Lord. In these four days the Lamb of God had been hidden in the bosom of the Father. Now the Lamb is brought out were He could be seen, and at Calvary, the Lamb of God was slain for the true Israel of God, for the redeemed of mankind. In other words, God had Israel to do typically and prophetically what He was going to do anti-typically and actually with His Lamb. Peter confirms to us that the Lamb was foreordained to die, but He was manifested in these "last times" (i.e., Last Days) for you" (1Pet.1:18-21). He was the Lamb slain from the foundation of the world (Rev.13:8; 17:8). Israel's four 24-hour days were prophetic of God's four 1000-year days.

7. **The Lamb of God in John's Gospel**
Because the Bible reveals that God has one unified plan and purpose, and because we believe in the total inspiration of Scripture, the Gospel of John adds thought to the truth of the manifested Lamb of God, the Lord Jesus Christ.

Keeping in mind the "four days" of the hidden Lamb (from Adam to Jesus, Ex.12:1-6), surely John's Gospel takes us on to the next time period in God's calendar. Isaac, the only begotten son of the Old Testament, had asked his father, Abraham, many years before, "Father, here is the fire and the wood, but **where is the Lamb** for the offering?" (Gen.22). It is hundreds of years later that John the Baptist, seeing Jesus, the New Testament only begotten Son, proclaims, "Behold, the Lamb of God who takes away the sin of the world" (Jhn.1:29,36). John actually answers Isaac's question as he points to the Lamb of God. This title, "Lamb of God" is peculiar to John's Gospel and Revelation, more than the Synoptic Gospels. It is for this reason that the word "day" would have some peculiar significance relative to the Lamb of God. Consider these references in John's Gospel in the light of the "four days" of the hidden Lamb from Adam to Jesus.

"The **next day** John sees Jesus coming to him, and he said, Behold, the Lamb of God, which takes (bears) away the sin of the world" (Jhn.1:29

Again, the **next day** after John stood…and looking upon Jesus as He walked, he said, Behold, the Lamb of God!" (Jhn.1:35-36).

And the **third day** there was a marriage" (Jhn.2:1). Here Jesus did His first miracle and manifested forth His glory and His disciples believe on Him.

One who believes in the inspiration of the Scripture should not fail to see something of God's overall plan relative to the Lamb of God. If the four days of the hidden Lamb are taken and then "the next day" (the fifth), and "again the next day" (the sixth), as in John's Gospel, it provides us with the picture of **six days**. In other words, the six Days of the Lord equal 6000 years of time as given over to man. The "third day" of the marriage would correspond with Hosea's prophecy concerning "the third day". Adding the four days and these three days of John's Gospel together makes seven days in all. This "third day" points to the "seventh day" of the Lord, the Millennial Kingdom, the Christian Millennium. Here the marriage of the Lamb to His Church, His Bride, is manifested in full glory in the earth (Rev.19:7). This "third day" would also correspond to the "third day" of Luke 13:31-33, concerning the Lord's walk and His perfection or the completeness of His healing ministry and power over demons.

[		]		]	]
[Adam	Old Testament	Jesus	New Testament	] Marriage	]
[	"The Hidden Lamb"	]	"The Revealed Lamb"	] Glory	]
[	Four Days of the Lord	]	Two Days	] Third Day	]

THE SEVEN DAYS OF THE LAMB
(The Week of Redemption)

Other examples of the "four days" may be seen in the "four days" of Lazarus' death until the Resurrection and the Life came (Jhn.11:39), and the "four days" of the Outpouring of the Spirit on the Gentiles (Acts 10:30). From Adam to Christ constitutes "four days". The Church is in the "last days", and the Millennial Age will be the "seventh day", thus completing God's plan in the Week of Redemption – Seven Days of the Lord, according to His calendar!

8. **The Last Days Pattern**
Another great confirmation of the theme of "The Days of the Lord" is that which concerns "The Last Days". Most expositors have reasonable agreement on this aspect of God's calendar, even though all may not accept things presented so far in this chapter. Our consideration is given as further support for the truth of the Days of the Lord and His plan in the Redemptive Week.

Both Old Testament and New Testament speak of "the last days", or "the latter days" or "the latter times", as a careful reading of Num.24:14; Isa.2:2-4; Mic.4:1-8 and Gen.49:1 confirm. Sometimes the Testaments just refer to "the last day" or "that day". These are similar and related terms, with some distinction with regards to the 'time element'. Only the passage context determines the 'time element' being spoken of. Most of the references, however, point to the "last days" as being the time period from Christ's first advent to His second advent. That is, they speak of some 2000 years of the Church Age. Other references speak of "the last day" or some equivalent day pointing to the seventh day of God's Week of Redemptive, the Millennial Day. A careful and thoughtful consideration of the following Scriptures should confirm this to the diligent student. The diagram helps to focus more sharply "the days of the Lord."

Adam → Jesus		
"Former Days" — Four "Days" of the Lord — Former Times, Old Testament Times	"Last Days" — Two "Days" of the Lord	Seventh Day
1. Four Days of the Hidden Lamb – Ex.12	1. Last Days – Heb.1:1	"Third Day" Hos.6:1-2
2. Four Days to Resurrection and Life	2. Last Days – Acts 2:17	"Third Day" Jhn.2:1-2
3. Four Days to Holy Spirit on Gentiles	3. Last Days – Isa.2:1-4	Sabbath Day Heb.4:9
4. Four Thousand cubits to God's River	4. Last Days – 2Tim.3:1	Lke.13:32-33
5. Four Thousand cubits in Brazen Altar of Solomon's Temple	5. Last Days – 2Pet.3:3	
Four = Number of Earth, Worldwide	6. Last Days – 1Pet.1:18-20	
	7. Last Time – 1Jhn.2:18	

9. **The Day of the Lord**

Following on from the pattern of God's Days, there is the theme of "the Day of the Lord" that runs throughout the whole of Scripture. This expression has much to teach us when it comes to the second coming of Christ.

A study of the Scripture references shows that there appears to be a three-fold application in the use of this term. This seems to be consistent in both Old and New Testaments.

A. **The Day of the Lord – Local**

The expression is used in a local and historical sense and fulfillment. When various judgments of the Lord fell on the nation of Israel, that was counted for them as "the day of the Lord". This is seen much in the Old Testament Prophets and the judgments that fell on the House of Israel and the House of Judah. The Assyrian Captivity and the Babylonian Captivity were a local and historical fulfillment of the Day of the Lord in judgments on the people of God for their sins (Examples may be seen in Joel 1-2 chapters, and the Prophecy of Obadiah, where "the day" is used some twenty times).

B. **The Day of the Lord – Universal**

This expression is also used with reference to the second coming of Christ and the judgments that will fall on the world at His advent. The coming of the Lord will be a literal or actual 24-hour day at the close of human history. But this day is also referred to as "the Day of the Lord" generally used in the singular to point to His coming. It is spoken of as:

(1) The Day of the Son of Man – Lke.17:26-27

Jesus spoke of the Days (plural) of Noah, and the Days (plural) of Lot. Noah entered the ark of safety in a certain day and the Flood came in judgment, taking away the wicked world. Jesus also mentioned the actual day Lot left Sodom and then the fire and brimstone fell on the evil cities (Lke.17:28-29). He also spoke of the Days (plural) of the Son of Man, but also the day (singular) when He returns again (Lke.17:22,26-37 with Matt.24:36-41). It is significant to note the use of the words "days" in the plural and then the use of the word "day" in the singular in each of these cases. It is used for the "days" and "day" of Noah's time. It is used for the "days" and the "day" of Lot's time. It is used for the "days" and "THE DAY" of Christ's coming the second time. The "days" speak of a period of time, in the end-times, and "THE day" speaks of an actual, literal 24-hour day when Christ again in judgment.

(2) The Great and Notable Day of the Lord (Acts 2:20).

(3) The Day of Christ (2Thess.2:2; Phil.1:10; 2:16).

(4) The Day of the Lord Jesus (1Cor.5:5; 2Cor.1:4).

(5) The Day of Jesus Christ (Phil.1:6).

(6) The Day of our Lord Jesus Christ (1Cor.1:8).

(7) The Great Day of God Almighty (Rev.16:14).
(8) The Day of Redemption (Eph.1:13-14; 4:30).
(9) His Day (Lke.17:24).
(10) That Day (Matt.7:22; Lke.10:12; 2Thess.1:10; 2Tim.1:18; 4:18; Isa.2:10-22; 1Cor.3:13; Heb.10:25).
(11) The Day of Vengeance (Isa.63:1-6 with Isa.61:1-2; 2Thess.1:7-10; Rev.6:9-10). In this Day, He takes vengeance on the Antichrist, the False Prophet and all those who have been deceived into Satan worship and His Satanic Mark, Name and Number.
(12) The Day of Wrath (Rom.2:5).
(13) The Day of Salvation (2Cor.6:2).

C. The Day of the Lord – The Seventh Day

The expression also has fulfillment in the seventh day of God's Redemptive Week, the Millennial Sabbath of Rest. This day is spoken of in Heb.4:9 where the writer speaks of the fact that "there remains a rest (Grk. **"Sabbatismos"**, Lit. "the keeping of a Sabbath") for the people of God." The writer is not talking only about spiritual rest found in Christ. He that believes has entered into rest. But he is also talking about God's rest in creation, and His rest in redemption, as well as the rest in Christ. But there is also a Sabbath rest for this earth. This is the Millennial Rest Day, the seventh day of God's redemptive week. This day is designated as:

(1) A keeping of Sabbath Rest (Heb.4:9).
(2) The Day of the Lord (2Pet.3:10).
(3) The Day of God (2Pet.3:12).
(4) The Day to the Lord as 1000 years (2Pet.3:8).
(5) The Day of Judgment and Perdition of the ungodly (2Pet.3:7).
(6) The Last Day (Jhn.6:39,40,44,54; 11:24; 12:48). The day of the first resurrection is the seventh or the last day of God's redemptive plan. The student needs to distinguish between "the last days" (Acts 2:17), and "the last day" (Jhn.11:24).

Since "a day unto the Lord is as a 1000 years and 1000 years as a day", then "the last days" began with Christ's first coming and will close with His second coming. "THE LAST DAY" brings us to the seventh day of God's Week of Redemption, to Christ's second coming and the first resurrection at the beginning of the Millennial Day. The reader is reminded of Hosea's prophecy. "After two days, He will revive us, and the third day (which is also the seventh), He will raise us up and we shall live in His sight."

The Christian Millennial Day is that final "Day of the Lord" in His dealings as pertaining to earth. At the close of this "Day", we look for the New Heavens and the New Earth wherein dwells eternal righteousness (Compare 2Pet.3 with Rev.20,21,22 chapters).

CHAPTER THREE

SIGNIFICANCE OF ONE HUNDRED AND TWENTY

There can be no doubt that, in the mind of God, numbers have great significance. Most Bible expositors realize this. The important thing is to beware of extremes in the use of numbers as in the Bible. The Bible does have meaning in numbers, "Bible Numerics", but not "Numerology", the worship and occultic use of numbers.

One of the most significant numbers in Scripture is the number 120. It is a multiple of the number 40 taken to its three-fold multiplication. The number 120 has the spiritual meaning and significance of, on the one hand, "the end of all flesh", and on the other hand, "the beginning of new life in the Spirit". The study of this number in Scripture is a remarkable study and it finds its ultimate meaning in the end of the age and the second coming of the Lord Jesus Christ. These examples show us the truth and significance of this number.

1. **The Days of Noah – Gen.6:3**
   The first specific reference to the number 120 is found in Gen.6:3. The context of Genesis Chapters 6-8 need to be read in the light of the comments here. The Lord said to Noah, the preacher of righteousness, "My Spirit shall not always strive with man, for that he also is **flesh**; yet his days shall be **120 years**…an end of all flesh is come before Me…"
   For some 120 years Noah preached righteousness and during this time prepared for the safety of his family. The Holy Spirit was striving with and convicting mankind of sin, righteousness and judgment. The time came when God's time limit was finished. God called Noah and his family to come into the Ark of Salvation. It was one ark, yet divided into three stories. All was significant of there being one God, but in the Godhead, there is Father, Son and Holy Spirit – the only means of salvation for mankind.
   The Flood came and destroyed all the ungodly, all sinful flesh. Once God shut the door, not another person was convicted of sin, not another soul could be saved. The door was shut. The preaching had ceased. The Holy Spirit was no longer at work in the godless, unrepentant and unbelieving world. All Adamic and corruptible flesh was destroyed. The number 120 meant the end of all flesh. The Flood was actually the 'water baptism' of the world, when all sinful flesh was buried beneath the waters. All sinful flesh perished.

   When the Flood period was ended, Noah and his family came back to a cleansed earth. It was a new beginning. God began anew in Noah and his family. It is here, however, that this picture ends. But Jesus told His disciples, "As it was in the days of Noah, so shall it be also in the days of the coming of the Son of Man" (Lke.17:26-27). When Christ comes the second time, it is an "end of all flesh", and "the beginning of a new age". Not another soul will be convicted or converted. The Gospel will no longer be preached. The door is shut. Only believers will enter into the new age, the Christian Millennium of 1000 years. Corruptible flesh and blood will not inherit the Kingdom of God (1Cor.15:50-55). The world will be cleansed by a baptism of fire in which all ungodly flesh will be destroyed. This is the significance of the number 120 in the Days of Noah. All points to the coming of Christ.

2. **The Life of Moses – Deut.34:5-7**
   The number 120 is also stamped upon the life of Moses. Moses life was divided into three forties (3 x 40=120). He was 120 years of age when death came. This was the end of his life in the flesh. Moses died, and the Bible tells us that God buried him. However, no one could find his burial place. It seems evident from the Scripture that God raised Moses from the dead. In his resurrection, the Devil (archangel of death) contended with Michael (archangel of resurrection) over **the body** of Moses (Jude 9). The Lord triumphed and Moses appeared on the Mt. of Transfiguration along with Elijah (Lke.9:30). Moses is expected to be one of the two witnesses to come again in the period of Great Tribulation (Rev.11:1-8).

   Moses had been in the very presence of the Lord, and his face shone with the Shekinah Glory. He had to wear a veil on his face when he spoke to the nation of Israel (2Cor.3 with Ex.33-34). Moses' life was seen in periods of 40 years. The first 40 years was in Egypt. The second 40 years was in the desert as a Shepherd. The third 40 years was in the Wilderness leading the Israel of God. At the close of his 120 years, his life in the flesh came to a close. He began life in the Spirit in the true sense of the word. From the glory of the world of Egypt, to the glory of the burning bush, he leaves for the glory of the Tabernacle and finally the glory of heaven. He went from 'glory to glory', being changed by the Spirit of the LORD. As in the days of

Noah (3 x 40 = 120 years), so it is in the life of Moses (3 x 40 = 120 years); the end of flesh life brings one to the beginning of life in the Spirit world. This will also be true for the redeemed of earth. Life after the flesh will finished, and life in the Spirit begins in the fullest sense of that truth.

3. The Temple of Solomon – 2Chron.5:11-14

One final picture from the Old Testament, with regard to the number 120, is that which is found in the dedication of the Temple of Solomon. In the passage given, the Temple has been finished. All is ready to be dedicated to the LORD for His presence and glory to dwell therein. The sacrifices have been offered. Solomon presents himself 'as a living sacrifice' on the brass scaffold in the outer court. There are 120 priests blowing with trumpets. When the priests and the singers were together, in one accord, in one place, making one sound in praising and magnifying the LORD, the Shekinah Glory of God fell. The Temple was filled with this Glory of the LORD. No one could minister by reason of that Glory. All ministry of the flesh ceased, and the Glory of God was supreme. The 120 priests, trumpeters and singers, fell before the LORD in true worship. This took place in the Feast of the seventh month, the Feast of Tabernacles. All of this scene finds its fulfillment in the New Testament Church.

4. The Day of Pentecost – Acts 1:15; 2:1-4

That which was seen in the dedication of the Temple of Solomon finds its spiritual fulfillment in the dedication of the New Testament Temple, the Church of the living God. There were 120 disciples in the upper room, all in one place and of one accord, making one sound before the Lord, as they waited for the power of the Holy Spirit to come. When the Day of Pentecost was fully come, they were all there and began to speak in tongues as the Holy Spirit gave them utterance. The flesh was set aside. The untamable member of the human body – the tongue – was now tamed by the power of the Holy Spirit. The Holy Spirit took control and tamed the untamable. It was an end of fleshly operations. The Spirit was to be supreme from now on as they were to live their lives in the power of the Spirit (Zech.4:6). Once again there is the great significance of the 120, but here it was in the Feast of Pentecost, not the Feast of Tabernacles, as in the Temple of Solomon. Both pictures are prophetic of the end of the age, when the Church becomes totally dedicated to Christ. All flesh activities cease and the Church lives life to the fulness of all God desires, 'in the Spirit'.

5. The Jubilees in Israel – Lev.25:8-17

The most wonderful truth seen in the number 120 is that which pertains to the Jubilees in the nation of Israel. Every 50th year in Israel was a Jubilee year. It was a year of liberty. All slaves were set free. All debts were cancelled. All possessions forfeited and lands lost were restored to the original owner. Families were re-united. There was freedom, liberty and a great time of rejoicing. It was the acceptable year of the LORD.
The year of Jubilee began on the Day of Atonement with the blowing of the trumpet of Jubilee, in the seventh month, in the Feast of Tabernacles. It was a year of rest. No sowing, no reaping, no labour or toil took place in this year. The LORD promised Israel that He would pour His blessing on the land so much that it would produce enough harvest-seed, and so forth, to carry Israel over the 49th, the 50th and on into the next year. It was a time of shouting, for 'Jubilee' means 'Shouting'. This was 'the joyful sound' heard throughout the land (Psa.89:15).

It has already been seen in "The Weeks of the Lord" the importance of the number seven in Scripture. The seventh Sabbath year preceded the Jubilee year (Lev.25:1-7; Deut.31:9-12). Both these years were a year of release. These years specially had special designations. Either or both were called:
- The Year of Release (7th year)
- The Year of Jubilee (50th year)
- The Acceptable year of the Lord (Isa.61:1-3; Lke.4:18-21)
- The Year of My redeemed (Isa.63:8), then the Day of Vengeance
- The Year of recompense and controversy (Isa.34:8), and the Day of the Lord's vengeance.

As mentioned, all these special years pointed to the end-times.

The greatest chronological revelation in the Bible, as it relates to the Jubilees, is found in superimposing the Jubilee years over man's Time period. The Jubilees are impressed on the Dispensations of Time as God has allotted to mankind. Because Father, Son and Holy Spirit are co-equal as Persons, so Time has been divided in the ministry of the Godhead in relation to the plan of redemption.

It may be said:
The Dispensation of the Father = 40 Jubilees (or, 40 x 50 = 2000 years)   )
The Dispensation of the Son = 40 Jubilees (or, 40 x 50 = 2000 years)   ) 6000 years in all.
The Dispensation of the Holy Spirit = 40 Jubilees (or, 40 x 50 = 2000 years)   )

In all, there are 120 Jubilees, or, 120 x 50 = 6000 years of Time God has allotted to man, working from His calendar. This is six days of the Lord, the number six being the number of man, as Adam was created on the sixth creative day. Wherever God's calendar begins or ends, God has allotted to mankind "six days" of the Lord. If one day with the Lord is as a 1000 years and a 1000 years as one day, then six "days" would equal 6000 years. And, 6000 years equals 120 Jubilees. Thus the number 120, "the end of all flesh" and "the beginning of new life in the Spirit" is also impressed on the periods of Time given by God over to man. When Christ comes again, His second coming will bring an end to all ungodly flesh and the Spirit life will be supreme (1Cor.15:50; 2Pet.3:7; 2Thess.1:7-10). "Flesh and blood will not inherit the Kingdom of God." The 120th Jubilee will bring us to the end of the age, and the beginning of a new age – the Christian Millennium. No unredeemed or sinful flesh will enter the Millennium, only those who have been born of the Spirit and are the new creations of God in Christ. The earth shall truly keep its Jubilee!

CHAPTER FOUR

THE AGE AND THE AGES TO COME

Another theme that flows throughout the Word of God is that which pertains to Time; past, present and future. The New Testament Scriptures speak of the various ages; the present evil age, the age to come and also the ages to come. The present age speaks of the time in which we live. The age to come points to the Millennial age, and the ages to come may either speak of the Millennial age or the eternal ages. The student of the Word needs to consider the language of the context in which the word, or its equivalent, is used.

Scriptures References	This Present Age Time Now	The Age to Come Millennial Age	The Ages to Come The Eternal Ages
Mark 10:30	100 fold in this Time	In the World to come	
Luke 20:34-36	Children of this age Marry, given in marriage	Worthy to obtain that age Resurrection of the dead No marriage, never die Equal to angels, children of the resurrection	
Ephesians 1:20-21	Name above every name Not only in this age	But also in that which is to come	
Ephesians 2:7	Quickened together Raised up together Sit together in heavenlies	In the age to come know the riches of His grace	In the ages to come the riches of His grace
Hebrews 6:4-5	Once enlightened Tasted heavenly gift Partakers of Holy Spirit Tasted good Word of God Powers of the age to come	The age to come	
Hebrews 2:5 1Corinthians 15:23-24		The age to come not subject to the Angels	Give the Kingdom back to the Father – God be all and in all
Matthew 13:22 Luke 16:8 Galatians 1:4 Titus 2:14 Romans 12:2	The cares of this age Children of this age This present evil age In this present age Not conformed to this age		
1Corinthians 10:11 Hebrews 9:26	End of the (OT) ages		
Matthew 12:39,40,49 Matthew 24:3 Matthew 28:20	Harvest end of the age End of the age With you to end of age		
Hebrews 4:9, 1-11 Matthew 11:28,30	Believers enter rest I will give you rest	There remains a Sabbath (Grk. Sabbatismos – 7th)	

Students of the Word also need to give attention to the word "end" as used in relation to the "ages". Sometimes it is asked, "How many 'ends' can there be?" Only the context can tell which 'end' is being referred to, as seen in the following references.

1. The "end" of the Old Testament Ages (Heb.9:26), Christ came as a sacrifice for sin.
2. The "ends" of the ages are on us (1Cor.10:11).
3. The "end" of Judaism in the destruction of the Temple, AD.70 (Matt.24:3,6).
4. The Gospel of the Kingdom to be preached in all the world for a witness and then the end of the age comes (Matt.24:14).

5. The "end" of this present age is a mixture in time of harvest. The harvest is the "end" of the age (Matt.13:19).
6. The ultimate "end" comes at the close of the Kingdom Day (the seventh day of the Lord), when the Son gives the Kingdom back to the Father that God may be all in all (1Cor.15:23-28).

The reader is referred to "The Chronometrical Principle" of Interpretation, in "**Interpreting the Scriptures**" (Conner/Malmin, pages 107-113), when the subject of "Ages" is dealt with more fully. The student of the Word needs to determine which "age" is being referred to into the verse or passage under consideration. Is it referring to the past age, the present age, the future age, or the eternal ages to come? Much confusion has come through not discerning the ages, or taking into a future age that which belongs to the present age, or, taking things from past ages (Old Testament age), and bringing them into this present age, and so on. Each age is greater than the previous as it moves on to a higher level in the eternal purpose of God. The Age of Law was greater than the Age of Promise. The Messianic Age is greater than both the Age of Promise and the Age of Law. The Age to Come and the Eternal Ages will supercede all previous Ages. This Principle must be used on conjunction with God's Covenantal purpose in the earth, relative to both creation and redemption.

CHAPTER FIVE

A STUDY IN "THOUSANDS"

Because the Holy Spirit is the inspirer of Scripture, we believe that He inspired the various writers in their use of numbers. Most Bible expositors recognize the Divine use of numbers throughout the Word of God.

From "**Interpreting The Scriptures**" (Conner/Malmin, page 146), some comments are adapted for the purpose of this chapter here. "It is impossible to read the Bible without noticing the continuous use of numbers. Practically every page of the Bible contains some usage of numbers. God Himself is the Divine Numberer and He has stamped His numerical seal on the whole of creation. The same seal is placed on redemption. It is also seen upon His Book – the Holy Bible!

In Dan.8:13, the saint who gives to Daniel the number of days concerning "the cleansing of the Sanctuary" (or, the Day of Atonement) is called **Palmoni, "the Numberer of Secrets, or "the Wonderful Number"** (Margin. Authorized Version).
- God numbers our steps (Job 14:16).
- God teaches us to number our days (Psa.90:12).
- God numbers the stars (Psa.147:4).

Numbers, as used in the Word of God, are not used promiscuously, but rather take on spiritual meaning and significance. They are used in both symbolic and figurative sense and also used in literal or actual sense. There is also use of numbers that have a prophetic significance." The student of the Word needs to discover which is used in the verse or passage context. Examples are provided here for consideration.

A. Significant Use of Numbers

1. **Literal/Actual Use of Numbers**
   In Gen.1:1-2:4 we have the first use of numbers in Scripture. These verses speaks of the seven days of creation. God worked for "six days" (whatever "time period" is mean by these "days"). The "seventh day" God rested. He blessed and sanctified the seventh day when He had finished His work. The first day, the second day, the third, fourth, fifth, sixth and seventh days were all literal or actual "days" known to God as to length. They cannot be allegorized away. It is evident, however, behind the literal/actual use of these seven days, there is symbolic truth. These "days" have some symbolic significance. This has been noted more especially in the chapter of "God's Week of Creation" and, "God's Week of Redemption."

2. **Symbolic/Figurative Use of Numbers**
   Numbers are used symbolically or in figurative sense also throughout Scripture. Example Scriptures are quoted in brief here.
   - The LORD owns the cattle on a thousand hills (Psa.50:10).
   - A day in Your courts is better than a thousand (Psa.84:10).
   - The LORD make you a thousand times so many more (Deut.1:11).
   - God's mercy extends to a thousand generations (Deut.7:9; Psa.105:8).

3. **Prophetic Use of Numbers**
   God also uses literal numbers in a prophetic sense. There are examples where an actual number of days are used in prophetic sense. Israel searched the land for forty literal/actual days. But, because of their unbelief and disobedience, these forty days became prophetic of the forty years wanderings in the wilderness. God said the forty days would be taken as "a day for a year." The forty actual days lengthened out to forty actual years (Read Num.13-14 chapters).

   The prophet Ezekiel had to lie on his left side 390 days, and then on his right side for 40 days. Both of these time periods were prophetic of the years of the iniquity of Israel and Judah. The Lord told Ezekiel the prophetic significance that He had "appointed a day for a year" (Ezek.4:1-7).

Bible expositors also see that the 2300 days of "the cleansing of the Sanctuary" has prophetic import for the House of Judah (Dan.8:13-14). The "many days" became prophetic of "many years", using "the day for a year" principle in Scripture, where appropriate.

As can be seen by these examples, sometimes there is an overlapping or blending of the literal/actual and symbolic/prophetic use of numbers.

It is the use of the number "one thousand" with which this specific chapter is concerned. There are many uses of the number 1000 and its multiples in the Word. It seems evident that there is the literal/actual and symbolic/prophetic use of this number, as the following Divine measurements recorded in Scripture would indicate. The examples given here have been chosen because of their prophetic and Dispensational import, as perhaps having some bearing on the 1000 year Kingdom Age. It is not that any doctrine is built of types and symbols, but these things may be used, within the bounds of sound theology, to illustrate Biblical teaching.

B. Actual, Symbolic, Prophetic Measurements

As study is given to the examples noted here, it should become evident that God used the literal or actual measurements, or given numbers, in these things, to show forth some symbolic and prophetic significance. If not, then these things can become meaningless in their use. As noted, God never used numbers promiscuously, but always with significance in His mind and purposes.

1. The Tabernacle of Moses Measurements

The Tabernacle of Moses is full of prophetic and symbolic significance. All was designed by the Lord and He gave to Moses the complete revelation of its details, furnishings and measurements. God was very particular about all the measurements of the furniture and its structure. He left nothing to the mind or the imagination of Moses. Everything had to be built according to God's pattern, and come up to Divine measurements.

There were two compartments in the Tabernacle. There was the Holiest of All, or the Most Holy Place, where the work of the atonement took place one day of the year, the great Day of Atonement. The High Priest went into this compartment but once a year, not without blood. The Most Holy Place was a compartment, its measurements being 10 x 10 x 10 = 1000 cubical content. The Holy Place was a compartment which measured 10 x 10 x 20 = 2000 cubical content.

The Holiest of All contained the lone article of furniture, the Ark of the Covenant. It was on this article that God's very Presence and Glory dwelt. In the Tabernacle of Moses, in the wilderness, this Glory 'covered the earth floor'. The Holy Place had three articles of furniture; the Golden Lampstand, the Altar of Incense, and the Table of Shewbread.

Then there was the Outer Court with its linen curtains. The height of the curtain wall was five cubits high, and the total length of the curtains was 100 + 100 + 50 + 50 = 300 cubits in these Divine measurements. When multiplied, 300 x 5 =1500 lineal curtain area. In the Outer Court, the blood sacrifices took place. There was the Brazen Altar and the Brazen Laver, the articles of furniture God wanted there. Blood and water were the things continually associated with these two Outer Court furnishings for some 1500 years (1Jhn.5:5-8).

"It is the glory of God to conceal a thing, but it is the honour of kings to search out a matter", says the Book of Proverbs (Prov.25:2). Surely God had something in mind when He gave these particular measurements to Moses and told him to make sure he built all things "according to the pattern shown him in the mount" (Ex.25:8). These measurements were literal or actual, as God commanded. Many expositors and teachers of the Tabernacle see that there is symbolic and prophetic truth therein. All, first of all, points to Christ, and then there is that which points to the believer's approach to God. In symbolic and prophetic significance, the measurements have some Dispensational significance:

- The 1500 lineal curtain measurements speak of the 1500 years of the Law Age, from Moses to Jesus, when the blood and water flowed from His side, fulfilling and abolishing all animal sacrifices, and ceremonial washings of the Law.
- The 2000 cubical content of the Holy Place, points to the some 2000 years of the Church Age, from Christ's first advent to His second advent, time as known to God. The

Lampstand, the Table of Shewbread and the Incense Altar find their spiritual fulfillment in the Church, the House of God.

- The 1000 cubical content of the Most Holy Place, points to the 1000 years of the Kingdom Age, the future Millennium, where, in fullest sense, "the glory of God covers the earth as the waters cover the sea" (Psa.72:19; Num.14:21). The Ark of the Covenant was the place of God's Presence and manifested Glory in the earth. No sinner or unredeemed would dare to enter this place. None could enter without the blood of atonement.

Who can say that these things have no meaning for the Church in the overall plan and purposes of God? These measurements were actual and literal, yet they take on prophetic and symbolic significance in the mind of God (Ex.26:7-25). (**Note**: The reader is referred to "**The Tabernacle of Moses**" by this author, and its Bibliography for other texts on this subject and fuller details).

2. **The Temple of Solomon Measurements**
There are similar truths in the measurements pertaining to Solomon's Temple and its articles. The Temple of Solomon was twice as large as the Tabernacle of Moses. Whereas the Tabernacle of Moses pointed especially to Christ, the Temple of Solomon points to both Christ and His Church.

Two articles of furniture stand out with significance as to the "thousands", these being the Brazen Altar and the Molten Sea.

The Brazen Altar measurements were 20 x 20 x 10 = 4000 cubical content. This was the only place of bloodshed. These measurements speak to us of the 4000 years (4 Days of the Lord: Psa.90:4; 2Pet.3:8; Job 24:1), from Adam to Christ, from the first Adam to the last Adam. In these 4000 years we have all the Divinely ordained animal blood sacrifices. These were all consummated in the sinlessly perfect and once-for-all sacrifice of the body and blood of Jesus.

The Molten Sea actually contained 2000 baths of water when in use. This speaks to us of the some 2000 years from Christ's first coming to His second coming, time known to God. This is the 2000 years of the dispensation of the Holy Spirit or "two Days of the Lord". It speaks of this Gospel Age. Then the Molten Sea received and held in total, 3000 baths of water in its fulness. This is another 1000 baths of water spoken of in Chronicles beyond that which is spoken of in King's account. This speaks to us of the dispensation of the fulness of time, bringing us to the 1000 year reign of Christ, in the Millennial Kingdom.

Therefore, we have, 4000 cubical content of the Brazen Altar,
>   2000 baths of the Molten Sea when in us, and
>   <u>1000</u> baths additional in its fulness, which all becomes symbolic of the
>   <u>7000</u> years in the Week of Redemption, from Adam to Christ's coming.

These two articles, in their distinctive truths, speak of the cleansings by blood and water. The blood and water flowed from His side on Calvary, the only possible means of cleansing from sin in time allotted to man by God (Jhn.19:33-34 with 1Jhn.5:5-8). When the blood and water flowed from His side at Calvary, this was the antitypical fulfillment of the Brazen Altar (blood) and the Molten Sea (water).

Once again, it may be asked, WHY did God given these measurements to David, by the Spirit, when He gave him the revelation of the Temple, God's habitation, which Solomon built "according to the pattern" given to his father David? What did God have in mind in the use of these "thousands" when He gave to David the vision of these two magnificent articles of furniture? (**Note**: The student is referred to the textbook, "**The Temple of Solomon**", by this author and its Bibliography for fuller details).

3. **Measurements of the River of God**
In Ezek.47 the Lord gave Ezekiel a vision of the rivers flowing from the Temple of God by way of the Altar of Sacrifice. Ezekiel was told to measure 1000 cubits from the source of the river, then another 1000 cubits, and another 1000 cubits, and then a final 1000 cubits. He came

to a river which could not be passed over. The total equals 4000 cubits in measurements. These measurements cannot just be spiritualized away to meaninglessness. They have some significance in the mind of God, for He does not do things promiscuously. It is significant that, from Adam to Christ and the rivers of the Holy Spirit flowing (Jhn.7:37-39) in the New Covenant Temple, the Church, there are some 4000 years of time. Or, in other words, four "Days of the Lord." Surely these measurements also have symbolic and prophetic import beyond that which is seen on the surface.

4. The Entrance to Canaan Land

In Josh.3:4 is given God's order for Israel crossing the Jordan into the Land of Promise. There was to be 2000 cubits between the Ark of the Lord and the people of Israel. The Ark of His Covenant symbolized the very Presence of God. It was carried on the shoulders of the Priests into the middle of Jordan. It held back the waters of the river while the people of God cross over from the Wilderness into Canaan Land. First the Ark of God, and then, 2000 cubits, the people behind. This was Divine order.

The 2000 cubits between the Ark of God and the people become a prophetic measurement of this entire Gospel Age, as time is known to God. Antitypically, this was fulfilled, when Jesus crossed the river of death ("Jordan") on the cross of Calvary. He was the fulfillment of the Ark of God personally. The Church is now some 2000 years further on in God's plan and purpose. The Church will pass through Jordan, the river of death, and enter into Canaan Land, the promised inheritance. All enemies will be totally conquered by Christ at His coming again. Once more there is that which is actual, yet has some symbolic and prophetic significance in its import.

5. The Destruction of the Swine

Another illustration of the use of "thousands" is seen in Mrk.5:13. Here Jesus ministered deliverance to a man possessed of 2000 demon spirits. These demon spirits entered into some 2000 swine (unclean animals to Jewry), and ran into the lake and were destroyed by the demon spirits who possessed their bodies temporarily.

Is there a symbolic and prophetic picture of the ultimate casting down, binding and sealing in the Abyss, the Bottomless Pit, of Satan at the end of this Gospel Age, the 2000 years, as time is known to the Father and the Son? The redeemed will be totally delivered from all Satanic influences. Read Rev.12:9. In God's appointed time, the Devil and all his hosts will be cast into the Lake of Fire eternally (Rev.20:11-15).

6. The 1000 Years Millennium

A consideration of each of these Divine measurements and "thousands" must have some significance beyond that of a surface reading! The Holy Spirit inspired the writers to record these measurements and numbers. The writer, along with other teachers, believes that these measurements each have some prophetic significance relative to God's "Time-Clock" and His dealings with mankind in the plan of redemption.

In Rev.20:1-10 there are six specific mention of 1000 years and some significant events taking place in conjunction with this period of time.

- Satan is bound with a chain by the Angel for 1000 years in the Bottomless Pit (vs.1-2).
- Satan is cast into the Bottomless Pit, shut up, and sealed that he cannot deceive the nations over the period of 1000 years (vs.3).
- Saints live and reign with Christ on thrones for 1000 years (vs.4). This is the first resurrection, that of the righteous.
- The rest of the dead – the wicked dead – lived not again until the 1000 years were finished, until that period of time was completed (vs.5).
- Those who are in the first resurrection are blessed and holy, and they reign as Kings and Priests with Christ over this 1000 years (vs.6).
- Satan is to be loosed for a little season at the expiration of the 1000 years (vs.7-10).

What the student of Scripture has to settle is whether this period of time is to be taken as an actual or literal time period, or whether it is only symbolic.

The Historic, Futurist and Dispensational teachers take these references to refer to an actual period of time, as does this writer. The Post-Millennialist would basically follow the same thought.

The A-Millennialist takes this passage to be a symbolic period of time between the first and second comings of Christ. This School contends that numbers in Revelation are not to be taken "literally" but "figuratively", or "symbolically" and not "actually". This is so for the four living ones, the twenty-four elders, the 144,000, and the 12,000's of the holy city, as well as for the 1260 days mentioned in Rev.11,12,13, and so forth.

This writer holds that numbers in Revelation cannot be dismissed merely and only as being symbolical. The seven Churches were actual Churches in Asia, even though they have some representative importance. The four living creatures, the twenty-four elders are actual beings, even though they may be and are also representative. The 144,000 have both actual and representative aspects, and not one at the expense of the other. The 1260 days, the time, times and half a time, or the 42 months (or, 3½ years) ought to be taken actually as seen in the exposition of the Seventy Weeks Prophecy. The measurements of the city of God should be taken in the same way. Most all references to numbers in Revelation can be taken literally. The writer, along with other Millennial Schools of thought, believes that this is so with regard to the 1000-year period in Rev.20. It is an actual and literal period of time, not merely a symbolic period of time. It is, of course, time known exactly to God and not to us.

The 3000 Israelites slain at Mt Sinai is to be taken actually (Ex.32:28). The 3000 foxes that Samson caught can be taken the same way (Jud.15:15). The 3000 souls saved at Pentecost can be taken actually and not made to be symbolic (Acts 2:41).

The A-Millennialist's argument against a future literal or actual Millennial Kingdom on earth is, Rev.20 is the **only passage** that mentions the 1000 year period in the whole Bible. How can a doctrine of a future Millennium be built on one passage, even though the 1000 years is mentioned six times in this passage? It has been said that neither Jesus nor any of the Old Testament prophets or New Testament apostles ever mentions a limited and temporary Kingdom of 1000 years. They are silent on such matters but all speak of "the Kingdom of God" as being "an everlasting Kingdom", and "eternal Kingdom" without end! The same comments are said about any truths concerning measurements in typical and symbolic structures, such as the Tabernacle of Moses and Temple of Solomon.

The argument from "silence" cannot be used to refute the 1000-year aspect of the Kingdom. The Lord's Table, the Communion, as well as the Gifts of the Spirit, speaking in tongues, as well as some other truths; these are not mentioned in any other Epistles in the New Testament, only in Corinthians. It may be asked, What does this "silence" prove? Nothing! Being "born again" is only mentioned in one Gospel, the Gospel of John, and that in one passage. It is never mentioned once in Acts or any of the Pauline Epistles. The only other reference would be 1 Pet.1:23. The virgin birth is only specifically mentioned in one verse (Isa.7:14). What does the "silence" prove? Nothing!

So it is with the 1000-year period. If the Lord did not mean 1000 years, why mention it six times in this one passage? If it is only symbolic, then, symbolic of what? The "chain" and "the key" have spiritual reality. The Devil is a real spirit being. The Abyss is a real place in the spirit realm. Then why cannot the 1000 years be a real period of time?

In studying the A-Millennial position (which has so much with which one can agree), the major reaction against any future 1000 year Kingdom on earth, is the re-institution of the Mosaic Covenant economy, taught by other Schools. Because Dispensational Pre-Millennialists teach a materialistic, political and nationalistic concept of the Millennium, the A-Millennialists have found this to be untenable. With that, this writer fully agrees. The Dispensational Pre-Millennialists teach a restoration of the Old Covenant in a Jewish Millennium. This has been fully covered in previous chapters.

This teaching contradicts the Book of Hebrews, as this writer has shown in the course of this exposition. The A-Millennialist has not considered the possible alternative to a Jewish Millennium – that is, a Christian Millennium! In other words, "do not throw out the baby (the Millennium) with the dirty bath water (restored Jewish economy)." This writer holds to a future Millennium, but not a Jewish Millennium with all the things that the Futurist/Dispensationalist Schools have put in it!

In a previous chapter, attention has been brought to the fact that Jesus and the apostles do speak of "an age" and "the ages to come". The only way to get around these passages is to place "the age to come" and "the ages to come" into eternity. The writer has endeavoured to show that there is a future Millennial Age, to finish God's purposes relative to this earth. There will be "ages to come" ushering the redeemed into the eternal states.

The Kingdom of God is indeed everlasting, from eternity to eternity, but there has been an unfolding manifestation on earth over the history of mankind. It is the final aspect of the Kingdom of God in earth, which the writer speaks of as a Christian Millennium. Every reference to "the Kingdom" cannot be "spiritualized", because God's Kingdom deals with mankind – human beings – as subjects of that Kingdom. There is both the literal and the spiritual aspects of the Kingdom in its earthly manifestation.

The 1000-year Christian Millennium will be a period of time, and will complete God's redemptive plan and purposes concerning this earth. This takes place before the Great White Throne Judgment and the ushering in of the eternal states.

Job asks the question" "Why seeing times are not hidden from the Almighty, do they that know Him not see **HIS DAYS**? (Job 24:1). To throw all these things as "only meaningless types and symbols" and "not to be taken in any literal sense" or prophetic sense is surely not good thinking for serious Bible students! The 6000 years, or six "Days of the Lord", given by God to man, is bounded by the seventh "Day of Rest" in creation, and also in redemption. At the end of God's work in creation, God rested the seventh day and sanctified it and blessed, setting it aside from the previous six days' work. The same is true in redemption. God works six days, and the seventh day, Millennial rest, is sanctified, set apart and blessed by God for Himself and the redeemed. When Satan is bound, and sinners are destroyed out of the earth, that will be rest indeed – the rest of redemption! Adam and his bride were created at the close of the sixth day of creation. They began life in the blessed seventh day. The sad story is that sin broke that rest of God and man. However, Christ and His bride (the Last Adam and Eve), enter the seventh day of redemption rest but sin will no longer be able to break that rest, for it is "eternal rest". This is the truth that God has shadowed forth in our study of "the thousands".

For the A-Millennialist, "the 1000 years" is a "symbolic number" speaking of an indefinite period of time between the first and second comings of Christ. For the Historic, Futurist, Dispensational Pre-Millennialist, "the 1000 years" is an actual period of time. The same would be true for the Post-Millennialist. For this writer, as a Christian Millennialist, "the 1000 years" is an actual period of time following the second coming of Christ and preceding the eternal states. It is ushered in by Christ's advent, the binding of Satan, and concludes with the Great White Throne Judgment and the incarceration of Satan in the Lake of Fire, and the ushering in of eternity. Each School believes in "the 1000 years". It is a matter of interpretation – whether it is a symbolic or actual period of time!

CHAPTER SIX

WHAT IS <u>NOT</u> IN A CHRISTIAN MILLENNIUM

In our previous chapter was mentioned the possibility of a Christian Millennium. This presents an alternative to a Jewish Millennialism (Futurist/Dispensational Schools), and a Realized Millennium (A-Millennium) as well as the thoughts of Historic and Post-Millennialism.

The reader will bear once more with the repetition of some things, owing to the possible 'newness' of some things presented in this view. By a "**Jewish Millennium**" is meant the restoration of the Mosaic Covenant economy and all the ritualism involved. It includes the restoration of a material Temple, in this time, called Ezekiel's Temple. The Jewish nation is the head all of Gentile nations. The Gentile nations are obliged to go up to earthly Jerusalem for worship festivals three times a year or else they will be plagued by the Lord. These teachings, as has already been seen, are based on interpretations of Ezek.40-48 chapters along with Zech.13-14 chapters.

By a "**Realized Millennium**" is meant there is no future 1000 years aspect of the Kingdom. The Kingdom is now. The Kingdom is a spiritual Kingdom, not a nationalistic or materialistic Kingdom. Satan is bound now and the 1000-year reign of Christ and the saints is that period of time between the first and second comings of the Lord. The Mosaic economy will never be restored. When Christ comes again, all believers are ushered into the eternal states, the Kingdom everlasting, and not into a temporary 1000 year Kingdom.

By a "**Utopian Millennium**" is meant, as Historic and Post-Millennialists would understand, a kind of Utopia that the world has been looking for. It will be a reign of peace, prosperity and happiness in all the nations of the earth. Evil will be subdued, though not eradicated. Christ will reign as King over all the earth, as mortals and immortals mingle together in harmony.

By a "**Christian Millennium**" is meant there will be an actual 1000 year manifestation of the Kingdom of God in the earth, this time known to God, as God counts time. The writer agrees with the points of the Pre-Millennial position as to this. But the writer also agrees with the A-Millennialist point of view that there will be no restoration of the Mosaic economy.

Where Pre-Millennial writers have sinners and unbelievers in the Millennium, this writer would disagree on this point. All sinners, all outside of Christ, are destroyed at Christ's coming, according to the A-Millennial point of view. With this the writer would agree. Whereas A-Millennialists say that all sinners are destroyed at Christ's coming, and all the righteous are taken into the New Heaven and New Earth, this writer would say all the righteous go into a Christian Millennium here on this earth.

Until the Lord comes and brings 'perfect light' on these things, there will be points of agreement and disagreement. All see through the glass very dimly and no one has perfect insight or full light on these future things. Therefore, Christian charity and kindness need to be exercised when considering these issues.

What a Christian Millennium is like and who will be blessed to be in it, and what things will not be in it, as the writer understands, is submitted here for the serious minded student's consideration. As the student carefully reads the Scriptures associated with the particular points, he should come to the conclusion that the 1000 years will indeed be a "Christian Millennium" – a Millennium that includes the believers of all ages. Let us consider then the things that are **NOT** in a Christian Millennium.

1. **There will be no Devil – Rev.20:1-6**
   Whichever view Millennial writers hold to, all agree that there will be no Devil in the Millennium. When Jesus comes the second time, Satan, the source and fountainhead of all sin and evil, corruption and death, is bound. He is chained and cast into the Bottomless Pit, shut up and sealed over the 1000 years. That will be rest indeed for the earth and all those who are blessed to enter the Millennium. Where no Devil is there is no temptation and no tempter to sin. The binding of Satan has already been covered in a previous chapter. In this period of time "the Mystery of Iniquity" is totally subjugated. It will be a Devil-less age.

2. **There will be no Demons or Fallen Angels**
It can be safely and Scripturally assumed that, when Satan is bound and cast into the Abyss, all his hordes are cast in with him. It would be very inconsistent to say that the King of the Kingdom of Darkness is bound in the Pit, yet all his hosts of demon spirits and fallen angels are left on the earth, or in the atmospheric heaven, to roam about over the 1000 years of the Kingdom. Our studies have shown that demonic powers were released from the Bottomless Pit when the Angel opened it with the key in Rev.9:1-20. It can be assumed that they are all bound in the Bottomless Pit when the key is used again to bind their leader, Satan, in this Pit (Rev.20:1-6).

The same would be true of fallen angels. When the Devil and his angels were cast out of heaven to the earth, by Michael and his angels, it was another step on the way to the Abyss. The Devil and fallen angels, the angels that fell with him, are evil angels. Scriptures also speak of angels bound in chains under darkness, reserved unto judgment of that great day (2Pet.2:4; Jude 6). Demon spirits begged Jesus not to send them to the Abyss (Bottomless Pit), or to torment them before the time. That time has now come and undoubtedly they are cast into the Abyss with their King – the Devil and Satan (Lke.8:26-36; Matt.8:28-34). It will indeed be peace when there is no Devil, demonic spirits or fallen angels around.

3. **There will be no Restored Mosaic Covenant Economy**
Contrary to Dispensationalists, there will not be any restoration or re-institution of the Mosaic Covenant economy in a Christian Millennium. As mentioned several times, these Schools hold for a Jewish Millennium; that is, a restored material Temple, animal sacrifices, Aaronic Priesthood, circumcision, Sabbath days and years, festival occasions and all that belonged to the Old Covenant. All of this is said to find fulfillment in Ezekiel's Temple, as yet to be built. Expositors know that there is no Temple in the New Heavens and the New Earth. The Lord God and the Lamb are the Temple there (Rev.21-22). Not knowing what to do with the vision of Ezekiel, it has caused them to place it in the Millennium, to be the central place of worship for all peoples of the earth.

A misunderstanding and misinterpetation (faulty hermeneutics) of Ezek.40-48 and Zech.13-14 and other supportive Scripture references are used to promulgate this kind of teaching. If the New Covenant is understood properly, it will be seen that the work of Jesus on the cross of Calvary fulfilled and abolished all that pertains to the Old or Mosaic Covenant. This is the whole truth of the Book of Hebrews. Otherwise, for God to re-institute the Old Covenant means that God will 'backslide' to the other side of the cross. It would be for God to restore the ceremonials of the Old Covenant, which He caused His Son to abolish when the New Covenant was brought in. This cessation of the Old Covenant was illustrated when God rent the veil of the Temple in two. In brief we list things of the Old Covenant never to be restored.

   (a) **There will be no material Temple**
   The Church is now God's Temple (1Cor.3:16; 2Cor.6:16; Eph.2:20-22; 1Pet.2:5-9). In the New Heavens and the New Earth, God and the Lamb are the true Temple (Rev.21:22). For God to go back to a material Temple in His Shekinah Glory means He would have to forsake the Church, His spiritual Temple, to which all material Temples pointed. God always and ever only wanted to dwell in His people, His Church, both individually and corporately.

   (b) **There will be no animal Sacrifices**
   Hebrews unquestioningly shows that Christ's once-for-all sacrifice and oblation brought an end to all animal sacrifices and oblations. To re-institute the animal sacrifices, or the body and blood of such, would be the greatest insult to Calvary. Millennialists say that these sacrifices in their Millennium are not for sin, but for "memorials" of Christ's sacrifice on the cross. Jesus has given the Church "memorials" in the bread and the cup. He would not forsake these to go back to the body and blood of animal sacrifices. There is no material Temple, and there is no need of animal sacrifices. Read again Heb.8-10 chapters.

   (c) **There will be no Aaronic/Levitical Priesthood**
   The same is true of the Priesthood as of the Temple and sacrificial system of the Old Covenant. When Jesus died on the cross, the veil of the Temple at Jerusalem was torn from top to bottom. It told the Aaronic and Levitical Priesthood, that their work and ministry was finished with – forever! Christ is the King-Priest, forever, after the Order of Melchisedek. He has been given the oath of an eternal Priesthood. The Levitical and Aaronic Priesthood could

not continue forever in their ministry by reason of sin and death and continual succession. Jesus was sinless. He died for sin and conquered death. He lives in the power of an endless life, never to be succeeded by any other Priest or Priesthood. His Priesthood is everlasting. The Church, His Body, are members of the same Order of King-Priests, with Him unto God (Rev.1:6; 5:9-10; 20:4-6 with 1Pet.2:5-9). For God to forsake the Priesthood after the Order of Melchisedek and go back to restore the Priesthood after the Order of Aaron is to violate His own New Covenant. This He will never do.

(d) There is no Restoration of the Mosaic Covenant
The ritualism and ceremonies of the Mosaic Covenant will not be restored. The vision of Ezekiel's Temple speaks of a Temple, the Aaronic Priesthood, the altars, the sacrifice and the oblation, the Feasts of the Lord, the Sabbaths, the New Moons, the rite of circumcision and so forth (Ezek.40-48).

The prophet Zechariah also speaks of the House of the Lord, the nations going up to worship at Jerusalem, the Feast of Tabernacles, the altar, the sacrifices, the pots and the bowls, and the plagues of judgment (Zech.13-14).

All of these things belonged to the Mosaic Covenant. The Lord Jesus established the New Covenant. The Old Covenant and all involved was abolished at Calvary. He took away the old to establish the new (Heb.8). The Lord is not going to have the Old and the New Covenants running parallel together in the Millennium. This would be 'Covenantal confusion' and God is not the author of confusion. Paul wrote to the Galatian believers to bring them out of such confusion over Covenants (Gal.3-4). To re-institute any or all of these things is a contradiction of all that God did in Christ in the New Covenant (Rom.2:28-29; Col.2:14-19).

(e) There will no Circumcision
The vision of Ezekiel speaks about circumcision. Paul clearly shows that the only circumcision God accepts is in the heart and of the spirit, not of the flesh (Rom.2:28-29). He is a Jew, which is inwardly, not of the flesh, but of the heart (Rev.2:9; 3:9).

(f) There will be no Sabbaths
Paul also tells us that Sabbaths, New Moons and Holy Days were all done away with at the cross. The reality is in the person of Christ, by the power of the Holy Spirit (Col.2:14-19).

4. There will be no Animals
Millennialists use Scriptures from Isaiah that speak of "the lamb and the lion" lying down together. "The cow and the bear", "serpent and the child", all will be at peace. There Isaiah mentioned the wolf, the lamb, the leopard, the calf and the lion – all will be led around as pets by a little child (Isa.11:6-9; 65:25). Even the serpent will be there. Nothing will be carnivorous, but all the animals will be at peace, as it was in Eden for Adam, and as it was for Noah in the Ark of safety.

Proper hermeneutics is to use the New Testament to interpret the Old Testament, but everything must be passed through the cross, and not the other way around. An overview of the Bible as to animals does provide some temporary purpose of God in the creation of animals and birds, as this outline helps us to see.

- When God created Adam, God caused him to name all the animals that God Himself had created on the sixth day. For Adam, however, there was no suitable helper. God then created Eve, and together, the man and the woman were king and queen over the animals and over creation. Man was made in the image and likeness of God. Man was created a triune being; spirit, soul and body. Animals were not created in the image of God, having soul and flesh body only. Animals were created for the pleasure of man in Eden. Animals do not have spirit and the intelligence of man to be worshippers of God, their creator (Gen.1-2 chapters). When man fell, the animals became wild and carnivorous in nature and instinct, as a whole. Animals fell into two classes; those beasts that are wild and carnivorous and those animals that are domestic and serve mankind.
- In the days of Noah, God caused Noah to take clean and unclean animals into the Ark of safety. There was no doubt about the fact that God must have moved on these animals and drew them into the Ark. Noah and his sons did not chase them in, whether wild or domestic in

nature. The Spirit of God subdued the natures of the animals while in the Ark. There indeed, the lion and the lamb dwelt together, the bear, the cow and all the other animals were at peace within the Ark during the Flood (Gen.6-7-8). God's Covenant with Noah also included the preservation of the animals against any Flood as in the days of Noah. After the Flood, God gave permission to mankind to kill animals for food. From Adam to Noah, man's food was fruit and produce of the earth. Now the eating of meats is permitted. Animals were also used for sacrifices offered to God.

- Under the Covenant given to Moses, God gave further laws concerning what meats were clean and unclean, and what meats the nation of Israel could eat. God gave further laws concerning animal sacrifices and oblations. Upon the altars of Israel, there was continual offering up of animal sacrifice to God in behalf of the nation (Book of Leviticus). The innocent, sinless animal sacrifices became substitutes for the guilty, sinful Israelites before God. Death penalty was placed on the innocent.
- Under the New Covenant, this would all change. When Christ died on the cross, His once-for-all sacrifice brought an end to all animal sacrifices and oblations. No animal body or blood could ever atone for sin. Up to Calvary, animals had served their purpose as a substitute for man's sin. There will be no animal sacrifices in the Millennium, as there is no Aaronic Priesthood and no material Temple. Christ is all and in all.
- In summary, we see that there has been basically a fivefold purpose in the creation of the animal kingdom.
    (1) Animals were created for man's pleasure in Eden, before the Fall.
    (2) Animals became substitute sacrifices for sin after the Fall; that is, domestic animals.
    (3) Animals became provision for man for clothing as man used the skins for such.
    (4) Animals became useful for food after the word of God to Noah.
    (5) Animals, whether wild or domestic, became symbols of the various nations, Israel or Gentile, in the earth. Daniel and Revelation both speak of various 'Beast Kingdoms'.

In the light of this, when Jesus comes the second time, will He take animals of this present state, wild and domestic, into a Millennial Kingdom? Will their natures be subdued in this age? Will all animals become herbivorous instead of carnivorous in this Millennium? This writer thinks not! God's purpose for animals will have finished.

(1) Animals will no longer be needed for man's food, as man will have eternal life. The Tree of Life at least symbolizes this truth. Man will eat of the Tree of Life, as it was possible in Eden. Man will not need to kill animals to live.
(2) Animals will not be needed for sacrifice, as Christ's sacrifice has forever finished with such.
(3) Animals will not be needed for clothing, as the redeemed will have a glorified body, and will not need 'coats of skin' to clothe nakedness.
(4) Animals will no longer be used for symbols; to represent the wild, rapacious Kingdoms of this world, for all will be in the perfect, sinless, Kingdom of God.

Other things that need to be considered are those things that pertain to redemption. Did Christ die to redeem animals and birds? Animals do not have a never-dying spirit as man does and therefore do not need redemption. No animal can be saved from sin. No animal can be born again. All animals have corruptible flesh and blood.

Paul presents the greatest argument in 1Cor.15:39-50, especially verses 39 and 50. Here Paul speaks of four kinds of "**flesh**". "All **flesh** is not the same flesh: but there is one kind of **flesh** of men, another **flesh** of beasts, another **flesh** of fishes, and another **flesh** of birds…Now this I say, brethren, that **flesh and blood** cannot inherit the Kingdom of God; neither does corruption inherit incorruption." Because of the nature of the Millennial Kingdom how then can animals, let alone human beings, with "flesh and blood" and "corruptible bodies" enter or inherit that Kingdom?

Because of this writer's understanding of the nature of that Kingdom, no one will enter that Kingdom without a new body, a glorified body like unto Christ's body (Phil.3:20-21). For this reason, there would be disagreement as to the Historic Pre-Millennial and Post-Millennial and the Futurist/Dispensationalist view of the Kingdom. In the view of these Schools, their Millennium has a mixture of **mortals and immortals corruptible and incorruptible** kinds of human beings on the earth. This is mixture indeed! "Flesh and blood" basically refers to the corruptible man, as a careful reading of these Scriptures confirm (Matt.16:15-19; 1Cor.15:50; Gal.1:16).

Corruptible, sinful flesh, or animal flesh cannot inherit the Kingdom of God. Christ did not die to redeem animals as they never sinned, nor can animals know God, the Creator. Any who enter the Millennial Kingdom need to have a redeemed body, a resurrection body, a spiritual body of honour and glory. Animals are never promised such. Before Calvary, animals were used for food, clothing, sacrifice and symbols of nations. At and after Calvary, animals are used for food and clothing but not for sacrifice for sin. They are still used in symbolic sense of the various nations of earth. So animals in their present state will not inherit the Kingdom of God, that is, unless God gives them a new and glorified body of some kind. No one knows whether God will create a new kind of animals or birds for the New Heavens and New Earth. Would these have 'eternal life' like redeemed human beings? Or, is God's purpose in the creation of animals now finished? This is the writer's view that this is so.

If this interpretation is true, then the Scriptures in Isaiah which speak of the lion and the lamb, the bear and the cow, and other animals living in peace, can only be taken in spiritual sense since the cross. Such harmony between animals has never been since Eden (Adamic Covenant) and Noah's time (Noahic Covenant). These things can be seen to be so spiritually, in the New Covenant. This is exemplified in Peter's vision. He saw the 'clean and unclean' animals in the great sheet let down from heaven. He misunderstood the voice, thinking he was to eat of the various meats, some of which were forbidden by the food laws of the Old Covenant. The vision, however, was nothing to do with the eating or not of forbidden meats, or unclean meats being now made clean. The vision, when interpreted by the Lord, referred to **the Gentiles** coming into the Kingdom of God, coming into the Church. Whether Jew or Gentile, all would be one in Christ. Here in the Church, on the spiritual plain, "the lion and lamb" dwell together, and so forth. Human and sinful natures are subdued in Christ as Jew and Gentile live in harmony by the Spirit of God. To make these things, since the cross, animal or "flesh and blood" inheriting the Kingdom is contrary to Pauline truth. So, according to these things, there will be no animals in the Millennial Kingdom, God's purpose in their creation now being accomplished.

5. **There will be no Curse in the Earth**
Paul also tells us in Romans 8 that the whole creation is groaning until now, waiting for the unveiling of the sons of God. The creation was subjected to bondage and corruption when Adam fell. Creation rises or falls with the man for whom it was created. When man is fully redeemed, then the earth will be liberated from the curse. It will come into the glorious liberty of the children of God (Read Gen.3:17-19; 4:12 with Rev.7:9-17; 21:1-8 and Romans 8). The Christian Millennium will be a time of total blessing, restoring the earth back to God's intended Edenic glory. There will be no more curse, as the curse is the result of sin. Sin brought sorrow and tears, sickness and pain, death and the curse of thorns, thistles and briers. All will be lifted by the revelation of the redeemed new creation race. Earth will resume its Edenic Glory.

6. **There will be no more Wars**
Isaiah speaks of time when nation shall not lift up sword against nation, neither shall they learn war any more. There has never been a time in human history when nations have not been in war and conflict. Swords will be turned into plowshares, and spears into pruning hooks. In other words, the weapons that once were instruments of destruction and death will now become instruments of productivity and life (Isa.4:1-4; Mic.4:1-4; Psa.72:7,16). Earth will be as the Garden of Eden. The redeemed out of all nations will live in harmony and peace.

7. **There will be no Darkness in Earth**
The human mind cannot imagine the Glory of the Millennial Kingdom. Isaiah speaks of the light of the sun being seven times its brightness, and the light of the moon will be as the light of the sun (Isa.30:26). All the saints in that Kingdom will be shining with light, in their various resurrection glories. It is a Kingdom of Light, not a Kingdom of Darkness. The saints will shine as the sun (Read Matt.13:43; 17:1-2; 1Cor.15:35-57; Dan.12:2-3; Jud.5:31). If these things are taken as the plain language of Scripture indicates, then how can there any darkness in the earth? The Glory of the Christian Millennium is the prelude to the Glory of the New Heavens and New Earth. If the glory of the sun is seven times its brightness, compared to now, and the glory of the moon as the brightness of the sun, then that means there is no day or night, as we understand it in this present state. And if the saints are shining with the light of their glorified bodies, even as Christ's body shone with the light on the Mt. of Transfiguration, how can there be darkness around? It is beyond

the human mind to understand this. The earth will be filled with the knowledge of the Glory of the Lord as the waters cover the sea (Hab.2:14).

Then, on top of this, the climate of the earth will be constant, as was the Garden of Eden. But there will be greater glory than ever as creation is delivered from the curse sin brought on it (Rom.8:19-23). How could any sinful, unredeemed and mortal human being stand the light of the glory of God in Christ and His saints in a Kingdom like this? Any of the saints who saw Christ in His unveiled glory fell as dead before His feet. How then can any sinner stand that glory in the Kingdom of God? They would become as ashes under His feet! Read Ezek.1:28; Dan.8:17; Rev.1:17.

8. **There will be no Sin, Transgression or Iniquity**
It is here in this Christian Millennium that the six clauses of Daniel's Seventy Weeks Prophecy are fully realized. This comes to completeness at Christ's second coming. That which happened judicially at Calvary on the cross will come into full manifestation actually in this Kingdom. We remind ourselves of those clauses.
- To finish the transgression,
- To made an end of sins,
- To make reconciliation for iniquity,
- To bring in everlasting righteousness,
- To seal up the vision and prophecy,
- To anoint the Most Holy (Place).

Here in this kind of a Kingdom, these things come to absolute fulness. All were made possible judicially at Calvary, but now all will be seen actually in the Millennial Age. Transgression, sin and iniquity are finished, made an end of, and more especially so, when the originator of sin – Satan himself – is bound in the Abyss. Reconciliation, made at Calvary, will be perfectly manifested in the redeemed with God through Christ, and with one another, as the saints of God. The faith righteousness that was brought in at Calvary will indeed be an everlasting righteousness. There will be no more need of vision and prophecy. At present, we know in part, we prophesy in part. But now that which is perfect, full and complete has come, there is no need for vision and prophecy. All the visions and prophecies that pointed to Christ and His Church are now fulfilled in His being and in His Body. There will be no more need of such in that Kingdom. And, this earth, like the Holiest of All in the Tabernacle (Measurements, 10 x 10 x10 = 1000 cubical content) will become the Most Holy Place, anointed by the Lord for the redeemed to dwell therein, with their Redeemer, Christ, the King of Kings and Lord of Lords! The Glory of the Lord covers the earth (Dan.9:24).

The Seventy Weeks Prophecy was to be fulfilled in that marked off period of 490 years. The final 3½ years was finished at the coming of Christ. Christ Himself, the main burden of this prophecy, brings the prophecy to an end, to its conclusion, to its absolute fulfillment. Again, what was done judicially at Calvary is now done actually at Christ's advent. The Seventy Weeks Prophecy must find its fulfillment in totality at the end of this age. Its benefits continue on through the Christian Millennium and on into eternity! The Tabernacle of God is with His redeemed!

9. **There will be no Sickness or Disease or Death**
Once again, the prophet Isaiah speaks of a time when "the inhabitant shall not say, I am sick: the people that dwell therein shall be forgiven their iniquity" (Isa.33:24). In verse 22, Isaiah says, "For the LORD is our Judge, the LORD is our Lawgiver, the LORD is our King; He will save us." (Read also the context of Isa.33:17-24). There has never been a time in human history when sickness and disease have not been evidenced in the human race. This Scripture will find its absolute fulfillment in this time, as the redeemed have a resurrection and a glorified body like Christ's (Phil.3:20-21). If there is no sickness or disease, there can be no death. It is a sick-less, disease-less, and death-less age, for all have resurrection life and immortality. Flesh and blood, in its corruption, is forever barred from this Kingdom. Once Satan is bound, there can be no death or sin, for he is the author of these things. He had the power of death and was stripped of his power by The Resurrection and The Life (Jhn.11:24; Heb.2:14). Mortality and immortality will not mix in that Kingdom. Neither will corruption and incorruption mix there. These things belong to this age, not the future age.

10. **There will be no Gospel Preaching**

In this Christian Millennium there will be no Gospel preaching. The fulness of the promises of the New Covenant will be realized. Jeremiah spoke of the New Covenant. Included in its promises were that, the time would come when they would no longer teach every man his neighbour, saying, Know the LORD, for all would know the LORD. Their sins and iniquities would be forgiven (Jer.31:31-34 with Heb.8:6-13). If there is no sin, no Satan, then there is no need for any preaching of the Gospel, no need for evangelism in that age. All the fruits and effect of sin are rooted out as the author of them is cast into the Bottomless Pit.

Paul, quoting from Isaiah, says, "NOW is the accepted time; behold, NOW is the day of salvation" (Read 2Cor.6:2 with Isa.49:8). The serious student will notice how Paul takes Isaiah's word of promise, and adds the word "**NOW**" to both clauses. It is "**Today**" that salvation and the accepted time is, not "**Tomorrow**", in the Millennium. There is no 'second chance' of salvation once Jesus Christ returns. All who enter that Kingdom will know the Lord. They will not need any preaching or teaching of the Gospel. That is needed now by the various ministries God has set in the Church.

The reader is reminded of the significance of the number 120, as in an earlier chapter. In the days of Noah, he preached the word of righteousness. The Holy Spirit was striving with mankind. Once, however, Noah and his family entered the Ark, God shut the door. There was not another person convicted of sin. There was not another person able to come to salvation. The time was finished for Noah's preaching. Jesus said it would be like the days of Noah in the time of His second coming. So, when Jesus returns, the Gospel preaching will be finished; the Holy Spirit will have finished His ministry, and the door of salvation will be shut. Not another person will be convicted or saved. The accepted time and the day of salvation are ended. (The student is referred back to comments on the chapter on "The One Hundred and Twenty").

One other picture is applicable here also. This relates to the Manna.

- **No Manna on the Seventh Day**
  In Israel's history, the manna in the wilderness fell for six days of the week. The Lord told Israel to gather the manna on a daily basis. On the sixth day, the Israelites were to gather twice as much, for there would be no manna falling on the seventh day, the Sabbath day. They were to gather a double portion on the sixth day, enough to carry them over the seventh day to the beginning of a new week (Ex.16:4-5,22-30). Surely there is significance here. The Gospel of salvation, the heavenly manna, has been available for mankind for "six days of the Lord" (i.e., 6000 years of time God has given to man). On the seventh day – the Millennial Sabbath Rest – there will be no Gospel preaching, no manna available. In this end of the age, mankind is living in the close of the "sixth day". It is now time to gather twice as much, a double portion of manna – so to speak – for there is no possible chance of salvation 'tomorrow'. NOW is the accepted time and NOW is the day of salvation. Some Israelites thought there would be manna on the seventh day, but they found none and were reproved of the Lord through Moses accordingly. So today, some Millennialists think there will be Gospel preaching in the coming Kingdom Age. But this is not to be, if we understand these things aright! The Gospel of the Kingdom will have been preached as a witness to all nations, and the end has come with the coming of Christ (Matt.24:14).

- **No Manna in the Temple**
  The golden pot of Manna was placed in the Ark of the Covenant as a memorial of the journeys in the Wilderness for 40 years, in the Tabernacle stage of Israel's history. When the Temple was built and set up in the land of promise under King Solomon, there was no Manna or Rod that budded in the Ark of God. The only thing remaining in the Ark of the Lord was the Ten Commandments on tables of stone. The Law of God stood. The staves were taken out of the Ark. The journeyings were over. Israel was in the land of rest under King Solomon and the glory of his Kingdom (1Kgs.8:1-11). Jesus Christ is King of Righteousness and King of Peace in Millennial Glory. He Himself is the Manna. There will be no other in the Millennium. His law will be on our hearts and minds. The journey of this life is over and all in that Kingdom have eternal life.

- **No Manna in the Promised Land**
  The third picture we have of the Manna is found in Josh.5:1-12. When Israel crossed the river Jordan, with the 2000 cubits between the people and the Ark of God, the Manna ceased the day they entered the promised land. After 40 years in the Wilderness, there was no more

Manna. They would eat of the fruit of the land of promise. So this becomes a prophetic picture of the Church, entering the Millennial "land of promise" at the end of some 2000 years of this Gospel Dispensation. The Gospel Manna will cease to be preached. It is all found now in the Lord Jesus Christ, who is "the Bread who came down from heaven, that a man may eat thereof and never die" (Jhn.6th chapter). In Him is eternal life. The Manna pointed to Christ Himself. The fathers ate manna in the Wilderness, and they died. But he who eats of the Lord Jesus Christ, as the heavenly Manna, will never die. Believers in the Millennium will enjoy the fruit of the land (Lev.25:8-24). Joshua typifies Jesus, who leads His people into "the rest that remains for the people of God."

In "**God and His Bible**", (page 199) W.H.Offiler writes: " With sin out of the earth, and Satan bound, the spirit of corruption is altogether destroyed. There will be no corruption, no changing seasons, the flowers will never fade, leaves will never fall. The Glory of the Lord will cover the earth as the waters cover the sea (Hab.2:14). No hunger, no thirst, no sorrow, no tears, no pain, no curse, no weariness, no night, no storms, no cold, no heat, no Devil, no sin, no fear, no sickness, no death, no grave, no sinners, no labour – Thank God. Nothing but love, rest, peace, joy, gladness, praise, Hallelujahs, holiness, fellowship, harmony, truth, living waters, river of life, loved ones, friends, reunion, redemption, restoration, perfection, fulness of glory, rewards and the Lord Jesus Christ, the fulness of the Godhead bodily. Amen!" (End quote)

Enough has been written in this chapter. Our next chapter needs to deal more fully with one thing not mentioned here. That is, There will be **no sinners** in a Christian Millennium! But, this needs a whole chapter owing to this being one of the major – if not, THE major – difference between the Christian Millennial view and all other Millennial views.

CHAPTER SEVEN

A CHRISTIAN MILLENNIUM
(No Sinners in The Millennium)

With the coming of Christ, the resurrection of the dead in Christ, the glorification of the living saints – most expositors of Pre-Millennial Schools would agree, whether Historic Pre-Millennialist or Futurist and Dispensational Pre-Millennialist. It is what happens to the wicked at Christ's advent is where the roads go into totally opposite directions.

For the Pre-Millennialist, whether Historic, Futurist or Dispensational – each believes that there will be some sinners who will be left over at Christ's coming. These will be taken into a Millennium. There they will be given a 'second chance' or an opportunity to accept Christ as King and Saviour in His Millennial reign. The textbooks are numerous when it comes to the Pre-Millennial Schools of thought. There are some slight variations in these Schools but the basic tenets are as follows. The reader will need to bear with some repetition as well as further enlarging on the Pre-Millennialist's position and their kind of Millennium.

- Unsaved people will be taken over into the Millennium.
- The nations that looked after the Jews in the Tribulation period are the "Sheep Nations" and these are rewarded by being taken into the Millennium.
- The Jews who are saved at the sight of Christ, or the 144,000 Jewish evangelists, are to be taken into the Millennium and will be the missionary-preachers of the Gospel during this time.
- Mortals and immortals will mingle together in the earth. Glorified saints and unregenerate sinners live together in earth.
- Jerusalem, as a city, will become the capital of the whole earth, both spiritually and politically. All nations will have to send representatives to Jerusalem for the Feast of Tabernacles. If disobedience is evident, then their nations will be cursed with no rains and other plagues of the Law. Yearly pilgrimages will take place in order to "keep the Feast" unto the Lord.
- The nation of Israel will be head of all Gentiles nations and fulfill the Old Testament prophecies of blessing on Israel for the nations of earth.
- The Temple of Ezekiel's vision will be built. The Aaronic and Levitical priesthood will function once again. Animal sacrifices will be offered again, and the whole of the Mosaic Covenant economy will be re-instituted. There will be one universal religion.
- Christ will sit on the throne of David in the Temple at Jerusalem and He will be king over all the nations of earth.
- The Millennium will be predominantly a Jewish Millennium.
- There will be marriage and giving in marriage. Children will be born, and need to come to salvation. There will be longevity of life. There will be marriages, births, deaths and funerals in the Millennium – much as life is now.
- There will be universal peace. Wars will cease.
- The whole earth will be as the Garden of the Lord, as the curse over the whole earth will be lifted from creation, which came on it when man fell.
- At the end of the 1000 years, Satan is loosed out of the Bottomless Pit for a little season. He deceives the nations, Gog and Magog, which shows that the heart of man is still rebellious even under the reign of Christ. Satan leads the hosts of the Millennial wicked and they surround the city of Jerusalem. Fire comes down from heaven and destroys them all.
- Following this final rebellion is the second resurrection, the Great White Throne Judgment and there eternal destinies are settled.
- The eternal states of Heaven and Hell are evident: for the wicked, Gehenna, and for the righteous, the New Heavens and New Earth.

As mentioned, there are some slight variations in the Pre-Millennial Schools. The Historic School does not hold to any restoration of the Mosaic economy. But, the basic tenets are as above. The Millennium is a mixture of good and evil, saints and sinners, mortals and immortals, Old and New Covenants, life and death – or simply, more of the present state. The resurrected and glorified saints will co-mingle with the mortal and earthly sinners. Some see the New Testament Church as God's heavenly people, and Israel as God's earthly people. They teach that God has two peoples for His purposes.

For the A-Millennialist School, Christ's second coming ushers us into eternity. Christ returns. There is the destruction of the wicked. There is the general resurrection, the general judgment at the Great White Throne. The Millennium is our present state and covers time between first and second comings. At Christ's coming, all the righteous are glorified and taken to the New Heavens and New Earth. The wicked are cast into the Lake of Fire. This brings us to the end of the Book of Revelation (Rev.21-22). The A-Millennial position, when it comes to the return of Christ, is certainly a much simpler approach, rather than the complicated Pre-Millennial position as seen here.

But this writer believes there is the possibility of an alternative view, which is what this text is all about and that is – The Christian Millennial point of view. This view holds that there will be **no sinners in the Millennium**, all the wicked being destroyed at Christ's second coming. To say it again, at the coming of Christ, all sin, transgression and iniquity are brought to an end. At the coming of Christ, all the unrighteous, the ungodly, the unredeemed, or, all sinners are judged. All are destroyed by the brightness of His coming. There will be no unsaved people left alive to enter the Millennial Kingdom. With this point, the A-Millennial would agree, except that this is applied to the eternal states, the New Heavens and New Earth, not to any earthly manifestation of a Millennial Kingdom.

All Schools of Millennialism do agree that there will be no unsaved or unredeemed left to enter the New Heavens and New Earth. Why? Because all have been judged at the Great White Throne and all unredeemed are cast into the Lake of Fire, while the righteous are taken to be with God and His Christ. Each School believes in the truth of these Scriptures used here as to the desolation of the wicked. It is the "**when**" that makes the difference. The "time element" in interpreting prophecy is the great dividing point and issue.

If the reader will keep these things in mind, they should be of great help. The writer believes that these Scriptures, on the whole, take place at Christ's advent. All unredeemed are judged by Christ's coming with physical death. No sinners will be left alive to enter the Millennial Kingdom. The saints possess the Kingdom. This is why it is called a "**Christian Millennium**". The student is encouraged to read fully, carefully and thoughtfully, the Scripture references listed here. They all speak of the separation of the wicked and the righteous, and the destruction of the wicked as the righteous enter the Kingdom in truest sense of that term. Our consideration goes from what the New Testament writers said, and to what the Old Testament prophets said, as well as what Jesus Himself said.

Because this is one of the major differences between Christian Millennialism and all other Pre-Millennial Schools of thought, a number of the passages or verses will be quoted in reasonable length. The Christian Millennial position believes that **there will be no sinners in the Millennium, and this is why the designation has been coined, "The CHRISTIAN Millennium"**. Old and New Testament saints, all are seen as "Christian", lovers and followers of Christ. The saints before the cross looked to the coming of Christ the first time, while the saints after the cross look to the second coming of Christ. The Old Testament saints had "the Spirit of Christ" in them. Moses valued the reproach of Christ more than the riches of Egypt. It is for this reason, all saints, of Old and New Testament times are gathered under that name, "Christian" (Read 1Pet.1:10-12 with Heb.11:24-26).

1. **What Paul Said in 2Thess.1:7-10**:
   " And to give you who are troubled rest with us when the Lord Jesus is revealed from heaven with His mighty angels, in flaming fire taking vengeance on those who do not know God, and on those who do not obey the gospel of our Lord Jesus Christ.
   These shall be punished with everlasting destruction from the presence of the Lord and from the glory of His power, when He comes, in that Day, to be glorified in His saints and to be admired among all those who believe, because our testimony among you was believed. (NKJ)

   Paul is very clear here. When Christ comes the second time, He is revealed from heaven with His mighty angels. He comes in flaming fire, taking vengeance of those who do not know God, on those who do not obey the Gospel of Christ. WHO does that exclude? They will be punished with everlasting destruction from the presence of the Lord and the glory of His power. This happens when He comes to be glorified in His saints and admired by all who believe. Note: They are not taken into a Millennium and given a second chance to receive and believe the Gospel. This Scripture is fulfilled at Christ's second coming – NOT at the ushering in of the New Heavens and New Earth! God is a consuming fire (Heb.12:29). The fire of God devoured even Aaron's sons when they presumed on God's presence (Lev.10:1-4).

2. **What Paul Said in Eph.5:3-6; Gal.5:19-21**
"But fornication and all uncleanness or covetousness, let it not even be named among you, as is fitting for saints; neither filthiness, nor foolish talking, nor coarse jesting, which are not fitting, but rather giving of thanks. For this you know, that no fornicator, unclean person, nor covetous man, who is an idolater, has **any inheritance in the kingdom of Christ and God."** (NKJ)

"Now the works of the flesh are evident, which are: adultery, fornication, uncleanness, lewdness, idolatry, sorcery, hatred, contentions, jealousies, outbursts of wrath, selfish ambitions, dissensions, heresies, envy, murders, drunkenness, revelries, and the like; of which I tell you beforehand, just as I also told you in time past, that those who practise such things **will not inherit the kingdom of God."** (NKJ)

Paul warns the believers in various Churches, that, if they persist in doing evil works of the flesh, they will "NOT inherit the Kingdom of God." What Kingdom? They are already in the Kingdom of God in its present form, a Kingdom that has mixture of good and evil in it. But the future aspect of the Kingdom will have no mixture in it. This teaching is also confirmed in the Parable of the Kingdom taught by Jesus. There will not be sinners and saints mingling in that future aspect of the Kingdom as there is now in the present state. Read also 1Cor.6:9-10; Matt.7:21-23.

3. **What Enoch Said in Jude 14-15**
The patriarch and prophet, Enoch, prophesied of the coming of the Lord and the judgment on the wicked. His prophecy pertains to Christ's second coming and not to the New Heavens and New Earth.
"And Enoch, the seventh from Adam, prophesied of these, saying, Behold, the Lord comes with ten thousands of His saints, To execute judgment on ALL, and to convince ALL that are ungodly among them of ALL their ungodly deeds which they have ungodly committed, and of ALL their hard speeches which ungodly sinners have spoken against Him." The student will notice the use of the words "ALL" and "UNGODLY", both being used four times in these verses. How will any of the ungodly be taken into the Millennium in the light of these prophetic words of Enoch? No! ALL the ungodly will be destroyed at the coming of Christ. This is exactly what Enoch is telling us. Who does the word "all" exclude in this prophecy? The answer is evident. It excludes no one. Only the godly will enter that Kingdom.

4. **What Isaiah Said in Isa.13:9-10**
Isaiah speaks of the Day of the Lord. "Behold, the day of the LORD cometh, cruel both with wrath and fierce anger, to lay the land desolate: and he shall **destroy the sinners thereof out of it.** For the stars of heaven and the constellations thereof shall not give their light: the sun shall be darkened in his going forth, and the moon shall not cause her light to shine. **And I will punish the world for their evil, and the wicked for their iniquity**; and I will cause the arrogancy of the proud to cease, and will lay low the haughtiness of the terrible" (KJV)
This is the language of the Book of Revelation also. The whole of Isa.13 should be read. Here, in conjunction with these verses, there are signs in the sun, moon and stars that take place in that day. If the Lord destroys sinners out of the land, and punishes the world for their evil and the wicked for their iniquity, how then shall they be taken into the Millennium?

5. **What Isaiah Said in Isa.24:1-23**
Once again, the whole of this chapter should be read in connection with our comments. There are clauses there that pertain to the coming of Christ and not to any previous human history. Some of these verses are quoted here, but the student needs to read the whole chapter.
"The Lord makes the earth empty, and makes it waste, and turns it upside down, and scatters abroad the inhabitants" (vs.1).
"The land shall be utterly emptied" (vs.3).
"The earth mourns and fades away, the world languishes and fades away, the haughty people of the earth do languish" (vs.4).
"The earth is defiled under the inhabitants, because they have also transgressed the laws, changed the ordinance, and broken the everlasting covenant" (vs.5).
"Therefore has the curse devoured the earth, and they that dwell there are desolate: therefore the inhabitants of the earth are burned, and few men left" (vs.6).

"The earth is utterly broken down, the earth is clean dissolved, the earth is moved away exceedingly" (vs.19).

"The earth shall reel to and fro like a drunkard, and shall be removed like a cottage…" (vs.20).

In vs.21-23 the Lord talks about punishing the ones on high and those that would be shut up in the pit as in the prison. He also talks about the moon and the sun being smitten in that day. Most expositors see this being fulfilled at Christ's second coming and the shake up of earth and the judgment on sinners. Who then is left to enter the Millennial earth after the terror of these verses is fulfilled?

6. **What Isaiah Said in Isa.34:1-10**

   Isaiah is very clear also on the events that take place here. The whole passage should be read. Most expositors see the totality of these verses fulfilled at Christ's advent. The passage is quoted in full here, so that the significance of the words is seen.

   "Come near, ye nations, to hear; and hearken, ye people: let the earth hear, and all that is therein; the world, and all things that come forth of it.
   For the indignation of the LORD is upon all nations, and his fury upon all their armies: he hath utterly destroyed them, he hath delivered them to the slaughter.
   Their slain also shall be cast out, and their stink shall come up out of their carcasses, and the mountains shall be melted with their blood.
   And all the host of heaven shall be dissolved, and the heavens shall be rolled together as a scroll: and all their host shall fall down, as the leaf falleth off from the vine, and as a falling fig from the fig tree.
   For my sword shall be bathed in heaven: behold, it shall come down upon Idumea, and upon the people of my curse, to judgment.
   The sword of the LORD is filled with blood, it is made fat with fatness, and with the blood of lambs and goats, with the fat of the kidneys of rams: for the LORD hath a sacrifice in Bozrah, and a great slaughter in the land of Idumea.
   And the unicorns shall come down with them, and the bullocks with the bulls; and their land shall be soaked with blood, and their dust made fat with fatness.
   For it is the day of the LORD's vengeance, and the year of recompenses for the controversy of Zion.
   And the streams thereof shall be turned into pitch, and the dust thereof into brimstone, and the land thereof shall become burning pitch.
   It shall not be quenched night nor day; the smoke thereof shall go up for ever: from generation to generation it shall lie waste; none shall pass through it for ever and ever." (KJV)

   Who can miss the language of John in Rev.19:11-21 as used from here, under the inspiration of the Holy Spirit, as well as other portions of Old Testament passages quoted or alluded to in the Book of Revelation? The second coming of Christ is the time of vengeance when the wicked of earth will be judged, not taken into a Millennial Kingdom to continue their evil in a subdued lifestyle!

7. **What Isaiah Said in Isa.30:27-30**

   "Behold, the name of the LORD cometh from far, burning with his anger, and the burden thereof is heavy: his lips are full of indignation, and his tongue as a devouring fire:
   And his breath, as an overflowing stream, shall reach to the midst of the neck, to sift the nations with the sieve of vanity: and there shall be a bridle in the jaws of the people, causing them to err.
   Ye shall have a song, as in the night when a holy solemnity is kept; and gladness of heart, as when one goeth with a pipe to come into the mountain of the LORD, to the mighty One of Israel.
   And the LORD shall cause his glorious voice to be heard, and shall shew the lighting down of his arm, with the indignation of his anger, and with the flame of a devouring fire, with scattering, and tempest, and hailstones. " (KJV)

   The passage speaks of the anger, indignation of Christ in His second coming. There were no such qualities in His first coming. Here He comes in flaming fire, taking vengeance on those who reject His so great a salvation. The New Testament writers confirm Isaiah's prophecy. How will any unredeemed sinner escape this anger and indignation and enter a Millennium?

8. What Isaiah Said in Isa.2:10-22

This passage also points to the second coming of the Lord. "The LORD alone will be exalted in that day. The LORD will arise and shake terribly the earth. Men will seek to hide themselves in the rocks and the caves of the earth for fear of the LORD, and the glory of His majesty. All the loftiness and the haughtiness of man will be brought down in that day. All the idols of man will be useless to help him when the LORD shakes terribly the earth. The final shaking is fulfilled in the Book of Revelation. Read again Rev.6:12-17 along with the Isaiah passage.

9. What Isaiah Said in Isa.60:12

" For the nation and kingdom that will not serve thee shall perish; yea, those nations shall be utterly wasted." (KJV) When is this verse fulfilled? Certainly not in our present state, but it shall be at Christ's return. There will be no unsaved people of nations enter the Millennial Kingdom.

10. What Malachi Said in Mal.4:1-6

The student should read the whole of this short chapter. Each and every verse relates to the second coming of Jesus. Comments on vs.4-6 relate to the ministry of the "two witnesses" as seen by John in Rev.11. Moses and Elijah are the last two prophets mentioned by name in the Old Testament, The LORD reminded Judah of the Law of Moses and His promise to send Elijah before the coming of the great and dreadful day of the LORD.

In vs.1-3 is seen the language of the day of the Lord's coming again. " For, behold, the day cometh, that shall burn as an oven; and all the proud, yea, and all that do wickedly, shall be stubble: and the day that cometh shall burn them up, saith the LORD of hosts, that it shall leave them neither root nor branch. But unto you that fear my name shall the Sun of righteousness arise with healing in his wings; and ye shall go forth, and grow up as calves of the stall. And ye shall tread down the wicked; for they shall be ashes under the soles of your feet in the day that I shall do this, saith the LORD of hosts." (KJV)

All the ingredients of the Lord's coming are in these several verses: Moses, Elijah, and the Day of the Lord's coming. The day will be hot as an oven. The wicked shall be burnt up, reduced to ashes under the feet of those who fear the name of the Lord. The wicked will have neither root or branch – that is, there is no possible chance of growth (root) or graft (branch). How then will any of the wicked, in the light of these verses, find a place to reproduce themselves in the Millennium? They become ashes at the Lord's coming, as they are destroyed by the brightness of His glory.

11. What Solomon Said in Prov.2:21-22

The words are clear and plain if they are taken just as they are written. "For the upright shall dwell in the land, and the perfect shall remain in it. But the wicked shall be cut off from the earth, and the transgressors shall be rooted out of it." (KJV)
When does this take place? At the end of the Millennium or the beginning of the New Heavens and New Earth, or at Christ's second coming? These verses harmonize with Malachi. The upright and perfect will dwell in the land – the cleansed earth. The wicked and transgressors will be cut off from the earth, rooted out of it, not left over to enter the Millennium.

12. What David Said in Psa.37:1-40

The whole Psalm should be read. Only the verses relating to our theme are mentioned. It is the Psalm of the Righteous and the Wicked.
"Fret not yourselves because of evil doers, neither be envious against the workers of iniquity. For they shall soon be **cut down** like grass, and wither as the green herb…For evil doers shall be **cut off**, but those that wait on the Lord shall **inherit the earth**. For yet a little while, and the wicked shall not be…but the meek shall **inherit the earth**; and they that be cursed of Him shall be **cut off**…But the transgressors shall be **destroyed** together: the end of the wicked shall be **cut off**…" (Psa.37:1,2,9,10,11,22,38).

When will this Psalm of David be fulfilled? It certainly was not in his time, nor even in this present age. Human history shows the wicked prospering and oftentimes the righteous suffering. Is the Psalm to be placed at the ushering in of eternity or is it relative to Christ's coming again and the Millennial Kingdom? The language simply confirms the previous references given. The wicked shall be cut off. The righteous shall inherit the earth. At least six times we are told that the righteous shall inherit the earth (vs.9,11,18,22,29,34). And at least six times we are also told that the wicked shall be cut off (vs.2,9,22,28,34,38). The prayer of Psa.105:35 is answered here. "Let the sinners be consumed out of the earth, and let the wicked be no more." And, "The Lord is King forever and ever: the heathen are perished out of His land" (Psa.10:16).

13. What Jeremiah Said in Jer.25:15-33

Undoubtedly there was some measure of fulfillment of this prophecy in Jeremiah's time. But this passage is one of those that point to a dual fulfillment, as the reader can see. The LORD told Jeremiah to take the wine cup of His fury from His hand. Jeremiah was to cause all the nations of earth to drink of it, beginning with Jerusalem and finishing with Babylon. The nations would drink themselves drunk. The prophecy ends with the sword coming to all nations. "A noise shall come even to the ends of the earth, for the LORD has a controversy with the nations. He will plead with all flesh. **He will give them that are wicked to the sword…and the slain of the LORD shall be at that day from one end of the earth even to the other end**…"(vs.31-33).

The second coming shows the LORD with that sword and all flesh is judged, along with the Antichrist and the False Prophet and their armies. Who will be left from this sword to enter into the Millennium? It is indeed an end to all ungodly flesh. From Jerusalem to Babylon and the nations round about and through the earth, the slain of the LORD will be many.

14. What Joel Said in Joel 3:11-17

Joel also prophesied of a time when multitudes will be in the Valley of Decision, or literally, the Valley of Threshing. It is in the Valley of Jehoshaphat. The nations are reaped by the sickle. The sun, moon and stars are affected in their shining. Even if there has been any measure of fulfillment, the language points ultimately to the second advent of the Lord Jesus Christ.

15. What Zechariah Said in Zech.12:9; 14:1-21

The passages are too lengthy to quote in full here. The student and reader should read them again and refresh the memory as to what the prophet Zechariah is saying and prophesying about. Whatever partial fulfillment there may have been in the past, the ultimate certainly points to Christ's coming again. Most expositors see this to be so. The important relative phrases are noted here rather than quoting passages in full.

"Behold, the day of the Lord is coming…" (vs.1).
"For I will gather all nations against Jerusalem to battle…" (vs.2).
"Then shall the Lord go forth and fight against those nations, as when He fought in the day of battle" (vs.3).
"And His feet shall stand in that day upon the Mt of Olives…and the Lord my God shall come, and all the saints with Him…And the Lord shall be King over all the earth; in that day there shall be one Lord and His Name one" (vs.4,5,9).

This passage, once again, is applicable to Christ's return. He returns to the Mt of Olives from whence He ascended (Acts 1:9-12). The Battle of Armageddon takes place in the Valley of Jehoshaphat, in the Valley of Megiddo. Antichrist and his armies are destroyed by the sword of His mouth. Jesus is King over all the earth in Millennial glory and His name is one Lord, one with the Father and the Holy Spirit in that triune Name of the LORD JESUS CHRIST (Rev.16:13-16; 19:11-21).

16. What Daniel Said in Dan.2

Daniel and Revelation belong to each other as twin volumes, each being incomplete without the other. Things unfulfilled in Daniel will find fulfillment in Revelation. John does not repeat all that Daniel has written; though he does some of the unfulfilled prophecies of Daniel (e.g., The Seventy Weeks, the Reign of Antichrist and Persecution of the saints).

In Dan.2, Daniel interprets the Dream of King Nebuchadnezzar. After seeing the Kingdoms of this world under the symbols of gold, silver, brass, iron and clay, he sees a stone cut out of the mountain without hands. This stone smites the great image on its ten toes, on the feet. The result is that the whole of the image – that is, the world Kingdoms – was destroyed and became as chaff in the wind. The Stone Kingdom represents the Kingdom of God and His Christ. This Stone Kingdom filled the whole earth. The smashing of the image on the ten toes speaks of Christ's coming as the crushing stone, smiting the ten kings of the Antichristal Empire at His coming.

There was no place found for any portion of this image. There is no place for another Kingdom in the Millennial Kingdom of Christ. The Kingdom is not left to other people, but the Stone Kingdom will stand for ever. Where will any one of the Kingdoms of this world be able to enter the Kingdom of Christ unless they belong to Christ? His Kingdom will fill the whole world and it will be a Christian Millennium.

17. **What Daniel Said in Dan.7**

The vision that Daniel has here follows the same truth of the dream of the image. Here additional details are given, all of which find their final fulfillment in Rev.13. Daniel sees the Beast Kingdoms of this world. The Son of Man receives a Kingdom from the Father, who is the Ancient of Days. He returns as the Son of Man and destroys these Beast Kingdoms. They are not taken into the Millennial Kingdom. This destruction takes place at the close of a Time, Times, and Half a Time, or, 3½ years of the persecution of the saints. Judgment takes place. The time has come that "the saints possess the Kingdom" (Dan.7:18,21,22,25,27). They possess the Kingdom forever and ever. World Kingdoms have been succeeded, but the Kingdom of God will never be succeeded or superceded by any other Kingdom. The Kingdom of God stands eternally. It shall never pass away. The Millennium will be a time when the saints – NOT the sinners – possess the Kingdom and reign with Christ for the 1000 years, and then on into eternity! There is no hint of any of the Kingdoms of this world being carried over into the Kingdom of the Son of Man.

18. **What Jesus Said in Matt.13:24-30,36-43**

Jesus confirmed the truth about the future aspect of the Kingdom of God and the separation of the wicked and righteous at His advent. This is seen in the Parable of the Wheat and Tares. The Parable of the Wheat and Tares reveals that there is mixture of good and evil in the Kingdom in its present mystery form and manifestation. At the end of the age, the Son of Man sends forth His angels. What will they do? They bind the tares into bundles, or, they gather out of His Kingdom all things that offend, and those who do iniquity. They cast them away into a furnace of fire, and there is wailing, weeping and gnashing of teeth. The words that follow this act are significant. "THEN shall the righteous shine forth as the sun in the Kingdom of their Father." No tares are taken into the Millennial Kingdom, the future aspect of God's everlasting Kingdom relative to earth. Wheat and tares are in the Kingdom in its present expression. But at Christ's coming, there comes the great separation of both. Only the righteous (the wheat) are taken into the Millennium – and this is why it will be a Christian Millennium. There will not be a mixture of wheat and tares, saints and sinners, mortals and immortals in the Kingdom to come!

19. **What Jesus Said in Matt.13:47-50**

The same truth as just considered is also seen and taught in the Parable of the Dragnet. The Gospel Net gathers in both good and bad fish. They both stay in the same net until the end. At the end of the age, the angels come and separate the wicked (bad fish) and the just (good fish). The bad fish are not taken into the Millennium. The mixture is in the Kingdom now, in its mystery form. There will be no mixture in the future aspect of the Kingdom. There will be no tares, no bad fish, no mixture of sinners and righteous, only the righteous will be there. These are the wheat and the good fish of the Kingdom of God. The process is: Ingathering, Mixture and then Separation at Christ's coming again.

20. **What Jesus Said in Matt.25:31-46**

Once again, Jesus teaches us the same truth in the Parable of the Sheep and Goats. A careful study of this Parable shows that the nations spoken of as "sheep" are those that are righteous and those who practiced that righteous in the Body of Christ. The nations spoken of as "goats" are those who were unrighteous and did not practice the words of Jesus or the works of the Kingdom of God. What was the reward of the sheep – the righteous? Jesus said to them, "Come, you blessed of My Father, inherit the Kingdom prepared for you from the foundation of the world" (vs.34). This is spoken to the sheep on His right hand, the hand of blessing. The only righteousness that God accepts is "faith-righteousness". There is no salvation by good works or even socially good works. Salvation is by grace, through faith, and it is the gift of God. It is not of works, lest any boast (Eph.2:5-8). To the goats on His left hand, the unrighteous, He tells them to "Depart from Me, you are cursed into everlasting fire, prepared for the Devil and his angels" (vs.41).

Christ's "brethren" are the members of the Body of Christ, not unregenerate Jewish brethren, after the flesh. To make these "brethren" Christ's brethren after the flesh, is to make good and social works of kindness the basis of entrance into the Kingdom. But, Jesus said, the only way to enter the Kingdom was to be "born again", or "born from above" and that by the Holy Spirit (Jhn.3:1-5).

The mixture of sheep and goats is in this age. It is not speaking of "sheep nations" or "goat nations", but it is speaking of those in all nations that are spiritually "sheep" or "goats"; that is, righteous or unrighteous, regenerate or unregenerate. The righteous are those individuals who responded to the Gospel when Jesus told His disciples to "Make disciples of all nations" (Matt.28:18-20). The goats are those who reject the Gospel and remain with their sinful nature.

The separation takes place when Jesus comes in all His glory, the holy angels with Him, and when He sits on the throne of His glory. All nations are gathered before Him. The great separation takes place of both sheep and goats.

SO – no tares, no bad fish, no goats, no mixture is to be found in the future aspect of the Kingdom in earth. If these parables do not speak of Christ's second coming at the end of the age, then when do they find fulfillment? The language of these parables point to Christ's advent. They either find fulfillment then or else must be postponed to the end of the Millennium!

21. What Jesus Said in Lke.17:20-37; Matt.24:36-41

Jesus spoke much about the days of His coming again. He likened these end-time days to the Days of Noah and to the Days of Lot. He spoke of the judgment that fell upon all and said that it would be like that when He comes again.

"As it was in **the days of Noah**, so shall it be also in **the days of the Son of Man**. They did eat, they drank, they married wives, they were given in marriage, until **the day** that Noah entered the Ark, and **the flood came and destroyed them ALL**.
Likewise also, as it was in **the days of Lot**; they did eat, they drank, they bought, they sold, they planted, they builded. But **the same day** that Lot went out of Sodom, it rained fire and brimstone from heaven, **and destroyed them ALL**, even so shall it be in **the day** when the Son of Man is revealed."

In the days of Noah, God said His Spirit would not always strive with man. At the end of the 120 years of Noah's preaching, the Holy Spirit ceased striving and convicting mankind. There was no more preaching. God called Noah and his family into the Ark. God – not Noah – shut the door! The end of all ungodly flesh had come (Gen.6). Not another person was saved. Not one unsaved person entered the Ark of safety. Not one unsaved person was left, after the Flood, to enter the cleansed earth. In Gen.7:3 we are told that "Noah only remained alive..." Compare this with Paul's word about "those who are alive and remain unto the coming of the Lord" (1Thess.4:15-18). Not another soul was saved after God shut the door. The Flood destroyed ALL, even as the fire and brimstone destroyed ALL in the days of Lot.

So shall it be when Christ returns again. ALL the ungodly will be destroyed. None shall inherit the cleansed earth or the Kingdom of God. Enoch said that ALL would be judged at Christ's advent. So, as it was in (a) the Days of Noah, and (b) the Days of Lot, SO shall it be in (c) the Days of the Son of Man. The student will note the emphasis on "**the days**" and "**THE DAY**". There was both a period of time ("the days"), and there was a final time ("**THE** day"). So in the end of this age, we are living in "the days of the Son of Man", but there is "THE DAY" when the Son of Man comes. It will be an actual, literal 24-hour-day when He returns in glory, judgment and separation. The diagram illustrates.

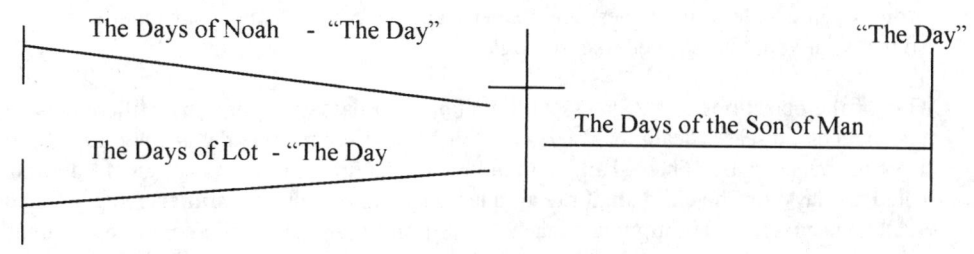

The Days of Noah - "The Day" "The Day"

The Days of the Son of Man

The Days of Lot - "The Day"

The picture given to us by Christ about the days of Noah and the days of Lot all pointed to the "last days" and the day of His coming.

22. What Jesus Said in Lke.20:37-38

The whole of this passage needs to be read by the serious student of these things. It is too full to be quoted here, except the salient and relevant points.

The Sadducees (Liberals, Modernists of that day) did not believe in the bodily resurrection, or angelic beings or spirit (Acts 23:8). They came to Jesus; tempting Him with the story of the wife who had seven husbands and all died without children. Last of all the woman died. Their trick question? "In the resurrection, whose wife of these is she, for the seven had her to wife?" Note Christ's answer! "The children of **this age** marry, and are given in marriage: But they which shall be accounted worthy to obtain **that age,** and **the resurrection of the dead**, neither marry, nor are given in marriage. Neither can they die any more, for they are equal to the angels, and are the children of God, being the children of the resurrection."

A number of important things are mentioned by Jesus here about the coming age in contrast to this present age.
- There is a present age – "this age"
- There is a future age – "that age"
- There is a resurrection of the dead
- Only those who are worthy enter that age
- In that future age there is no marriage, and no one is given away in marriage
- In that future age there is no death; neither can any one die any more
- Those who are worthy to enter that age are equal to the angels as spiritual beings
- They are the children of God
- They are the children of the resurrection.

There should be no mistaking the words of Jesus. In the coming Millennial age, there is no marriage and no death. There will be no "Registrar of Births, Deaths and Marriages" in that age, as each of those things belongs to this age.

If there is no marriage or being given in marriage, then no children will be born. All children born in the past and present ages have been born in sin and iniquity and in need of redemption. This will not be so in the age to come. It will be a marriage-less age. Again, if there is no death, there can be no sinners, for "the wages of sin is death." It means that the last enemy has been conquered, which is death. It means that the sting of death, which is SIN, has been taken out. It is therefore, a sinless and deathless Millennium. The Devil, who was the author of sin and had the power of death, has been bound in the Bottomless Pit. The greatest power that Satan had over mankind was death, and that because of sin.

The prophet Isaiah, along with the apostle Paul, saw that death would be swallowed up in victory. Paul saw that all believers would not die. They would escape that appointment with death, should they be the ones who "are alive and remain unto the coming of the Lord" (1Thess.4:13-18 with Isa.25:8-10; 1Cor.15:50-57; Heb.2:13-14). If there is no sin, there is no sickness or disease or death or anything that causes death. Isaiah writes: "And the inhabitant shall not say, I am sick: the people that dwell therein shall be forgiven their iniquity" (Isa.33:20).

Psalm 103:1-5 will find total fulfillment. "Bless the Lord, O my soul, and all that is within me, bless His holy name. Bless the Lord, O my soul, and forget not ALL of His benefits. Who forgives ALL your iniquities, who heals ALL your diseases; Who redeems your life from destruction; Who crowns you with loving kindness and tender mercies; Who satisfies your mouth with good things; so that your youth is renewed like the eagle's."

One of the objections to a "Sinless Millennium" is a passage quoted by Millennialists who have sin, sickness, disease, death, marriages and births, and funerals, is the passage found in Isa.65:20. Here the verse reads: "There shall be no more there an **infant of days**, nor an **old man** that has not filled his days: for the **child shall die** an hundred years old; but the **sinner** being an hundred years shall be **accursed**." The argument teaches that in the Millennium, there will be children born, and there will be death and the curse on sinners who refuse to come under Christ's rule. These things, such as "infants, children, old age, sinners and the curse and death" all belong to this age. Jesus said there would be no marriage, or death in the future age. Therefore, there can be no children, no sinners born, no death and nothing will be accursed of God, in that age. If this verse is seen in its apparent context, it speaks of the New Heavens and New Earth and New Jerusalem where none of these things will be. It is because of this that most Millennialists make this "a Millennial Scripture". The fact of the matter is, it is faulty hermeneutics to use an Old Testament passage for a future age that would contradict a New Testament passage, and what Jesus said, as this interpretation would. This passage must be taken in the light of the clear teaching of Jesus. He taught that, in the age to come, there would be no marriages, which means no births, no sinners, and there would be no deaths. All in that age will have a glorified body, that will never grow old, for all have eternal life. With this, the A-Millennialist would agree, although this School would place this all in eternity, and not in any future Millennium.

23. What Jesus Said in Lke.19:11-27

Because of a wrong conception and understanding of the Kingdom of God, and because the people thought the Kingdom of God should immediately appear, Jesus, enroute to Jerusalem, gave the hearers another parable.

"And as they heard these things, He **added** and spoke this parable, **because** He was near to Jerusalem, and **because** they thought the Kingdom of God should immediately appear" (vs.11). Jesus had already told them that "the Kingdom of God is among you" (Lke.16:16; Lke.17:20-21). Here in Lke.10:11-27, He **added** a parable to show them that there was, not only a present aspect of the Kingdom, but also a future aspect. He told of a certain nobleman (Himself), who went into a far country (a Heavenly Country, Heb.11:10-16), to receive for Himself a Kingdom (vs.12). Later on He would return. Once He received that Kingdom (vs.15), He returned and took account of His servants. These servants were rewarded or disciplined accordingly. All of this accords with other Scriptures, where the Son receives the Kingdom from the Father. He establishes the Kingdom on earth, and His saints possess the Kingdom and reign with Christ for a 1000 years (Dan.7:9-10,13-14, 22-27; Psa.2:6-8; 1Cor.15:27; Rev.20:1-6). The Kingdom is "now, but not yet", as has been drawn to our attention previously. There is the Kingdom now, but there is also the Kingdom future– in the Millennial age and then the eternal ages to come.

24. What John Said in Revelation

In the Book of Revelation, the judgments of God are unleashed in the earth. These judgments are seen in the Seven Seals, the Seven Trumpets and the Seven Bowls of God's Wrath. These things are seen unfolding through Church history right on down to the end of the present age. Without doubt, the greatest judgments take place in the final years prior to the coming of the Lord. In outline form we consider the judgments of God in Revelation that decimate earth's population, leaving no sinners or unregenerate people alive to enter the Millennial Kingdom of God.

(a) Under the second seal, world wars destroy many peoples of the earth (Rev.6:3-4).
(b) Under the third and fourth seals, famine, pestilence and death destroyed a fourth part of earth's population (Rev.6:5-8).
(c) Under the seven trumpet judgments, many are slain and under the second and third trumpets, many people die, as one third of things in nature are struck (Rev.8:1—9:18).
(d) Under the seventh trumpet, 7000 are killed by a great earthquake (Rev.11:13).
(e) Under the seven vials of wrath, thousands are killed by these Divine judgments (Rev.15-16).
(f) Under the 3½ years of wrath, untold numbers of the saints are martyred (Rev.12:17; 13:1-5).
(g) In Rev.13-14 "ALL the world wondered after the Beast", and "ALL receive the Mark of the Beast and his number and worship his image." No one can buy or sell without the Mark of the Beast. To take the Mark of the Beast is the unpardonable sin, yet to refuse to take it means death. All who take the Mark will be tormented in the Lake of Fire and Brimstone eternally (Rev.14:9-11). The word "**all**" should be especially noted in the passage in Rev.13.
ALL the world wonders after the Beast" (vs.3,4).
ALL kindreds, and tongues and nations are ruled over by the Antichrist (vs.7b).
ALL that dwell on the earth worship him, whose names are not written in the book (vs.8).
ALL the saints, the believers in Christ, are persecuted and overcome (vs.7a).
ALL who will not worship the Beast are killed (vs.15).
ALL others, both small and great, rich or poor, bond or free, must receive a Mark in their right hand, or in their foreheads in order to be able to live (vs.16).

None of these Beast-worshippers will enter the Millennium to get a second chance. They have blasphemed God and His Name and repented not because of their sins. The False Prophet

causes all the earth to take the Mark or perish. Saints are martyred, and none will be able to live without worshipping the image of the Antichrist.
- (h) The Battle of Armageddon takes place at Christ's coming. Christ smites the nations with the sword of His mouth. All are destroyed by the brightness of His coming (Rev.16:12-16; 19:11-21 with 2Thess.2:1-10).
- (i) The second coming is the harvest of the vine of the earth. It is the end of the age. All the ungodly are cast into the winepress of God's wrath and their life-blood poured out in death is the result (Rev.14:20; 11:15-19). None will be taken into the Millennial Kingdom.
- (j) The Antichrist and the False Prophet are cast alive into the Lake of Fire at Christ's advent (Rev.19:11-21). The Antichrist, as the Beast, or the Little Horn is destroyed by the Son of Man, King of Kings and Lord of Lords (2Thess.2:1-8; Dan.7; Dan.8).
- (k) The ten Kings, or the ten toes, or the ten horns – all speaking of the same thing – are slain by Christ at His coming. They make war with the Lamb but the Lamb overcomes them (Rev.17:14; 19:11-21; Psa.2; Psa.110). He smashes them with the rod of iron, the sword of His mouth, by the power of His spoken word! There is no physical combat on His part. He but speaks the word of power and all are destroyed.
- (l) All who know not God and obey not the Gospel of the Lord Jesus Christ will be destroyed by the brightness of Christ's coming. "The remnant are slain" by the sword (2Thess.1:7-10; 2:8; Rev.19:11-21).
- (m) The tribes of the earth mourn at His coming, as well as the Jewish people who crucified Him (Rev.1:7). For the believers alive at this time, it will be a time of rejoicing and shouting.

In the light of all of these Scriptures considered here, it should be seen that the populations of the earth are decimated at this time. These Scriptures should be taken together as they belong to each other. When Christ returns again, an end is made of sin, transgression, and iniquity. All sinners, everyone outside of Christ, are destroyed. He will destroy the sinners out of the earth, according to the prophetic word. The saints will possess the Kingdom. The Kingdom will not be left to other people, to the unregenerate. Man's "days" are ended. God has given man his "week of days", but this "day" is God's day – the seventh day of rest from Satan and sin and sinners! It will indeed be a Christian Millennium, for none but Christians inherit the earth in this Millennial age.

At His coming, the dead in Christ arise, the living saints are changed. Together they are caught up in the air to meet their Lord. The unregenerate are destroyed. The earth is cleansed and made as the Garden of the Lord. Together, Christ and His saints enjoy Millennial rest over that 1000 years. Mortals and immortals will not dwell together. Saints and sinners will not be together in that Kingdom. The Kingdom is the Lord's. Of the increase of His government there shall be no end. There will be righteousness, peace and joy in the Holy Spirit (Rom.14:17).

Summary:
For the Historic, Futurist and Dispensational Millennarians, there would be disagreement on these things, as each School teaches there will be sinners in the Millennium, and life will be much like it is now. There will be a mixture of mortals and immortals, unredeemed and redeemed in that age.

For the Post-Millennialist, the Millennium will be much the same as conditions in this present life, but the world will be 'Christianized', at least in this Utopian age of peace and righteousness.

For the A-Millennialist, these Scriptures, on the whole, would take place at Christ's second coming. At this time, there is the general resurrection and the general judgment, where eternal issues are settled. After this Great White Throne Judgment, there is a New Heavens and New Earth, and Gehenna for the unredeemed.

It may be seen why the A-Millennialists react against the kind of Millennium that those of the Ultra-Dispensationalist School present by the several brief quotations from those of that School noted here.

In **"The Basis of Millennial Faith"** (page 99), Floyd E.Hamilton points out that if Paul's words in 1Cor.15:50-54 are understood as having "reference to an alleged Millennial Kingdom, then this passage asserts that all those, Jews and Gentiles, who 'inherit the Kingdom of God' that follows the resurrection of the righteous, will have glorified bodies. There is no room here for the assertion that the Jews will enter the Millennial Kingdom with mortal bodies, for 'flesh and blood cannot inherit the Kingdom of God.' This cannot refer to the Church as distinct from the Jewish remnant, for according to

Pre-Millennialists, those Jews decidedly do 'inherit the Kingdom.' Anyone, Jew or Gentile, who inherits this Kingdom in the text, following immediately upon the resurrection of the righteous, will be like the angels in heaven. There is no room for unsaved people in that Kingdom, for they will not be present in mortal bodies. Whoever is will have immortal bodies. There will be no people there whom Satan could deceive at the end of the alleged Millennium."

Arthur H.Lewis, in, "**The Dark Side of the Millennium**" presents very fully the problem of evil in a future Millennium of the Dispensationalist kind. The problems he points out may be seen in the things listed here:

- The mixture of saints and sinners in the Millennium.
- Children born with sinful natures, who rebel even under Christ's rule and reign
- Sin and death in that future age
- The blending of the new and the old, the good and the evil, blessing and cursing
- Forced worship of the nations, and forced submission to Christ, the King
- Preaching to sinners, who receive another chance to be saved in this future age
- Sinners experiencing longevity of life, along with immortalized saints
- Sinners, who marry, have children, live and die but not the resurrected saints there
- Christ on His throne of glory and evil men able to behold that glory
- A rebuilt Temple and a relapse into the religion of Judaism
- Israel now fulfilling the Old Testament promises and purpose of God

Lewis points out that none can enter that Kingdom unless born again in true sense of the word, spoken by John (Jhn.3:1-5). "NOW" is the day of salvation, and not "tomorrow" (2Cor.6:2). Lewis sees that ALL the wicked are destroyed at Christ's coming, and provides many Scriptures confirming that truth. The tares are burned, the wicked are banished, all the Beast-worshippers are destroyed by the sword of the Lord's mouth, the Stone Kingdom smites the world Kingdoms, the wicked are ashes under the feet of the righteous, Antichrist is slain and the armies who served him (Matt.13:41-42; 24:39; 2Thess.1:7-10; Jude 14-15; Rev.19:11-21; Psa.2; Psa.110; 2Thess.2:8; Mal.4:1-4, etc). Lewis, however, rejects the idea of any future Millennium, and this, undoubtedly because of the kind of Millennium that most Pre-Millennialists hold to in their teaching..

Lewis Berkhof, also an A-Millennialist, writes in "**Systematic Theology**" (page 715) concerning the mingling of mortals and immortals in an earthly Kingdom. He says: "The Pre-Millennial theory entangles itself in all kinds of insuperable difficulties with its doctrine of the Millennium. It is impossible to understand how a part of the old world and of sinful humanity can exist alongside of a part of the new earth and of a humanity that is glorified. How can perfect saints in glorified bodies live in this sin-laden atmosphere and amid scenes of death and decay? How can the Lord of Glory, the glorified Christ, establish His throne on earth as long as it has not yet been renewed? The twenty-first chapter of Revelation informs us that God and the Church of the redeemed will take up their dwelling place on earth after heaven and earth have been renewed. How then can it be maintained that Christ and the saints will dwell there a 1000 years before this renewal? How will sinners and saints in the flesh be able to stand in the presence of the glorified Christ, seeing that even Paul and John were completely overwhelmed by the vision of Him (Acts 26:12-14; Rev.1:17)." While not agreeing with all that Berkhof writes here, he presents challenging questions as to the kind of Millennium Dispensationlists teach about.

From a Post-Millennarian's point of view, David Brown ("**The Second Coming**", page 384) writes these words. "What a mongrel state of things is this! What an abhorrent mixture of things totally inconsistent with each other…This system almost inevitably engenders much confusion. The fundamental principle of the system – contemporaneousness and co-existence of the state of grace and the state of glory – of mortality and immortality – of an upper and a lower - a celestial and a terrestrial department of one and the same Kingdom – this principle destroys the real nature of both and the things which it places in juxtaposition."

So much agreement there is with these thoughts in the Christian Millennialist's viewpoint. Perhaps the possibility of a Millennium without this kind of mixture is the kind of Millennium these writers were looking for. Perhaps, if they could hold to a future Millennium, but not have in it all the things that the Dispensationalist teachers placed in it! A Christian Millennium would be an alternative for them.

For the Christian Millennialist, these Scriptures must find fulfillment either at (1) the second coming of Christ and beginning of the Millennium, or at (2) the New Heavens and New Earth, and the New Jerusalem, ushering in the eternal state. It is either one or the other. For the writer, these Scriptures on the destruction of the wicked find fulfillment at Christ's return. There will be no mixture of mortals and immortals, saints and sinners in a Christian Millennium. For this reason - that no sinners will be left alive to enter any future Kingdom - the writer has coined this term as being the most suitable to designate his belief, and that is, "The Christian Millennium."

CHAPTER EIGHT

REIGNING ON THE EARTH

Attention needs to be given to the matter of the saints "reigning on the earth" in the future Millennium. The Post-Millennialists and A-Millennialists see the Scriptures that speak of the saints "reigning on (or over) the earth" as being fulfilled in spiritual sense. Some hold that this reigning is now taking place on the earth, living a victorious Christian life, over the world, the flesh and the Devil. Some would see this reigning as taking place in heaven after departure from this life. They understand that this speaks of the intermediate state of the believers, between the first and second comings of Christ, in a "present Millennium." It is a reigning in heaven over the earth in the spiritual realm of the Kingdom of God. For them there is no future Kingdom where Christ and His saints reign here on this earth.

For the Historic, Futurist and Dispensationalists, each hold that there is a reigning here on the earth, which is fully experienced when Christ returns again in His glory.

Do the Scriptures teach that Christ will rule and reign on and over this earth in a coming future Millennium? The chapters so far have sought to establish that there is a coming "new age", a seventh day of the Lord, the 1000 years Millennial Age. In this present chapter, our consideration is given to those Scriptures that would point to this reign of Christ with His saints as taking place on this earth, and not just in the New Heavens and New Earth, in the eternal states. With the latter part, all Schools are in agreement. But what about "reigning on the earth?"

This writer believes that there will be a 1000 years reign of Christ and his saints, the true believers of all ages, right here on this earth. This is the seventh day and will complete God's Week of Redemption as it pertains to this planet earth. The seventh day in the Week of Creation, as already seen, pertained to this earth. This becomes the shadow in creation of what God would do and what would take place in the Week of Redemption.

1. **Paradise Restored**
   The first pointer to a coming future age is found in Genesis. God created Adam and Eve and placed them in a beautiful Garden of Eden. It was an earthly Paradise. It was God's will and plan that the man and woman reproduce themselves, with a perfect offspring, and fill the whole earth. It would seem that Eden was but a small part of this planet earth. As man was given dominion over the earth, to subdue it through his offspring, then the whole earth would have become a Paradise.

   Man had dominion over the earth, the fishes of the sea and the fowl of the air and beasts of the earth. God gave the man and woman dominion. God blessed them and told them to be fruitful and multiply and replenish the earth. Adam and his bride were given rule over a sinless creation where there was no sin, no sickness, no disease and no death. Adam and Eve sinned, and lost this blessing. Sin entered, and so creation fell with the man over it. In their Fall, they took, not only the human race, but they also took the whole of creation with them in that Fall. They brought sin, sickness, disease and death and every evil condition in the world today. Adam and Eve forfeited their earthly Paradise and this whole earth over to Satan, the Deceiver. They sold out the whole of the unborn human race and the inheritance of this earth to the Devil. The seed of the woman, the Lord Jesus Christ, was to bruise the head of the serpent, and restore all that was lost – and more – to redeemed mankind. Part of this restoration is the forfeited inheritance of this earth.

   The Millennial Kingdom will be a restored earth as Paradise and made to be the Garden of the Lord. The student should read these inter-related Scriptures (Gen.3:22-24; Matt.4:8-9; Jhn.12:30; 16:11; 2Cor.4:4; Eph.2:2; Gen.3:15; Rom.8:19-21; Isa.32:15; 35:1-10; 55:12; 65:25. These Scriptures show that Satan became the god of this world system and its kingdoms, but Jesus Christ conquered him in order to restore to man the lost inheritance. Redemption is restoration! What was lost in Adam is restored in Christ. God is determined that the promise and command He gave in Eden, to the whole earth, will be fulfilled. Those who are blessed and holy and have part in the first resurrection will complete what Adam and his bride failed to do. What the First Adam and bride failed to do because of the entrance of sin, the Last Adam and His bride will do because of righteousness.

It will be a perfect earth, without sin, sickness, disease, the curse or death. There will be no serpent there as he is bound in the Bottomless Pit for 1000 years. There will be no Tempter or any temptation. No Fall will be repeated in this Edenic bliss. All that was involved in the Covenant of Eden – the Covenant made before the entrance of sin – will come to pass. All of this will be made possible because of the NEW Covenant. It is the New Covenant that brings man back to all that was lost in the Edenic Covenant! Some Millennialists would place these things in the New Heavens and New Earth, but the Edenic Covenant pertained to **this earth**, and the New Covenant will finish that plan as it pertains to **this earth**! That plan will continue in the New Heavens and New Earth once God's plan for this earth is completed, at the end of the Millennial Age.

2. **Abraham – Heir of the World**

   God promised Abraham, Isaac and Jacob that they would "inherit the land" as seen in these Scripture references.
   - God promised Abraham the land (Gen.15:6-21; 17:4-8; 24:7).
   - God promised Isaac the land (Gen.26:2-6).
   - God promised Jacob and his seed the land (Gen.28:13; 35:12; 48:4).

   Abraham, Isaac and Jacob never ever personally possessed the land of Canaan. Yet, in Ex.6:2-4, the Lord says, "I am the Lord, and I appeared unto Abraham, unto Isaac, and unto Jacob, by the Name of God Almighty, but by My Name JEHOVAH was I not known to them. And I have also established My Covenant with them, **to give them the land of Canaan, the land of their pilgrimage, wherein they were strangers**." The fathers never ever possessed the land of promise. When the apostle Paul takes it up, he tells us that Abraham was actually **heir of the world**, not merely the land of Canaan (Rom.4:13-14). Abraham is the father of all who believe (Rom.4:16). In full sense of the promise, it extends to the seed of Abraham, which is Christ (Gal.3:16-19), and to the Church (Gal.3:29), which is the spiritual seed of Abraham, the true Israel of God. The promise is sure to all the seed, that is, those who are of the same faith as Abraham (Gal.6:16; Rom.2:29; Phil.3:3). Jesus told His generation that Abraham, Isaac and Jacob would sit down in the Kingdom of God with those of like faith (Matt.8:11-12; Lke.13:28-30). Salvation is by faith, and the promise to inherit the land – the world – is also through faith. Both these promises are in one and the same Covenant that God made with Abraham and his seed. The promise of "inheriting the land" will be fulfilled in the Millennial Kingdom, right here on this earth, an earth redeemed from the curse of Adam's fall. The eternal fulfillment will be in the New Heavens and New Earth, the better and the heavenly country and city (Heb.11:10-16).

3. **The Promised Land of Rest**

   The land of Canaan, as possessed by the seed of Abraham, was also a shadow of the promised rest in the Millennial Age. As Joshua entered the land, Israel had the promise of all enemies being under their feet. That the theme of "rest" points to the Millennial day is confirmed in the Book of Hebrews 3-4 chapters. This is seen by the several ways in which the writer speaks of "rest" for the believer in Christ. Note how this theme is covered in these chapters.
   - There is the rest of God in creation. God worked for six days, then the seventh day was a day of rest. Adam and his bride were created at the close of the sixth day, and they began their life with the day of rest. It was sin that broke their rest and God's rest, and God began work again in the work of redemption. The seventh creative day was sanctified, set apart, and blessed as a day of rest (Gen.2:1-4 with Heb.4:3-4).
   - There was the Sabbath day of rest for Israel. Israel would work for six days, and then the seventh day was rest. Their seven-day week was following the pattern of God's seven-day week in creation. The Sabbath was made for man and not man for the Sabbath. The day was made for the man and not man for the day (Ex.20:9-11; 31:12-17; Heb.4:9).
   - There was Canaan rest (Num.13-14 with Heb.3-4). This land of promise was the land of Canaan. It was promised to Abraham, Isaac and Jacob, as seen previously (Gen.13:14-15; 17:8; 26:3; 28:13). The fathers were pilgrims and strangers in it. Israel possessed it under Joshua and David (Psa.106:33; Dt.3:23-27; Psa.95). However, the Psalmist, along with Hebrews says that Canaan land was not the true rest God had in mind.
   - There is a spiritual rest in Christ. Jesus called those who were weary to come to Him and He would give them rest, and as they were yoked to Him and learnt of Him, they would also find rest (Heb.11:28-30). Those who believe on Christ come into that spiritual rest (Heb.4:3-11), It is a rest from works and a trust in Christ. This is what Hebrews says; that, if Joshua had given Israel the true rest, then the Holy Spirit would not have spoken of another day, in David (Psa.95).

- There is also a coming day of rest. In Heb.4:4,8,9 it speaks of this day of rest to come. "There remains therefore, a **rest** to the people of God." The Greek word here for "rest" is **"Sabbatismos"** and means 'A Sabbath". When is this Sabbath Day of Rest fulfilled? It is in the seventh Millennium, the seventh Day of the Lord. The Psalmist, Moses, says, "A day unto the Lord is as a 1000 years and a 1000 years as one day" (Psa.90:4 with 2Pet.3:8). God has worked six days in creation, and now He has worked six days in redemption. The seventh day – the Millennial Day – is the Sabbath Rest for God and for the people of God. When Satan is bound in the Abyss, that will be true rest for the redeemed, for the earth and for God! Creation's rest pointed to Redemption's rest! This finds its fulfillment in the Kingdom Age here on earth, and not only and ultimately as seen in the New Heavens and New Earth.

4. **The Kinsman Redeemer**
The Book of Ruth provides a beautiful picture of the work of redemption in Christ. Boaz was found to be a kinsman redeemer. When he redeemed Ruth to be his bride, he also redeemed the lost inheritance of the land. He could not redeem the bride without redeeming the land. They belonged to each other. So Christ, our kinsman redeemer, has purchased for Himself the Church, as His bride. With her redemption comes the redemption of the forfeited inheritance, this earth (Ruth 3:11-13; 4:1-12). The Millennial reign of Christ on a redeemed earth will be with His bride, the perfect Church. Christ Jesus, our kinsman redeemer of the New Testament, has fulfilled all the laws that a kinsman redeemer was required to fulfill in the Old Testament.

A similar picture is found in Jer.31-32 chapters. Jeremiah is a kinsman redeemer. He is told by the Lord to purchase the forfeited inheritance of land as the people go into Babylonian Captivity. After many days (i.e., many years), the land would be restored to its rightful owners. The price of the redemption was written in the books; an open book and a sealed book. The Lord is the Lord of the land – He is the "Land-Lord" and He will restore the land to its owners, having paid the price of redemption for it. This finds it fulfillment in the Millennial reign of Christ with His saints on this earth also.

5. **The Meek inherit the Earth**
There are many promises about the "meek shall inherit the earth" found in the Word of God. David said, "For evil doers shall be cut off, but those that wait upon the Lord, they shall inherit the earth. For yet a little while, and the wicked shall not be; yes, you shall diligently consider his place, and it shall not be. But the meek shall inherit the earth, and shall delight themselves in the abundance of peace." (Psa.37:7-11, and note vs.7,9,11,22,29,34,38).

Jesus also said, "Blessed are the meek, for they shall inherit the earth" (Matt.5:5). Again, the Psalm says, "What man is he that fears the Lord? Him shall He teach in the way that he shall choose. His soul shall dwell at ease, and his seed shall inherit the earth" (Psa.25:12-13). Psalm 37 also tells us that the wicked will be cut off (Psa.37:2,9,22,28,34,38). The Book of Proverbs tells us that the upright will dwell in the land, but the wicked shall be rooted out (Prov.2:21-22). Malachi says the righteous shall see the wicked as ashes under their feet (Mal.4:1-4). These promises should not be put off to the New Heavens and New Earth. The meek have never inherited this earth, but the Kingdom in earth will fulfill the promise to them. The righteous inherit the Kingdom of God in this earth, not merely "in the sweet bye and bye", as often promised.

6. **The Stone Kingdom**
Daniel, as he interprets the Dream of Nebuchadnezzar, sees the stone cut out of the mountain without hands. This Stone becomes a great Kingdom and fills the whole earth, after smashing all the Kingdoms of this world, as seen in the metals of the image. They become as the chaff of the threshing floor and are blown away. His Kingdom fills the whole earth. Here the Kingdoms of this world become the Kingdom of our God and His Christ, and He shall reign for ever and for ever (Dan.2:34-35, 44-45 with Rev.11:15-19; 16:17-21). Here at His coming again, Jesus will destroy those who **destroy the earth**. He will bring an end to those who corrupt the earth. In Dan.7:18-22, Daniel sees in vision how the Son of Man comes to the Ancient of Days, and receives a Kingdom. The saints possess the Kingdom for ever. It is in the days of these ten kings, of the Antichrist rule, that the Lord comes as the smiting stone and then His Kingdom fills the whole earth. This promise should not be put off to the New Heavens and New Earth, but it relates to this present earth, cleansed by the Lord at His second coming (Matt.16:15-19 with Matt.21:41-44; Gen.49:24).

7. **The Glory of God in the Earth**
The Word tells us that the glory of God is to cover the earth as the waters cover the sea (Isa.40:9-11; Isa.11:9; Num.14:21; Psa.72:18-19; Isa.6:3; Hab.2:14). There is not just the spiritual fulfillment of this promise in the measure seen now, but in full sense, the glory of God will cover this earth after Jesus returns and establishes His Kingdom of Light and Glory. The whole of the Millennial Kingdom will be a time of manifested glory and light of God and His saints.
- The sun will shine in sevenfold strength, and the light of the moon will be the light of the sun (Isa.30:26). This makes for no night or day, as we understand it in this present time.
- Christ will reign in all His glory, not veiled as in His first coming, but now, unveiled, as seen on the Mt. Of Transfiguration (Matt.17:1-7). This glory was manifested after six days, pointing to the fullness of His glory being seen by the redeemed after "six days" of the Week of Redemption. John saw that glory on Patmos (Rev.1:16-17).
- The Church, as His bride, will be clothed with the glory of the sun, the moon and the stars (Rev.12:1). She is clothed with light.
- The righteous shine forth as the sun in the Kingdom of the Father once the Kingdom in its present state has been cleansed of tares (Matt.13:43; Isa.60:1-2; Dan.12:3).
- God is the source of all light, whether natural light or spiritual light. He dwells in light that no man can approach to. It is unspeakable glory and light (1Tim.6:15-16). How could any sinner stand in the blaze of that unveiled glory and light? Read 1Jhn.1:6; Gen.1:14-19; Rev.1:16; Jud.5:31; Psa.84:11; Rev.10:1).
- God is a consuming fire and who could stand unredeemed in the midst of this burning fire and light (Heb.12:29; Ex.3:1-15; Isa.33:14-17; 24:22-23; 60:19-20; Mal.4:1-3)?

The earth also is likened to "the Holiest of All" or "the Most Holy Place" in the Tabernacle of Moses. The measurements were 10 x 10 x 10 = 1000 cubits, and become prophetic of the 1000 years of the Millennial Age. In the Tabernacle of Moses, the priest walked on the 'earth floor' that was covered with the Glory of the Lord. So shall it be in the Millennial Kingdom. All will be light, love, glory and fire. Only the redeemed will be able to dwell with such a God and His Christ. The only way to reject these Scriptures as applicable to a Millennial Kingdom is to set them in the New Heavens and New Earth. But these things pertain, first of all, to a cleansed and redeemed earth.

8. **The Age to Come**
This truth has been covered in previous chapters. The writer to the Hebrews tells us "the world to come, whereof we speak, is not subject to angels." God has subjected the world to come, that is, "the age to come" to redeemed mankind. The "age to come" is the Millennial Age, here on this earth. The eternal states are "the ages to come" at the close of the Millennium. The earth was made subject to man (Gen.1-2). Man lost his dominion through sin (Gen.3). The earth is redeemed by the Man Christ Jesus, and so "the world to come" (Lit."the age to come") has been subject to man once more, that is, redeemed man and this through the Lord Jesus Christ (Psa.8 with Heb.6:5; Eph.2:7; 3:21; Matt.12:32; Mrk.10:30; Lke.18:30; 20:35). The Kingdom Age is "the age to come" and that here on this earth, and eternity speaks of "the ages to come" in the New Heavens and the New Earth.

9. **The Earth Cleansed**
As one reads through the various Scripture references given here, it will be seen that, when Jesus comes the second time, this present earth is to go through a great cleansing, a purging by fire. The earth is to be cleansed of sin and sinners, and all the works of mankind are to be burned up. The earth will be set free from the bondage of the curse and the groans of creation. The earth will be renovated, and mighty changes, upheavals and re-adjustments will take place in nature. This will restore the earth to its former glory, and greater. All creation will right itself with the restoration of man to the image of God. Earth and man rise and fall together. They were created together and came under the curse together. They were judged together and will be redeemed together. Man is of the earth, the natural creation. Through new birth, he is of heaven, the new creation. The restored earth will be "heaven on earth" as God promised to Israel. Earth will once again be the Paradise that God intended it to be. The climate will change. There will be no storms, no hot, no cold, no labour or travail. All will be perfection. There will be perfect conditions, perfect climate, because man is now perfect by the redemptive and restorative power of God in Christ. Earth will be fruitful and filled with the glory of the Lord (Psa.67:1-7; Rev.6:14; Mic.1:3-4; Isa.55:10-12).

That the earth is to have cleansings by fire is found in 2Pet.3 with Heb.12:27-29; Mal.4:1-3; 2Thess.1:7-10). It would seem by a careful study of 2Pet.3 that the earth experiences a cleansing by fire at the beginning of the 1000-year period, and then at the end of that time, and then become the Lake of Fire. After this God takes the redeemed to a New Heavens and a New Earth wherein righteousness dwells – forever!

10. The Disciple's Prayer

Some Millennialists say that Jesus never said anything about a 1000 year Kingdom on earth. The argument of the "silence" of Jesus on this is no argument. Jesus never mentioned a lot of things in the Gospel, but He did send the Holy Spirit to finish His unfinished work of revealing truth. But Jesus did teach His disciples to pray: "Our Father in heaven, Hallowed be Your Name, Your Kingdom come, Your will be done **in earth as it is in heaven**..." (Matt.6:9-13). The will of God has never been done perfectly in earth, only ever in the Lord Jesus Christ. His will shall be done perfectly in earth in the Millennium. There will be no need to pray this prayer in the New Heavens and New Earth!

11. Reign on the Earth

In Rev.5:9-10, there is a prophetic song of the twenty-four elders. They, as Kings and Priests, after the Order of Melchisedek, sing a new song to God and the Lamb. "You were slain, and have redeemed us to God by Your blood out of every kindred, tongue, tribe and nation, and has made us unto our God, kings and priests, and **we shall reign on the earth**." It is not just a spiritual reign in the intermediate state, or in the Kingdom of God. It is a song sung to the kinsman redeemer, the Lord Jesus Christ, the Lamb of God. He has paid the price. He has redeemed the earth. He will destroy those who destroy the earth at His advent. The saints, with Christ, shall reign on the earth (Rev.11:15-19; Psa.67:1-7).

The opening of the seals is significant of the Lamb taking steps to repossess and reclaim the earth, which He has redeemed for redeemed man. It is the lost and forfeited and now, the reclaimed inheritance. The seven seals, the seven trumpets, the seven bowls of wrath are all judgments in the earth pertaining to this fact. He alone is worthy to take the Book of Redemption, for He alone has the rights of redemption, as the kinsman redeemer. Under these judgments, and at His coming, He evicts Satan and his hosts off the redeemed property, and restores the rightful inheritance to those He has redeemed. Satan and his evil hosts are "the squatters" that are to be evicted at His coming again. This is what the Millennial reign on the earth is also about. The fact that, at the end of the 1000 years, Satan and the wicked resurrected dead are like the sand of the sea, and come up on the breadth of the earth, also confirms that this reign of Christ and His saints is on the earth.

12. The Groans of Creation

Paul tells us in Rom.8 of the groans of this creation, groaning for deliverance. This deliverance from corruption is linked with the unveiling or "the manifestation of the sons of God." Note the major thoughts Paul presents to us in this great redemptive chapter.

- Creation groans – vs.20-22.
  Creation groans because of the curse that was brought upon it through man's sin. It was subjected to the hope of being redeemed from the curse. The creation is groaning and travailing in pain waiting for the unveiled sons of God. Adam was a created son of God (Lke.3:38). Jesus was the only begotten Son of God. He came to undo the evil work that Adam did and to make possible the groanings of creation to cease.
- Believer's groans – vs.23-25.
  The believer also groans. The believer has the firstfruits of the Spirit in new birth and baptism of the Spirit, but he awaits the full redemption, that of the body. This takes place either in the resurrection of "the dead in Christ" or else in the immortalization of "the alive and remaining in Christ" (1Thess.4:13-18). This is the hope of the believer, to experience the redemption of the mortal body from death by immortality.
- Holy Spirit groans – vs.26-30.
  Not only does creation groan, and the believer groans, the Holy Spirit also groans within the redeemed, making intercession according to the will of God. This 'groaning' will cease when Christ returns, and creation and the saints are fully redeemed and the work of the Holy Spirit is completed in the believer.

This Scripture pertains to this earth and to the saints. It is not speaking of the New Heavens and the New Earth. There is no groaning for redemption in that eternal state. The earth is still groaning under the wickedness of man and its fallen state. When the Millennial Kingdom is established, the curse on the earth is lifted. Creation will rise with THE MAN who redeemed it, and enjoy the fruits of blessing with Christ and His saints reigning over the earth in glory, as before the Fall.

13. King over all the Earth

Many, many Scriptures speak of Christ being King over all the earth. "And the LORD shall be King over **all the earth: in that day** there shall be one LORD and His Name one" (Zech.14:4-8,9). It is not enough to say that Christ is King now. This is true in His sovereignty. But the Scriptures point to His Kingship right here on this earth, not just His reigning from heaven in spiritual reality. Some brief references are noted here.

"Unto us a child is born, unto us a Son is given: and the government shall be upon His shoulder...Of the increase of His government and peace there shall be no end, upon the throne of David, and upon His kingdom, to order it, and to establish it in judgment and with justice, from henceforth even for ever. The zeal of the Lord of Hosts will perform it" (Isa.9:6-7).

"...when the Lord of Hosts shall reign in Mt.Zion, and in Jerusalem, and before His ancients gloriously..."(Isa.24:23).

"Behold, a King shall reign in righteousness, and princes shall rule in judgment..." (Isa.32:1).

"I have set My King upon My holy hill of Zion..." (Psa.2).

"The LORD said to my LORD, Sit on My right hand until all Your enemies are Your footstool...Rule in the midst of Zion..." (Psa.110).

"When the Son of Man shall come, He shall sit on the throne of His glory..." (Matt.25:31).

The Father promised the Son that He would sit on the throne of His father David, and of His Kingdom there would be no end (Lke.1:30-33; Psa.89:19-37; Ezek.37:24-25; 34:24). This reigning is all a part of the Davidic Covenant, the Covenant of Kingship (Hos.3:5; 2Sam.7:12-18; Jer.23:5; 30:29). The Lord Jesus Christ is King now, reigning in heaven, but when he returns the second time, He will be King over **all the earth**. He comes as King of Kings and Lord of Lords (Rev.19:16; Psa.47:2-3). The Word of God has both spiritual and literal aspects to it. The fact that Christ reigns now in spiritual reality does not nullify the promises that He shall reign actually over the earth in the Millennial Kingdom. Otherwise, these promises of "reigning on the earth" have to be spiritualized away, or else put off to the New Heavens and New Earth. This cannot be so, for when the total plan of redemption is accomplished, the Son delivers up the Kingdom to the Father and He Himself became subject to the Father (1Cor.15:24-28).

Conclusion:

For the Historic Pre-Millennarian, the Futurist and Dispensationalist, there will be no difficulty in seeing Christ reigning on this earth. The difficulty has been discussed as to the nature and character of Christ's Kingdom on the earth in the Millennium.

For the A-Millennialist, there is no future aspect of the Kingdom on this earth. Christ reigns as King now and when He comes, He will turn all rule and authority back to the Father. Therefore, the A-Millennialist would see this array of Scriptures of the Lord reigning on or over the earth as in fulfillment now, and the saints reigning in victory on the earth, or reigning in the intermediate state in heaven.

For the Christian Millennialist, these Scriptures point to Christ's actual reigning on and over this earth, cleansed by fire at His return, with His saints. This will complete the "Week of Redemption" and when finished, all will be ushered into the eternal states. This writer holds to a sinless Millennium, a death-less age, a Devil-less age and a time of earth experiencing the glory of Paradise, as God originally intended when He created the first Adam and his bride. What the first Adam and bride failed to do in this earth, the Last Adam and His bride, the Church, will fulfill. The lost and forfeited inheritance is returned to those who are in Christ. This becomes the foyer, the prelude to the New Heavens and New Earth and the blessed eternal states for the redeemed, while the unredeemed are cast into the final Hell. The Christian Millennium will be the Kingdom Age indeed. His glory covers the whole earth. Jesus, as the greater Son of David reigns literally and actually over this fully redeemed earth in the final purposes of God here.

CHAPTER NINE

THE GLORY OF THE CHRISTIAN MILLENNIUM

The Scriptures do not provide over many details about the Millennial aspect of God's everlasting Kingdom. John's passage in Rev.20:1-6 provides some important truths about this period of time, but beyond that, he gives no details about the nature, character and conditions of such a Millennium. It is to other passages of Scripture that have not been fulfilled in this age that the student turns. Full and complete details are not spelled out for us, but enough clues have been given to give some idea of Kingdom glory and order. The same would be true also, when it comes to the nature, character and service of the New Heavens and New Earth. Not much detail has been provided as to all that believers will do in eternity.

There are, however, some questions that need to be addressed. What will believers be doing in the Millennium? What will the Millennial Kingdom be like? If there are no sinners in the Millennium, over whom do the saints rule and reign? These and other questions naturally arise in the hearts and minds of serious students of Eschatology, and those who see the possibility of a "Christian Millennium" as an alternative view to Ultra-Dispensationalism.

The same questions, however, could be raised about the New Heavens and New Earth. For those in the A-Millennial School of thought, who believe that Christ's second coming ushers us straight into eternity, these same questions are also applicable. If eternity follows the second coming, and there is no intermediary Millennial state, then what will believers be doing in eternity? There are no details given in particular. The eternal states definitely tell us there will be no pain and sorrow; there will be no tears, no death and no curse. But what we will be doing in the New Heavens and New Earth and the New Jerusalem for all eternity, God has not told us. All will enjoy eternal life in worship of God and the Lamb. But as to activity in eternity, the Bible takes us so far and no further. This is basically so of the Millennial state. The following passages of Scripture do, however, provide some clues as to the glory and order of the Millennial Kingdom. The reader will bear with some things mentioned in this chapter on the Glory of a Christian Millennium, as there will be some overlap with previous comments.

1. **Christ the King of Kings**
   Christ will indeed be King over all the earth. "And the LORD shall be King over all the earth: in that day there shall be one LORD and His Name one" (Zech.14:9). This has been amply commented on in our previous chapter. When the Lord comes the second time, His feet stand on the Mt. of Olives. The earth experiences geographical and topographical changes. Read carefully Zech.14:4-8. He ascended to heaven from the Mt of Olives. He will descend from heaven to the Mt of Olives (Acts 1:9-12). He reigns as King of Kings and Lord of Lords. He came from heaven to earth the first time as the Lamb of God, the sacrifice and victim. He comes from heaven to earth the second time as the Lion of the tribe of Judah, the conqueror and victor. He reigns on the throne of David as David's Lord and David's greater Son (Lke.1: 30-33).

2. **Saints Possess the Kingdom**
   As already noted, the Kingdom is not left to others. Daniel is very clear when he speaks of "the time came when the saints possessed the Kingdom" – not the sinners (Dan.7: 13,14,17,18,21,22,27 with Dan.2: 34,35,44,45). Subsequent World Kingdoms have continually succeeded the Kingdoms of this world. Kingdoms rise and fall according the rulers and peoples. At Christ's advent, the Kingdoms of this world, which Satan offered Jesus in the Temptation, all become the Kingdom of our God and His Christ. He is the Stone Kingdom personified. He is the Son of Man who receives the Kingdom from the Father. This is an unshakeable Kingdom and with Christ, the saints possess the Kingdom as they reign on this earth (Heb.12:28-29; Lke.4:5-8).

3. **Saints Born again enter the Kingdom**
   Jesus said, "Except a man be born again (born from above), he cannot see (or enter) the Kingdom" (Jhn.3:1-5; 1Pet.1:23). If that is true in spiritual sense, of this present time, and the Kingdom is in its mystery manifestation here, how much more in the glories of the Millennial Kingdom? If people have to be born again, born of the Spirit and the Word to enter into spiritual reality now, how can sinners, unregenerate people – people NOT born again – enter that Kingdom with the full manifestation of God's glory and the unveiled glory of Christ manifested? Sinners must be born again to enter the Kingdom now, yet, according to Ultra-Dispensationalists, they do not have to be

born again to enter that Kingdom then. This is totally contradictory to the revelation of God's Kingdom both now and in the future. No one could enter the New Heavens and New Earth unless they are born again. It has been proven, hopefully, that no unregenerate sinners will ever enter the Kingdom of God in Millennial glory. Only those who have truly been "born from above", truly "born again" will enter that Kingdom, for they will receive a glorified body in order to be able to stand in the Presence and Glory of the risen Christ!

4. **Saints in Resurrection Glories**
    The Millennial Kingdom is the age of the resurrection. When Christ returns, the saints rise into resurrection power and glory. They receive immortalized bodies, bodies like unto Christ's (Phil.3:20-21; 1Thess.4:13-18). The living saints are transfigured and glorified also in the change-over from mortality to immortality (1Cor.15:1-28). The last enemy, death, has been destroyed in and for them (Heb.2:13-15; Jhn.8:50-59; Heb.11:5-6; 11:15-19; Jhn.11:24-25; 5:29). Resurrection life and glorified bodies have been promised to the saints, NOT to the sinners. It would be impossible for anyone to get into that Kingdom without a glorified and immortal body. No mortal or corruptible flesh will enter there. Between the first and second resurrections, there is a 'great gulf fixed' and no one can pass from one to the other without Christ.

    Paul tells us that, in the resurrection, "there is one glory of the sun, another glory of the moon, and another glory of the stars. For as the stars differ from one another in glory, so also is the resurrection of the saints" (1Cor.15:42-46). The saints will rise from the dead in various glories. Some will have the glory of the sun, some of the moon and some of the stars. All saints will not have the same glory. The saints will shine as the sun in the Kingdom of the Father (Dan.12:2-3; Matt.13:36-43). And Jud.5:31 says, "Let them that love You be as the sun..." The resurrection glory of the saints will be determined by their obedience to the measure of light God gave them in their generation. The Christian Millennium will be a time of unveiled resurrection glories in Christ and His saints. All will be shining lights through glorified bodies, even as Christ's body shone with light on the Mt. of Transfiguration (Matt.17:1-6).

5. **Saints are Rewarded**
    In the resurrection, and the establishment of the Kingdom on earth, the saints appear at the "Bema Seat" of Christ. There they are rewarded according to their works. This is not to do with salvation, as that has been settled. No one is saved by works, but all are rewarded according to works. In 1Cor.3:9b-15 Paul speaks of the various materials representing the works of the saints. Some works are likened to "wood, hay and stubble". All will be put through the fire and reduced to ashes. There will be no rewards, but there is no loss of salvation. Undoubtedly at this time, the Word will be fulfilled where Jesus wipes tears from their eyes, when saints see the worthlessness of some much "work for Christ" once it passes through the fire. Some saints will have "nothing but ashes". There are some saints whose works are likened to "gold, silver and precious stones". These things will go through the fire. The fire does not destroy them but simply purifies them. These saints receive a reward from the Lord accordingly. Whatever is the full significance of these truths, it should challenge the believer to make sure that all works done for the Lord (not for salvation!) are works according to the Word of God, energized by the Spirit of God and done in the love of God! These will stand the fire test in that day when all give an account to the Lord. The Millennium is a time when the saints have received their rewards; some more, some less, and some nothing at all!

6. **Saints are Crowned**
    At the Lord's coming, the saints receive crowns from the Lord. Some lose their crowns. They do not forfeit their salvation as that is settled. They forfeit their crowns. This is to say that not all saints will be rulers in the Kingdom of God. Many saints will be subjects of the Kingdom. This should answer the question as to "who do the saints rule over" if there are no sinners in the Millennium?" The answer is" All saints will not be ruling and reigning; many will be subjects of the Kingdom order. The elders in Revelation receive their crowns to cast them before the Lamb in worship and adoration. All glory belongs to Him. In Rev.3:11, the Lord does warn His people to "hold fast that which you have, that no man take your crown", while John also writes to the believers to encourage them to "receive a full reward" (2Jhn.8). The rewards and the crowns of the saints are linked in their truths. Read 1Cor.9:24-27.

7. **Saints in Kingdom Order**
In the Kingdom, the saints will be given their positions in Kingdom order. These positions will be of authority, in varying degrees according to the will of the Lord. The fulness of Isa.9:6-7 will be seen in Millennial glory. "For unto us a child is born, unto us a Son is given; and the government shall be upon His shoulder. And His name shall be called Wonderful, Counsellor, the Mighty God, the Everlasting Father, the Prince of Peace. Of the increase of His government and peace there shall be no end, upon the throne of David, and upon his Kingdom, **to order it, and to establish it**, with judgment and with justice, from henceforth even for ever. The zeal of the Lord of Hosts will perform it."

Whatever measure of this government and order that Jesus exercises on the throne of David and his Kingdom, there will be a fuller manifestation of it all in the Millennial Kingdom order. In David's Kingdom, there was order. So will it be in the Kingdom of Christ. Some saints will rule and reign. Some will be crowned and enthroned. Many will be subjects of the Kingdom. Many lose their crowns and have little or no rewards, as already seen. The order would seem to be: Christ (the King and Bridegroom), and the Church (the Queen, His Bride), then the Four Living Ones and the Twenty-Four Elders, and then the untold millions of the redeemed of all ages.

Jesus spoke of those in the Kingdom who will rule over ten cities, some over five cities and some will be ruled over (Lke.19:11-27). The Parable has to do with the nobleman going into the far country to receive for Himself a Kingdom. When He receives it, He returns and takes account of His servants. Whatever the full significance of this Kingdom Parable may be, it shows that some will be rulers in the Kingdom and other will be subjects in God's will and order.

Whatever that glory and order in the Millennial state is, there will be peace, joy, rest, love, praise and worship in spirit and in truth. There will be the union and reunion of all saints of all ages. It will be a foretaste of heaven on earth and the blessedness of the eternal states in the New Heavens and New Earth.

8. **Saints of Old and New Testament Times**
All the Old Testament saints will be in that Kingdom, along with all New Testament saints. Jesus Himself said of that time and his coming, "There shall be weeping and gnashing of teeth, when you see Abraham, and Isaac and Jacob, and all the prophets in the Kingdom of God, and you yourselves thrust out. And they shall come from the east, and from the west and from the north and from the south, and shall sit down in the Kingdom of God" (Lke.13:24-30 with Matt.8:11-12; 13:42; 24:51). The patriarchs will be there. The prophets will be there. The Gentiles who came to Christ from the four quarters of the earth will be there. All will be there with the New Testament saints. Multitudes of the redeemed of Old Testament and New Testament times will sit down in the Kingdom of God; not merely in its present state, but in the day when Jesus comes.

9. **Saints of Old Testament Israel**
What about the promises given to the nation of Israel as seen in the Old Testament? This is a question that is often asked. A careful study of Rom.11 shows that the Jewish nation (Israel) will experience a visitation of the Lord, and their blinded eyes will be opened to their long-rejected Messiah. They will be grafted back into the faith-olive tree when the fulness of the Gentiles has come in. This takes place under a final outpouring of the Holy Spirit on this nation in the end of the age. It is through Christ "all Israel shall be saved", understanding that "they are not all Israel which are of Israel." The Israel after the flesh must become the Israel after the Spirit. This can only be by the new birth. Natural birth makes them Israel after the flesh. Spiritual birth makes them Israel after the Spirit. Jesus told Nicodemus that, as a Jew, he MUST be born again to enter the Kingdom. No unconverted Jew or Israelite will enter the Millennial Kingdom, even as no unconverted Gentile will enter that Kingdom.

Ezekiel shows that the two houses, the House of Israel and the House of Judah, will become one in the hand of the Son of Man. They will no longer be "two sticks", or two nations, but they will become "one stick" in Christ's hand. The prophets prophesied of this reunion of the two nations. This can only be through Christ (Ezek.37), the greater Son of David. The vision of Ezekiel can only find its fulfillment in the true Israel of God – those who are one in Christ. His rule is not over the unregenerate of either the House of Israel or the House of Judah. It is the spiritual Israel even though they may have been born of natural birth in Israel. There has always been an Israel within

Israel, even in Old Testament times. They are not all spiritual Israel which are of national Israel. Many were Israel after the flesh, and the seed of Abraham after the flesh, but they were not the Israel after the Spirit, nor the seed of Abraham by faith in Christ. Abraham is the father of all who believe, Jew or Gentile. No unredeemed Jew, Israelite or Gentile will enter the Millennial Kingdom. In the truest sense, as already seen, all would have to be born again, born from above. This was the message of Jesus to Nicodemus, a ruler of the Jews, of the chosen nation. The only Israel of the Old Testament that enter the Millennium are those of faith, who follow and walk in the steps of faithful Abraham (Jhn.8 chapter). The Jews must come in through the cross of Jesus and His shed blood, and this must be this side of Christ's coming, NOT in the Millennium. This side of His coming, Jewry will have its eyes opened and mourn for Christ to come to them (Zech.12-13 chapters).

It means that Israel will become, as a whole, a converted nation. Their sins will be taken away by reason of opened eyes, and faith in the blood of the New Covenant. They enter the Millennium as a converted nation, and as one people in the Body of Christ, with the believing Gentiles. There will not be any middle wall of partition between Israel and the Gentiles. This wall was broken down at the cross, so God will not have Israel as "an earthly people" and "the Church" as His heavenly people", for all are one in Christ (Eph.2:14-15). To have "two peoples of God" in the Millennium, or in eternity, is to contradict the work of the cross, where two peoples were made one "in Christ." Whether Jew or Gentile, bond or free, male or female, all are one in Christ. This is so of every believer out of every kindred, tongue, tribe and nation.

Jesus gave a very distinctive promise to the Twelve Apostles of the Lamb in Matt.19:28, relative to the saved Israel of God. "So Jesus said to them, Assuredly I say to you, that in the regeneration, when the Son of Man sits on the throne of His glory, you who have followed Me will also sit on twelve thrones, judging the twelve tribes of Israel" (NKJ).

The Amplified NT, puts it this way. "Jesus said to them, Truly, I say to you, in the new age – the Messianic rebirth of the world – when the Son of Man shall sit down on the throne of His glory, you (who have become My disciples, sided with My party and followed Me) will also sit on twelve thrones and judge the twelve tribes of Israel." Read Matt.25:31-46 and Matt.19:28. These verses together show the relationship of these things, as both concern "the throne of His glory."

Where will this promise be fulfilled? Who or what are the twelve tribes of Israel over which the Twelve Apostles of the Lamb rule? What is the regeneration, or the "new age" the Lord is speaking about here? It points, not to the New Heavens and New Earth, but to the Millennial Kingdom. It does not speak of the Twelve reigning in heaven over Israel in heaven. It speaks of the age after Christ comes, when the twelve tribes of redeemed Israel take their place in the Millennium under the rule of Christ and the Twelve Apostles of the Lamb (Rev.21:12).

10. The New Jerusalem

Rev.20:9 speaks of "the camp of the saints" and "the beloved city". Many expositors see this city referring to earthly Jerusalem. They see that Christ will make His throne in Jerusalem as the capital city of the earth, and all nations will have annual pilgrimages to this city. This writer sees that there are some difficulties in holding this view. These are set out here for the student to consider.

- Earthly Jerusalem, where our Lord was crucified, is spiritually seen in God's eyes as Sodom and Gommorah (Rev.11:8).
- Earthly Jerusalem is in bondage with her children and is likened to Hagar and Ishmael, Abraham's children after the flesh (Gal.4:22-31).
- Earthly Jerusalem has been set aside as the place of worship, and this by the Lord Jesus Himself (Jhn.4:20-24).
- Earthly Jerusalem experiences a great earthquake under the judgments of God in Revelation (Rev.11:13; 16:19).
- Earthly Jerusalem was certainly not the city that Abraham, Isaac and Jacob were looking for. They looked for a city whose Builder and Maker is God (Heb.11:10-16). Could any believer say they were looking for earthly Jerusalem?
- Earthly Jerusalem was for earthly people. The writer told the Hebrew believers that they had no continuing or abiding city. They were to look for one to come (Heb.13:14). The Hebrew believers were to go "outside the camp" of Judaism, and look for the city of God.

Were they to look for a renovated "Old Jerusalem" as cleaned up by the Lord at His coming? Or were they looking for the "New Jerusalem" whose Builder and Maker truly is God? In Rev.21-22 John sees the NEW Jerusalem, the HOLY city of God, descending from heaven above. It is a holy city. It is a heavenly city. It is a NEW city.

Of course, the Lord could cleanse the earthly city, but in the light of these Scripture references here, that speak of its spiritual and present state, it seems very unlikely. There are a few writers and expositors of Revelation that see the NEW Jerusalem being the capital of the Millennial Kingdom. Some hold that the New Jerusalem, will be suspended over the Old Jerusalem, and that both are connected by "Jacob's Ladder", or (Jacob's Staircase). Time will tell.

The present writer believes that, possibly, the New Jerusalem will be suspended over the earth and "the saved nations" walk in the light of it (Rev.21:24-27). The only "saved nations" are those who are saved by grace, through faith in the Lord Jesus Christ. There will be no unsaved nations in the Kingdom Age. Heaven and earth are therefore connected in these thoughts. Undoubtedly, the fulness of this passage will be seen in the New Heavens and New Earth. But, it is a worthy and possible thought to think that the New Jerusalem will descend from heaven and be suspended over the Millennial earth, and those who are indeed "saved" through Christ, will walk in its light and glory! When Jesus comes, all will be clear to us then. But these thoughts are worthy of consideration and meditation. Is "the beloved city" OLD or NEW Jerusalem?

The heavenly city is the city of righteousness and peace. It is from this city that the King-Priest Melchisidek came, for He is "King of Righteousness and King of Peace". He came from Salem, or Jeru-Salem; that is, the heavenly Jerusalem and not the earthly Jerusalem. Heaven is God's throne. Earth is His footstool. Jerusalem is the city of the "Great King" (Matt.5:34-35; Psa.72; Heb.7:1-2). It is difficult to see this as referring to the earthly city which "spiritually is Sodom and Egypt", both cities being destroyed by plagues and fire and brimstone. Time will tell which city it refers to, whether the OLD or the NEW Jerusalem.

Conclusion:
There is not much that can be written of the Millennium. But, as already mentioned, the same is true of the eternal states. The details provided for us of what the eternal states will be like are found for us in the description of the New Jerusalem, in the New Heavens and New Earth (Rev.21-22) What we will be doing in eternity, we are not told. We know that we will worship and serve God, but what that service is to be is not written. Whatever eternity holds for the redeemed, all will be righteousness, peace and joy in the Holy Spirit. The Kingdom is like the King. He is KING of Righteousness and KING of Peace, and the Kingdom is "righteousness, peace" and for good measure, "joy in the Holy Spirit" (Rom.14:17; Psa.110; Heb.7:1-4).

The same is true of the Christian Millennium. It is a foretaste of eternity and its glories. It is heaven on earth. It is the prelude to eternity. This is our faith! This is our hope! This is our joy!

CHAPTER TEN

END OF MILLENNIUM EVENTS
(Satan Loosed, Second Resurrection, Great White Throne)

In bringing our text to its final chapter, some exposition and attention needs to be given to Rev.20:3,7-15; events that take place at the end or the close of the Millennium. The reader is encouraged to refresh their thoughts on comments given on Rev.20:1-6, concerning:

1. The Binding of Satan for 1000 years – Rev.20:1-3 (Refer Part 2, Chapter 11).
2. The Resurrection and Reigning of the Saints with Christ for a 1000 years – Rev.20:4-6 (Refer Part 2, Chapter 12).
3. The Millennial Kingdom of 1000 years – Rev.20:1-6 (Refer Part 2, Chapter 14).
4. The Christian Millennium - Who and What are not in it (Refer Part 3, Chapters 6-7).
5. End of Millennium Events – Rev.20:3,7-15 (Refer Part 3, Chapter 10 – this present chapter).

Together, these chapters provide some exposition of this most controversial chapter for all Millennial Schools, Revelation Chapter Twenty.

All Millennial Schools are faced with questions when it comes to the passage under consideration. What about Gog and Magog? Why is Satan loosed for " a little season" to deceive the nations of earth? What is God's purpose in this? How come that there is this final revolt of Satan and the wicked hosts of earth innumerable as the sand of the seashore? And for the Christian Millennialist, IF there are no sinners in the Millennium, then who does Satan deceive at the end of this period? To the natural mind, the whole scene of events seems unreasonable, senseless and purposeless. These are good questions and need some serious consideration, and this is the purpose of this final chapter. Some possible alternative answers from a Christian Millennial point of view will be given in the course of our exposition of these verses from Rev.20.

"...and he cast him into the bottomless pit, and shut him up, and set a seal on him, so that he should deceive the nations no more till the thousand years were finished. But after these things he must be released for a little while"
Now when the thousand years have expired, Satan will be released from his prison and will go out to deceive the nations which are in the four corners of the earth, Gog and Magog, to gather them together to battle, whose number is as the sand of the sea. They went up on the breadth of the earth and surrounded the camp of the saints and the beloved city. And fire came down from God out of heaven and devoured them. The devil, who deceived them, was cast into the lake of fire and brimstone where the beast and the false prophet are. And they will be tormented day and night forever and ever" (vs.3, 7-10. NKJ).

In these verses, John provides us with the briefest details of events that take place at the close of Millennium and immediately before the Great White Throne Judgment and the ushering in of eternal states. The facts are noted from the clauses in these verses.

1. At the conclusion of the 1000 years, Satan is released from the Bottomless Pit, his prison, his place of confinement and this but for a little season ("a short time". Amp.NT) – vs.3,7.

2. Satan goes out to deceive, seduce and lead astray the nations in the four quarters of the earth, designated as Gog and Magog – vs.8.

3. He gathers them for battle, their number being as innumerable as the sand of the sea – vs.8 (Compare with Ezek.38:2,9,15,22).

4. Satan and his hosts cover the earth and encircle the camp of the saints and the beloved city –vs.8.

5. Fire comes down from heaven and destroys them – vs.9 with 2Kgs.1:10-12; Ezek.38:2,22.

6. The Devil who deceived them is cast into the Lake of Fire and Brimstone, where the Beast and the False Prophet are and where they were cast at the beginning of the 1000 years – vs.10.

7. The Satanic trio; the Antichrist Beast, the False Prophet and the Devil will be tormented day and night, forever and ever; that is, eternally – vs.10.

8. John then sees the Great White Throne Judgment take place and all the dead are judged out of the books – vs.11-12. Compare vs.5 where "the rest of the dead lived not again until the 1000 years were fulfilled." The wicked dead are in the second resurrection and appear before this Great White Throne for judgment.

9. The sea and death and Hades surrendered their dead for judgment also – vs.13.

10. Death and Hades and all whose names were not found in the Book of Life were all cast into the Lake of Fire. This is the second death – vs.14-15.

These are the basic facts and order of events given to John pertaining to the end of the Millennium. The passage has provoked much thought and discussion among all expositors of Revelation, as to the purpose behind the whole scenario. Perfect understanding into the purposes of God will come when the Lord returns. In the meantime, one studies these things in order to be a good student of the Word, endeavouring to rightly divide the Word of truth, as Paul exhorted Timothy (2Tim.2:15).

Who then is Gog and Magog, as innumerable as the sad of the sea? What is this final revolt against the saints and the city of God; and more especially, if there are no sinners in a Christian Millennium? As the writer understands this passage, there are **two major events** that take place at the close of the Millennium, and these immediately precede the Great White Throne Judgment and eternal states. That is: (1) the loosing of Satan and (2) the resurrection of the wicked dead. These are considered, and what may be seen as the Divine purpose for such. The diagram illustrates.

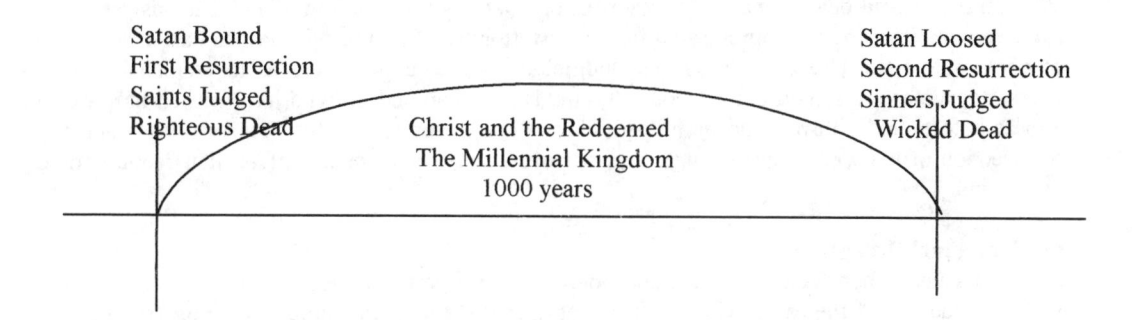

```
Satan Bound                                              Satan Loosed
First Resurrection                                       Second Resurrection
Saints Judged                                            Sinners Judged
Righteous Dead      Christ and the Redeemed              Wicked Dead
                    The Millennial Kingdom
                         1000 years
```

1. **Satan is Loosed out of his Prison**
   Vs.3 says, "And after that (the 1000 years) he must be loosed for a little season."
   Vs.7 also says, "And when the 1000 years are expired, Satan shall be loosed out of his prison."

It may be seen by the diagram that, at the beginning of the 1000 years, there is the first resurrection of the righteous and they are judged and rewarded, and Satan is bound for a 1000 years. Then, at the end of the 1000 years, there is the second resurrection of the wicked and this is in conjunction with the loosing of Satan. The 1000 years is therefore, bounded by the binding and loosing of Satan and the first and second resurrections. This is consistent at each end of the Millennium.

It will be remembered that Satan was bound in the Bottomless Pit at Christ's second coming. It is the next step in God's progressive dealings with Satan over the centuries. There is but one final step for Satan's final judgment, which is the Lake of Fire. God, in His sovereignty could have cast Satan straight into the Lake of Fire. This could have been done way back in eternity. He could have done this at Christ's second coming, instead of casting him into the Abyss for the 1000 years. The Antichrist and the False Prophet were cast straight into this Lake of Fire at Christ's advent, but not Satan. Why did God do this? There is no doubt that, in His sovereignty, God does nothing without some purpose in mind. Satan is not sovereign but is subject to God's control and power. He is a created angelic spirit being and owes his very existence to God.

It would appear that the major purpose of Satan being released from prison is to come before the Great White Throne Judgment. He is the original sinner, the first rebel against the government of

God. He is the author of sin. In his case, God does not consign Satan to the Lake of Fire without a just trial. This takes place in the Divine Court Room before the Divine Judge. God did not need to hold Satan's Court Case up for 1000 years while Satan is in the Abyss. But Satan is to come up for judgment and his case tried before the whole universe of created beings, angelic or human. After this, he is justly cast into the Lake of Fire. Theologically, God will never do anything with His creatures that is inconsistent with His holy character. So God's judgment is done in perfect justice and all the universe of created beings will acknowledge this truth as they see Satan cast into the Lake of Fire for all eternity. This is because of who he is and all he has done in the realm of angels and mankind, and the resultant havoc in the universe. With this, most Millennialists would agree.

2. **The Second Resurrection – The Wicked Dead**
The next major event to take place, and this in conjunction with the loosing of Satan, is the second resurrection, the resurrection of the wicked dead. The first resurrection took place in conjunction with the binding of Satan. The second resurrection takes place in conjunction with the loosing of Satan. It should be remembered that Satan was the one who once had the power of death. He is the author of sin and death is the wages. These things cannot be disassociated from each other. Satan, sin and death belong together. Once Satan was bound, then the righteous are resurrected. Once Satan is loosed for judgment, then the wicked dead are raised for judgment.

When it comes to the resurrection of the wicked dead, the same thing is applicable here as to the binding of Satan for the 1000 years. God could have judged the wicked dead at Christ's coming. There could have been a general resurrection and a general judgment at Christ's return, as A-Millennialists hold. But, in His sovereign plan and purpose, "the rest of the dead lived not again until the 1000 years were finished."

Why do the wicked dead come up for resurrection? Why are they raised at all? The answer is the same reason as for the loosing of Satan from the Bottomless Pit. The wicked dead are resurrected to come before the Great White Throne Judgment and be judged there as to eternal destinies. Eternal destinies are settled before God's throne. Both Satan and all who have served him are to appear before God's throne and be judged. This is the major reason for Satan's release and the resurrection of the wicked dead. There are, however, some other details given that require some comments.

(a) **The Final Deception**
It is asked, when Satan is loosed and goes up on the earth, he deceives those nations in the four quarters of the earth (This confirms the fact that the Millennium is here **on the earth**!), then who are these nations? It is certain that Satan could never deceive the resurrected righteous dead. They have been blood-washed, redeemed, resurrected and perfected and have glorified and immortal bodies. In the resurrection and that age, there is no sin, no temptation, for they are raised in the likeness of Jesus Christ. All in that age have passed beyond the possibility of deception – forever! They are perfected in holiness and glorified, redeemed in spirit, soul and body totally. Then what nations are deceived by Satan in this short time?

The student needs to remind himself that the moment of the second coming of Jesus was the exact moment of the first resurrection of all the righteous dead. So the loosing of Satan from his prison is the exact moment of the second resurrection, the resurrection of all the wicked and unholy dead. The wicked dead are raised from the four quarters of the earth, from the sea and from death and Hades, and these are "the nations" who Satan deceives for the final time.

(b) **Gog and Magog**
The wicked dead come under the designation of "Gog and Magog." This title becomes, as it were, a representative title for the wicked resurrected dead. "Gog" means "Prince" and "Magog" means "The People or Land of the Prince" as the following would confirm.

- Gog and Magog are mentioned in the genealogy of the sons of Noah, the sons of Japheth (Gen.10:1-5).
- Gog and Magog are mentioned in Ezek.38:1-3, referring to the Prince of the north and his armies from the north.

- Gog and Magog are mentioned for the final time here in Revelation as being a name that represents all the hosts of the wicked and unholy dead (Rev.20:8).

The ultimate "Gog" or "Prince" is Satan himself, who is the Prince of the power of the air, and Prince of demon spirits and fallen angels, and wicked mankind. Satan is the God of this world system (2Cor.4:4). "Magog" becomes the representative title for the hosts of Satan, those who belong to him and are in his Kingdom, the unredeemed peoples of the earth. Gog and Magog then are the hosts of the wicked resurrected dead, under the deceptive headship of Satan.

What then happens? Satan has been loosed from his Pit. The wicked dead have been resurrected. These are "the nations in the four quarters of the earth" whom Satan deceives. He deceived them in life. He deceives them in their resurrection for judgment. He gathers the wicked resurrected dead to battle. The wicked resurrected dead, from Cain down to the last Antichristal worshipper, go up on the breadth or face of the earth. They are as innumerable as the sand of the sea; sand being the symbol of the earthly, the fleshly and unregenerate seed of Adam's race.

It is to these unholy resurrected ones that the Prince of Devils goes in a last effort to deceive them into attacking the camp of the saints and the holy city. It is the final revolt, the final rebellion of Satan and the wicked dead. Satan leads them to surround the camp of the saints. It would be like the flesh-seed of the Ammonites and Moabites surrounding the camp of Israel in Old Testament times. They surround the camp of the saints and the beloved city. There really is no battle. The account simply says that, "fire came down from heaven and devours them" (vs.10). It cannot be imagined that Christ, in His full unveiled glory, and the saints who are in glorified bodies of perfection have any fleshly conflict with Satan and his resurrected hosts of wicked! The warfare is not against flesh and blood. It is a warfare of the spiritual realm.

The situation will be similar, in a small way, to the days of the prophet Elisha. The captains of fifties came to take Elisha captive. There was no physical conflict or battle. Elisha simply said, "If I am a man of God, let fire come down from heaven and consume you and your fifty." Fire came down from heaven and consumed the captain and his fifty. This happened at least on two occasions and it would have happened the third time unless the captain pled for mercy from Elisha (2Kgs.1:1-15). So will it be like this in Rev.20. There will be, however, no mercy, for Satan and the wicked resurrected dead are beyond redemption. There is no physical conflict. There is no battle. Fire descends from heaven and destroys them.

3. **The Great White Throne Judgment**
It is then that John sees the Great White Throne Judgment taking place on Satan and on all the wicked dead. All are judged according to their works. After this, all are cast into the Lake of Fire and eternal states are settled – forever! This has been amply dealt with in Part 2, Chapter 13, to which the student is referred.

4. **The Earth – The Lake of Fire**
As one reads 2Pet.3 along with Rev.20:11-15 and Rev.21:1-2 it would seem that this earth, once the purposes of God have been completed, at the close of the Millennium, will then become the Lake of Fire. The loosing of Satan and the second resurrection of the wicked dead, as in vs.3,7-10 must coincide with vs.11-15 and the throne judgment of God. It is after this that all are cast into the Lake of Fire and Brimstone.

In the events here, fire falls from heaven, ignites the fires of the earth and the earth becomes a world on fire. Peter tells us that the heavens and the earth, which are now in existence, at this present time, **are reserved unto fire at the Day of Judgment and Perdition of ungodly men**. This all takes place at the Great White Throne Judgment. The earth was judged by water once, and now the earth is to be judged by fire (2Pet.3:7).

Everything in this present earth has the elements of fire in them. The very atmosphere is explosive. The earth is filled with oils, gases, coal and other inflammable substances. Scientists tell us that the core of the earth is already burning with untold heat. People speak of "hell on earth", and so it will be for all who rejected the blessed Lamb of God. At the end of the Millennial age, and after the Great White Throne Judgment, the earth will become a flaming world, a Lake of Fire revolving among the planets in its appointed orbit. It will become like a comet, a world on fire. God will, as it were, put a notice on this planet, "Crime does not pay!" It will be a sign for all eternity that sin is not worth the price and the penalty that angels and mankind have paid. It pays to serve God and His Christ.

At this time, the camp of the saints will rise above this flaming planet and be taken away to the new capital of the universe, the New Heavens, the New Earth and the New Jerusalem (Rev.21-22). This earth, the Hell-hole and Gehenna of the universe will be "outside of the New Jerusalem" and the elect angels and the redeemed will forever remember God's grace in redemption. Never again will any rebellion against God and His word take place. This flaming, burning planet of earth will be a reminder of the terribleness and horror of sin and rebellion against a loving, holy and righteous God.

It is at the end of the Millennium, as we have seen, Jesus will give the Kingdom back to the Father, that God may be all in all. Jesus will take His place as the head of all His redeemed for whatever the Father has for us in eternity (1Cor.15:24-28).

In Conclusion:
This then provides an alternate answer to who the nations are that Satan deceives in the end of the 1000 years. Satan is loosed at the end of the Millennium. The wicked dead are resurrected at the end of the 1000 years. These things God purposes for one reason and that is, all are to appear at His throne of judgment and eternal destinies are to be justly settled there.

So IF there are no sinners or unregenerate or wicked in a Christian Millennium, then the only ones that Satan could deceive would be the wicked resurrected dead, and certainly not the righteous saints of the first resurrection. Of course, as our study has noted, IF there are sinners in the Millennium, then it means the mixture of mortals and immortals, saints and sinners, unregenerate and glorified all mingling together in the unveiled glory of the risen Christ. It means a violation and contradiction of the many Scriptures that point to the destruction of the wicked at Christ's coming again.

The student has these options to consider. What kind of a Millennium does one hold to? Is it a mixed Millennial age of saved and unsaved, of righteous and unrighteous, of mortals and immortals, and of corruption and incorruption – like as it is now? Or is it a sinless, Devil-less, glorious Millennium where Christ and the saints – not the sinners – possess the Kingdom?

Why then have a Millennium? What is the purpose of it all? The same questions could be asked of the creation of God in Genesis. Why did God work six days, then rest the seventh day? Was He tired and weary? Or was there a Divine purpose in that Week of Creation, with the First Adam and His bride, which purpose sin seemed to frustrate? So God has a purpose in the Week of Redemption. God is working "six days" again in the work of dealing with sin and evil. He will have a perfect bridegroom, Christ, the Last Adam and a perfect bride, the Church, and together they will enter the "seventh day" of rest. It will be perfect rest indeed. There will be no serpent to cause any further fall. The Christian Millennium will complete the plan and purposes of God for this earth, and prepare for the New Heavens and New Earth and eternal bliss and happiness for the redeemed!

CONCLUSION

Our studies are at an end, though not exhausted! In **Part One** the various Millennial views were briefly considered and a Bibliography provided. In **Part Two**, the fifteen areas of Eschatological controversy – some more, some less – were worked through, the writer presenting a study on each, from his point of view. In **Part Three**, the Christian Millennium was considered. As the reader will have seen, there are some things in each of the Schools that appear to be in harmony with the whole of the Bible, and some things that are not. An endeavour has been constantly made in the text to ground any exposition on sound theology and sound hermeneutics.

Once again, where there is difference of opinion and understanding, the writer asks for Christian grace and tolerance, as all Millennial Schools seek to discern truth on end-time events. The reader is reminded of "The Six Blind Men and The Elephant." Each disputed loud and long, Each in his own opinion, Exceeding stiff and strong; Though each was partly in the right, They all were in the wrong!

When we all, as teachers, preachers and expositors of the Word stand before the Lord, undoubtedly this will be the case. All see through a glass faintly and dimly, but there we will see Him clearly and face to face. We know in part, and we teach and preach in part, but when the perfect and complete is come, then all that we know in part will be dissolved into the whole.

Until that time, let us serve the Lord in a spirit of grace and humility, and in righteousness, peace and joy in the Holy Spirit, for this is the Kingdom of God (Rom.14:17).

AMEN & AMEN

OVERVIEW CHART OF MILLENNIAL VIEWS

No	Eschatological Area	Historic Pre-Millennial	Futurist Pre-Millennial	Dispensational Pre-Millennial	Post-Millennial	A-Millennial	Christian Millennial
1	Seventy Weeks Prophecy	Fulfilled by Christ	Unfulfilled 70th Week	Unfulfilled 70th Week	Fulfilled by Christ	Fulfilled by Christ	Half Week Unfulfilled
2	The Kingdom	Kingdom Now but Not Yet	Kingdom Postponed	Kingdom Postponed	Kingdom now, Eternal	Kingdom now, Eternal	Kingdom Now, Not Yet
3	The Church	Church-Spiritual Israel	Parenthetical Purpose	Seven Dispensations	Church-Eternal Purpose	Church-Eternal Purpose	Church-Eternal Purpose
4	The Nation of Israel	Visitation – Eyes be opened	Nation's eyes to be opened	Nation's Eyes to be opened	Promises forfeited	Promises forfeited	Eyes to be opened
5	The New Covenant	Established by Christ	Yet to be made with Israel	Yet to be made with Israel	Established by Christ	Established by Christ	Established by Christ
6	The Mosaic Covenant Economy	Fulfilled, Abolished forever	Re-instituted in Millennium	Restored in Millennium	Fulfilled, Abolished	Fulfilled, Abolished	Fulfilled, Abolished
7	The Rapture	Rapture at His Coming	Imminent Secret Rapture	Secret Rapture as Thief	No Secret Rapture	No Secret Rapture	No Secret Rapture
8	The Antichrist	Antichrist Forces	Individual Antichrist	Personal Antichrist	Satan's Wicked Forces	Satan's Wicked Forces	Person, Spirit, System
9	The Great Tribulation	Church always Suffered	Seven Years Tribulation	Seven Years Tribulation	Church always Suffers	Church always Suffers	Always & To Intensify
10	The Second Coming of Christ	Revelation of Christ	Personal Coming of Christ	Personal Coming	Rapture & Coming	Rapture & Coming	Rapture & Revelation
11	The Binding of Satan	Bound at Christ's Coming	Bound at Christ's Coming	Satan is yet to be Bound	Progressive Binding	Bound at Calvary	Yet to be Bound
12	The Resurrection	First & Second Resurrection	Two Resurrections	Two Resurrections	General Resurrection	General Resurrection	Two Resurrections
13	The Judgment	Saints & Sinners Judged	Two Judgments	Two Judgments	General Judgment	General Judgment	Two Judgments
14	The Millennial Kingdom	Christ's Kingdom on Earth	Jewish Millennium	Jewish Millennium	World Christianized	Millennium is now	Christian Millennium
15	The Eternal States	Heaven or Hell Destiny	Heaven & Hell	Heaven or Hell Destiny	Heaven or Hell Destiny	Heaven or Hell Destiny	Heaven or Hell Destiny

BIBLIOGRAPHY

Conner, Kevin J., The Seventy Weeks Prophecy
Conner, Kevin J., Interpreting the Book of Revelation
Conner, Kevin J., The Foundations of Christian Doctrine
Conner, Kevin J., An Exposition of the Book of Revelation
Conner, Kevin J., The Tabernacle of Moses
Conner, Kevin J., The Tabernacle of David
Conner, Kevin J., The Temple of Solomon
Conner, Kevin J., The Church in the New Testament
Conner, Kevin J., New Covenant Realities
Conner, Kevin J., & Malmin, Ken., The Covenants
Conner, Kevin J., & Malmin, Ken., Interpreting the Scriptures
Offiler, W.H., Harmonies of Divine Revelation